LISTENING TO MUSIC

LISTENING TO MUSIC

Craig Wright
Yale University

West Publishing Company

St. Paul   New York   Los Angeles   San Francisco

Copy Editor: Elaine Levin
Composition: Parkwood Composition
Musical Examples: Igor Popovic
Index: Lavina Miller
Production, PrePress, Printing, and Binding: West Publishing Company

Cover Image: "Liszt at the Grand Piano" by Josef Danhauser, 1840

Student Study Guide

A study guide has been developed to assist students in mastering the concepts presented in this text. It reinforces chapter material presenting it in a concise format with review questions. An examination copy is available to instructors by contacting West Publishing Company. Students can purchase the study guide from their local bookstore under the title *Study Guide to Accompany Listening to Music*, prepared by LaVaun Salaets-Beyer.

West's Commitment to the Environment

In 1906, West Publishing Company began recycling materials left over from the production of books. This began a tradition of efficient and responsible use of resources. Today, up to 95 percent of our legal books and 70 percent of our college texts are printed on recycled, acid-free stock. West also recycles nearly 22 million pounds of scrap paper annually—the equivalent of 181,717 trees. Since the 1960s, West has devised ways to capture and recycle waste inks, solvents, oils, and vapors created in the printing process. We also recycle plastics of all kinds, wood, glass, corrugated cardboard, and batteries, and have eliminated the use of styrofoam book packaging. We at West are proud of the longevity and the scope of our commitment to the environment.

COPYRIGHT © 1992   By WEST PUBLISHING COMPANY
610 Opperman Drive
P.O. Box 64526
St. Paul, MN 55164-0526

Printed in the United States of America

99 98 97 96 95 94 93 92   8 7 6 5 4 3 2 1

Library of Congress Cataloging-in-Publication Data

Wright, Craig M.
  Listening to music / Craig Wright.
    p.   cm.
  Includes index.
  ISBN: 0-314-91106-5 (soft)
  1. Music appreciation.   I. Title.
MT6.W94L6   1992
781.1'7—dc20

∞ 91-36216
CIP
MN

CONTENTS

Chapter 5 | RENAISSANCE   85

Chapter 6 | EARLY BAROQUE MUSIC   98

Chapter 9 | CLASSICAL FORMS 166

Chapter 10 | CLASSICAL GENRES 188

Chapter 11 | THE BRIDGE TO ROMANTICISM: LUDWIG VAN BEETHOVEN 212

Chapter 12 | THE ROMANTIC SPIRIT (1820–1900)   233

Chapter 13 | THE EARLY ROMANTICS   246

Chapter 14 | ROMANTIC OPERA   279

Chapter 15 | LATE ROMANTICISM   298

LISTENING EXERCISE LIST

PREFACE

The painting that serves as the cover for this book is a fascinating artifact. Indeed, one could write a book about it alone. Executed in 1840 by a minor Austrian painter, Josef Danhauser, it is a fanciful depiction of a gathering of some of the greatest artistic luminaries of the nineteenth century. Engaged at the piano is the imposing figure of Franz Liszt, perhaps the most formidable pianist who ever lived. Standing immediately behind him are Gioachino Rossini, the famous opera composer, and Niccolò Paganini, a violin virtuoso whose playing was so extraordinary that he was widely thought to be in league with the devil. With arm on chair, book in hand, is the French nineteenth-century lion of letters, Victor Hugo. Below sits Alexandre Dumas, author of *The Three Musketeers* and *The Count of Monte Cristo*. To his left, cigar in hand, is Aurore Dudevant, the prototype of the nineteenth-century feminist, and a novelist of more than two dozen volumes under the pen name George Sand. Reclining under the sway of the music is Marie d'Agoult, herself a novelist, playwright, and historian of distinction. Finally, radiating the very spirit of music from Olympian heights, a bust of the great Beethoven sits atop the piano. Although most of the listeners are poets, playwrights, and novelists, it is the art of music that dominates the scene. By the faces of the guests we can see that they are profoundly affected by what they hear. Music touches their emotions. They are transfixed by its power.

Pedagogical Goals

The aim of this textbook is to help the student of today discover and be moved by the great expressive power of music, as in the painting by Danhauser. As this scene suggests, music can be the most compelling of the arts. Yet ironically, most beginning students feel more comfortable with the visual arts than with music. The reason for this is not difficult to fathom: Painting, sculpture and architecture have an immediate appeal to our visual senses. But music cannot be seen or held. It is intangible, ephemeral, and more mysterious. Because of this, our ways of thinking and talking about music are different from those used to address the visual arts. A new and separate set of concepts and vocabulary is needed. The notion of scales, chords, meters, and rhythms, for example, involves a technical understanding that can be intimidating to the beginning student. This book aims to present these concepts in simple, straightforward terms so as to remove this technical barrier. Pursuing the same desire for clarity, it will also use the language of the visual arts whenever possible to explain musical concepts. The more than two hundred lavish illustrations contained herein are present in great measure to help transfer concepts already understood in the visual arts to the art of music.

A course in music should be a qualitatively different experience than that which the student receives elsewhere in the university. It should involve feelings, personal interpretations, taste, and notions of beauty, not precise formulas, equations, figures, and dates. The student should be encouraged to express feelings and to be sincerely moved by music as a way of developing the ability to judge this art more critically. But most textbooks of this sort treat music not as an expressive art, but more as a history of that art. The student is required to learn something of the technical workings of music (what is a tonic chord? for example) and specific facts (how many symphonies did Beethoven write?) but is not asked to become personally engaged in the act of listening to music. What listening there is is passive, not active and participatory.

This book makes use of a new and different approach, one that the author has used for many years in his own teaching. By means of forty-five Listening Exercises, the student is asked to embrace hundreds of specific passages of music and make critical decisions about them. The exercises begin by developing basic listening skills—recognizing rhythmic patterns, graphing melodies, distinguishing major keys from minor ones, differentiating various kinds of textures. They then move on to entire pieces in which the student is required to become a participant in a lengthy artistic exchange, the composer communicating with the listener, and the listener reacting over a long span of time. Ultimately, equipped with these listening skills and a new-found capacity for critical judgment, the student will move comfortably to the concert hall to listen to classical and popular music with equal facility and enjoyment.

Pedagogical Aids: Listening Exercises, Listening Guides, CDs and Tapes

The Listening Exercises are the most novel and important part of this text and the student should be assigned at least two of them each week. When they have been completed, they can be photocopied and then handed to the instructor. (Duplicate copies are also contained in the Study Guide prepared by Professor La Vaun Salaets-Beyer of Cypress College.)

In addition to the Listening Exercises, a total of seventy-four Listening Guides appear regularly throughout the text to help the novice enjoy extended musical compositions. Within each guide is a "time log" that allows the listener to follow along as the piece unfolds. The advent of the compact disc makes this especially easy since all that is required is a glance at the minute and second counter to know how far the piece has progressed. The discussion in the text, the Listening Exercises, and the Listening Guides have been carefully coordinated, minute by minute, second by second, with a set of six CDs. Whenever feasible, students should read the text and do their assignments at a CD player, using a set of CDs they have purchased or one available in the college library. By watching the minute and second counter, the student will easily be able to coordinate the description of the music in the text with what he or she hears. Repeated hearing also can be carried out quickly and accurately with CD players. Of course many students will prefer to work with the less expensive set of tapes. This will require that they follow the music with a digital watch or a watch or clock with a sweep hand. This is more awkward, but it is still workable. Tapes are available in a six-tape set (6-Tape), which contains all of the music on the CDs, as well as in a more limited and selective two-tape set (2-Tape).

Finally, Professor Matt McCready of Jefferson College, Jefferson, Missouri, has written an imaginative Teacher's Manual which includes core material for lectures as well as ancillary aids to make the teaching of this course more effective. The author of the text has contributed to the list of useful teaching pieces and secondary readings suggested in Professor McCready's manual.

Acknowledgments

In the process of writing this text I have been blessed with the assistance and good will of many persons. My editor, Clark Baxter, and production supervisor, Kent Baird, have encouraged and cajoled with equal vigor. Igor Popovic set the musical examples with a steady hand and sure eye. Sally Hilger helped edit the text, saving me from many of my usual embarrassments. The staff of the Yale Music Library, especially Professor Harold Samuel and Ken Crilly, made that extraordinary resource work to my very best advantage. My colleagues at Yale, among them Jonathan Berger, Allen Forte, Joel Galand, Eva Linfield, Daniel Melamed, Robert Morgan, Leon Plantinga, Claude Palisca, and Richard Rephann, let me pester them with an endless stream of trivial questions and special requests. Michael Tenzer and Ramon Satyendra were especially helpful in guiding me with respect to non-Western music. James Ross and Curt Hancock put the resources of the Yale Symphony Orchestra at my disposal in several useful ways. Karl Schrom was an unending source of valuable information about recordings, and Larry Lash rescued the audio portion of the project when it seemed in danger of foundering. Finally, my thanks to my wife Sherry, who read and reread my text—she remains my sharpest and most enduring critic.

The following instructors also evaluated material or provided helpful information during the writing of this book:

Mary Jenifer Bloxam
Williams College

John Chiego
Memphis State University

Fredric T. Cohen
University of Massachusetts

Michael Coolen
Oregon State University

J. Phillip Dalby
Hillsborough Community College

Daniel Dunavan
Southeast Missouri State University

David Grayson
University of Minnesota

Annmarie George
Gannon University

Barbara Haagh
University of Maryland, Baltimore Campus

Laurie Hasselman
Loyola College, New Orleans

William E. Hettrick
Hofstra University

Jerome Laszloffy
University of Connecticut

Matthew A. McCready
Jefferson College

Keith Polk
University of New Hampshire

Lee A. Rothfarb
Harvard University

La Vaun Salaets-Beyer
Cypress College

Marian Smith
University of Oregon

Andrew Tomasello
Baruch College, CUNY

New Haven, Connecticut
January 1992

LISTENING TO MUSIC

W hy do we listen to music? Because it gives us pleasure. Why does it give us pleasure? We don't know, though psychologists have spent a great deal of time trying to find out. By some inexplicable means, music has the power to intensify and deepen our feelings, to calm our jangled nerves, to make us sad or cheerful, to incite us to dance, and even, perhaps, march proudly off to war. The ancient Greeks recognized the effective powers of music; indeed, Plato thought the proper sort of music would encourage the young men of Athens to study diligently and avoid the eternal temptations of wine, women, and wanton song. We in the modern world have made music a part of our most important religious, social, and artistic activities. Music adds to the solemnity of our ceremonies, arts, and entertainments, and thus "moves" or heightens the feelings of all those who watch and participate. If you doubt this is so, try looking at a motion picture without listening to the musical score, or imagine a parade or a funeral procession without music and think how empty these events would be.

When we listen to music, physically speaking, we are reacting to an organized disturbance of our environment. A voice or an instrument emits energized sounds that set the air in motion, creating waves that carry the sound to our ears. Inside the inner ear, these vibrations are transformed into electrochemical impulses that, in turn, are transferred to the brain. What happens there is not certain, but it appears that the impulses are sorted and recognized as patterns and shapes, perhaps not unlike visual patterns or geometric shapes. In the end, the way we perceive a musical composition may not be much different than our perception of an impressive work of architecture, the harmonious shapes of a beautiful painting, or the gently moving contours of a lovely landscape. We respond emotionally to, and are moved by, musical relationships that are pleasing, novel, or even disturbing. Responding to the endless patterns of music—by tapping our feet, moving our bodies, or humming along—is an experience common to all of us.

This book aims to improve your ability to listen to music and thus your enjoyment of it. "But I listen to music every day," you may say, "why must I *learn* to listen"? Because hearing music in the way that most of us do and

FIGURE 1–1

Outdoor concert at the Hollywood Bowl. The shell focuses sound and projects it to the listener. Although sound can also be picked up by microphones and electronically amplified, it is not as pleasing as natural, acoustical sound.

truly listening to music in an attentive, perceptive way are two different things. Ironically, the more we are surrounded by music—with the Walkman, car radio, or MTV, say—the less we actually hear. The very technology that has engulfed us with music has tended to make us poor listeners. We are so accustomed to music in our daily lives that we pay little attention to it.

Now is your opportunity to tune into music. If you eagerly embrace the material that follows, you will soon discover a whole new world of sound opening before you. You will find yourself hearing things in music that you never heard before; sounds that had passed right by you will take on new and exciting significance. Your experience with this important part of life will be richer, deeper, more intense. Music has been on this earth for as long as humans themselves, and it shows no signs of going away. Perhaps until now you have let this art form pass in one ear and out the other. Here is your chance to improve your capacity to understand and appreciate music, and thereby add an important new dimension to your personality.

B ECOMING A GOOD LISTENER

Part of listening well is knowing what to listen for and what to expect in music. To do this, we should all have some knowledge of how music works. What are the standard operating procedures of this art? What are its usual components, styles, and forms? How do melodies unfold, how do musical phrases and endings work together to mark the progress of a piece, how does a composer get from one section to the next, and how does he or she signal that the conclusion is near? Becoming familiar with the common patterns of musical behavior makes it possible for the listener to make sense out of any musical composition. One of the aims of this book is to give you an understanding of what these common musical processes are so that you

FIGURE 1–2
A musical instrument produces regular waves of sound that pass through the air to the listener's ear. The listener sorts and tries to make sense of the sound patterns.

become comfortable with what you hear and can even anticipate what may come next. In this way, knowledge will increase your enjoyment.

Along with learning how music works, you will soon begin to develop good listening skills. Most of us listen passively and inattentively. Instead, we should be active participants in an artistic exchange, making use of an arsenal of listening techniques that allow us quickly and surely to make sense of what the composer is trying to communicate. We should be able to recognize which instruments are playing, sort out the melody from the harmony, identify how many distinctive layers or lines of music are present, feel the meter and the rhythm of the piece, and sense the formal plan that the composer is unfolding. Once such listening skills have been mastered, they can be applied equally well to both classical and popular music. Hearing a bass line in a Beatles tune, for example, is not a radically different process from hearing one in an **aria*** of Bach.

improve listening skills

Focus Solely on the Music

The first step toward improving your listening skills is to focus your attention solely on the music. You may be able to listen to a rock tune or some blues while doing your class assignments, paying only slight attention to the music, just as you are perhaps able to read a newspaper and keep a conversation going at the same time. But for more serious music, this sort of "background" listening won't do. Instead, your total concentration will be needed.

Hearing music as a work of art, just as properly viewing a sculpture or painting, requires thought. With most popular music, we need only respond to the music emotionally, and perhaps physically if we wish to dance. But classical music and much jazz requires that we open our minds as well as hearts to the music. We have to recognize various musical events, retain these in our memory, and relate them to one another over a span of time. If we don't make these mental connections, we will fail to see the musical genius of the composer and miss what is artful in the composition. Concen-

FIGURE 1–3
The new compact disc (CD) technology is only the latest development in audio techniques in the twentieth century, superseding phonograph and magnetic tape machines.

*Terms marked with an asterisk are defined both in the text and in the Glossary.
 Aria—an elaborate lyrical song for solo voice.

FIGURE 1–4

The early phonograph used a stylus, or needle, to cut the patterns of sound waves into a wax or vinyl disk.

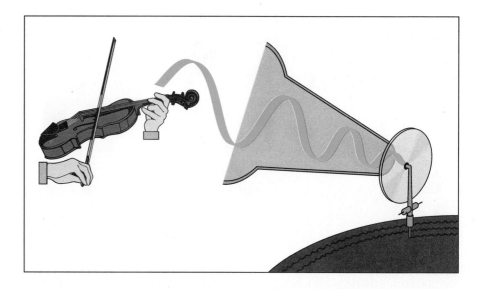

tration, then, encourages us to focus on the music and think intelligently about what we hear.

Improving Your Memory

Memory, too, is important to good listening. Unlike the visual arts, music moves by in time. When we look at a painting, for example, it stands still before us, to be taken in all at once. The challenge to the viewer is to bring some knowledge of painting techniques, subject matter, and symbolism to bear in order to appreciate the work of art in terms of its technical execution and its meaning. Our approach to a musical composition is much different. We are not given the entire object at once. Rather, it comes to us gradually, bit by bit, as the seconds and minutes go by. To make sense of the musical object, we have to remember what came before. Trying to remember and relate sounds that seem to pass by all too quickly is perhaps the greatest challenge for the beginning listener. How do we deal with this rush of musical ideas? Simply said, the listener must learn how to seize a few key musical events and hold them firmly in the consciousness. The Listening Exercises in this book are designed to improve your capacity to remember sounds. And, like most physical and mental exercises, the more you use your musical memory, the better it becomes.

Hearing the Important Sounds

seize the important ideas

Unless we happen to have a talent like Mozart's, our minds cannot retain all that our ears hear. The music simply passes too quickly, no matter how good our memory, how hard we concentrate, or how well prepared for listening we may be. But composers have central ideas or themes they wish to express, and they also have moments of preparation, transition, and just plain filler. Some parts of their music should be strongly locked in our consciousness and other parts less so. Being able to differentiate between the

FIGURE 1–5

A tape recorder transfers sound waves into magnetized particles on the tape. A CD player uses a laser to read the specifics of sound which have been encoded as digital information on a small metal disc.

important and the unimportant in music is thus indispensable to good listening. The Listening Guides in this book are designed to sharpen your critical faculties by showing you what the author thinks you should listen for. But reading another's description of what is important is only a start toward hearing and evaluating by yourself. The Listening Exercises at the end of the chapters are intended to get you actively involved in the decision-making process. Both Guides and Exercises make use of tapes and the new compact disc technology. With either, you can go back quickly to an important musical event and play it again and again. You have at your fingertips a way to listen, learn, and improve your critical skills in a controlled musical environment. Later, you will begin to make critical judgments about music by yourself, when you attend a concert or hear a new piece on the television or radio.

Listen Regularly

When everything is said and done, all this work on developing listening skills will be in vain if you do not listen to music regularly. We perceive music aurally, with our ears, not visually, with our eyes. And for some unknown reason, the rate at which we can absorb sounds is different from that of visually received information—facts and figures, dates, and abstract designs. The student of music cannot expect to cram large amounts of material in a few intense sessions, the way one might prepare for an exam in American history, for example. Learning to listen to music is much like learning the sounds of a foreign language. It must be done gradually, a small amount every day, and with much repetition.

FIGURE 1–6

Trumpeter Wynton Marsalis can record a collection of Vivaldi trumpet concertos one week, and an album of Dixieland jazz the next.

CLASSICAL MUSIC—POPULAR MUSIC

There is an astonishing variety of music in the world, and there is good and bad in all of it. Most of the music that will be discussed in this book is what we refer to as "classical" music. It is also called "art" music or "serious" music. Whatever its name, this is the music that we hear in the concert hall, on certain FM radio stations, sometimes on public television, and occasionally as background music for movies, cartoons, and television commercials. Most of it was created by composers living in Europe and Russia and by Americans using European traditions. It also tends to be old. That is to say, most of what we hear in the way of classical music—the music of Bach, Handel, Mozart, Haydn, Beethoven, Schubert, and Tchaikovsky, for example—was written between 1700 and 1900, and thus was created at least a century ago. Indeed, one thing that makes a cultural artifact a "classic" is that it possesses certain qualities of expression, proportion, and balance that are timeless in their appeal. Classical music has given pleasure to music lovers generation after generation.

Popular music, which we also discuss here from time to time, can be just as artful and just as serious as classical music, and often the musicians who perform it are just as talented and skilled as classical musicians. Some performers are equally at home in both the classical and popular repertoire, as is the case with trumpeter Wynton Marsalis (Fig. 1–6). Popular music can be highly useful in learning good listening skills. When trying to hear how and when chords change in music, for example, it can be helpful to listen to a rock 'n' roll tune where the chords are uncomplicated, the chords change at regular time intervals, and the bass, which carries the chords, is played very loud and thus is easy to hear.

But popular music, unlike classical, rarely contains multiple levels of musical activity, and for this reason does not require, and does not reward, concentrated thought. What we hear the first time is more or less what we get. Perhaps this inability to reward repeated hearings or to allow for a different interpretation each time we listen accounts for the fact that the listening public quickly tires of particular popular songs and then moves on to new ones. Only when a popular song does give pleasure to more than one generation, over a span of twenty or thirty years, do we say that that tune has become a "classic."

CLASSICAL CONCERTS

If this book is successful, you will find yourself listening to more and more classical music. You may discover yourself searching for classical music programs on the radio, buying a tape or CD of some new symphony you have learned, or perhaps going to a concert of classical music. Let's say you opt for a concert. What kinds of music are you likely to hear? That, of course, depends on where you go.

Some theaters are designed specifically for the production of operas and ballets. In these the action—whether sung or danced—takes place on the stage, and the musicians of the orchestra accompany this from beneath the

FIGURE 1–7
Opera Theater, Indiana University, with a production of Peter Tchaikovsky's opera *Eugene Onegin* in progress.

front of the stage, in the orchestral pit as it is called. A **ballet** is a dance form featuring one or more dancers who usually use conventional movements to tell a tale. An **opera** is a dramatic work in which the actors sing some or all of their parts. It usually makes use of elaborate stage sets and costumes. Some operas have great dramatic content. Some are written solely to exploit, or showcase, the vocal skills of the principal singers. Yet when all of the elements of opera—music, word, drama, dance, and scenery—work together harmoniously, there is no more powerful medium of artistic expression.

ballet and opera

FIGURE 1–8
Concert Hall, Kennedy Center, with a concert in progress as played by the National Symphony Orchestra.

FIGURE 1–9

Kilbourn Hall, Eastman School of Music, Rochester, New York, is the site of many chamber music performances.

FIGURE 1–10

Maurice Ravel working at the piano ca. 1925. Ravel habitually composed at the piano, even when writing music for full orchestra.

Should you venture into a large concert hall, like the Concert Hall (Fig. 1–8) of the Kennedy Center in Washington, D.C., you will likely hear a symphony orchestra performing a symphony*, a concerto*, or an overture*. These are all genres, or general types, of symphonic music, which are explained in the chapters that follow. All are performed by a symphony orchestra that may have nearly a hundred players and in an auditorium that may seat as many as three thousand listeners. Concert halls can accommodate a large symphony orchestra on the stage, but they do not have the space or theatrical machinery to make possible the production of opera and ballet.

If more intimate classical music becomes your passion, then perhaps you will head for a recital hall where a few hundred connoisseurs might gather to hear a string quartet play string quartets* or a pianist play piano sonatas*. These more intimate genres of classical music make up what we call **chamber music,** because of the smaller, more personal surroundings in which they take place.

But why wait until the spirit moves you? Let's get started with the listening experience by discussing, and hearing, a piece that often opens a program of classical music in a large concert hall, Maurice Ravel's *Bolero*.

Maurice Ravel (1875–1937): *Bolero*

The composer of *Bolero* came from the Basque region in southwestern France, though he spent most of his life in and around Paris. Diminutive in size—he was smaller than the five-foot-four-inch Napoleon—Maurice Ravel cultivated the image of a dandy, always appearing publicly in the latest, color-coordinated fashions. For the most part, he earned his living as a pianist, teacher, and composer. In many of his compositions Ravel tried to capture the musical flavor of far-off places: Spain, Arabia, ancient Greece, and the Far East. But Ravel had little personal knowledge of any of these distant lands. As one writer said of his life of the imagination, "He was the eternal traveler who never went there."

One trip that Ravel did make—and it was by far the longest of his life—was to the United States in 1928. Lured to America by the guarantee of $10,000 for a two-month visit, Ravel arrived in New York City and began to criss-cross the continent, playing and conducting his music before large, enthusiastic crowds in twenty-five different cities. He heard jazz in Harlem with American composer George Gershwin (1898–1937), and had breakfast in Hollywood with actor Charlie Chaplin (1889–1977); he visited Niagara Falls and the Grand Canyon. In the end, Ravel's American tour lasted nearly four months and earned him what was then the enormous sum of $27,000. He left the United States financially secure for the remainder of his life.

The first thing Ravel did on his return to Paris was to begin planning the music for a new ballet. It was to be called *Bolero* and to feature Spanish dancing. The work had been commissioned by ballerina Ida Rubinstein (1880–1960), a woman of legendary beauty and great wealth who used her money to sponsor new ballets in which she appeared (Fig. 1–12). *Bolero* had its premiere at the Paris Opera on November 22, 1928, with Ida Rubinstein dancing the principal role, a seductive gypsy.

Bolero draws its title from the stately Spanish dance of the same name. For the first performance in Paris, the stage was set to represent the interior of a Spanish inn of the sort found not far from Ravel's own Basque country. Located at center stage is a large table. Above it hangs a huge chandelier that not only casts bright light but also creates dark shadows on the colorful scene below. On the floor languishes a group of male dancers. At first they seem unaware of the gypsy dancer's presence, but as she mounts the table and moves with greater passion, they, too, join in her seductive dance. With growing abandon, the entire company is inspired to sway to the hypnotic music, moving toward a frenzied climax of sound, motion, and color.

Most of the audience that first night in Paris cheered the composer and his new work, but at least one woman yelled, "He's mad!" What excited the passions of the crowd was that Ravel had written a work with only one melody repeated over and over. It didn't develop or progress, as melodies in classical music usually do; it just got louder and louder each time it recurred. Ravel himself was ambivalent about his creation. "I have written only one masterpiece. That is the *Bolero*. Unfortunately, it contains no music." What Ravel meant by this paradox was that *Bolero* is an exercise in the creation of a gigantic orchestral **crescendo** (a progressive increase in volume), but is devoid of musical contrasts and melodic invention. Here the volume and color of the orchestra grow while the melody remains constant.

The first sound you hear when listening to Ravel's *Bolero* is a rhythmic pattern played on a snare drum. This represents the sound of the castanets carried by the ballerina. The rhythmic pattern is only two measures long, but it repeats over and over. (In the examples below, the variously shaped notes show the rhythm, while the short, vertical lines indicate the beginning of a new **measure**—a group of beats, or musical pulses. Musical notation will be explained much more fully in Chapter 2.)

EXAMPLE 1–1

While the drum moves inexorably forward, a few string instruments are heard plucking softly in the background. This accompaniment sets up a second two-measure rhythm.

EXAMPLE 1–2

Soon a flute enters and plays a soft, enchanting melody. This theme came to Ravel one day when he was working at the piano, perhaps inspired, as he said, by the Spanish folk songs his mother used to sing to him. The melody,

FIGURE 1–11

Spanish dancer Lola de Valence painted by Manet, 1862. Spanish music and Spanish dancing had a powerful influence on French musicians and painters beginning in the 1860s.

FIGURE 1–12

Ida Rubenstein, who commissioned and first danced the role of the seductive gypsy in Ravel's *Bolero*.

or theme, actually appears in two different guises: One is somewhat bland as well as rhythmically square (we'll call it A); the other is more colorful and rhythmically complex (let's call that B):

EXAMPLE 1–3 Melody A:

EXAMPLE 1–4 Melody B:

Both versions of the melody are sixteen measures long, and they, too, repeat again and again, according to the following arrangement: **AABBAABB** (etc.) **AB.**

A rhythm, melody, or harmony that repeats over and over in music is called an **ostinato** (from the Italian word meaning "obstinate" or "stubborn"). We will have occasion to hear many musical ostinatos. Here in *Bolero* Ravel has created two rhythmic ostinatos (examples 1–1 and 1–2) and two melodic ostinatos (examples 1–3 and 1–4). As *Bolero* proceeds, more and more instruments join in playing these patterns, just as more and more of the men on stage become excited and join in the dance. The music grows louder and more insistent, and a musical form begins to emerge. Form in music, simply said, is the general shape of a composition as perceived by the listener. The form of *Bolero* might be represented by the following diagram. The work not only increases in volume (gets louder) but also in density as more and more instruments are added.

Finally, after nearly fourteen minutes of repetition and rising tension, the melody changes (at 13:46). It is extended by several measures and moves up to a new, higher group of pitches. This shift breaks the hypnotic spell of the music, and soon the work comes to a crashing conclusion. Listen now to *Bolero* and follow the Listening Guide below.

LISTENING GUIDE	Maurice Ravel Ballet music, *Bolero* (1928)	CD 1/1 Introduction to Listening tape, Side A

This is the first of seventy-four Listening Guides contained in this book. It is intended to lead you through the fourteen and a half minutes of *Bolero* and begin to give you a feeling of what to listen for in music. *Bolero* is marked by the gradual appearance of several different instruments of the orchestra, each playing in turn as a soloist. Some of these instruments, like the trumpet and

the flute, you may be familiar with already. Others, like the oboe and bassoon, are likely to be foreign to you. But don't worry too much about the
sounds of the various instruments or what they look like. This will all be
explained in Chapter 3. For the moment, just sit back and enjoy the music.

The numbers in the left-hand column tell you where you are in the composition. If you are listening to a CD, the numbers will appear on the machine
and are easy to follow. If you are listening to a tape, you will need a digital
watch or a watch or clock with a sweep hand. This "time log" is here to help
you follow the music. It shouldn't detract or interfere with your listening
pleasure.

0:00	Snare drum accompanied by low strings begin two-measure rhythmic ostinatos
0:10	Flute enters quietly with melody **A**
0:55	Clarinet presents melody **A**
1:42	Bassoon enters with melody **B** harp added to accompaniment
2:29	High clarinet presents melody **B**
3:08	Bassoon joins with snare drum in playing rhythmic ostinato
3:13	Low oboe plays melody **A**
4:00	Trumpet (with mute) and flute together play melody **A**
4:45	Saxophone plays melody **B**
5:32	High saxophone repeats melody **B**
6:18	Two flutes, a French horn, and a celesta (a keyboard instrument that produces a sound like a bell) together play melody **A**
7:03	Several woodwind instruments play melody **A**
7:48	Trombone plays melody **B**
8:33	Woodwinds and French horn play melody **B** loud
9:13	Large drum (a timpani) added to accompaniment
9:19	First violins and woodwinds play melody **A**
10:03	First and second violins and woodwinds play melody **A**
10:48	Violins, woodwinds, and trumpets play melody **B**
11:33	Violins, violas, cellos, woodwinds, and trumpets play melody **B**
12:19	Melody **A** played mainly by first violins, trumpets, and piccolos (small, high flutes)
13:05	Same instruments, now with trombone added, play melody **B**
13:46	Musical climax: melody **B** moves to higher pitches and is extended
14:06	Melody settles back down to original pitch level
14:11	End: no melody, just rhythmic ostinato and cymbal crashes

When Ravel completed his *Bolero,* he predicted that no symphony orchestra would dare to play the work. He was wrong. Its initial popularity was so
great that symphony conductors jumped at the chance to perform it, though
usually just as a musical work without the accompanying dance. One Hollywood producer, thinking mistakenly that *Bolero* was an opera, paid Ravel a
handsome sum for the movie rights to the work; and in the end Ravel's score

popularity of Bolero

served as background music for a film entitled *Bolero* (1934). More recently, it was used in the same fashion for the movie *10* (1979), starring Dudley Moore and Bo Derek, in which Ida Rubinstein's sexually suggestive conception receives an updated treatment. Ravel's strikingly original way of whipping up tension and holding the listener in a trancelike state has lost none of its broad appeal: The allure of the endlessly repeating melody continues to fascinate lovers of both classical and popular music alike. Now do Listening Exercise 1, which asks you some specific questions about *Bolero* as well as about your general reaction to this unusual musical creation.

LISTENING EXERCISE

1	Maurice Ravel Ballet music, *Bolero* (1928)	CD 1/1 Intro. tape, Side A

Read the discussion of Maurice Ravel's *Bolero* in the text (pages 8–10) and listen to the piece while following the Listening Guide (page 11). Now listen to it again and answer the questions below. As we noted, your task will be easier if you are able to listen by means of a compact disc player that has a built-in clock to keep track of the minutes and seconds as the work unfolds. If you are listening to a tape, you will need a digital watch or a watch or clock with a sweep hand to follow the time. This first exercise is designed to be "user friendly"—the questions are not too difficult.

1. (0:00–0:50) Which is an accurate description of the opening of *Bolero?*
   a. opens with a solo flute playing the melody (**A**) loudly while snare drum and strings play loudly in the background
   b. opens with a loud melody (**A**) in the snare drum while flute and strings play loud accompaniment
   c. opens with a quiet background of snare drum and strings, and then a flute enters quietly with the melody (**A**)
2. (0:51–0:55) When the flute ends its solo, is there a gap between its last sounds and the first sounds of the clarinet, or does the clarinet come in immediately? _____

1:42 Bassoon enters with melody **B.**

3. (2:29–3:08) Clarinet enters with melody **B.** Is the sound of this clarinet higher or lower than that of the bassoon which just ended? _____

3:13 Oboe enters with melody **A.**

4. (4:00–4:40) A trumpet (with mute) and a flute play melody **A** together. Are the snare drum and the low strings still audible in the background, or have they stopped playing? _____
5. (4:45–5:26) A saxophone now enters with melody **B.** Is this a true solo, or is some other instrument also playing the tune at this point? _____
6. (5:32–6:12) A higher saxophone plays melody **B.** What about now, have the snare drum and strings stopped playing their ostinato rhythm in the background? _____

6:18 Two flutes, a French horn, and a celesta (bell-like instrument) enter with melody **A.**

7:03 Several woodwind instruments play melody **A.**

7. (7:48–8:27) A trombone comes in with melody **B.** The trombone is an instrument provided with a slide. Does the performer make use of it by sliding between notes? _____

Now just listen to the music to the end and answer these questions.

8. As the music progresses, what is happening?
   a. music gets louder and texture gets thicker as more and more instruments are added
   b. music gets softer and texture gets thinner as more and more instruments are added
9. At the very end, which is true about the music?
   a. it sounds loud, harsh, and dissonant
   b. it sounds soft, bland, and consonant
10. Now on a scale of 10, how would you characterize your response to Ravel's *Bolero*?
    1. Constant beating made me ill.
    2. Left me cold and a little bored.
    3. Found it interesting but unnecessarily repetitious.
    4. Would enjoy it more if I could see the dancers.
    5. Astonished that a musician can get so much mileage out of just one idea.
    6. Decided that Ravel had an odd notion of what erotic music ought to be.
    7. Liked the piece, but now can't get that ostinato rhythm out of my head.
    8. Found myself moving around the room in step with the beat.
    9. Vowed to learn how to dance a bolero.
    10. Felt a sense of exhilaration, even power as I listened to the growing swell of sound.

KEY WORDS

aria	crescendo	opera
ballet	Ida Rubinstein	ostinato
Bolero	Maurice Ravel	Wynton Marsalis
chamber music	measure	

2

RHYTHM, MELODY, AND HARMONY

Music can be defined as sound that moves through time in some organized fashion. Sounds and silences can be shaped, given a profile, as they pass through time. Musical pitches can be placed one after the other in a purposeful way to form a melody. And durations can be organized in repeating patterns to form rhythms. When more than one pitch sounds at a time, the potential exists for musical harmony. Rhythm, melody, and harmony, then, are the most basic musical elements. They are the building blocks of music, and how they are arranged determines the color, texture, and form of every musical composition.

In discussing rhythm, melody, and harmony, we depend greatly on a terminology that has grown up around the practice of notating music. Musical notation is simply music put down on paper by means of special signs or symbols. By recording a piece in musical notation, we, in effect, "freeze dry" the musical work so that it can be exactly reproduced by performers at some later date. In addition, musical notation allows us to stop at any point, to look at a composition as it is standing still, talk about its various parts, and learn something about how it is put together. A listener does not have to know musical notation to derive great pleasure from music, nor will you have to read it to be highly successful in using this book. But the enjoyment of music can be enhanced if one understands how music works, and to explain this we need to know something of the technical language of music. This allows us to talk about the music we hear in a specific, meaningful way, rather than in vague generalities.

RHYTHM

Rhythm is arguably the most fundamental element of music. When asked to sing a favorite song, most of us will recall the rhythm better than the melody. Similarly, when hearing a piece of music for the first time, we are more likely to be struck by, and remember, a catchy rhythm than a catchy tune. We have a direct, even physical, response to rhythm.

Rhythm, in its broadest definition, is the organization of time in music. It divides up long spans of time into smaller, more easily comprehended units. It gives a shape or profile to the melody or tune. Basic to rhythm is the principle of the beat. The **beat** is an even pulse that divides the passing of time into equal segments. It may be strongly felt, as in a waltz or a straight-ahead rock 'n' roll tune, or it may be only dimly heard (because no instrument plays it strongly), as in much of the Impressionistic music of the late nineteenth century (Chapter 16). But whether immediately or distantly heard, almost all music has a beat to it. When we tap our foot to music, we are reacting to such a beat.

the beat

The beat in music is most often carried by a unit of measurement called the quarter note (♩), a basic duration in music. Normally, the quarter note will move along roughly at the rate of the average person's heartbeat, sometimes faster, sometimes slower. As you might suspect from its name, the quarter note is shorter in length than the half and the whole note, but longer than the eighth and the sixteenth note. These other note values account for durations that are longer or shorter than the beat. Here are the symbols for the most-used musical notes and an indication of how they relate to one another in length:

note values

EXAMPLE 2–1

(whole note) 𝅝 = ♩ ♩ (2 half notes)

(half note) 𝅗𝅥 = ♩ ♩ (2 quarter notes)

(quarter note) ♩ = ♪ ♪ (2 eighth notes)

(eighth note) ♪ = ♬ ♬ (2 sixteenth notes)

To help the performer keep the beat when playing or singing, the smaller note values, specifically, those with flags on the vertical stem, are beamed, or joined together, in groups of two or four:

EXAMPLE 2–2

♩ ♪♪♩ ♬♬ becomes ♩ ♫♩ ♬

In vocal music, however, the beaming is broken when a syllable of text is placed below a note:

EXAMPLE 2–3

Jin - gle bells, jin - gle bells,   jin - gle all the way

FIGURE 2–1

rests

In addition to notes that signify the duration of sound, there are other signs, called rests, that indicate silence. For each note there is a corresponding rest of the same value:

EXAMPLE 2–4

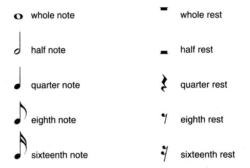

𝗈	whole note	▬	whole rest
𝅗𝅥	half note	▬	half rest
𝅘𝅥	quarter note	𝄽	quarter rest
𝅘𝅥𝅮	eighth note	𝄾	eighth rest
𝅘𝅥𝅯	sixteenth note	𝄿	sixteenth rest

dotted notes

You will have noticed that, in their basic form, the note values (and rests) in music all have a 2:1 ratio to one another: one half note equals two quarter notes, and so on. But triple relationships can and do exist, and these are created by means of the addition of a dot after a note which increases the duration of the note to one and one half its original value:

EXAMPLE 2–5

$$\mathsf{o \cdot} \; = \; \mathsf{o} \; + \; \text{𝅗𝅥}$$
$$\text{𝅗𝅥} \cdot \; = \; \text{𝅗𝅥} \; + \; \text{𝅘𝅥}$$
$$\text{𝅘𝅥} \cdot \; = \; \text{𝅘𝅥} \; + \; \text{𝅘𝅥𝅮}$$

Let's take a look at how the various note values can reflect the rhythm of an actual piece of music. For this we choose a simple, well-known tune, *Yankee Doodle*. First the text is given to refresh your memory as to how the song goes, next the rhythm of the tune in linear form to show how long each pitch lasts, then the rhythm in musical notation, and finally the position of the beat in *Yankee Doodle* as indicated by quarter notes:

EXAMPLE 2–6

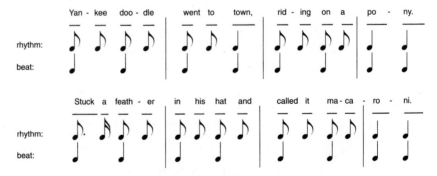

Here's the patriotic song *America* (first known in England and Canada as *God Save the King*) arranged the same way:

EXAMPLE 2–7

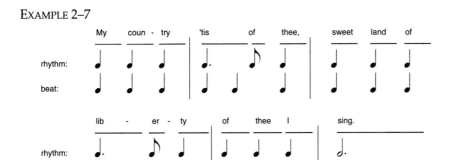

Listening Exercise 2a at the end of the chapter will help you to focus on the many musical rhythms you already have in your ear.

Meter

Notice how in the preceding examples vertical lines divide the music into groups of two beats, in the case of *Yankee Doodle*, and into groups of three beats in *America*. These strokes are called measure lines, or bar lines. A measure*, or bar, is a group of beats. Usually, there are two or three, sometimes four or more beats per measure. The gathering of beats into regular groups is called **meter.** Instead of having a steady stream of undifferentiated beats, we instinctively stress some more than others in a regular and repeating fashion. If we stress every other beat–ONE two, ONE two, ONE two—we have two beats per measure and therefore duple meter. The stressed beats are called strong beats and the unstressed beats weak beats. Similarly, if we emphasize every third beat–ONE two three, ONE two three, ONE two three—we have three beats per measure and thus triple meter. Triple meter has one strong beat and two weak beats per bar. In addition, there are other meters with four or six beats per measure. Here is a familiar folk song in the more common quadruple meter (four beats per measure):

EXAMPLE 2–8

And here is an equally well-known tune in sextuple meter:

EXAMPLE 2–9

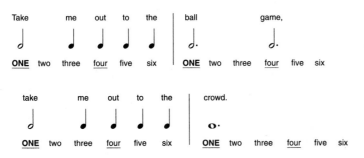

Most music, however, is written in duple ($\frac{2}{4}$), triple ($\frac{3}{4}$), or quadruple ($\frac{4}{4}$) meter.

Meter in music is indicated by a **time signature,** two numbers, one on top of the other, placed at the beginning of the music to tell the performer how the beats of the music are to be grouped. The top number of the signature *time signatures* indicates how many beats there are per measure; the bottom number tells what note value is the beat. Since, as we have said, the quarter note most often carries the beat, most time signatures have a "4" on the bottom. The three most frequently encountered time signatures are given here:

EXAMPLE 2–10

Having a time signature at the beginning of the music may be of great value *duple and triple meter* to the performer, but it doesn't help the listener, unless he or she happens to be following along with the musical notation—following the **score** as musicians call it. Without a score, the listener must of necessity hear and feel the meter. Most music, as we have said, is written in $\frac{2}{4}$, $\frac{3}{4}$, or $\frac{4}{4}$. Since $\frac{4}{4}$ is in most (but not all) ways merely a multiple or extension of $\frac{2}{4}$, there are really only two meters that the beginning listener should be aware of: duple meter ($\frac{2}{4}$) and triple meter ($\frac{3}{4}$). But how do we hear these and differentiate between them?

Hearing Meters

One way the listener can more easily come to hear a given meter is to establish some sort of physical response to the music: Obvious as it seems, start tapping the beat with your foot and moving with the music in a way that groups beats into measures of two or three. Perhaps the most graceful way to move with the music is to adopt the same patterns of motion that conductors use to lead symphony orchestras and other musical ensembles. These are patterns cut in the air with the right hand (a baton is optional!). Here are the patterns that conductors use to show $\frac{2}{4}$ and $\frac{3}{4}$ meter:

Example 2–11

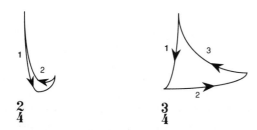

$$\frac{2}{4} \qquad \frac{3}{4}$$

Notice that in both of these patterns, and indeed in all conducting patterns, the first beat is indicated by a downward movement of the hand. This is called the **downbeat.** It is always the first and by far the strongest beat in the measure. In $\frac{2}{4}$ the downbeat is stronger, or more accented, than the upbeat (the beat signaled by an upward motion); in $\frac{3}{4}$ it is more accented than either the middle beat (2) or upbeat (3). When listening to a piece of music, then, tap the beat with your foot, listen for the downbeat, and try to get your conducting pattern synchronized with the music. If you hear only one weak beat between each strong beat you are in duple meter and should be conducting in $\frac{2}{4}$ time. If you hear two weak beats between each downbeat, on the other hand, you are listening to a piece in triple meter and should be using the $\frac{3}{4}$ pattern. Try conducting *Yankee Doodle* and *America* in $\frac{2}{4}$ and $\frac{3}{4}$, respectively.

feel the downbeat

Example 2–12

Yan - kee	doo - dle	went to	town	rid - ing	on a	po -	ny.
ONE	two	**ONE**	two	**ONE**	two	**ONE**	two

My	coun - try	'tis	of thee,	sweet land of	lib -	er - ty	of	thee I	sing.
ONE two three	**ONE** two three	**ONE** two three	**ONE** two three	**ONE** two three	**ONE** two three	**ONE** two three

One final observation about meters and conducting patterns: Almost all music that we hear, and especially dance music, has a clearly identifiable meter and a strong downbeat. But not all music *starts* with the downbeat. Often a piece will begin with an upbeat. An upbeat at the very beginning of a piece is called a pickup. The **pickup** is usually only a note or two, but it gives a little momentum or extra push into the first downbeat, as can be seen in the following examples:

the pickup to the downbeat

Example 2–13

She'll be	com-in'	round the	moun-tain	when she	comes	
two	**ONE**	two	**ONE**	two	**ONE**	two

Oh	say can you	see	by the	dawn's ear - ly	light	
three	**ONE** two three	**ONE** two	three	**ONE** two three	**ONE**	two

Turn now to the end of the chapter and complete Listening Exercise 2b. Then go on to Listening Exercises 3 and 4, which ask you to identify the meter of several musical works and give you a chance to practice conducting in $\frac{2}{4}$ and $\frac{3}{4}$ time.

Syncopation

One of the ways to add variety and excitement to music is by the use of syncopation. In most music the **accent,** or musical stress, falls on the beat with the downbeat getting the greatest accent of all. **Syncopation** places the accent either on a weak beat or between the beats. The note that is syncopated sounds accented because it is played louder or held longer than the surrounding notes. A good example of syncopation is found at the end of the first phrase of Stephen Foster's *Camptown Races* where the "dah" of "doo-dah" is syncopated.

EXAMPLE 2–14

Syncopation gives an unexpected bounce or lift to the music and is a prominent feature in jazz. Indeed, part of the fun of playing jazz is to obscure the beat by means of syncopation and thereby tease or tantalize the listener.

Tempo

tempo: the speed of the beat

If meter is the grouping of beats, and rhythm the durational patterns superimposed on the meter, **tempo** is the speed at which the beats occur. Obviously, the tempo, or speed, of the beat can be fast or slow, but it usually falls somewhere in the neighborhood of 60 to 100 beats per minute. Tempo is indicated to the performer by means of tempo markings placed at the beginning of the piece. Because they were first used in Italy in the seventeenth century, at the beginning of the Baroque period in music, tempo markings are most often written in Italian. The following are a few of the most common tempo indications, arranged from slow to fast:

grave (grave) *lento* (slow)	very slow
largo (broad) *adagio* (slow)	slow
andante (moving) *andantino* (slightly faster than *andante*) *moderato* (moderate)	moderate
allegretto (moderately fast) *allegro* (fast)	fast

vivace (fast and lively)   very fast
presto (very fast)
prestissimo (as fast as possible)

Naturally, general terms such as these allow for a good deal of interpretive freedom. Conductors like Leonard Bernstein (1918–1990), Arturo Toscanini (1867–1957), and Seiji Ozawa (b. 1935), for example, have had different *varying the tempo* notions of just how fast a movement of Beethoven marked *allegro* (fast) should really go. In addition, composers often call for fluctuations in tempo within a piece by placing commands such as *accelerando* (getting faster) and *ritardando* (getting slower) in the score. One particularly colorful term is *rubato* (robbed), meaning that the performer is given license to steal some additional time for the passage of music in question and thus slow it down. Frequent changes in tempo make it more difficult for the listener to follow the beat, but they add much in the way of expression and feeling to the music.

MELODY

A **melody** is a series of notes arranged in order to form a recognizable unit. The more beautiful the melody, the more we are drawn to the music. When supported by its companions rhythm and harmony, melody can produce an overwhelming emotional experience. Yet one of the wonders of music is that we are hard pressed to explain in precise terms why this is so. What is it about the shape of a melody, its balance and contour, that makes one so moving and another so very forgettable? The pursuit of this question, however, would carry us off into the realm of aesthetic theory. Instead, let us simply describe how melodies are put together so that we can more readily grasp them.

Pitch

Just as a grammatical sentence is made up of building blocks we call words, so a melody is composed of individual units called pitches. **Pitch** is the relative position, high or low, of a musical sound. When sound comes in regular vibrations, it produces a musical **tone.** If it occurs in irregular vibrations, then it is merely noise of the sort generated by a crashing plate or a barking dog. Musical tones are usually produced when a string or a column of air is set in motion on a musical instrument, and this motion, in turn, creates vibrating air waves that reach the ear at equal time intervals. The faster a string vibrates, for example, the higher the pitch. Normally, humans will hear sounds produced in a range between a low of about 20 vibrations (or cycles) per second to a high of about 16,000. (Some animals can hear sounds twice this high.) In theory, pitch can occur anywhere on this wide band of sound—think of a fire siren starting low, rising, and then falling back down. But when making music, we take this broad spectrum of sound and divide it into individual steps or degrees of pitch. We then string these units together in time to produce a melody.

EXAMPLE 2–15

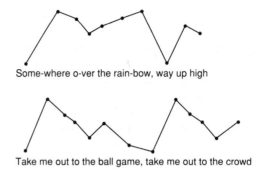

Some-where o-ver the rain-bow, way up high

Take me out to the ball game, take me out to the crowd

The Octave

dividing the octave

One of the remarkable qualities of pitch is that, when singing or playing a succession of tones up or down, a performer often comes to a tone that sounds like an exact duplication of an earlier pitch, but at a higher or lower level. For a reason that will become clear shortly, the duplicating pitch is called an **octave.** Pitches an octave apart sound similar because the frequency of vibration of the higher pitch, or note, is precisely twice that of the lower. Middle C on the piano, for example, vibrates at 256 cycles per second, while the C an octave above does so at 512 cycles. When men and women sing a song or hymn together without harmony, they invariably sing at the octave; it sounds as if they are all singing the same notes, but, in fact, the men are an octave below the women. Almost all musical cultures, Western and non-Western, make use of the principle of octave duplication in their melodies. But not all cultures agree as to how the octave should be divided, that is, how many notes there should be within an octave. In many traditional Chinese melodies the octave is divided into five separate pitches. Many Arabic and Turkish melodies, however, make use of fourteen. Judging from our earliest written music, which dates back more than a thousand years, we in the West have always preferred melodies that were built on seven pitches within the octave. The eighth pitch duplicated, or doubled, the sound of the first, and thus it was called the octave.

At first, the seven notes within the octave corresponded to the white keys of the keyboard. Eventually, five additional notes were inserted within the span of the octave, and these correspond to the black keys.

EXAMPLE 2–16

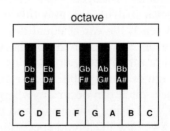

To get the sound of the octave in your ear, try singing *Over the Rainbow* and *Take Me Out to the Ball Game*. Both begin with a leap up of an octave no matter on what pitch you choose to start.

Notating Melodies

The type of notation used for the two tunes in example 2–15 is useful if you merely need to be reminded of how a melody goes, but it is not precise enough to allow a singer to produce the tune if he or she didn't know it already. When the melody goes up, how *far* up does it go? More precision for musical notation began to appear in the West as early as the eleventh century, when notes came to be situated on lines and spaces so that the exact distance between pitches could be judged immediately. This gridwork of lines and spaces came to be called a **staff.** The higher on the staff the note is placed, the higher the pitch.

EXAMPLE 2–17

The staff is always provided with a **clef sign** to indicate the range of pitch in which the melody is to be played or sung. One clef, called the **treble clef,** designates the upper range and is appropriate for high instruments like the trumpet or violin, or a woman's voice. A second clef, called the **bass clef,** covers the lower range and is used for lower instruments like the trombone or cello, or a man's voice.

EXAMPLE 2–18

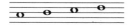

For a single vocal part or a single instrument, a melody could easily be placed on either one of these two clefs. But for two-hand keyboard music with greater range, both clefs are used, one on top of the other. The performer looks at this combination of clefs, called the **great staff,** and relates the notes to the keys beneath the fingers. The space between the two clefs is filled in by a short, temporary line called a ledger line. On the keyboard it indicates middle C (the middle-most note on the piano).

EXAMPLE 2–19

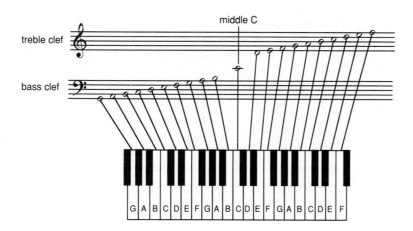

Each musical pitch can be referred to by a letter name, like C, as well as represented by a note placed on the great staff. Only seven letter names are used because, as we have said, melodies were originally made up of only seven pitches within each octave—the seven white notes of the keyboard. When the pitch is duplicated at the octave, the letter name repeats (see example 2–19). But gradually, the spaces between the white keys were divided and additional (black) keys inserted. This increased the number of pitches within the octave from seven to twelve. Since they were not originally part of the staff, the five additional pitches were not represented by a line or space, nor were they given a separate letter name. Instead, they came to be indicated by a symbol, either a sharp or a flat, applied to one of the existing notes. A **sharp (#)** raises the note to the key immediately above, usually a black one, whereas a **flat (♭)** lowers it to the next key below, again usually a black one. A **natural (♮),** on the other hand, cancels either of the two previous signs. Here, as an example of musical notation on the great staff, is a well-known melody as it might be notated for a chorus of male and female voices, the women an octave higher than the men. To keep things simple, the melody is notated in equal whole notes (without rhythm).

EXAMPLE 2–20

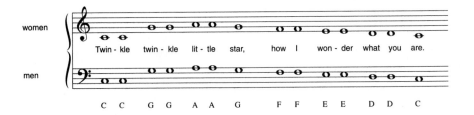

Tonality, Keys, and Scales

Melodies have a central pitch, called the **tonic,** around which they gravitate and on which they usually end. The organization of music around a central tone, the tonic, is called **tonality.** In the case of *Twinkle, Twinkle,* C is the tonic—the tune not only ends on C but happens to begin on C as well. A melody may, in fact, have C or D or F#, or any other of the twelve notes within the octave, as the tonic. In addition, we say that *Twinkle, Twinkle* is written in the tonality, or key, of C major, meaning that it has the tonic C, but also that it makes use of a C major scale. A **key,** then, is a tonal center built on a tonic note and making use of a scale.

But what is a scale? A **scale** is an arrangement of pitches that ascends and descends in a fixed and unvarying pattern. Almost all Western melodies are written in one of two types of scales, either major or minor. To understand the difference between the major and minor scale, it's necessary to go back and look at a keyboard for a moment (see example 2–19). Notice that there are no black keys between B and C and between E and F. All the white notes of the keyboard are not the same distance apart. The difference, or distance, in sound between B and C is only half of that between C and D. B to C is the interval of a half step, while C to D is the interval of a whole step. The major and minor scales, in turn, are built on two distinctly different patterns of whole and half steps, each starting on a tonic note. The major scale has a succession of whole and half steps that proceeds 1–1–1/2–1–1–1–1/2. The minor scale goes 1–1/2–1–1–1/2–1–1. Every scale uses only seven of the available twelve pitches within each octave, and once the octave is reached, the pattern can start over again. A major or minor scale may begin on any of the twelve notes within the octave, and thus there are twelve major and twelve minor scales and keys. Here are the notes of the major and minor scales as they start on C and then on A. Next time you pass by a piano, try playing these in order to get the sound of major and minor in your ear.

major and minor scales

EXAMPLE 2–21

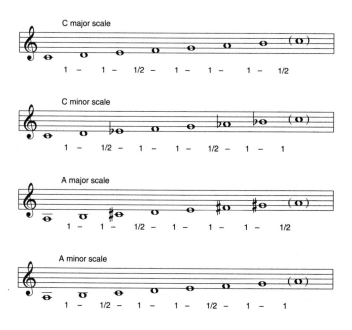

A major scale built on C uses only the white notes of the keyboard, as does a minor scale constructed on A. When begun on a note other than C, for the major scale, or A, for the minor scale, however, sharps and flats are needed so that the pattern of whole and half steps does not vary. For example, a major scale may begin on A and ascend up the octave, but to keep the major scale pattern intact, the notes C, F, and G must be sharped (see example 2–21). Similarly, starting the minor scale pattern on C will require that E be lowered to E♭, A to A♭, and B to B♭ (see example 2–21). Composing a piece in A major would require writing out many sharps, just as one in C minor would require writing many flats. To avoid this labor, musicians have developed the custom of "preplacing" the sharps and flats at the beginning of the staff. The sharps and flats are then active throughout the piece. Preplaced sharps or flats are called a **key signature.**

key signatures

EXAMPLE 2–22

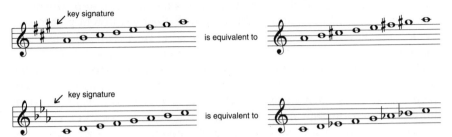

Key signatures indicate to the performer the key in which a piece is written, that is, they show what scale is about to be employed and what the tonic note is.

MODULATION.   Modulation is the change from one key to another. Most short pieces—folk songs, hymns, and the like—don't modulate; they stay in one key. But longer pieces need to modulate or the listener is soon bored. Modulation gives a dynamic sense of movement to music. As the composer Arnold Schoenberg (1874–1951) has said, "Modulation is like a change of scenery." The beginning listener will find modulations difficult to hear. You may not recognize precisely when they occur, but you will sense, however subconsciously, that the music is changing from one key to another.

HEARING MAJOR AND MINOR. Scales are like colors on an artist's palette. A composer will choose what he or she believes is the right scale to achieve the desired musical mood or feeling for the composition. The differences in mood or color within each of the two principal melodic types, major and minor, are small and are not commonly agreed on even by professional musicians. Some say D major is a bright key, F major comfortable and restful, D♭ major dark and rich. But what may seem rich to one listener may sound bright to the next. Taste in music, as in the other arts, is a very personal matter.

One thing we can all agree on, however, is that a melody in a major key sounds decidedly different from one in minor. Major melodies seem bright, cheery, optimistic, while minor ones are dark, somber, even ominous. Try singing the beginning of the following familiar major and minor songs to establish firmly in your mind's ear the difference between major and minor:

EXAMPLE 2–23

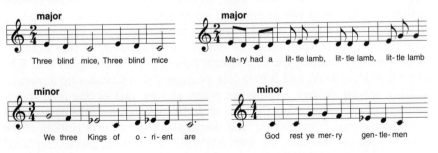

Dances, school songs, hymns, and marches are overwhelmingly in major, whereas laments, Masses for the Dead, and funeral marches have traditionally been written in minor. But the major and minor scales are constructed according to distinctly different patterns of whole and half steps (see example 2–21), and this is why they affect us in different ways. The change from a major key to a minor one with the same tonic (C major to C minor, for example), or from minor to major (F minor to F major, for example) is called a change of **mode.** Lest there be any doubt that a change in mode can change how you feel about a melody, listen to the following familiar tunes (your instructor will play them for you). The mode in each has been changed from major to minor by inserting a flat into the scale near the tonic note (C). Notice here how all the happiness, joy, and sunshine have disappeared from these formerly major tunes.

changing the mode

EXAMPLE 2–24

Now turn to Listening Exercise 5, which asks you to distinguish between melodies in the major and minor mode.

DIATONIC VERSUS CHROMATIC.   Most of the melodies we know are what we call **diatonic** melodies. Meaning that they make use only of the seven notes of the major or minor scale, the so-called diatonic notes. A scale using all twelve notes within the octave, however, is called a **chromatic** scale. In a chromatic scale all twelve pitches are a half step apart.

EXAMPLE 2–25

Chromatic (from the Greek *chroma,* "color") is a good word for this scale because the additional five pitches do indeed add color and richness to a melody. Here is a popular tune that begins by using a chromatic scale.

EXAMPLE 2–26

In general, chromatic melodies sound more intense, tight, and angular than diatonic ones.

Melodic Structure

Beethoven's Ode to Joy

Difficult as it is to say why some melodies are so pleasing and others so dull, all good melodies seem to have a few essential qualities: a strong tonic note, forward motion, a goal or climax, and ultimately a feeling of repose or completion. These qualities are all found in abundance in the *Ode to Joy* by Ludwig van Beethoven (1770–1827). Beethoven originally composed this music for the last movement of his Symphony No. 9 (1824), but in more recent times the melody has been used as a Christmas carol, a hymn for the United Nations, a movie score *(Die Hard)*, and even a pop-rock tune. Here the melody is notated in the bass clef in D major, the key in which Beethoven composed it.

EXAMPLE 2–27

We can make a few general observations about Beethoven's melody: First, notice that it moves mainly by **step,** from one letter name of the scale to the next (D to E, for example), and rarely moves by **leap,** a jump of one or more letter names (D to F#, or D to G, for example). Melodies that move predominantly by step are called **conjunct** melodies, while those that move mainly by leap are called **disjunct** ones. *Ode to Joy* may be the most conjunct melody ever written! The only leaps of any importance are the two at the end of phrase **c** (measure 12).

Next, notice that there are, in fact, four melodic phrases here. A **phrase** in music functions much like a dependent phrase or clause within a grammatical sentence; it constitutes a dependent idea within a melody. Here four four-measure phrases form a complete sixteen-bar melody. Let's concentrate for a moment on the first two phrases. The opening phrase **(a)** begins on the third step of the D major scale, F#, and ends on the second step, E. If you try to sing, hum, or whistle this first phrase, you will notice that when you get to the end ("Elysium") the music doesn't sound complete or finished—it wants to go on. By the end of the second phrase **(b),** however, you arrive on the tonic note ("welcome") and now do have a feeling of arrival and completion. Many melodies begin this way: The initial phrase opens the melody and ends on some note *other* than the tonic; the second phrase answers this idea and returns the melody to the tonic. Two phrases that work in tandem this way are called **antecedent** and **consequent** phrases. Both end with a cadence. A **cadence** is a musical resting place at the end of a phrase. The cadence at the end of Beethoven's antecedent phrase does not sound final, and therefore is called a **half cadence;** the one at the end of his consequent phrase, because it ends on the tonic, does sound complete and is called a **full cadence.**

Ode to Joy then pushes off in a new direction **(c).** The music gains momentum by means of a repeating rhythm in measures 10–11 and reaches a musical climax in measure 12 with the two leaps. The fourth and final phrase is an almost exact repeat of the second phrase **(b),** with the exception of one interesting detail (see *in example 2–27). Beethoven brings the return of this phrase in one beat early—a bit of rhythmic syncopation—thereby giving an unexpected lift to the melody.

The melodic structure of Beethoven's *Ode to Joy*—balanced groups of four-bar phrases arranged antecedent–consequent–extension–consequent—is found frequently in music, from the works of Haydn, Mozart, and Beethoven in the eighteenth and early nineteenth centuries to popular songs of nineteenth- and twentieth-century America. You may have been singing antecedent–consequent phrases and using full and half cadences all your life and not been aware of it. To prove the point, sing the following two well-known tunes:

The Saints Go Marching In (traditional)

"Oh when the saints, go marching in, oh when the saints go marching in" (antecedent phrase)	(half cadence)
"Oh how I want to be in that number, when the saints go marching in." (consequent phrase)	(full cadence)

Oh Suzanna (Stephen Foster)

"Oh I come from Alabama with my banjo on my knee" (antecedent phrase)	(half cadence)
"I'm bound for Louisiana my true love for to see." (consequent phrase)	(full cadence)

Now do Listening Exercise 6, which invites you to become more familiar with the melodic structure of Beethoven's famous *Ode to Joy.*

Hearing Melodies

Hearing melodies may be the single most important part of listening to music. Melodies contain the main musical ideas the composer wishes to communicate. Once a composer has hit on a good melody, he or she is likely to repeat or elaborate on it several times in the course of a composition. Beethoven, for example, brings back his *Ode to Joy* in various guises at least a half-dozen times in his Symphony No. 9. Indeed, by reintroducing a melody at certain important moments in a work, the composer reveals the form, or structure, of the musical creation. It is important, therefore, that the listener be able to seize on the melody, to remember it over a span of time, and to recognize its return, as if welcoming an old friend.

How do we improve our ability to hear melodies and recognize their return? The best way is perhaps not to try to take in an entire melody, or even a full phrase, at once. A melody can move by rapidly, and the beginning listener can expect to absorb only three to four seconds of it at a time. Instead of trying to grasp everything at once, grab hold of some small part of the melody. Find a distinctive rhythmic figure of three or four notes, or a *melodic motives*   salient melodic motive. A **motive** in music is a short, distinctive melodic figure that stands by itself. Concentrate on this one figure and lock it into your mind by asking: What is it doing? Does it jump up rapidly? If so, by a lot or just a little? Does it move down by step? Does it repeat a note in some distinctive way? Does it end on the same pitch as it began? To do this it is helpful to visualize, even draw a picture of, the melodic motive that you seize on. Listening Exercise 7 is designed to help you construct a visual image of the musical sounds you hear. While taking hold of some striking feature of the melody, you may come to discover some broader aspects of the music, such as its meter (duple or triple) or its mode (major or minor).

FIGURE 2–2

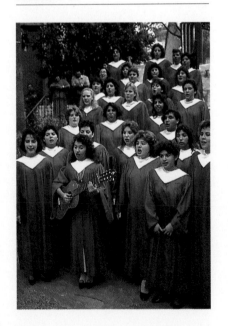

H ARMONY

Melody provides a lyrical voice for music, rhythm gives vitality and definition to that voice, while harmony adds depth and richness to it, just as the dimension of depth in painting adds a rich backdrop to that art. Although melody can and does sometimes stand by itself, most often it is closely bound to, and, indeed, grows out of, the harmony. The two work gracefully in tandem, the harmony supporting and amplifying the melody. Sometimes, however, discord arises—as when a folksinger strumming a guitar suddenly hits a wrong chord—and the result can be startling. The melody and harmony now clash: They are out of harmony. The double sense of this last statement shows that the term **harmony** has several meanings. Broadly speaking, harmony means the peaceful cohabitation of diverse elements; the ancient Greeks, for example, spoke of the unheard harmony of the planets and of the soul. When applied specifically to music, harmony is said to be the sounds that provide a support and enrichment—an accompaniment—for melody. Finally, we often speak of harmony as if it was a specific musical event, as when we say the harmony changes, meaning that one chord in the accompaniment changes to another. Thus, we say that the cowboy ballad *The Streets of Laredo* is a harmonious piece, harmonized in the key of F major, and that the harmony changes fifteen times:

EXAMPLE 2–28

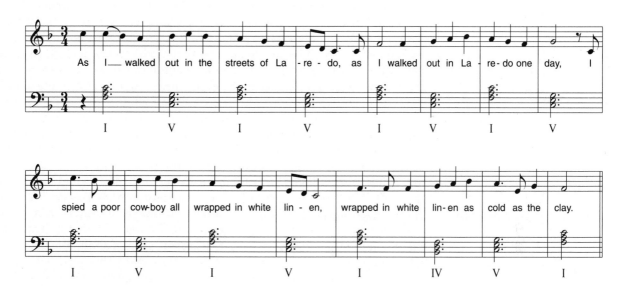

Building Harmony

Chords are the building blocks of harmony. A **chord** is simply a group of two or more pitches that sound at the same time. When we learn to play guitar or jazz piano, we first learn mainly how to construct chords. The basic chord in music is the **triad,** so called because it consists of three pitches arranged in a very specific way. Here is a C major triad:

EXAMPLE 2–29

Note that it comprises the first, third, and fifth notes of the C major scale. The distance between each of these notes is called an **interval.** C to E, spanning three letter names (C,D,E) is the interval of a third. E to G, again spanning three letter names (E,F,G) is another third. Triads always consist of two intervals of a third placed one on top of another. Here are triads built on every note of the C major scale:

EXAMPLE 2–30

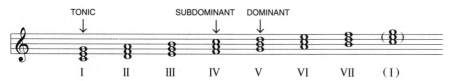

These triads provide all the basic chords that are necessary to harmonize a melody in C major. Notice that each of the chords is given a Roman numeral, indicating on which note of the scale the triad is built, and that the triads built on I, IV, and V are called the **tonic, subdominant, dominant** chords. We have already met the tonic note in our discussion of melody—it is the pitch around which a tune gravitates and on which it ends. Similarly, the tonic chord, or triad, is the "home" chord of the harmony. It is the most stable and the one toward which the other chords move. The **dominant** triad, always built on the fifth note of the scale, is next in importance. Note in *The Streets of Laredo* how most of the melody is harmonized simply by changing back and forth between tonic and dominant triads. Dominant triads are especially likely to move to tonic triads at the ends of a musical phrase where such a movement (V–I) helps create the strong effect of a full cadence*. The **subdominant** triad is built on the note below the dominant, and it frequently moves to the dominant which, in turn, moves to the tonic (IV–V–I). A movement of chords in a purposeful fashion like this is called a

chord progressions
    chord progression. The end of *The Streets of Laredo* is marked by a subdominant–dominant–tonic chord progression (IV–V–I), one that is heard frequently in music and, perhaps for that reason, gives a solid, reliable feeling to the harmony.

The notes of a triad need not always enter together but can be spaced out over time. Such a broken or staggered triad is called an **arpeggio.** Arpeggios can appear either as part of the melody or in the harmony that supports a melody. An arpeggio used in an accompaniment usually gives the listener the sense that the harmony has more substance than it really does. In example 2–31, the beginning of *The Streets of Laredo* is harmonized with the triads spaced out as arpeggios (beneath the brackets). The supporting triads are the same as in example 2–28, but now the accompaniment seems more active because one note of the triad is sounding on every beat:

EXAMPLE 2–31

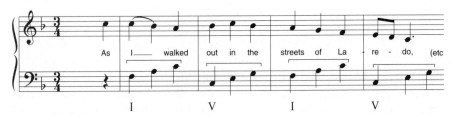

Consonance and Dissonance

You have undoubtedly noticed, when pressing the keys of the piano at one time or another, that some combinations of keys produce a harsh, jarring sound, while others are pleasing and harmonious. The former chords are characterized by **dissonance** (pitches sounding disagreeable and unstable) and the latter by **consonance** (pitches sounding agreeable and stable). Generally speaking, chords that contain pitches that are very close together, just a half or a whole step apart, sound dissonant. On the other hand, chords that involve a third, a somewhat larger interval, are usually consonant. Each of the triads built on the notes of the major scale (see example 2–30), for example, contains two intervals of a third and therefore is consonant. Dissonant chords add a feeling of tension and anxiety to music; consonant ones produce a sense of rest and stability. Composers have traditionally used dissonant chords sparingly, like a hot spice. They prepare them carefully in a bed of consonance and then immediately resolve them—move them—back to a consonance. Our musical psyche demands this constant ebb and flow between the tension of dissonance and the stability of consonance.

Hearing the Harmony Change

Chords move from consonance to consonance, from consonance to dissonance, from dissonance to consonance, and sometimes, in modern music, from dissonance to dissonance. The rate of change may be rapid or slow, regular or irregular. In *The Streets of Laredo* (example 2–28), the rate of harmonic change is moderately fast and regular. There are three beats for each chord and then a new chord appears, without exception, at the beginning of each group of three (each new measure). Composers can alter the rate at which new chords appear in order to achieve particular effects. A rapid rate of change communicates to the listener a feeling of movement and perhaps tension. A deceleration in the speed with which chords change from one to the next can convey a sense of slowing down and relaxation, even though the tempo of the piece (the real speed at which it is moving) remains the same. Handel (1685–1759) and Beethoven (1770–1827) were especially fond of slowing down the rate of harmonic change toward the end of a piece in order to give it a feeling of conclusion, to tell the listener that the piece, in fact, is at an end.

varying the rate of harmonic change

The first step to listening to harmony is to focus your attention on the bass, separating it from the higher melody line. Chords are often built upon the bass note, and a change in the bass from one pitch to another may signal a change in chord. Concentrating on the bass at first will not be easy. Most of us have always thought that listening to music is listening to melody. Certainly, hearing melody is crucial. But the bass is next in importance, and it rules supreme in a sort of subterranean world. It carries the chords and determines where the harmony is going, more so than the higher melody. Baroque music (1600–1750) usually has a clear, driving bass line, and hard rock music perhaps even more so. Next time you listen to a piece of rock, follow the bass guitar line instead of the melody and lyrics. See if you don't begin to sense when the chords are changing and when you have reached a chord that feels like the home key (the tonic triad). Listening Exercise 8 helps you to focus on the bass and begin to recognize when the harmony changes form one chord to the next.

importance of the bass line

LISTENING EXERCISES

2 Identification of Rhythm

(a) In this exercise you are asked to recall and listen to rhythms that are already in your musical memory. Following are the opening text and rhythm of several well-known songs. Place the correct note values above the unnotated portion of the text in order to complete the rhythm for the entire phrase. For example:

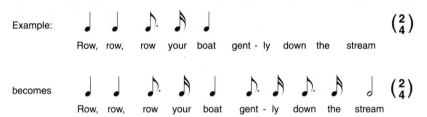

(If you are unfamiliar with one or more of these tunes, feel free to substitute your own. Simply write out the text and then try to indicate the musical rhythm above it by writing in the note values.)

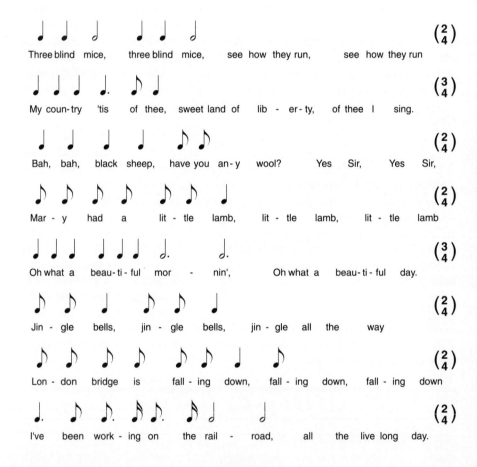

(b) Now that you have read about meters and times signatures (pages 17–18), complete this exercise by inserting the bar lines and beats (1 2, or 1 2 3) for each of the preceding examples. The meter for each example is either $\frac{2}{4}$ or $\frac{3}{4}$, and each begins with a downbeat, not a pickup. For example:

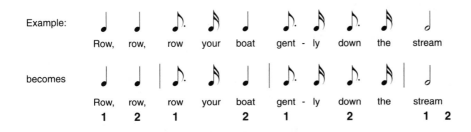

Identification of Meters

3

On your Introduction to Listening tape (side A), you have ten short musical excerpts each played once (you'll probably want to rewind the tape for additional hearings). Identify the meter of each excerpt. To do this, you should listen for the beat, count 1–2 or 1–2–3, and get your conductor's beat pattern in synchrony with the music (downbeat of the hand with the downbeat of the music). If you have done it correctly, the completion of each full conductor's pattern will equal one measure. All the pieces are in duple ($\frac{2}{4}$) or triple ($\frac{3}{4}$) meter, and all begin with the downbeat.

1. Meter —————— (Chopin, Grande Valse brillante in E♭)
2. Meter —————— (Sousa, March: *Stars and Stripes Forever*)
3. Meter —————— (Beethoven, Variations on *God Save the King*)
4. Meter —————— (Schubert, Scottish Dance in A♭)
5. Meter —————— (Johann Strauss, *Blue Danube Waltz*)
6. Meter —————— (Beethoven, Symphony No. 8, first movement)
7. Meter —————— (Beethoven, Symphony No. 8, second movement)
8. Meter —————— (Mozart, Symphony No. 36, fourth movement)
9. Meter —————— (Scott Joplin, *The Entertainer*)
10. Meter —————— (Schubert, *Original Dance*, No. 36)

Identification of Meters

4

Below are listed eight pieces of classical music and jazz that are found on the CDs and tapes for this book. Your task is to listen to each and identify the meter of the piece. Find the music on the CDs or tapes and begin listening. Try to feel the beat. Then get your conducting pattern in sync with the music, making sure that your downbeat comes with the strongest beat in the music. Remember, if you have just one weak beat between each strong beat, then the piece is in duple meter ($\frac{2}{4}$), if you have two, it is in triple meter ($\frac{3}{4}$).

1. Handel, "Hallelujah" chorus from *Messiah* (1741) (CD 2/6; 6–Tape 2A, 2–Tape 1A): meter —————
2. Mozart, Symphony No. 40 in G minor (1788), first movement (CD 2/15; 6–Tape 2B, 2–Tape 1B): meter —————

3. Ravel, *Bolero* (1928) (CD 1/1; Introduction to Listening tape, side A): meter _____

4. Louis Armstrong, *Droppin Shucks* (1926) (CD 6/17; 6–Tape 6B): meter _____

5. Medieval dance, *The Spanish Tune* (ca. 1470) (CD 1/5; 6–Tape 1A): meter _____

6. Mozart, minuet from *A Little Night Music* (1787) (CD 2/10; 6–Tape 2B): meter _____

7. Jean-Joseph Mouret, *Rondeau* from *Suite de symphonies* (1729) (CD 2/7; 6–Tape 2A, 2–Tape 1A): meter _____

8. Haydn, minuet from Symphony No. 94 (1791) (CD 2/12; 6–Tape 2B): meter _____

---

5 Hearing Major and Minor Melodies

On your Introduction to Listening tape (side A) you will find ten musical excerpts that will help you begin to differentiate a piece in a major key from one in a minor key. Each is preceded by the major or minor scale that is used for the excerpt, so you can more readily identify whether the piece is in major or minor. For most listeners, melodies in major are bright, cheerful, sometimes bland, whereas those in minor tend to be darker, more somber, sometimes exotic, even oriental, in sound. Again, each excerpt is played just once, but you can rewind the tape to hear it as many times as you like.

1. _____ (Mozart, Piano Sonata, K. 331)
2. _____ (Chopin, Mazurka, Opus 7, No. 3)
3. _____ (Beethoven, Variations on a theme of Paisiello)
4. _____ (Schumann, *Träumerei (Dreaming)* from *Kinderszenen*)
5. _____ (C. P. E. Bach, *Polonaise*)
6. _____ (J. S. Bach, Three-part Invention)
7. _____ (Schubert, Piano Sonata, D. 959)
8. _____ (Beethoven, Piano Sonata, Opus 13)
9. _____ (Chopin, Piano Sonata, Opus 35)
10. _____ (J. S. Bach, Prelude, *The Well-Tempered Clavier*, Book I)

---

6 Hearing Melodic Structure
Ludwig van Beethoven, *Ode to Joy* from Symphony No. 9 (1824)

On your Introduction to Listening tape (side A), you have an excerpt from the last movement of Beethoven's Symphony No. 9, in which his famous *Ode to Joy* can be heard. You are likely familiar with the tune already, but look at it again as it is given on page 28. Try to get the antecedent **(a)**, consequent **(b)**, and extension **(c)** phrases firmly in your ear. Now listen to the music on your tape. The melody is actually heard four times, first played softly by the low string instruments, then more loudly by the higher strings, then louder still by yet higher strings, and finally loudest of all by the trumpets and full orchestra.

Your task is to prepare a listening guide indicating when each phrase occurs. Get a digital watch or one with a sweep hand, and indicate in the blanks the minute and second when each phrase occurs. (Notice that Beethoven actually repeats the extension **(c)** and consequent **(b)** phrases at the end of each of the four presentations of the melody.) Some of the timings have already been inserted to help you along.

After you have filled in the blanks, go back and treat yourself to one final hearing in which you listen unencumbered to the growing power of Beethoven's melody.

Playing Number:	1 Low strings (double basses)	2 Higher strings (2nd violins)	3 Higher strings (1st violins)	4 Trumpets with full orchestra
Antecedent	**a** 0:00	**a** 0:49	**a** 1:40	**a** 2:30
Consequent	**b** 0:08	**b** :___	**b** :___	**b** :___
Extension	**c** :___	**c** :___	**c** :___	**c** :___
Consequent	**b** :___	**b** :___	**b** :___	**b** :___
	(repeat)	(repeat)	(repeat)	(repeat)
Extension	**c** 0:32	**c** 1:23	**c** 2:13	**c** 3:03
Consequent	**b** :___	**b** :___	**b** :___	**b** :___

---

7 Melodic Graphing

One of the biggest challenges for any listener is to lock onto the important motives and melodies as they unfold in a musical composition. Constructing a visual image of the music is often a good way of grasping more surely what you hear. In this assignment we once again make use of melodies that you know. For the following melodies, sing, whistle, or hum the tune and then try to construct a melodic graph that shows the relative distance between the pitches. You don't have to get the exact proportions between pitches, just the general contour or shape of the tune. Nor do you have to be concerned at this point with the rhythm. Here are two completed examples to give you the idea. Later, when you listen to a symphony of Mozart or Beethoven, you will be better prepared to draw a picture, either actual or mental, of the melody that you hear. Again, if you don't know one or more of these tunes, substitute one of your own. Simply write down the text and draw a melodic graph of the melody above it.

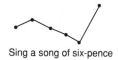

Sing a song of six-pence

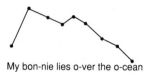

My bon-nie lies o-ver the o-cean

1. Joy to the world, the Lord has come

2. Jin-gle bells, jin-gle bells, jin-gle all the way

3. Should old ac-quain-tance be for-got and nev-er brought to mind (*Auld Lang Syne*)

4. Row, row, row your boat gent-ly down the stream.

5. Yes-ter-day, all my trou-bles seemed so far a-way (Lennon/McCartney)

6. Ru-dolph the red-nosed rein-deer, had a ver-y shin-y nose

7. The hills are a-live, with the sound of mu-sic (*Sound of Music*)

8. Oh say can you see, by the dawn's ear-ly light *(Star Spangled Banner)*

9. Oh beau-ti-ful, for spa-cious skies *(America)*

10. For he's a jol-ly good fel-low

8	Hearing Chord Changes in the Harmony
	Listening to Music Blues

The following exercise encourages you to focus on the bass and the chords that support a melody, rather than the melody itself. The music you hear (Introduction to Listening tape, side A) consists of three improvisations on a standard blues chord progression. The rate at which the chords of the harmony change is slow to moderately slow. It is also irregular, meaning that sometimes a chord is held for many beats and sometimes only for a few. In this performance the left hand of the electronic keyboard player holds one chord until it is time to move on to the next. Each time it stops holding and moves elsewhere, we have a new chord. Below you are asked to fill in a time log for the chord changes in this repeating blues harmony. Get a digital watch or one with a second hand and record the minute and second that each chord changes. A few of the correct times are already filled in to make your task easier.

There are several traditional blues harmonies. The one employed here is an old standard that uses the repeating chord progression tonic (I), subdominant (IV), tonic (I), dominant (V), subdominant (IV), tonic (I) to carry the blues tune. The blues and its history are discussed in Chapter 19, but for now let's just concentrate on the harmony.

1. 0:00 ____   ____   ____   ____   ____
    I   IV   I   V   IV   I

2. 0:25 ____   ____   ____   ____   ____
    I   IV   I   V   IV   I

3. 0:50 ____   ____   ____   ____   1:10
    I   IV   I   V   IV   I

KEY WORDS

arpeggio	downbeat	modulation
bass clef	great staff	motive
beat	harmony	pickup
cadence	key	rhythm
chord	key signature	syncopation
chord progression	major scale	tonality
chromatic	melody	tonic
diatonic	meter	treble clef
dominant chord	minor scale	triad

MUSICAL COLOR,
TEXTURE, AND FORM

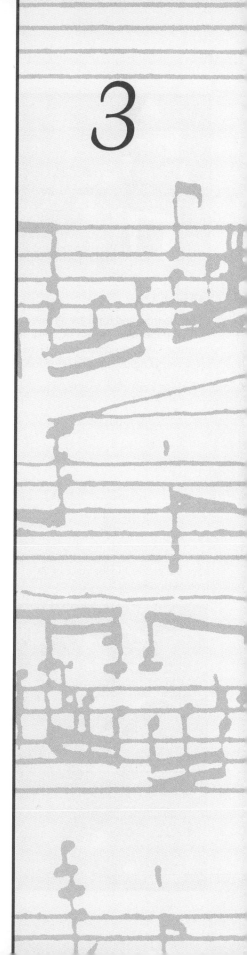

3

Every musical composition is made up of a number of elements, just as every painting has a number of components to it. Color, texture, and form are important in both these arts. They are the broad, general qualities of a work that help give it its meaning and structure. Form in music is the general shape of a composition as perceived by the listener. It usually becomes apparent only gradually as the work progresses from beginning to end. Color and texture, on the other hand, are qualities that may be obvious to the listener immediately. We may be struck by a particular melody, not so much because of its pitches or rhythm, but because it is played on a brilliant-sounding instrument like the trumpet. Or we may be captivated by a musical climax, not because the melody at that point is particularly original, but because the full sound of a large orchestra is heard for the first time—the musical texture has gained impressive substance. Color and texture, then, are less musical ideas in themselves and more ways of expressing ideas. Nonetheless, color and texture can be crucial to the success of a work. Imagine how boring Ravel's *Bolero* would be if the melody returned each time in the same instrument or if the texture remained the same because no new instruments were added. The interest in *Bolero* lies not in the melody itself but in the changing colors and textures in which that melody is clothed (see page 8).

COLOR

Simply said, **color** in music is the tone quality of any sound produced by a voice or an instrument. **Timbre** is another term for the tone quality of musical sound. Instruments produce sounds of different colors, or timbres, because they are constructed in different ways and of different materials. We need not go into the acoustical reasons why this is so—instinctively, we all recognize that the sound of a flute has a different tone quality than that of a trombone. Similarly, the voice of pop singer Bruce Springsteen has a different timbre to it than that of opera star Luciano Pavarotti (Fig. 3–2), even

FIGURE 3–1

Color, texture, and form are all essential components in Picasso's Cubist painting *Three Musicians* (1921). Here color works rigidly to elucidate form.

FIGURE 3–2

Opera singer Luciano Pavarotti, perhaps the greatest tenor voice of the twentieth century.

when the two produce the same pitches. Since the human voice was probably the first "instrument" to make music, let's start our investigation of musical color with it.

The Voice

The human voice is an instrument of a very special sort that naturally generates sound without the aid of any kind of mechanical contrivance. It is highly expressive, in part because it can produce an enormously wide range of sounds.

When we sing we force air up through our vocal chords causing them to vibrate. Men's vocal chords are longer and thicker than women's, and for that reason the sound of the male voice is lower. (This principle is also at work with the string instruments: The longer and thicker the string, the lower the pitch.) Voices are classified by range into four principal parts. The two women's vocal parts are the **soprano** and **alto,** and the two men's parts the **tenor** and the **bass.** The soprano is the highest voice and the bass the lowest. When many voices join together, they form a **chorus;** the soprano, alto, tenor, and bass constitute the four standard choral parts. In addition, the area of pitch shared by the soprano and alto is sometimes designated as a separate vocal range called the **mezzo-soprano,** just as the notes adjoining the tenor and bass are said to be encompassed by the **baritone** voice.

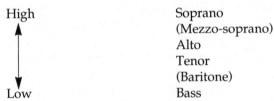

| High ↕ Low | Soprano (Mezzo-soprano) Alto Tenor (Baritone) Bass |

The voice is capable of producing many different styles of singing: the raspy sound of a blues singer, the twang of the country balladeer, the gutsy belt of a Broadway songster, or the lyrical tones of an operatic soprano. We all try to sing, and we would like to sing well. How well we do, and what kind of sound we produce, depends on our training and our physical makeup—the lungs, vocal chords, throat, nose, and mouth are all involved in the production of vocal sound.

Musical Instruments

Musical instruments come in groups, or families. The symphony orchestra traditionally includes four such groups. The first is the string family, so called because these instruments produce sound by plucking or bowing a string. The second and third groups are the woodwind and brass families, both of which generate music by blowing air through a pipe or tube of one sort or another. The fourth group is the percussion family, which makes music—and sometimes just plain noise—usually by striking a stick of some kind on a suspended membrane (a drum), a block of wood, or a piece of metal. In addition, there is a fifth group of instruments, the keyboard instruments, which are not normally part of the symphony orchestra. The organ, harpsichord, and piano are the main keyboard instruments, and they make sound by means of keys and pipes (organ) or keys and strings (harpsichord and piano). The organ is usually played alone, while the piano is most often heard either by itself or as an accompaniment to another solo instrument.

Why does a composer choose a particular instrument to present a melody and not some other? In general, one instrument is chosen over another because of its capacity to express what the composer feels about the music that he or she intends to create. Invariably, the instrument with the tone color best able to portray the composer's feeling about a given musical line—and what the composer wishes to express to the listener—is the one selected. To be able to hear these subtle emotional shadings in music, it is important that we sharpen our awareness of the separate tone colors of the various instruments.

STRINGS. Generally speaking, when we speak of string instruments we broadly include all instruments that produce sound by means of vibrating strings: the guitar, banjo, ukulele, and the harp, as well as the violin and its close relatives, the viola, cello, and double bass. But the guitar, banjo, ukulele, and harp usually produce their sound when plucked, whereas the violin and its relatives are normally played with a bow, not just plucked. Indeed, it is their use of a bow, along with their distinctive shape, that identifies the four members of the violin group. We traditionally associate these instruments with classical music. The guitar, banjo, ukulele, and harp, on the other hand, have their origins in folk music.

Violin Group. The violin group constituted the original core of the symphony orchestra when it was first formed during the Baroque era (1600–1750). In numbers of players, the violins, violas, cellos, and double basses still make up the largest part of any orchestra. A large symphony orchestra can easily include as many as a hundred members, at least sixty of whom play one of these four instruments.

The **violin** is chief among the string instruments. It is also the smallest—it has the shortest strings and therefore the highest pitch. Because of its high range and singing tone, it often is assigned the melody in orchestral and chamber music. The violins are usually divided into groups known as firsts and seconds. The seconds play a part slightly lower in pitch and subordinate in function to the firsts.

The sound of the violin is produced when a bow is pulled across one of four strings held tightly in place by tuning pegs at one end of the instrument and by a tailpiece at the other (Fig. 3–3). The strings are slightly elevated above the wooden body by means of a supporting bridge. Different sounds or pitches are produced when a finger of the left hand shortens or "stops" a string by pressing it against the fingerboard—again, the shorter the string, the higher the pitch. Because each of the four strings can be stopped quickly in many different places, the violin possesses both great range and agility. The strings themselves are made either of animal gut or of metal wire. The singing tone of the violin, however, comes not so much from the strings as from the wooden body, known as the sound box, which amplifies and enriches the sound. The better the design, wood, glue, and varnish of the sound box, the better the tone.

FIGURE 3–3
Violinist Midori

FIGURES 3–4, 3–5, AND 3–6
(left) Violist Yuri Bashmet (center) Cellist Yo-Yo Ma (right) Double bass player Gary Karr.

The **viola** (Fig. 3–4) is about six inches larger than the violin and it produces a somewhat lower sound. If the violin is the string counterpart of the soprano voice, then the viola has its parallel in the alto voice. Its tone is darker, richer, and more somber than the brilliant violin.

You can easily spot the **cello** (violoncello) in the orchestra because the player sits with the instrument placed between the legs (Fig. 3–5). The pitch of the cello is well below that of the viola. It can provide a low bass sound as well as a singing melody. When played in its middle range by a skilled performer, the cello is capable of producing an indescribably rich, expressive tone.

The **double bass** (Fig. 3–6) joined the orchestra to give weight and power to the bass line. Since at first it merely doubled the notes of the cello an octave* below, it was called the double bass. As you can see, the double bass is the largest, and hence lowest sounding, of the string instruments. Its job in the orchestra, and even in jazz bands, is to help set a firm base for the musical harmony.

String Techniques. The members of the violin group all generate pitches in the same way: A bow is drawn across a tight string. This produces the traditional, penetrating string sound. In addition, a number of other effects can be created by using different playing techniques.

pizzicato: Instead of bowing the strings, the performer plucks them. With this technique, the resulting sound has a sharp attack, but it dies away quickly. For a good example of pizzicato, listen again to the beginning of Ravel's *Bolero* where the soft string accompaniment is plucked rather than bowed (CD 1/1; Introduction to Listening tape, side A).

vibrato: By shaking the left hand as it stops the string, the performer can produce a sort of controlled wobble in the pitch. This adds richness to the tone of the string because, in effect, it creates a blend of two or more pitches.

tremolo: The performer creates a musical "tremor" by rapidly repeating the same pitch with quick up and down strokes of the bow. Tremolo creates a feeling of heightened tension and excitement when played loudly, and a velvety, shimmering backdrop when performed quietly.

double-stopping: Normally, a string player will play just one pitch (or note) at a time and then go on to the next. It is possible, however, to bow two adjacent strings simultaneously, and when this is done two notes sound together. This technique is called double-stopping.

mute: If a composer wants to dampen the penetrating tone of a string instrument, he or she can instruct the player to place a mute (a metal or rubber clamp) on the strings of the instrument.

Harp. Although originally a folk instrument, one found in virtually every musical culture, the **harp** (Fig. 3–7) is sometimes added to the modern symphony orchestra. Its role is to add color to the orchestral sound and sometimes to create special effects, the most striking of which is a rapid run up or down the strings called a *glissando*.

WOODWINDS. The name "woodwind" was originally given to this family of instruments because they emit sound when air is blown through a wooden tube or pipe. The pipe has holes along its length, and the player covers or uncovers these to change the pitch. Nowadays, however, some of these woodwind instruments are made entirely of metal. Flutes, for example, are constructed of silver, and sometimes of gold or even platinum. As with the violin group, there are four principal woodwind instruments in every modern symphony orchestra: flute, oboe, clarinet, and bassoon. In addition, each of these has a close relative that is larger or smaller in size and which possesses a somewhat different timbre and range. The larger the instrument or length of pipe, the lower the sound.

FIGURE 3–7

A harp

FIGURE 3–8

(from left to right) A flute, two clarinets, an oboe, and a bassoon.

The lovely, silvery tone of the **flute** is probably familiar to you. The instrument can be rich in the lower register and then light and airy on top. It is especially agile, capable of playing tones rapidly and moving quickly from one range to another.

The smaller cousin of the flute is the **piccolo.** ("Piccolo" comes from the Italian *flauto piccolo,* meaning "little flute".) It can produce higher notes than any other orchestral instrument. And though very small, its sound is so shrill that it can always be heard, even when the full orchestra is playing loudly.

The **clarinet** produces sound when the player blows against a single reed fitted to the mouthpiece. The tone of the clarinet is more mellow than that of the other woodwinds, especially in the lower register of the instrument. It also has the capacity to slide or glide smoothly between pitches, and this allows for a highly expressive style of playing. The flexibility and expressiveness of the instrument have made it a favorite with jazz musicians. A lower, larger version of the clarinet is the **bass clarinet.**

The **oboe** is equipped with a double reed—two reeds tied together with an air space in between. When the player blows into the instrument through the double reed, a nasal, slightly exotic sound is created. It is invariably the oboe that gives the pitch at the beginning of every symphony concert. Not only was the oboe the first nonstring instrument to be added to the orchestra, but it is a difficult instrument to tune. Better have the other instruments tune to it than to try to have it adjust to them.

Related to the oboe is the **English horn.** Unfortunately, it is wrongly named, for the English horn is neither English nor a horn. It is simply a larger variety of the oboe which originated on the continent of Europe. The English horn produces a dark, haunting sound, one that was especially favored by composers of the Romantic period (1820–1900).

The **bassoon** functions among the woodwinds much like the cello does among the strings. It can serve as a bass instrument, adding weight to the lowest sound, or it can act as a soloist in its own right. When playing moderately fast or rapid passages as a solo instrument, it has a dry, almost comic tone. If you are unfamiliar with the sound of the bassoon, go back and listen to *Bolero* where the bassoon presents the melody (at 1:42).

There is also a double bassoon, usually called the **contrabassoon.** Its sound is deep and sluggish. Indeed, the contrabassoon can play lower notes than any other orchestral instrument.

The bassoon, contrabassoon, and English horn are all double reed instruments, just like the oboe. Their tones, therefore, may sound more vibrant, even exotic, than those of the single reed instruments like the clarinet and saxophone.

Strictly speaking, the single reed **saxophone** is not a member of the symphony orchestra, though it can be added on occasion, as Ravel chose to do in *Bolero* (at 4:45). Its sound can be mellow and expressive but also, if the player wishes, shrill and raucous. The expressiveness of the saxophone makes it a welcome member of most jazz ensembles, while the shrill, penetrating tone of the instrument is prized by rock musicians.

BRASSES. Like the woodwind and string groups of the orchestra, the brass family consists of four primary instruments: French horn, trumpet, trom-

FIGURE 3–9

Members of the Canadian Brass.

bone, and tuba. Brass players use no reeds but instead blow into their instruments through a cup-shaped **mouthpiece** (Fig. 3–10). By adjusting valves or moving a slide, the performer can make the length of pipe on the instrument longer or shorter, and hence the pitch lower or higher.

The **French horn** was the first brass instrument to join the orchestra. Its sound is rich and mellow, yet somewhat veiled or covered. Because of this, composers have traditionally used the horn to add warmth and fullness to the orchestral texture. During the Romantic period (1820–1900), the horn not only provided a sonorous glue to bind the tones of the other instruments but also began to emerge as a solo instrument in its own right.

Everyone has heard the high, bright, cutting sound of the **trumpet.** Whether on a parade ground or in an orchestral hall, the trumpet is an excellent solo instrument because of its agility and penetrating tone. When provided with a mute (a plug placed in the bell of the instrument to dampen the sound), it can produce a softer tone that blends well with other instruments. Witness the effective combination of muted trumpet with flute early on in *Bolero* (at 4:00).

Although distantly related to the trumpet, the **trombone** plays in the middle range of the brass family. Sometimes it is possible to confuse the sound of the trombone with that of the French horn, because they are both full and majestic. But the tone of the trombone is somewhat clearer and more focused than that of the horn. Because of its slide, the trombone also has the capacity to glide easily between pitches. A good example of the slide at work can be heard in the trombone solo, once again, in *Bolero* (at 7:48).

The **tuba** is the lowest-sounding instrument of the brass family. It produces a full, though surprisingly muffled tone. Like the double bass of the violin group, the tuba is most often used for setting a base, or foundation, of sound, but not for serving as a solo melodic instrument. In fact, the tuba is perhaps more spectacular in the way it looks, concealing the performer as it does, than in the way it sounds.

FIGURE 3–10

Mouthpieces for brass instruments.

FIGURES 3–11 AND 3–12

(left) A timpanist (right) A xylophone, celesta, and glockenspiel.

PERCUSSION. Percussion instruments are those that are struck in some way, either by hitting the head of a drum with a stick or by banging or scraping a piece of metal or wood in one fashion or another. Some percussion instruments, like the timpani (kettledrums), produce a specific pitch, while others just generate noise without a recognizable musical tone. It is the job of the percussion instruments to sharpen the rhythmic contour of the music. They can also add color to the sounds of other instruments and, when they play loudly, can heighten the sense of climax in a piece. In *Bolero* the snare drum is used to carry the primary rhythmic pattern from beginning to end, the timpani (starting at 9:13) adds color to the accompaniment in the low strings, while the cymbals heighten the intensity of the final climax.

The **timpani** (Fig. 3–11) is the percussion instrument most often heard in classical music. Whether struck in single, detached strokes or hit rapidly to produce a thunderlike roll, the function of the timpani is usually to add depth, tension, and drama to the music. Timpani usually come in pairs, one instrument to play the tonic* note and the other to play the dominant*.

The crashing ring of the **cymbals,** the dull thud of the **bass drum,** and the rat-ta-tat-tat of the **snare drum** are sounds well known from marching bands and jazz ensembles, as well as the classical orchestra. None of these instruments produces a specific musical tone.

On the other hand, a wide spectrum of musical pitches are created by a trio of instruments that generate sound in a rather similar way: the xylophone, glockenspiel, and celesta. The **xylophone** is a set of wooden bars which, when struck by two hard mallets, produce a dry, wooden sound. The **glockenspiel** works the same way, but the bars are made of metal so that the tone is brighter and more ringing. The **celesta,** too, produces sound when hammers strike metal bars, but the hammers are activated by keys, as in a piano; the tone of the celesta is bright and tinkling—a delightful, "celestial" sound, as the name of the instrument suggests.

KEYBOARD INSTRUMENTS. The pipe organ, harpsichord, and piano are our most familiar keyboard instruments. The **pipe organ** (Fig. 3–13), which traces its ancestry back to ancient Greece, is by far the oldest. It works according to a simple principle: The player depresses a key which allows air to rush into or over a pipe, thereby producing sound. The pipes are arranged in separate groups according to their shape and material. Each group produces a full range of musical tones with one special tone quality or color. When the organist wants to bring a particular group of pipes into play, he or she simply pulls a switch, called a **stop.** The most colorful, forceful sound occurs when all the stops have been activated (thus the expression "pulling out all the stops"). The several keyboards of the organ make it possible to play several musical lines at once, each with its own timbre. There is even a keyboard for the feet!

The **harpsichord** (Fig. 3–14) was known in northern Italy as early as 1400, but it reached its heyday during the Baroque era (1600–1750). It produces sound, not by means of pipes, but by strings. When a key is depressed, it drives a lever upward which, in turn, forces a pick to pluck a string. The plucking process creates a bright, jangling sound. Some harpsichords are equipped with two keyboards so that the player can change from one group of strings to another, each with its particular tone color and volume of sound. The harpsichord has one important shortcoming, however: The lever mechanism does not allow the performer to control the force with which the string is plucked, so each string always sounds at the same volume. (For more on the harpsichord, see page 103.)

The **piano** (Fig. 3–15) was invented in Italy in 1709, in part, to remove the dynamic limitations of the harpsichord. In a piano, strings are not plucked but hit by soft hammers. A lever mechanism makes it possible for the player to regulate how hard each string is struck, thus producing softs and louds (the original piano was called the *pianoforte,* the "soft-loud"). During the lifetime of Mozart (1756–1791), the piano replaced the harpsichord as the favorite domestic musical instrument. By the nineteenth century every aspiring household had to have a piano, whether as an instrument for real musical enjoyment or as a symbol of affluence.

If the organ's familiar home is the church where it is heard in association with religious services, the versatile piano is found almost everywhere. With

FIGURE 3–13

A pipe organ found in the Chapel of St. Thomas Aquinas at the University of St. Thomas, Minnesota.

FIGURES 3–14 AND 3–15

(left) A two manual harpsichord built by Pascal Taskin (Paris, 1770) preserved in the Yale University Collection of Musical Instruments. (right) Pianist André Watts.

equal success it can accompany a school chorus or an opera singer; it can harmonize with a rock band when in the hands of an Elton John or a Billy Joel; or it can become a powerful, yet expressive, solo instrument when played by a master such as Vladimir Horowitz or André Watts. The harpsichord, on the other hand, is used mainly to recreate the music of the time of Johann Sebastian Bach (1685–1750).

ELECTRONIC INSTRUMENTS. In addition to these natural musical instruments—acoustical instruments as they are called—machines that produce musical sounds by electronic means have been invented in the twentieth century. The electric keyboard synthesizer has recently gained great favor among rock and jazz musicians because of the variety of sounds it can create and the ease with which it can be moved from job to job. Electronic instruments such as the keyboard synthesizer and electric organ and guitar, as well as the sound-processing computer, are discussed in Chapter 18.

The Orchestra

The modern symphony orchestra is one of the largest and certainly the most colorful of all musical ensembles. It originated in the seventeenth century and has continually grown in size since then. When at full strength, the symphony orchestra can include upward of one hundred performers and nearly thirty different instruments, from the high piping of the piccolo down to the rumble of the contrabassoon. A typical seating plan for an orchestra is given in Figure 3–16. Strings are placed toward the front and the more powerful brasses at the back. Other seating arrangements are also used, according to the composition to be played and the personal preferences of the conductor.

Surprisingly, a separate conductor was not originally part of the orchestra. For the first two hundred years of its existence (1600–1800), the sympho-

FIGURE 3–16

Seating plan of an orchestra.

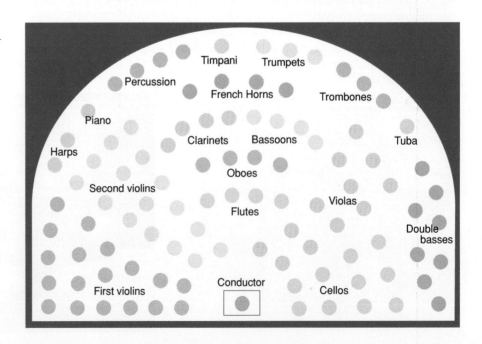

ny was led by one of the performers, often by the principal first violinist. By the time of Beethoven (1770–1827), however, the group had so grown in size that it was thought necessary to have someone stand before it and lead, not only to keep the players together, but also to help draw out and elucidate the important musical ideas. The conductor follows an **orchestral score,** a composite of all the instrumental parts for a particular piece (Fig. 3–17).

the conductor

When hearing a symphony orchestra perform, the listener's first task is to pick out the instruments that are playing the melodies, or main themes, and to differentiate them from the instruments that provide an accompaniment or play some other subordinate role. If you are fortunate enough to attend a "live" performance, the gestures of the conductor can be an aid to your listening, for he or she will usually turn to, and communicate directly with the instruments that are playing the most important musical lines (Fig. 3–18). Listening Exercise 9 gives you the chance to gain greater familiarity with the instruments of the orchestra.

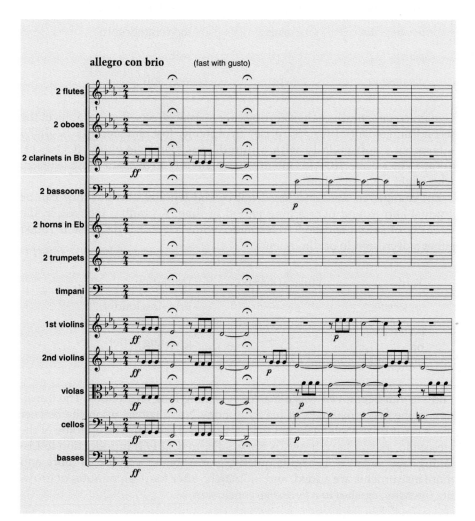

FIGURE 3–17

The orchestral score of the beginning of Beethoven's Symphony No. 5, first page, with instruments listed.

FIGURE 3–18
Conductor Seiji Ozawa of the Boston Symphony Orchestra. By watching the gestures of the conductor, the listener is often able to follow the principal themes as they are passed from player to player or section to section.

Dynamics

Dynamics in music are the various levels of volume, loud and soft, at which sounds are produced. Dynamics work together with tone colors to affect the way we hear and react to musical sound. A high note in the clarinet has one quality—shrill and harsh—when played *fortissimo* (very loud) and quite another—vague and other worldly—when played *pianissimo* (very soft). Below are the names of the most common musical dynamics. Since they were first used by composers working in Italy, these terms are traditionally written in Italian.

Term	Musical Symbol	Definition
fortissimo	ff	very loud
sforzando	sfz	a sudden, loud attack on one note or chord
forte	f	loud
mezzo forte	mf	moderately loud
mezzo piano	mp	moderately soft
piano	p	soft
pianissimo	pp	very soft

Dynamics sometimes change abruptly for special effects. For example, in the second movement of his "Surprise" Symphony, Joseph Haydn (1732–1809) interrupts a soft melody with a thunderous *sforzando* chord (CD 2/11; 6–Tape 2B; 2–Tape 1B)—his intent was apparently to awaken those listeners who might have dozed off!

But changes in dynamics need not be sudden and abrupt. They can be gradual and extend over a long period of time. A gradual increase in the intensity of sound is called a crescendo, while a gradual decrease is called either a decrescendo or diminuendo.

Term	Musical symbol	Definition
crescendo	<	growing louder
decrescendo or *diminuendo*	>	growing softer

Ludwig van Beethoven was a master at writing long crescendos. The transition to the last movement of his Symphony No. 5 comes upon the listener like a great tidal wave of sound (CD 3/9–10; 6–Tape 3B). The epitome of the crescendo, as you have heard, is Ravel's *Bolero* (CD 1/1; Introduction to Listening tape, side A). It begins quietly, gains greater volume as more and more instruments are added, and ultimately, after fourteen minutes of growing intensity, crashes to a *fortissimo* conclusion.

TEXTURE

Texture in music is the density and disposition of the musical lines that make up a musical composition. To understand this better, picture in your mind a tapestry or some other type of woven material. The individual strands, or lines, can be dense or thin; colors can be bunched toward the center or spread out more or less evenly; the lines may have either a strong vertical or a horizontal thrust. Just as a weaver or painter can fabricate a particular texture—dense, heavy, light, or thin, with independent or interdependent strands—so, too, can the composer create similar effects with musical lines. *Bolero* begins with a few, well-spaced lines and hence a thin texture. As more and more instruments are added, the density of the texture increases. By the end, the texture is dense, with the density being about equal from the top instruments to the bottom ones.

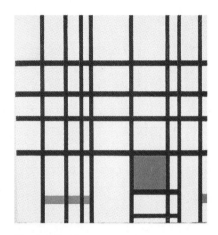

FIGURE 3–19

Piet Mondrian's *Composition with Red, Yellow and Blue* (1939–1942) has a rather thin texture with uneven linear spacing and occasional zones of dense color.

Monophonic, Polyphonic, and Homophonic Textures

There are three primary textures in music—monophonic, polyphonic, and homophonic—depending on the number of musical lines and the way they relate to one another. Often we call these lines, or parts, "voices" even though they may not actually be sung.

Monophonic texture is the easiest to hear. As the name "one sounding" indicates, there is only a single line of music with no accompaniment. When you sing by yourself, you are creating monophonic music. The largest body of monophonic music in the West is Gregorian chant*, one-line melodies created during the Middle Ages as music for the Church (see page 71). Most Gregorian chants were intended to be sung by a group of clerics, all chanting the same pitches together—singing in **unison** as it is called. This adds richness to the otherwise sparse sound of monophonic music.

As you may suppose from the name "many sounding," **polyphonic** texture requires two or more lines in the musical fabric. In addition, the term "polyphonic" also implies that each of the lines will be autonomous and independent. They compete equally for the listener's attention. Usually, they move against one another, and when this happens they create what is called counterpoint. **Counterpoint** is simply the harmonious opposition of two or more independent musical lines. Because counterpoint presupposes polyphony, the terms "contrapuntal texture" and "polyphonic texture" are often used interchangeably.

counterpoint

What is more, there are two types of counterpoint: imitative and free. In imitative counterpoint the individual voices enter separately and the followers duplicate at least a part of what the first, or lead, voice had presented. If they reproduce exactly, note for note, what the first part plays or sings, then a **canon** results. Think of *Three Blind Mice, Are You Sleeping*, or *Row, Row, Row Your Boat*, and remember how each voice enters in turn and then exactly imitates the first voice from beginning to end. These are all short canons, or rounds. Among the more famous longer canons in music is the well-known canon of Johann Pachelbel (1653–1706) that goes on for several minutes. Example 3–1 shows the beginning of a brief canon for three voices:

canon

EXAMPLE 3–1

Free counterpoint is counterpoint without any sort of imitation among the voices. The voices, or lines, may begin all together or begin separately, but they go their separate ways. Much jazz improvisation is done in free counterpoint.

Homophony means "same sounding." In this texture the voices, or lines, move to new pitches at roughly the same time. Homophony, then, differs from polyphony in that the strands are not independent but interdependent; they proceed in a tight, interlocking fashion. Usually, the lines form harmonious blocks of sound, called chords, which support and draw attention to a higher voice that carries the melody. Hymns, Christmas carols, popular songs, and folk songs almost always have a homophonic texture because they consist of a simple melody and blocks of accompanying chords below. Melody plus accompaniment then—perhaps the most common musical arrangement—produces homophonic texture. As the arrows in examples 3–1 and 3–2 show, in polyphonic texture the musical fabric has lines with a strong linear (horizontal) thrust, whereas in homophonic texture the fabric is marked by lines that are more vertically conceived, as blocks of accompany chords.

EXAMPLE 3–2

changing textures

Of course, composers are not limited to just one of these three musical textures within any given work. They can change from one texture to another to add variety and contrast to their music. A monophonic solo can be saved for a particularly expressive moment, a homophonic passage may be needed to create a feeling of comfort and solidity, and a polyphonic section may be desirable to give the piece a sudden sense of movement and tension owing to the independent action of several parts. Usually, the longer the piece, the greater the number of changes. But changes of texture can come in rapid succession in short pieces as well. George Frideric Handel (1685–1759) is perhaps best known as the composer of *Messiah,* a large work for chorus and orchestra usually performed just before Christmas. By far the most familiar number within *Messiah* is the "Hallelujah" chorus for which the audience traditionally rises to its feet.[†] To get the sound of the various textures securely in your ear, listen to this famous chorus. Notice how rapidly and how smoothly the composer moves back and forth among homophonic, polyphonic, and monophonic textures. The following Listening Guide makes it clear where the changes come.

LISTENING GUIDE	George Frideric Handel "Hallelujah" Chorus from *Messiah* (1741)	CD 2/6 6–Tape 2A 2–Tape 1A

0:01	"Hallelujah! Hallelujah!"—homophony
0:25	"For the Lord God Omnipotent reigneth"—monophony
0:32	"Hallelujah! Hallelujah!"—homophony
0:37	"For the Lord God Omnipotent reigneth"—monophony
0:44	"Hallelujah! Hallelujah!"—homophony
0:49	"For the Lord God Omnipotent reigneth" together with "Hallelujah"—polyphony
1:16	"The Kingdom of this world is become,"—homophony
1:35	"And He shall reign for ever and ever"—polyphony
1:58	"King of Kings and Lord of Lords" together with "Hallelujah"—homophony
2:39	"And He shall reign for ever and ever"—polyphony
2:51	"King of Kings and Lord of Lords" together with "Hallelujah"—homophony
3:01	"And He shall reign for ever and ever"—polyphony
3:07	"King of Kings and Lord of Lords" together with "Hallelujah"—homophony

When you have finished, turn to Listening Exercise 10, which asks you to compare the textures of three rather dissimilar musical works.

F ORM

Form in art is the purposeful organization of the artist's materials. It is present in every medium of creative expression. In architecture, sculpture, and painting, for example, the formal design imposes a shape and definition on physical space. In poetry the meter, the rhyme, and the stanza give a sense of logic and coherence to the sounds, ideas, and images. And in music the melody, harmony, rhythm, tone color, and texture can be arranged to create a sequence of events that the composer and listener find pleasing and convincing.

A composer needs formal principles to help in the process of selecting and arranging materials. Nothing is more frightening to a creator than absolute freedom of choice. How to begin? What to write now? What next? When

---

[†] It seems that King George II (ruled 1727–1760) stood up at this point during a performance of *Messiah* in London. If the King stood, so did everyone else, hence the tradition of the audience standing.

and how to end? The selection of a musical form can help with these decisions by suggesting an overall shape as well as a set of operating procedures. Sometimes a composer will create a unique design because the musical material seems to develop in new and surprising ways. Ravel's *Bolero,* for example, continues to grow in the shape of an ever-enlarging wedge. But more often a composer will fall back on a time-honored form. Using a traditional form does not tell the composer what to do at every step, but it does suggest plausible paths that might be taken—paths that other composers at other times have used and with which the listener is likely to be familiar.

composers need formal principles

From the listener's standpoint, an awareness of form is perhaps the most important tool he or she can employ while listening to music. If the composer needs help in setting a broad musical plan, the listener needs formal guideposts as a means of following what the composer is trying to communicate. What has happened? Where am I? What is about to come? These questions are invariably asked, consciously or unconsciously, when hearing a piece for the first time. By working through the discussion and diagrams that follow, you will acquire a mental picture of the most commonly used musical forms. You will more easily comprehend the material that you hear, and be comfortable with it, because you will have met these forms before and now know what to expect. You may also gain satisfaction from hearing the composer deviate from your expectations by treating the traditional time-honored form in some new and surprising fashion.

listeners need formal guideposts

Creating Formal Designs: Repetition, Contrast, and Variation

How are formal designs created in music? By means of repetition, contrast, and variation. **Repetition** establishes the most obvious formal units. When a distinctive melody returns, for example, it strikes the ear as an important event. Such repeating events set forth the outlines of a musical design in the same way that a steel framework outlines and holds together the materials of a building. Repetition is essential to music, perhaps because music is the most abstract of all the arts. Instead of creating tedium or boredom, each return helps to establish weight, balance, and symmetry. Because the musical material is familiar, repetition conveys to the listener a feeling of comfort and security.

repetition

Contrast, on the other hand, takes us away from the familiar and into the unknown. A quiet melody in the strings can suddenly be followed by an insistent theme blasting from the French horns, as happens, for example, in the third movement of Beethoven's well-known Symphony No. 5 (CD 3/9; 6–Tape 3B). Contrasting melodies, rhythms, textures, and moods can be both exciting and disquieting. They are most effective when used as a foil to familiar material, to provide variety, even conflict. In many aspects of our lives we have a need to balance comfort and security with novelty and excitement. In music this human need is given expression through the juxtaposition of the familiar and the unknown—through the interplay of repeating and contrasting musical units.

contrast

Variation stands midway between repetition and contrast. The original melody returns, but it is altered in some way. The tune may now be more

variation

complex or new instruments added against it to create counterpoint, for example. The listener has the satisfaction of hearing the familiar melody, yet is challenged to recognize in what way it has been changed.

Needless to say, memory plays an important role in hearing musical form. In architecture, painting, and sculpture, form is taken in all at once by a single glance. But in music, as to some extent in poetry and literature, formal relationships only become obvious over the course of time. Here our memory must put the pieces together and show us the relationships. For this to happen, we must be able to recognize an exact repetition, a varied repetition, and a contrasting musical event. To help in this process, musicians have developed a simple system to visualize forms by labeling musical units with letters. The first prominent musical idea is designated **A.** Subsequent contrasting sections are each labeled **B, C, D,** and so on. If the first, or any other musical unit returns in varied form, then that variation is indicated by a superscript number: A^1, B^2, for example. Subdivisions of each large musical unit are shown by lower case letters (**a, b,** etc.). How this works will become clear in the following examples.

role of memory

Musical Forms

Most musical forms transcend musical epochs—they are not unique to any one period in the history of music. The following musical forms are universal as well as timeless.

STROPHIC FORM. This is the most familiar of all musical forms because our hymns, carols, folk tunes, and patriotic songs invariably make use of it. In strophic form several musical phrases, each setting a line of text, flow into a single, broad melody that is repeated over and over. A good example is the Welsh holiday carol *Deck the Halls.* Notice how the first phrase **(a)** of the musical unit **(A),** or stanza, is repeated.

	a	Deck the halls with boughs of holly, fa, la, la, la, etc.
	a	'Tis the season to be jolly, fa, la, la, la, la, etc.
A	**b**	Don we now our gay apparel, fa, la, la, la, la, etc.
	c	Troll the ancient Yule-tide carol, fa, la, la, la, etc.

The basic musical unit, **A,** with the subdivision **a, a, b, c,** is then heard four more times for each of the remaining stanzas, or strophes, of text. The overall form is thus:

A	**A**	**A**	**A**	**A**
a a b c	a a b c	a a b c	a a b c	a a b c

THEME AND VARIATIONS. If, in the preceding example, the music of the first strophe **(A)** is altered in some way each time it returns, then theme and variations form is present. Additions to the melody, new chords in the supporting accompaniment, and more density in the texture are the sort of changes that might occur. The return of the basic musical unit **(A)** provides a

FIGURE 3–20

Sydney Opera House seen from Sydney harbor. There is a theme, the rising pointed arch, and many variations of it.

unifying element, while the changes add variety. Theme and variations form can be visualized in the following scheme:

Statement of theme	Variation 1	Variation 2	Variation 3	Variation 4
A	**A**^{1}	**A**^{2}	**A**^{3}	**A**^{4}

A good example of theme and variation form can be found in the second movement of Joseph Haydn's String Quartet, Opus 76, No. 3. Here the composer created a theme **(A)**, which was later to become the Austrian national anthem, and then wrote a set of four variations on it. (For more on this piece, see page 195).

LISTENING GUIDE

Joseph Haydn
String Quartet, Opus 76, No. 3 (1797) Second movement

CD 2/16
6–Tape 2B
2–Tape 1B

0:00	**A**	Theme: theme in first violin supported by homophonic accompaniment
1:19	**A**^{1}	Variation 1: theme varied in second violin
2:35	**A**^{2}	Variation 2: theme varied in cello
4:04	**A**^{3}	Variation 3: theme varied in viola
5:31	**A**^{4}	Variation 4: theme in first violin supported by polyphonic accompaniment

---

BINARY FORM. As the name indicates, binary form consists of two contrasting units, **A** and **B**. In length and general shape, **A** and **B** are constructed so as to balance and complement each other. Variety is usually introduced in **B** by means of a dissimilar mood, key*, or melody. Normally, both **A** and **B** are immediately repeated, note for note. Musicians indicate exact repeats by means of the following sign: | :: |. Thus, the binary form | : **A** : | | : **B** : | is performed **A A B B**.

Johann Sebastian Bach's famous "Air" from his Orchestral Suite No. 3 is a lovely example of binary form. The end of the **A** section—and hence the division between the two units—is easy to hear because the bass, which had been plodding along, suddenly moves faster. As you listen to this piece, see if you can recognize the repeat of **A**, then the beginning of **B**, and finally the repeat of **B**. (This "Air" is discussed further on page 135.)

LISTENING GUIDE

Johann Sebastian Bach
"Air" from Orchestral Suite No. 3 (1730)

CD 1/14
6–Tape 1B
2–Tape 1A

0:00	**A**
0:51	**A** (repeat)
1:41	**B**
3:20	**B** (repeat)

FIGURES 3–21 AND 3–22

(left) Barbara Hepworth, *Two Figures (Menhirs)* (1964). Here the two units of sculpture are distinctly different, yet mutually harmonious. This is the essence of binary form. (right) The cathedral of Salzburg, Austria, where Mozart and his father frequently performed during the 1760s and 1770s. It clearly reflects a ternary, or **ABA** form.

TERNARY FORM. Ternary form in music is even more common than binary. It consists of three sections. The second is a contrasting unit, and the third is a repeat of the first—hence the formal pattern is **ABA**. As we will see later (page 166), ternary form has appeared at many different times in the history of music. It is an especially satisfying arrangement because it is simple yet rounded and complete. It, too, often uses musical repeats, first of the **A** section, then of both **B** and **A** together (| : **A** : | | : **B A** : |). Listen to Robert Schumann's short piano piece *Of Foreign Lands and People* and notice how the **B** section contrasts with **A.** It has a different melody and a darker, more somber mood. Notice, too, that the return to **A** is signaled to the listener each time by a pause at the end of **B.** (For more on this piece, see page 266.)

LISTENING GUIDE		Robert Schumann Piano solo, *Of Foreign Lands and People* from *Kinderszenen* (*Scenes from Childhood*, 1838)	CD 4/6 6–Tape 4A
0:00	**A**	Melody and homophonic texture	
0:15	**A**	(repeat)	
0:30	**B**	Different melody and darker mood	
0:45	**A**	Repeat of opening music	
1:00	**B**	(repeat)	
1:15	**A**	(repeat)	

RONDO FORM. Rondo form is almost as old as music itself. It uses a simple principle: A refrain alternates with contrasting music. Perhaps because of this simplicity, rondo form has been favored by musicians of every age—Medieval songsters, Classical symphonists like Mozart and Haydn, and even contemporary rock stars like Elton John and Sting. Although the principle of a recurring refrain is a constant, composers have written rondos in several different formal patterns including the following:

A B A B A   A B A C A   A B A C A B A

FIGURE 3–23

The chateau of Chambord, France, has a formal design equivalent to **ABACABA** structure, a pattern often encountered in music in the rondo.

You may already be familiar with a rondo composed by Jean-Joseph Mouret (1682–1738), for it is used as the theme music for "Masterpiece Theater" on PBS. Mouret was a composer at the French court during the reign of Louis XV (1715–1774) and his well-known *Rondeau* typifies the ceremonial splendor of the royal household during the Baroque era (1600–1750). Here the refrain **(A)**, played by full orchestra with brilliant trumpets and drums, alternates with two contrasting ideas (**B** and **C**) to form a neatly symmetrical pattern. The divisions between sections are clearly audible because each unit is played by a distinctive group of instruments. As you listen to Mouret's rondo, perhaps you will agree that here a simple, effective formal principle is at work.

LISTENING GUIDE		Jean-Joseph Mouret *Rondeau* from *Suite de symphonies* (1729)	CD 2/7 6–Tape 2A 2–Tape 1A
0:00	**A**	Refrain played by full orchestra including trumpets and drums and then repeated (at 0:12)	
0:24	**B**	Quieter contrasting section with oboes prominent	
0:37	**A**	Refrain returns but without repeat	
0:50	**C**	New contrasting section with oboes and violins	
1:22	**A**	Refrain returns and is repeated (at 1:34)	

Although these examples of musical form are all short, they clearly show that an internal logic and cohesiveness is at work in each piece. More complex musical forms, of course, do exist, and these give rise to longer, more complex compositions. Sonata-allegro form and fugal form are the principal ones. These we will discuss when we come to the music of the Baroque and Classical periods. In addition, there are also free musical forms, such as the fantasy and the prelude, which give free reign to the composer's imagination without tight formal restraints. These, too, we will meet in good time.

LISTENING EXERCISES

9 Instruments of the Orchestra
Benjamin Britten, *The Young Person's Guide to the Orchestra* (1946)

On your Introduction to Listening tape (beginning of side B), you will find a performance of Benjamin Britten's *The Young Person's Guide to the Orchestra.* Britten (1913–1976) wrote this piece in 1946, though he used as his main theme a melody written in 1695 by another English composer, Henry Purcell (1659–1695). *The Young Person's Guide* was originally composed to provide musical examples for a film entitled *The Instruments of the Orchestra.* Britten's intent was to demonstrate first the sounds of the four instrumental families of the orchestra and then the distinctive colors of the individual instruments.

The work begins with the full orchestra playing the theme. This is followed by a presentation of the same theme, in turn, by the woodwind family alone, by the brasses, by the strings (including harp), and finally by the percussion. After the percussion holds forth, the full orchestra returns with a sweeping statement of the theme.

Next comes a series of thirteen variations of the theme (1–13), each of which exposes the special tone colors of one or two instruments. We begin with the flutes (1) and work our way to the percussion (13).

Finally, *The Young Person's Guide* ends with all of the instruments of the orchestra engaged in a fugue. We discuss the fugue at length in Chapter 7. For now, notice simply that the texture of the fugue is polyphonic, meaning that there are several quickly moving lines and they proceed independently of one another.

Your task is to fill in the blanks below by indicating the time at which each musical event occurs, specifically, the minute and second at which the various families of instruments or individual instruments enter. To do this you will need a digital watch or a watch or clock with a sweep hand.

Introduction to the theme:

0:00   Full orchestra
_____   Woodwinds
_____   Brass
_____   Strings (with harp)
_____   Percussion
_____   Full Orchestra

Short transition (string tremolo and harp)

Variations on the theme:

1. 1:56   Flutes and piccolo (with harp accompaniment)
2. _____   Oboes (with string accompaniment)
3. _____   Clarinets (with tuba accompaniment)
4. _____   Bassoons (with string accompaniment)

5. 5:00   Violins sweep forward

6. _____   Violas play more quietly (with brass and woodwind accompaniment)

7. _____   Cellos offer lovely melody (with clarinet/string accompaniment)

8. _____   Double basses play comical melody (with light woodwind and percussion accompaniment)

9. _____   Harp solo (with string tremolo accompaniment)

10. _____   French horns (with string and harp accompaniment)

11. _____   Trumpets play a light gallop

12. _____   Trombones blast forth with tuba down below (with woodwind accompaniment)

13. _____   Percussion, beginning with the timpani, and then cymbals, snare drum, xylophone, and so on; ends with xylophone solo

Fugue based on the theme:

13:39   (very fast) Fugue begins with piccolo and flutes, followed by clarinets, bassoons, violins, violas, cellos, double basses, harp, horns, trumpets, trombones, and tuba

---

10   Hearing Musical Textures

This exercise asks you to become familiar with the three basic textures of music: monophonic, polyphonic, and homophonic. On your Introduction to Listening tape (toward the end of side A), you have eight excerpts which represent these various textures. Monophonic texture, you will find, is easy to hear because it has only one line of music. More difficult is to differentiate between polyphonic texture and homophonic texture. Polyphonic texture embodies many active, independent lines. Homophonic texture, on the other hand, usually uses blocks of chords that accompany and support a single melody. Identify the texture of each of the excerpts in the spaces below.

1. _____ (Saint-Saëns, *Carnival of the Animals*)
2. _____ (Schubert, Overture to *Rosamunde*)
3. _____ (Bach, Fugue, *The Well-Tempered Clavier*, Book I)
4. _____ (Mahler, Symphony No. 5, first movement)
5. _____ (Strauss, *Blue Danube Waltz*)
6. _____ (Beethoven, Piano Sonata, Opus 110)
7. _____ (Brahms, Rhapsody for Piano, Opus 119)
8. _____ (Beethoven, Symphony No. 8, fourth movement)

---

11   Hearing Musical Textures

This assignment asks you to listen to three different pieces performed by three different musical forces. All are found on your Listening CDs or tapes.

The following questions will help you to focus on the texture of each.

A. Let's return for a moment to Ravel's *Bolero* (CD 1/1; Intro tape, side A). Instead of commencing at the beginning, this time start the music somewhere toward the end, perhaps two or three minutes from the end.

1. Is Ravel's *Bolero* performed by one instrument or many?

    _____

2. Does the texture involve just one melody at a time and an accompaniment or many different melodies played simultaneously?

    _____

3. How would you describe this melody-plus-accompaniment texture of *Bolero:* monophonic, homophonic, or polyphonic? _____

B. Now find the Organ Fugue in G minor of Baroque composer Johann Sebastian Bach (CD 2/4; 6–Tape 2A; 2–Tape 1A). Listen to just the first minute of the music. Can you hear four musical lines or voices enter during this opening passage (at 0:00, 0:18, 0:42, and 1:00)?

1. Are they all being played on one instrument or several?

    _____

2. As the voices enter, does each come in with the same melody or does each enter with a new and different tune? _____

3. How would you characterize the texture of this piece: monophonic, homophonic, or polyphonic? _____

4. Is this an example of imitative or nonimitative counterpoint?

    _____

C. Finally, turn to CD 6/17, or 6–Tape 6B, and listen to the opening (the first forty-seven seconds to be precise) of Louis Armstrong's rendition of *Droppin' Shucks.* This is a fine example of classic New Orleans–style jazz. Can you hear the three principal melodic instruments: trumpet, trombone, and clarinet? _____

1. Are the three melodic instruments all playing the same melody, or are they playing different-sounding lines? _____

2. How would you characterize the texture of this piece: monophonic, homophonic, or polyphonic? _____

3. Is this imitative or nonimitative counterpoint? _____

KEY WORDS

binary form	orchestral score	texture
canon	*piano*	theme and variations
color	*pianissimo*	timbre
counterpoint	pizzicato	tremolo
forte	polyphony	vibrato
fortissimo	rondo form	unison
homophony	strophic form	
monophony	ternary form	

HEARING MUSICAL STYLES

O ne of the pleasures of learning more about music is being able to evaluate and appreciate what we hear. But before we can make value judgments about a musical composition and begin to enjoy its beauty, we must have a sense of what it is—its identity in relation to other music and to a particular time. When we hear an unknown work for the first time, we try to make an educated guess, however subconsciously, to identify the period of the music and perhaps the composer. Is it Baroque music or Romantic music, New Orleans–style jazz or bebop, Bach or Beethoven? Identifying the period of a composition, and even the composer, is the first step toward true musical enjoyment. This recognition is mainly an exercise in hearing musical style. But what is musical style?

Style in music is the surface sound produced by the inner action of the elements of music: melody, rhythm, harmony, color, texture, and form. It is the shape of the melody, the arrangement of the rhythm, the choice of the harmony, the disposition of the texture, the treatment of form, and the use of instrumental color that, taken in sum, determine musical style. Each composer, like each painter and poet, has a personal style, one that makes his or her music different from all the rest. Take a work by Mozart (1756–1791), for example. A trained listener will recognize it as a piece of the Classical period (1750–1820) because of its generally symmetrical melodies, light texture, and dynamic ebb and flow. A truly experienced ear will identify Mozart as the composer, perhaps by recognizing the sudden shifts to minor keys, the intensely chromatic melodies, or the colorful writing for bassoon or clarinet—all hallmarks of Mozart's musical style.

Each period in the history of music has a musical style, too. That is to say, the music of one epoch will possess qualities common to much other music of that same time. A common set of musical practices and procedures are at work. Many symphonies* of the Romantic period (1820–1900), for example, exhibit long, vocally inspired melodies, chromatic* harmonies, languid rhythms, and uniformly dense orchestral textures. A sinfonia* from the late Baroque period (1700–1750), on the other hand, is more likely to possess an instrumentally inspired melody, diatonic* harmonies, driving rhythms, and a texture that is heavy on both top and bottom but thin in the middle.

As you might suspect, the boundaries between any two periods in the history of music are arbitrarily drawn. Musical styles do not change overnight; usually they evolve and overlap. Composers can stand midway between periods. For example, Guillaume Dufay (ca. 1400–1474) is a composer of the Middle Ages in his use of texture, but of the Renaissance in regard to his harmonies. Ludwig van Beethoven (1770–1827) straddles the Classical and Romantic periods, being somewhat conservative in his choice of harmonies but radically progressive in his use of form and rhythm. Despite such contradictions, historians of music, like historians of art, find it useful to discuss style in terms of historical periods. It makes it possible to conceptualize and appreciate these arts in a more convenient way. Below are the stylistic periods that are discussed in the following chapters:

Middle Ages: 400–1475   Classical: 1750–1820
Renaissance: 1475–1600   Romantic: 1820–1900
Early Baroque: 1600–1700   Impressionist: 1880–1920
Late Baroque: 1700–1750   Modern: 1900–present

Check List of Musical Style by Periods

Middle Ages: 400–1475

Melody	Moves mostly by step within a narrow range; uses diatonic and not chromatic notes of the scale
Harmony:	Most surviving medieval music is monophonic Gregorian chant or monophonic *troubadour* and *trouvère* songs—hence there is no harmony
	Medieval polyphony (Mass, motet, and chanson) has dissonant phrases ending with open, hollow-sounding chords
Rhythm:	Gregorian chant as well as *troubadour* and *trouvère* songs sung mainly in notes of equal value without clearly marked rhythms; medieval polyphony is composed mostly in triple meter and uses repeating rhythmic patterns
Color:	Mainly vocal sounds (choir or soloists); little instrumental music survives
Texture:	Mostly monophonic—Gregorian chant as well as *troubadour* and *trouvère* songs are monophonic melodies
	Medieval polyphony (two, three, or four independent lines) is mainly contrapuntal
Form:	Strophic form of *troubadour* and *trouvère* songs; ternary form of the Kyrie; rondo form of the French *rondeau*

Principal composers: Hildegard von Bingen, Leoninus, Perotinus, Machaut, Countess of Dia, Dufay, Binchois

Principal genres: Gregorian chant, polyphonic Mass, *troubadour*, and *trouvère* songs, secular chanson, instrumental dance

Renaissance: 1475–1600

Principal composers: Desprez, Weelkes, Palestrina, Byrd, Lasso

Principal genres: sacred Mass and motet, secular chanson and madrigal, instrumental dance

Melody:	Mainly stepwise motion within a moderately narrow range; still mainly diatonic, but some intense chromaticism found in madrigals from end of period
Harmony:	More careful use of dissonance than in the Middle Ages as the triad, a consonant chord, becomes the basic building block of harmony
Rhythm:	Duple meter is now as common as triple meter; rhythm in sacred vocal music (Mass and motet) is relaxed and non-pulsating; rhythm in secular vocal music (chanson and madrigal) and in instrumental dances is usually lively and catchy, with frequent use of syncopation
Color:	Although there is more surviving music for instruments, the predominant sound remains that of unaccompanied vocal music, whether for soloists or for choir
Texture:	Contrapuntal, polyphonic texture for four or five vocal lines is heard throughout Mass, motet, and madrigal, though occasionally passages of chordal homophonic texture are inserted for variety
Form:	Strict musical forms are not often used; most Masses, motets, madrigals, chansons, and instrumental dances are through-composed—have no musical repetitions and hence no standard formal plan

Early Baroque: 1600–1700

Principal composers: Gabrieli, Monteverdi, Purcell, Corelli, Vivaldi

Principal genres: polychoral motet, cantata, opera, sonata, concerto grosso, orchestral suite

Melody:	Less stepwise movement, larger leaps, wider range, and more chromaticism reflect influence of virtuosic solo singing; melodic patterns idiomatic to particular musical instruments emerge; introduction of melodic sequence
Harmony:	Stable, diatonic chords played by *basso continuo* support melody; clearly defined chord progressions begin to develop; tonality reduced to major and minor keys
Rhythm:	Relaxed, flexible rhythms of the Renaissance transformed into regularly repeating, driving rhythms
Color:	Musical timbre becomes enormously varied as traditional instruments are perfected (e.g., harpsichord, violin, and oboe) and new combinations of voices and instruments are explored; symphony orchestra begins to take shape; sudden shifts in dynamics (terraced dynamics) reflect dramatic quality of Baroque music
Texture:	Chordal, homophonic texture predominates; top and bottom lines are the strongest as *basso continuo* creates a powerful bass to support the melody above

Form: Arias and instrumental works often make use of *basso ostinato* procedure; ritornello form emerges in the concerto grosso; binary form regulates most movements of the sonata and orchestral suite

Late Baroque: 1700–1750

Melody: Grows longer, more expansive, and more asymmetrical; idiomatic instrumental style influences vocal melodies

Harmony: Functional chord progressions govern harmonic movement—harmony moves purposefully from one chord to the next; *basso continuo* continues to provide strong bass

Rhythm: Exciting, driving, machinelike rhythms propel music forward with vigor; "walking" bass creates feeling of rhythmic regularity

Color: Instruments reign supreme; instrumental sounds, especially of violin, harpsichord, and organ, set musical tone for the era; one tone color used throughout a movement or large section of movement

Texture: Homophonic texture remains important, but polyphonic texture reemerges because of growing importance of the contrapuntal fugue

Form: Binary form in sonatas and orchestral suites; *da capo* aria (ternary) form in arias; fugal procedure used in fugue

Principal composers: Bach, Handel, Telemann, Vivaldi

Principal genres: cantata, opera, oratorio, sonata, orchestral suite, concerto grosso

Classical: 1750–1820

Melody: Short, balanced phrases create tuneful melodies; melody more influenced by vocal than instrumental style; frequent cadences produce light, airy feeling

Harmony: The rate at which chords change (harmonic rhythm) varies dramatically, creating a dynamic flux and flow; simple chordal harmonies made more active by "Alberti" bass

Rhythm: Departs from regular, driving patterns of Baroque era to become more stop and go; greater rhythmic variety within a single movement

Color: Orchestra grows larger; woodwind section of two flutes, oboes, clarinets, and bassoons becomes typical; piano replaces harpsichord as principal keyboard instrument

Texture: Mostly homophonic; thin bass and middle range, hence light and transparent; passages in contrapuntal style appear sparingly and mainly for contrast

Form: A few standard forms regulate much of Classical music: sonata-allegro, theme and variations, rondo, ternary (for minuets and trios), and double exposition (for solo concerto)

Principal composers: Mozart, Haydn, Beethoven

Principal genres: symphony, sonata, string quartet, solo concerto, opera

Romantic: 1820–1900

Principal composers: Beethoven, Schubert, Berlioz, Mendelssohn, Schumann, Chopin, Liszt, Verdi, Wagner, Brahms, Tchaikovsky, Musorgsky, Mahler, Strauss

Principal genres: symphony, program symphony, symphonic poem, concert overture, opera, *Lied*, orchestral song, solo concerto, character piece for piano

Melody:	Long, singable lines with powerful climaxes and chromatic inflections for expressiveness
Harmony:	Greater use of chromaticism makes the harmony richer and more colorful; sudden shifts to remote chords for expressive purposes; more dissonance to convey feeling of anxiety and longing
Rhythm:	Rhythms are flexible, often languid and therefore meter is sometimes not clearly articulated
Color:	The orchestra becomes enormous, reaching upward of one hundred performers: trombone, tuba, contrabassoon, piccolo, and English horn added to the ensemble; experiments with new playing techniques for special effects; dynamics vary widely to create different levels of expression; piano becomes larger and more powerful
Texture:	Predominantly homophonic but dense and rich because of larger orchestra; sustaining pedal on the piano also adds to density
Form:	No new forms created, rather traditional forms (strophic, sonata-allegro, and theme and variations, for example) used and extended in length; traditional forms also applied to new genres such as *Lied*, symphonic poem, and orchestral song

Impressionist: 1880–1920

Principal composers: Debussy, Ravel, Fauré

Principal genres: symphonic poem, string quartet, orchestral song, opera, character piece for piano

Melody:	Varies from short dabs of sound to long, free-flowing lines; chromatic scale, whole-tone scale, and pentatonic scale often replace usual major and minor scales
Harmony:	Primarily homophonic; triad is extended to form seventh chords and ninth chords, and these frequently move in parallel motion
Rhythm:	Usually free and flexible with irregular accents, making it sometimes difficult to determine the meter; rhythmic ostinatos used to give feeling of stasis rather than movement
Color:	More emphasis on woodwinds and brass and less on the violins as primary carriers of melody; more soloistic writing to show that the color of the instrument is as important as the melody line it plays
Texture:	Can vary from thin and airy to heavy and dense; sustaining pedal of the piano often used to create a wash of sound
Form:	Traditional forms involving clear-cut repetitions rarely used; composers try to develop a form unique and particular to each new musical work

Modern: 1900–present

Melody: Wide-ranging disjunct lines, often chromatic and dissonant, angularity accentuated by use of octave displacement

Harmony: Highly dissonant; dissonance no longer must move to consonance but may move to another dissonance

Rhythm: Vigorous, energetic rhythms; conflicting simultaneous meters (polymeters) and rhythms (polyrhythms) make for temporal complexity

Color: Color becomes an agent of form and beauty in and by itself; composers seek new sounds from traditional, acoustical instruments, from electronic instruments and computers, and from noises in the environment

Texture: As varied and individual as the men and women composing music

Form: A range of extremes: sonata-allegro, rondo, theme and variations benefit from a neo-Classical revival; twelve-tone procedure allows for an almost mathematical formal control; yet chance music permits random happenings and noises from the environment to shape a musical work

Principal composers: Stravinsky, Schoenberg, Berg, Webern, Bartók, Messiaen, Penderecki, Ives, Copland, Varèse, Cage, Glass

Principal genres: symphony, solo concerto, string quartet, opera, electronic music, chance music

4

MEDIEVAL MUSIC

Historians use the term "Middle Ages" as a catch-all phrase to refer to the thousand years of history between the fall of the Roman Empire (late 400s) and the age of reawakening and discovery, exemplified by the voyages of Christopher Columbus (late 1400s). It was a period of triumphs and tragedies, of soaring cathedrals and murderous plagues, of sublime spirituality and abject poverty, of knightly chivalry and barbarous warfare. Seen from our modern perspective, the medieval period appears as a vast chronological expanse whose bleak vista is only occasionally broken by the beauty of its churches, paintings, poems, and music.

MUSIC IN THE MONASTERY

There were many kinds of music in the Middle Ages: songs for the knights as they rode into battle, songs for the men in the fields and the women around the hearth, songs and dances for the nobles in their castles, and chants for the priests to accompany the Christian service in the monasteries and cathedrals. Unfortunately, most of this music, and virtually all of it emanating from the common folk, is now lost because it was never written down. Only the music of the Church is preserved in any significant amount because at that time only the men of the Church, and to a lesser degree the nuns, were educated. Even the nobility was more or less illiterate. The reading and copying of texts was the private preserve of the rural monasteries and, somewhat later, the urban cathedrals. The monks were encouraged to read and write as a means of becoming more familiar with the scriptures, and it was they who devised a system to notate and copy music. In this way, the music of the Church could be spread to other monastic communities and taught to succeeding generations of novices.

Life was rigorous in a medieval monastery. The founder of the principal monastic order, St. Benedict (died ca. 547), prescribed a code of conduct, or rule, for his followers. The Benedictines rose at about four in the morning for the night office (matins), at which they sang psalms and read scripture. After a break "for the necessities of nature" the brethren returned at daybreak to sing another service in praise of the Lord. Thereafter, the monks dispersed to farm and otherwise attend to their lands, though they came together again at six other times for services of prayer and song and for two communal meals.

Gregorian chant

The music sung at the eight monastic hours of prayer and at the daily Mass was what we today call Gregorian chant, named in honor of Pope Gregory the Great (540?–604). Ironically, Gregory wrote little, if any, of this music. Being more a church administrator than musician, he merely decreed that certain chants should be sung on certain days of the liturgical year. Melodies for the Christian service had, of course, existed since the time of the apostles, some taken over directly from the Jewish Temple. What we now call **Gregorian chant** (also called **plainsong**) is really a large body of unaccompanied vocal music, setting Latin texts, composed for the Western Church over the course of fifteen centuries, from the time of the earliest Fathers to the Council of Trent, which ended in 1563. The names of most of the creators of Gregorian chant, the cantors of the church, are lost in the mists of bygone eras, but a few are known to us. They were forceful personalities whose creative energies carried them into many fields of intellectual and artistic endeavor.

Hildegard von Bingen

One of the most remarkable contributors to the repertoire of Gregorian chant was Abbess Hildegard von Bingen (1098–1171). Hildegard was born of noble parents and raised by a group of nuns attached to a Benedictine monastery established a few miles west of the Rhine River near Mainz, Germany. In the course of time, she manifested her extraordinary intellect and imagination as a playwright, poet, musician, naturalist, pharmacologist, and visionary. During intense religious experiences, she saw images such as the breath of Satan in the guise of a serpent, the fiery descent of the Holy Spirit, and the blood of Christ streaming in the heavens. These she recorded in a collection of visionary writings called *Scivias*. The images of her visions were often transferred to her poetry, much of which was set to music as liturgical chant. Thus, her song to the Virgin Mary, *O viridissima virga* (*O Greenest Branch*, Ex. 4–1), vividly depicts Mary as the most verdant branch of the tree of Jesse through whom the heat of the sun radiates like the aroma of balm.

Hildegard's *O Greenest Branch* possesses many qualities typical of Gregorian chant. The musical phrases are of differing lengths because the phrases of text vary from just a few syllables to many words. They all gravitate, however, toward a single tonal center, here the pitch G. The first phrase starts on G and works its way up a fifth to D for the hail "ave." The second commences on that D and descends a full octave before returning to the central pitch. Most of the short third phrase ("sanctorum prodisti") is occupied with circumscribing a cadence on G. Like most pieces of Gregorian chant, *O Greenest Branch* is a predominantly stepwise melody, one without large leaps. Nor does it make use of chromatic* twists—added sharps and flats—that might make the chant more difficult to perform. This was, after all, choral music to be sung in unison* (all together) by the full community of monks or nuns, not by trained specialists. This chant, as all Gregorian chant, is also a good example of monophony* or music of one line. There are no additional instrumental or vocal parts sounding at the same time. (On our recording the twentieth-century performers have added a string instrument to surround the melody at the interval of a fifth, producing what sounds like a continu-

FIGURE 4–1

Nuns in choir singing the divine service, from an illumination in an early fifteenth-century English manuscript.

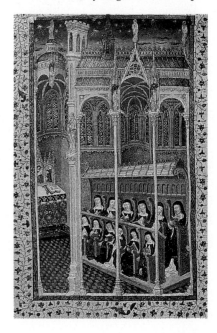

ous musical halo.) Perhaps most important, the melody is conceived without rhythm or meter. The notes are all of one basic value, something close to our eighth note in length. The unaccompanied, monophonic line and the absence of rhythmic drive allow a restful, contemplative mood to develop. The music is meant to float unfettered as it bears the transcendent spirit aloft.

EXAMPLE 4–1: Hildegard von Bingen, *O Greenest Branch*

O vi - ri - dis - si - ma vir - ga, a - ve que in ven - to - so

flab - ro scis - ci - ta - ti - o - nis san - cto - rum pro - di - sti.

LISTENING GUIDE

Hildegard von Bingen
Gregorian chant, *O Greenest Branch* (ca. 1150)

CD 1/2
6–Tape 1A

Choir

| 0:00 | O viridissima virga, ave que in ventoso flabro sciscitationis sanctorum prodisti. | Hail, o greenest branch who sprang forth in the airy breeze of the prayers of the saints. |

Soloist

| 0:24 | Cum venit tempus, quod tu floruisti, in ramis tuis, ave, ave sit tibi, quia calor solis in te sudavit sicut odor balsami. | So the time has come that you flourished in your boughs, hail, hail to you, because the heat of the sun radiated in you like the aroma of balm. |

Choir

| 0:56 | Nam in te floruit pulcher flos qui odorem dedit omnibus aromatibus que arida erant. | For in you bloomed the beautiful flower which scented all parched perfumes. |

Soloist

| 1:18 | Et illa apparuerunt omnia in viriditate plena. | And all things have been manifested in their full verdure. |

Choir

| 1:34 | Unde celi dederunt rorem super gramen et omnis terra leta facta est, quoniam viscera ipsius frumentum protulerunt et quoniam volucres celi nidos in ipsa habuerunt. | Whence the skys set down dew on the pasture, and all the earth was made more joyful because her womb produced grain, and because the birds of Heaven built their nests in her. |

Soloist

| 2:08 | Deinde facta est esca hominibus et gaudium magnum epulantum; inde, o suavis virgo, in te non deficit ullum gaudium. | Then the harvest was made ready for Man, and a great rejoicing of banqueters, because in you, o sweet Virgin, no joy is lacking. |

Choir

| 2:43 | Hec omnia Eva contempsit. Nunc autem laus sit altissimo. | All these things Eve rejected. Now let there be praise to you in the Highest. |

MUSIC IN THE CATHEDRAL

If the monastery was primarily a rural establishment, one of solitude and spiritual contemplation, the cathedral was an urban institution. For only in a city could a bishop, the religious leader of the people, effectively minister to a flock of any size. During the twelfth and thirteenth centuries, the population of the urban centers of Europe—Milan, Paris, and London, among others—grew significantly owing to a healthy revival of trade and commerce. Much of the commercial wealth that flowed to the cities was channeled toward the construction of splendid new churches which served not only as houses of worship but also as civic auditoriums. So substantial was this building campaign that the period 1150–1350 is often called "the Age of the Cathedrals." In these years, the great urban cathedrals of England, France, Italy, and Germany rose above the city skyline, and many of them are still visible today. Most were constructed in what we call the Gothic style, with pointed arches, high ceiling vaults, supporting buttresses, and richly colored stained glass.

Gothic architecture began in France and radiated in all directions to foreign lands, even to the Christian-held territories of the Near East. In a similar way, France was the wellspring of other intellectual and artistic developments at this time. Paris, which by the end of the thirteenth century counted eighty thousand inhabitants, had become the leading university town in Europe for the study of the arts and theology. Young clerical scholars from distant countries flocked to the Parisian schools, and when they returned to their native diocese they took with them the teachings of philosophers like Peter Abelard (1079–1142) and Thomas Aquinas (1225?–1274) and also the music they had heard at the cathedral of Notre Dame (Our Lady) of Paris (Fig. 4–2).

Paris, an intellectual center

Notre Dame of Paris

Notre Dame of Paris was begun in the 1160s, yet not completed in its final form until more than a hundred years later. Throughout this period the cathedral was blessed with a succession of churchmen who were not only theologians and philosophers but poets and musicians as well. Foremost among these were Master Leoninus (fl. 1169–1201) and Master Perotinus, called the Great (fl. 1198–1236). Leoninus wrote a great book of religious music *(Magnus liber organi)* to adorn the Gregorian chant sung at Notre Dame on high feasts. Perotinus revised the book of Leoninus and also composed many additional pieces of his own.

What is new about this Gothic church music is that it is written in polyphony* (two or more voices, or lines, sounding simultaneously) and not merely monophonic (one-voice) Gregorian chant. In truth, earlier church musicians had attempted to enhance the sound of the plainsong of the Church by adding another voice to it, but these efforts often required the new voice to move in exact parallel motion, usually at the interval of a fourth, fifth, or octave, with the preexisting chant. Leoninus, however, seized the opportunity to create an autonomous second voice, one that did not merely duplicate and amplify the plainsong but that complemented and graced it. Indeed, the added voice became the center of attention itself. In

FIGURE 4–2

The cathedral of Notre Dame of Paris, begun ca. 1160, was one of the first to be built in the new Gothic style of architecture.

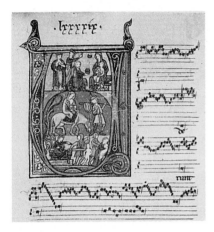

FIGURE 4–3

A thirteenth-century manuscript preserving Leoninus's organum for Christmas, *Viderunt omnes.* Leoninus's newly created voice is on each of the upper four-line staffs, while the Gregorian chant, with the text below, is on each of the lower staffs.

this musical development, we see an early instance of an artistic spirit breaking free of the constraints of the ancient authority of the Church.

LEONINUS: ORGANUM *VIDERUNT OMNES.* The expressive freedom Leoninus imparted to the new voice can be seen in his setting of the Gregorian chant *Viderunt omnes* for Mass on Christmas Day. By adding his own musical line above the chant, Leoninus created a two-voice **organum,** the name given to early church polyphony. The old chant is strung out in the lower voice and Leoninus's newly created line is on top. Soloists were assigned to the organum. Yet they sang in this new polyphonic style only for the first two words of the chant, "Viderunt omnes," which are greatly extended because of the addition of the new voice. Thereafter, the full clerical choir entered to continue and complete the remaining music in monophonic Gregorian chant. Try listening to this piece twice, first as it is given in the musical example below, which has the lower line in full and a graphic representation of Leoninus's added part. Then listen again, now trying to follow both lines of the organum as they appear in an original thirteenth-century manuscript from Paris (Fig. 4–3). As you can see in the manuscript, Leoninus's newly created upper voice undulates and even cascades in a virtuosic way as the lower one holds the chant in long notes. Only at the beginning of the word "omnes" is any sort of rhythmic precision introduced. At this time medieval musical notation could indicate pitches accurately, but was only beginning to deal with matters of rhythm. What Leoninus has fashioned here is a rather free, rhapsodic hymn in praise of the Christ child. Imagine how these new sounds struck the ear of the medieval citizen of Paris as they rebounded around the bare stone walls of the vast, newly constructed cathedral of Notre Dame.

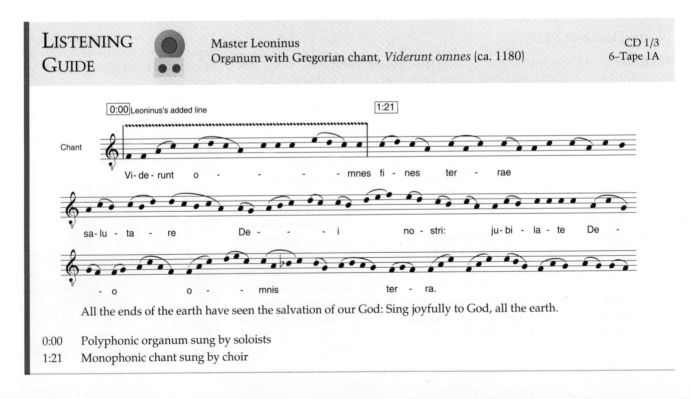

LISTENING GUIDE

Master Leoninus
Organum with Gregorian chant, *Viderunt omnes* (ca. 1180)

CD 1/3
6–Tape 1A

All the ends of the earth have seen the salvation of our God: Sing joyfully to God, all the earth.

0:00   Polyphonic organum sung by soloists
1:21   Monophonic chant sung by choir

Notre Dame of Rheims

Notre Dame of Paris was not the only important cathedral devoted to Our Lady in northern Europe. The city of Rheims, one hundred miles east of Paris in the Champagne region, was graced with a monument equally large and impressive (Fig. 4–4). In the fourteenth century it, too, benefited from the service of a poetically and musically talented churchman, Guillaume de Machaut (1300?–1377). Judging by his nearly 150 surviving works, Machaut was the most important composer of the fourteenth century. And he was equally esteemed as a narrative and lyric poet. Today historians of literature place him on a pedestal with his slightly younger English counterpart, Geoffrey Chaucer (1340?–1400), author of the *Canterbury Tales*.

MACHAUT: *MASS OF OUR LADY.* Machaut's *Messe de Nostre Dame (Mass of Our Lady)* is deservedly the best-known work in the entire repertoire of medieval music. It is impressive for its length and innovative in the way music is applied to the texts of the **Mass**—the central and most important service of the Roman Catholic Church. Before Machaut's time, composers writing polyphony for the Mass had set only one or two sections of what is called the Proper of the Mass (chants whose texts changed to suit the feast day). Leoninus's *Viderunt omnes,* for example, is a setting of the Gradual (see below) of the Proper of the Mass for Christmas Day. Machaut, on the other hand, chose to set all of the chants of the Ordinary of the Mass (chants with unvarying texts that were sung virtually everyday), and he united, or linked, these together by placing a distinctive musical motive, a descending scale, in each of the five movements. Setting the Ordinary of the Mass had the obvious practical advantage that the composition could be heard more than on just one feast day of the church year. Machaut's *Mass of Our Lady,* for example, could be sung any time a Mass in honor of the Virgin Mary was celebrated. Following are given the musical portions of the Mass and the order in which they are sung.

FIGURE 4–4

Interior of the cathedral of Rheims looking east to west. The high, ribbed vaults and pointed arches give this Gothic cathedral a feeling of great upward movement.

the Mass

Musical Portions of the Mass

Proper of the Mass	Ordinary of the Mass
1. Introit (an introductory chant for the entry of the celebrating clergy)	
	2. Kyrie (a petition for mercy)
	3. Gloria (a hymn of praise to the Lord)
4. Gradual (a reflective chant)	
5. Alleluia or Tract (a chant of thanksgiving or penance)	
	6. Credo (a profession of faith)
7. Offertory (a chant for the offering)	
	8. Sanctus (an acclamation to the Lord)
	9. Agnus Dei (a petition for mercy and eternal peace)
10. Communion (a chant for communion)	

The figure of St. John the Evangelist sculpted for the cathedral of Rheims about 1230. Notice the serene, almost abstract quality of the face.

Although Machaut's innovation—creating a unified setting of the Ordinary of the Mass—was not embraced immediately by all composers in all regions, by the early fifteenth century his idea had come to be adopted universally in the West. Henceforth, to write a polyphonic Mass for the Church meant that a composer would set the five texts of the Ordinary and find some way to bind or shape them musically into an integrated unit. This is true, not only for later masters like Bach, Mozart, Beethoven, and Schubert, but also for more modern composers like Igor Stravinsky, whose Mass of 1948, by his own admission, owes much to the model of Machaut.

The *Kyrie* of Machaut's *Mass of Our Lady* is a threefold petition for mercy ("Kyrie eleison" means "Lord have mercy upon us"). As in the previous example by Leoninus, it is built upon a preexisting Gregorian chant which is held in longer notes than the surrounding material. Because the men who sang the chant sustained it, they came to be called the "tenors" (from the Latin *tenere*, "to hold"). Around them Machaut added not one new line but three, thereby creating four-voice polyphony. The two voices added above the tenor came to be called the *superius* and the *contratenor altus*, whence we get our terms "soprano" and "alto." The voice added below the tenor was called the *contratenor bassus*, whence our term "bass" (for more on the four standard voice parts, see page 42). By writing for four voices and spreading these over a range of two and a half octaves, Machaut was able to create truly sonorous choral polyphony.

When you listen to Machaut's *Kyrie* for the first time, you will be struck by its dark, dissonant sound. The dark quality is present because only male voices are employed here, and hence the range is rather low. Only men and boys were allowed to sing in medieval cathedrals. Singing by women was confined to nunneries (for more on this point, see pages 77 and 95). As to the dissonant, biting sound, it is caused by the fact that Machaut makes use of many unusual dissonances, ones later forbidden in Western polypohonic music by music theorists. In stark contrast to these dissonances, each section of polyphony ends with an open, somewhat hollow-sounding consonant chord. These chords use only the intervals of a fifth and an octave. Such open, hollow final chords sound especially rich in buildings with very resonant, or "lively," acoustics of the sort universally found in medieval cathedrals.

LISTENING GUIDE	Guillaume de Machaut *Kyrie* of the *Mass of Our Lady* (ca. 1360)	CD 1/4 6–Tape 1A 2–Tape 1A

0:00	Kyrie eleison	Lord have mercy upon us
1:00	Kyrie eleison	Lord have mercy upon us
1:23	Kyrie eleison	Lord have mercy upon us
2:22	Christe eleison	Christ have mercy upon us
2:42	Christe eleison	Christ have mercy upon us
3:36	Christe eleison	Christ have mercy upon us
3:57	Kyrie eleison	Lord have mercy upon us
4:41	Kyrie eleison	Lord have mercy upon us
5:00	Kyrie eleison	Lord have mercy upon us

(Listening Exercise 12 asks you to differentiate the polyphonic sections from the sections of monophonic plainsong.)

MUSIC AT THE COURT

Machaut wrote music for the cathedral of Rheims, but he composed for the court as well. At various times in his career, he was employed by powerful nobles such as the king of Bohemia, the king of Navarre, and the duke of Berry. It may seem strange that a man of the cloth was active in affairs at court, but in the Middle Ages learned churchmen were much in demand for their ability to read and write. And because of their skill with letters and music learned in the church, clerics were inevitably drawn to the poetry and music of the courtly song. Indeed, most of the polyphonic love songs emanating from the court in the late Middle Ages were written by ordained priests.

The court first emerged as a center for the patronage of the arts during the years 1150–1400. The fourteenth century in particular witnessed a general decline in the authority of the Church, epitomized by the "Babylonian captivity" (1309–1377) during which the popes, driven from Rome, lived as exiles in France. Kings, dukes, counts, and lesser nobles now assumed responsibility for the defense of the land as well as for affairs of commerce and justice. The aristocratic court became a small city-state, yet one continually on the move within the lord's lands, from town to town or chateau to chateau. To enhance the ruler's prestige and show that he or she was a person of refinement and sensitivity, the noble often engaged bands of trumpeters to herald an arrival, instrumentalists to provide dance music for the festivals of the court, and singers and poets to create lyric verse.

growing importance of the court

The first composer-poets to appear at court in any number in the West were the musicians who graced the castles of southern France and northern Spain and Italy in the late twelfth and thirteenth centuries. They were called **troubadours** because they were thought to be "finders" or "inventors" of words and melodies (*trobar* means "to find" in the medieval French of southern France). Their art was devoted mainly to the creation of songs of love which extolled the courtly ideals of faith and devotion, whether to the ideal lady, to the just seigneur, or to the Christian cause in the Moslem East. Their songs were not in the Latin of the Church, but in the vernacular tongue: medieval Italian, Catalan, and Provençal (medieval French of the South). The origins of the *troubadours* were equally varied. Some were sons of bakers and drapers, others were members of the nobility, many were clerics living outside the church, and not a few were women.

the troubadours

In the Middle Ages and later during the Renaissance (1475–1600), women were not allowed to sing in church, except in convents, owing to the early injunction of the Apostle Paul ("A woman must be silent in the church"). But at court women often appeared as reciters of poetry, singers, and performers on the so-called *bas* (soft) instruments like the harp, lute, rebec (medieval fiddle), and flute (Fig. 4–6). Women *troubadours* were not merely performers, but creators in their own right. One such composer was the Countess of Dia (Fig. 4–7), about whom we know virtually nothing, except that she was a member of the minor nobility. Her song *A chantar m'er (I Must Sing)* laments her failure in love, despite her self-proclaimed charms. It is composed of five strophes, or stanzas, each with seven lines of text and seven musical phrases. The seven-phrase melody, which owes much to the music of the Church in its stepwise movement and strong tonal feeling, displays a clear musical form, **ABABCDB** (the use of letters to indicate musical

women troubadours

FIGURES 4–6 AND 4–7

(left) A thirteenth-century Spanish miniature showing a medieval fiddle (the rebec) on the left and a lute on the right. (right) The Countess of Dia as depicted in a manuscript of *troubadour* and *trouvère* poetry.

form is explained on page 57). Also in common with the chant of the Church, this *troubadour* song, as true of most, has no clearly articulated meter and rhythm, but is sung in notes of more or less equal length.

EXAMPLE 4–2: Countess of Dia: *I Must Sing*† (ca. 1200), first strophe

† Recorded by the Clemencic Consort on *Troubadours*, vol. 2, Harmonia Mundi France, 397; the Studio der Frühen Musik on *Chansons der Troubadours*, Telefunken SAWT 9567-B; and by Hesperion XX on *Cansos de Trobairitz*, Odeon/Reflexe IC065-30941Q.

(I must sing of that which I'd rather not,
So vexed am I by him to whom I am a friend,
Because I love him more than anything that be,
But with him kindness and courtliness get me nowhere:
Neither my beauty, nor my worth, nor my wits.
In this way am I thwarted and betrayed,
Just as I would be if I were ugly.)

Gradually, the musical traditions created by the *troubadours* were carried to the north of France where such composer-performers came to be called *trouvères*, and even to Germany where they were called *Minnesingers*. Around 1300, some of the *trouvères* began to mix the traditions of the *troubadours* with the learned vocal polyphony coming from the Church. Soon churchmen like Guillaume de Machaut (see above) adopted the musical forms and poetic style of the *trouvères* to fashion a new genre of music, the polyphonic **chanson** (French for "song"). The chanson is simply a love song, normally in French, for two, three, or four voices, which usually follows a set poetic and musical form. At its best, the chanson is a small jewel of poignant lyricism.

the chanson

During the fifteenth century, Gilles Binchois (1400?–1460) and Guillaume Dufay (1400?–1474) excelled at writing chansons (Fig. 4–8). Both men were ordained priests, yet both moved easily between ecclesiastical and courtly circles in northern France. Dufay's *Craindre vous vueil (I Wish to Honor You)* is a lovely three-voice chanson with the structure of a *rondeau*—a musical and textual form with a recurring refrain like the rondo* (see page 59). All three voices may be sung, or the lower two may be played on accompanying instruments like the lute or rebec (medieval fiddle). Notice that the composer, who undoubtedly was the author of the text, has linked himself amorously to a certain woman named "Cateline" by means of an acrostic. The first letters of each line spell out "Cateline-Dufay" (*i, j,* and *y* being interchangeable in the Middle Ages). A rather daring act for a priest!

FIGURE 4–8

Guillaume Dufay and Gilles Binchois. Dufay, who spent most of his life employed at various churches, stands next to an organ to symbolize his role as a church musician, while Binchois holds a secular harp to suggest his position as a musician at the worldly court of Burgundy.

EXAMPLE 4–3: Guillaume Dufay: Chanson, *I Wish to Honor You*† (ca. 1430)

Crain - dre vous vueil, dou - ce da - me de pris,

† Recorded by the Medieval Ensemble of London on *Guillaume Dufay: Complete Secular Music,*
 L'Oiseau-lyre 237D 3.

Craindre vous vueil, douce dame de pris,
Amer, doubter, louer en fais, en dis,
Tout mon vivant, en quelque lieu que soye.   **refrain**
Et vous donner, m'amour, ma seule joye,
Le cuer de moy tant que je seray vis.

Iamais ne suy annuieux ne pensis
Ne douleureux, quant je voy vo clair vis
Et vo maintieng en alant par la voie.

Craindre . . .   (repeat **refrain**)

De vous amer cel m'est un paradis,
Vëu les biens qui sont en vous compris;
Faire le doy quoy qu'avenir en doye.
A vous me rens, lÿes meiux que de soye,
Ioieusement, en bon espoir toudis.

Craindre . . .   (repeat **refrain**)

                           *   *   *   *   *   *   *

(I wish to honor you, sweet worthy lady,
To love, esteem, and praise you in word and deed,
All my life, no matter where I may be.   **refrain**
And to give you, my love, my only joy,
My heart as long as I shall live.

I am never anxious or melancholy,
Or sad when I see your bright face,
And I will stand by you through life.

I wish to honor . . .   (repeat **refrain**)

To love you is paradise for me
Such are your charms.
I must do so, no matter what the future brings.
To render myself to you, in a bond tighter than silk
Joyfully, in bliss forever.

I wish to honor . . .)   (repeat **refrain**)

the court of Burgundy   At various times, both Guillaume Dufay and his colleague Gilles Binchois
were employed at the court of a French nobleman, Philip the Good, duke of
Burgundy (ruled 1419–1467). Owing to a succession of marriages and terri-
torial conquests in France, Germany, and the Low Countries, the dukes of
Burgundy had become the most powerful rulers in Europe and their ostenta-
tious court the envy of all the West. Here fashions, including conical head-
dress for women and long pointed-toed shoes for men, attained bizarre proportions (Fig. 4–9). Equally fanciful were the evening entertainments of the
court. At one banquet in Lille, in 1454, twenty-eight persons "playing on
diverse instruments" were placed in a round tower, and a costumed stag
with a boy on its horns sang a two-voice love song (*I've Never Seen the Likes of*

FIGURES 4–9 AND 4–10

(left) Dance scene at a wedding at a French court in the mid-fifteenth century. The musicians, who play shawms and a sackbut, are placed on high in a balcony. (right) A later scene, ca. 1600, showing musicians in a procession as painted by Denis van Alsloot. The instruments are, from left to right, a cornetto, two shawms, and a sackbut.

You) variously attributed to Dufay or Binchois. Dancing was an inevitable part of such courtly displays, and for this a standard band of two or three shawms* (ancestor of the oboe), a sackbut* (parent of the trombone), and a drum provided the music. The sackbut played the tune in long notes while the shawms or other instruments wove ornamental lines, much like a contemporary jazz quartet in which a piano and saxophone improvise above the fundamental bass notes provided by the double bass or the guitar. The late fifteenth-century tune entitled *La Spagna (The Spanish Tune)* is typical of the dance melodies played at the court of Burgundy during the waning years of the Middle Ages.

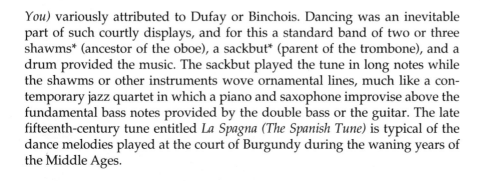

LISTENING GUIDE		Anonymous Instrumental Dance, *The Spanish Tune* (ca. 1470)	CD 1/5 6–Tape 1A

0:00   Two instruments and drum begin
0:05   Third instrument inters
1:04   An exact repeat of the previous music

(Listening Exercise 13 asks you to focus in greater detail on the individual parts.)

LISTENING EXERCISES

	Guillaume de Machaut	CD 1/4
12	*Kyrie* of the *Mass of Our Lady* (ca. 1360)	6–Tape 1A
		2–Tape 1A

Guillaume de Machaut composed the *Kyrie* of the *Mass of Our Lady* so as to make use of both monophonic Gregorian chant and polyphony. The chant, or plainsong, is used within the polyphonic sections as well as by itself. On this recording, when the chant is heard alone it is sung by men in unison. Also, this twentieth-century recording uses instruments to double the vocal lines, although Machaut originally wrote his Mass for voices alone. Your task in this listening assignment is straightforward: to identify which sections are in four-voice polyphony and which are in monophonic Gregorian chant. Do so by writing either "polyphony" or "plainsong" in the blanks below.

0:00   Kyrie eleison   _____
1:00   Kyrie eleison   _____
1:23   Kyrie eleison   _____

2:22   Christe eleison   _____
2:42   Christe eleison   _____
3:36   Christe eleison   _____

3:57   Kyrie eleison   _____
4:41   Kyrie eleison   _____
5:00   Kyrie eleison   _____

Finally, which sections are consistently longer?
      a. those in polyphony   b. those in plainsong

	Anonymous	CD 1/5
13	Instrumental Dance, *The Spanish Tune* (ca. 1470)	6–Tape 1A

The Spanish Tune is a three-voice dance piece with added drum rhythms. On this recording, the top line is played by a cornetto (a late-medieval instrument that sounds something like a cross between a trumpet and a clarinet; see Fig. 4–10), the middle voice by a shawm (predecessor of the oboe), and the bottom line by a sackbut (ancestor of our modern trombone). Try to keep these distinctly different sounds separate in your ear as you respond to the following questions.

Let's start by concentrating on the drum.

1. What is the meter of the piece, duple or triple? (Listen to the accents in the drum.) _____
2. Does the drummer play the same rhythm throughout, or does he vary it? _____

Now let's go back to the beginning.

3. Which instrument comes in last (at 0:05), the cornetto (top), shawm (middle), or sackbut (bottom)? _____
4. Which instrument is playing the longest notes, the cornetto, shawm, or sackbut? _____
5. Which instrument is playing every note the same length, the cornetto, shawm, or sackbut? _____
6. At 0:51 what is the sackbut playing?
   a. an ascending diatonic scale
   b. an ascending chromatic scale
   c. a descending diatonic scale
7. At what moment in the repeat does this scale recur?
   a. 1:14   b. 1:37   c. 1:54
8. At the end of the dance which instrument is left playing while the others hold their pitches?
   a. drum   b. sackbut   c. shawm
9. Is this dance an example of monophony or polyphony? _____

Extra Credit: Assuming that the sackbut on the lowest part is playing one note for every measure, how many measures are there in the dance before the entire piece begins to repeat? (The repeat starts at 1:04.)
   a. 35   b. 45   c. 55

KEY WORDS

chanson	organum	shawm
Gregorian chant	plainsong	*troubadour*
Mass	Proper of the Mass	*trouvère*
Minnesinger	*rondeau*	
Ordinary of the Mass	sackbut	

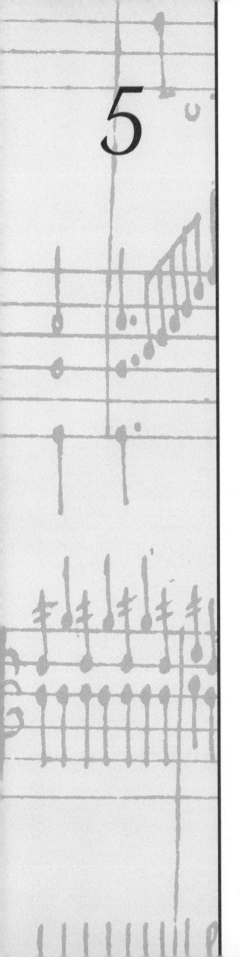

RENAISSANCE

enaissance" means rebirth or reawakening. As an historical designation, the term was first used in the nineteenth century to characterize a great flowering of intellectual and artistic activity that occurred first in Italy and then in France, Germany, England, and the Low Countries during the years 1350–1600. In music the term is more narrowly applied to musical developments in those countries between the years 1475 and 1600. Although the Renaissance did not represent a radical split with an earlier period of darkness and ignorance, as has sometimes been assumed, it was, nonetheless, a time in which new ideas and new attitudes sprang forth and flourished in an hospitable Italian climate. As the Florentine philosopher Marsilio Ficino said in the eventful year 1492:

> If then we are to call any age golden, it is beyond doubt that age which brings forth golden talents in different places. That such is true of this our age he who wishes to consider the illustrious discoveries of this century will hardly doubt. For this century, like a golden age, has restored to light the liberal arts, which were almost extinct: grammar, poetry, rhetoric, painting, sculpture, architecture, and music, the ancient singing of songs to the Orphic lyre.

The restoration of the philosophy, literature, and art of ancient Greece and Rome could take place, particularly in Italy, because many classical texts still survived and the ruins of the mighty Roman colonnades and arches were everywhere to be seen. But for musicians in Italy and elsewhere, the process of reviving things classical—singing songs to the Orphic lyre—was less obvious and immediate, for almost no music from classical antiquity survived for them to emulate, and what little there was could not be deciphered. Hence, for musicians, rebirth meant not copying earlier musical styles but adopting the attitudes about music that the ancients had possessed. This was done, in part, by writing books about music—on melody, harmony, counterpoint, and rhythm—in which the author adopted the format and vocabulary of the ancient authors.

The ancient Greek writers, especially Homer and Plato, had spoken of the great emotional power of music. Their stories told how music had calmed

FIGURES 5–1 AND 5–2

(left) The expressive grief of the Virgin and St. John mark this portion of an altarpiece painted by Mathias Grünewald in 1510–1515. (right) Virgin and Child with St. Anne by Leonardo da Vinci (1509–1510). Notice the human expression and near complete absence of traditional religious symbolism, as well as the highly formalistic composition of the painting—the figures form successively larger triangles.

the agitated spirit, made brave the warrior, and even induced the wanton wife to chastity. The musicians of the Renaissance eagerly embraced this notion that music could sway the emotions, even the behavior, of the listener. To heighten the emotional intensity of music, they selected a mode (major, minor, or one of several others then in use) and a musical style that would amply suit the meaning of the text they wished to set. A hymn would be set in one style, a lament in another, a love song in yet a third. The belief in the persuasive power of music and the capacity of music to reinforce the meaning of the text were two primary articles of faith held by musicians of the Renaissance. When transformed into real compositions, these beliefs produced pieces in a great variety of musical styles and a wide range of moods. In this way music mirrored the visual arts of the Renaissance, which now likewise allowed for a great range of emotional expression. Compare, for example, the serene and abstract quality of the medieval statue from the cathedral of Rheims (page 76, Fig. 4–5) with the intense expressiveness of the Renaissance figures in the altarpiece from the parish church at Issenheim (Fig. 5–1), or with the warm human glow of Mary, St. Anne, and the Christ child as painted by Leonardo da Vinci (Fig. 5–2).

Attending the rebirth of the arts and letters of classical antiquity was a renewed interest in man himself. We have come to call this enthusiastic self-interest humanism. Simply said, **humanism** is the belief that people have the capacity to shape their world, to create many things good and beautiful; that they are something more than a mere conduit for gifts descending from Heaven. Even the human form, in all its physical fullness, has aesthetic value (Fig. 5–3). This attitude, with its emphasis on self-esteem and human worth, differs markedly from the prevailing view in the Middle Ages when the individual was seen as a covered, almost faceless object in a great, divine pageant. The culture of the Middle Ages was fostered by the Church; it

FIGURE 5–3

Michelangelo's David (1501–1504) expresses the heroic nobility of man in a near perfect form.

emphasized the group and contemplation of the Almighty within a cloistered setting. The culture of the Renaissance, on the other hand, with its focus on personal achievement, looked outward and indulged its passion for travel, adventure, and discovery.

New meaning and value were given to what musicians produced in the Renaissance, and this affected the way in which society viewed the composer and the listener appreciated the composer's work. In the Middle Ages most compositions were preserved anonymously in manuscripts, but from the fifteenth century on, the name of the creator was usually placed at the head of each piece. One composer even went so far as to insert his own name in a setting of a liturgical text in honor of the Virgin, a novel act of self-aggrandizement. Musicians also gained an increased awareness of the monetary value of their art. This can be seen, not only in the high salaries they commanded at court, but also in the astute way in which they played one patron off against another to gain other economic benefits.

music becomes a fine art

One reason for the new estimation of music was that it was now viewed as an art rather than a craft or a science, an art that could be a source of delight in and of itself. No longer was music just an abstract medium for divine worship, one in which the skill of the humble craftsman could be judged only by his or her sincerity toward God. Music in the Renaissance was created by proud artists whose aim was to give pleasure to listening men and women. Their music was judged good or bad only to the degree that it accomplished this humanistic end. Music, as the other arts, could now be freely measured in the secular world for its quality, just as the worth of one human being could be measured against the worth of another. The process of artistic evaluation, appreciation, and criticism enters Western thought for the first time in the Renaissance.

JOSQUIN DESPREZ (CA. 1440–1521) AND THE RENAISSANCE MOTET

FIGURE 5–4

The only surviving portrait of Josquin Desprez.

Josquin Desprez was one of the greatest composers of the Renaissance or, indeed, of any age (Fig. 5–4). He was born somewhere near the present border between France and Belgium about 1440, and died in the same region in 1521. Yet, like so many musicians of northern France, he was attracted to Italy for reasons of professional and monetary gain. Between 1459 and 1504 he worked successively as a singer at the cathedral of Milan, in the chapel of a cardinal in Rome, in the Sistine Chapel of the pope, and finally in the chapel of the duke of Ferrara. Several contemporary accounts, as well as his frequent movement from one employer to another, suggest that he possessed a temperamental, egotistical spirit typical of many artists of the Renaissance: He composed only when he, not his patron, wished; he demanded a salary twice that of composers only slightly less gifted; and he would break into a rage when singers tried to tamper with the notes he had written. Yet Josquin's contemporaries and immediate successors recognized his genius. Castiglione (*The Book of the Courtier*, 1528) and Rabelais (*Pantagruel*, 1535) praised him. He was the favorite of Martin Luther, who said, "Josquin is master of the notes, which must express what he desires; other

composers can do only what the notes dictate." The Florentine humanist
Cosimo Bartoli compared him to the great Michelangelo (1475–1564), who
had decorated the ceiling of the chapel where Josquin once sang (Fig. 5–5):

> Josquin may be said to have been a prodigy of nature, as our Michelangelo
> Buonarroti has been in architecture, painting, and sculpture; for, as there has
> not thus far been anybody who in his compositions approaches Josquin, so
> Michelangelo, among all those who have been active in these his arts, is still
> alone and without a peer; both one and the other have opened the eyes of all
> those who delight in these arts or are to delight in them in the future.

Josquin wrote more than twenty settings of the Ordinary of the Mass and
a large number of French chansons (see pages 75–79). But he especially
excelled in the genre of the motet. Composers had written motets in different forms and musical styles since the thirteenth century and continued to
do so into the nineteenth. The **motet** in the Renaissance can be defined as a
composition for a choir, setting a Latin text on a sacred subject, and intended
to be sung in a church or chapel or at home in private devotion. Most motets
in the Renaissance, as well as most Masses for the church, were sung **a cappella** (literally, "in the chapel"), meaning that they were performed by voices alone without any sort of instrumental accompaniment. (Instruments
other than the organ were generally not allowed in churches during the
Middle Ages and Renaissance.) This, in part, accounts for the often serene
quality of the sound of Renaissance sacred music. Indeed, the Renaissance
has been called "the golden age of *a cappella* singing."

Josquin's motet *Ave Maria* was written about 1485 when the composer was
in Rome in the service of Cardinal Ascanio Sforza. It is composed in honor of
the Virgin Mary, and employs the standard four voice parts: soprano, alto,
tenor, and bass. As the motet unfolds, the listener hears the voices enter in
succession with the same musical motive. This process is called **imitation,** a

the motet

imitation

FIGURE 5–5

The "Creation of Adam" by
Michelangelo, part of the ceiling of
the Sistine Chapel. Michelangelo
began painting in the Sistine Chapel
in 1508, a few years after Josquin
Desprez had sung there as a member
of the papal chapel.

procedure whereby one or more voices duplicate in turn the notes of a melody:

EXAMPLE 5–1

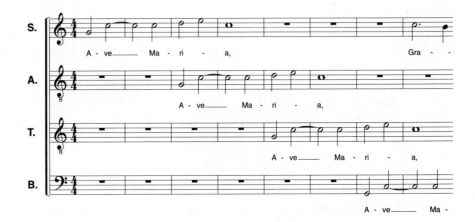

Josquin will also sometimes have one pair of voices imitate another, the tenor and bass, for example, imitating what the alto and soprano have just sung:

EXAMPLE 5–2

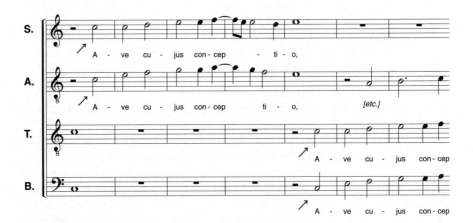

In imitative writing the voices all have a chance to present equally the melodic material and thus are all of equal importance. Moreover, because they all enter independently, imitative writing invariably produces counterpoint*—independent voices working with and against one another in a harmonious fashion. In Josquin's *Ave Maria* sections in imitative counterpoint (polyphony*) alternate with passages of chordal writing (homophony*) in order to achieve musical variety. Josquin and his contemporaries favored imitative writing because the quality of balance and proportion that could be achieved by four equal voices was harmonious with the notion of balance and symmetry much prized in the visual arts during the Renaissance (see Fig. 5–2).

As to the overall structure of Josquin's *Ave Maria,* it is organized in something akin to the way a humanistic orator would construct a persuasive speech or address. It begins with an introductory salutation to the Virgin sung in imitation. Thereafter, a key word "Ave" ("Hail") sparks a series of salutes to the Virgin, each making reference to one of her principal feast days during the church year (Conception, Nativity, Annunciation, Purification, and Assumption). At the end of this series of hails comes a final exclamation, "O mother of God, be mindful of me. Amen." These last words are set in a striking succession of imposing chords, with each syllable of text getting its own chord. The chordal, homophonic treatment allows this final sentence to stand out with absolute clarity. In this way is fulfilled the humanistic ideal that text and music work together to persuade and move the listener, in this case toward greater devotion to the Virgin Mary.

LISTENING GUIDE

Josquin Desprez
Motet, *Ave Maria* (ca. 1485)

CD 1/6
6–Tape 1A
2–Tape 1A

0:00	All four voices present each two-word phrase in turn	Ave Maria, gratia plena, Dominus tecum, virgo serena.	Hail Mary, full of grace. The Lord be with you, serene Virgin.
0:46	Soprano and alto are imitated by tenor and bass; then all four voices work to a peak on "laetitia" ("joy")	Ave cujus conceptio, Solemni plena gaudio, Coelestia, terrestria, Nova replet laetitia.	Hail to you whose conception, With solemn rejoicing, Fills heaven and earth With new joy.
1:20	Imitation in pairs; soprano and alto answered by tenor and bass	Ave cujus nativitas Nostra fuit solemnitas, Ut lucifer lux oriens, Verum solem praeveniens.	Hail to you whose birth Was to be our solemnity, As the rising morning star Anticipates the true sun.
1:58	More imitation by pairs of voices; soprano and alto followed by tenor and bass	Ave pia humilitas, Sine viro foecunditas, Cujus annuntiatio, Nostra fuit salvatio.	Hail pious humility, Fruitful without man, Whose annunciation Was to be our salvation.
2:26	Chordal writing (no imitation); meter changes from duple to triple	Ave vera virginitas, Immaculata castitas, Cujus purificatio Nostra fuit purgatio.	Hail true virginity, Immaculate chastity, Whose purification Was to be our purgation.
3:03	Return to duple meter; soprano and alto imitated by tenor and bass	Ave praeclara omnibus Angelicis virtutibus, Cujus fuit assumptio Nostra glorificatio.	Hail shining example Of all angelic virtues, Whose assumption Was to be our glorification.
3:58	Strict chordal writing; clear presentation of the text	O Mater Dei, Memento mei. Amen.	Oh Mother of God, Be mindful of me. Amen.

(Listening Exercise 14)

POPULAR MUSIC IN THE RENAISSANCE: THE MADRIGAL

The chordal section that catches the listener's attention at the end of Josquin's *Ave Maria* is both distinctive and new. Yet chordal writing first rose to prominence during the Renaissance, not in the Masses and motets of the church, but in the secular, more popular music of the middle class. The appearance of a middle class—and a musical repertoire for it—was an important social phenomenon of the sixteenth century. Whereas medieval society had been structured in a two-tier hierarchy with the clergy and aristocracy on top and the vast mass of common laborers at the bottom, now in the sixteenth century a third class arose. It was made up of tradesmen, merchants, bankers, lawyers, physicians, and civil servants. This "third estate" was concentrated in the cities and constituted a small but growing percentage of the population. Naturally, the urban middle class had different, more popular musical tastes than did the churchmen and the nobles.

Of course, there had always been popular music for the less exalted members of society. Yet we know much less about its history than we do of the music of the church and the aristocratic court. The reason for this is simple: Popular music usually was not written down and only rarely survived in written form. It was most often improvised on the spot, created on the spur of the moment by musicians who had learned their art orally from master teachers rather than by studying written manuscripts. Like jazz artists, blues singers, and rock musicians today, they performed without benefit of written musical notation. Music manuscripts had to be copied laboriously by hand, making them expensive. Written music was traditionally the private preserve of a wealthy, educated elite.

music printing

All of this changed, however, with the invention of music printing during the Renaissance. Music printing was first undertaken in Venice in 1501, and its effect for that art was as revolutionary then as the introduction of the computer has been in modern times. Mass production drastically reduced the cost of the individual book, putting notated music within the reach of the banker and merchant as well as bishop and noble. In addition, the new consumers lured to the market by a lower-cost product wanted a more immediately accessible sort of entertainment. They wanted music they could learn to sing and play in their homes—music in a simpler, more chordal, more tuneful style.

the madrigal

As a product of this demand for a more popular musical style, there arose in Italy about 1530 a new genre of music called the madrigal. Apparently derived from the Latin word *matricale* ("something in the mother tongue"), the **madrigal** was a musical setting of some vernacular (non-Latin) verse, usually a love poem, in which the various lines, or even single words, were sung in a highly expressive way in a mixture of imitative counterpoint and homophonic chords. Within a few short lines the range of emotional expression of the madrigal might move from the airy heights of a starry night to the depths of a lover's despair.

Nowhere in all of music does sound so artfully depict, even mimic, text as in the sixteenth-century madrigal. Each individual phrase, sometimes each word of an extravagant text, will receive its own musical painting. Thus, when the madrigal text says "chase after" or "follow quickly," the music becomes fast and one voice chases after another in musical imitation. Should the text say "arise, awake" or "clouds in showers descending," the music will ascend or descend. For words such as "pain," "anguish," "death," or "cruel fate," invariably the madrigal composer will employ a twisting chromatic* scale or a biting dissonance*. The practice of depicting the text in music, be it subtly, overtly, or even jokingly as a musical pun, is called **word painting.** Word painting became all the rage with madrigal composers in Italy and England. Even today such musical clichés as sighs and dissonances for "harsh" words are called **madrigalisms.**

word painting

The madrigal was born in Italy, but popular favor soon carried it over the Alps to Germany, Denmark, the Low Countries, and England. The first madrigals to be printed in England appeared in a publication of 1588 called *Musica transalpina (Music from across the Alps)*, a collection of more than fifty madrigals, mainly by Italian composers, with the texts translated into English. Soon English composers—all contemporaries of Shakespeare—were writing their own madrigals to new English poems. One of the best of the English madrigalists was Thomas Weelkes (1576–1623), an organist who spent most of his days in rural Chichester but ended his career in London.

the English madrigal

Weelkes's five-voice madrigal *O Care Thou Wilt Dispatch Me* (1600) has been called a madrigalian masterpiece. Here the text, evidently Weelkes's own creation, consists of two stanzas each subdivided into two pairs of lines, or couplets. The two lines within each couplet are arranged to express opposing sentiments—the cares of the world are pitted against the healing power of music. Phrases dealing with "Care," its "deadly sting," or its "cruel pain" are set in long notes with harsh dissonances or tense chromaticism. These "painful" phrases are each followed, in turn, by a lighter thought and sound to show how Care can be banished by Music; the music becomes faster and more sprightly, and ultimately breaks into a light-hearted "Fa la la" refrain. Text and sound in *O Care Thou Wilt Dispatch Me* work together in the true spirit of Renaissance humanism. They give voice once again to the belief of the ancient Greeks that music has the power to cure the sorrowful human soul.

LISTENING GUIDE

Thomas Weelkes
Madrigal, *O Care Thou Wilt Dispatch Me* (1600)

CD 1/7
6–Tape 1A

0:00	Slow, melancholy sounds with painful dissonances	O Care thou wilt dispatch me,
0:33	Notes get shorter, hence sound faster; general elevation of pitch and mood	If Music do not match thee,
0:43	Fast notes, bright major key	Fa la la la la la.
0:53	Long notes and biting dissonance return	So deadly dost thou sting me,
1:37	Lighter, faster sound; the melody moves upward	Mirth only help can bring me,
1:57	Light, tripping refrain	Fa la la la la la.
2:09	Tight chromatic lines create even greater dissonances	Hence Care, thou art too cruel,
2:46	Dissonance suddenly gives way to consonance; soprano descends diatonic scale	Come Music, sick man's jewel,
3:06	Light, fast descents down diatonic (not chromatic) scale	Fa la la la la la.
3:21	Long notes and painful dissonances return	His force had well nigh slain me,
3:51	Faster, more consonant sound	But thou must now sustain me,
4:14	Refrain this time tinged with melancholy dissonance	Fa la la la la la la.

(Listening Exercise 15)

FIGURE 5–6

Singers of a four-part madrigal during the middle of the sixteenth century. Women were very much a part of this secular, non-religious music making.

The madrigal was a truly social art, one for both men and women (Fig. 5–6). It was meant to be sung, usually with just one singer on a part, though a lute or a harpsichord might sometimes provide a background accompaniment. Most madrigals were not difficult to perform, for above all else they were intended to provide recreation for cultivated amateurs. Skill in singing such pieces was thought to be a necessary social grace for members of the upwardly mobile middle class—just as playing the piano would become in the nineteenth century. And it was meant to be fun for the performer! Vocal lines were written within a comfortable range, melodies were often triadic, rhythms were catchy, and musical puns plentiful. More than a thousand prints or collections of madrigals, each containing approximately twenty pieces, were printed in Europe before 1620. The pleasure it gave the performers accounts for its widespread popularity in the Renaissance as well as the existence of madrigal groups and societies even today.

THE COUNTER-REFORMATION AND PALESTRINA (1525–1594)

On October 31, 1517, an obscure Augustinian monk named Martin Luther nailed his ninety-five theses to the door of the castle church at Wittenberg, Germany, the first defiant act in what was to become the Protestant Reformation. Luther and his fellow reformers sought to bring an end to the persistent corruption within the Roman Catholic Church: the increased opulence and worldliness of the papacy, the selling of indulgences (spiritual grace in exchange for money), and the abuse of power in church appointments (one pope rewarded the fifteen-year-old keeper of his pet monkey by making him a cardinal). By the time the Protestant Reformation had run its course, most of Germany, Switzerland, the Low Countries, and all of England, as well as parts of France, Austria, Bohemia, Poland, and Hungary had gone over to the Protestant cause. The established Roman Catholic Church was shaken to its very foundations.

church reform

In response to this religious challenge and its attendant social and economic upheaval, the Church of Rome began to clean its own house. The cleansing applied not only to matters of spirituality and church administration but to art, liturgy, and music as well. Nudity in religious paintings, musical instruments within the church, secular tunes in the midst of polyphonic Masses, and married church singers were now deemed inappropriate to a truly pious environment.

the Council of Trent

The movement that fostered this counter reform and a more conservative and austere art within the established Church is called the Counter-Reformation. Its spirit was institutionalized in the Council of Trent (1545–1563), a congress of bishops and cardinals held at the small town of Trent in the Italian Alps. Although the assembled prelates debated many aspects of reform within the Church of Rome, the liturgy and its music occupied much of their time. What bothered the Catholic reformers most about the church music of the day was that the incessant entry of voices in musical imitation caused an overlapping of lines that obscured the text—excessively dense counterpoint was burying the sacred word of the Lord. As one well-placed bishop said derisively:

> In our times they [composers] have put all their industry and effort into the writing of imitative passages, so that while one voice says "Sanctus," another says "Sabaoth," still another says "Gloria tua," with howling, bellowing, and stammering, so that they more nearly resemble cats in January than flowers in May.

Initially, the assembled prelates considered banning music altogether from the service or limiting it to just the old, monophonic Gregorian chant. But the timely appearance of a few sacred compositions by Giovanni Pierluigi da Palestrina (1525–1594), among them his *Mass for Pope Marcellus* (1562), demonstrated to the council representatives that sacred polyphony for four, five, or six voices could still be written in a clear, dignified manner. For his role in maintaining a place for composed polyphony within the established Church, Palestrina came to be called "the savior of church music."

Palestrina was born in the small town of that name outside Rome, and spent almost his entire professional life as a singer and composer at various churches in and around the Vatican: the Sistine Chapel (Fig. 5–8), St. Peter's Basilica, St. John Lateran, and St. Mary Major. Although Paul IV, one of the more zealous of the reforming popes, dismissed him from the Sistine Chapel in 1555 because he was a married layman not conforming to the rule of celibacy, Palestrina returned to papal employment at St. Peter's in 1571 holding the titles *maestro di cappella* (master of the chapel) and ultimately *maestro compositore* (master composer).

The *Sanctus* of Palestrina's *Missa Aeterna Christi munera (Mass: Eternal Gifts of Christ)* epitomizes the musical spirit of the Counter-Reformation which then radiated from Rome. (Remember, a *Sanctus* is the fourth of five parts of the Ordinary of the Mass* which composers traditionally set to music.) Palestrina's *Sanctus* unfolds slowly and deliberately with long notes gradu-

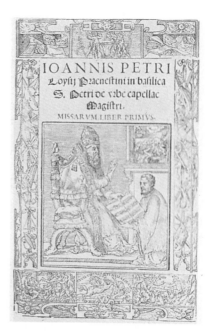

FIGURE 5–7

Palestrina presents his first published volume of Masses to Pope Julius III in 1554.

FIGURE 5–8

Interior of the Sistine Chapel. The high altar and Michelangelo's "Last Judgment" are at the far end, the balcony for the singers at the lower right.

ally giving way to shorter, faster-moving ones, but without catchy rhythms or a strong beat. As is true for Gregorian chant*, the melodic lines move mainly in stepwise fashion avoiding large leaps or chromatic turns. The sober mood is created in part by the careful use of imitative counterpoint. Each phrase of text is assigned its own motive*, which appears, in turn, in each voice. A motive used in this fashion is called a **point of imitation.** Palestrina's *Sanctus* has four points of imitation (see examples in the following Listening Guide). The first enters in the order soprano, alto, tenor, and bass, and the music works to a cadence*. While the soprano and bass conclude the cadence, the alto and tenor begin the second point of imitation. Soon this section cadences in the soprano and alto as the bass and tenor enter with the third point. Palestrina was a master of sewing a cadence to the beginning of a new point of imitation. The listener experiences not only a sense of satisfaction on arrival at the cadence but also a feeling of on-going progress as the new point pushes forward. As you listen to the *Sanctus*, follow the diagram in the Listening Guide and see if you can hear when the voices are cadencing and when a new point of imitation begins.

point of imitation

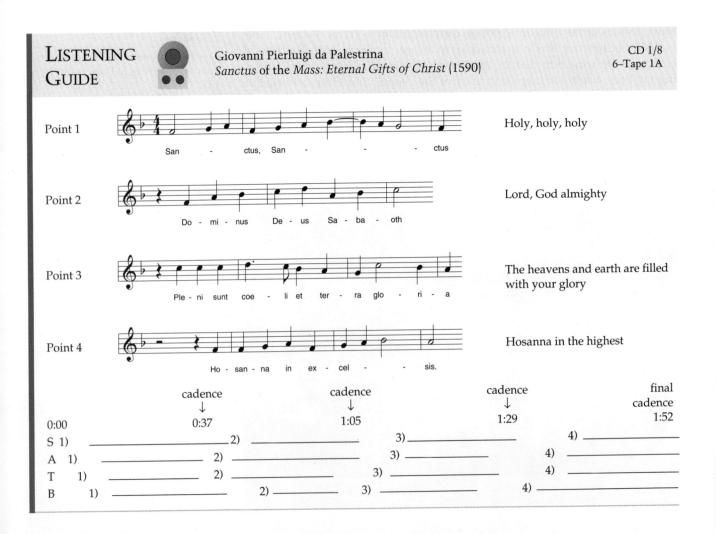

LISTENING GUIDE

Giovanni Pierluigi da Palestrina
Sanctus of the *Mass: Eternal Gifts of Christ* (1590)

CD 1/8
6–Tape 1A

Point 1 — San - ctus, San - - - ctus — Holy, holy, holy

Point 2 — Do - mi - nus De - us Sa - ba - oth — Lord, God almighty

Point 3 — Ple - ni sunt coe - li et ter - ra glo - ri - a — The heavens and earth are filled with your glory

Point 4 — Ho - san - na in ex - cel - sis. — Hosanna in the highest

	cadence ↓	cadence ↓	cadence ↓	final cadence
0:00	0:37	1:05	1:29	1:52
S 1) ———	2) ———		3) ———	4) ———
A 1) ———	2) ———		3) ———	4) ———
T 1) ———	2) ———	3) ———		4) ———
B 1) ———		2) ———	3) ———	4) ———

Male Choirs

Notice on our recording of Palestrina's *Sanctus* that the soprano part is performed by males singing in head voice, or what is called *falsetto* voice. This is an historically authentic manner of performance. Following an early decree of the Apostle Paul, women in the Middle Ages and Renaissance were not allowed to sing in the Roman Church, except in convents. Similarly, women were not allowed to appear in public in theatrical productions, tragic or comic, in territories under strict church control. Their participation in musical activities was limited to secular music making at court and at home, singing madrigals, for example, in a more domestic environment. Thus, polyphonic church choirs in the Renaissance were exclusively male, the soprano part being performed by either choirboys or by adult males singing in *falsetto*. Beginning in 1565, however, castratos (castrated males) were introduced into the papal chapel, mainly as a money-saving measure. A single castrato could produce as much volume as two falsettists or three or four boys. Surprisingly, castrati sopranos remained a hallmark of the papal chapel until 1903 when they were officially banned by Pope Pius X.

All-male choir with choirboys for the soprano part as depicted in a sixteenth-century Italian fresco.

Palestrina's music best captures the serene, sober spirit of the Counter-Reformation, embodying all that Roman authority thought proper church music should be. After his death in 1594, the legend of Palestrina, "savior of church music," continued to grow. Later composers such as Bach (Mass in B minor, 1733) and Mozart (Requiem Mass, 1791) incorporated elements of Palestrina's style into their sacred compositions. Even in our universities today, courses in counterpoint for advanced music students usually include some practice in composing in the pure, contrapuntally correct style of Palestrina. Thus, the spirit of the Counter-Reformation, distilled into a set of contrapuntal rules, continued to influence musicians long after the Renaissance had come to an end.

LISTENING EXERCISES

14	Josquin Desprez	CD 1/6
	Motet, *Ave Maria* (ca. 1485)	6–Tape 1A
		2–Tape 1A

Ave Maria by Josquin Desprez is a fine example of a motet using imitative counterpoint, a texture that dominated the musical style of sacred motets and Masses during the Renaissance. As you work through this exercise, you will become more familiar with how the voices unfold in this imitative, polyphonic texture.

1. (0:00) What is the order in which the voices enter?
   a. bass, tenor, alto, soprano
   b. soprano, tenor, alto, bass
   c. soprano, alto, tenor, bass
2. (1:05–1:14) What is the general direction of the music during the phrase "Coelestia, terrestria" ("heaven and earth")?
   a. rises from "heaven" to "earth"
   b. falls from "heaven" to "earth"
3. (1:18) Which voice sings the final "laetitia"?
   a. soprano   b. male alto   c. bass
4. (2:26) Not only does this section change from imitative to chordal writing, but it also changes from duple to triple meter. Which meter is more clearly pronounced—which do you feel more strongly—the previous duple or the new triple?
   a. duple   b. triple
5. (2:57) Which voice ends this section (on the word "purgatio")?
   a. bass   b. male alto   c. soprano
6. (3:58) Is this final, chordal section written in homophony or counterpoint? _____
7. (4:23) On the last word ("Amen"), do the voices change pitches on the two syllables ("A" and "men") or do they repeat their pitches?
   _____

8. Which is true throughout this motet?
   a. in the imitative sections the soprano and alto always enter before the tenor and bass
   b. in the imitative sections the tenor and bass always enter before the soprano and alto
9. Are there any instruments accompanying the voices in this performance? _____
10. What is this style of performance called? _____

| | Thomas Weelkes | CD 1/7 |
| 15 | Madrigal, *O Care Thou Wilt Dispatch Me* (1600) | 6–Tape 1A |

Thomas Weelkes's madrigal *O Care Thou Wilt Dispatch Me* consists of four couplets, each followed by a "Fa la la" refrain. The mood within each three-line unit gradually changes from a dark, somber feeling, to a lighter one, and ultimately to a carefree state of mind, once the refrain is reached. The following questions are intended to illuminate this structure, showing how the composer makes four successive journeys from the depths of despair to a happier realm:

(O Care thou wilt dispatch me)
1. (0:00) Which voice starts this madrigal, the tenor or the soprano?
   _____

(If Music do not match thee)
2. (0:31) Is there a noticeable pause or silence between the lines of this first couplet? _____

(Fa la la la la la la)

3. (0:52–0:56) Which voice is holding a note so as to provide a bridge or link into the next couplet?
   a. soprano   b. alto   c. bass

(So deadly dost thou sting me)

4. (0:53–1:36) For this dissonant section, do the voices sing long, sustained pitches or rapidly fly up and down the scale? _____

(Mirth only help can bring me)

(Fa la la la la la la)

5. (2:05–2:08) Is the chord that ends this first stanza of two couplets a bright major chord or a dark minor chord? _____

6. Is there a pause or cessation of sound here between the two stanzas? _____

(Hence Care, thou art too cruel)

7. (2:09) Which voice starts the second stanza? _____
   a. soprano   b. tenor   c. bass

(Come Music, sick man's jewel)

(Fa la la la la la la)

(His force had well nigh slain me)

(But thou must now sustain me)

8. (3:51–4:13) Which phrase more accurately describes this passage?
   a. imitative counterpoint   b. chordal homophony

(Fa la la la la la la)

9. (4:14–4:36) Which is true of this final statement of the refrain?
   a. it has gotten even faster in order to drive toward the final cadence
   b. it has slowed down to signal that the end is near

10. (4:31–4:36) Is the final chord major or minor? _____

KEY WORDS

a cappella	humanism	motet
castrato	imitation	point of imitation
Council of Trent	madrigal	Sistine Chapel
Counter-reformation	madrigalism	word painting
falsetto voice		

6 EARLY BAROQUE MUSIC

I t is a fact of historical evolution that the fruits of any cultural period have grown from seeds sown in the preceding epoch. So it is
with the Baroque era that certain qualities in the music of the late
Renaissance were cultivated to the exclusion of all others. These
aspects of musical style developed to the point that the art they
embodied was fundamentally different from that of the preceding epoch,
and soon this new art was given a new name.

"Baroque" is the term used to describe the art, architecture, dance, and
music of the period 1600–1750. It is taken from the Portuguese word *barroco*,
meaning a pearl of irregular shape then used in jewelry and fine decoration.
During the eighteenth century the term "Baroque" was applied by various
observers to indicate a rough, bold instrumental sound in music and excessive ornamentation in the visual arts. To the philosopher Jean-Jacques
Rousseau (1712–1778), "A baroque music is that in which the harmony is
confused, charged with modulations and dissonances, the melody is harsh
and little natural, the intonation difficult, and the movement constrained."
Thus, originally, "Baroque" had a pejorative meaning. It signified distortion,
excess, and extravagance. Only during the twentieth century, with a new-
found appreciation of the painting of Peter Paul Rubens (1577–1640), the
sculpture of Gian Lorenzo Bernini (1598–1680), and the music of Johann
Sebastian Bach (1685–1750), among others, has the term "Baroque" come to
assume a positive meaning in Western cultural history.

Baroque art and architecture have several distinctive characteristics. These
qualities are observable in the music of the period as well. What strikes us
most when we encounter a monument of Baroque planning, such as the
basilica of St. Peter in Rome or the palace of Versailles outside of Paris, is
that everything is constructed on a massive scale. The plazas, gardens, foun-
tains, colonnades, and buildings are all of the grandest design. Similarly,
human forms, as presented in the painting and sculpture of the time, are
larger than life. Look at the ninety-foot-high baldachin inside St. Peter's and
imagine how it dwarfs the priest at the altar below (Fig. 6–1). The nearby
statue of St. Helena with Cross is almost twenty feet tall. Outside the basilica
a circle of colonnades forms a courtyard large enough to encompass several

FIGURES 6–1 AND 6–2

(left) Bernini's baldachin in St. Peter's, Rome. Standing more than ninety feet high, this canopy above the high altar is marked by twisted columns and curving shapes, color, and movement, all typical of Baroque art. (right) St. Peter's Square, designed by Bernini in the mid seventeenth century, here shown in a drawing by G. B. Piranesi (ca. 1720–1778).

FIGURE 6–3

The chapel of the palace of Versailles (1699–1710) exhalts the power of the French monarch as much as it does the Lord. Note the organ in the background.

football fields (Fig. 6–2). Or consider the French king's palace of Versailles, constructed during the reign of Louis XIV (1643–1715), so monumental in scope that it formed a small independent city, home to several thousand court functionaries (Fig. 6-3).

The music composed for performance in such vast expanses was also grandiose. Instrumental groups approaching the size of the modern orchestra came into being, and choral works for twenty-four, forty-eight, and even fifty-three separate vocal parts were written. Mostly intended for spacious churches, these compositions for multiple choruses with instrumental accompaniment have come to epitomize the grand or colossal Baroque.

Once the exteriors of these large Baroque palaces and churches were built, the artists of the time went to the opposite extreme, filling the long lines with an overabundance of small, decorative details. It is as if monumental space had created a vacuum into which the artist rushed with a certain nervous energy. The *Rape of the Sabine Women* by Nicolas Poussin (1594–1665), for example, has the spatial proportions of colossal Baroque art, anchored by the towering figure of Romulus on the left and massive Roman pillars on the right; yet it has energy, power, and movement, mainly because of the great number of participants in the drama, the positioning of the figures, and the detail with which they are drawn (Fig. 6–4). The painting is at once spacious and cluttered. When filling the interior of a church the sculptor or carver employed decorative scrolls, floral capitals, and multiple layers of adornment to complete and add warmth to a large expanse (Fig. 6–5).

Similarly, when expressed in the music of the Baroque era, this love of busy detail within large-scale compositions took the form of vigorous, pulsating rhythms with strong, regular beats and many smaller subdivisions. It also was expressed by the use of musical ornaments, whether for instruments such as the violin or harpsichord (see page 103) or for voice. Notice, in figure 6–6, the abundance of ornaments and figural patterns in just a few bars of music for violin by Arcangelo Corelli (1653–1713). Such ornaments were equally popular with the singers of the early Baroque era when the cult of the vocal virtuoso first began to emerge.

FIGURES 6–4 AND 6–5

(left) Nicolas Poussin, *Rape of the Sabine Women* (1647). The painter said of this work that "it is violent and furious, very severe and calculated to produce amazement." (right) Church of the monastery of St. Florian, Austria (1686–1708). The powerful pillars and arches provide a strong structural framework, while the painted ceiling and heavily foliated capitals provide decoration and warmth.

We observed in the music of the Renaissance (1475–1600) a growing awareness of the capacity of this art to sway, or affect, the emotions. This belief in the powers of music to move the listener intensified in the Baroque period. Musical moods now came to be called the "affections," and it was the task of the composer to fashion a musical language that could vividly express many and varied affections.

Painters and sculptors, too, sought to increase emotional expression, which they did by means of exaggeration and distortion. The new emotionalism in Baroque art can easily be seen by comparing the *David* of Gian Lorenzo Bernini (1598–1680), with its fierce visage and twisted body (Fig. 6–7), with Michelangelo's serenely balanced treatment of the same subject done about a hundred years earlier (see page 85). Moreover, the spirit of the Baroque age required of both artist and composer that the emotional "units" they created be large, or long-lasting, and clearly defined. Baroque music does not change hurriedly from one mood to another as was the practice, for example, in the Renaissance madrigal where the musical feeling changed to reflect the meaning of each new phrase or word (see page 91). Instead, in the newer Baroque style each piece or each large section of a piece carried a single mood or affection throughout—joy, jealousy, resignation, agony, triumph, and others. What is perhaps unique about Baroque music and Baroque art in general is not only its intense expression but also the clear-cut way in which one emotion, color, or spatial unit is kept separate and distinct from the next.

FIGURE 6–6

Corelli's sonata for violin and *basso continuo*, Opus 5, No. 1. The continuo provides the structural support while the violin adds elaborate decoration above.

CHARACTERISTICS OF BAROQUE MUSIC

The hundred and fifty years encompassed by the Baroque era (1600–1750) witnessed significant changes in musical style, from the straightforward homophony of Giovanni Gabrieli (ca. 1557–1612) to the complex polyphony of Johann Sebastian Bach (1685–1750). It also saw the introduction of many new musical forms and genres, which we discuss later in this chapter and the next: the sonata, suite, concerto, cantata, opera, oratorio, and fugue. Yet despite such stylistic evolution and formal innovation, there was one musical element that remained constant throughout the Baroque—the *basso continuo,* or "thorough bass" as it was called in seventeenth-century England.

The *Basso Continuo*

The **basso continuo** was a small ensemble of at least two instrumentalists who provided a foundation for the melody or melodies above. One performer played an instrument that could produce chords, usually the organ or harpsichord, but sometimes even a large lute. The other played a low-sounding instrument, like the cello, the cellolike *viola da gamba* (Fig. 6–8) or the bassoon, which played the bass line. By having the harpsichord, for example, generate the basic chords of the piece, a composition acquired a solid harmonic foundation. At the same time, the bass instrument always doubled the lowest note played by the left hand of the harpsichordist, thereby giving the bass line new and greater power.

The additional weight that the *basso continuo* lent to the bass reflected the fact that the music of the early Baroque period had assumed a new structure. In the Mass and motet of the Renaissance, the voices spin out a web of imitative counterpoint, and the character and importance of each of the lines is equal:

FIGURE 6–7

Gian Lorenzo Bernini's *David* (1623) displays a vitality and restless energy of the sort that can be heard in the music of the Baroque era.

FIGURE 6–8

Basso continuo and violin. The continuo consists of a harpsichord and a large string instrument, the *viola da gamba,* or bass viol as it was called in England. The viol had six strings and produced a slightly darker less brilliant sound than members of the violin family. The gambist playing here is Eva Linfield.

In early Baroque music, however, the voices are no longer equal. Rather, there is a polarity of force directed toward the top and bottom:

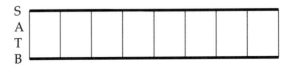

The soprano carries the melody, the bass provides a strong harmonic support. In between, the middle voices often do little more than fill out the texture. If Renaissance music is conceived polyphonically and horizontally, line by line, that of the early Baroque period is organized homophonically and vertically, chord by chord. The *basso continuo* helps establish a strong bass and assures that the fundamentally chordal structure of the music hold tight.

universal use of the basso continuo

The sound of the *basso continuo* (or simply continuo in English) pervaded almost all Baroque music. When a solo violinist or flutist played a sonata, or when a singer performed a recitative or aria (see page 108), the continuo was there; thus, three performers were involved, a principal and an accompanying cast of two (Fig. 6–8). As we shall see, the continuo also held together soloists and orchestra in the Baroque concerto, just as it unified multiple choirs in polychoral motets for the church. For church music it was the organ—the traditional instrument of the church—that played the keyboard continuo, while in virtually all other music that chord-supplying function was provided by the harpsichord. Indeed, it is the continual tinkling of the harpsichord, in step with the bass sounds of a cello or bassoon, that signals to the listener that the music being played comes from the Baroque era.

Treatment of Musical Elements

Baroque music, as we have seen, is marked by spaciousness and grandeur, by the desire to create a powerful, unified mood within each work or large section of a work, and by its chordal framework and strong bass line, both generated by the *basso continuo*. These are qualities to be heard in all Baroque music. But there are others as well which appear as distinctive treatments of familiar musical elements. (In the next chapter we see how the stylistic traits of early Baroque music were modified and extended by Bach and Handel in the late Baroque period.)

MELODY. In the Renaissance melody was more or less all of one type. It was a direct, uncomplicated line that could be either sung by the voice or played on an instrument, according to the wishes of the performer. Now in early Baroque music, beginning about 1600, two different melodic styles begin to develop: a dramatic, virtuosic style in singing and, by contrast, a more mechanical, repetitious style in instrumental music. Despite the increasing virtuosity of vocal music, attention is no longer focused exclusively on the voice. Throughout the Baroque era there is a new emphasis on writing melodies specifically for instruments such as the harpsichord and violin, melodies that were idiomatic (well-suited) to the technical demands of these instruments.

The Harpsichord

The harpsichord has been called the workhorse of the Baroque era because it served both as the main instrument for accompaniment and as a solo instrument in its own right (see Figs. 3–14 and 6–8). In this sense the harpsichord functioned much like the piano would later in the Classical and Romantic periods, as an accompanying and a solo instrument. The sound of the harpsichord is produced by depressing a key which pushes up a quill or (nowadays) a plastic "pick" to pluck a taut wire string. This abrupt plucking of wire is what creates the tinkling sound of the instrument. Unlike the piano, in which a complicated mechanism permits different levels of finger pressure to achieve a wide range of dynamics, the harpsichord cannot produce a louder or softer sound because the plucking mechanism transmits a constant level of force to the string. There are, therefore, no subtle gradations of sound on the harpsichord. When greater volume is needed, an additional full set of strings is brought into play to double the sound, and all the music thereafter will be loud until this set of strings is disengaged. Thus, the harpsichord typifies the way in which sound was produced in the Baroque period. There are no gradual swells and decreases, but only abrupt changes in the amount or volume of sound. The harpsichord was invented in the late Middle Ages, reached the peak of its popularity in the Baroque era, and went out of fashion in the time of Mozart (1756–1791), replaced by the more flexible, responsive, and potentially powerful piano.

Early in the Baroque period a new melodic technique called sequence was applied to melody. A melodic **sequence** is the repetition of a musical motive at successively higher or lower degrees of the scale. Example 6–1 shows a sequence, indeed an exceptionally long sequence, from the music of the early Baroque composer Claudio Monteverdi (1567–1643). Notice how the initial motive is repeated seven times, each time one step lower than before.

melodic sequence

EXAMPLE 6–1

The sequence first appears in the music of the Baroque era and continues to be a standard melodic device into the twentieth century.

HARMONY. Baroque harmonies are chordally conceived and tightly bound to the *basso continuo*. As the seventeenth century progresses, harmonies unfold more and more in familiar patterns as standard harmonic progressions—chord progressions*—begin to emerge. The shortest and most frequent of these is the V–I (dominant–tonic) cadence (see page 32). The advent of standard harmonic progressions like the V–I cadence gives added direction and cohesion to the music.

chord progressions

Attending this development is the growing importance—and eventual total domination—of the major and minor system of keys. These two scale patterns, major and minor, replaced the dozen or so scales (or "modes" as they were called) used during the Renaissance and before. Moreover, by reducing music to just two qualities of sound, the listener could more easily distinguish one from the other. Composers could play minor off against major, or vice versa, to create the emotional effects so important in Baroque music.

major and minor keys

RHYTHM. Rhythm in Baroque music is characterized by uniformity. Just as a single mood, or affect, is carried from the beginning to the end of a piece, so the rhythmic patterns heard at the beginning will surface again and again, right to the end. This tendency toward rhythmic uniformity and rhythmic drive becomes more and more pronounced as the Baroque era proceeds.

DYNAMICS. Baroque music, like Baroque art, is organized in units of distinctly different, yet independent, moods and colors. Dynamics do not change gradually from one section or piece to the next. Rather, a single dynamic range, whether loud or soft, will hold fast until abruptly replaced by another. This phenomenon of shifting the volume of sound suddenly and dramatically from one level to another is called **terraced dynamics.** Changing dynamics in this fashion, especially when combined with equally abrupt changes in orchestration and shifts to major or minor tonality, helps create the clearly sectionalized sound of Baroque music.

The Rise of Instrumental Music

Composers of the early Baroque period were the first to think of instrumental music as different from vocal music. As we have said, musical lines in the Renaissance were assigned indiscriminately to any voice or any instrument. Baroque composers not only started to differentiate between a vocal style of writing and an instrumental one but they also began to assign specific musical lines to specific instruments, according to their natural strengths and weaknesses. The brasses, for example, were often given short figures with dotted rhythms which maximized their capacity for sharp attacks. They would not, however, be assigned rapid running scales because of the difficulties in pitch they would encounter. Fast scales were most often given over to the more agile violins. Thus here in the early Baroque era, the practice of writing idiomatically for the instruments first appears. The first composer to conceive of musical lines in terms of particular instruments was Giovanni Gabrieli (ca. 1557–1611), who spent his entire career in Venice.

T HE VENETIAN POLYCHORAL MOTET

Venice, the Queen of the Seas, was—and remains—a city of canals, arching bridges, and colorful palaces. Reaching its zenith of commercial and economic importance in the fifteenth century, it owed its success partly to its truly republican form of government and partly to its strategic location at the head of the Adriatic Sea, which made it a natural center of trade (Fig. 6–9). The focus of civic and spiritual life in Venice was the palace of the doge (or mayor) and the adjoining basilica of St. Mark with its spacious piazza in front (Fig. 6–10). St. Mark's, which preserves the remains of the Apostle Mark beneath the high altar, has an architectural plan unique among the major churches of the West. It is built in the form of an equal-sided Greek cross, probably because for centuries Venice was under the political and artistic domination of the Byzantine Empire.

Beginning in the mid-sixteenth century, musicians exploited the unusual architectural plan of St. Mark's by composing motets for it for two or more choirs. At first these separate ensembles were placed in the two singing gal-

FIGURE 6–9

A map of Italy showing Milan, Venice, Rome, Bologna, and Florence.

FIGURE 6–10

Piazza San Marco painted by Gentile Bellini (ca. 1429–1507). St. Mark's was the focal point of all religious and civic activities in Venice.

leries on opposite sides of the main aisle (Fig. 6–11). Later they were also stationed in the other elevated galleries that adjoined the central dome. By situating groups of musicians in these separate, elevated lofts—or loggias as they are called—composers were able to create new sonic effects that astonished the listeners seated or standing below. To a visitor to St. Mark's in the early seventeenth century, the novelty of the musical environment must have been as striking as the twentieth-century change from mono to stereophonic or even to quadrophonic sound.

Giovanni Gabrieli (ca. 1557–1612)

The composer who made the most of the opportunities afforded by the architecture of St. Mark's was Giovanni Gabrieli, a native of Venice. Gabrieli wrote little secular music and few Masses for the church. Most of his creative energy was devoted to the composition of ceremonial motets for the semireligious occasions of state which took place beneath the domes of St. Mark's. One such piece is his polychoral motet *In ecclesiis (In the Churches)* written for three choirs. Gabrieli's first musical group consists of a quartet of vocal soloists; the second is a vocal chorus; and the third is an ensemble of six instruments: a violin, two trombones, and three cornettos (see page 81, Fig. 4–10). Accompanying all three groups is the *basso continuo*, here supplied by an organ.

Not only was Gabrieli the first composer to prescribe specific instruments, he was also one of the first to indicate in the score a dynamic level at which the music was to be played, either *piano* (soft) or *forte* (loud). The volume of sound was not changed gradually but suddenly, being added or subtracted in blocks, as is typical of Baroque music. As you listen to the motet *In the Churches,* notice how exuberant and virtuosic the vocal writing of the soloists (Choir 1) has become and how this unit of music differs in style from the block created by the instruments (Choir 3). Notice also that the chorus (Choir 2) regularly inserts a refrain on the word "Alleluja." This serves as a solid counterweight to keep the extravagant lines of the solo singers in balance. Energetic expression within solidly constructed formal units is a hallmark of Baroque art.

FIGURE 6–11

Interior of the basilica of St. Mark with a view of the upper galleries where musicians sometimes performed polychoral motets.

LISTENING GUIDE

Giovanni Gabrieli
Motet, *In the Churches* (1612)

CD 1/9
6–Tape 1A

0:00	Soprano soloist of Choir 1 plus organ *basso continuo*	In ecclesiis, benedicite Domino	In the churches, bless the Lord
0:16	Choir 2 and soprano echo, rising rapid notes on third and final time	Alleluja	
0:31	Bass soloist of Choir 1 plus continuo; peaks on "anima mea" ("my soul")	In omni loco dominationis, benedic anima mea Dominum	In every holy place, may my soul bless the Lord
1:09	Choir 2 and bass echo	Alleluja	
1:21	An instrumental interlude; begins solemnly but changes to lively dotted rhythms, ends with descending sequence	Sinfonia played by Choir 3	
1:53	Tenor and alto of Choir 1 sing duet accompanied by the instrumental ensemble and continuo	In Deo salutari meo, et gloria mea	In God is my salvation and my glory
2:35	Duet continues; notes become more rapid and rise in a sequence	Deus, auxilium meum et spes mea in Deo est	Lord, my help and my hope is in God
3:20	Choir 2 with alto and tenor echos	Alleluja	
3:35	Soprano and bass duet with imitation and echos	Deus noster, te invocamus, te laudamus, te adoramus	Our Lord, we call to you, we praise you, we adore you
4:17	Duet continues; change to lively triple meter on "vivifica nos" ("revivify us")	Libera nos, salva nos, vivifica nos	Deliver us, save us, revivify us
4:46	Choir 2 with soprano and bass echo	Alleluja	
5:03	Rich-sounding chords for all three choirs on "Deus," followed by long notes in the bass	Deus, adjutor noster in aeternum (repeated)	Lord, our judge forever
6:25	Choirs 2 and 3 with echoes by Choir 1 (soloists); third statement of "Alleluja" repeated; strong final cadence added	Alleluja	

(Listening Exercise 16)

The contrast between Gabrieli's instrumentally supported motet of the early Baroque and Palestrina's *a cappella* (unaccompanied) *Sanctus* of the Renaissance (see page 94) could not be more striking. As it moves from large section to section, Gabrieli's motet displays dramatic changes of texture, dynamics, and musical color, all for bold effect. A prominent place is now given to a colorful instrumental ensemble (Choir 3). *In the Churches* sounds exuberant, brash, even prideful, like the city of Venice itself.

E ARLY BAROQUE OPERA

Opera was created in Italy around 1600. Literally, opera means "work": The word first appeared in the Italian phrase *opera drammatica in musica* (a dramatic work set to music). Thus, opera implies an association of music and drama—music is to heighten the emotional intensity of the action that unfolds on the stage. Turning away from the Renaissance notion that the emotions of an individual could be best expressed by a group of singers, opera stressed solo singing at the expense of the polyphonic choir. Choral singing might be a useful way to convey abstract religious thought in a Mass or motet, but to communicate raw human emotion, the solo song, allowing greater freedom and flexibility, was a more effective vehicle. One individual could express his or her feelings in a more direct, personal way. Tying together a succession of solo songs and recitations so as to create a large-scale musical drama satisfied the Baroque desire for grandiose form as well as its need for intense, even exaggerated, personal expression.

FIGURE 6–12

Portrait of Claudio Monteverdi by Bernardo Strozzi (1581–1628).

Claudio Monteverdi (1567–1643)

Claudio Monteverdi was the first great composer of opera. He succeeded Giovanni Gabrieli as the principal composer at St. Mark's in Venice in 1613 and held that post until the time of his death thirty years later. Although he was skilled at writing polychoral motets for the church, it was in opera that Monteverdi made his greatest contribution to the history of music. Monteverdi's first opera, entitled *Orfeo,* was composed in 1607. The subject was drawn from ancient Greek folklore and relates how Orpheus, on learning that his wife had been bitten by a snake and carried off to Hell, undertakes a perilous descent into the Inferno to bring her back to earth. Along the way he encounters the many deadly spirits, gods, and goddesses who inhabit the underworld of Greek mythology. By the end of Monteverdi's life, however, the composer had turned to a different sort of drama. His *L'Incoronazione di Poppea (The Coronation of Poppea),* written in 1642, is based on real historical figures and explores the theme of human sexual desire.

Perhaps this new emphasis on human emotions was due to a growing popular interest in opera. The first public opera house, San Cassiano, opened in Venice in 1637, and by the end of the century there were no fewer than seven such theaters offering opera to an eager populace in this city of about 150,000 (Fig. 6–13). It is clear from contemporary reports that the

public opera in Venice

FIGURE 6–13

Teatro Grimani was one of seven theaters given over exclusively to opera in seventeenth century Venice. The orchestra is immediately before the stage.

Baroque opera house had none of the solemn atmosphere that we associate with opera today. Those who could afford it bought boxes in the galleries where they talked, played cards, ate and drank, and occasionally spat on those who walked around the less expensive, open floor below. Under these circuslike conditions an opera had to be of exceptionally fine quality to hold the audience's attention.

Such an opera is Monteverdi's masterpiece *The Coronation of Poppea*, perhaps the greatest opera written before those of Mozart. The opera might be subtitled "The Triumph of Lust," for here vice is victorious over virtue. The **libretto,** or text of the drama, may be summarized as follows: Roman emperor Nero feels the most carnal sort of desire for the beautiful courtesan Poppea. To achieve a union with her, he sentences to death his wise but prudish counselor Seneca, banishes his wife Ottavia, and places the ambitious Poppea on the throne of all Rome.

We will listen to only one scene (Act II, Scene 6) of this nearly three-hour work, but it will be sufficient to gain a sense of the structure and flavor of Baroque opera. Act II, Scene 6, of *Poppea* begins with a very brief recitative in which Nero announces that his bothersome adviser Seneca is now dead.

recitative **Recitative,** from the Italian word *recitativo* ("something recited"), is musically heightened speech. It is used in opera for dialogue, to report dramatic action, and generally to advance the plot. Because recitative attempts to mirror the natural stresses of oral delivery, it is often made up of rapidly repeating notes followed by one or two long notes, as at the very beginning of the scene from *Poppea:*

EXAMPLE 6–2

Hor che Se - ne - ca è mor - to
(Now that Seneca is dead)

Recitative in Baroque opera is accompanied only by the *basso continuo* playing simple chords. Such a sparsely accompanied recitative is called **secco** recitative, from the Italian for "dry." (By the nineteenth century, recitative will be accompanied by the full orchestra and called *accompagnato*.) A good example of *secco* recitative is found toward the middle of the scene (4:12) when Lucan, Nero's faithful servant, addresses his master "Tu vai, signor" ("My lord, you delight").

In contrast to the declamatory recitatives, the most lyrical portion of Act II, Scene 6, comes toward the end, when Nero sings an aria "Son rubini *aria* preziosi" ("Precious rubies are your lovely lips") in tribute to his beloved Poppea. An **aria,** Italian for "song" or "ayre," is more expressive, more expansive, and more tuneful than a recitative. It is sung with a less rapid-fire delivery and more in the way of vocal **melisma** (one vowel luxuriously spread out over many notes as in example 6–3).

EXAMPLE 6–3

Can-tia - mo
(Let us sing)

If a recitative relates action, an aria expresses feeling. Its poetry is not narrative but lyrical, and its musical form not open-ended but closed—there is a clear beginning, climax, and conclusion. Look at the text of Nero's aria "Precious rubies" (5:34) as it appears at the end of the following Listening Guide and notice how it is full of romantic images. Moreover, as poetry, it is very tightly constructed since the Italian text is arranged as three rhymed couplets. The aria strikes the hearer as a self-contained unit, not only because it is set off by a *sinfonia* (a short instrumental piece, here beginning at 5:12), but also because it starts on one pitch (G), ascends into a range an octave above, and gradually returns to the opening pitch. Operatic arias are nearly always accompanied by full orchestra to intensify the emotion of the moment.

Recitative and aria are the two main structural units and styles of singing in Baroque opera and in opera in general. In addition, there is a third, somewhat shorter structural unit called the arioso. An **arioso** is a brief passage sung in a style about half way between aria and recitative. It is more declamatory than an aria but has fewer quickly repeating notes than a recitative. Nero's arioso "Idolo mio, Poppea" ("My idol, Poppea"; 4:40) serves to connect the preceding recitative to the following aria, a task often performed by the arioso.

Monteverdi wrote the part of Nero for a castrato, a voice given many leading operatic roles in the Baroque theater (see page 95 and also Fig. 6–14). Not only were women still proscribed from singing in church choirs but also they were not allowed to appear on stage in some church-dominated cities in Italy. This encouraged the use of the castrato, whose voice combined the power of a male frame with the agility and brilliance of the high female register. So enamored were Baroque audiences with the castrato sound that they did not think it incongruous to hear the greatest heroic male roles of the operatic stage sung by men with "womanly" voices (attending an opera has always required that the patron leave his or her credulity at the front door). Castrati fell out of fashion in the nineteenth century and disappeared completely in the early twentieth. That is why contemporary performances have women sing the castrato roles. On the recording you will hear, the part of Nero is sung by the Swedish operatic soprano Elisabeth Söderström.

FIGURE 6–14

Caricature of Carlo Broschi, one of the greatest castrati of the Baroque era, here seen playing a female role in Rome in 1724.

LISTENING GUIDE		Claudio Monteverdi *The Coronation of Poppea* (1642) Act II, Scene 6	CD 1/10 6–Tape 1B

Characters: Nero, emperor of Rome; Lucan, Nero's servant
Situation: Having disposed of his counselor Seneca, the intoxicated Nero, joined by Lucan, sings of his love for Poppea. He does so first in a duet (an aria for two), then an arioso, and finally a solo aria.

BRIEF RECITATIVE   **Nero**

0:00	*Secco* recitative (accompanied by continuo only)	Or che Seneca è morto.	Now that Seneca is dead

ARIA (DUET)   **Nero and Lucan**

0:08	Accompanied by full orchestra	Cantiam, cantiam Lucano, amorose canzoni in lode di quel viso che di sua mano Amor nel cor m'ha inciso.	Let us sing, Lucan, amorous songs in praise of that face, which Love etched upon my heart with his own hand.

0:44	Melodic sequences and strong harmonic movement	Cantiam di quel viso ridente, che spira glorie ed influisce amor.	Sing of that laughing face, which inspires to glory and goads to love.
1:31	Singing gradually grows more impassioned	Cantiam di quel viso beato in cui l'idea d'Amor se stessa pose, e seppe su le nevi, con nova maraviglia animar, incarnar la granatiglia.	Sing of that beatific face in which the idea of Love placed itself, and was able, in the snow, by another of his miracles to give life to the passion-flower.
2:19	Descending scale in bass	Cantiam di quella bocca a cui l'India e l'Arabia le perle consacrò, donò gli odori.	Sing of that mouth to which India and Arabia dedicated their pearls and offered their perfumes.
2:50	Continuo only, then flutes enter; bass repeats descending four-note motive again and again	Bocca, ahi destin, che se ragiona, o ride, con invisibil arme punge, e all'alma dona felicità mentre l'uccide. Bocca che se mi porge, lasciveggiando, il tenero rubino m'inebria il cor di nettare divino.	Mouth, ah destiny! when it speaks or laughs it wounds with invisible weapons and gives the soul bliss while it kills. Mouth, when it lasciviously offers to me its soft ruby, it makes my heart drunk with divine nectar.

RECITATIVE

			Lucan
4:12	*Secco* recitative (accompanied by continuo only)	Tu vai, signor, tu vai nell'estasi d'amor deliciando, e ti poivon dagl'occhi stille di tenerezza, lacrime di dolcezza.	My lord, you delight in the ecstasy of love, while from your eyes are falling drops of tenderness, tears of sweetness.

ARIOSO

			Nero
4:40	More expression; accompanied by continuo only	Idolo mio, Poppea, celebrati io verrei, ma son minute fiaccole, e cadenti, dirimpetto al tuo sole i detti miei.	My idol, Poppea, I want to sing your praises, but my words are merely pale fire while you are the sun.
5:12	Sinfonia: orchestra plays a light, triple-meter piece as an introduction to Nero's aria		

ARIA

			Nero
5:34	Accompanied by full orchestra; soprano works up an octave to climax on "il mio core" and then gradually descends to the end	Son rubini preziosi i tuoi labbri amorosi, il mio core costante di saldo diamente così le tue bellezze ed il mio core da care gemme ha fabbricato Amore.	Precious rubies are your lovely lips, my faithful heart is a hard diamond, thus Love has built your beauties and my heart from rare stones.

Henry Purcell (1659–1695)

An equally famous, though smaller and less grand, example of Baroque opera is *Dido and Aeneas* written in 1689 by the English composer Henry Purcell. Purcell was an organist at London's Westminster Abbey and a singer in the king's Royal Chapel. His *Dido and Aeneas* was one of the first operas composed in the English language. Yet it was not written for the king's court, but for a private girls' boarding school in the London suburb of Chelsea. The students apparently served as the singers of the chorus, while professionals from London sang the principal roles. The libretto of the opera, one appropriate for a school curriculum steeped in classical Latin, is drawn from Virgil's *Aeneid*. The Trojan hero Aeneas, fleeing his conquered homeland, sails west to found the city of Rome, but is blown off course and onto the shores of Carthage where the widowed Dido rules as queen. No sooner does the proud queen surrender herself to the soldier of fortune than the gods command him to depart for Italy and fulfill his divine destiny—to found the city of Rome. Betrayed and alone, Dido vents her feelings in an exceptionally beautiful aria, "When I am laid in earth," and then expires of a broken heart.

Dido's aria is introduced by a brief bit of recitative, "Thy hand Belinda." As recitative goes, this is one of the more expressive examples of what is at heart a declamatory, businesslike style. In the stepwise scale that descends an octave, one can feel the resignation of the abandoned Dido as she slumps into the arms of her servant Belinda:

EXAMPLE 6–4

Thy hand, Be - lin - da! Dark - ness shades me; on thy bo - som let me

rest. More I would, but Death in - vades me: Death is now a wel - come guest.

The aria that follows is constructed of two beautifully shaped musical phrases which carry the following two lines of text:

When I am laid in earth, may my wrongs create
　no trouble in thy breast.
Remember me, but ah! forget my fate.

Each of the lines is repeated, as are many individual words and pairs of words within them. Repetition of text is typical of an aria but not a recitative. It is one means by which the composer depicts emotion—the heroine can vocalize but cannot clearly articulate her feelings in complete sentences. No fewer than six times does Dido plead with Belinda, and with us, to remember her. And, indeed, we do remember, for this plaintive aria is one of the most moving in all of opera.

Purcell constructs his aria "When I am laid in earth" on a *basso ostinato*. The term **basso ostinato** is an extension of the Italian word *ostinato* (meaning "obstinate," "stubborn," or "pig-headed") and refers to the fact that a phrase in the bass, whether just a few notes or several measures, repeats over and over. English composers of the seventeenth century called the *basso ostinato* the **ground bass** because the repeating bass provided a solid foundation on which an entire composition could be built or grounded. *Basso ostinato* is a common feature of Baroque music, often used to symbolize grief.

The ostinato, or ground bass, Purcell composed for Dido's lament is five measures long. It consists of two sections (see the Listening Guide): a chromatic descent over the interval of a fourth (G, F#, F, E, E♭, D) and a two-measure cadence returning to the tonic G (B♭, C, D, G). The aria begins with one statement of this ostinato pattern played by low string instruments alone. When Dido enters she sings her phrase "When I am laid in earth, may my wrongs create no trouble in thy breast" above two statements of the ostinato.

FIGURE 6–15

Henry Purcell by an anonymous painter.

This music and text is then repeated. Statement and repeat is next applied to the second and last phrase, "Remember me, but ah! forget my fate." At the end of the repeat of this final line, the singer breaks off, as if unable to articulate further her grief. But the strings press on, carrying Dido's highly charged emotion across two final statements of the ostinato.

LISTENING GUIDE

Henry Purcell
Dido and Aeneas (1689)
Aria, "When I am laid in earth"

CD 1/11
6–Tape 1B
2–Tape 1A

Characters: Dido, queen of Carthage; Belinda, her servant
Situation: Having been deserted by her lover, Aeneas, Dido sings farewell to Belinda (and to all) before dying of a broken heart.

BRIEF RECITATIVE

0:00   Continuo played by harpsichord and cello

Thy hand, Belinda! Darkness shades me; on thy bosom let me rest. More I would—but Death invades me: Death is now a welcome guest.

ARIA

0:55   *basso ostinato* alone on cellos and double basses

1:13   *basso ostinato* with voice and strings

1:35   *basso ostinato* repeats

1:59   *basso ostinato* repeats

2:20   *basso ostinato* repeats

When I am laid in earth, may my wrongs create no trouble in thy breast. Remember me, but ah! forget my fate.

2:45	*basso ostinato* repeats
3:07	*basso ostinato* repeats
3:30	*basso ostinato* repeats
3:52	*basso ostinato* repeats
4:19	*basso ostinato* alone with strings
4:40	*basso ostinato* alone with strings

(Listening Exercise 17)

Elton John and *Basso Ostinato*

For an up-to-date example of ostinato bass, we can look at a modern aria-lament by a more recent English composer, Elton John. Although not built exclusively on an ostinato figure, John's song *Sorry Seems to Be the Hardest Word* (*Live in Australia*, MCA2-8022) nonetheless has one striking affinity to the aria by Purcell—it, too, makes use of a *basso ostinato* incorporating a chromatically descending fourth as a way of setting a very, very sad text. The ostinato pattern begins on G with a chromatically descending fourth followed by a one-measure cadence.

It's sad (so sad), it' a sad, sad situation
Bass
G   F#   F   E

              And it's getting more and more absurd
          E♭   D   F#GAD
                               (cadence)

This *basso ostinato*, and a slightly varied form of it, is then repeated several times for this and other lines of text. Compare Elton John's bass line with Purcell's *basso ostinato* (see page 112) and note that both laments are set in the key of G minor. Was the pop artist, who studied at the Royal Conservatory in London, inspired by the famous aria of his well-coiffured countryman (see Fig. 6–15)?

Elton John

THE RISE OF INSTRUMENTAL MUSIC: SONATA AND CONCERTO GROSSO

The Baroque period, as we have seen, was one in which instrumental music—music without text—rose to new prominence. Indeed, during the seventeenth century, instrumental music came to rival and ultimately surpass vocal music in importance. Idiomatic instrumental music—music written specifically to exploit the technical strengths of a particular instrument—came to be cultivated by most composers. These creators likewise demanded virtuosity—the ability to play technically demanding passages rapidly and surely—of the performer. Many of the most renowned composers of the Baroque era, including Corelli (1653–1713), Vivaldi (1678–1741), and Bach (1685–1750), were themselves virtuosos on a particular instrument. Naturally, their passion for instrumental music led to the creation of new musical forms, like the fugue (see page 137), and new musical genres, such as the sonata and concerto.

The Baroque Sonata

A **sonata** is a type of chamber music to be played on an instrument. The term was first used in Venice around 1600 to indicate a composition intended specifically to be played or sounded, as opposed to one that was to be sung. Hence, a sonata is "something sounded" in distinction to a cantata (see page 128), which is "something sung."

Usually, a sonata consisted of a collection of short pieces, each of which is called a **movement.** In the Baroque era these collections of movements were of two types. One, called the **sonata da camera** (chamber sonata), was made up of a series of dancelike movements which had the name and character of a particular dance. A typical chamber sonata might consist of an allemand, sarabande, gavotte, and gigue—all dances. The second type of sonata was called the **sonata da chiesa** (church sonata), but its movements were designated only by a tempo marking such as *grave, vivace, adagio,* or *allegro* (grave, fast and lively, slow, fast)—it was thought inappropriate to have the movements of a piece destined for the church associated with secular dances. Indeed, as the names *sonata da camera* and *sonata da chiesa* indicate, the church sonata was intended to provide background music for religious services, while the chamber sonata, with its links to the dance, was usually heard at court or in the private homes of the well-to-do.

A sonata might be written for a solo keyboard instrument like the harpsichord. Or it might be composed for a solo melody instrument like the violin, in which case three performers would be involved—the violinist and two persons playing the continuo (Fig. 6–8). But whether for solo keyboard or solo melody instrument plus continuo, the work was called a **solo sonata.** Similarly, many Baroque sonatas were written for two melody instruments, two violins or violin and oboe, for example, plus continuo. Such a force was called a **trio sonata** because the composer wrote only three musical lines, even though four performers were involved—two soloists and two players on the *basso continuo.*

chamber sonata

church sonata

trio sonata

Arcangelo Corelli (1653–1713)

The composer-virtuoso who made the Baroque solo and trio sonata internationally popular was Arcangelo Corelli. Corelli was born in 1653 near Bologna, Italy, then an important center for violin instruction and performance. By 1675 he had moved to Rome, where he remained for the duration of his life as a teacher, composer, and performer on the violin. Although Corelli's musical output was small, consisting only of five sets of sonatas and one of concertos, his works were widely admired. Such diverse composers as Johann Sebastian Bach in Leipzig, François Couperin (1668–1733) in Paris, and Henry Purcell in London either borrowed his melodies directly or more generally studied and absorbed his style.

The most remarkable aspect of Corelli's music is its harmony. It sounds modern to our ears. That is to say, we have heard so much classical and popular music that we have come to possess an almost subconscious sense of how a succession of chords, or harmonic progression, should sound. Corelli was the first in a long line of composers to establish that harmonic norm. He was the first to write fully functional harmony; in other words, in his sonatas each chord has a specific function or role in the succession of chords. Not only does the individual chord constitute an important sound in itself but it also prepares or leads toward the next, thereby helping to form a tightly linked chain of chords. They sound purposeful, well-directed. The most basic link in the chain is the V–I (dominant–tonic) cadence (see page 32). In addition, Corelli will often construct a bass line that moves upward chromatically by half step. This chromatic, stepwise motion pulls up and into the next higher note, increasing the sense of direction and cohesiveness we feel in Corelli's music.

FIGURE 6–16

Arcangelo Corelli

TRIO SONATA IN C MAJOR, OPUS 4, NO. 1 (1694)

The Trio Sonata in C major, Opus 4, No. 1, is a chamber sonata written by Corelli in 1694 for two violins and *basso continuo*, here played by a harpsichord and cello. Corelli called this sonata Opus 4, No. 1. (Composers frequently use **opus**, the Latin word meaning "work," to enumerate and identify their compositions.) This chamber sonata is in four movements, the second and fourth of which are dance movements in binary form* **(AB)**, the most common musical form for Baroque dances.

The opening *preludio* (prelude) gives the players a chance to warm up as well as establishes the general musical mood of the sonata. Note that the prelude makes use of what is called a **walking bass,** a bass that moves at a moderate, steady pace, mostly in equal note values and often stepwise up or down the scale:

walking bass

EXAMPLE 6–5

The second movement, a dance called the *corrente* (from the Italian *correre,* "to run") is rather fast and in triple meter. Here the first violin engages in a rapid dialogue with the cello. The second violin is scarcely audible as it helps fill in the chords, literally playing "second fiddle" to the first violin. The short *adagio* ("slow" movement) merely serves as a bridge that links the *corrente* with the final movement—the brisk, duple meter *allemanda* (literally, "the German dance"). This last movement, too, has a walking bass, but the tempo is so fast *(presto)* that it sounds more like a running or a sprinting bass. Of course, the dances of this chamber sonata were not actually danced; they were stylized abstractions intended only to be listened to—just as one would listen, but not dance, to a minuet by Beethoven or a waltz by Chopin.

LISTENING GUIDE

Arcangelo Corelli
Trio Sonata in C major, Opus 4, No. 1 (1694)

CD 1/12
6–Tape 1B

PRELUDE

0:00	"Walking bass" descends stepwise below dotted rhythms in violins
0:28	Cadence
0:32	Bass now moves twice as fast
0:41	Bass returns to original slow pace

CORRENTE

1:17	First violin and cello lead lively dance in triple meter
1:34	Repeat of **A**
1:49	**B** section begins with sequences in cello and violins
2:10	Rhythmic syncopation signals arrival of final cadence
2:19	Repeat of **B** including syncopation (2:40)

ADAGIO

2:53	Stationary chords in violins; only the cello moves in a purposeful fashion
4:05	Cadential chords prepare way to next movement

ALLEMANDA

4:25	Two violins move together above a racing bass
4:46	Repeat of **A** and pause
5:07	**B** section begins with sudden shift to minor key
5:23	Moves back to tonic major key for final cadence
5:27	Repeat of **B** including final shift back to major (5:43)

The Baroque Concerto

Abrupt contrast within a unity of mood—this is a hallmark of Baroque music, just as striking change between the zones of light and darkness often characterize a Baroque painting (Fig. 6–19). This aesthetic doctrine of sectional contrast within overall unity can most vividly be heard in the Baroque concerto.

A **concerto** (from the Latin *concertare*, "to strive together") is a musical composition marked by a friendly contest or competition between a soloist and an orchestra. When only one soloist confronts the orchestra, the work is a **solo concerto.** When more than one is present and they function as a unit, *concerto grosso* the piece is a **concerto grosso.** The soloists in a concerto grosso constitute a subgroup called the **concertino** ("little concert"), and the full orchestra is called the **tutti** ("all" or "everybody"). A typical concerto grosso had a concertino of two or four violins and continuo. The soloists were not highly paid masters imported from afar, but rather the regular first chair players who, when they were not serving as soloists, joined with the tutti to play the orchestral string parts. The contrast in sound between the heavy tutti and the lighter, more virtuosic concertino is the most distinctive feature of the concerto grosso.

The Baroque Violin

The most important string instrument in the Baroque period was the violin. During the seventeenth century the violin, along with its larger cousins, the viola and cello, came to form the core of the orchestra. Before that time it had been the poor man's string instrument, used mainly for playing dances in taverns. But the violin had two special virtues: First, it produced a more powerful, penetrating sound than had the earlier viol (Fig. 6–8); and second, it was more versatile and expressive. Of all the instruments the violin comes closest to the sound of the human voice in its agility, flexibility, and expressiveness. It can play a gentle lullaby with great tenderness, just as it can a loud fanfare with splendor. By 1650 the violin had become the instrument of preference for the opera, the solo and trio sonata, and the concerto.

As the violin's popularity increased, so did the number of makers producing the instrument. The earliest of these were centered in northern Italy in small towns such as Cremona and Brescia (both near the Italian Alps). The most gifted of the Cremonese craftsmen was Antonio Stradivari (1644–1737), in whose hands the violin assumed its definitive form. Stradivari produced more than a thousand instruments in his lifetime, including violas, cellos, lutes, and guitars, and about 650 of his violins have survived. They not only exhibit the highest quality of materials—including a miraculous varnish made according to a now-lost formula—but also reflect years of practice and experimentation. In fact, Stradivari was still making violins in his last year, at the age of ninety-two. So rich and singing is the tone of a Stradivari violin that for two centuries most of the world's great artists have preferred this instrument. Unfortunately, in recent times the Stradivari has become the darling of commercial auction houses where collectors and speculators have pushed up the price of his best instruments to more than a million dollars, well beyond the means of all but a very few performing musicians.

Front of a Stradivari violin photographed in ultraviolet light.

As written by Vivaldi, Bach, and Handel, the solo concerto and the concerto grosso had three movements: fast, slow, fast. The serious first movement is composed in a carefully worked-out structure called ritornello form (see page 118); the second movement is invariably more lyrical and tender; while the third movement, though usually using ritornello form, tends to be lighter, more dancelike, sometimes even rustic in mood. Both the solo concerto and the concerto grosso originated in Italy toward the end of the seventeenth century. Solo concertos for violin, flute, recorder, oboe, trumpet, and harpsichord were especially popular. The vogue of the concerto grosso peaked about 1730 and then all but came to an end about the time of the death of Bach (1750). But the solo concerto continued to be cultivated during the Classical and Romantic periods, becoming increasingly a showcase in which a single soloist could display his or her technical mastery of an instrument.

solo concerto

Antonio Vivaldi (1678–1741)

No composer was more influential, and certainly none more prolific, in the creation of the Baroque concerto than Antonio Vivaldi. Vivaldi, like Gabrieli,

a native of Venice, was the son of a barber and part-time musician at the church of St. Mark (Figs. 6–10 and 6–11). Surprisingly, it was not unusual in the seventeenth and eighteenth centuries for barbers to be semiprofessional musicians, since their shops were frequently supplied with musical instruments with which waiting customers could amuse themselves. Young Vivaldi's proximity to St. Mark's naturally brought him into contact with the clergy. Although he became a skilled performer on the violin, he also entered Holy Orders, ultimately becoming a priest. Vivaldi's life, however, was by no means confined to the realm of the spirit: He concertized on the violin throughout Europe; he wrote and produced nearly fifty operas, which brought him a great deal of money; and for fifteen years he lived with a French soprano. The worldly pursuits of *il prete rosso* (the red-haired priest) eventually got him into trouble with the authorities of the Roman Church, and in 1737 Vivaldi was forbidden to practice his musical artistry in papally controlled lands. This ban affected his income as well as his creativity: He died poor and obscure in Vienna in 1741 where he had gone in search of a post at the imperial court.

From 1703 until 1740 Vivaldi worked in Venice at the *Ospedale della Pietà* (Hospice of Mercy), first as a violinst and music teacher and then as its musical director. The *Ospedale* was an orphanage for the care and education of young women, one of several such charitable institutions in Venice. The orphaned girls received rigorous instruction in music, and they regularly gave public concerts on Sundays and feast days (Fig. 6–18). These were often attended by foreign visitors—Venice was already a tourist city—among them a French diplomat who wrote in 1739:

> These girls are educated at the expense of the state, and they are trained solely with the purpose of excelling in music. That is why they sing like angels and play violin, flute, organ, oboe, cello, bassoon; in short, no instrument is so big as to frighten them. They are kept like nuns in a convent. All they do is perform concerts, always in groups of about forty girls. I swear to you that there is nothing as pleasant as seeing a young and pretty nun, dressed in white, with a little pomegranate bouquet over her ears, conducting the orchestra with all the gracefulness and incredible precision one can imagine.

music in Venetian orphanages

CONCERTO GROSSO IN A MINOR, OPUS 3, NO. 8 (1711)

It was for the orchestra of the Hospice of Mercy that Vivaldi wrote his Concerto Grosso in A minor. It belongs to a set of twelve concertos that Vivaldi called *L'Estro armonico (The Harmonic Whim)*, which he dedicated to a wealthy prince in Florence (Fig. 6–19).

As is usually the case in the three-movement concerto grosso, the first movement of the Concerto Grosso in A minor is in **ritornello** form. The Italian word *ritornello* means "return" or "refrain." In ritornello form all or part of one main theme—the ritornello—returns again and again, invariably played by the tutti, or full orchestra. Between the tutti's statements of the ritornello, the concertino—the small group of soloists—inserts fragments and extensions of the theme presented in virtuosic fashion.

ritornello form

The ritornello in the first movement of Vivaldi's Concerto Grosso in A minor is in four sections. The first begins with three strong chords (called "Vivaldi hammerstrokes"), a descending scale, and then a rising scale in a

strongly marked rhythm (see the Listening Guide). Section 2 has a repeated figure with a similarly strong rhythm which grows into a clearly audible sequence that descends by step. Section 3 is characterized by typical violin sawing (up-down, up-down, and so on) above a **pedal point**—a long held note in the bass in imitation of an organist holding down a foot pedal. The use of such a mechanical up-down, up-down figure as this is typical of the new style of idiomatic writing for the violin in the Baroque era. Finally, section 4 continues this violin motion above a strikingly rich chord that grabs the listener's attention (it is a B♭ chord in the key of A minor, to be specific). At this point (0:36) a concertino of two solo violins and continuo emerges from the orchestra. It interjects an insistent, repeated figure, but then goes on to play sequences and rapid sixteenth notes. Thereafter, the entire movement is simply a succession of elaborate violin patterns played by the light concertino, which are interrupted periodically by a loud return of the tutti playing one or more of the sections of the ritornello. The plan of this movement can be diagramed as follows:

T = tutti (full orchestra)   c = concertino (two violins plus continuo)

	T	c	T	c	T	c	T	c	T	c	T	c	T	c	T
Ritornello section:	1–4		4		2		1		3		1		2&4		4

The oft-heard sections of the ritornello begin to function as familiar friends whose return we welcome. The more virtuosic concertino, having borrowed melodic motives from the ritornello, departs unexpectedly on exciting flights of fancy, the destinations of which never seem certain. In large measure it is the tension between the musical known and the unknown that makes listening to a concerto grosso such a satisfying experience.

FIGURES 6–18 AND 6–19

(left) A public concert by young women at the Venetian *Ospedale* where Vivaldi had worked. Note how the performers are placed in special galleries to the left. (right) Musicians of Prince Ferdinando de Medici. The prince was a fine amateur keyboard player himself and the patron to whom Vivaldi dedicated his set of concerti grossi called *The Harmonic Whim*.

LISTENING GUIDE

Antonio Vivaldi
Concerto Grosso in A minor, Opus 3, No. 8 (1711)
First movement, *Allegro* (fast)

CD 1/13
6–Tape 1B
2–Tape 1A

0:00	Ritornello section 1
0:07	Ritornello section 2
0:19	Ritornello section 3
0:30	Ritornello section 4

0:36   Concertino: Borrows rhythmic motive from ritornello section 1
0:50   Ritornello section 4
0:56   Concertino: Begins like first concertino but first violin goes on to play sequences and figural patterns, strong *basso continuo*
1:22   Tutti returns to add weight to the cadence
1:28   Ritornello section 2: Extended by a descending cascade of sound in the violins and a quick modulation (1:46)
1:50   Concertino: Borrows rhythmic motive from ritornello section 2
1:58   Ritornello section 1
2:04   Concertino: Second violin reiterates same rhythmic motive but now in a sequence
2:21   Ritornello section 3
2:27   Concertino: Starts like very first concertino but is immediately interrupted by ritornello
2:34   Ritornello section 1
2:42   Concertino: Rhythmic motive again appears in second violin now as part of a long sequence that descends by step
2:57   Ritornello sections 2 and 4
3:16   Concertino: Rhythmic motive is pushed upward by step
3:24   Ritornello section 4: Movement ends abruptly without any cadential padding

(Listening Exercise 18)

Vivaldi's more than 450 concertos were widely admired in the early eighteenth century, especially by German composers. No less a figure than Johann Sebastian Bach arranged this A minor concerto for organ as a means of assimilating Vivaldi's style. But within a few years Vivaldi was largely forgotten, a victim of rapidly changing musical tastes. Not until the revival of Baroque music in the 1950s did the listening public again come to hear his music and enjoy its energy, exuberance, and daring.

LISTENING EXERCISES

| 16 | Giovanni Gabrieli
Motet, *In the Churches* (1612) | CD 1/9
6–Tape 1A |

The text of this motet is given below. First listen to the motet following the text, then answer the questions that follow:

In ecclesiis, benedicite Domino Alleluja	In the churches, bless the Lord
In omni loco dominationis, benedic anima mea Dominum Alleluja	In every holy place, may my soul bless the Lord
In Deo salutari meo, et gloria mea Deus, auxilium meum et spes mea in Deo est Alleluja	In God is my salvation and my glory Lord, my help and my hope is in God
Deus noster, te invocamus, te laudamus, te adoramus Libera nos, salva nos, vivifica nos Alleluja	Our Lord, we call to you, we praise you, we adore you Deliver us, save us, revivify us
Deus, adjutor noster in aeternum Alleluja	Lord, our judge forever

1. (0:08 and 0:13) At the repeat of the words "benedicite Domino," the soprano repeats the music:
   a. on a higher pitch   b. on the same pitch   c. at a lower pitch
2. (0:16–0:30) Is this "Alleluja" (and, indeed, all statements of the "Alleluja") in duple or triple meter? _____
3. (0:31–0:59) In this bass solo the words "In omni loco," "dominationis," and "benedic" are each *repeated*:
   a. once   b. twice   c. three times
4. (1:43–1:52) What melodic device is used at the end of the sinfonia?
   a. sequence   b. pizzicato   c. pedal point
5. (1:53–3:20) Do you ever hear more than two voices singing in this section?
   _____
6. (3:35) What happens at the beginning of this section ("Deus, te invocamus")?
   a. soprano sings first and bass answers
   b. bass sings first and soprano answers
7. (4:46) Is the instrumental choir playing during this "Alleluja"?
   _____
8. (5:03–5:14) Do the instruments accompany the singers on the important word "Deus"? _____
9. (6:58) Is the final chord major or minor (does it sound bright or dark and gloomy)? _____
10. Finally, is *In the Churches* an example of an *a cappella* motet?
    _____

17 Henry Purcell
Recitative, "Thy hand Belinda" and aria, "When I
am laid in earth" from *Dido and Aeneas* (1689)

Your selection begins with about a minute of recitative (see page 111).
Notice how Dido's deflated spirits are reflected in the music: She gradually
sinks down from the C above middle C to middle C itself, touching the chromatic notes of the scale along the way. Begin, however, with the aria that follows, "When I am laid in earth." The opening is easy to recognize because it
starts with a chromatically descending ostinato bass.

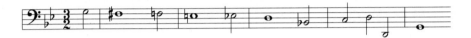

First draw a schematic diagram of the aria showing the statements of the
basso ostinato and how it relates to the text. Start by drawing a line beneath
the text to show where each statement of the ostinato pattern begins and
ends. Then number all the lines (1–11). The lines and numbers for the opening continuo statement and the final two statements are provided for you, as
is the first statement beneath the text. The repetitions in the text are included
to facilitate your efforts.

1 _____ 2 When I am laid (am laid) in earth, may my wrongs
create no trouble (no trouble) in thy breast. (When I am laid, am laid
in earth, may my wrongs create no trouble, no trouble in thy breast.)
Remember me (remember me), but ah! forget my fate. (Remember me, but
ah! forget my fate. Remember me, remember me, but ah! forget my fate.
Remember me, but ah! forget my fate.) 10 _____
11 _____

Now answer the following questions:

1. Is the recitative "Thy hand Belinda" an example of *secco* recitative (accompanied only by *basso continuo*) or *accompagnato* recitative (accompanied by
   full orchestra)? _____

2. In the aria "When I am laid in earth," is the meter duple or triple?
   _____

3. Is the mode of the aria major or minor? _____

4. Listen once again to the end of the aria, to the last two statements of the
   ground bass after Dido has fallen silent. The strings play with the continuo but without the voice. Compare this to the first statement of the ostinato at the very beginning of the aria. In what way is the texture thicker
   now than at the beginning? _____

5. In the final two statements of the ground bass (10–11), what is the general
   direction of the melody?
   a. up by step
   b. up by leaps
   c. down by step
   d. down by leaps

18 | Antonio Vivaldi
Concerto Grosso in A minor, Opus 3, No. 8 (1711)
First movement, *Allegro* (fast)

CD 1/13
6–Tape 1B
2–Tape 1A

Listen once to the opening movement of this concerto grosso, and answer the following general questions regarding instrumentation, tempo, and meter.

1. Do you hear any woodwinds, brass, or percussion playing in Vivaldi's orchestra in this concerto?
2. Is the harpsichord or the organ used as the keyboard instrument in the *basso continuo?*
3. How would you describe the tempo of this movement?
   a. *grave*   b. *adagio*   c. *allegro*
4. Is the meter duple or triple?

Now listen again to the movement, this time concentrating on details of the ritornello and concertino.

5. In the second appearance of the concertino (0:56–1:21), does the harpsichord play continually or does it come in and go out? _____
6. Is the cascade of violins at 1:35–1:45 loud or soft? _____
7. In the third appearance of the concertino (1:50–1:57), how many musical lines do you hear?
   a. one violin   b. two violins   c. two violins plus continuo
8. In the fourth appearance of the concertino (2:04–2:20), which rhythmic figure best represents what the bass is playing?

   a.    b.

9. In the final appearance of the concertino (3:16–3:23), is the continuo playing?

Finally, here is a general question:

10. Ritornello form is closest in structure to which of the following forms discussed in Chapter 3?
   a. strophic form   b. binary form   c. rondo form

KEY WORDS

Antonio Stradivari	libretto	sequence
aria	melisma	*sinfonia*
arioso	movement	*sonata da camera*
basso continuo	opera	*sonata da chiesa*
basso ostinato (ground bass)	opus	terraced dynamics
concertino	pedal point	trio sonata
concerto grosso	recitative	tutti
harpsichord	*secco* recitative	*viola da gamba* (bass viol)
	ritornello	walking bass

7

LATE BAROQUE MUSIC: BACH AND HANDEL

The music of the late Baroque era (1700–1750), represented by the two great figures Johann Sebastian Bach and George Frideric Handel, is the earliest musical repertoire with which most music lovers are familiar. While only a few connoisseurs might have heard a motet of Josquin Desprez (ca. 1440–1521) or an aria of Claudio Monteverdi (1567–1643), virtually everyone has listened to some of Handel's *Messiah,* knowingly or unknowingly. Why is it that our common musical experience begins with late Baroque music when, as we have seen, there were many masterpieces written during earlier periods?

One reason is our modern dislike for sameness. A Mass of the Renaissance composer Palestrina, for example, despite its serene beauty, may continue with the same four unaccompanied voices singing in the same style for twenty-five minutes. It took a century of development, roughly from 1600 to 1700, for music with more varied textures and colors to come into its own. By 1700 there are many genres of music like the opera, the sonata, and the concerto that allow for a multitude of moods, sounds, timbres, and dynamics within individual sections of one large composition. All these satisfy today's obsession with change and varied stimuli.

Yet while the innovations of the early Baroque period brought greater variety of musical expression, the new musical genres of the opera, the sonata, and the concerto had not reached maturity. They possess a certain roughness and imbalance, no matter how exciting and vital these novel sounds may be. The late Baroque, by contrast, is not a period of innovation, but one of perfection. Bach and his contemporaries did not, in the main, invent new harmonies, forms, and techniques, but rather gave unity and polish to those established during the course of the seventeenth century. Arcangelo Corelli (1653–1713), for example, had introduced functional harmony in his sonatas, but Bach and Handel smoothed away the occasional jarring chord and made the harmony work so as to tie together small units of music without any visible seams. Bach and Handel approached the art of composition with unbounded self-confidence, maturity, and wisdom because they were building on a century of musical experimentation. For this reason, as well as their own genius, their music has a sense of rightness, wholeness, and perfection. Each time we choose to hear one of their compositions, we offer further witness to their success in bringing a hundred years of musical development to a glorious culmination.

ASPECTS OF LATE BAROQUE MUSICAL STYLE

Treatment of Musical Elements

During the years 1700–1750 Bach, Handel and their contemporaries continued to develop the distinctive elements of musical style that appeared in the early Baroque era (see pages 100–104), now amplifying and extending them. In brief, melodies became longer, rhythms more driving, harmonies more purposeful, and textures more contrapuntal.

MELODY. Melody in late Baroque music is governed by the principle of continuing development. An initial motive or theme is set forth and then continually expanded, or spun out, over an ever-lengthening line. Such a melody tends to be long and ornate. Often the notes are propelled forward by melodic sequence*, the repetition of a motive or phrase on a successively higher or lower degree of the scale. Sequence helps the melody fly higher and farther and postpones the time when it must arrive at a cadence, as is the case in this example from Handel's *Messiah:*

EXAMPLE 7–1

The exuberant quality of late Baroque melody, however, makes it more impressive than memorable, that is, it is hard to sing or hum, even after repeated hearings. This is due, in part, to the fact that the phrases are frequently not short, narrow, and symmetrical, but rather long, expansive, and irregular. They are also often instrumental in nature, meaning that melodic patterns that can easily be played on instruments are frequently transferred to the voice where they can be difficult to sing. Bach, for example, often wrote difficult vocal lines that are instrumental in character.

RHYTHM. Rhythm is the most distinctive and exciting element of late Baroque music. If a concerto of Bach or Handel seems to chug along with an irrepressible optimism and vitality, it is because of the almost unstoppable quality of the rhythm. A piece will begin with one prominent rhythmic idea, and it or a complementary one will keep going in machinelike fashion to the end of the movement. In this context meter is firmly established by regular accents and a steady beat. Indeed, meter is more easily recognized in late Baroque music than in the music of any other period. One or two prominent instruments, often those assigned the bass line, usually play a regular rhythmic pattern that sets a strong beat. This clear, regular beat, in turn, makes the meter immediately audible. The strong beat and powerful bass are elements of late Baroque music that make it appealing to modern listeners. In these it has a certain affinity to contemporary rock and jazz.

driving rhythms

HARMONY. The pull of forceful chord progressions and the use of just major and minor keys were qualities of harmony found earlier in the music of Corelli (see page 115). They continue to be embodied in the music of the late Baroque era. So, too, does the *basso continuo* (see page 101), that small ensemble of usually keyboard and a bass instrument that gives added weight to the bass and generates chords, thereby providing the harmonic support for the melody above. What chords the keyboard player is to construct are suggested to him or her by means of a **figured bass**—a numerical shorthand placed in the music that tells the player which unwritten notes to fill in above the written bass note. (Figured bass is similar in intent to the numerical code found in "fake books" used by modern jazz pianists that indicates which chords to play beneath the written melody.)

figured bass

EXAMPLE 7–2A AND 7–2B

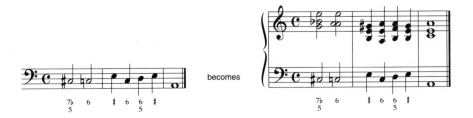

What is new in the harmony of the late Baroque is the regularity with which it moves. Specifically, chords appear at regular intervals and produce a constant rate of harmonic change. Chord changes may occur every beat, every other beat, or just once in each measure, but usually the rate of change is stable. Regular harmonic change and repetitious rhythms are what give the music of this period its sense of relentless, unstoppable movement.

TEXTURE: THE RETURN OF COUNTERPOINT. We have seen that imitative counterpoint with independent polyphonic lines dominated the church music of the Renaissance and that, partly as a reaction to this, composers of the early Baroque era began to avoid counterpoint. Now in the late Baroque period, however, they returned to contrapuntal writing, in part to add richness to the middle range of what was otherwise a top–bottom (soprano–bass) dominated texture. German composers were particularly fond of counterpoint, perhaps because of their traditional love of the organ, an instrument with several keyboards and thus well suited to playing many musical lines at once. The gradual reintegration of counterpoint into the fabric of Baroque music culminates in the rigorously contrapuntal vocal and instrumental music of Bach.

The Late Baroque Orchestra

During the seventeenth century changes occurred in the makeup of the orchestra. The trumpet, which had formerly been used alone (or with drums) as a purely ceremonial or military instrument, was now welcomed into the ensemble for its bright sound, while the older, duller wooden cor-

FIGURE 7–1

Detail of an orchestra playing for a Baroque opera. From left to right are a bassoon, two French horns, a cello, double bass, harpsichord and then violins, violas, and oboes. The full orchestra and the complete painting can be seen in figure 7–8.

netto (see page 82) quickly disappeared. At the same time the horn left the hunting field and watchtower and took a place in the orchestra. Similarly, the oboe, usually appearing in pairs, was admitted as the principal wood-wind instrument because of its penetrating sound, though it might be replaced by one or two flutes, especially if no trumpets or horns were present. Members of the violin family replaced those of the viol (see page 117), whose "still music," as Shakespeare called it, was thought too delicate, and other soft plucked instruments from the Renaissance, like the lute, were sent packing. The core of the orchestra was now provided by the violins, violas, cellos, and double basses (which doubled the cello line an octave below). They were supported, still, by a continuo group of harpsichord (or organ in church) and cello, perhaps with a double bass playing as well. The bassoon, a low woodwind, joined the continuo group in this period to give yet more strength to the bass line (see Fig. 7–1).

Many concerti grossi*, opera overtures (see page 135), and dance suites (see page 134) of the late Baroque period were written for an orchestra of just string instruments and continuo. Pieces for especially festive occasions, however, would normally include a greater number of instruments for greater brilliancy. Yet never were all available instruments heard at once, even in the largest orchestral scores. If there were trumpets, there were usually no horns; if there were oboes, there were no flutes, and vice versa. Hence, by modern standards, the late Baroque orchestra was at best a mid-size group. Rarely did it include more than thirty-five players, about twenty of whom belonged to the nucleus of strings.

Johann Sebastian Bach (1685–1750)

In the creations of Johann Sebastian Bach, the music of the Baroque reaches its greatest glory. Bach was born to a musical dynasty, though one originally of common standing. For nearly two hundred years members of the Bach family served as musicians in small towns in Thuringia, a province in south-central Germany. Johann Sebastian was merely the most talented of the ubiquitous musical Bachs, though he himself had four sons who achieved international fame. Although he received an excellent formal education in the humanities, as a musician Bach was largely self-taught. To learn his craft he studied, copied, and arranged the compositions of Corelli, Vivaldi, Pachelbel, and even Palestrina. He also learned to play the organ, in part by emulating others, once traveling two hundred miles on foot to hear a great performer. By the time of his maturity he had become the most renowned

FIGURE 7–2

Portrait of Johann Sebastian Bach painted by Elias Gottlob Haussmann in 1748.

FIGURE 7–3

Leipzig, St. Thomas's Church (center) and choir school (left) from an engraving of 1723, the year in which Bach·moved to the city.

virtuoso of the organ in Germany, and his improvisations on that instrument became legendary. Although Bach held several positions as an organist and composer during his youth, in 1723 he was appointed cantor of St. Thomas's Church and choir school in Leipzig, Germany, a post that he retained until his death in 1750 (Fig. 7–3). He seems to have been attracted to Leipzig, then a city of about thirty thousand inhabitants, because of the excellent schools and university in which his sons might enroll.

The position of cantor of St. Thomas's Church in Leipzig has been compared with that of director of music at St. Mark's in Venice (see page 105) in regard to its great prestige. Bach's job, however, seems to have been more demanding. As an employee of the town council of Leipzig, Bach was charged with superintending the liturgical music of the four principal churches of that city. He was also to direct the music of the university and teach Latin grammar to the boys at the choir school of St. Thomas. But by far the most exacting aspect of his job as cantor was to provide new music for the church for each Sunday and religious holiday, a total of about sixty days in the year. In so doing, Bach brought an important genre of religious music, the cantata, to the highest point of its development.

The Cantata

Like the opera*, the sonata*, and the concerto*, the **cantata** was a genre of music that arose in Italy in the seventeenth century. Originally, a cantata ("something sung") was simply a sung aria, as opposed to the sonata that was a piece played or sounded on instruments. Gradually, the cantata was expanded to several movements, including one or more arias*, ariosos*, and recitatives*, all with instrumental accompaniment. As was true of the sonata, the cantata was heard by audiences in both the aristocratic salon and in the church. Secular chamber cantatas on themes of love, morality, and politics were favored by the Italians, while the Germans preferred religious subjects. Composers like Bach and Georg Philipp Telemann (1681–1767) made the German church cantata the musical centerpiece of the German Protestant service, and their works include music for chorus as well as solo arias and recitatives.

In Bach's time St. Thomas's Church celebrated a Sunday Mass as prescribed by Martin Luther (1483–1546) nearly two centuries earlier. The service began at seven o'clock in the morning and lasted nearly four hours. The musical high point was the cantata. It came after the reading of the Gospel and provided a commentary on the Gospel text, allowing the congregation to meditate on the word of the Lord. The preacher then delivered an hour-long sermon, which also expounded on the scriptural theme of the day. Bach wrote almost three hundred cantatas for the citizens of Leipzig (five annual cycles), though only about two-thirds of these survive. His musical forces consisted of singers from the St. Thomas choir school and instrumentalists from the university and town. The ensemble was placed in a choir loft above the west door (Fig. 7–6), and Bach himself conducted the group, beating time with a roll of paper.

A MIGHTY FORTRESS IS OUR GOD (begun 1715)

Although Bach was a devoted husband, loving father to twenty children, and respected burgher of Leipzig, he was above all else a religious man who believed that all music was composed for the greater glory of God. Perhaps no cantata of Bach expresses the strength of his faith and bond with his church more clearly than *Ein feste Burg ist unser Gott (A Mighty Fortress Is Our God)*. It was composed for the annual Reformation festival (October 31) which celebrated Luther's separation from the Church of Rome. Bach began it in 1715 and continued to add and subtract movements over the course of fifteen years. Even after his death, his eldest son, Wilhelm Friedemann Bach (1710–1784), added parts for trumpets and timpani. In its final form the cantata *A Mighty Fortress* has eight movements. Those for chorus provide the structural framework, coming at the beginning, middle, and end:

Movement:

1	2	3	4	5	6	7	8
Chorus	Aria (duet)	Recitative	Aria	Chorus	Recitative	Aria (duet)	Chorus
1st stanza	2nd stanza			3rd stanza			4th stanza

FIGURE 7–4

Looking toward the altar in the interior of St. Thomas's Church, Leipzig, as it was in the mid-nineteenth century.

Movements 1, 2, 5, and 8 make use of the four stanzas of text of the Reformation hymn *A Mighty Fortress*, whence the cantata derives its name. The text of items 2 (in the bass of the duet), 3, 4, 6, and 7 were written by a contemporary of Bach and are paraphrases and elaborations of the Gospel text and of the text of this German hymn. Thus, it is mainly the chorus that sings the verses of the traditional hymn, or chorale, while the soloists present newly created text.

A Mighty Fortress is a chorale cantata, meaning that the work is built around a chorale. A **chorale** is a well-known spiritual melody or religious folksong of the German Protestant (Lutheran) church, what other denominations would simply call a hymn. In this case both melody and text were penned by Martin Luther himself in 1529. The structure of *A Mighty Fortress* is typical of chorale melodies (see Listening Guide). It begins with two short phrases that move first from the tonic* note down to the dominant* and then from the initial tonic down by step to the tonic an octave below (on tonic and dominant, see page 31). These two phrases are then repeated. Phrases 3 and 4 reverse this procedure, working from the lower tonic up to the dominant and then from the lower tonic up to the tonic an octave above. Phrases 5 and 6 allow for tonal contrast. The final phrase is simply a repeat of phrase 2, the scale descending tonic to tonic. As is appropriate for the meaning of the text, this melody sounds firm and secure—a musical fortress—in part because it is so strongly rooted in tonic and dominant.

Of the eight movements of the cantata *A Mighty Fortress*, the most remarkable is the first, a gigantic choral fantasy that displays a polyphonic mastery exceptional even for Bach. Here Bach takes each phrase of the chorale and transforms it into a musical theme that is worked out contrapuntally in all four voices of the chorus. One voice presents Bach's transformation of the chorale tune and the others then imitate it in turn:

EXAMPLE 7–3

At the end of each section of vocal counterpoint, the unchanged chorale melody is sounded on high in long notes by the trumpet and then immediately below in exact imitation (canon*) by the low pedal notes of the organ. Thus, at times Bach has two contrapuntal works going at once, one in the trumpet and organ using the simple form of the chorale, and one in the four voices of the chorus employing his own thematic transformation of that phrase of the chorale tune. The architectural complexity of a movement such as this shows why musicians, then and now, view Bach as the greatest contrapuntalist who ever lived.

| LISTENING GUIDE | Johann Sebastian Bach Cantata, *A Mighty Fortress Is Our God* (begun 1715) First movement | CD 2/1 6–Tape 2A 2–Tape 1A |

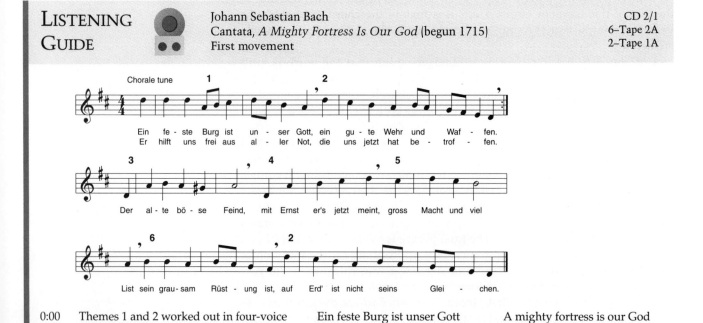

0:00	Themes 1 and 2 worked out in four-voice imitation beginning with tenors	Ein feste Burg ist unser Gott	A mighty fortress is our God
0:30	Chorale phrase 1 enters first in trumpet and then in organ pedal		
0:43	Themes 1 and 2 worked out further in four-voice imitation	Ein gute Wehr und Waffen	A bulwark never failing

1:06	Chorale phrase 2 enters first in trumpet and then in organ pedal		

Repeat of opening music (0:00–1:20) with new text as required by repeat in chorale tune

1:23	Themes 1 and 2	Er hilft uns frei aus aller Not	Our helper he amid the flood
1:53	Chorale phrase 1		
2:06	Themes 1 and 2	Die uns jetzt hat betroffen	Our mortal ills prevailing
2:29	Chorale phrase 2		
2:46	Theme 3 worked out in four-voice imitation	Der alte böse Feind	For still our ancient foe
3:12	Chorale phrase 3 in trumpet and then in organ pedal		
3:22	Theme 4 worked out in four-voice imitation	Mit Ernst er's jetzt meint	Does seek to work us woe
3:42	Chorale phrase 4 in trumpet and then in organ pedal		
3:48	Theme 5 worked out in four-voice imitation	Gross Macht und viel List	His craft and power are great
4:06	Chorale phrase 5 in trumpet and then in organ pedal		
4:14	Theme 6 worked out in four-voice imitation	Sein grausam Rüstung ist	And armed with cruel hate
4:30	Chorale phrase 6 in trumpet and then in organ pedal		
4:41	Theme 1 (beginning varied) worked out in four-voice imitation	Auf Erd' ist nichts seins Gleichen	On earth is not his equal
5:04	Chorale phrase 2 in trumpet and then in organ pedal		

(Listening Exercise 19)

Movement 2: Aria (duet) for soprano and bass, with oboe, violin, viola, and continuo. The soprano sings the text of stanza 2 of *A Mighty Fortress* and a thematic transformation of the chorale tune. The bass sings new text and music.

Movement 3: Recitative and arioso for bass voice and continuo; no use of chorale tune.

Movement 4: Aria for soprano and continuo; no use of chorale tune.

Movement 5: This movement of the cantata *A Mighty Fortress* is another extraordinary choral work, one less contrapuntal but more grand than the first. The four voices of the chorus do not work polyphonically, but rather are brought together in unison to sing the third stanza of the chorale in long notes. Bach does this for symbolic purposes, for the text of this stanza reads: "And tho' this world with devils filled, should threaten to undo us, we will not fear, for God hath willed, His truth to triumph through us." The orchestra, though it starts in a gentle 6/8 meter, soon changes into an assault force of running and leaping sixteenth notes that attempts to overwhelm the united forces of the chorale. Here Bach creates in music a battle scene that depicts the conflict between the earthly devils (played by the increasingly agitated strings and woodwinds) and the true believers of God (the chorus and brilliant trumpets), the latter strong and secure in their heavenly fortress.

LISTENING **GUIDE**	Johann Sebastian Bach *A Mighty Fortress* Fifth movement		CD 2/2 6–Tape 2A

0:00   Orchestra begins with a lilting 6/8 transformation of phrase 1 of the chorale tune accompanied by trumpet fanfares

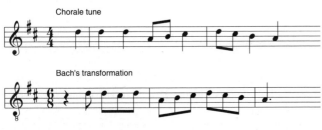

0:22   Chorus sings chorale phrase 1
0:40   Chorus sings chorale phrase 2
0:48   Trumpets play chorale phrase 1 and are answered by oboes
1:14   Repeat of chorale phrase 1
1:32   Repeat of chorale phrase 2
1:39   Trumpets play chorale phrase 1 in imitation
2:03   Chorus sings chorale phrase 3
2:21   Chorus sings chorale phrase 4
2:38   Chorus sings chorale phrase 5
2:56   Chorus sings chorale phrase 6
3:16   Chorus sings chorale phrase 2

Movement 6: Recitative and arioso for tenor and continuo; no use of chorale tune.

Movement 7: Aria (duet) for alto and tenor, oboe, violin, and continuo; no use of chorale tune.

Movement 8: Bach's cantatas usually end with a simple four-voice homophonic setting of the last stanza of the chorale. The instruments of the orchestra double these four vocal parts. But more important, the members of the congregation join in the singing of the chorale tune, thereby providing each believer the chance to confirm in song his or her faith. Giving the congregation the opportunity to participate in the music of the service was one of the church reforms instituted by Martin Luther in the 1520s. The last stanza of *A Mighty Fortress* rings like a Protestant warrior's oath of fidelity to both the heavenly God and the German nation.

LISTENING GUIDE

Johann Sebastian Bach
A Mighty Fortress
Eighth and last movement

CD 2/3
6–Tape 2A

Phrases 1 and 2 of chorale *A Mighty Fortress* in a four-voice setting

0:00	Das Wort sie sollen lassen stahn	The Word of God will firm abide
	Und kein Dank dazu haben	Against our foes assailing,
0:19	Er ist bei uns wohl auf dem Plan	For He will battle on our side,
	Mit seinem Geist und Gaben.	An ally never failing.
0:38	Nehmen sie uns den Leib,	Tho' they take from me here
	Gut, Ehr, Kind und Weib,	All that I hold dear
	Lass, fahren, dahin,	I will not complain,
	Sie haben's kein Gewinn;	Their vantage will be vain,
	Das Reich muss uns doch bleiben.	God's realm is all prevailing.

The Orchestral Suite

In 1729 Bach became director of the Collegium Musicum of Leipzig, in addition to his position of cantor of St. Thomas's Church. The Collegium was an organization of university students and town musicians who voluntarily came together to give weekly concerts in a local coffeehouse (one run by a certain Herr Zimmerman), where the patrons sipped beer and puffed long pipes (Fig. 7–5). By means of such societies, middle-class musical culture flourished in the eighteenth century. (The Collegium has persisted in European and American universities down to the present day, though now it exists mainly to promote "early music"—the music of Bach's time and before.) Bach's association with the Collegium of Leipzig gave him the opportunity to compose and perform purely orchestral works, compositions

FIGURE 7–5

An orchestra and small chorus perform in a German coffeehouse in the mid eighteenth century. The *basso continuo* is comprised of harpsichord, cello, and bassoon.

not tied to a religious text. His famous set of six concerti grossi*, the Brandenburg concertos, though written before his arrival in Leipzig, were likely performed by the Collegium. And his dozen or so harpsichord concertos and four orchestral suites were either written or revised for the ensemble.

Most of Bach's music is serious, sometimes even severe, and its aim is to enlighten or instruct the listener. When Bach wished to "lighten up," to have fun in music, he did so through his dance suites. By the eighteenth century a collection of dances had come to be called by the French term *suite,* a succession of pieces. The **dance suite,** no different from the older *sonata da camera* (see page 113), was a collection of dances, usually varying from four to seven, all in one key and for one group of instruments, be it full orchestra, trio, or solo, all usually with continuo. The listeners did not dance the music of Bach's suites. These were stylized, abstract dances. But it was the job of the composer to bring each one alive, to make it recognizable to the audience by incorporating the salient elements of rhythm and style of each particular dance. Among the dances that Bach recreated in his suites for orchestra or for harpsichord solo are the following:

the dance suite

Allemande: a stately dance in 4/4 meter with gracefully interweaving lines

Courante: a lively dance in 6/4 with an upbeat* and frequent changes of metrical accent

Baroque dances

Saraband: a slow, elegant dance in 3/4 with a strong accent on the second beat

Gavotte: a moderate dance in 2/2 with full upbeat and prominent rhythm

Bourrée: a fast dance in 2/2 with a quick upbeat and rapidly running eighth notes

Minuet: a moderate dance in 3/4, though actually danced in patterns of six steps, with no upbeat but with highly symmetrical phrasing

Gigue: a fast dance in 6/8 or 12/8 with a constant eighth-note pulse that produces a galloplike effect

But no matter what the rhythm or style of the dance, the form of each dance movement was invariably the same: binary form* (see page 58). Binary form is simply a musical form with two sections. The first, which we traditionally call **A**, takes the movement from tonic to dominant; the second, called **B**, brings it back home to the tonic. Both sections are repeated immediately, producing an **AABB** structure.

binary form

ORCHESTRAL SUITE NO. 3 IN D MAJOR (1730)

Bach's Orchestral Suite No. 3 in D major was composed for the Leipzig Collegium Musicum in 1730. It is scored for string orchestra plus two oboes, three trumpets, timpani, and continuo. D major is the key that Bach favored when writing for trumpets because most trumpets at that time were natural instruments of a length and size that easily produced the pitch D. (Valves, which allow the trumpet to play equally well in all keys, were not introduced until the nineteenth century.) One wonders what effect Bach's brilliant orchestral work had on the patrons of Herr Zimmermann's coffeehouse!

Movement 1: Overture. Each of Bach's orchestral suites begins with a **French overture,** so called because the genre was first popularized by Jean Baptiste Lully (1632–1687) in the overtures to his French operas. The French overture consists of two sections: the first, slow in duple meter with dotted rhythms that give a certain majestic, even fanfarelike quality to the music; and the second, fast and light with imitative counterpoint much like a fugue (discussed in the next section). The purpose of the overture is to create a festive atmosphere for what follows.

French overture

Movement 2: Air. This air is not really a dance at all, but rather a tender, lyrical aria for the violins of the orchestra, and it is one of Bach's loveliest and most famous creations. (In an arrangement for violin solo it is known as the "Air for the G string.") For this movement, the woodwinds, brass, and percussion drop out, leaving only a four-part string ensemble. The score of the **A** section of the binary form is given in the Listening Guide. As you listen to the "Air," follow the score and see if you can hear the different lines. The ear finds the two violin parts the most difficult to distinguish because they are in the same high range and play similar sixteenth-note figurations. The next-to-bottom part, played by the viola, stands out more clearly, and the bass line is easiest to hear because of its separate, low range and regular eighth-note pulse. This bass is a good example of a walking bass*—the line moves steadily along in identical note values and proceeds usually by step or repeated notes (the repeats are disguised by octave leaps). The only time the regular pulse is broken is at the end of bar 6 where the introduction of sixteenth notes signals the repeat of the **A** section. As you listen to **B,** see if you can continue to hear the unfolding of the four lines even though you no longer have the musical score to follow.

LISTENING GUIDE

Johann Sebastian Bach
Orchestral Suite No. 3 in D major (1730)
Second movement, "Air"

CD 1/14
6–Tape 2B
2–Tape 1A

0:00   "Air" begins above walking bass
0:46   Bass breaks into faster sixteenth notes
0:51   Repeat of **A**
1:41   **B** section begins
3:20   Repeat of **B**

Movement 3: Gavotte. Here Bach actually composes two gavottes and then returns to the first to create a rounded structure: Gavotte I, Gavotte II, Gavotte I. Aside from this aspect of form, the listener is struck by the frequent contrast between passages for full orchestra and sections without trumpets and drums. It is as if Bach had the sound of the concerto grosso (see page 116) in his ear when composing this movement.

Movement 4: Bourrée. The lively bourée is noteworthy for its brevity (it's barely more than a minute long) and its symmetry (**A** = 8 bars, **B** = 12 + 12 bars), something unusual for Bach.

Movement 5: Gigue. We would think of this final gigue as a rollicking peasant's dance were it not for the regal sound of the trumpets, an instrument traditionally associated with the nobility. The beat of the dance has a strong impact here because of the recurrent rhythmic pattern in the bass.

LISTENING GUIDE

Johann Sebastian Bach
Orchestral Suite No. 3 in D major (1730)
Fifth movement, Gigue

CD 1/15
6–Tape 1B
2–Tape 1A

( ) = repeats

0:00	(0:28)	**A** section: brilliant trumpets
0:20	(0:47)	Chromatic descent in strings: trumpets at end
0:54	(1:50)	**B** section begins
1:05	(2:01)	Passing through different keys
1:34	(2:30)	Long ascent
1:43	(2:38)	Chromatic descent in strings; trumpets at end

Fugue

If the suites of Bach have a lighthearted, playful mood, it is partly because they are usually devoid of rigorous counterpoint. But Bach was the master of counterpoint, and it is his love of contrapuntal writing that gives his music unparalleled substance and complexity. Bach excelled above all other composers in writing fugues.

A fugue is a contrapuntal form and procedure that flourished during the late Baroque era. The word "fugue" itself comes from the Latin *fuga*, meaning "flight." Within a fugue one voice presents a theme and then "flies away" as another voice enters with the same theme. The theme in a fugue is called the **subject.** At the outset each voice presents the subject in turn, and this successive presentation is called the **exposition** of the fugue. As the voices enter, they do not imitate or pursue each other exactly—this would produce a canon* (see page 53). Rather, passages of exact imitation are interrupted by sections of free writing in which the voices more or less go their own ways. These freer, nonimitative sections are called **episodes.** Episodes and further presentations of the subject alternate throughout the remainder of the fugue.

subject, exposition, episode

Fugues have been written for two to as many as thirty-two voices, but usually the norm is three, four, or five. These may be actual voices in a chorus or choir, or they may be simply lines or parts played by a group of instruments, or even by a solo instrument like the piano, organ, or guitar, which has the capacity to play several "voices" simultaneously. Thus, a formal definition of a **fugue** might be as follows: a composition for three, four, or five parts played or sung by voices or instruments, which begins with a presentation of a subject in imitation in each part (exposition), continues with modulating passages of free counterpoint (episodes) and further appearances of the subject, and ends with a strong affirmation of the tonic key. Fortunately, the fugue is easier to hear than to describe: The unfolding and recurrence of one subject makes it easy to follow.

ORGAN FUGUE IN G MINOR (CA. 1710)

Bach has left us nearly one hundred keyboard fugues, about a third of these for organ. The organ was Bach's favorite instrument, and in his day he was known more as a performer and improviser on it than as a composer. Bach's G minor organ fugue was composed rather early in his career, sometime between 1708 and 1717. It is written for four voices, which we will refer to as soprano, alto, tenor, and bass, and it begins with the subject appearing first in the soprano:

EXAMPLE 7–4

As fugue subjects go, this is a rather long one, but it is typical of the way Baroque composers liked to "spin out" their melodies. It sounds very solid in regard to its tonality. That's because the subject is clearly built around the notes of the G minor triad (G, B♭, D), not only in the first measure but on the strong beats of the final measures as well. The subject also conveys a sense of gathering momentum. It starts moderately with quarter notes, and then seems to gain speed as eighth notes and finally sixteenth notes are introduced. This, too, is typical of fugue subjects. After the soprano gives forth the subject, it is then presented, in turn, by the alto, the tenor, and the bass. The voices need not appear in any particular order; here Bach just decided to have them enter in succession from top to bottom.

Once Bach has each voice present the subject and join the polyphonic complex, his exposition is at an end. Now a short passage of free counterpoint follows—the first episode—which makes use of just bits and pieces of the subject. Then the subject returns, but in a highly unusual way: It begins in the tenor, but continues and ends in the soprano (see [†] in the following Listening Guide). Thereafter, Bach's G minor fugue unfolds in the usual alternation of episodes and statements of the subject. The episodes sound unsettled and convey a sense of movement. They modulate from one key to another. The subject, on the other hand, doesn't modulate. It is *in* a key, here the tonic G minor or the dominant D minor or some other closely related key. This tension between unsettled music (the episode) and stationary music (the subject) is what creates the exciting, dynamic quality of the fugue. Ultimately, Bach modulates back to the tonic key G minor for one final statement of the subject in the bass, and the fugue is ended. Note that, although this fugue is in a minor key, the final chord has been changed to major. This is common in Baroque music, composers preferring the brighter, perhaps more conclusive, sound of major in the final chord.

To hear this and other fugues, then, the listener is encouraged to proceed in the following manner: Follow the unfolding of the subject as it appears in rapid succession in each voice in the exposition; identify the episodic material as distinct from the subject (sense that the subject is no longer present and that the music is changing key); listen for the subsequent alternation between episodes and further appearances of the subject, and, finally, recognize that the home key has been reached when the subject enters in strong fashion for the last time.

FIGURE 7–6

The organ presently in the choir loft of St. Thomas's Church, Leipzig. It was from this loft that Bach played and conducted.

hearing fugues

LISTENING GUIDE

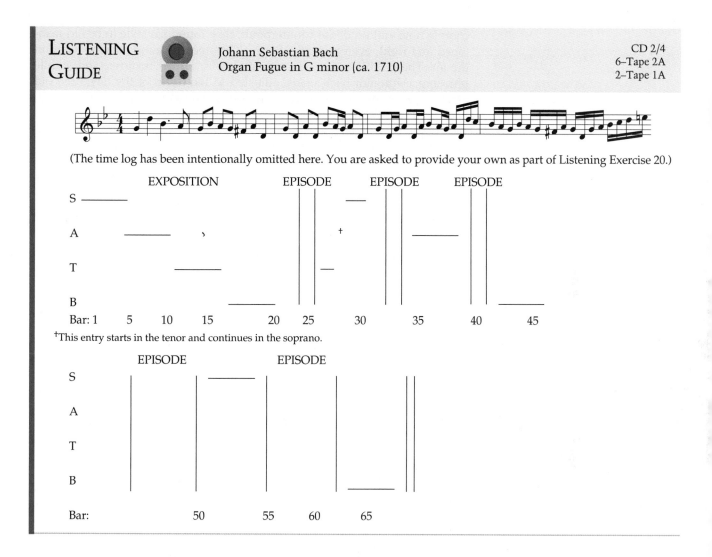

Johann Sebastian Bach
Organ Fugue in G minor (ca. 1710)

CD 2/4
6–Tape 2A
2–Tape 1A

(The time log has been intentionally omitted here. You are asked to provide your own as part of Listening Exercise 20.)

†This entry starts in the tenor and continues in the soprano.

Perhaps the best-known collection of fugues by Bach is *The Well-Tempered Clavier* (1720–1742), "clavier" simply being Bach's word for keyboard. It consists of two sets of twenty-four preludes and fugues. The **prelude** is a short improvisatory-like piece that sets a mood and serves as a technical warm-up for the player before the fugue. In both sets of twenty-four there is one prelude and fugue in each of the major and minor keys: the first pair in C major, the next in C minor, the next in C# major, then C# minor, and so on. Through this arrangement Bach showed that it was possible to write a piece—in this case a prelude and fugue—in every key, something that had not been done in a systematic fashion up to that time.

The Well-Tempered Clavier

Such rigorous, systematic music was not always popular in the eighteenth century. Indeed, Bach was not fully appreciated by the citizens of Leipzig or the music critics of the time. With his heavy reliance on the traditional

Bach and posterity

chorale tune and on dense counterpoint, they found his style to be old-fashioned and rigid, even pedantic. By the 1730s new musical currents were in the air. The public wanted singable melodies, lighter textures, and simple phrasing. Although Bach's sons adjusted to the tastes of the day, "the old Wig," as one of them irreverently called him, did so only sporadically. When Bach died in 1750 he was soon forgotten, and mention of the name "Bach" shortly thereafter conjured up the image of one or the other of his fashionable sons, not the great polyphonic master. Yet a small group of musicians, including Mozart, Beethoven, Schumann, and Mendelssohn, kept the knowledge of his extraordinary music alive. When Mendelssohn performed Bach's *St. Matthew Passion* (an oratorio*) in 1829 on the centenary of its first performance, a "Bach revival" was underway. From that time on, the listening public has never ceased to admire Bach's music for its stylistic integrity, grand design, and superhuman craftsmanship.

GEORGE FRIDERIC HANDEL (1685–1759)

The careers of Bach and Handel could hardly have been more different. While Bach spent his life confined to towns in central Germany, his cosmopolitan countryman Handel traveled the world from Rome, to Venice, to Hamburg, to Amsterdam, to London, and to Dublin. If Bach was most at home conducting chorale cantatas and playing organ fugues from the church choir loft, Handel was a man of the public theater, a denizen of the orchestra pit, by training and temperament a composer of opera. And if Bach fell into virtual obscurity at the end of his life, retreating into a world of esoteric counterpoint, Handel's stature only grew larger on the international stage. He became the most famous composer in Europe and a treasured national institution in England.

George Frideric Handel (as he styled himself after becoming a naturalized English citizen) was born in the town of Halle, Germany, in 1685, and died in London in 1759. Although his father had decreed a program of study in law, the young Handel managed to cultivate his intense interest in music, sometimes secretly by candlelight. At the age of eighteen he got his first taste of opera in the city of Hamburg, where he had gone to take a job as violinist in the public opera theater. But since the musical world around 1700 was dominated by things Italian, he, too, set off for Italy to learn his trade and broaden his horizons. He moved between Florence and Venice, for which cities he wrote operas, and Rome, where he composed mainly secular cantatas. In 1710 Handel returned to North Germany to accept the post of chapel master to the elector of Hanover, but on the condition that he be given an immediate leave of absence to visit London. Although he made one additional voyage back to his employer in Hanover in 1711 and many subsequent visits to the Continent, Handel conveniently forgot about his obligation to the Hanoverian court. London became the site of his musical activity and the place where he won his fortune.

After four years in Italy, London must have seemed a cultural backwater to Handel. Many of the streets were unpaved, the buildings were black with the soot of coal fires, and there was none of the art and architecture that graced Venice, Florence, or Rome. But there was opportunity. Handel soon found employment in the homes of the aristocracy and became the music

tutor to the English royal family. As fate would have it, his continental employer, the elector of Hanover, became King George I of England in 1714, when the Hanoverians acceded to the throne on the extinction of the Stuart line. Fortunately for Handel, the new king bore his truant musician no grudge, and he was called on frequently to compose festival music to entertain the court or mark its progress. For these events Handel produced such works as *The Water Music* (1717), *The Royal Fireworks Music* (1749), and *The Coronation Service* (1727), parts of which have been used at the coronation of every English monarch since its first hearing.

Handel in London

But it was not the chance to entertain the English royal family, and certainly not the climate or cuisine, that had lured Handel to London, but the opportunity to compose opera. With the rare exception of a work such as Purcell's *Dido and Aeneas* (see page 110), there was no English opera. Nor were there offerings imported from France, Germany, or Italy. Instead, spoken plays with occasional musical interludes dominated the stage. What few tunes the audience heard were sung in English by English performers.

Handel and Opera

Handel enjoyed great success when he first composed and mounted full-blown Italian opera in London during 1711–1718, and this inspired a bolder venture. In 1719 he became the musical force behind a remarkable capitalistic enterprise: the formation of a publicly held stock company for the production of Italian opera. In truth, most of those who purchased shares in the new opera company were members of the nobility, including the king (hence, the company was called the Royal Academy of Music). Handel was empowered to round up the best singers that could be found on the Continent, at almost any cost. Then, as now, the fees commanded by the great male leads and the prima donnas were enormous. The castrato Senesino, who joined the Royal Academy in 1720, ultimately received an annual salary equal

Italian opera in London

FIGURES 7–8 AND 7–9

(left) Interior of an opera theater in Turin, Italy, painted in 1740 by Pietro Domenico Olivero. Notice not only the orchestra before the stage, with continuo groups on both the left and right, but also the vendors of wine and fruit walking the floor. (right) Title-page of an English edition of Handel's *Julius Caesar*.

A caricature of a scene from an opera by Handel showing the castrato Senesino (left) and soprano Cuzzoni (center).

opera seria

Beverly Sills singing Cleopatra in the New York City Opera Company production of *Julius Caesar*.

to twice that of the entire orchestra of approximately thirty-five players. Although Handel's fees are not recorded, they, too, must have been sizable, for he was charged to write most of the operas, oversee rehearsals, and finally, conduct the finished product from the harpsichord in the orchestra pit.

JULIUS CAESAR (1724)

One of the operas Handel wrote for the Royal Academy of Music, indeed, one of its most successful productions, was *Giulio Cesare (Julius Caesar)*, first given in 1724. The libretto* picks up the story of Caesar's life late in his career, as he pursues and then defeats his rival, Pompey, in Egypt. Cleopatra, who rules Egypt jointly with her brother, Ptolemy, conspires to seduce the newly arrived Caesar and gain his help in eliminating her despised brother. All of this she accomplishes, aided by a generous supply of confidants, servants, disguises, and theatrical tricks. She ends, like Monteverdi's Poppea (see page 107), as queen to a Roman emperor.

Julius Caesar is the epitome of a type of opera, called **opera seria** (literally, serious, as opposed to comic, opera), that dominated the Baroque stage. The plots of *opera seria* are usually derived from historical or mythological material and involve larger-than-life figures. There is little drama on stage. The action is not seen by the audience, but reported by third parties normally in the form of recitatives. The characters do not so much act as react. One after the other, the principals come forward to sing a self-contained aria, each expressing one of several stock emotions—hope, anger, hate, frenzy, despair, and lust, to name a few. What is more, the castrati and prima donnas of the time demanded that each principal be given a set number of show-stopping arias, along with suitably grand entrances and exits. Such a formulaic and dramatically static opera would make an audience weary to the point of slumber. What keeps *opera seria* alive is the great beauty of the arias and the opportunity these give the singers to display their vocal virtuosity.

"V'adoro, pupille" ("I Adore You") from Act II of *Julius Caesar* shows just how glorious such arias can be. Here Cleopatra must exert all her charm to win the heart of Caesar, and her music, accordingly, must enchant and captivate. To accomplish this, Handel not only constructed an exquisite melody but also engaged unusual instruments—the harp, the theorbo (a large lute), and the old bass viol (see page 101)—to create a special effect. As is true in most arias in *Julius Caesar*, and in *opera seria* in general, "I Adore You" is a **da capo aria**. A *da capo* aria has two musical sections, **A** and **B**. When the singer reaches the end of part **B**, he or she is instructed by the words "da capo" to "take it from the top," or "start from the head," and sing section **A** once more. What results is **ABA**, another example of ternary form* in music. Composers of Baroque opera rigidly adhered to *da capo* form for two reasons: It allowed the audience to hear an exciting or beautiful melody once again, and it permitted the soloist to exhibit his or her vocal virtuosity by means of ornamentation added to the repeat of section **A**.

The melody for the first presentation of **A** in "I Adore You" is given in the Listening Guide. This is followed by a short **B** section, and, after an interruption, the reappearance of **A**. As you listen to the return of **A**, follow the written melody, but notice how much more ornate this repeat is. Here convention required that the singer improvise and show talent as a creative artist. The soprano in the original production was the Italian diva Francesca Cuzzoni (Fig. 7–10). On our recording the role of Cleopatra is sung by Beverly Sills, once the leading lyric soprano of the New York City Opera and more recently its artistic director (Fig. 7–11). Listening Exercise 21 asks you to listen again to this ravishing aria which, perhaps better than any other, vividly expresses in music the process of seduction.

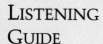

LISTENING GUIDE

George Frideric Handel
Aria, "I Adore You" from *Julius Caesar* (1724)

CD 2/5
6–Tape 2A

Characters: Cleopatra, queen of Egypt; Julius Caesar, emperor of Rome
Situation: Cleopatra tries to seduce Caesar so as to become empress of Rome.

A

0:00   (3:23)   The lilting effect of the rhythm is created by a dotted rhythm and strong second beat

V'a - do - ro,   pu - pil - le,   sa - et - te____ d'a - mo - re,   le vo - stre fa - vil - le son gra - te nel sen,
(I adore you, oh eyes, darts of love, your rays are pleasing to my heart.)

0:33   (4:00)   Notice how this second statement of the text "I adore you" gains momentum by the use of an ascending sequence

v'a - do - to, pu - pil - le, le vo - stre fa - vil - le son gra - te,   son gra - te nel sen____,
(I adore you, ...)

1:08   (4:39)   The end of this third statement is extended and the last words are repeated

v'a - do - ro,   pu - pil - le,   sa - et - te d'a - mo - re,   le vo - stre fa - vil - le son____ gra - te nel sen____,
(I adore you, ...)

B

2:18– 3:00	Shift to a minor key and a new musical mood; the dotted rhythms are replaced by slowly moving eighth notes	Pietose vi brama il mesto mio core ch'ogn'ora vi chiama l'amato suo ben.	My sad heart, which never ceases calling you beloved, begs for your mercy.
3:02	Recitative; the anticipated return of **A** is delayed by Caesar who exclaims that even the heavens have never heard such a beautiful melody	Non ha in cielo il Tonante melodia, che pareggi un si bel canto.	The Thunderer in heaven lacks a melody to rival so lovely a song.

A (*da capo*)

3:23   Return of **A** now with vocal ornamentation; see above at times in ( ).

(Listening Exercise 21)

Despite the general success of Italian opera in London and the popularity of *Julius Caesar* in particular, Handel's academy went bankrupt in 1728. The excessive fees and temperamental natures of the soloists were a primary cause. (At one rehearsal Handel tried to throw the uncooperative Cuzzoni out a window.) Rivalries between the prima donnas and competition from other operatic companies added to the composer's woes. Handel continued to write opera into the 1730s, but faced with these and other obstacles, he increasingly turned his attention to a musical genre similar in construction to opera, oratorio.

The Oratorio

An **oratorio** is literally "something sung in an oratory," an oratory being a hall or chapel used specifically for religious devotion as expressed in prayer and music. Thus, the oratorio as it first appeared in seventeenth-century Italy was an extended musical setting of a sacred text intended for the spiritual edification of the faithful and performed in a special hall or chapel. By the time it reached Handel's hands, however, the oratorio had become in most ways nothing but an opera with a religious subject. Both Baroque oratorio and opera were begun with an overture*, were divided into acts, and were composed primarily of recitatives and *da capo* arias. But there were a few important differences, aside from the obvious fact that oratorio treated a religious subject. Oratorio, being a quasi-religious genre, was performed in an oratory, theater, or concert hall, but made no use of staging and costumes. Because of the sacred subject, it also possessed more vocal decorum; that is, composers tended to avoid writing lines that gave the singers a chance to engage in extravagant displays of vocal showmanship. If the soloists were somewhat less important in oratorio, the chorus was more so. It sometimes served as a narrator, but more often functioned, like the chorus in ancient Greek drama, as the voice of the people, commenting on, or moralizing about, the action that had transpired. Add to these the fact that oratorio in England is sung in English (not Italian), and its potential impact on a large segment of English society becomes obvious.

advantages of oratorio

By the 1730s oratorio appeared to Handel as an attractive alternative to the increasingly unprofitable opera in London. He could do away with the irascible and expensive castrati and prima donnas. He no longer had to pay for elaborate sets and costumes. He could draw on the ancient English love of choral music, a tradition that extended well back into the Middle Ages. And he could exploit a new, untapped market—the faithful of the Puritan, Methodist, and growing evangelical sects in England who had viewed the pleasures of operatic theater with distrust and even contempt.

MESSIAH (1741)

Beginning in 1732 and continuing over a twenty-year period, Handel wrote upward of twenty oratorios. The most famous of these is his *Messiah*, composed in the astonishingly short period of three and a half weeks during the summer of 1741. It was first performed in Dublin, Ireland, the following April as part of a charity benefit with Handel conducting. Having heard the dress rehearsal, the local press waxed enthusiastic about the new oratorio, saying it "far surpasses anything of that Nature, which has been performed

premiere in Dublin

FIGURE 7–12

The chapel of the Foundling Hospital, London, where *Messiah* was performed annually for the benefit of the orphans.

in this or any other Kingdom." Such a large crowd was expected for the work of the famous Handel that ladies were urged not to wear hoopskirts, "as it will greatly encrease the Charity, by making Room for more company."

Buoyed by his artistic and financial success in Dublin, Handel took *Messiah* back to London, made minor alterations, and performed it in Covent Garden Theater. In 1750 he again offered *Messiah*, this time in the chapel of the Foundling Hospital for orphans in London (Fig. 7–12), and again there was much popular acclaim for Handel as well as profit for charity. This was the first time one of his oratorios was sung in a religious setting rather than a theater or concert hall. The annual repetition of *Messiah* in the Foundling Hospital chapel during Handel's lifetime and long after did much to convince the public that his oratorios were essentially religious music to be performed in church.

early performances

In a general way, *Messiah* tells the story of the life of Christ. It is divided into three parts (instead of three acts): (I) the prophecy of His coming and His Incarnation; (II) His Passion and Resurrection, and the triumph of the Gospel; and (III) reflections on the Christian victory over death. In *Messiah* dramatic confrontation is replaced by a mood of lyrical meditation and, ultimately, exaltation. The music consists of fifty-three numbers: Nineteen are for chorus, sixteen are solo arias, sixteen are recitatives, and two are purely instrumental pieces.

Although there are many beautiful and stirring arias in *Messiah* (among them "Every valley shall be exalted" and "O thou that tellest good tidings to Zion"), its true glory is found in the choral numbers. Handel was arguably the finest composer for chorus who ever lived. As a world traveler with an unsurpassed ear, he had absorbed the German tradition of the fugue and the Lutheran chorale; he knew the Venetian polychoral style of Gabrieli (see page 104) and the powerful English church anthems* (extended motets) of Henry Purcell; and, of course, he had a flair for the dramatic, gained from a lifetime in the theater. Nowhere is Handel's choral mastery more evident than in the justly famous "Hallelujah" chorus which concludes Part II of *Messiah*. Here a variety of choral styles are displayed in quick succession:

Handel's choruses

chordal, unison, chorale, fugal, and fugal and chordal together. So moved was King George II when he first heard the great opening chords, as the story goes, that he rose to his feet in admiration, thereby establishing the tradition of the audience standing for the "Hallelujah" chorus—for no one sat while the king stood. Indeed, this movement would serve well as a royal coronation march, though in *Messiah*, of course, it is Christ the King who is being crowned.

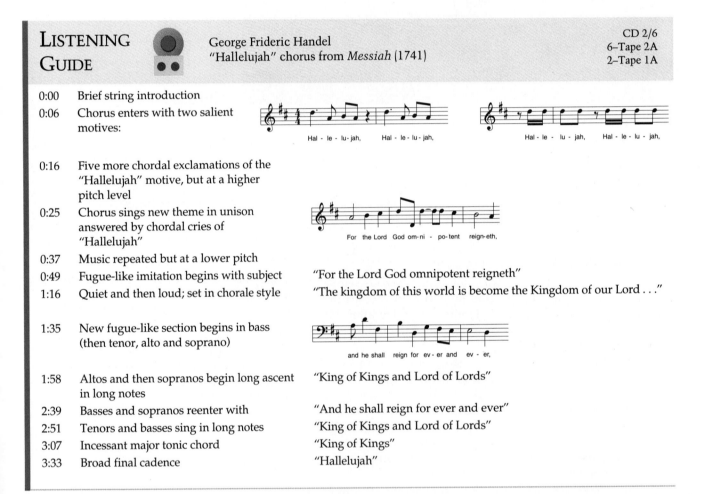

LISTENING GUIDE

George Frideric Handel
"Hallelujah" chorus from *Messiah* (1741)

CD 2/6
6–Tape 2A
2–Tape 1A

0:00	Brief string introduction	
0:06	Chorus enters with two salient motives:	*Hal - le - lu - jah, Hal - le - lu - jah, Hal - le - lu - jah, Hal - le - lu - jah,*
0:16	Five more chordal exclamations of the "Hallelujah" motive, but at a higher pitch level	
0:25	Chorus sings new theme in unison answered by chordal cries of "Hallelujah"	*For the Lord God om-ni - po-tent reign-eth,*
0:37	Music repeated but at a lower pitch	
0:49	Fugue-like imitation begins with subject	"For the Lord God omnipotent reigneth"
1:16	Quiet and then loud; set in chorale style	"The kingdom of this world is become the Kingdom of our Lord . . ."
1:35	New fugue-like section begins in bass (then tenor, alto and soprano)	*and he shall reign for ev - er and ev - er,*
1:58	Altos and then sopranos begin long ascent in long notes	"King of Kings and Lord of Lords"
2:39	Basses and sopranos reenter with	"And he shall reign for ever and ever"
2:51	Tenors and basses sing in long notes	"King of Kings and Lord of Lords"
3:07	Incessant major tonic chord	"King of Kings"
3:33	Broad final cadence	"Hallelujah"

The "Hallelujah" chorus is a strikingly effective work mainly because the large choral force creates a sense of heavenly power and strength. In point of fact, however, Handel's chorus for the original Dublin *Messiah* was much smaller than those used today. It included no more than four singers on the alto, tenor, and bass parts and six choirboys singing the soprano. The orchestra was equally slight. For the Foundling Hospital performances of the 1750s, however, the orchestra grew to thirty-eight players. Then, in the course of the next hundred years, the chorus progressively swelled to as

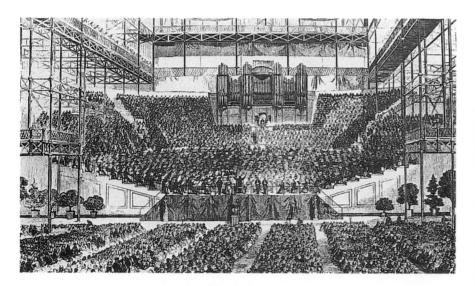

many as four thousand with a balancing orchestra of five hundred in what were billed as "Festivals of the People" in honor of Handel (Fig. 7–13).

And just as there was a continual increase in the performing forces for his *Messiah*, so too Handel's fortune and reputation grew. Toward the end of his life he owned a squire's house in the center of London, bought paintings including a large and "indeed excellent" Rembrandt, and, on his death, left an enormous estate of nearly twenty thousand pounds, as the newspapers of the day were quick to report. More than three thousand persons attended his funeral in Westminster Abbey on April 20, 1759, and a sculpture of the composer holding an aria from *Messiah* was erected above his grave and is still visible today (Fig. 7–14). As a memento of Handel's music, *Messiah* was an apt choice, for it is still performed each year at Christmas by countless amateur and professional groups throughout the world.

FIGURES 7–13 AND 7–14

(left) An enormous orchestra, and even larger chorus, performing an oratorio of Handel at the Great Handel Festival, London, 1859. (right) Handel's funeral monument at Westminster Abbey. The composer holds the aria "I know that my Redeemer liveth" from *Messiah*.

LISTENING EXERCISES

19	Johann Sebastian Bach Cantata, *A Mighty Fortress Is Our God* (begun 1715) First movement	CD 2/1 6–Tape 2A 2–Tape 1A

The purpose of this listening exercise is to have you learn to identify the entry of a theme or motive and become more familiar with the range and sound of the voices of a choir. As discussed on page 130, for the opening movement of this cantata Bach has fashioned a theme out of each of the phrases of the chorale tune *A Mighty Fortress*. He then presents each theme in imitation, making use of the four voices of the choir and rounding off each imitative unit with a phrase of the original chorale tune played first in the trumpet and then organ. You are asked to fill in the blanks by indicating the sequence in which the voices enter in each imitative unit. Some of these are difficult to hear because the great density of Bach's contrapuntal web makes individual strands hard to identify. These more obscure entries have been filled in for you.

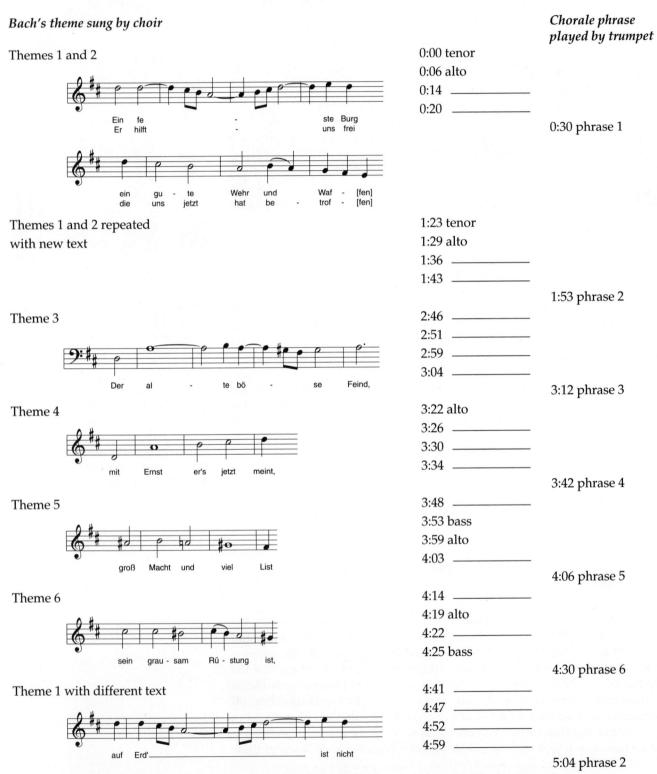

Bach's theme sung by choir

Chorale phrase played by trumpet

Themes 1 and 2

0:00 tenor
0:06 alto
0:14 _____
0:20 _____

0:30 phrase 1

Themes 1 and 2 repeated
with new text

1:23 tenor
1:29 alto
1:36 _____
1:43 _____

1:53 phrase 2

Theme 3

2:46 _____
2:51 _____
2:59 _____
3:04 _____

3:12 phrase 3

Theme 4

3:22 alto
3:26 _____
3:30 _____
3:34 _____

3:42 phrase 4

Theme 5

3:48 _____
3:53 bass
3:59 alto
4:03 _____

4:06 phrase 5

Theme 6

4:14 _____
4:19 alto
4:22 _____
4:25 bass

4:30 phrase 6

Theme 1 with different text

4:41 _____
4:47 _____
4:52 _____
4:59 _____

5:04 phrase 2

20	Johann Sebastian Bach	CD 2/4
	Organ Fugue in G minor (ca. 1710)	6–Tape 2A
		2–Tape 1A

The following diagram is essentially the same as that found on page 139. It charts the flow of the music as Bach's Organ Fugue in G minor unfolds from the straightforward exposition, through the increasingly lengthy episodes, to the final statement of the subject in the bass. For this problem set, you are asked to make your own time log, or listening guide, for the nine entries of the subject. Above the blank line that shows each subject entry (_____), write in the time at which the subject appears. The first, of course, will be "S0:00." You don't have to indicate times during the episodes, but see if you can sense that modulations are occurring.

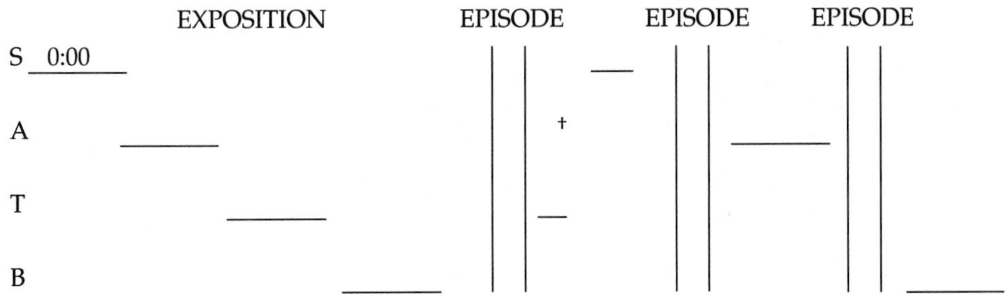

	EXPOSITION	EPISODE	EPISODE	EPISODE

S 0:00 _____

A _____ †

T _____

B _____

†This entry starts in the tenor and continues in the soprano.

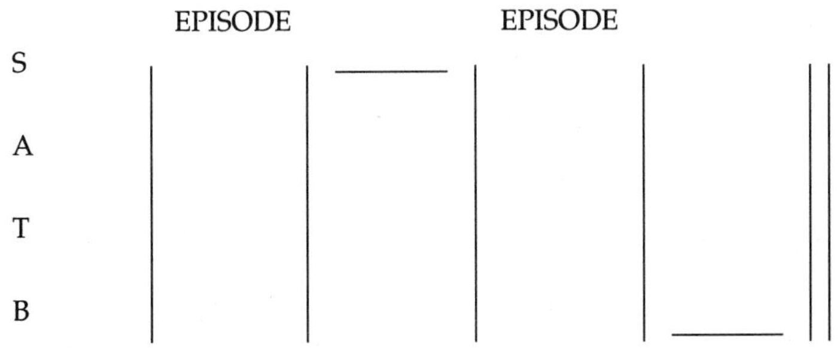

	EPISODE	EPISODE

S

A

T

B

21	George Frideric Handel	CD 2/5
	Aria, "I Adore You" from the opera *Julius Caesar* (1724)	6–Tape 2A

Before beginning this listening exercise, be sure that you have listened to the aria at least once and followed the listening guide on page 143. This will give you an idea of the overall shape of the *da capo* form and will prepare you to answer the more specific questions that follow:

1. What is the meter of the aria, duple or triple? _____
2. What is the tonality, major or minor? _____

3. Is the harpsichord or the organ used here as the basic keyboard instrument of the *basso continuo?* _____
4. What two plucked string instruments begin to become audible at 0:37?
   a. organ   b. harp   c. theorbo   d. bassoon
5. At the beginning of the **B** section of the *da capo* form (2:18), what is the rhythm of the bass? (circle one)

6. What is this kind of Baroque bass called?
   a. running bass   b. walking bass   c. pedal point
7. Is the tonality at the end of the **B** section (2:57) major or minor?
   _____

8. When Caesar interrupts with his recitative (3:02), is he accompanied by just the continuo (harpsichord and cello) or by the full orchestra?
   _____

9. In the return to the **A** section (3:23–end), is the soprano voice more or less ornamented than the first presentation of **A** (does she sing more notes)? _____
10. In this repeat of **A** the soprano generally sings
    a. in a lower register   b. in the same register   c. in a higher register

KEY WORDS

cantata	exposition	oratorio
chorale	figured bass	prelude
da capo aria	French overture	subject
dance suite	fugue	*The Well-Tempered*
episode	*opera seria*	*Clavier*

Classical Ideals:
The World of Haydn and Mozart

8

"Classical" as a musical term has two separate, though related, meanings. We use the word "classical" to signify the "serious" or "art" music of the West as distinguished from folk music, popular music, jazz, and the traditional music of various ethnic cultures. We call this music "classical" because there is something about the excellence of its form and style that makes it enduring, just as a finely crafted watch or a vintage automobile may be said to be a "classic" because it has a timeless beauty. Yet in the same breath we may refer to "Classical" music (now with a capital C), and by this we mean the music of a specific historical period, 1750–1820, a period of the great works of Haydn and Mozart and the early masterpieces of Beethoven. The creations of these men have become so identified in the public mind with musical proportion, balance, and formal correctness that this comparatively brief period has given its name to all music of lasting aesthetic worth.

"Classical" derives from the Latin *classicus*, meaning "something of the first rank or highest quality." To the men and women of the eighteenth century, no art, architecture, philosophy, or political institutions were more admirable, virtuous, and worthy of emulation than those of ancient Greece and Rome. Other periods in Western history have been inspired by classical antiquity—the Renaissance heavily, the early Baroque less so, and our own century to some degree—but no period more than the eighteenth century. This was the time of the discovery of the ruins of Pompeii (1748), of the publication of Winkelmann's *History of Ancient Art* (1764) and Gibbon's *Rise and Fall of the Roman Empire* (1788). It was also the period in which young English aristocrats made the "grand tour" of Italy and carted back to their country estates Roman statues, columns, and parts of entire villas. Classical architecture, with its formal control of space, geometric shapes, balance, and symmetrical design, became the only style thought worthy for domestic and state buildings of consequence. European palaces, opera houses, episcopal residences, and country homes all made use of it. Thomas Jefferson also traveled to Italy in these years while American ambassador to France, and later was instrumental in establishing Classical design in this country. Our nation's capitol, many state capitols, and countless other governmental and

FIGURES 8–1 AND 8–2

FIGURES 8–1 AND 8–2

(left) A view of Thomas Jefferson's design for the library at the University of Virginia. The portico with columns, triangular pediment, and central rotunda are all qualities of Classical style in architecture. (right) Thomas Jefferson by the French sculptor Houdon, 1789.

FIGURE 8–3

Voltaire by the French sculptor Houdon, 1778.

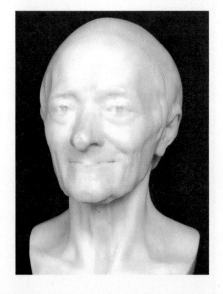

university buildings abound with the well-proportioned columns, porticos, and rotundas of the Classical style.

THE ENLIGHTENMENT

The Classical era in music, art, and architecture coincides with the period in philosophy and letters called the Enlightenment. During the Enlightenment, also referred to as the Age of Reason, thinkers gave free rein to the pursuit of truth and the discovery of natural laws. This is the era that saw the rise of a natural religion called Deism, which believes that a Creator made the world, set it in motion, and has left it alone ever since. This is also the age of such scientific advances as the discovery of electricity and the invention of the steam engine. The first *Encyclopedia Britannica* appeared in 1771 and the French *Encyclopédie* between 1751 and 1772, a twenty-four volume set whose authors discarded traditional religious convictions and superstitions in favor of more rational scientific, philosophical, and political beliefs. In France the encyclopedists Voltaire (1694–1778), Rousseau (1712–1778), and Diderot (1713–1784) espoused the principles of social justice, equality, religious tolerance, and freedom of speech. These Enlightenment ideals subsequently became fundamental to all democratic governments and were enshrined in our American constitution.

Needless to say, the notion that all persons are created equal and should enjoy full political freedom put the thinkers of the Enlightenment on a collision course with the defenders of the existing social order. The old political structure had been built on the mysteries of the church, the privileges of the nobility, and the divine right of kings. Voltaire attacked the habits and prerogatives of both clergy and aristocracy, and championed middle-class virtues: honesty, common sense, and hard work. The extravagant gestures, sword, and wig of the frivolous courtier were an easy target for his pen. A more natural appearance, one appropriate to a tradesman, merchant, or manufacturer, now became the paradigm. Spurred on by economic self-interest and the principles of the philosophers, an increasingly numerous and self-confident middle class in France and America rebelled against the monarchy and its supporters. The Age of Reason gave way to a newer Age of Revolution.

Music and Social Change: Comic Opera

Music was affected by these profound social changes, and in some ways it helped to precipitate them. A new form of opera, comic opera, proved to be a powerful vehicle for social reform. Opera in the Baroque period had been dominated by *opera seria** of the sort we have seen in Handel's *Julius Caesar* (see page 142). It was beautiful, grandiose, somewhat stiff, and expensive to mount. Portraying the deeds of mythological heros, gods, and goddesses, emperors and kings, it was the quintessential opera of the aristocracy. By contrast, the new comic opera was the opera of the middle class. It made use of everyday characters and situations; it employed spoken dialogues and simple songs in place of recitatives and *da capo** arias; and it was liberally spiced with sight gags, slapstick comedy, and bawdy humor. The librettos, such as they were, either poked fun at the nobility for its pomposity and incompetence or criticized it for being heartless. Like seditious pamphlets, comic operas appeared in every country; among them were John Gay's *The Beggar's Opera* (1728) in England, Giovanni Pergolesi's *La serva padrona* (*The Maid Made Master*, 1733) in Italy, and Jean-Jacques Rousseau's *Le devin du village* (*The Village Soothsayer*, 1752) in France. And composers of greater stature were seduced by the charms of this middle-class entertainment. Mozart, who was treated poorly by the nobility throughout his short life, set one libretto in which a barber outsmarts a count and holds him up to public ridicule, *Le nozze di Figaro* (*The Marriage of Figaro*, 1786), and another, *Don Giovanni* (1787), in which the villain is a leading nobleman of the town. The play that served as the basis for Mozart's *Figaro* was banned by the authorities when it first appeared in Paris. By the time of the French Revolution (1789), comic opera, a rebellious upstart, had nearly driven the established *opera seria* off the eighteenth-century stage.

FIGURE 8–4

An illustration from a 1785 edition of Pierre Beaumarchais's play *The Marriage of Figaro* showing a scene in Act I. It was on this play that Mozart based his opera of the same name.

Public Concerts

FIGURE 8–5

A public concert in the Vauxhall Gardens, London. A singer performs from the balcony with an accompanying orchestra behind her.

The social changes of the eighteenth century, in turn, affected who listened to music. In an earlier day a citizen might only hear sacred vocal music in a church or a bit of instrumental music at court, if he or she happened to be lucky enough to be an invited guest. But by mid-century the bookkeeper, physician, cloth merchant, and customs agent collectively had enough disposable income to organize and patronize their own concerts. In Leipzig, for example, the merchants got together to form the *Gewandhaus* ("Clothiers' House") concerts, which were held in the great hall of that guild, and this *Gewandhaus* orchestra is still active today. Entrepreneurs in London offered concerts in the Vauxhall Gardens, where music could be heard inside in the orchestra room and outside as well (Fig. 8–5). And in Paris, then a city of 500,000, one could attend, as a citizen of the day said, "the best concerts everyday with complete freedom." The most successful Parisian concert series was the *Concert spirituel*, which was advertised to the public by means of flyers or handbills distributed in the streets. To make its offerings accessible to a broad stratum of society, it also instituted a two-tiered system of prices (four livres for boxes and two livres for the pit). Thus we can trace to the middle of the eighteenth century the tradition of middle-class citizens

attending public performances in return for an admission fee. The institution of "concerts" as we know them and the development of a broadly based listening audience dates from this time.

FIGURE 8–6

Mozart's piano preserved in the house of his birth in Salzburg. Note that the keyboard spans only five octaves, typical for the late eighteenth-century piano.

THE ADVENT OF THE PIANO

The newly affluent middle class did not only wish to listen to music but to play it as well. Most of this music making was centered in the home and around an instrument that first entered public consciousness in the Classical period: the piano. Invented in Italy about 1700, the piano gradually replaced the harpsichord as the keyboard instrument of preference (Fig. 8–6). And with good reason, for the piano could play at more than one dynamic level (hence the original name *pianoforte*, "soft-loud"). Compared with the harpsichord, the piano could generate music that was more dramatic—because of the possibility of sudden contrast—and at the same time more subtle—because of the way phrases could be graded and shaped by increasing or diminishing the volume of successive notes. Those who played this new domestic instrument were mostly amateurs, and the great majority of these were women. Young ladies were encouraged to show skill on the piano as a means of demonstrating their refinement. This social requirement, in turn, encouraged a simpler, more homophonic keyboard style, one that would presumably not tax the technical limitations of the female performer. The spirit of democracy may have been in the air, but this was still very much a sexist age. It was assumed that ladies would not wish, as one publication said, "to bother their pretty little heads with counterpoint and harmony," but would be content with a tuneful melody and a few rudimentary chords to flesh it out. Collections such as *Keyboard Pieces for Ladies* (1768) were directed at these new musical consumers.

ROCOCO STYLE

Many keyboard works of the mid-eighteenth century were composed in a charming, graceful style called Rococo, a style that predates mature Classical style. **Rococo** derives from the French *rocaille* ("shell-work") and is applied to a light, yet highly decorative, style of art, architecture, and furniture design that arose in France during the early years of the eighteenth century. It drew its inspiration from natural objects with curved and flowing lines— flowers, leaves, seashells, and the like—and it played out these curves and double curves in pastel colors and soft hues. Rococo painters, notably Antoine Watteau (1684–1721), François Boucher (1703–1770) and Jean Honoré Fragonard (1732-1806), created pastoral scenes populated by elegantly dressed men and women enjoying their leisure (Fig. 8–7). Like all things

French in this period, Rococo style spread to other regions of Europe, its curvesome playfulness being particularly favored for the interiors of palaces and churches in parts of southern Germany and in Austria (Fig. 8–8).

When associated with music, Rococo style suggests a flowing, tuneful melody, simple chordal accompaniment (though the notes of these chords may be played in succession), and light texture. These same qualities of mid-eighteenth-century music are sometimes referred to more broadly as the "gallant" style or even the "pre-Classical" style, the pre-Classical manner being thought of as a bridge between the heavy seriousness of the Baroque and the more graceful, transparent Classical.

A clear example of this transitional style can be found in the opera of Giovanni Battista Pergolesi (1710–1736), *La serva padrona (The Maid Made Master)*, which appeared in 1733. As we have noted, this is a comic opera, an **opera buffa,** as the Italians call this comic genre. In it, the clever maid Serpina outwits her master, Uberto, to become his wife and mistress of his house. Serpina's aria "Stizzoso, mio stizzoso" ("Peevish man, oh peevish man") has one important vestige of Baroque *opera seria—da capo* form. Yet in its simple phrase structure and transparent texture, it is entirely in the new Classical manner. The phrases of melody are short, invariably three or four bars long, and each is usually repeated immediately. The texture consists of only two musical strands, the voice (accompanied by the violins) and the bass. The intent here is not to educate or elevate the listener but to provide a pleasant diversion, a fashionable amusement. The aria is pretty, but it does not aspire to the higher realm of art. When *The Maid Made Master* reached Paris in 1752, it enjoyed a *succès de scandale,* attacked by the traditionalists and defended by progressives such as Jean-Jacques Rousseau, the outspoken champion of simplicity and all things natural.

FIGURE 8–7

The Music Lesson attributed to François Boucher (1759). A lightness and grace attends two musical dilettantes in this oil painting in Rococo style.

FIGURE 8–8

Delicate twists and turns, and elaborate floral patterns are hallmarks of Rococo design, as can be seen in the interior of the pilgrimage church Vierzehnheiligen (The Fourteen Saints), located in southern Germany.

LISTENING GUIDE

Giovanni Battista Pergolesi
Aria, "Peevish man, oh peevish man,"
from the *opera buffa, The Maid Made Master* (1733)

CD 2/8
6–Tape 2A

Characters: Serpina, the young servant of Uberto; Uberto, a grumbling old bachelor

Situation: The clever maid Serpina refuses to do her master's bidding. Uberto is made to realize that it is Serpina he loves.

Stiz - zo - so,   mio   stiz - zo-so,   Voi   fa - te il   bo - ri - o-so,

A

0:00   "Ma" ("but") and "non" ("no") are treated in comic fashion

Stizzoso, mio stizzosó,
Voi fate il borioso,
Ma non vi pù giovare.

Peevish man, oh peevish man,
you play the lord,
but it will do you no good.

0:22   "Zit, zit" is also given comic treatment

Bisogna al mio divieto,
Star cheto, e non parlare.
Zit, zit, Serpina vuol così.

You'll follow my command,
and be silent, not speak.
Zit, zit, Serpina wants it so.

0:35   The above text is repeated to somewhat varied music

B

1:24   Music becomes more serious with hints of minor key

Cred'io che m'intendete, sì
Da che mi conoscete
Son molti e molti dì.

I believe you understand me,
since you have known me for
many, many days.

A

1:50   *Da capo* return to the beginning with **A** text and music repeated

VIENNA: A CITY OF MUSIC

Whereas pre-Classical music in the Rococo or gallant manner flourished in Paris and London, it was Vienna that provided a home for the development of the mature Classical style. Indeed, Vienna became so important as a center of musical composition that the late eighteenth century is often called the age of the Viennese Classical style. The city owed its prominence to a fortuitous location. As the capital city of the old Holy Roman Empire, Vienna was the administrative center for portions of modern-day Germany, Yugoslavia, Czechoslovakia, Hungary, and Italy, in addition to all of Austria, and thus was a cultural crossroads for Central Europe (see Fig. 8–9). Musicians such as Christoph Gluck (1714–1787) from Bohemia (Czechoslovakia), Antonio Salieri (1750–1825) from northern Italy, Franz Joseph Haydn (1732–1809) from Rohrau in lower Austria, Wolfgang Amadeus Mozart (1756–1791) from Salzburg in upper Austria, and Ludwig van Beethoven (1770–1827) from the German Rhineland gravitated toward Vienna for its rich musical life. There

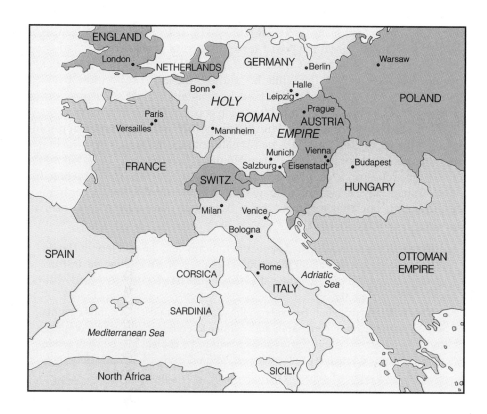

FIGURE 8–9

A map of eighteenth-century Europe showing the Holy Roman Empire and the principal musical cities.

were theaters for German and Italian opera, concerts in the streets on fine summer nights, and ballroom dances where as many as four thousand persons might sway to a minuet, a contradance, or even a waltz by Mozart or Beethoven. In a city of nearly 200,000 inhabitants (the fourth largest in Europe behind London, Paris, and Naples), there were estimated to be 300 piano teachers. "There cannot be many cities in which musical amateurism is as widespread as it is here. Everybody plays, everybody takes music lessons," reported a journal of the day. And the musical allure of Vienna continued into the nineteenth century. In addition to native-born Franz Schubert (1797–1828), outsiders such as Anton Bruckner (1824–1896), Johannes Brahms (1833–1897), and Gustav Mahler (1860–1911) spent many of their most productive years there. Even today Vienna remains the capital of a nation (Austria) that spends nearly as much money on its state opera as it does on its national defense.

Franz Joseph Haydn (1732–1809)

Thus, it was only natural that Franz Joseph Haydn, the son of a wheelwright from Rohrau in lower (eastern) Austria, should be sent to the capital to nurture his obvious musical talent. Haydn was born in 1732, and by the age of eight his pleasing voice had caught the attention of local church authorities. Soon he was singing among the choirboys at the cathedral of St. Stephen in Vienna. After nearly ten years of service his voice broke and he was abruptly

FIGURE 8–10

A portrait of Franz Joseph Haydn painted in 1791 when the composer was in London.

dismissed. For most of the 1750s Haydn eked out a meager living as a free-lance musician: He gave keyboard lessons, accompanied singers, and sang or played violin or organ at three churches each Sunday, moving quickly from one to the next. All the while he studied musical composition. By 1761 he had progressed to the point where he was able to obtain a position as composer and leader of the orchestra at the court of Prince Esterházy.

The Esterházy were a noble Hungarian family with extensive landhold-ings southeast of Vienna and a passionate interest in music. As did many wealthy aristocrats of the time, Prince Nikolaus Esterházy (1714–1790) main-tained an orchestra, a chapel for singing religious music, and a theater for opera. When Haydn was first engaged he was required to sign a contract of employment, one that suggests the subservient place of the composer in eighteenth-century society:

> [He] and all the musicians shall appear in uniform, and the said Joseph Haydn shall take care that he and all the members of the orchestra follow the instruc-tions given, and appear in white stocking, white linen, powdered, and with either a pigtail or a tiewig....
>
> The said [Haydn] shall be under obligation to compose such music as his Serene Highness may command, and neither to communicate such composi-tions to any other person, nor to allow them to be copied, but he shall retain them for the absolute use of his Highness, and not compose for any other per-son without the knowledge and permission of his Highness.

Thus, not only did Haydn lead the life of a liveried servant at court, eating with the other domestics, but he also was prohibited from circulating his music without the express permission of his patron. But Nikolaus Esterházy was a benign ruler, and Haydn's symphonies, quartets, and sonatas came to be known not only in Vienna but in foreign capitals as well. In the 1770s they surfaced in Amsterdam, London, and Paris in "pirated" editions. Since there was no international copyright in these years, a publisher might sim-ply print a work from a copyist's score without the composer's knowledge or consent. When Haydn signed another contract with Prince Nikolaus in 1779, there was no such "exclusive use" provision, and he now began to sell his works to various publishers, sometimes consigning the same piece to two or three at the same time!

composing before the time of copyright laws

For a period of nearly thirty years Haydn served Nikolaus Esterházy, writing symphonies and divertimentos* for evening entertainment, operas for the court theater (see Fig. 10–3), and string trios in which the prince him-self might participate. When Nikolaus died in 1790, the Esterházy orchestra was dismissed in favor of a smaller military band. Haydn retained his title as court composer as well as his full salary, but he was now free to travel as he wished. After settling briefly in Vienna, he journeyed to London where he had been engaged at a substantial fee to compose and conduct. From this commission resulted the twelve "London symphonies," which were first performed in the Hanover Square Rooms (see Fig. 9–7), a large public con-cert hall built in part with capital supplied by Johann Christian Bach, old Bach's youngest son. Haydn stayed in London during 1791–1792 and returned again for the concert season 1794–1795. He was presented to the king and queen, received the honorary degree of doctor of music at Oxford,

Haydn in London

and generally accorded the status of a visiting celebrity, as a letter written within a fortnight of his arrival attests:

> Everyone wants to know me. I had to dine out six times up to now, and if I wanted, I could have an invitation every day; but first I must consider my health and second my work. Except for the nobility, I admit no callers 'til 2 o'clock in the afternoon.

After Haydn returned home to Vienna for good in the summer of 1795, he wrote mainly Masses for chorus and orchestra and two oratorios, *The Creation* (1798) and *The Seasons* (1801)—it seems that he had been deeply impressed by the performances of Handel's oratorios which he had heard while in England. His last public appearance was in 1808 for a performance of *The Creation* given in his honor in the festival hall of the university and conducted by court chapel master Antonio Salieri (Fig. 8–11). He died the following spring, on May 31, 1809, just two weeks after the besieging armies of Napoleon had conquered Vienna.

Haydn's long life, commitment to duty, and unflagging industry resulted in an impressive number of musical compositions: 104 symphonies, about 70 string quartets, nearly a dozen operas, 52 piano sonatas, 15 Masses, and 2 oratorios. He began composing before the death of Bach (1750) and did not put down his pen until about the time Beethoven set to work on his Fifth Symphony (1808). Thus, Haydn not only witnessed but, more than any other composer, helped to create the mature Classical style.

Haydn's accomplishments

Despite his accomplishments, he did not rebel against the modest station assigned to him in traditional eighteenth-century society: "I have associated with emperors, kings, and many great people," he said, "and I have heard many flattering things from them, but I would not live in familiar relations with such persons; I prefer to be close to people of my own standing." And though keenly aware of his own musical gifts, he was quick to recognize talent in others, especially Mozart: "Friends often flatter me that I have some genius, but he [Mozart] stood far above me."

FIGURE 8–11

A public performance of Haydn's oratorio *The Creation* given at the university in Vienna in 1808 to mark the composer's 76th birthday. The orchestra, which can be seen on the podium at the rear, is conducted by Antonio Salieri.

FIGURE 8–12

An unfinished portrait of Mozart executed by his brother-in-law Joseph Lange during 1789–1790.

WOLFGANG AMADEUS MOZART (1756–1791)

Indeed, Wolfgang Amadeus Mozart may be the greatest musical genius the world has ever known. Mendelssohn (1809–1847) and Schubert (1797–1828) were perhaps his equals as youthful composers, but who except possibly Bach can match the diversity, breadth of expression, and perfect formal control present in the best works of Mozart? The stories of Mozart's prodigious musical talent are many. As a child he could identify the notes played in any chord, judge the pitch of an instrument within an eighth of a tone, or pick out a wrong note in a musical score while crawling on his back across a table. As a youth he heard a motet sung in the papal chapel in Rome, went to his room, and wrote it down by memory, note for note. He frequently copied one of his finished compositions onto a score while working out a new piece in his head. Little wonder that the great German poet Goethe (1749–1832), who had heard Mozart play as a child, referred to him as "the human incarnation of a divine force of creation."

Mozart was born in Salzburg, Austria, in 1756. His father, Leopold, was a violinist in the orchestra of the archbishop of Salzburg, and his older sister, Nannerl, was also a talented performer (Fig. 8–13). Leopold was quick to recognize the musical gifts of his son, who by the age of six was playing the piano, violin, and organ as well as composing. The Mozart family coached off to Vienna where the children displayed their musical wares before Empress Maria Theresa (1717–1780). They then embarked on a three-year tour of Northern Europe that included extended stops in Munich, Brussels, Paris, London, Amsterdam, and Geneva. In London, Wolfgang sat on the knee of Johann Christian Bach (1735–1782) and improvised a fugue, and here, at the age of eight, his first two symphonies were performed. Eventually, the Mozarts made their way back to Salzburg. But in 1768 they were off

travels of Mozart's youth

FIGURES 8–13 AND 8–14

(left) Young Mozart at the keyboard with his sister Nannerl and father Leopold painted in Paris 1763–1764 during their three-year tour of Europe. (right) Archbishop Colloredo, the unsympathetic patron of both Wolfgang Mozart and his father Leopold.

Mozart and *Amadeus*

Perhaps you have seen the extraordinary film *Amadeus* (1985) by Milos Forman, based on a play of Peter Schaffer, and wondered if the Mozart portrayed there bore any relation to the real Mozart. The answer is, in a few ways, yes; in most ways, no. To be sure, Mozart's life-style was somewhat chaotic, he had expensive tastes, and he was often downright silly in his behavior. Yet there is no hint of drunkeness in the contemporary documents; he had an excellent, if erratic income; and his childish behavior, according to his brother-in-law Joseph Lange was the way in which he released excess tension built up during concentrated periods of creative activity. Mozart did not die poor. Indeed, his income from two major operas in 1791 and the famous Requiem Mass made his last year one of his most lucrative. Nor was he abandoned to suffer a pauper's funeral. He received the same sort of burial (placed in a common grave) as eighty-five percent of the upper-middle-class in Vienna at that time. Nor, finally, was Mozart poisoned by his principal rival in Vienna, the composer Antonio Salieri (1750–1825). Salieri, court composer to Emperor Joseph II and his two successors, was a universally respected, if not supremely gifted, musician who later went on to become, at various times, the teacher of Beethoven, Schubert, Liszt, and even one of Mozart's two sons. As court composer to his imperial majesty, Salieri had little to fear from Mozart, no matter how enormous the latter's genius.

A scene from *Amadeus*.

again to Vienna where the now twelve-year-old Wolfgang staged a production of his first opera, *Bastien und Bastienne*, in the home of the famous Dr. Franz Anton Mesmer (1733–1815), the inventor of the theory of animal magnetism (hence, "to mesmerize"). The next year father and son visited the major cities of Italy, including Rome where the pope dubbed Wolfgang a Knight of the Golden Spur. Although the aim of this globe-trotting was to acquire fame and fortune, the result was that Mozart, unlike Haydn, was exposed at an early age to a wealth of musical styles—French Rococo, English choral, German polyphonic, and Italian vocal. His extraordinarily keen ear absorbed them all, and ultimately they increased the breadth and substance of his music.

A period of relative stability followed: For much of the 1770s Mozart resided in Salzburg where, like his father, he had been taken on as a violinist and composer to the archbishop. Unfortunately, the reigning archbishop, Colloredo (Fig. 8–14), was a stern, somewhat miserly man who had little sympathy for Mozart, genius or not. As was the custom since medieval times, this prince of the Church, whom Mozart refers to in his letters as "the Archboobie," was as much a political figure as a spiritual leader. Mozart was given a place in the orchestra, a small salary, and his board. Like Haydn and the other musicians at the court of Esterházy, those at Salzburg ate with the cooks and valets. For a Knight of the Golden Spur who had played for kings and queens across Europe, this was humble fare indeed, and Mozart chafed

FIGURE 8–15

Antonio Salieri (1750–1825).

FIGURE 8–16

St. Stephen's Cathedral, Vienna, where Mozart was married in 1782 and where his funeral was held in 1791.

under this system of aristocratic patronage. After several unpleasant scenes in the spring of 1781, the twenty-five-year-old composer cut himself free of the archbishop and determined to make a living as an independent musician in Vienna.

Mozart chose Vienna partly because of the city's rich musical life and partly because it was a comfortable distance from his overbearing father. In a letter to his sister written in the spring of 1782, Wolfgang spells out his daily regimen in the Austrian capital.

> My hair is always done by six o'clock in the morning and by seven I am fully dressed. I then compose until nine. From nine to one I give lessons. Then I lunch, unless I am invited to some house where they lunch at two or even three o'clock. . . . I can never work before five or six o'clock in the evening, and even then I am often prevented by a concert. If I am not prevented, I compose until nine. Then I go to my dear Constanze.

Against the advice of his father, Wolfgang married his "dear Constanze" (Weber) in the summer of 1782 but, alas, she was as romantic and impractical as he, though less given to streaks of hard work. In addition to his composing, teaching, and performing, Mozart now found time to study the music of Bach and Handel, play chamber music with his friend Joseph Haydn, and join the Freemasons. Although still very much a practicing Catholic, he was attracted to this fraternity of the Enlightenment because of its belief in tolerance and universal brotherhood. His opera *Die Zauberflöte* (*The Magic Flute*, 1791) is viewed by many as a hymn in praise of masonic ideals.

The years 1785–1787 witnessed the peak of Mozart's success and the creation of many of his greatest works. He had a full complement of pupils, played several concerts a week, and enjoyed lucrative commissions as a composer. Piano concertos, string quartets, and symphonies flowed from his pen, as well as his two greatest Italian operas, *The Marriage of Figaro* and *Don Giovanni*. But *Don Giovanni*, a huge success when first performed in Prague in 1787, was little appreciated when mounted in Vienna in the spring of 1788. "The opera is divine, perhaps even more beautiful than *Figaro*," declared Emperor Joseph II, "but no food for the teeth of my Viennese." Mozart's music was no longer in vogue. His pupils began to dwindle and the elite failed to subscribe to his concerts. His style was thought to be too dense, too intense, too dissonant. One publisher warned him: "Write in a more popular style or else I cannot print or pay for more of your music."

Although now in declining health, Mozart was still capable of creating the greatest sort of masterpieces. In his last year (1791) he composed a superb clarinet concerto and the German comic opera *The Magic Flute*, and began work on a Requiem Mass, one he was never to finish. Mozart died on December 5, 1791, at the age of thirty-five. The precise reason for his death has never been determined, though kidney failure made worse by needless bloodletting was the most likely cause.

Mozart's last year

CLASSICAL STYLE IN MUSIC

Even for a music lover of many years' experience, it is sometimes difficult to distinguish the sound of Haydn from that of Mozart or, similarly, to differentiate late Haydn or Mozart from early Beethoven. This easy confusion points up the fact that music in the Classical period is more homogeneous in style than in any other period in the history of music—pieces in the same genre, but by different composers, tend to sound like one another. Clearly, there was then a consensus of opinion among creative musicians as to what music was supposed to sound like, an ideal tacitly agreed to, not only by Haydn, Mozart, and Beethoven in Vienna, but also by lesser men working in Milan, Paris, London, and elsewhere. The Viennese Classical style embodied universal principles in an age that greatly valued universal ideals.

Much has been written about the Classical style in music: its quiet grace, noble simplicity, purity, and serenity. It is certainly "classical" in the sense that extreme emphasis is placed on formal clarity, order, and balance. Compared with the relentless, grandiose, sometimes pompous sound of the Baroque, Classical music is lighter in tone, more natural, yet less predictable. It is even capable of humor and surprise, as when Mozart again and again leads up to, but carefully avoids, a cadence, or when Haydn explodes with a thunderous chord in the midst of a sea of quiet. But what is it in precise musical terms that creates this feeling of levity and grace, of clarity and balance, in Classical music?

MELODY. Perhaps the first thing that strikes the listener about the music of Haydn or Mozart is that the theme is often tuneful, catchy, even singable. Not only are melodies simple and short but also the phrases tend to be organized in antecedent–consequent*, or question–answer, pairs. The melody usually progresses by playing out these short phrases in symmetrical groups of two, three, four, eight, twelve, or sixteen bars. The brevity of the phrase and frequent cadences allow for ample light and air to penetrate the melodic line. Following is the theme from the second movement of Mozart's Piano Concerto in C major (1785). It is composed of two three-bar phrases–an antecedent and a consequent phrase. The melody is light and airy, yet perfectly balanced. It is also singable and quite memorable—indeed, it has been turned into a popular movie theme (the "love song" from *Elvira Madigan*). Compare this with the long, asymmetrical melodies of the Baroque that were often instrumental in character (see page 125).

Classical balance and symmetry

EXAMPLE 8–1

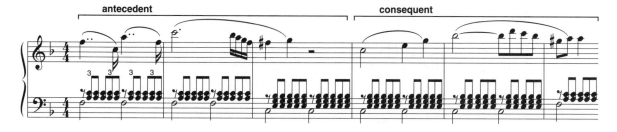

HARMONY. After about 1750 all music assumed a more homophonic, less polyphonic character. The new tuneful melody was supported by a simple harmony. In the preceding example only two chords, tonic and dominant, support Mozart's lovely melody. The bass still generates the harmony, but it does not always move in the regular, constant fashion typified by the Baroque walking bass. Rather, the bass might sit on the bottom of one chord for several beats, even several measures, then move rapidly, and then stop

flexible harmonic rhythm

again. Thus, the rate at which chords change—the harmonic rhythm as it is called—is much more fluid and flexible with Classical composers.

To avoid a feeling of inactivity when the harmony is static, Classical composers invented new accompanying patterns. Sometimes, as in example 8–1, they simply repeat the accompanying chord in a uniform triplet rhythm. *Alberti bass*   More common is the pattern called the **Alberti bass,** named after the minor Italian keyboard composer Domenico Alberti (1710–1740) who popularized this figure. Instead of playing the pitches of a chord all together, the notes are spread out to provide a continual stream of sound. Mozart used an Alberti bass at the beginning of his famous C major piano sonata (1788):

EXAMPLE 8–2

The Alberti pattern serves essentially the same function as the modern "boogie-woogie" bass. It provides a feeling of harmonic activity for those moments when, in fact, the harmony is stationary.

RHYTHM. Rhythm, too, is more flexible in the hands of Haydn and Mozart. It animates the stop-and-go character of their melodies and harmonies. Rapid motion may be followed by repose and then further quick movement, but there is little of the driving, perpetual motion of Baroque musical rhythm.

TEXTURE. Musical texture was also transformed in the latter half of the eighteenth century, mainly because composers began to concentrate less on writing dense counterpoint than creating charming melodies. No longer are independent polyphonic lines superimposed, layer upon layer, as in a fugue of Bach or a polyphonic chorus of Handel. The lessening of counterpoint, *light, homophonic textures*   then, made for a lighter, more transparent sound, especially in the middle range of the texture. Mozart, after a study of Bach and Handel in the early 1780s, infused his symphonies, quartets, and concertos with greater polyphonic content, but this seems to have caused the pleasure-loving Viennese to think his music too dense!

The Classical Orchestra

The development of the orchestra during the Classical period is discussed in connection with the creation of the Classical symphony in Chapter 10. For the moment, suffice it to say that during the late eighteenth century the orchestra grew in size as a direct response to the larger audience that crowded into the new public concert halls. The strings still constitute the core of the orchestra, but the woodwinds—oboes, flutes, bassoons, and the new clarinets—gain increased autonomy. They no longer merely double or echo the violins and the bass line as they had during the Baroque era. Henceforth, they enter and depart, seemingly at will, now to play a theme as a solo, now to thicken momentarily the musical texture or to add a dash of instrumental color.

The Dramatic Quality of Classical Music

What is perhaps most revolutionary in the music of Haydn, Mozart, and their younger contemporary Beethoven is its capacity for rapid change and endless fluctuation. Recall that in earlier times a work of Purcell, Corelli, Vivaldi, or Bach would establish one "affect" or mood to be rigidly maintained from beginning to end—the rhythm, melody, and harmony all progressing in a continuous, uninterrupted flow. Such a uniform approach to expression is part of the "single-mindedness" of Baroque art. Now with Haydn, Mozart, and the young Beethoven, the mood or character of a piece may change radically within a few short phrases. An energetic theme in rapid notes may be followed by a second one that is slow, lyrical, and tender. Similarly, textures may change quickly from light and airy to dense and more contrapuntal so as to create tension and excitement. For the first time composers began to call for crescendos and diminuendos, a gradual increase or lessening of the dynamic level, so that the volume of sound might continually fluctuate. When skilled orchestras made use of this technique, audiences were fascinated and rose to their feet. Keyboard players, too, now took up the crescendo and diminuendo, assuming that the new multidynamic piano was at hand in place of the old monodynamic harpsichord. These rapid changes in mood, texture, color, and dynamics give to Classical music a new sense of urgency and drama. The listener feels a constant flux and flow, not unlike the continual swings of mood we all experience.

frequent changes in mood

Classical Forms

How did composers of the Classical period reconcile their desire to express changing moods, colors, and textures with the Classical principles of grace, order, and balance? They did so, in a word, by means of form. All of the elements of expression—themes, harmonic relationships, colors, textures, dynamics—are arranged within the boundaries of strict musical forms. Limits are set as to where the changing or conflicting elements may be placed, how intense they may be, and how long they may last. By placing the musical events in a carefully regulated form, grace, balance, and proportion are achieved. Indeed, so important is form in Classical music, that the subject requires a chapter unto itself.

KEY WORDS

Alberti bass	Nikolaus Esterházy	Salzburg
Antonio Salieri	*opera buffa*	*The Magic Flute*
comic opera	*pianoforte*	*The Marriage of Figaro*
London symphonies	rococo	

CLASSICAL FORMS

To understand and appreciate Classical music, it is especially important to understand musical form. For in the Classical period, more so than any other, a small number of forms—ternary, sonata-allegro, rondo, and theme and variations—regulated nearly all music. Indeed, there are few compositions written during the years 1750–1820 that are not shaped according to one of these. At the same time, it is important to realize that none of these forms was unique to the Classical period. Ternary form can be found in the earliest examples of Gregorian chant* as well as in all *da capo** arias of the Baroque era (1600–1750). The rondo had its origins in the popular dances and songs of the Middle Ages, though its repetitive structure has made it attractive to such diverse musicians as Mozart, Beethoven, Elton John, and Sting. And theme and variations, as both a musical and a literary process, is at once ancient and eternal. Only sonata-allegro form actually came into being in the Classical period. It dominated musical structure during the time of Mozart and Haydn, but it also remained a potent force in the works of most composers of the Romantic era (1820–1900) and in the creations of some twentieth-century musicians as well. Thus, the forms discussed in this chapter should not be thought of as belonging to the Classical period alone, but in the broader meaning of the term "classical." With the single exception of the more recent sonata-allegro form, they are all timeless and universal.

TERNARY FORM

Ternary structure **(ABA)** is a form often encountered in the history of music. Yet the simple principle of presentation, contrast, and return was especially favored by Classical composers for its simplicity and directness. Everyone is familiar with the tune *Twinkle, Twinkle Little Star* (also the tune of *Bah, Bah, Black Sheep*, and *A, B, C, D, E, F, G*). Less well known is the fact that it began life as a French folk song, *Ah, vous dirai-je Maman (Ah, Let Me Tell You, Mama)*. Wolfgang Amadeus Mozart (1756–1791) came to know the melody

FIGURE 9–1

A ball at the Redoutensaal in the emperor's court in Vienna ca. 1800. Mozart and his wife frequently danced at these, and during the last four years of his life he composed many minuets for officially sponsored events here. The orchestra can be seen in the gallery at the left.

when he toured France as a youth, and he wrote it down in a keyboard version. Here is his setting of it:

EXAMPLE 9-1

Notice that both units (**A** and **BA**) are repeated. Observe also that **A** is in the tonic, **B** emphasizes a contrasting key (here the dominant), and the returning **A** is again in the tonic. If a piece in ternary form is in a minor key, the contrasting **B** section will usually be in what is called the relative major[†]. Needless to say, most pieces in ternary form are more complex than *Twinkle*,

[†]Relative keys are keys that share the same key signature, E♭ major and C minor (both with three flats), for example.

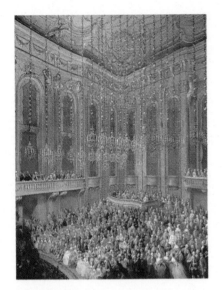

FIGURE 9–2

The Redoutensaal was also used for the production of opera. Here the audience, which included the six-year-old Mozart, is assembled for a production of an *opera seria* in 1762.

Mozart's A Little Night Music

Twinkle. Most have more contrast of melody, key, and/or mood between the **B** section and the surrounding units of **A**.

Minuet and Trio

The most common use of ternary form in the Classical period is found in the minuet and trio. Strictly speaking, the **minuet** is not a form, but rather a genre of dance implying an elegant musical style, stately tempo, and constant triple meter. It first appeared at the French royal court early in the reign of King Louis XIV (1643–1715) and soon became the most popular social dance of aristocratic society. By 1770 the minuet was usually written in ternary form and grouped with a second minuet possessing a much lighter texture. Because this second minuet had originally been played by only three instruments, it was called the **trio,** a name that persisted into the nineteenth century, no matter how many instrumental lines were required in this second minuet. Once the trio was finished, convention dictated that there be a return to the first minuet, now performed without repeats. Since the trio also was composed in ternary form, a threefold **ABA** pattern resulted. (Here in the trio the **ABA** structure is represented by **CDC** to distinguish it from the minuet.)

A (minuet)	**B** (trio)	**A** (minuet)
|: **A** :||: **BA** :|	|: **C** :||: **DC** :|	**ABA**

Mozart's *Eine kleine Nachtmusik (A Little Night Music),* written in the summer of 1787, is among his most popular works. It is a **serenade,** a light, multi-movement piece for strings alone or small orchestra, one intended for public entertainment and often performed outdoors. Although we do not know the precise occasion for which Mozart composed it, we might well imagine *A Little Night Music* providing the musical backdrop for a torch lit party in a formal Viennese garden. The *Menuetto* appears as the third of four movements in this serenade, and is a model of grace and concision.

EXAMPLE 9-2

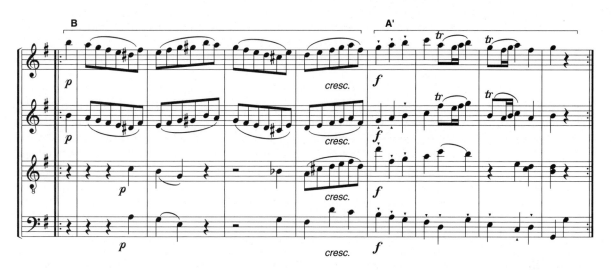

As you can see, the **B** section is only four measures long, and the return to **A** does not produce the full eight bars of the original but only the last four—thus, this pattern might be viewed as **ABA'**. In the trio that follows a lighter texture is created as the first violin plays a solo melody quietly above a soft accompaniment in the lower strings. The **B** section of the trio is distinguished by a *forte* stepwise run up and down the scale, and then the quiet melody of **A** returns to complete the ternary form. Finally, the minuet appears once again, but now without repeats.

LISTENING GUIDE

Wolfgang Amadeus Mozart
Serenade, *A Little Night Music* (1787)
Third movement, Minuet and Trio

CD 2/10
6–Tape 2B

MINUET

		Form	Number of bars
0:00	Strong violin melody with active bass	**A**	8
0:10	Repeat of **A**		
0:20	Softer violin scales	**B**	4
0:26	Return of violin melody	**A'**	4
0:30	Repeat of **B** and **A'**		

TRIO

0:41	Soft, stepwise melody in violins	**C**	8
0:52	Repeat of **C**		
1:03	Louder violins	**D**	4
1:09	Return of soft stepwise melody	**C**	8
1:20	Repeat of **D** and **C**		

MINUET

1:37	Return of **A**	**A**	8
1:48	Return of **B**	**B**	4
1:54	Return of violin melody	**A'**	4

We have said that Classical music is symmetrical and proportional. Note here how both minuet and trio are balanced by a return of the opening music **(A)** and **(C)** and how all the sections are either four or eight measures in length.

If Mozart's *Menuetto* represents the minuet in its most succinct form, the minuet of Haydn's Symphony No. 94 (The "Surprise" Symphony) offers a more typically symphonic presentation of this ternary design. The form is considerably extended, in part because Haydn was writing for a full orchestra rather than a small string ensemble as in Mozart's serenade. (It is axiomatic in music that the larger the performing force, the more extended the musical form.) But keeping the model of Mozart's simple ternary minuet in our ears, we can easily follow Haydn's more expansive formal plan.

LISTENING GUIDE		Franz Joseph Haydn Symphony No. 94, The "Surprise" Symphony (1791) Third movement, Minuet and Trio	CD 2/12 6–Tape 2B

			Form
MINUET [] = repeats			
0:00		Rollicking dance in triple meter begins	**A**
0:19		Repeat of **A**	
0:40	[1:33]	Imitation and lighter texture	**B**
0:50	[1:43]	Strong harmonic movement	
0:58	[1:51]	Bass sits on dominant note	
1:05	[1:59]	Return of **A**	**A'**
1:13	[2:07]	Pause on dominant chord	
1:23	[2:17]	Gentle rocking over tonic pedal point	
TRIO			
2:27		Light descending scales for violins and bassoon	**C**
2:37		Repeat of **C**	
2:46	[3:08]	Two-voice counterpoint for 1st and 2nd violins	**D**
2:58	[3:21]	Bassoon reentry signals return of **C**	**C**
MINUET			
3:30		Return to minuet	**A**
3:51		Return of **B**	**B**
4:16		Return of **A**	**A'**

S ONATA–ALLEGRO FORM

Sonata–allegro form is at once the most complex and most satisfying of musical forms. It is also the only form to originate during the Classical period (1750–1820). We must keep in mind, however, the distinction between the general term "sonata" and the more specific term "sonata-allegro form"—that is, between the multimovement composition called the sonata and the single-movement form called sonata–allegro.

Recall that in the Baroque period a multimovement work was often called a sonata, either a solo sonata or a trio sonata. These consisted of a succession of binary-form movements that often proceeded slow–fast–slow–fast (see, for example, the trio sonata by Corelli discussed on page 115). By the early Classical period, however, the usual arrangement of movements for a sonata had become fast–slow–minuet–fast, or occasionally just fast–slow–fast. When played by a solo instrument like the piano, this group of movements is called a solo sonata. When this same sort of three- or four-movement composition is written for string quartet or quintet, it is simply called a string quartet or quintet. And when intended for a full symphonic orchestra, it is called a symphony.

Yet no matter what the performing force, the form of each of these movements can be one of several different types. As we have seen, if there are four movements the third is usually a minuet with trio. The second and fourth movements might be, for example, in rondo form or theme and variations form (both discussed later in the chapter). The fast first movement, however, is almost invariably written in what is called sonata–allegro form. Thus, the term "sonata–allegro" derives from the fact that sonata–allegro form was usually applied to the fast (allegro) first movement. Slow second movements and fast finales sometimes make use of sonata–allegro form as well. To show at least two typical arrangements, here are the movements and forms of Mozart's *A Little Night Music* and Haydn's Symphony No. 94:

FIGURE 9–3

A portrait of the young Mozart at the keyboard painted during his first trip to Italy in 1770.

Mozart, *A Little Night Music* (1787)

Fast (sonato–allegro)	Slow (rondo)	Minuet and Trio (ternary)	Fast (rondo)

Haydn, Symphony No. 94 (1791)

Fast (sonata–allegro)	Slow (theme and variations)	Minuet and Trio (ternary)	Fast (sonata–allegro)

Sonata–allegro form came into being around 1750 as a means of incorporating more drama and conflict into a single movement of music. Like a great play, sonato–allegro form has the potential for dramatic presentation, conflict, and resolution. That sonata–allegro form would prove useful for composers of the Classical and Romantic periods, as well as for many of the modern era, attests to its inherent logic and great flexibility.

The Shape of Sonata-Allegro Form

To get a sense of what might happen in a typical first movement of a sonata, string quartet, symphony, or serenade, look at the following diagram. As with all models of this sort, this one is an ideal, an abstraction of what commonly occurs in sonata–allegro form. It is not a blueprint for any composition. Composers have exhibited countless individual solutions to the task of writing in this and every other form. Yet such a model can be of great use to the listener because it gives a clear picture of what we might expect to hear. Ultimately, once we have embraced the form and are familiar with its workings, we will take as much delight in having our musical expectations foiled or delayed as in having them fulfilled.

SONATA-ALLEGRO FORM

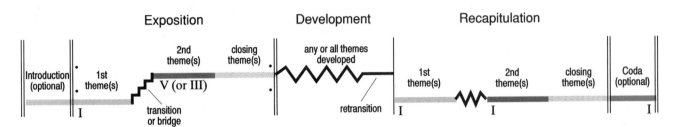

In its broad outline sonata–allegro form looks much like ternary form. It consists of an **ABA** plan with the **B** section providing contrast in mood, key, and thematic treatment. The initial **A** in sonata–allegro form is called the exposition, the **B** the development, and the return to **A** the recapitulation. In the early Classical period the exposition (**A**) and the development and recapitulation (**BA**) were repeated, as in ternary form. But Haydn and Mozart eventually dropped the repeat of the development and recapitulation, and composers of the Romantic period gradually dispensed with the repeat of the exposition. Let's take each of these sections in turn and see what we are likely to hear.

presentation   EXPOSITION. The purpose of the **exposition** is to present or expose the main thematic material of the movement, just as the exposition of a fugue exposes the subject.

First theme: The exposition begins with a first theme, or group of themes, and can be anywhere from four to forty measures or more in length. If not easily singable, the first theme is at least distinctive, memorable enough so that later returns and references to it will be recognized by the listener and enjoyed.

Transition: The aim of the **transition,** or bridge as it is sometimes called, is to carry the music from the tonic to the dominant (from tonic to relative major if the movement is in minor key) and prepare the arrival of the second theme. The transition is usually made up of rapidly moving figural patterns— runnings scales, arpeggios,* and the like— which are frequently put forth as melodic sequences*. In order to effect the I–V modulation, the bass becomes active and generates quick chord changes. This lively harmonic movement may subside if the transition ends with a solid cadence.

Second theme: Not only does a new melody usually appear at this point but it enters in the fresh context of a new key, the dominant or, less frequently, relative major. The second theme often contrasts in mood with the first: If the first is rapid and assertive, the second may be more languid and lyrical. Because a clear-cut theme holds center stage here, the accompanying harmonic material is stable, not modulatory. The listener's attention is focused on melody, not on harmonic movement.

Closing theme: The second theme usually gives way to a closing theme, one that is normally light and carefree in style. It often ends in a harmonically simple way, merely rocking back and forth between dominant and tonic chords. The static harmony and repeated full cadences* signal the conclusion of the exposition. The piece has stopped moving forward, and therefore the exposition is at an end. Tradition requires that the exposition now be repeated note for note.

DEVELOPMENT. As the name indicates, the **development** is a section in which there is a further working out, or developing, of the thematic material presented in the exposition. Both the first or second theme may be manipulated, and occasionally even the closing theme is exploited as well. A theme may be elaborated on and expanded or, just as often, it may be taken apart, *confrontation* reduced to just a few notes to be tossed around from instrument to instrument. One typical technique is for the composer to show the contrapuntal possibilities lurking within a theme by using it as the subject of a brief fugue.* (A fugue within a movement of a sonata is called a **fugato,** meaning "little fugue.") Like the transition, the development tends to have unstable harmonies. The use of both melodic and harmonic sequence is plentiful and this encourages rapid modulation from one key, or tonal center, to another. Only toward the end of the development, in the area called the **retransition,** does tonal stability return, often in the form of a pedal point* on the dominant note. The retransition helps prepare the ear for the return of the tonic key and the restatement of the first theme.

RECAPITULATION. After the dramatic disruptions of the development, *resolution* the listener greets the return of the first theme and other material from the exposition with a sense of welcome relief. Though the recapitulation is not an exact note-for-note repetition of the exposition, it nonetheless presents the same musical events in the same order, reaffirming the logic and integrity of the original. The only change that regularly occurs in this restatement is the rewriting of the transition, or bridge. Because the movement must end in the tonic, the bridge must not modulate to the dominant (or relative major) as before but stay at home in the tonic key. Thus, the recapitulation imparts to the listener not only a feeling of return to familiar surroundings but also an increased sense of harmonic stability, as all themes are now heard in the tonic key.

The following two elements are optional to sonata–allegro form.

INTRODUCTION. About half the mature symphonies of Haydn and Mozart have brief introductions before the exposition begins. These are, without exception, slow and stately, and usually filled with ominous or puz- *optional elements* zling chords designed to set the listener wondering what sort of musical excursion he or she is about to undertake. That the introduction is not part of the exposition is shown by the fact that it is never repeated.

CODA. As the name *coda* (Italian for "tail") indicates, this is a section added to the end of the sonata–allegro movement. It may be just a few bars long, as is most often the case with Mozart, or it may, in the hands of Beethoven, for example, expand into an independent section, one equal in size to the development. The melodic material is usually no more than a short motive extracted from the first theme, or sometimes from the closing theme, or it may be a newly created motive. But whatever the source, normally this motive is sounded again and again in conjunction with repeating dominant–tonic chords, or merely the tonic chord alone played over and over, all intended to create a grand effect and announce to the listener that the movement is at an end. Again, thematic repetition at the same pitch level and static harmony are two ways a composer can signal the end of a section or the end of a piece. The more of this that goes on, the greater the feeling of conclusion.

Hearing Sonata–Allegro Form

the challenge of sonata–allegro form

Given its central place in the music of Mozart and Haydn, and later in Beethoven, Schubert, Brahms, and Mahler, among others, sonata–allegro is perhaps the most important of all musical forms. But it is also the most complex and the most difficult for the listener to follow. A sonata–allegro movement tends to be long, lasting anywhere from a minimum of four minutes in a simple piece of the Classical period to twenty minutes or more in a full-blown movement of the Romantic era. Moreover, it embodies many kinds of musical events and many styles of writing—thematic and transitional, for example. And finally, sonata–allegro form does not merely involve one theme but incorporates several, and all of these have to be remembered and their development followed.

four styles of music in sonata–allegro form

How does one get the better of this musical beast? First of all, be sure that you have the model of sonata–allegro form clearly in mind. This will help you know what to expect, what you are likely to hear. Next, sharpen your ability to grasp and remember melodies, or at least the beginnings of melodies. If necessary, return to Chapter 2 and practice some melodic graphing. And finally, think carefully about the four principal styles of writing found in sonata–allegro form. Each has its own distinct character. A thematic section has clearly recognizable themes or melodies, sometimes even singable tunes. The transition is full of melodic movement, sequences, and rapid chord changes. The development is also disjunct, agitated, contrapuntal, and harmonically active, but it makes use of a recognizable theme, albeit extended or cut up into small pieces. And a concluding passage, whether at the end of the exposition, in the retransition at the end of the development, or in the coda at the end of the movement, tends to repeat motives or cadential phrases over and over above a static harmony. Much of your success in hearing sonata–allegro form will come from your ability to differentiate thematic, transitional, developmental, and concluding sections. With this by way of preparation, let's listen to a movement in sonata–allegro form.

For this we once again turn to the familiar sound of Mozart's *A Little Night Music*. The first movement (*Allegro*) of this four-movement serenade offers a concise, graceful example of sonata–allegro principle. Yet even a straightforward sonata–allegro-form movement such as this requires the listener's full attention. The Listening Guide below is not typical of this book. It is unusually lengthy so as to lead you through the difficult process of hearing sonata–allegro form. First read the description in the center column, then listen to the music, stopping where indicated to rehear each of the principal sections of the form.

LISTENING GUIDE

Wolfgang Amadeus Mozart
A Little Night Music (1787)
First movement, *Allegro* (fast)

CD 2/9
6–Tape 2A
2–Tape 1B

FIRST THEME GROUP [] = repeats

0:00 [1:37]   The movement opens aggressively with a leaping, fanfare-like motive. It then moves on to a more confined, pressing melody with sixteenth notes agitating beneath, and ends with a relaxed, stepwise descent down the G major scale which is repeated with light ornamentation.

STOP: LISTEN TO THE FIRST THEME GROUP AGAIN

TRANSITION

0:30 [2:08]   This starts with two quick turns and then races up the scale in repeating sixteenth notes. The bass is at first static, but when it finally moves it does so with great urgency, pushing the modulation along until a cadence. The stage is then cleared by a brief pause, allowing the listener an "unobstructed view" of the new theme that is about to enter.

0:30 Rapid scales
0:40 Bass moves
0:45 Cadence and pause

STOP: LISTEN TO THE TRANSITION AGAIN

SECOND THEME

0:48 [2:26]   With its *piano* dynamic level and separating rests, the second theme sounds soft and delicate. It is soon overtaken by a light, somewhat humorous closing theme.

STOP: LISTEN TO THE SECOND THEME AGAIN

CLOSING THEME

1:01 [2:39]   The light quality of this melody is produced by its repeating note and the simple rocking of dominant-to-tonic harmony below. Toward the end of it more substance is added when the music turns *forte*, and good counterpoint is inserted in the bass. The closing theme is then repeated, and a few cadential chords tacked on to bring the exposition to an end.

1:09 Loud; more counterpoint in bass
1:17 Closing theme repeated
1:31 Cadential chords

STOP: LISTEN TO THE CLOSING SECTION AGAIN

1:37   The exposition is now repeated.

DEVELOPMENT

3:15   Just about anything can happen in a development, so the listener   3:15 First theme developed
            had best be on guard. Mozart begins with the fanfare-like first   3:20 Quick modulation
            theme again in unison, as if this were yet another statement of   3:25 Closing theme developed
            the exposition! But abruptly the theme is altered and the tonal   3:32 More modulations
            center slides up to a new key. Now the closing theme is heard,   3:41 Rising scale in unison
            but soon it, too, begins to slide tonally, down through several   3:48 Held note (dominant) in violins
            keys that increasingly sound remote and bizarre. From this   and then bass
            arises a unison scale (all parts move up stepwise together) in a
            dark sounding minor key. The dominant note is held, first on top
            in the violins and then in the bass. This begins the retransition. The
            mode changes from dark minor to bright major, and the first
            theme returns with force in the tonic key, signaling the beginning
            of the recapitulation.

STOP: LISTEN TO THE DEVELOPMENT AGAIN

RECAPITULATION

3:52   It is this "double return" of both the tonic key and the first theme   3:52 Loud return of first theme
            that makes the arrival of this and all recapitulations so satisfying.   4:23 Transition much abbreviated
            We expect the recapitulation to more or less duplicate the   4:38 Second theme
            exposition, and this one holds true to form. The only change comes,   4:51 Closing theme
            as usual, in the transition, or bridge, where the modulation to the   5:05 Closing theme repeated
            dominant is simply omitted—there's no need to modulate to the   5:23 Cadential chords
            dominant since tradition demands that the second theme and the
            closing theme appear in the tonic.

CODA

5:26   After the cadential chords that ended the exposition are heard again,
            a brief coda begins. It makes use of a fanfare motive that strongly
            resembles that of the opening theme, but this one is supported by a
            pounding tonic chord that drives home the feeling that the movement
            has come to an appropriate end.

What we have just heard is an example of sonata–allegro form in minia-ture. Rarely is this design produced in less time, or space, and almost never as artfully. But sonata–allegro is a dynamic, flexible form, one that can serve equally well as an appropriate vessel for a large symphonic movement, a dramatic overture to an opera, or a Romantic tone poem*. We will meet it again in several later compositions. Listening Exercise 22 presents another, even more dramatic, unfolding of sonata–allegro form: the overture to Mozart's tragic–comic opera *Don Giovanni.*

THEME AND VARIATIONS

After the complexity of sonata–allegro form, a movement in theme and vari-ations form seems relatively simple and straightforward. This is partly because just one theme is used and that theme is subjected to only one sort

FIGURE 9–4

The autograph manuscript of *A Little Night Music* (1787). Mozart was composing here with a score of four staves: First and second violins are on the top two staves, violas on stave three, and cellos and double basses on four. One can sense with what extraordinary speed, yet accuracy, Mozart could set music on paper.

FIGURE 9–5

Emperor Joseph II with two of his sisters. Mozart made a point of meeting the musically knowledgeable emperor in 1781. The score on the piano is by Mozart's rival at court, Antonio Salieri.

of compositional treatment: variation. For theme and variations to be effective, the theme itself must be easy to grasp and clearly stated at the outset. As the Enlightenment philosopher Jean–Jacques Rousseau said in his *Dictionnaire de musique* (1768): "Through all the embroidery, one must always be able to recognize the essence of the melody." To that end composers of the Classical period and beyond chose themes that were often already well-known to the listener: folk songs, popular tunes, and favorite arias and marches from successful operas, for example. Patriotic songs have always seemed especially apt for musical variation. Those so treated include *God Preserve Franz the Emperor* (Haydn), *God Save the King* (Beethoven), *Rule Britannia* (Beethoven), and later *Yankee Doodle* (Vieuxtemps) and *America* (Ives). Such tunes are popular, in part, because they are simple, and this, too, is an advantage for the composer. Melodies that are spare and uncluttered can more easily be dressed in new musical clothing. The essence of theme and variations, then, is to present a simple, direct melody and restate it again and again, each time musically varying or disguising the theme in some novel fashion.

How is variation of a theme brought about? It is done one of two ways: either by merely ornamenting the theme, overlaying it with figural patterns, or, what produces a more radical transformation, by altering its shape—changing its rhythmic, harmonic, or melodic profile in some way. In the two examples that follow, one by Mozart and one by Haydn, the specific techniques of ornamentation and alternation of a melody will become apparent. You will be challenged to retain a familiar tune in your ear as the composer embellishes or transforms it.

In the Classical period it was common for a composer-pianist to improvise in concert a set of variations on a well-known tune, perhaps one called out from the audience. Contemporary reports tell us that Mozart was especially skilled in this art of spontaneous variation. In 1778 he published a set of such improvised variations built on the French folk song *Ah, vous dirai-je Maman*, which we know as *Twinkle, Twinkle Little Star*. With a tune as well-known as this, it is easy to follow the melody as it is subjected increasingly to ornamentation and transformation in the course of twelve variations. (Only the first eight bars of the theme are given here; for the complete melody, see page 167; the music can be heard on CD 2/13 and 6–Tape 2B.)

EXAMPLE 9–3a

Variation 1 ornaments the theme and almost buries it beneath an avalanche of sixteenth notes. Would you know that *Twinkle, Twinkle* lurks herein (see the asterisks) if you did not have the tune securely in your ear?

EXAMPLE 9–3b

In variation 2 the rushing sixteenth notes are transferred to the bass, so that the theme surfaces again rather clearly in the upper voice.

EXAMPLE 9–3c

Now, in variation 3, triplets appear in the right hand, and only the general contour of the melody is audible. Thus, the melody here is transformed.

EXAMPLE 9–3d

After the same technique has been applied to the bass (variation 4), a thematic alteration again occurs in variation 5. Here the rhythm of the melody is "jazzed up" by placing part of it off the beat in syncopated fashion.

EXAMPLE 9–3e

Of the remaining seven variations, some change the tune to minor, others add Bach-like counterpoint against it, while the final variation presents this duple-meter folk tune reworked into a triple-meter waltz! Yet throughout all of Mozart's magical embroidery, the theme remains clearly audible, so well ingrained is *Twinkle, Twinkle* in our musical memory.

Joseph Haydn (1732–1809) was the first composer to take theme and variations form and use it for a movement inside a symphony. His Symphony No. 94 (The "Surprise" Symphony) has been his most celebrated composition ever since it was first performed in London early in 1792. We have already discussed the third movement, the minuet (see page 170). But the work owes its popularity, and its nickname to the slow second movement *(Andante)*, written in theme and variations form. The famous opening theme possesses both simplicity and immediate appeal. Notice how the beginning is shaped by laying out in succession the notes of a tonic triad (I) and a dominant chord (V) in C major. The chordal implications of the tune account for its folk song–like quality and make it easy to remember during the variations that follow (see the first example in the Listening Guide). These first eight bars **(A)** are stated and then repeated quietly. And just when all is ending peacefully, the full orchestra comes crashing in with a *fortissimo* chord, as if to shock the drowsy listener back to attention. What better way to show off the latent dynamic power of the large Classical orchestra? The surprise *fortissimo* chord is a dominant chord that leads into the **B** section of the theme (second example in the Listening Guide), another eight-bar phrase which is also repeated but with added flute and oboe accompaniment. With the simple yet highly attractive binary theme now in place, Haydn proceeds to compose four variations on it, adding then a superb coda at the end.

FIGURE 9–6

A portrait of Joseph Haydn at work. His left hand is trying an idea at the keyboard while his right is ready to write it down.

LISTENING
GUIDE Joseph Haydn
Symphony No. 94, The "Surprise" Symphony (1791)
Second movement, *Andante* (moving)

CD 2/11
6–Tape 2B
2–Tape 1B

THEME

0:00   First part **(A)** of the theme
       A repeated softly, then *fortissimo* chord

0:33   Second part **(B)** of the theme
       B repeated with flute and oboe added

VARIATION 1

1:06   Loud chord, then **A** ornamented above by first violins and flutes
       A repeated
1:39   **B** with ornamentation continuing above in violins and flutes
       B repeated

VARIATION 2

2:11   **A** played loud and in minor key, shift (2:19) to rich major chord
       A repeated
       (Variation of **B** omitted)
2:43   Full orchestra develops **A** in minor key
3:11   First violins alone, playing in unison

VARIATION 3

3:20   **A** ornamented rapidly by oboe
       A repeated; melody in strings with oboe and flute ornamenting above

3:50   **B** now in strings with oboe and flute ornamenting above
       B repeated

VARIATION 4

4:23   **A** loud, in full orchestra, with violins playing running scales
       A repeated with theme rhythmically varied

4:55   **B** varied further by the violins
       B repeated loudly by full orchestra
5:27   Transition to coda, pause (5:35)

CODA

5:40   Reminiscences of theme in its original form

(Listening Exercise 23)

FIGURE 9–7

The Hanover Square Rooms in London, the hall in which Haydn's "Surprise" Symphony was first performed in 1792.

After listening to this movement by Haydn, you can now understand that hearing theme and variations form requires listening to discrete units of music. Each block (variation) is marked by some new treatment of the theme. In the Classical period all the units are usually the same size, that is, the same number of measures. The variations become progressively more complicated as more ornamentation and transformation is applied. The addition of a coda after the last variation gives extra weight to the end, so that the listener feels the set of variations has reached an appropriate conclusion. If such extra bars were not appended, the audience would be left hanging, expecting yet another variation to begin.

R ONDO FORM

Rondo form is an ancient musical structure in which a refrain continually alternates with contrasting material. We have previously seen this formal plan at work in the music of the Middle Ages (see page 79) and of the Baroque era (see pages 59 and 118). During the Classical period composers like Haydn and Mozart took the principle of rondo form and expanded and enlivened it. Not only were simple designs like **ABABA** and **ABACA** used but sometimes more complex arrangements as well, such as **ABACABA** and **ABACADA.** What is more, they borrowed a style of writing found in sonata–allegro form. The more expansive and dramatic musical treatment of the transitions and development sections of sonata–allegro form was brought into the rondo. The rondo of the Classical period, therefore, is not merely a collection of short sections linked back to back, as is usually true of the Baroque rondo (see page 59) but an elastic, flexible form in which the recurring theme and the subordinate ideas develop and expand to new proportions. The subordinate ideas may be themes in their own right (lettered **B, C,** and **D**), or they may simply be digressions **(X)** away from the periodic refrain. Haydn uses the latter approach—refrain–digression—in the last movement of his Symphony No. 88 (1789). Here the theme (refrain) is a carefree tune in bright G major and, although lengthy, it has a clear ternary (**aba'**) shape to it. You can remember the beginning more easily if you hear it as a descending triad (D, B, G) with each note quickly repeated.

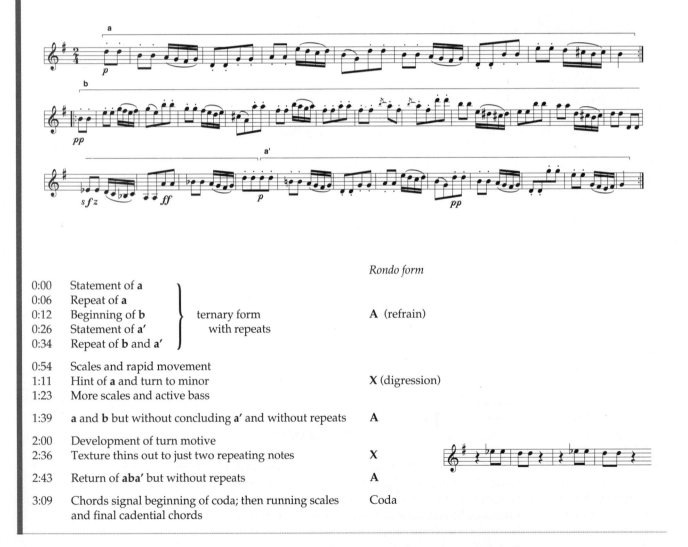

LISTENING GUIDE

Joseph Haydn
Symphony No. 88 (1789)
Fourth movement, *Allegro con spirito* (fast with spirit)

CD 2/14
6–Tape 2B

Rondo form

0:00	Statement of **a**		
0:06	Repeat of **a**		
0:12	Beginning of **b**	ternary form	**A** (refrain)
0:26	Statement of **a'**	with repeats	
0:34	Repeat of **b** and **a'**		
0:54	Scales and rapid movement		
1:11	Hint of **a** and turn to minor		**X** (digression)
1:23	More scales and active bass		
1:39	**a** and **b** but without concluding **a'** and without repeats		**A**
2:00	Development of turn motive		
2:36	Texture thins out to just two repeating notes		**X**
2:43	Return of **aba'** but without repeats		**A**
3:09	Chords signal beginning of coda; then running scales and final cadential chords		Coda

A RONDO BY STING

While the rondo may have enjoyed its greatest favor in the sphere of art music during the Baroque and Classical periods, it has continued to live on in the realm of folk and popular song, undoubtedly because the refrain–digression pattern has such universal appeal. Traditional ballads such as *Tom Dooley* make use of it, and so do more recent pop songs by artists such as Arlo Guthrie in *City of New Orleans*. Sting's *Every Breath You Take* produces a rondo pattern (**ABACABA**) that in its symmetrical, indeed palindromic, shape would do any Classical composer proud:

Every breath you take	Every single day	
Every move you make	Every word you say	
Every bond you break	Every game you play	**A**
Every step you take	Every night you stay	
I'll be watching you.	I'll be watching you.	

O can't you see, you belong to me	
How my poor heart aches, with every step you take.	**B**

Every move you make	
Every vow you break	
Every smile you fake	**A**
Every claim you stake	
I'll be watching you.	

Since you've gone I've been lost without a trace	
I dream at night I can only see your face	
I look around but it's you I can't replace	**C**
I keep crying baby please.	

Instrumental interlude (no text) to **A** music,	**A**
O can't you see, you belong to me . . . (etc.)	**B**
Every move you make . . . (etc.)	**A**
	Coda (fade out)

(Available on A & M Records SP-3735)

Sting

The general mood of this movement is typical of the lively rondo, which tends to be lighter and more jovial in spirit than does a movement in sonata–allegro form. Classical composers most often used rondo form as the final movement (finale) of a sonata, quartet, or symphony. The tuneful refrain and easily grasped digressions produce a light-hearted ending intended to leave the audience, if not euphoric, at least in a pleasant state of mind.

FORM, MOOD, AND THE LISTENER'S EXPECTATIONS

The audience of the late eighteenth century brought to the concert hall certain expectations, not only about the structure, but also about the mood of the music that was to be performed. Listeners had a notion of what the form, tempo, and general character would be of each movement of a sonata, quartet, or symphony. For the Classical period we might summarize these as follows:

Movement:	1	2	3	4
Tempo:	Fast	Slow	Lively	Fast
Form:	Sonata–allegro	Large ternary, theme and variations, or rondo	Minuet and trio in ternary form	Sonata–allegro, theme and variations, or rondo
Mood:	Serious and substantive despite fast tempo	Lyrical and tender	usually light and elegant, sometimes spirited	Bright, light-hearted, sometimes humorous

lasting influence of the Classical model

Ludwig van Beethoven (1770–1827) and later composers of the Romantic period (1820–1900) modified somewhat this conventional format—the third movement, for example, was often treated as a boisterous scherzo (see page 225) rather than an elegant minuet, and the finale became more serious, with the result that the lighthearted rondo fell out of fashion. Yet the Classical model was well established in the mind of the listener. For unlike previous periods in the history of music, succeeding generations did not forget the music of Haydn, Mozart, and their contemporaries. Their sonatas, quartets, and symphonies enjoyed undiminished favor with the listening public, and the formal designs they created or popularized have remained, with a few exceptions, the norm for the concert hall down to the present day.

LISTENING EXERCISES

22	Wolfgang Amadeus Mozart Overture to the opera *Don Giovanni* (1787)	CD 3/2 6–Tape 3A 2–Tape 1B

As is typical of overtures in the Classical period, the one Mozart wrote to precede his opera *Don Giovanni* (1787) is composed in sonata–allegro form. (The opera itself is discussed at length in the following chapter.) Mozart begins his overture with a slow introduction that incorporates many of the musical motives he will later use within the opera. This ominous beginning is written in D minor which brightens to D major at the start of the exposition. Since this is an overture and not a symphony, there is no repetition of the exposition.

In the exercise that follows, the sections of the exposition are identified for you so that you become familiar with the main thematic material of this piece. Then, beginning with the development and continuing through the recapitulation and brief coda, you are asked a series of questions that follows the unfolding of sonata form.

0:00   Slow, portentous introduction that makes use of a fateful dotted rhythm, twisting chromaticism, and, finally, writhing scales.

1:56   Exposition begins fast but quietly in major key with first theme in the strings.

2:15   Cadential pattern brings first theme group to a close.

2:20   Transition starts with scalar theme presented in sequence.

2:30   Continues with unstable chords that build tension.

2:35   Transition ends with strong cadence.

2:41   Second theme marked by scalar descent and then "birdlike fluttering" in woodwinds.

3:00   Light closing theme.

3:10   Static, cadential harmony signals end of exposition.

Questions:

1.   3:20   Which theme is used at the beginning of the development? _____

2.   3:31   This same theme is now heard in the woodwinds in which guise?
              a. as a cadence
              b. in overlapping imitation
              c. as a chorale

3.   3:40   Which theme enters? _____

4.   3:54   Which theme now returns? _____

5.   4:16–4:26   Would you call this passage one of movement and agitation or one of stasis and quietude? _____

6.   4:16–4:26   In this section is the harmony active or static?_____
              (Can you sing one basic consonant pitch throughout it? If so, it is static.)

7.   4:27   Now the recapitulation begins. Does it commence as expected with the first theme? _____

8.   4:49   Does the transition return again at this point? _____

9.   5:08   Do both the descending scale and the "flutter" motive appear as the second theme returns? _____

10. 5:29   Does the closing theme return? _____

11. 5:45   A brief coda begins here. A reminiscence of which theme is heard as the main melodic material? _____

N.B. There are no *forte* cadential chords to produce a "big bang" ending for this overture. Rather, Mozart writes an orchestral fade out designed to coincide with the raising of the curtain and to lead into the music of the first scene.

23   Joseph Haydn   CD 2/11
         Symphony No. 94, The "Surprise" Symphony (1791)   6–Tape 2B
         Second movement, *Andante* (moving)   2–Tape 1B

The theme of the famous slow movement of this symphony has a simple
binary shape (**AB;** see page 180). Both **A** and **B** are eight measures long, and
both are repeated immediately each time they are heard. By repeating the
two sections of the theme, Haydn gives himself the opportunity to change it,
not only from one variation to the next, but also during the repeats within
each variation. Your task in this listening exercise is to hear when the repeats
begin (fill in the blanks in the time log below) and then to note whether the
repeat changes what you have heard immediately before. Has Haydn varied
the theme or changed the orchestration in the repeat?

Theme
0:00   First part **(A)** of theme
 :   Repeat of **A**
       Is the theme varied further or the orchestration changed in the repeat?
       _____

 :   Surprise *fortissimo* chord
0:33   Second part **(B)** of theme
 :   Repeat of **B**
       Is the theme varied further or the orchestration changed in the repeat?
       _____

Variation 1
1:06   Loud chord, then dancing counter melody above in violins and flutes
 :   Repeat of **A**
       Is the theme varied further or the orchestration changed in the repeat?
       _____

1:39   **B** proceeds; violins and flutes ornamenting above
 :   Repeat of **B**
       Is the theme varied further or the orchestration changed in the repeat?
       _____

Variation 2
2:11   **A** loud and in minor
 :   Repeat of **A**
       Is the theme varied further or the orchestration changed in the repeat?
       _____

2:43   Development of **A;** no **B;** violins lead to variation 3
Variation 3
3:20   **A** ornamented in oboe
 :   Repeat of **A**
       Is the theme varied further or the orchestration changed in the repeat?
       _____

3:50   **B** in strings; oboe and flute ornamenting above
 :   Repeat of **B**
       Is the theme varied further or the orchestration changed in the repeat?
       _____

Variation 4

4:23 **A** loud in full orchestra

_:___ Repeat of **A**

Is the theme varied further or the orchestration changed in the repeat?

_____

4:55 **B** varied by the violins

_:___ Repeat of **B**

Is the theme varied further or the orchestration changed in the repeat?

_____

5:40 Coda

KEY WORDS

coda	recapitulation	sonata–allegro form
development	relative major	transition (bridge)
exposition	relative minor	trio
fugato	retransition	
minuet	serenade	

10 CLASSICAL GENRES

G enre" in music is a general term that refers to that special quality of musical style, form, performing medium, and even place of performance that we associate with one class or general type of music. The string quartet is a genre of music just as is the country music ballad, the cabaret song, the military march, and even the straight-ahead rock 'n' roll tune. When we choose to hear pieces of one genre or another, we listen with certain expectations as to how these works will sound, how they will progress, and how long they will last. We may even go to a special place, a theater or perhaps a bar, and dress a certain way, depending on the genre of music we will hear.

In the Classical period there were five main genres of art music: the symphony, string quartet, sonata, concerto, and opera. Though performed by different forces and usually in different environments, the same sort of audience might attend each. One of these genres, the opera, was taken over from the Baroque era and, though modified by Classical composers, retained its fundamental structure. Two others, the sonata and concerto, had also existed during the Baroque period, but were so changed by Haydn, Mozart, and their contemporaries that they were now tantamount to new genres. And still two others, the symphony and the string quartet, had no immediate ancestors in the Baroque era but were created wholly new during the Classical period.

THE SYMPHONY

It was during the Classical era that the symphony sprang forth to become the preeminent musical genre. That Haydn composed so many (104) and Mozart an even more astonishing number (41), given his short life, shows that the symphony had become, and would remain, the genre through which an aspiring composer might test his mettle and start on the road to international fame.

The symphony traces its origins to the late seventeenth-century Italian opera overture called the *sinfonia* ("an harmonious sounding together").

Around 1700 the typical Italian *sinfonia* was a one-movement instrumental work in three sections, fast–slow–fast. Soon Italian musicians and foreigners alike took the *sinfonia* out of the opera house and expanded it into three separate and distinct movements. A fourth movement, the minuet, was inserted by composers north of the Alps beginning in the 1740s. Thus, by mid-century the symphony had emerged as an independent genre and assumed its familiar four-movement format, fast–slow–minuet–fast.

The public favor the symphony came to enjoy was tied directly to certain revolutionary social changes that swept Europe during the Enlightenment. Not the least of these, as we have seen, was the impressive growth of public concerts (see page 153). The center of musical life in such cities as London, Paris, and, to a lesser degree, Vienna gradually shifted from the aristocratic court to the newly constructed or refurbished public concert hall. Larger audiences and greater financial gain for the composer could be had at public concerts like those mounted in the Hanover Square Rooms in London (see page 181) or the Burgtheater in Vienna (Fig. 10–1), where commoner and aristocrat met on more-or-less equal footing. Although some members of the nobility, notably the elector at Mannheim and the Esterházy princes, were important patrons of the early symphony, the genre ultimately flourished in an upper-middle-class environment. All but a few of Haydn's last twenty symphonies were composed for public performance in Paris and London, and Mozart apparently wrote no symphonies for a court patron during the last ten years of his life. Henceforth, the concert-going public, and not the aristocratic prince, provided the principal support for the symphony and for the instrumental ensemble that performed it, the symphony orchestra.

Naturally, as the place of performance of the symphony moved from the aristocratic salon to the public auditorium, the size of the audience and the concert hall increased. The orchestra of Haydn's patron, Prince Nikolaus Esterházy, was never larger than twenty-five, and the audience at court was

FIGURE 10–1

At the right, the Burgtheater, Vienna, where many symphonies, concertos, and operas by Mozart were first heard. The building to the left now serves as the famous Spanish Riding School.

FIGURE 10–2

The interior of the Burgtheater which could accommodate an audience of about seven hundred.

often only the prince and his staff (Fig. 10–3). But when Haydn went to London to appear before the public in 1791, his "London Symphonies" were performed in the Hanover Square Rooms (see page 181) which accommodated between eight and nine hundred persons. Indeed, for one of his public concerts in the spring of 1792, nearly 1,500 eager patrons crowded in. To fill these larger halls with sound, a larger orchestra was needed. Mozart mentions an orchestra of at least eighty players, including forty violins, ten violas, eight cellos, and ten double basses, for a public concert in the Burgtheater in Vienna in 1781 (Fig. 10–2). And although this ensemble was unusually large, orchestras of fifty or sixty players for public performance were not uncommon in Paris and London by the end of the century.

the Classical orchestra

The heart of the Classical orchestra, as had been true of the earlier Baroque orchestra, was the string section: the ensemble of violins, violas, cellos, and double basses. But not only were there now more instruments in the group, the violin was modestly different as well. To produce a larger, more penetrating tone, metal strings, which could be strung to greater tension, began to replace those of animal gut. The winds were also increased in number so as to be heard in the midst of the large string sound. Now, instead of just one flute or one bassoon, there were usually pairs. And one new woodwind was introduced, the clarinet. Mozart was particularly delighted when he first heard the clarinet used as an orchestral instrument during a visit to the Mannheim court in 1778. "Ah, if only we had clarinets too! You cannot imagine the glorious effect of a symphony with flutes, oboes, and clarinets," he wrote to his father back in provincial Salzburg. Later Beethoven and Schubert would share his love for the rich color of this instrument. By the 1780s, then, the full Classical orchestra consisted of strings, two oboes, two flutes, two clarinets, two bassoons, two horns, and for especially festive symphonies, two trumpets and timpani.

FIGURE 10–3

Haydn leading the orchestra at the court of the Esterházy princes during a performance of a comic opera. The composer is seated at the keyboard surrounded by the cellos. The higher strings and woodwinds are seated at the desk.

Mozart: Symphony No. 40 in G Minor (1788)

Mozart's celebrated symphony in G minor requires all of the full instrumental sound and disciplined playing the late eighteenth-century orchestra could muster. This is not a festive composition (hence no trumpets and drums), but rather an intensely brooding work that suggests tragedy and feverish despair. While we might be tempted to associate the minor key and despondent mood with a specific event in Mozart's life, apparently no such causal relationship exists. This was one of three symphonies, his last three, that Mozart produced in the incredibly short span of six weeks during the summer of 1788, and the other two are sunny, optimistic works. Rather than responding to a particular disappointment, it is more likely that Mozart invoked the tragic muse in this G minor symphony by drawing on a lifetime of disappointments and a premonition—as his letters attest—of an early death.

FIRST MOVEMENT *(MOLTO ALLEGRO)*

Exposition: Although Mozart begins his G minor symphony with a textbook example of Classical phrase structure (four-bar antecedent, four-bar consequent phrases), an unusual sense of urgency is created by the repeating, insistent eighth-note figure at the beginning. This urgent motive is immediately grasped by the listener and, indeed, is the most memorable theme of the work.

EXAMPLE 10–1

What is not so quickly seized, but yet contributes equally to the sense of urgency, is the accelerating rate of harmonic change. At the outset chords are set beneath the melody at an interval of one chord every four measures, then one every two bars, then one every measure, then two chords per measure, and finally four. Thus, the harmony, or harmonic rhythm, is moving sixteen times faster at the end of this section than at the start. This is how Mozart creates the drive and urgency we all feel, yet may not be able to explain. After this quickening start, the first theme begins once again, but soon veers off its previous course and into the transition. Transitions are filled with motion, especially running scales, and this one is no exception. What is unusual is that a motive is inserted, one so distinctive we might call it a transition theme (see the example in the Listening Guide). As if to reciprocate for an extra theme here, Mozart dispenses with one toward the end of the exposition, at the point where we would expect a closing theme to appear. Instead, as closing material he makes use of the persistent motive and rhythm from the beginning of the first theme, and this rather nicely rounds off the exposition. Finally, a single, isolated chord is heard, one that leads back to a repeat of the exposition, or, second time through, launches into the development.

accelerating harmonic rhythm

Development: In the development Mozart employs only the first theme (and then only the first four bars), but subjects it to a variety of musical treatments. First he carries it through several distantly related keys, next shapes it into a fugue subject for use in a fugato*, then sets it in descending sequence, and finally inverts it melodically:

The retransition is suddenly interrupted by *sforzandi* (loud attacks). But soon a dominant pedal point* is heard in the bassoons, and above it the flute and clarinets begin to cascade down to the tonic note. This use of soloistic woodwinds in the retransition* is a hallmark of Mozart's symphonic style.

Recapitulation: As expected, the recapitulation offers the themes in the same order in which they appeared in the exposition. But now the transition theme, which Mozart has left untouched since its initial appearance, receives extended treatment, creating something akin to a second development section as it is pulled through one new key after another, only to end up back in the original tonic minor. When the lyrical second theme finally reappears, it has a more somber, plaintive mood now that it is in minor. Because the repeating figure of the first theme rounds off the recapitulation by way of a closing theme, only the briefest coda is needed to end this passionate, haunting movement.

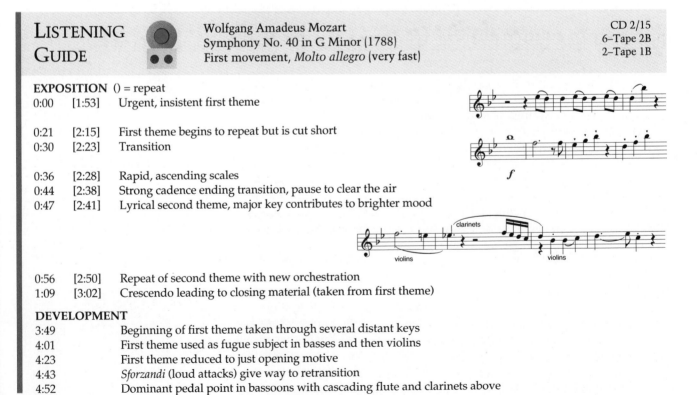

| LISTENING GUIDE | Wolfgang Amadeus Mozart
Symphony No. 40 in G Minor (1788)
First movement, *Molto allegro* (very fast) | CD 2/15
6–Tape 2B
2–Tape 1B |

EXPOSITION () = repeat

0:00	[1:53]	Urgent, insistent first theme
0:21	[2:15]	First theme begins to repeat but is cut short
0:30	[2:23]	Transition
0:36	[2:28]	Rapid, ascending scales
0:44	[2:38]	Strong cadence ending transition, pause to clear the air
0:47	[2:41]	Lyrical second theme, major key contributes to brighter mood
0:56	[2:50]	Repeat of second theme with new orchestration
1:09	[3:02]	Crescendo leading to closing material (taken from first theme)

DEVELOPMENT

3:49		Beginning of first theme taken through several distant keys
4:01		First theme used as fugue subject in basses and then violins
4:23		First theme reduced to just opening motive
4:43		*Sforzandi* (loud attacks) give way to retransition
4:52		Dominant pedal point in bassoons with cascading flute and clarinets above

RECAPITULATION

4:59	Return of first theme
5:19	First theme begins to repeat but cut off by transition
5:27	Transition theme returns but is greatly extended
5:55	Rapid, ascending scales
6:04	Cadence and pause
6:07	Return of second theme now in (tonic) minor
6:17	Repeat of second theme with new orchestration
6:30	Return of crescendo leading to closing material (taken from first theme)

CODA

7:11	Begins with rising chromatic scale
7:18	Return of opening motive, then three final chords

(Listening Exercise 24)

SECOND MOVEMENT *(ANDANTE)* After the feverish excitement of the opening movement, the slow, lyrical *Andante* comes as a welcome change of pace. What makes this movement exceptionally beautiful is the extraordinary interplay between the light and dark colors of the woodwinds against the constant tone of the strings. If there is not thematic contrast and confrontation here, there is, nonetheless, heartfelt expression brought about by Mozart's masterful use of orchestral color.

THIRD MOVEMENT *(MINUETTO: ALLEGRETTO)* We expect the aristocratic minuet to provide elegant, graceful dance music. But much to our surprise, Mozart returns to the intense, somber mood of the opening movement. This he does, in part, by choosing to write in the tonic minor key—a rare minuet in minor.

FOURTH MOVEMENT *(ALLEGRO ASSAI)* The finale starts with an ascending rocket that explodes in a rapid, *forte* flourish—and only carefully rehearsed string playing can bring off the brilliant effect of this opening gesture. The contrasting second theme of this sonata–allegro form movement is typically Mozartean in its grace and charm, a proper foil to the explosive opening melody. Midway through the development musical compression takes hold: There is no retransition, only a pregnant pause before the recapitulation; the return dispenses with the repeats built into the first theme; and a coda is omitted. This musical foreshortening at the end produces the same psychological effect that we experienced at the very beginning of the symphony—a feeling of urgency and acceleration.

THE STRING QUARTET

If the symphony is the ideal genre for the public concert hall and aims to please a large listening public, the string quartet is intended for the private chamber and sometimes for an audience of just the performers themselves. Unlike the symphony, which even in the Classical era might have a dozen violinists joining on the first violin line, the string quartet has only one player

FIGURE 10–4

The New Market in Vienna as painted in 1759. The building on the right housed the city casino and it was here that Mozart's G minor symphony was first performed in 1788.

FIGURE 10–5

A representation of a string quartet at the end of the eighteenth century.

chamber music: one player per part

emergence of the string quartet

per part: one first violinist, one second violinist, one violist, and one cellist (Fig. 10–5). Moreover, there is no conductor. All performers function equally and communicate directly among themselves. No wonder the German poet Johann von Goethe (1749–1832) compared the string quartet to a conversation among four intelligent people. Although chamber music can include many modes of performance, ranging from a solo piano or violin to a piano trio, wind quintet, or even a string octet, all employ just one player on a part. Of these chamber media, the string quartet is historically the most important.

In the Baroque era the favored ensemble for chamber music was the trio sonata*, a group of two melody instruments, usually violins, and a *basso continuo** (including keyboard) which set the harmonies from below. With the emphasis shifting from the bottom-heavy Baroque to the lighter, simpler melodies of the early Classical period, the trio sonata ceded pride of place in the 1750s to the string quartet. The *basso continuo* gradually disappears and a new type of bass line emerges, one played by an agile cello alone. Moreover, the middle of the texture is given greater substance by assigning an active role to the viola, the instrument playing immediately above the cello.

Joseph Haydn created this new style of chamber music. In his mature quartets the spectrum of sound from top to bottom is covered evenly by four instruments that participate more or less equally in a give and take of theme and motive. As with most Classical quartets, Haydn's have the usual sequence of four movements, fast–slow–minuet–fast. But in a set he wrote in 1772 Haydn dubbed each minuet a **scherzo** (Italian for "joke"), suggesting the high-spirited style of playing intended for this movement and the string quartet in general.

It was the chance to play string quartets together that gave rise to a lasting friendship between Haydn and Mozart. During the summer of 1784 and winter of 1785, the two men met in Vienna, sometimes at the home of an aristocrat, sometimes in Mozart's own apartments. Haydn played first violin, Mozart viola in their quartet. As a result of this experience, Mozart was inspired to dedicate a set of his best works in this genre to the older master, which he published in 1785 (Fig. 10–6). Yet in this convivial, domestic music making, Haydn and Mozart merely joined in the fashion of the day. For whether in Vienna, Paris, or London, aristocrats and members of the well-to-do middle class were encouraged to play quartets with friends as well as to engage professional musicians to entertain their guests. Haydn, Mozart, Beethoven, and young Schubert wrote some of their finest works for these amateur and professional ensembles. Their trios, quartets, and quintets have come to occupy such an important part of the repertoire that Classical chamber music has become almost synonymous with chamber music itself.

Title page of six string quartets by Mozart dedicated to Haydn (1785). Mozart offers them to Haydn as "six children," asking Haydn to be their "father, guide, and friend."

Haydn: Opus 76, No. 3, The "Emperor" Quartet (1797)

Haydn's "Emporer" Quartet, written in Vienna during the summer of 1797, is counted among the best works of the string quartet genre. It is known as The "Emperor" because it makes liberal use of *The Emperor's Hymn*, a melody Haydn himself composed the previous January in honor of Emperor Franz II. The invasion of imperial lands by the armies of Napoleon in that year had started a patriotic firestorm in Vienna, and Haydn's tune, set to the text "Gott erhalte Franz den Kaiser" ("God preserve Franz the Emperor"), was all the rage. (It subsequently became, in addition to a Protestant hymn, the Austrian national anthem.) Although the charming minuet makes no use of the emperor's tune, and the opening and closing movements of this quartet only allude to it, the slow second movement uses the majestic melody as the basis of a theme and variations set. The theme (see the example in the following Listening Guide) is first presented by the first violin, and harmonized in simple chords. Four variations follow. In these all four instruments are given equal opportunity to hold forth with the tune. Example 10–2 shows how in the Classical string quartet the melodic profile of each of the lines is pretty much the same, a far cry from the melody–walking bass* polarity that typified the earlier Baroque trio sonata.

equality of instruments

EXAMPLE 10–2

Had Haydn been writing for a symphony orchestra, he could not have composed his bass line in this fashion. For the lowest string instrument in the symphony is the low double bass, which plays an octave below the cello and

active role of the cello in that range produces a resonant, yet slightly muddled sound. But the more flexible fingering and singing tone of the cello make it possible for even the lowest instrument of the string quartet to participate as an equal partner. What the quartet gives up by way of depth and richness of sound, it gains in increased motivic interaction and in a more transparent texture.

| LISTENING GUIDE | Joseph Haydn
String Quartet, Opus 76, No. 3, The "Emperor" Quartet (1797)
Second movement, *Poco adagio cantabile* (rather slow, songlike) | CD 2/16
6–Tape 2B
2–Tape 1B |

Theme

(repeat)

(repeat)

0:00   Theme played slowly in first violin; lower three parts provide chordal accompaniment
Variation 1
1:19   Theme in second violin while first violin ornaments above it
Variation 2
2:35   Theme in cello while other three instruments provide counterpoint against it
Variation 3
4:04   Theme in viola; other three instruments only gradually enter
Variation 4
5:31   Theme returns to first violin, but now the accompaniment is more contrapuntal than chordal

(Listening Exercise 25)

THE SONATA

The sonata was another important genre of chamber music that flourished during the Classical period. No longer was it a succession of four or five dance movements, as was usually the case with the sonata during the Baroque era. Now the sonata was a three-movement work (fast–slow–fast), each of which might make use of one or other of the forms favored by Classical composers: sonata–allegro, ternary, rondo, or theme and variations.

the piano sonata   The sonata came to enjoy great popularity during the Classical period. According to publishers' inventories from the end of the eighteenth century, more sonatas were printed than any other type of music. The explanation for this sudden vogue is tied to the equally sudden favor experienced by the piano. Indeed, the word "sonata" has become so closely associated with the piano that unless otherwise qualified as "violin sonata," "cello sonata," or the like, we usually assume that "sonata" refers to a three-movement work for piano.

Who played this flood of new sonatas for the piano? Amateur musicians, mostly women, who practiced and performed for polite society in the comfort of their own homes. As we have seen (page 154), in Mozart's time the ability to play the piano, to do fancy needlework, and to utter a few selected words of French were thought by male-dominated society all that was necessary to be a cultured young lady. To teach the musical handicraft, instructors were needed. Both Haydn and Mozart served as piano teachers in fashionable circles early in their careers. When Mozart arrived in Vienna in 1781 he took on four pupils, charged them a hefty fee, and wrote some of his best sonatas for the more talented of them. One of these, Josephina Auernhammer, rose above societal expectations for her sex to become a respected composer and public performer in her own right. But the piano sonatas that Mozart, Haydn, and Beethoven composed for their numerous pupils were not intended to be played in the public concert halls. Sonatas were to provide students with material that they might practice to develop technique and that they might play as musical entertainment in the home. Even among the splendid thirty-two piano sonatas that Beethoven composed, only one was ever performed at a public concert in Vienna during his lifetime.

sonatas for women

(An example of a Classical piano sonata by Beethoven is found on CD 3, tracks 5–6, on 6–Tape 3A, and on 2–tape 1B. It is discussed in detail on page 214.)

THE CONCERTO

With the genre of the concerto we leave the salon or private chamber and return once again to the public concert hall. For the Classical concerto is a large-scale, three-movement work for instrumental soloist and orchestra, and thus of the same magnitude as the symphony itself. And while the symphony might provide the greatest musical substance at a concert, more often than not the audience was lured to the hall by the prospect of hearing a virtuoso performer play a concerto. Audiences then as now had a special fascination with personal virtuosity and all the daring and excitement that a stunning technical display might bring. The soloist in such concertos was a single performer whose place in the musical firmament was that of a star. Gone was the Baroque tradition of the concerto grosso* which pitted an orchestra (*tutti**) against a *group* of soloists (the *concertino**). From now on the concerto was a **solo concerto,** usually for piano, but sometimes for violin, cello, or wind instrument.

solo concerto

Development of the solo concerto for piano had begun with the two sons of Johann Sebastian Bach, one living in Berlin, the other in London. The Berlin Bach, Carl Philip Emanuel Bach (1714–1788), was the keyboard player for the flute-playing King Frederick the Great (1712–1786) of Prussia, who drilled his troops during the day and played concertos in the evening (Fig.

FIGURE 10–7

FIGURE 10–7

King Frederick the Great of Prussia performing a flute concerto at his court in Berlin. C. P. E. Bach, the second son of J. S. Bach, is at the keyboard.

FIGURE 10–8

One of the few surviving tickets to a concert mounted by Mozart in Vienna.

10–7). Johann Christian Bach (1735–1782), the London Bach as he was called, experimented with the piano concerto in connection with a series of public concerts he gave both in London and Paris during the 1760s and 1770s. But no one did more to bring the form and style of the piano concerto to maturity than Wolfgang Amadeus Mozart.

Mozart wrote twenty-three piano concertos, more than any other important composer. He did so mainly because his economic livelihood depended on it, especially after he took up residence in Vienna as a free-lance musician in 1781. Most of his masterpieces in this genre were composed so that Mozart himself might showcase his talents at a public concert that he alone had organized. For to attract attention in this period, a composer had not only to write the music but also serve as performer, concert manager, and ticket seller all in one (see Fig. 10–8). It was up to Mozart to rent the hall (see Figs. 10–1 and 10–2), hire the orchestra, solicit an audience, and offer his paying public a collection of his newest creations. A musical journal for March 22, 1783, reports one of Mozart's more successful ventures of this sort:

> Today the celebrated Chevalier Mozart gave a musical concert for his own benefit at the Burgtheater in which pieces of his own music, which was already very popular, were performed. The concert was honored by the presence of an extraordinarily large audience and the two new concertos and other fantasies which Mr. Mozart played on the Forte Piano were received with the loudest approval. Our Monarch [Emperor Joseph II], who contrary to his custom honored the entire concert with his presence, joined in the applause of the public so heartily that one can think of no similar example. The proceeds of the concert are estimated at sixteen hundred gulden.

With a take such as this, Mozart could, at least for a time, indulge his expensive tastes.

Mozart: Piano Concerto in A Major (1786)

Mozart composed his Piano Concerto in A major for the concert season of 1786. In it the Classical love of balance is immediately evident, for the piano and orchestra appear in equal measure. Of all the solo instruments, the piano, with its capacity for melody, for speed of execution, and for full sound, is perhaps most up to the task of competing with an orchestra in a spirited give and take of musical material. When the orchestra comes forward with a rich full sound or varied instrumental color, the piano can counter with a line of tender expression, a virtuosic run, or a passage of *fortissimo* chords. The constant exchange between orchestra and soloist requires special attention on the part of the listener. As a biographer of Mozart has said: "Listeners who can really appreciate Mozart's piano concertos are the best audience there is."

FIRST MOVEMENT *(ALLEGRO)* As with all of Mozart's concertos, this one is in three movements (there is never a minuet or scherzo in a concerto). And, as is invariably the case, the first movement is written in sonata–allegro form. However, here it is modified to meet the special demands and opportunities of the concerto. What results is **double exposition form,** an extension of sonata–allegro form in which the orchestra plays one exposition and the soloist then plays another. First the orchestra presents the first, second, and closing themes, all in the tonic key. Then the soloist enters and, with orchestral assistance, offers the piano's version of the same material, but now modulating to the dominant before the second theme. After the piano expands the closing theme, part of the first theme group returns, a throwback to the ritornello* principle of the old Baroque concerto grosso.

FIGURE 10–9

Another view of Mozart's piano. Mozart purchased this instrument in Vienna in 1784 and had it transported wherever he played in the city. His Concerto in A major was composed and first performed on this piano.

Then, in this concerto in A, a surprise: Instead of the usual closing chords, Mozart ends this second exposition with a lyrical new melody presented by the strings. This is another feature of the Classical concerto—a melody held back, or saved, for presentation by the soloist at some unexpected moment in the second exposition.

DOUBLE EXPOSITION FORM

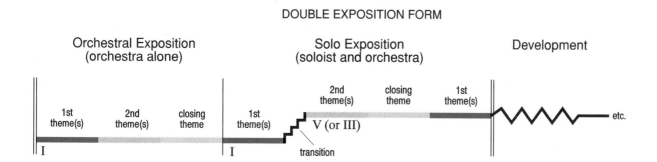

The development here is concerned exclusively with exploiting the new theme that had appeared at the end of the second exposition. The recapitulation compresses the two expositions into one, presenting the themes in the same order as before but now all in the tonic key. Finally, toward the end of the movement the orchestra suddenly stops its forward motion and comes *the cadenza*   to rest on a single chord for several moments. Using this chord as a point of departure, the pianist plunges headlong into a flight of virtuosic fancy called a cadenza. In a **cadenza** the soloist, playing alone, mixes rapid runs, arpeggios, and snippets of previously heard themes into a fantasy-like improvisation. Indeed, Mozart didn't write down this cadenza when he first performed it, but improvised it on the spot, just as in our own century a talented jazz musician might improvise an extended solo. After a minute or so of this virtuosic dazzle, the pianist plays a trill* in the right hand and a V–I cadence in the left to signal the orchestra that it is time for it to reenter the competition. From here to the end the orchestra holds forth, making use of the original closing theme. There is much to follow in the Listening Guide for this movement in double exposition form, but the glorious music of Mozart will more than reward your efforts.

LISTENING GUIDE

Wolfgang Amadeus Mozart
Piano Concerto in A major (1786)
First movement, *Allegro* (fast)

CD 3/1
6–Tape 3A

EXPOSITION 1 (orchestra)

0:00	Strings present first theme, part **a**

0:16	Woodwinds repeat first theme, part **a**
0:34	Full orchestra presents first theme, part **b**

0:56	Strings present second theme, part **a**

1:12	Woodwinds repeat second theme, part **a**
1:27	Strings present second theme, part **b**

1:32	Strings present closing theme, part **a**

1:57	Woodwinds present closing theme, part **b**

EXPOSITION 2 (piano and orchestra)

2:07	Piano enters with first theme, part **a**
2:35	Orchestra plays first theme, part **b**
3:05	Piano plays second theme, part **a**
3:20	Woodwinds repeat second theme, part **a**
3:36	Piano plays and ornaments second theme, part **b**
3:41	Piano and orchestra in dialogue play closing theme, part **a**
4:15	Piano trill heralds return of first theme, part **b**
4:29	Strings quietly offer lyrical new theme

DEVELOPMENT

4:54	Woodwinds transform the new theme as piano interjects scales and then arpeggios
5:25	Woodwinds offer the new theme in imitative counterpoint
5:37	Pedal point on dominant note in low strings signals beginning of retransition
5:50	Piano takes over dominant pedal point
6:07	Piano flourish above held dominant chord leads to recapitulation

RECAPITULATION

6:17	Orchestra plays first theme, part **a**
6:31	Piano repeats first theme, part **a**
6:45	Orchestra plays first theme, part **b**
6:54	Scales in piano sound beginning of transition
7:13	Piano plays second theme now in tonic, part **a**
7:28	Woodwinds repeat second theme, part **a**
7:43	Piano plays second theme, part **b**
7:48	Piano and orchestra divide closing theme, part **a**
8:15	Piano plays the new theme
8:28	Woodwinds play the new theme while piano offers scales and arpeggios against it
8:54	Trill in piano announces return of first theme, part **b**
9:21	Orchestra stops and holds chord
9:25	Cadenza for piano
10:36	Trills signal reentry of orchestra
10:47	Orchestra plays closing themes, parts **a** and **b**
11:05	Final cadential chords

SECOND MOVEMENT *(ANDANTE).* The essence of this movement rests in Mozart's exquisitely crafted lines and colorist harmonies. This is the only work the Viennese master ever wrote in the key of F# minor, and the daring harmonic changes it contains prefigure those of the Romantic era. Musicians who have lived with Mozart from childhood to old age continue to be profoundly moved by this extraordinary movement. It is at once sublimely beautiful but distantly remote, its ending as cold and desolate as death itself.

THIRD MOVEMENT *(PRESTO).* The sublime pessimism of the *Andante* is suddenly shattered by a boisterous rondo refrain in the piano. As Mozart was well aware, this movement, not the previous slow one, has the kind of music the fun-loving Viennese would pay to hear. And in this rondo his subscribers got more than their money's worth, for the refrain alone has no fewer than five separate and distinct parts. The feeling that pervades throughout is not so much a tug of war between soloist and orchestra but rather a high-spirited race to see which party can finish first the wealth of musical ideas.

PERA

Opera in the Classical period maintained the broad features passed on to it from the Baroque era. It still began with an overture, was divided into two or three acts, and made use of a succession of arias and recitatives along with an occasional choral number. Also, needless to say, it still was performed in a theater, one large enough to accommodate both an orchestra and elaborate stage sets.

comic opera

Yet while the genre of opera retained its overall shape, it nonetheless underwent important internal changes during the second half of the eighteenth century. Italian comic opera *(opera buffa)*, a powerful voice for social change in the Enlightenment (see page 153), came to dominate the stage and gradually replace the serious opera *(opera seria)* of the Baroque period. The statuelike gods and goddesses, emperors and queens, of the older style have departed, replaced by more natural, realistic characters drawn from everyday life. Gone, too, are the rigid sectional divisions between aria, recitative, and chorus set in place to segregate one emotion from another. Although aria and recitative were still differentiated, in Classical opera they now flow more easily one to another. The mood of the music changes rapidly to reflect the fluctuating emotions of the characters. The new Classical style, marked by fluid changes of mood, is well suited to comic situations that invariably involve a quick give and take between characters.

the vocal ensemble

Comic opera also brought a new element into the opera house, the **vocal ensemble.** While recitatives are still used to narrate action and arias to express emotion, now a variety of emotions can be expressed simultaneously by means of a vocal trio, quartet, or even sextet of soloists. One character might sing of her love, another of his fear, another of her outrage, while a fourth pokes fun at the other three. Vocal ensembles are especially favored at the ends of acts. No longer does the curtain fall after a solo "exit aria" from a famous prima donna (leading lady), but after a vocal ensemble including the principals—another manifestation of the collective spirit, and better dramatic sense, of the late eighteenth century.

The master of Classical opera, and of the vocal ensemble in particular, is Wolfgang Amadeus Mozart. While Haydn wrote more than a dozen operas and conducted others (see Fig. 10–3, page 190), he lacked Mozart's instinct for what would work in the theater and what would not. Nor did he have Mozart's uncanny ability to depict and differentiate characters through music. With its lightening-quick changes in mood and color, and juxtaposition of themes of different character, Mozart's music is inherently theatrical and perfectly suited to the genre of opera.

Mozart wrote Italian *opera seria* of the old Baroque sort as well as German comic opera, which was called *Singspiel*. Like a Broadway musical, a **Singspiel** is made up of spoken dialogue (instead of recitative) and songs. Mozart's best work of this type is *Die Zauberflöte* (*The Magic Flute*, 1791), recently popularized in a film version by the Swedish director Ingmar Bergman. But Mozart also wrote operas more in the tradition of Italian comic opera. These include his masterpieces *Le nozze di Figaro* (*The Marriage of Figaro*, 1786), *Don Giovanni* (1787), and *Cosi fan tutte* (*Thus Do They All*, 1790), all three with text (libretto) by Lorenzo da Ponte.

Mozart: *Don Giovanni* (1787)

Don Giovanni has not only been called Mozart's greatest opera but also the greatest opera ever written. The story tells the tale of a wicked philanderer, a Don Juan, who seduces and murders his way across Europe before being pursued and finally dragged down to hell by the ghost of a man whom he

Lorenzo da Ponte: Librettist to Mozart

Mozart's principal librettist during the 1780s was Lorenzo da Ponte, whose own life was more unbelievable than the theatrical characters he created. Born in northern Italy of Jewish parents, he received his only formal education in a Catholic seminary. He became a teacher of Italian and Latin literature and then an ordained priest, but was banned from his native Venice for his unreligious thinking and adulterous liaisons. Having made his way to Vienna in 1781, he was introduced to Emperor Joseph II by the imperial court composer Antonio Salieri (see page 161). Da Ponte became the official court librettist ("Poet to the Imperial Theaters"), and both Salieri and Mozart made use of his talents. But when Joseph died in 1790 and Mozart the following year, da Ponte's fortunes in Vienna declined. After passing time with another famous Venetian adventurer, Giovanni Casanova (1725–1798), da Ponte made his way to London where he opened a bookstore. But he was soon charged with shady financial dealings, so in 1805 da Ponte stole away from London for America, one step ahead of his creditors. After a brief stop in New York, he established himself in Sunbury, Pennsyl-

vania, as a trader, distiller, and occasional gunrunner during the War of 1812. Eventually, he gave this up and returned to New York, becoming the first professor of Italian literature at Columbia University in 1825. The high point of his final years came in May 1826, when he helped bring *Don Giovanni* to the stage in New York, the first opera by Mozart to be performed in America.

Lorenzo da Ponte (1749–1838).

has killed. Since the seducer and mocker of public law and mortality is a nobleman, *Don Giovanni* is implicitly critical of the aristocracy, and Mozart and da Ponte danced quickly to stay one step ahead of the imperial censor before production. Mozart's opera was first performed on October 29, 1787, at the Nostitz Theater (Fig. 10–10) in Prague, a city in which his music was especially popular. As fate would have it, the most notorious Don Juan of the eighteenth century, Giovanni Casanova (1725–1798), was in the audience that first night in Prague. It turns out that he had had a small hand in helping his friend da Ponte shape the libretto.

The overture to *Don Giovanni*, as we have seen (Listening Exercise 22), is written in sonata–allegro form. It begins with a slow introduction that incorporates several themes or motives important later in the opera. Just as an author postpones writing a preface until after a book is finished, so a composer saves the overture for the end of the creative process. In this way the overture can not only prefigure important themes in the opera but can also characterize the overall tone of the work. Mozart, as was his custom, postponed much of the writing of *Don Giovanni* to the last minute and the overture was not completed until the night before the premiere, the copyist's ink still wet on the page as the music was handed to the orchestra.

As the last strains of the overture die away, the curtain rises on the comic figure Leporello, Don Giovanni's faithful, though somewhat reluctant, servant. He has been waiting all night outside the house of Donna Anna while his master is at work inside. Grumbling as he paces back and forth, Leporello sings about how he would gladly trade places with the fortunate aristo-

overture

FIGURE 10–10

A view of the Nostitz Theater, Prague, where *Don Giovanni* was first performed on October 29, 1787.

character depiction by music

crat ("I would like to play the gentleman"). Immediately, we see Mozart working to establish the musical character of Leporello: He sets this opening song in F major, a traditional key for the pastoral in music, showing that Leporello is a rustic fellow; he gives him a purely diatonic scale, but no fancy chromaticism; and he has him sing quick repeated notes, almost as if he was stuttering. This last technique, called "patter song," is a stock device used to depict low-caste characters in comic opera.

As Leporello concludes his complaint, the masked Don Giovanni rushes on stage, chased by the virtuous Donna Anna. Here the strings rush up the scale and the music modulates up a fourth (at 1:32) to signify that we are now dealing with the highborn. It seems that the Don has been checked in his advances toward Donna Anna, and the affronted lady wants him captured and unmasked. While the gentleman and lady carry on a musical tug of war in long notes above, the cowering Leporello patters away fearfully below. The vocal ensemble makes clear the conflicting emotions of each party.

Now the cast of characters in the ensemble changes as Donna Anna runs to get help and her father enters to challenge Don Giovanni. The listener senses that this bodes ill—there is an ominous tremolo* in the strings, and the music shifts from major to minor (2:50). Our fear is immediately confirmed as the Don, first refusing to duel, draws his sword and attacks the aging Commandant. In the brief exchange of steel, Mozart depicts the rising anxiety by means of ascending chromatic scales and tight, tense chords (3:32). At the very moment Don Giovanni's sword pierces the Commandant, the action stops and the orchestra holds on a painful diminished chord* (3:44)—a chord made up of all minor thirds. Mozart then clears the air of discord with a simple texture and accompaniment as Don Giovanni and Leporello gaze in horror on the dying Commandant. The listener can feel the Commandant expire, his life sinking away through the slow descent of a chromatic scale (4:52). In its intensity and compression, the opening scene of *Don Giovanni* has no equal outside of Shakespeare's *King Lear*.

LISTENING GUIDE	Wolfgang Amadeus Mozart Opera, *Don Giovanni* (1787) Act I, Scene 1	CD 3/3 6–Tape 3A

Characters: Don Giovanni, a rakish lord; Leporello, his servant; Donna Anna, a virtuous noblewoman; the Commandant, her father, a retired military man

ARIA

<table>
<tr><td></td><td></td><td colspan="2" align="center">Leporello</td></tr>
<tr>
<td>0:00</td>
<td>The watchful Leporello grumbles as he awaits his master Don Giovanni</td>
<td>Notte e giorno faticar,
per chi nulla sa gradi,
piova e il vento sopportar,
mangiar male e mal dormir.
Voglio far il gentilumo
e non volgio più servir . . .</td>
<td>On the go from morn til night
for one who shows no appreciation,
sustaining wind and rain,
poorly fed and poorly paid.
I would like to play the gentleman
and no more a servant be . . .</td>
</tr>
</table>

(Leporello continues in this vein)

1:32	Violins rush up the scale and music modulates upward as Don Giovanni and Donna Anna rush in

ENSEMBLE (TRIO)

<table>
<tr><td></td><td></td><td colspan="2" align="center">Donna Anna</td></tr>
<tr>
<td>1:38</td>
<td>Donna Anna trys to hold and unmask Don Giovanni while Leporello cowers on the side</td>
<td>Non sperar, se non m'uccidi,
ch'io ti lasci fuggir mai'.</td>
<td>Do not hope you can escape
unless you kill me.</td>
</tr>
<tr><td></td><td></td><td colspan="2" align="center">Don Giovanni</td></tr>
<tr>
<td></td><td></td>
<td>Donna folle, indarno gridi,
chi son io tu no saprai.</td>
<td>Crazy lady, you scream in vain,
you will never know who I am.</td>
</tr>
<tr><td></td><td></td><td colspan="2" align="center">Leporello</td></tr>
<tr>
<td></td><td></td>
<td>Che tumulto, Oh ciel, che gridi
il padron in nuovi guai.</td>
<td>What a racket, heavens, what screams,
my master in a new scrape.</td>
</tr>
<tr><td></td><td></td><td colspan="2" align="center">Donna Anna</td></tr>
<tr>
<td></td><td></td>
<td>Gente! Servi! Al traditore!
Scellerato!</td>
<td>Everyone! Help! Catch the traitor!
Scoundrel!</td>
</tr>
<tr><td></td><td></td><td colspan="2" align="center">Don Giovanni</td></tr>
<tr>
<td></td><td></td>
<td>Taci et trema al mio furore!
Sconsigliata!</td>
<td>Shut up and get out of my way!
Fool!</td>
</tr>
<tr><td></td><td></td><td colspan="2" align="center">Leporello</td></tr>
<tr>
<td></td><td></td>
<td>Sta a veder che il malandrino
mi fara recipitar. . . .</td>
<td>We will see if this malefactor
will be the ruin of me. . . .</td>
</tr>
</table>

(The trio continues in this manner with liberal repeats of text and music.)

2:50	String tremolo and shift from major to minor as the Commandant enters

ENSEMBLE (TRIO)

<table>
<tr><td></td><td colspan="2" align="center">Commandant</td></tr>
<tr>
<td>The Commandant comes forward to fight; Don Giovanni first refuses, then duels; Leporello tries to flee</td>
<td>Lasciala, indegno!
Battiti meco!</td>
<td>Let her go, villain!
Fight with me!</td>
</tr>
<tr><td></td><td colspan="2" align="center">Don Giovanni</td></tr>
<tr>
<td></td>
<td>Va! non mi degno
di pugnar teco!</td>
<td>Away, I wouldn't deign
to fight with you!</td>
</tr>
<tr><td></td><td colspan="2" align="center">Commandant</td></tr>
<tr>
<td></td>
<td>Così pretendi
da me fuggir!</td>
<td>So you think
you can get away thus?</td>
</tr>
<tr><td></td><td colspan="2" align="center">Leporello (aside)</td></tr>
<tr>
<td></td>
<td>Potessi almeno
di qua partir!</td>
<td>If I could only
get out of here.</td>
</tr>
</table>

Don Giovanni

Misero! attendi	You old fool! Get ready then,
se vuoi morir!	if you wish to die!

3:32   Musical duel (running scales and
        tense diminished chords)
3:44   Climax on intense chord (the
        Commandant falls mortally wounded),
        then a pause

ENSEMBLE (TRIO)

3:50   Don Giovanni and Leporello look
        on the dying Commandant

Commandant

Ah, soccorso! son tradito.	Ah, I'm wounded, the traitor.
L'assassino m'ha ferito,	The assassin has run me through,
e dal seno palpitante	and from my heaving breast
sento l'anima partir.	I feel my soul depart.

Don Giovanni

Ah, gia cade il sciagurato,	Ah, already the old fool falls,
affannoso e agonizzante,	gasping and writhing in pain,
gia del seno palpitante	and from his heaving breast
Veggo l'anima partir.	I can see his soul depart.

Leporello

Qual misfatto! qual eccesso!	What a horrible thing, how stupid!
Entro il sen dallo spavento	I can feel within my breast
palpitar il cor mi sento.	my heart pounding from fear.
Io non so che far, che dir.	I don't know what to say or do.

4:52   A slow, chromatic descent as the last
        breath seeps out of the Commandant

FIGURE 10–11

Don Giovanni (Sherrill Milnes) and
Zerlina (Teresa Stratas) sing the duet
"Là ci darem la mano" from *Don Gio-
vanni.*

When we next meet the unrepentant Don Giovanni, he is in pursuit of the country girl Zerlina. She is the betrothed of another peasant, Masetto, and the two are to be married the next day. Don Giovanni quickly dismisses Masetto and turns his charm upon the naive Zerlina. First he tries verbal persuasion carried off in *secco* recitative* (the harpsichord is still used to accompany *secco* recitatives in Classical opera, a vestige of the older Baroque practice). Zerlina, he says, is too lovely for a common swain like Masetto. Her beauty demands a higher state: She will become his wife.

This preliminary discussion in *secco* recitative now gives way to more passionate expression in the form of a charming duet, "Là ci darem la mano" ("Give me your hand, oh fairest"). Don Giovanni begins with a seductive melody **(A)** cast squarely in the Classical mold of two four-bar phrases. Zerlina repeats and extends this, but is still singing alone and untouched. The Don becomes more insistent in a new phrase **(B),** and Zerlina, in turn, becomes flustered as her quick sixteenth notes reveal. The initial melody **(A)** returns but is now sung together by the two principals, their voices intertwining—musical union accompanies the act of physical touching that occurs on stage. Finally, as if to further affirm this coupling through music, a concluding section **(C)** is added in which the two characters skip off arm in arm ("Let's go, my treasure"), their voices linked together, mainly in parallel-moving thirds.

LISTENING GUIDE

Wolfgang Amadeus Mozart
Opera, *Don Giovanni* (1787)
Act I, Scene 7

CD 3/4
6–Tape 3A
2–Tape 1B

Characters: Don Giovanni and the peasant girl Zerlina
Situation: Don Giovanni tries, and apparently succeeds, in the
seduction of Zerlina.

RECITATIVE

0:00

Don Giovanni

Alfin siam liberati, Zerlinetta gentil,
da quel sioccone.
Che ne dite, mio ben,
so far pulito?

At last, gentle Zerlina,
we are free of that clown.
And say, my love, didn't
I handle it well?

Zerlina

Signore, é mio marito . . .

Sir, he is my fiance.

Don Giovanni

Chi? Colui?
Vi par che un onest'uomo,
un mobil cavalier, qual io mi vanto,
possa soffrir che quel visetto d'oro,
quel viso inzuccherato
da un bifolcaccio vil sia strapazzato?

Who? Him?
Do you think that an honorable
man, a noble cavalier as I
believe I am, could let such a
golden face, such a sweet
beauty, be profaned by that
clumsy oaf?

Zerlina

Ma, signore, io gli diedi
parola di sposarlo.

But sir, I have already given
my word to marry him.

Don Giovanni

Tal parola non vale un zero.
Voi non siete fatta per essere paesana;
un altra sorte vi procuran quegli
occi bricconcelli, quei labretti si
belli, quelle dituccia candide e
odorose, par me toccar giuncata e
fiutar rose.

Such a promise counts for
nothing. You were not made
to be a peasant girl, a higher
fate is in store for those
roguish eyes, those beautiful
lips, those milkly, perfumed
hands, so soft to touch,
scented with roses.

Zerlina

Ah! . . . Non vorrei . . .

Ah! . . . I do not wish . . .

Don Giovanni

Che non vorreste?

What don't you wish?

Zerlina

Alfine ingannata restar.
Io so che raro colle donne voi
altri cavalierisiete onesti e sinceri.

In the end to be decieved.
I know that rarely with
women are you noblemen
honest and sincere.

Don Giovanni

Eh, un'impostura della gente plebea!
La nobiltà ha dipinta negli occi
l'onestà. Orsù, non perdiam tempo;
in questo istante io ti voglio sponsar.

A vile slander of the low
classes. Nobility can be
seen in honest eyes. Now
let's not waste time. I
will marry you immediately.

Zerlina

Voi?

You?

Don Giovanni

Certo, io. Quell casinetto è mio.	Certainly I. That villa
Soli saremo, e là, gioiello mio,	over there is mine. We
ci sposeremo.	will be alone, and there, my
	little jewel, we will be married.

ARIA (DUET)

A

1:45

Don Giovanni

Là   ci da-rem la   ma - no,   là   mi di-rai di   sì.

Là ci darem la mano,	Give me your hand, oh fairest,
là mi dirai di sì.	whisper a gentle "yes."
Vedi, non è lontano:	Come, if for me you carest,
partiam, ben mio, da qui.	with joy my life to bless.

Zerlina

Vorrei, e non vorrei,	I'd like to but yet I would not.
mi trema un poco il cor;	My heart will not be still.
felice, è ver, sarei,	Tis true I would be happy,
ma può burlarmi ancor.	yet he may deceive me still.

B

Don Giovanni

Vie - ni, mio bel   di - let - to!

2:26	Vieni, mio bel diletto!	Come with me my pretty!

Zerlina

Mi fa pietà Masetto!	May Masetto take pity!

Don Giovanni

Io cangierò tua sorte!`	I will change your fate!

Zerlina

Presto, non son più forte.	Quick then, I can no longer resist.

A'

2:51   repeat of first eight lines

B'

3:14   repeat of next four lines

C

3:42   Change of meter to 6/8

Together

(Zerlina)
An - diam, an-diam, mio be-ne,   a   ri - sto-rar   le   pe-ne   d'un' in - no - cen-te a - mor!

(Don Giovanni)
An - diam, an-diam, mio be-ne,   a   ri - sto-rar   le   pe-ne   d'un' in - no - cen-te a - mor!

Andiam, andiam mio bene,	Let's go, let's go, my treasure,
a ristorar le pene	to soothe the pangs
d'un innocente amor!	of innocent love.

Ultimately, in the duet "Give me your hand, oh fairest," Don Giovanni persuades Zerlina to extend her hand and the prospect of a good deal more. The tune, perhaps the most memorable of the opera, became a popular favorite in the nineteenth century. No less so *Don Giovanni*. From the moment of its first performance in Prague, Mozart's tragic–comic opera has enjoyed enormous favor with all who are moved by alluring melodies and passionate drama. *Don Giovanni* is one of those rare instances in the fine arts of a work that has immediate popular appeal, yet is universally judged to be a masterpiece of the highest order.

LISTENING EXERCISES

| 24 | Wolfgang Amadeus Mozart
Symphony No. 40 in G minor (1788)
First movement, *Molto allegro* (very fast) | CD 2/15
6–Tape 2B
2–Tape 1B |

Mozart's Symphony No. 40 in G minor has been discussed in detail (page 191) as has the development of the symphony orchestra in the Classical period. The following questions focus on the various instruments and instrumental families of the orchestra as they work within the context of sonata–allegro form. This is not a festive symphony, so there are no trumpets and drums. Mozart is writing for French horns, woodwinds, and strings. How does he use these instrumental forces to achieve his musical aims?

0:00–0:20   Beginning of first theme

1. Which instruments are playing the melody here?
   a. violins   b. violas   c. cellos
2. At which time do the woodwinds finally enter? ——————————

0:30–0:45   Transition

3. Which instruments dominate the transition?
   a. cellos   b. flutes   c. violins

0:47–1:04   Second theme

4. Which is true?
   a. The strings dominate this second theme area.
   b. The strings and woodwinds participate equally.

1:22–1:32   Echoes of the first theme provide a closing

5. Which woodwind instrument can be heard playing the main motive of the first theme?
   a. French horn   b. trumpet   c. bassoon

1:53–3:45   Repeat of exposition

3:49–4:28   Development section, first of two parts

6. Which family of instruments dominates this contrapuntal working out of the first theme?
   a. strings   b. woodwinds   c. brass

4:52–4:58   Retransition at the end of the development

7. Which family of instruments dominates this retransition?
   a. strings   b. woodwinds   c. brass

4:59–5:26   Beginning of recapitulation

8. Which of the following is true?
   a. The orchestration here at the beginning of the recapitulation is mostly the same as that at the beginning of the movement (strings followed by later woodwind entry).
   b. Mozart has radically changed the orchestration. The woodwinds come in first with the theme, and the strings come in later.

5:27   Transition

9. Which family of instruments dominates this extended transition?
   a. strings   b. woodwinds   c. brass

6:07–6:25   Second theme

6:48   Echoes of first theme provide a closing

10. Which of the following is true generally about this movement?
   a. The woodwinds never introduce a new theme. They only repeat and elaborate themes presented by the violins as well as add instrumental color.
   b. The woodwinds introduce new themes in this movement just as often as the violins. They also add instrumental color.

	Joseph Haydn	CD 2/16
25	Opus 76, No. 3, The "Emperor" Quartet (1797), Second movement, *Poco adagio cantabile* (rather slow, songlike)	6–Tape 2B 2–Tape 1B

The string quartet is a type of chamber music, and its musical style is different from that of the symphony. Here we have a quartet by the aging Haydn in which the slow movement is composed in the form of theme and variations. Go back and have another look at the melody that constitutes the theme (page 196) and then answer the following questions.

0:00–1:17   Theme
1. Listen to the theme as it is played by the first violin. Is it in a major or a minor key? _____
2. Why does this melody sound so secure and firm?
   a. because all the notes are the same length
   b. because each phrase ends on a dominant or a tonic note
   c. because there are many modulations

1:19–2:33   Variation 1
3. The second violin has the theme while the first violin rapidly ornaments above. Do the viola and cello (the lowest two instruments) play at all during this variation? _____

2:35–4:02   Variation 2

4. The cello has the theme in this variation. Would you say the instrument is playing in the higher or lower part of its range? (Listen especially to the last section of the melody.) _____

4:04–5:29   Variation 3

5. The viola has the melody but is gradually joined by the other instruments. Which instrument is the *last* to enter in this variation?
   a. first violin   b. second violin   c. cello

6. Is the style of writing in this variation homophonic or polyphonic (chordal or contrapuntal)? _____

5:31–6:55   Variation 4

7. The theme now returns to the first violin. When the violin repeats the first phrase of the melody, it does so
   a. an octave higher.   b. an octave lower.   c. at the same pitch level.

8. (6:57) Is there a brief coda added here? _____

9. This ending sounds suddenly darker; why?
   a. because a minor chord is heard
   b. because the tempo gets faster
   c. because the theme now is played on the lowest instrument

10. A general question about this movement: Which of the following is true?
   a.   In this set of theme and variations Haydn keeps the theme pretty much intact and changes, or varies, the context in which it appears.
   b.   In this set of theme and variations Haydn radically transforms the theme while keeping its context pretty much intact.

KEY WORDS

cadenza	prima donna	string quartet
diminished chord	scherzo	*The Emperor's Hymn*
double exposition	*Singspiel*	vocal ensemble
form	solo concerto	
Lorenzo da Ponte	sonata	

11

THE BRIDGE TO ROMANTICISM: LUDWIG VAN BEETHOVEN

No composer is more revered than Ludwig van Beethoven (1770–1827), no music more loved than his. Indeed, when one conjures up the image of a composer of music, most likely it is the figure of Beethoven that comes to mind—the angry, defiant, disheveled Beethoven. Is it not the bust of Beethoven, rather than the elegant Mozart or the stalwart Bach, that sits atop the piano in the comic strip *Peanuts*? Is it not Beethoven who is the butt of all "decomposing" jokes? Such observations are not mere trivialities. The image of Beethoven is deeply ingrained in our popular culture. For many, Beethoven personifies the ideal of "the musician as artist," for some he is the consummate "artist as hero."

His music, too, enjoys great public favor. Statistics show that Beethoven's symphonies, sonatas, and quartets are performed in concert halls and heard on radio more than those of any other classical composer. His works are tender but powerful, perfectly balanced yet bursting with energy. And just as Beethoven the composer struggled to overcome personal adversity—his growing deafness—so his music imparts a feeling of struggle and ultimate victory. It has a sense of rightness, even morality, about it. It elevates and inspires the listener, and for that reason it has an immediate and universal appeal.

Beethoven's life spanned the last quarter of the eighteenth century and the first quarter of the nineteenth. For the most part his music belongs to the tradition of the Viennese Classical masters. He composed predominantly in the Classical genres of symphony, piano sonata, concerto, string quartet, and opera; and he wrote within the Classical forms of sonata–allegro, rondo, and theme and variations. Yet even in the compositions of his youth, there is unmistakably a new spirit at work in his music, one that foreshadows the musical style of the Romantic period (1820–1900). An intense, lyrical expression is heard in his slow movements, while his allegros abound with striking themes, pounding rhythms, and startling dynamic contrasts. He stays within the bounds of Classical forms, yet he pushes their confines to the breaking point, so great is his urge for personal expression. Though a pupil of Haydn and a lifelong admirer of Mozart, he nonetheless elevated music to new heights of eloquence and dramatic power. For this reason he can rightly be called the prophet of Romantic music.

THE EARLY YEARS (1770–1802)

Like Bach and Mozart before him, Beethoven came from a family of musicians. His father and grandfather were performers at the court of the Elector at Bonn, Germany, a small town on the Rhine River where Beethoven was born on December 17, 1770. Seeing great musical talent in his young son, Beethoven's father, a violent, alcoholic man, forcibly made him practice at the keyboard all hours, day and night. Soon he tried to exploit his son as a child prodigy, a second Mozart, telling the world the diminutive boy was two years younger than he actually was. At the age of seventeen Beethoven was packed off to far-away Vienna to study with Mozart himself, but no sooner had he arrived and played for the master than his mother became seriously ill and he was forced to return to Bonn. Five years later, in 1792, Beethoven finally went off to Vienna for good. As one of his benefactors said, "You are going to Vienna in fulfillment of your long frustrated wishes . . . you will receive the spirit of Mozart from the hands of Haydn."

FIGURE 11–1

Ludwig van Beethoven in an oil painting of 1819.

Indeed, Mozart had died since Beethoven's last visit, so he now took up the study of musical composition with Haydn. But the aging Haydn and the youthful, impetuous Beethoven were not compatible. So when Haydn set off for his second sojourn in London in 1794 (see page 158), Beethoven began to work with other teachers including a certain Johann Albrechtsberger (1736–1809), with whom he studied fugue, and the ever-present Antonio Salieri (1750–1825; see page 161), who taught him the Italian vocal style. At the same time Beethoven tried to make himself acceptable to polite society in Vienna: He bought new clothes, located a wigmaker, and found someone who could give him dancing lessons.

Beethoven's aim was to gain an entrée into the homes of the wealthy of the Austrian capital. And this he soon did, not because of his skill as a composer, and less because of his social graces, but because of his phenomenal talent as a pianist. His playing was louder, more violent, more forceful, yet more expressive than the aristocrats of the salons had ever heard. He possessed an extraordinary technique—even if he did hit occasional wrong notes—and this he put to good use, especially in his fanciful improvisations. As a contemporary witness observed: "He knew how to produce such an impression on every listener that frequently there was not a single dry eye, while many broke out into loud sobs, for there was a certain magic in his expression."

Beethoven and the aristocracy

The aristocracy was captivated. One patron put a string quartet at his disposal, another made it possible for Beethoven to experiment with a small orchestra, and all showered him with gifts. He acquired well-to-do pupils; he sold his compositions ("I state my price and they pay," he said with pride in 1801); and he requested and eventually received an annuity from three noblemen so that he could work undisturbed. The text of this arrangement includes the following lines:

It is recognized that only a person who is as free as possible from all cares can consecrate himself to his craft. He can only produce these great and sublime works which enoble Art if they form his sole pursuit, to the exclusion of all unnecessary obligations. The undersigned have therefore taken the decision to ensure that Herr Ludwig van Beethoven's situation shall not be embarrassed

FIGURE 11–2

Beethoven's study in the last year of his life (1827). The piano was given him by the English maker Broadwood in 1818.

by his most necessary requirements, nor shall his powerful genius be hampered.

What a contrast between Beethoven's contract and the one signed by Haydn four decades earlier! Music is no longer merely a craft and the composer a servant. It is now an exalted Art, and the great creator a Genius who must be protected and nurtured—this is a new notion of the value of music, one of the Romantic age. And Beethoven did his best to encourage a belief in the exalted mission of the composer as artist. He would not stand at the beck and call of a master. When one patron demanded that he play for some visiting French officers, Beethoven stormed out of the salon and responded by letter: "Prince, what you are, you are through the accident of birth. What I am, I am through my own efforts. There have been many princes and there will be thousands more. But there is only one Beethoven!"

Piano Sonata, Opus 27, No. 2, The "Moonlight" Sonata (1801)

The bold originality in Beethoven's music can be seen in one of his most celebrated compositions, the piano sonata that has come to be called the "Moonlight" Sonata. It is written in C# minor, a key foreign to most Classical composers who made use of less remote keys (keys with fewer sharps or flats) when writing in minor. The unusual key may account, in part, for the eerie, almost extraterrestrial sound of the sonata. Moreover, Beethoven breaks with formal convention by foregoing the traditional fast opening movement in sonata–allegro form. Instead, he begins with a lyrical *Adagio* (slow) and follows this with a minuet and a lively finale. Beethoven subtitled this work "Sonata quasi una fantasia" ("Sonata like a fantasy"), and this vision of a romantic fantasy may explain the special nature of the first movement.

FIRST MOVEMENT: This famous *Adagio* is built around a beautiful, singing melody (see second example in the Listening Guide). But the composer's aim here is not so much to work out melodic material as it is to evoke a mood, an atmosphere, and this he does by creating a background of changing harmonies carried along in a flowing triplet accompaniment. The harmonies are rich, sometimes dissonant, and frequently involve changes from major to minor, as if a nocturnal cloud has darkened the face of the moon. Although the form of the movement is the **ABA'** pattern familiar from the Baroque and Classical periods, the mood is distinctly Romantic.

LISTENING GUIDE		Ludwig van Beethoven Piano Sonata, Opus 27, No. 2, The "Moonlight" Sonata (1801) First movement, *Adagio* (slow)	CD 3/5 6-Tape 3A 2-Tape 1B

0:00	Introduction: repeated triplets in the middle range and octaves in the bass set the mood	

| 0:24 | **A** | Melody marked by dotted rhythm sounds on high; starts in minor and moves to major |

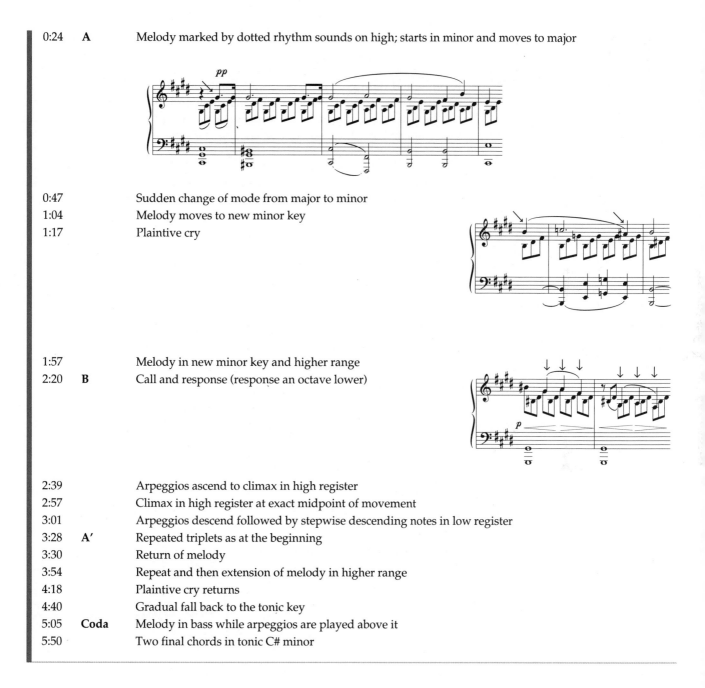

0:47		Sudden change of mode from major to minor
1:04		Melody moves to new minor key
1:17		Plaintive cry
1:57		Melody in new minor key and higher range
2:20	**B**	Call and response (response an octave lower)
2:39		Arpeggios ascend to climax in high register
2:57		Climax in high register at exact midpoint of movement
3:01		Arpeggios descend followed by stepwise descending notes in low register
3:28	**A′**	Repeated triplets as at the beginning
3:30		Return of melody
3:54		Repeat and then extension of melody in higher range
4:18		Plaintive cry returns
4:40		Gradual fall back to the tonic key
5:05	**Coda**	Melody in bass while arpeggios are played above it
5:50		Two final chords in tonic C# minor

SECOND MOVEMENT: Beethoven designated the second movement of the "Moonlight" Sonata simply *Allegretto* (lightly moving), though the mood is that of an animated minuet in 3/4 time. As expected, the minuet-like *Allegretto* is followed by a trio, in this case one in which the right hand plays a game of cat and mouse with the left: The right sounds mainly on beat three of each measure, and the left reacts by playing immediately on the next downbeat. True to Classical form, the trio then gives way to a return of the opening *Allegretto*.

THIRD MOVEMENT: The third and final movement of the "Moonlight" Sonata is a technical tour de force for the pianist. No previous sonatas of Haydn or Mozart, and indeed none of Beethoven himself, involve such bravura and daring. If we can picture Beethoven playing this movement in an aristocratic salon in Vienna, we can better understand why he took the city by storm. Rapid arpeggios leap up the keyboard, Alberti bass* figures move at a blistering pace, and scales that race up the keyboard alternate with crashing chords down below. Yet all of this electrifying energy is kept within the bounds of strict sonata–allegro form. Exposition, development, recapitulation, and coda unfold according to Classical "rules" (see page 172). Here Beethoven harnesses his explosive technical power by means of tight formal control and thereby produces a near perfect interaction between form and content.

LISTENING GUIDE	Ludwig van Beethoven Piano Sonata, Opus 27, No. 2, The "Moonlight" Sonata (1801) Third movement, *Presto agitato* (very-fast and agitated)	CD 3/6 6-Tape 3A

EXPOSITION () = repeats

0:00	(1:38)	Rapidly ascending arpeggios against rocking bass (first theme, part 1)

0:11	(1:50)	Rapid tremolo (fluttering) in the right hand (first theme, part 2) followed by a *fermata* (hold)
0:21	(2:00)	More rising arpeggios (transition)
0:30	(2:08)	Songlike second theme in right hand above Alberti bass in left

0:50	(2:28)	Rapid scales prepare arrival of closing theme
1:04	(2:42)	Quick, repeating chords (closing theme, part 1)
1:13	(2:50)	Quick, repeating chords played again and become more insistent
1:25	(3:03)	Lyrical ending (closing theme, part 2)

(1:38 – 3:15)		Repeat of exposition

DEVELOPMENT

3:16	Sudden shift to major and reappearance of rising arpeggios (first theme, part 1)
3:26	Songlike second theme, part 1, in minor key
3:33	Second theme, part 1, now in bass
3:40	Second theme, part 1, again in bass but now in a major key
3:53	Rumbling pedal point in bass; general release of tension (retransition)
4:16	Two long chords mark end of development

RECAPITULATION

4:21	Rapidly ascending arpeggios of first theme, part 1
4:32	Tremolo figure of first theme, part 2, followed by pause
4:44	Jump to songlike second theme now in minor
5:05	Racing scales lead to closing theme
5:18	Quickly repeating chords of closing theme, part 1
5:26	Closing theme repeated
5:40	Lyrical ending (closing theme, part 2)

CODA

5:52	Rising arpeggios from first theme, part 1
5:58	Prolonged rising arpeggios, then pause
6:10	Second theme, part 1, in bass and then in treble
6:30	Descending triplets but rising tension
6:44	A race up the scale to a trill
6:48	Trill and ornamental descent from it
7:10	Lyrical ending (closing theme, part 2, returns)
7:20	Arpeggios on the tonic triad rise and then fall in both hands followed by two concluding tonic chords

(Listening Exercise 26)

At the time he wrote the "Moonlight" Sonata, the thirty-year-old Beethoven was in love with one of his young piano pupils, Countess Giulietta Guicciardi (see Fig. 11–3), and he dedicated this sonata to her. The mood of nocturnal romance in the opening *Adagio* may have something to do with the composer's state of mind. This infatuation was just one of Beethoven's many ultimately unsuccessful relationships. None of the women he pursued was able to reciprocate his love to the point of agreeing to marriage. His total absorption in his art, his slovenly habits, and his somewhat unstable personality made him a less-than-ideal domestic mate.

Beethoven's social difficulties were compounded by the fact that he was gradually going deaf—a serious handicap for any person, a tragic condition for a musician. The symptoms first manifested themselves in the late 1790s and, quite understandably, the victim suffered considerable anguish and depression. His deafness perhaps least affected his work as a composer—good musicians can hear with an "inner ear" and do not need actual sound. But it caused him to retreat from society even more, and it all but ended his career as a performer since he could no longer gauge how hard to press the

FIGURE 11–3

Countess Guilietta Guicciardi (1784–1856).

Beethoven's Confession: The Heiligenstadt Testament

Beethoven was a physically powerful, proud, egotistical man who suffered no fools and had few doubts about his own worth as a musician. The loss of his hearing, which began in 1798, was a near fatal blow. It not only jeopardized his profession but also caused him to withdraw increasingly from society, creating the image of Beethoven the loner, the outcast, the misanthrope. The Heiligenstadt Testament is a lengthy, public letter which Beethoven, having finally decided against suicide, wrote in the fall of 1802. It is a remarkable document—part plea for understanding, part artistic manifesto. The name "Heiligenstadt" derives from the fact that Beethoven penned it in the village of that name, just to the north of Vienna, where he had gone in 1802 for a "cure" for his deafness. Here are a few lines of Beethoven's public declaration.

Oh my fellow men who consider me an unfriendly, hostile, peevish man or even misanthropic, how greatly you wrong me. For you do not know the secret reason why I appear to be so to you. . . . Though endowed with a passionate and lively temperament and even fond of the distractions offered by society, I was soon obliged to withdraw and live in solitude. . . . I could not bring myself to say to people: "Speak up, shout, for I am deaf." Alas, how could I possibly mention the loss *of a sense* which in me should be more perfectly developed than in other people, a sense which at one time I possessed in the greatest perfection, even to a degree few in my profession possess or have ever possessed . . . But how humiliated I have felt if somebody standing beside me heard the sound of a flute in the distance and *I heard nothing!* Such experiences made me despair. I would have ended my life—it was only *my art* that held me back.

piano keys. By late 1802 Beethoven recognized that he would suffer a gradual, though ultimately total, loss of hearing. Yet he emerged from his period of depression with a renewed conviction to do great things. His music had sustained him: "I would have ended my life—it was only *my art* that held me back," he said. He would now "seize Fate by the throat."

The "Heroic" Period (1803–1813)

the "Eroica" symphony

It was in this resurgent, defiant mood that Beethoven entered what we call his "heroic" period of composition (1803–1813). His works became longer, more assertive, full of broad themes and grand gestures. A watershed is his "Eroica" Symphony (Symphony No. 3, 1803). It is forty-five minutes long, about twice the length of the average symphony of Haydn or Mozart. Themes and motives are endlessly manipulated, crescendos gradually swell over long spans of time, and repeating syncopations are played *sforzando* (with a loud attack) to create a novel, almost shocking, rhythmic effect. Unprecedented in a symphony is the slow second movement, entitled *Marcia funèbre (Funeral March)*. It is composed in the style of many funeral marches created in Paris in these years to honor the fallen heroes of the French Republic. Although Austria was at war almost continually with France early in the nineteenth century, Beethoven was much taken with the enemy's revolutionary call for liberty, equality, and fraternity. Napoleon Bonaparte became his hero, and the composer entitled this, his third symphony, *Bonaparte*. But when Napoleon declared himself emperor, Beethoven flew into a rage and ripped the title page in two saying, "Now he, too, will trample on all the rights of man and indulge only his ambition." When the work was published, Napoleon's name had been removed in favor of the more general title, "Heroic" Symphony.

Beethoven wrote nine symphonies in all, six of them in his "heroic" period. Although few in number compared with earlier Classical composers, Beethoven's symphonies nonetheless set the standard for the genre of the symphony for the remainder of the nineteenth century. Noteworthy, in addition to the "Eroica" (Third), are the famous Fifth Symphony, the Sixth (called the "Pastoral" because it tries to evoke the ambiance of the Austrian countryside), the Seventh, and the monumental Ninth. In these Beethoven introduces new orchestral colors by bringing new instruments into the symphony orchestra: the trombone (Symphony No. 5, 7, and 9), the contrabassoon (Symphony No. 5 and 9), the piccolo (Symphony No. 5, 6, and 9), and even the human voice (Symphony No. 9). He also changes the nature of the four principal movements of the symphony: The first movement becomes even larger as the development section and coda are expanded; the slow movement assumes a solemn, hymnlike, sometimes tragic quality; the third movement loses the dance character of the minuet and becomes a faster, driving scherzo* (see page 194); and the finale, which had previously been marked by lightness and gaiety, takes on a weightier, often triumphant tone, one sufficient to balance the general seriousness of the opening movement.

Symphony No. 5 in C Minor (1808)

The four movements of Beethoven's well-known Symphony No. 5 have these characteristics and something more. The movements work together in a new way to convey a sense of psychological progression. An imaginative listener might feel the following sequence of events: (1) a fateful encounter with elemental forces, (2) a period of quiet soul-searching followed by (3) a further wrestling with the elements, and, finally, (4) a triumphant victory over the forces of Fate. Beethoven himself is said to have remarked with regard to the famous opening motive of the symphony: "There Fate knocks at the door!"

FIGURE 11–4

Napoleon as a Young Officer. Napoleon seized control of the government of France and established a new form of Republic in 1799. When he elevated himself to emperor in 1804, Beethoven changed the title of his Symphony No. 3 from "Bonaparte" to "Eroica."

FIGURE 11–5

Interior of the Theater an der Wien, Vienna, where Beethoven's Symphony No. 5 was first performed on December 22, 1808.

The rhythm of the opening—perhaps the best-known moment in all of classical music—animates the entire symphony. Not only does it dominate the opening *Allegro* but it reappears in varied form in the three later movements as well, binding the symphony into a unified whole.

EXAMPLE 11–1

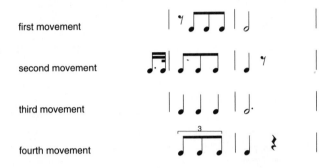

FIRST MOVEMENT: At the very outset the listener is jolted to attention, forced to sit up and take notice by a sudden explosion of sound. And what an odd beginning to a symphony—a blast of three short notes and a long one, followed by the same three shorts and a long, all now a step lower. The movement can't quite get going. It starts and stops, then seems to lurch forward and gather momentum. And where is the theme or melody? This three-shorts-and-a-long pattern is more a motive or musical cell than a melody. Yet it is striking by virtue of its power and compactness. As the movement unfolds, the actual pitches of the motive prove to be of secondary importance. Beethoven is obsessed here with rhythm. He wants to demonstrate the enormous latent force that lurks within even the simplest rhythmic cell just waiting to be unleashed by a composer who understands the secrets of rhythmic energy.

a basic four-note motive

To control the sometimes violent forces that will emerge, the musical processes unfold within the traditional confines of sonata–allegro form. The basic four-note motive provides all the musical material for the first theme area:

EXAMPLE 11–2

There is a brief transition played by a solo French horn. It is only six notes long and is formed simply by adding two notes to the end of the basic four-note motive. As expected, the transition moves the tonality from the tonic (C minor) to the relative major* (E♭ major):

EXAMPLE 11–3

The second theme seems to offer a moment of escape from the rush of the motive, but even here the pattern of three shorts and a long is heard underneath in the low strings:

EXAMPLE 11–4

The closing theme, too, is none other than the motive once again, now presented in a somewhat different guise:

EXAMPLE 11–5

With the development, the opening motive returns and assumes all, if not more than all, of the force it had at the beginning. It soon takes on different melodic forms, as it is tossed back and forth between instruments, though the rhythmic shape remains constant:

EXAMPLE 11–6

Following a rhythmic climax and a brief imitative passage, Beethoven reduces the six-note motive of the transition down to merely two notes, and then just one, and he passes these around *pianissimo* between the strings and the winds:

EXAMPLE 11–7

Beethoven was a master of the process of musical fragmentation–stripping away all extraneous material to get to the core of a musical idea. Here in this mysterious *pianissimo* passage he holds up the irreducible minimum of his motive: a single note. In the midst of this quiet the original four-note motive tries to reassert itself *fortissimo*, yet at first cannot do so. Its explosive force, however, cannot be held back. A thunderous return of the opening chords signals the beginning of the recapitulation.

Although the recapitulation offers a repeat of the events of the exposition, Beethoven has one surprise in store. No sooner has the motive regained its momentum than an oboe enters to play a tender, languid, and wholly unexpected solo. Though a deviation from the usual path of sonata–allegro form, this brief oboe cadenza* allows for a momentary release of excess energy. The recapitulation then resumes its expected course.

What is not expected is the enormous coda that follows. It is even longer than the exposition! A new form of the motive appears and it, too, is subjected to development. In fact, what Beethoven does here is write a second development section, so great is his urge to exploit the latent power of this one simple musical idea.

LISTENING GUIDE		Ludwig van Beethoven Symphony No. 5 in C minor (1808) First movement, *Allegro con brio* (fast with gusto)	CD 3/7 6-Tape 3B 2-Tape 2A

EXPOSITION () = repeats

0:00	(1:22)	Two statements of the motive	
0:06	(1:29)	Motive builds momentum in a crescendo working up to climax and three chords, the last of which is held	
0:20	(1:44)	Another crescendo begins as motive is piled upon itself in imitative counterpoint	
0:40	(2:03)	Loud climax on two chords	
0:41	(2:05)	Short transition played by solo horn	
0:45	(2:07)	Quiet second theme in new major key (relative major)	
0:58	(2:20)	Crescendo	
1:04	(2:27)	Loud string passage prepares arrival of closing theme	
1:13	(2:36)	Closing theme	
(1:22 – 2:44)		Repeat of exposition	

DEVELOPMENT

2:46		Motive played *fortissimo* by horn and strings and then passed back and forth between woodwinds and strings
3:07		Another crescendo or "Beethovenian swell"
3:13		Rhythmic climax in which motive is pounded incessantly

3:20	Short passage of imitative counterpoint using transition motive
3:30	Two notes of transition motive passed back and forth
3:40	One note passed back and forth between winds and strings; gets quiet
3:50	Basic four-note motive tries to reassert itself loudly
3:54	More *pianissimo* one-note alternation between winds and strings
3:58	Motive reenters insistently

RECAPITULATION

4:04	Return of motive
4:10	Motive gathers momentum and cadences with three chords
4:18	Unexpected oboe solo

4:36	Motive returns and moves hurriedly to a climax
4:56	Transition now played by bassoon instead of horn
4:59	Quiet second theme with timpani now playing rhythm of motive
5:15	Crescendo leading to closing theme
5:23	Closing theme

CODA

5:43	Motive pounded *fortissimo* on one note, then again a step higher
5:53	Imitative counterpoint
6:07	Rising quarter notes form new four-note pattern

6:19	New four-note pattern alternates between strings and wood-winds
6:39	Pounding on a single note, then motive as at beginning
6:55	Succession of I–V–I chords brings movement to abrupt end

SECOND MOVEMENT: After the pounding we have been subjected to in the explosive first movement, the calm, noble *Andante* comes as a welcome change of pace. The key is now major (A♭), the mood serene, and the melody expansive—instead of beginning with a four-note motive, the opening theme here runs on for twenty-two measures. The musical form is also a familiar one: theme and variations (see pages 176–177). But this is not the simple, easily audible theme and variations of Haydn. There are, in fact, two themes, and the first one has three parts. Not only do the variations become more complex as the movement progresses but also, beginning with variation 2, Beethoven shuffles the order in which the themes and parts of themes appear. The listener should become familiar with the themes by repeated hearings and then, in the variations, try to sense which theme is being varied. Is it theme 1 or theme 2? If theme 1 is being used, which of its three parts? A guide to the unfolding of this movement is offered below. Listening Exercise 27 will help you develop additional skill in hearing more advanced variation pieces of this sort.

a more complex theme and variations

**LISTENING
GUIDE**

Ludwig van Beethoven
Symphony No. 5 in C minor (1808)
Second movement, *Andante con moto* (progressing with movement)

CD 3/8
6-Tape 3B

THEMES

0:00   Violas and cellos play beginning of theme 1

0:24   Woodwinds play middle of theme 1

0:38   Violins play end of theme 1

0:54   Clarinets, bassoons, and violins play theme 2

1:16   Brasses play theme 2 in fanfare style

1:34   Mysterious *pianissimo*

VARIATION 1

2:01   Violas and cellos vary beginning of theme 1 by adding sixteenth notes

2:24   Woodwinds play middle of theme 1

2:34   Strings play end of theme 1

2:53   Clarinets, bassoons, and violins play theme 2

3:14   Brasses return with fanfare (theme 2)

3:32   More of the mysterious *pianissimo*

VARIATION 2

4:00   Violas and cellos overlay beginning of theme 1 with rapidly moving orna-
        mentation

4:36   Pounding repeated chords with theme below in cellos and basses

4:53   Rising scales lead to a fermata (hold)

5:12   Woodwinds play fragments of beginning of theme 1

5:54   Fanfare (theme 2) now returns in full orchestra

6:43   Woodwinds play beginning of theme 1 detached and in a minor key

VARIATION 3

7:23   Violins play beginning of theme 1 *fortissimo*

7:48   Woodwinds play middle of theme 1

7:58   Strings play end of theme 1

CODA

8:12	Tempo quickens as bassoons play reminiscence of beginning of theme 1
8:28	Violins play reminiscence of theme 2
8:37	Woodwinds play middle of theme 1
8:48	Strings play end of theme 1
9:09	Ends with repetitions of the rhythm of the very first measure of the movement

(Listening Exercise 27)

THIRD MOVEMENT: In the Classical period the third movement of a symphony or quartet was usually a graceful minuet and trio (see page 168). Haydn and his pupil Beethoven wanted to infuse this third movement generally with more life and energy, so they often wrote a faster, more rollicking piece and called it a scherzo, meaning "joke." There is nothing really humorous about the mysterious and sometimes threatening sound of the scherzo of Beethoven's Symphony No. 5, yet it is certainly far removed from the elegant world of the courtly minuet.

The formal plan of Beethoven's scherzo, **ABA'** is taken over from the ternary form of the minuet, as is the triple meter heard here. The scherzo, **A,** is in the tonic key of C minor, while the trio, **B,** is in C major. This conflict, or juxtaposition, of major and minor, of dark and light, is just one of several confrontations that is resolved in the course of the four-movement symphony.

The scherzo opens with a theme in the cellos and double basses. They creep up from the bottom of their register and pass the musical line on to the higher strings. Suddenly, the horns burst in with a second theme, one built on the short-short-short-long pattern of the first movement—evidently, that fateful motive has not yet been put to rest in Beethoven's mind. For the remainder of the scherzo **(A),** the two contrasting themes vie with each other for pride of place, with theme 2 winning out in the end. *the scherzo*

The trio begins true to the spirit of a scherzo—the theme is a comical bustle of sound in the cellos and basses. But the treatment of this theme soon becomes anything but humorous. It is worked out as a brief fugato* as the higher strings, one by one, present the subject (or theme). *the trio*

The scherzo does not so much reenter as it does sneak back in, played quietly by the cellos and double basses. And the powerful second theme has become merely a ghost of its former self, tiptoeing around in short, detached notes. Now comes one of Beethoven's greatest strokes of genius. He has decided to link the third and fourth movements by means of a musical bridge. He starts by creating a foreboding, eerie sound. The violins hold a single note as quietly as possible while the timpani beats ominously in the background. A three-note motive grows from the violins and is repeated over and over as a wave of sound begins to swell from the orchestra. With enormous force the wave finally crashes down, and from it emerges the triumphant beginning of the fourth movement—one of the most thrilling moments in all of music. *a bridge to the finale*

LISTENING GUIDE

Ludwig van Beethoven
Symphony No. 5 in C minor (1808)
Third movement, *Allegro* (fast)

CD 3/9
6-Tape 3B

SCHERZO

0:00	Cellos and basses creep in with theme 1 and pass it on to higher strings
0:08	Repeat
0:21	Horns enter with theme 2
0:38	Cellos and basses come back with theme 1
0:52	Crescendo
0:59	Full orchestra again plays theme 2 *fortissimo*
1:18	Development of theme 1
1:41	Ends with theme 2 *fortissimo*, then *piano*

TRIO

1:47	Cellos and basses present subject of fugato
	Violas and bassoons enter with the subject
	Second violins enter with the subject
	First violins enter with the subject
2:01 – 2:22	Repeat of these imitative entries
2:23 – 2:49	Subject enters imitatively again: cellos and basses, violas and bassoons, second violins, first violins, and then flutes are added
2:50 – 3:17	Subject enters imitatively again in the same instruments and the flutes extend it

SCHERZO

3:15	Quiet return of theme 1 in cellos and basses
3:24	Pizzicato (plucked) presentation of theme 1 in cellos accompanied by bassoons
3:36	Ghostlike return of theme 2 in short notes in winds and pizzicato in strings

BRIDGE TO FOURTH MOVEMENT

4:26	Long note held *pianissimo* in strings with timpani beating softly below
4:40	Repeating three-note pattern emerges in the first violins
5:00	Great crescendo leads to fourth movement

FOURTH MOVEMENT: When Beethoven arrived at the finale, he was faced with a nearly impossible task: How to write a conclusion that would lift the tension of the preceding musical events, yet provide an appropriate, substantive balance to the weighty first movement. He did so by fashioning a monumental work in sonata–allegro form, the longest movement of the symphony, and by bringing some unusual forces into play. To his orchestra he added three trombones, a contrabassoon (low bassoon), and a piccolo

FIGURE 11–6

Beethoven at work on the second movement of his Symphony No. 5. The many corrections in different colored inks and red pencil suggest the turmoil and constant evolution involved in Beethoven's creative process.

(high flute), the first time any of these instruments had been used in a symphony. He also wrote big, bold, and in most cases, triadic themes, assigning these, often as not, to the powerful brasses. It is these instruments and these themes, along with the final turn from C minor to C major, that cause the finale to project a strong feeling of optimism, a sense that a superhuman will has triumphed over adversity.

Although the finale is a model of sonata–allegro form, the unfolding of the form can be difficult to hear or follow. Beethoven has written a movement without seams. There are no big, obvious cadences that clearly mark off the various sections. The transition moves without pause into the second theme, the exposition into the development, the recapitulation into the coda. We can hardly miss the beginning of the recapitulation, however, because the composer has prepared it in a surprising way. In the retransition (the section that sets up the return of the first theme in the recapitulation), he brings back the ghostlike *pianissimo* scherzo theme of the third movement with its short–short–short–long rhythm. What is a theme from the third movement doing here in the fourth? Obviously, Beethoven wishes to bind tightly movements 3 and 4 as well as evoke again the fateful motive from the beginning of the symphony. Because of this *pianissimo* preparation, the *fortissimo* return of the first theme at the beginning of the recapitulation is unmistakable.

binding the movements

The lengthy coda, too, has its share of surprises including a change of tempo and a "false ending"—we hear what sound like final chords but instead the piece continues. In fact, there have been so many surprises in this astonishingly original symphony that when Beethoven finally reaches the end, he is compelled to write an exceptionally obvious and repetitious cadence to assure the skeptical listener that this is, in fact, the end.

LISTENING GUIDE

Ludwig van Beethoven
Symphony No. 5 in C minor (1808)
Fourth movement, *Allegro* (fast)

CD 3/10
6-Tape 3B

EXPOSITION

0:00   Full orchestra with prominent brasses plays first theme

0:36   Horns play transition theme

1:04   Strings play second theme

1:33   Full orchestra plays closing theme

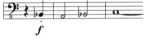

(Repeat of exposition omitted)

DEVELOPMENT

2:06   Loud string tremolo (fluttering)

2:11   Strings and woodwinds pass around fragments of second theme
         in different keys

2:36   Double basses begin to play countermelody against the second
         theme

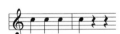

2:46   Trombones play countermelody

3:13   Woodwinds and brasses play countermelody above dominant
         pedal point in cellos and basses

3:30   Climax and pause on dominant triad

3:48   Ghostlike theme from the scherzo with four-note rhythm

RECAPITULATION

4:17   Full orchestra plays first theme *fortissimo*

4:54   Horns bring in transition theme

5:26   Strings play second theme

5:54   Woodwinds play closing theme

CODA

6:26   Violins play second theme

6:37   Brasses and woodwinds play countermelody

6:50   V–I, V–I chords sound like final cadence

6:59   Bassoons, horns, flutes, clarinets, and then piccolo continue with
         transition theme

7:27   Trill high in piccolo

7:50   Tempo changes to *presto* (very fast)

8:14   Brasses recall first theme but now twice as fast

8:21   V–I, V–I cadence followed by pounding tonic chord

Almost all the qualities we associate with Beethoven's heroic symphonic style are present in his Symphony No. 5. A single theme or short motive is presented and continually elaborated, modified, and developed. It may be fragmented or broken down to just a note or two in the process of development. Small, cell-like units are repeated over and over to build momentum. Long crescendos swell like tidal waves of sound. Climaxes are reached and a rhythmic motive or fragment of a theme is pounded incessantly. In this way, great tension and excitement are created. Extremes of expression, of range, and of mood are accommodated within a single movement. In the quiet string music of the *Andante* (second movement), for example, we are never far from an heroic brass fanfare. Everywhere there is a feeling of raw, elemental power pushed forward by a newly enlarged orchestra. No wonder that during World War II (1939–1945) both sides used the music of this symphony to symbolize "Victory."[†]

Beethoven's symphonic style

THE FINAL YEARS (1814–1827)

By 1814 Beethoven had become totally deaf and had withdrawn almost completely from society. His music, too, took on a more remote, inaccessible quality, placing heavy demands on both the performer and auditor. In these late works Beethoven requires the listener to connect musical ideas over long spans of time, to follow the variation of a theme when that variation has become quite remote from the original theme itself. Most of these late works are piano sonatas and string quartets—intimate, introspective chamber music. But two pieces, the Mass in D (*Missa solemnis*, 1823) and the Symphony No. 9 (1824), are large-scale compositions for full orchestra and chorus. In these works for larger forces, Beethoven seems again to wish to communicate directly to a broad spectrum of humanity.

Beethoven's Symphony No. 9, his last, was the first work in the history of this genre to include a chorus. It is as if the composer's need for expression in his final symphonic work was so great that the instruments of the orchestra alone were no longer sufficient. Something more was necessary: text and voices. And so they enter in the finale of this four-movement work. The text, *An die Freude (Ode to Joy)*, was written by the German poet Frederick Schiller in 1786. It is a hymn, in the spirit of the French Revolution, in honor of universal brotherhood, a theme that had been important to Beethoven since his earliest years. Beethoven set Schiller's text to a melody that has become well known to all of us as his *Ode to Joy*. (In recent times the tune has been popularized in a TV commercial, a movie score, as a Christmas song, and, more appropriately, as an anthem for the United Nations.) Beethoven intentionally constructed a melody that is folk song–like, even commonplace in shape, a fitting musical companion to a text extolling the commonality of mankind. (For a discussion of the structure of the melody, see page 28 and Listening Exercise 6.)

Symphony No. 9

Ode to Joy

[†]In Morse code short–short–short–long is the letter "V" as in "Victory."

EXAMPLE 11–8

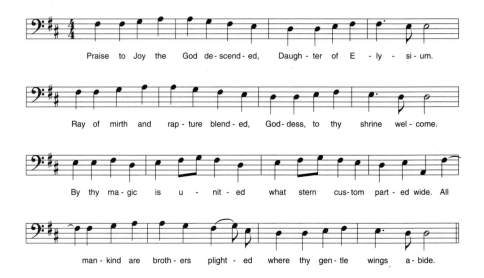

Praise to Joy the God de-scend-ed, Daugh-ter of E - ly - si - um.

Ray of mirth and rap-ture blend-ed, God-dess, to thy shrine wel-come.

By thy ma-gic is u – nit-ed what stern cus-tom part-ed wide. All

man-kind are broth-ers plight-ed where thy gen-tle wings a-bide.

In the course of this twenty-five-minute finale, the *Ode to Joy* serves as a theme for a magnificent set of variations which marches toward a grandiose climax. Beethoven pushes the voices to sing louder and louder, higher and higher, faster than they can enunciate the text. The instrumentalists, too, are driven by the *presto* tempo to go so quickly they can scarcely play the notes. All performers strain to exceed the limits of their physical abilities, to accomplish the impossible. The sound is not so much beautiful as it is overwhelming, for the chorus and orchestra speak as all humanity. Their message is Beethoven's message: great art can be achieved by a quest for fulfillment above mortal reach.

LISTENING EXERCISES

26

Ludwig van Beethoven   CD 3/6
Piano Sonata, Opus 27, No. 2, "Moonlight" (1801)   6–Tape 3A
Third movement, *Presto agitato* (fast and agitated)

In the finale of his "Moonlight" Sonata, Beethoven has written a virtuosic movement in sonata–allegro form that pushes the technical skills of the pianist to the limit. For this assignment, first read the discussion of the movement on page 216 of your text and listen to the piece while following the Listening Guide. Now listen to the movement again, perhaps several more times, and answer the following questions.

0:00–1:37 Exposition
1. Does the movement begin in C# major or C# minor? ——————
2. Is the tempo fast or slow? ——————————

3. (0:11) Is the first theme, part 2, played *piano* or *forte*? _____
4. (0:50) While the right hand executes these rapid scales, the left hand below adds a few:
   a. chords in syncopation   b. triplet arpeggios
5. The closing theme enters (1:04) and then is repeated (1:13). The repeat is:
   a. higher and louder   b. lower and softer

1:38–3:15   Now comes the repeat of the exposition. As you listen, check your answers.

3:16–4:20   Development
6. (3:16) Which theme is heard at the beginning of the development?
   a. the arpeggios of theme 1, part 1
   b. the repeating chords of the closing theme

3:26–3:50   Now the second theme begins to dominate the development.
7. (3:53–4:20) The retransition to the recapitulation has a special mood of its own. How would you describe it?
   a. loud and repetitious   b. quiet and pensive

4:21–5:51   Recapitulation

5:52–end   Coda
8. (5:58–6:09) Is there a *ritardando* (slow down) and pause at the end of the rising arpeggios? _____
9. (6:44–6:50) A rapidly rising scale leads to which of the following?
   a. a trill (rapid alternation of two notes)
   b. an ostinato bass
   c. a fugue
10. (7:20–7:27) Are the final arpeggios and chords in C# major or C# minor? _____

| 27 | Ludwig van Beethoven
Symphony No. 5 (1808)
Second movement, *Andante con moto* (progressing with movement) | CD 3/8
6–Tape 3B |

The slow second movement of Beethoven's Symphony No. 5 is in theme and variations form. Yet it differs from the examples of this form we have heard by Mozart and Haydn (see pages 176–181 and 196) in two respects. First, Beethoven uses two themes instead of just one. And second, the two themes do not come back each time in their complete form. Some parts of a theme are omitted entirely and others greatly expanded. Obviously, this is a more complex use of variation technique than we have previously experienced, one that asks more of you, the listener. Try to answer the questions below without recourse to the Listening Guide on page 224. If you get stuck, then have a look at it.

Themes

0:00   Violas and cellos play theme 1
0:54   Clarinets, bassoons, and violins play theme 2

1:16 Brasses play theme 2 in fanfare style
2:01 Variation 1 of theme 1
2:53 Variation 1 of theme 2
3:14 Brasses play theme 2 in fanfare style

1. (4:00) Variation 2 of _____ (which) theme?
2. (5:54) Variation 2 of _____ (which) theme?
3. (7:23) Variation 3 of _____ (which) theme?

8:12 Coda

4. Although at the outset both themes are allotted about the same amount of time, as the movement progresses the time devoted to each changes drastically. Which theme gradually gets *less* attention? _____ In what way does this occur? Specifically, is there more or less of theme 2 in variation 2 (4:00–7:22)? _____ Do you hear the brass fanfare in variation 3 (7:23–8:11)? _____ Do you hear it in the coda? _____

Now listen to the movement again and answer the following question about musical instruments.

5. The first time the brasses play the fanfare version of theme 2 (1:16), what does Beethoven write as counterpoint against it?
   a. rising scales in the woodwinds   b. triplets in the violins
6. At the beginning of variation 1 (2:01), the violas and cellos ornament theme 1 by means of rapidly moving notes. Which combination of instruments is used against the theme?
   a. clarinet and pizzicato violins   b. muted horns and trombones
7. In variation 1 the brasses return with the fanfare (3:14). Are the violins playing counterpoint against it? _____ Extra credit: Are the triplets still there? _____

KEY WORDS

"Eroica" Symphony	"Moonlight" Sonata	*Ode to Joy*
Heiligenstadt Testament		

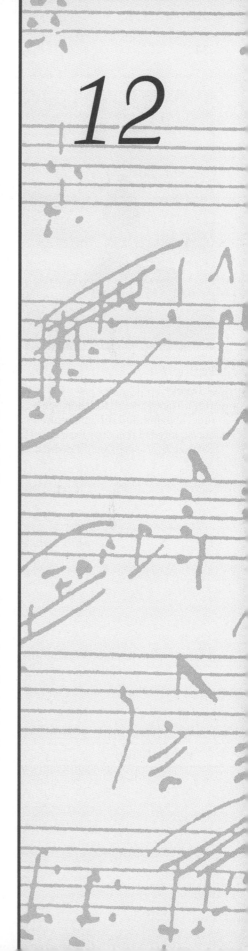

THE ROMANTIC SPIRIT (1820–1900)

12

T he mature music of Beethoven, with its powerful crescendos, pounding rhythms, imitations of nature, and larger, more colorful orchestra, announces the arrival of an important change in music in the first decades of the nineteenth century. This is the change from Classicism to Romanticism. It coincides with similar changes in style in the poetry, literature, and painting of the period. In all the arts revolutionary sentiments were in the air: a new desire for liberty, self-expression, bold action, passionate feeling, and a love of nature. And just as the impatient Beethoven finally cast off the wig and powdered hair of the eighteenth century, so now the formal constraints of the old Classical art were thrown aside.

R EVOLUTIONARY SENTIMENT AND ROMANTIC CREATIVITY

Romanticism is often defined as a revolt against the Classical adherence to reason, rules, forms, and traditions. Whereas artists of the eighteenth century sought to achieve unity, order, proportion, and a balance of form and content, those of the nineteenth century strove for self-expression, to communicate with passion no matter what sort of imbalance, contradiction, or formal inconsistency might result. If Classical architecture, painting, and music drew its inspiration from the monuments of ancient Greece and Rome, Romantic literature, poetry, painting, and music found creative encouragement in the newly proclaimed liberty of man and in the wonders of nature. The Romantic artist exalted instinctive feelings, human and natural, above all else. These were not the feelings of Beethoven's masses of his Ninth Symphony, however, but individual, personal, private feelings. Music and her sister arts now withdrew from Beethoven's vision of humanity. They became at the same time more intensely expressive, yet highly personal and introspective.

If there was a single feeling or sentiment that pervaded the Romantic era it was love. Indeed, love or "romance" is at the very heart of the word "Romantic." The loves of Romeo and Juliet and of Tristan and Isolde, for

FIGURE 12–1

A Traveler looking over a Sea of Fog (ca. 1818). The themes of isolation, solitude, oblivion, and sublime nature are explored in this early Romantic painting by Casper David Friedrich.

Romantic nature

the Romantic Wanderlust

Romantic fantasy

example, captured the imagination of the Romantic century. These were ardent tales in which desire, anguish, longing, and despair were felt far more powerfully than any enjoyment or happiness in love. The endless pursuit of love, the search for the unattainable, became an obsession which, when expressed as music, produced the sounds of longing and of yearning heard in so much of Romantic music. Berlioz, Liszt, and Wagner not only wrote about the pursuit of ideal love through their music but also lived this quest in their personal lives.

Yet love was only one of many emotions strongly felt by the Romantics. Despair, revenge, pride, frenzy, and heavenly exaltation were a few of the others they communicated effectively in their music and poetry. Classical music had, in general, exhibited only a narrow range of emotional expression. Romantic music, on the other hand, was marked by wide swings of mood, just as the composers themselves sometimes indulged in wild extremes of behavior. Just how the range of expression was broadened in Romantic music can be seen in the "expression marks" that came into being at this time: *expressivo* (expressively), *dolente* (sadly), *presto furioso* (fast and furiously), *con forza e passione* (with force and passion), *misterioso* (mysteriously), and *maestoso* (majestically). Although these are directives to the performer explaining how a passage is to be played, they also reveal what the composer felt about the music.

Feelings about nature also received unprecedented attention with the Romantics. Nature came to be seen as a source of knowledge and goodness, of certainty and perfection, a reflection of God, of the Eternal Mind. Romantic painters like J. M. W. Turner (1775–1851) and Caspar David Friedrich (1774–1840), stood in awe of her powerful, mysterious forces (see Fig. 12–1). The English Romantic poets John Keats (1795–1821), William Wordsworth (1770–1850), and Lord Byron (1778–1824) communed with her verdant woods, dissolving mists, and tender twilights. Musicians, too, paid homage to nature through sounds that sought to capture her lyrical song, spacious majesty, and destructive fury. Beethoven's "Pastoral" Symphony (Symphony No. 6), with its bird calls and summer storm, was the first of these evocative pieces. Schubert's "Trout" Quintet, Liszt's *Lake of Wallenstadt*, Schumann's "Spring" Symphony, and Strauss's "Alpine" Symphony are just a few of the musical works that continue the tradition.

Associated with this desire to be at one with nature was a passion for travel, what the Germans call a *Wanderlust*. Far-off places and people stirred the imagination of the Romantics. The German composer Felix Mendelssohn (1809–1847) journeyed to Italy, to Scotland, and to the Hebrides Islands to find inspiration for his symphonies and overtures. The English poet Byron sailed to Greece and Turkey in order to infuse his art with a sense of the exotic.

Fantasy, imagination, dreams, even nightmares—this was the creative stuff of the Romantics. Composers gave free rein to their musical imagination in countless pieces called "fantasies" and "romances." Writers like the brothers (Jakob and Wilhelm) Grimm wrote fairy tales whose themes expressed the dark side of human nature. Other authors were swept away by the bizarre, the macabre, and the demonic. Johann von Goethe's *Faust* (1808 and 1831), perhaps the most influential work of the nineteenth century, tells the tale of a scholar who sells his soul to the devil, finding beauty in

Lord Byron's *Know You the Land*

George Gordon, Lord Byron, was the epitome of the Romantic hero: dashing, passionate, self-absorbed, idealistic, and guilt ridden (he had had an affair with his half sister). He climbed the Swiss Alps, swam the Hellespont

A portrait of the English poet, Lord Byron, in the dress of an Albanian adventurer.

(separating Europe from Asia Minor), and died, at age thirty-six, fighting for Greek independence from Turkish rule. His poem *Know You the Land* (from *The Bride of Abydos: A Turkish Tale*) possesses several of the sensibilities dear to the hearts of the Romantics: the colors and sounds of nature, the sights and perfumes of the exotic East, and a hint of forbidden love.

Know you the land of the cedar and vine,
Where the flowers ever blossom, the beams ever shine;
Where the light wings of Zephyr, oppress'd with perfume,
Wax fain o'er the gardens of Gul in her bloom;
Where the citron and olive are fairest of fruit,
And the voice of the nightingale never is mute:
Where the tints of the earth, and the hues of the sky,
In colour though varied, in beauty may vie,
And the purple of Ocean is deepest in dye;
Where the virgins are soft as the roses they twine,
And all, save the spirit of man, is divine?

from Lord Byron's *Know You the Land* (1813)

horror and pain. In 1818 Mary Shelley (1797–1851) published her novel *Frankenstein,* and in 1831 Victor Hugo (1802–1885) gave to his readers *The Hunchback of Notre Dame.* In music, as we shall see, magic bullets (in Weber's *Der Freischutz,* 1821), an evil elfking (in Schubert's *Erlkönig,* 1815), and a witches' black Mass (in Berlioz's *Symphonie fantastique,* 1830) reflect the attraction of the supernatural for the Romantic temperament.

As the many parallel developments in music and literature attest, word and sound were never more closely allied than during the nineteenth century. The poets viewed music as the womb from which sprang all true art; tones were capable of expressing emotions and feelings more powerfully, more subtly, more perfectly than could mere words. For their part, composers were as much enraptured by literature as they were by music—Berlioz, Schumann, Liszt, and Wagner were writers of poetry and aesthetic criticism as well as music. They sought to bring external stimuli—poetic and literary themes—into their musical creations as if thereby to double the emotional impact of pure sound. Byron, Goethe, and, above all, Shakespeare struck resonant chords with Romantic composers who turned the poetry and plays of these writers into overtures, symphonic poems, and operas. Now for the first time Shakespeare became widely read on the Continent, in part because of the publication of an authoritative German translation of his works in 1801. Rare was the Romantic composer who failed to capture in music the spirit of one of the Bard's great plays.

literature and music

FIGURE 12–2

Witches' Sabbath by Francisco de Goya. Images of the fantastic and demonic were created not only by the early Romantic painters such as Goya but by musicians as well. In his *Symphonie fantastique* the composer Hector Berlioz wrote a final movement which he entitled *Witches' Sabbath* (see page 258).

The Musician as Artist, Music as Art

Besides fostering a tight bond between sound and word, the spirit of Romanticism encouraged a new attitude about music as an art. The forceful pens of musician-writers like Berlioz, Schumann, and Wagner persuaded the public that the composer was no longer a mere craftsman but an artist, someone above an ordinary mortal. Bach had been a municipal civil servant, devoted and dutiful, to the town government in Leipzig. Haydn and Mozart served, and were treated, as domestics in the homes of the great lords of Europe. But Beethoven began to break the chains of submission. He was the first to demand, and receive, the respect and admiration due a great creative spirit. Ultimately, Franz Liszt and Richard Wagner, as much through their literary works as through their musical compositions, caused the public to view the artist as a sort of demigod, a prophet able to inspire the audience through the creation of music that was morally uplifting as well as beautiful. They fostered the idea that the artist was a superior being, endowed with exceptional powers of expression. Never was the position of the creative musician loftier than in the mid-nineteenth century.

Just as the musician changed from craftsman to artist in the public mind at this time, so the music he or she produced changed from handicraft to work of art. Classical music had been created for the immediate gratification of patron and audience, with little thought given to its lasting value. With the mature Beethoven and the early Romantics, this attitude began to change. Symphonies, quartets, and piano sonatas sprang to life, not to give immediate pleasure to a listener, but to gratify a deep-seated creative urge within the composer. They became extensions of the artist's personality. These works might not be understood by the creator's contemporaries, as was true of the late piano sonatas of Beethoven and the orchestral works of Hector Berlioz, for example, but they would be understood by posterity, by future generations of listeners. The idea of "art for art's sake"—art free of all functional concerns—was born of the Romantic spirit.

The new exalted position of the composer and his work of art soon brought a more serious tone to the concert hall. Before 1800 people gathered to listen to music more for the opportunity for social interchange than for the chance to enjoy an aesthetic experience. They talked, drank, ate, played cards, flirted, and wandered about. By the 1830s, however, this had changed. With the revered figure of the Romantic composer-performer now before them, the members of the audience sat in respectful silence. The work of art was surrounded by a sacred aura of devotion and absolute attention (see cover). More was expected of the listener, partly because symphonies and sonatas were longer and more complex. But the listener, in turn, expected more from the music: not mere entertainment but an emotionally satisfying encounter that would leave the attentive person exhausted, yet somehow purified and uplifted by the artistic experience.

concerts assume a more serious tone

The Style of Romantic Music

The Romantic spirit rebelled against Classical ideals in ways that allow us to generalize these two artistic movements as pairs of opposites: rational against irrational, intellect opposed to heart, conformity versus originality, and the masses in contradistinction to the individual. Yet in purely musical terms, the works of the Romantic composers represent not so much a revolution against Classical ideals as an evolution that goes beyond them. Romantic music is an expansion and amplification of the style created by the Classical masters. The Romantics introduced no new musical forms and only one or two new genres. Instead, Romantic composers took the musical materials received from the hands of Haydn, Mozart, and young Beethoven and made them more intensely expressive, more original, more personal, and, in some cases, more bizarre.

Romantic Melody

The Romantic period witnessed the apotheosis of melody. Melodies become broad, powerful streams of sound intended to sweep the listener away. They go beyond the neat symmetrical units of two plus two, four plus four, inherent in the Classical style. They become longer, rhythmically more flexible, and more irregular in shape. At the same time, Romantic melodies continue a trend that developed in the late eighteenth century in which themes became vocal in conception, more singable. Melodies of Chopin, Tchaikovsky, and Rachmaninoff have been turned into popular songs in our own day. Similarly, today's popular collections of "40 All-Time Favorite Classical Melodies" draw primarily from the symphonies, sonatas, and operas of the Romantic period, simply because these themes are so profoundly expressive. They sigh and lament. They grow and become ecstatic. They start haltingly and then build to a grandiose climax, sublime and triumphant. We will soon have ample opportunity to hear the sumptuous melodic creations of Berlioz and Brahms, of Verdi and Tchaikovsky, of Wagner and Mahler, to name only a few of the best composers of Romantic melody.

Colorful Harmony

Part of the emotional intensity of Romantic music is generated by a new, more colorful harmony. Classical music had, in the main, made use of chords built only on the seven notes of the major or minor scale—the so-called diatonic* notes of the scale (see page 27). Romantic composers went farther by constructing chords on the five additional notes within the full twelve-note chromatic scale—the so-called chromatic* notes. This gave more colors to their harmonic palette. It also gave fluency to the sound as chords and inner voices glide smoothly to notes only a half step away. Using chromatic chords similarly made it easier for the composer to modulate to distant keys, to carry the music tonally away to some far-off, exotic land of six flats or seven sharps.

more chromaticism

The rich, lush sounds of the Romantics are also created by setting up novel relationships between chords. In the Baroque and Classical periods, harmony often moved along in chord progressions in which the roots of the chords were an interval of a fifth apart. Now chords only a third apart are frequently set in close proximity, and these can require radically different key signatures*—a harmony with four sharps might be followed immediately by one with four flats, for example. The striking sound that results from

bold chord progressions

these unusual relationships is appropriate for music that seeks to express a wider range of feeling.

more dissonance

Finally, much of the sound of pain and anguish that we hear in Romantic music comes about because of a greater use of dissonance. Dissonant notes are not only more numerous but they are held for longer periods of time as well. Since dissonance always wants to move, or resolve, to consonance, the delay of the resolution produces a feeling of anxiety, longing, and searching, all sentiments appropriate for music that often deals with the subject of love.

Here are three examples that show aspects of the new, expressive harmony of the Romantics as typified in the Nocturne in C# Minor of the composer Frédéric Chopin (1810–1849). You undoubtedly won't hear this music simply by looking at it. To hear it you will have to turn to your CDs (disc 4, track 8) and tapes (6: 4B/2: 2A). You can, however, visualize here some of its inner workings—the chords a third apart, the chromatic lines, and the long-held dissonance—so that when you hear the richness and poignance of Romantic music, you will have a sense of how these new sounds are created.

EXAMPLE 12–1: bold harmonies heard at 2:43

Another splendid example of the richness of Romantic harmony can be heard at the end of Richard Strauss's orchestral song *Red Glow of Sunset* (CD 5/7, 6–Tape 5B).

EXAMPLE 12–2: chromaticism heard at 3:12

EXAMPLE 12–3: dissonance heard at 4:58

Expressive Tone Colors, Greater Volume

From the listener's perspective, perhaps the most striking aspect of Romantic music is the color and sheer volume of the sound. It is this, more than any other quality, that makes Romantic music easily distinguishable from the music of earlier periods. The orchestra now becomes larger and more varied, the piano bigger and more powerful. Composers demanded, and received, musical forces equal to the task of expressing the extremes of emotion, changing moods, and extravagant gestures of the Romantic spirit.

The Industrial Revolution brought with it mechanical innovations that gave several woodwind and brass instruments a better sound and made them easier to play. The wood of the flute was replaced by silver, and the instrument was supplied with a new fingering system which added to its agility. Similarly, the trumpet and French horn were provided with valves which improved technical facility and accuracy of pitch in all keys. These brass instruments were now capable of playing intricate, chromatic melodies as well as providing the traditional backdrop of sonic support for the rest of the orchestra. The horn, in particular, became an object of special affection during the Romantic period. Its rich, dark tone and its traditional association with the hunt—and by extension nature—made it the Romantic instrument par excellence. Composers often called on a solo horn when they wished to express something mysterious or distant.

Besides improvements to existing instruments, several new instruments were added to the symphony orchestra during the nineteenth century. We have seen how Beethoven brought the piccolo (a high flute), the trombone, and the contrabassoon (a bass bassoon) into the orchestra in his famous Symphony No. 5 (1808). In 1830 Hector Berlioz went even farther, requiring an ophicleide* (an early form of the tuba), an English horn* (a low-pitched oboe), a cornet*, and two harps in his *Symphonie fantastique*. Berlioz, the embodiment of the Romantic spirit, had a typically grandiose notion of what the ideal symphony orchestra should contain. He wanted no fewer than 467 instrumentalists including 120 violins, 40 violas, 45 cellos, 35 double basses, and 30 harps. Needless to say, such a gigantic instrumental force was never assembled, but Berlioz's utopian vision indicates the direction in which Romantic composers were headed. By the second half of the nineteenth century, orchestras with nearly a hundred players were not uncommon. Compare the instruments and their number required for a typical eighteenth-century performance of Mozart's G minor symphony (1788) with the symphony orchestra called on to play the Prelude (overture) to Richard Wagner's *Tristan und Isolde* (1865) (Fig. 12–4). Our ears today have become so desensitized by constant exposure to electronically amplified sound that we can hardly imagine the overwhelming impact that the newly enlarged orchestra had on listeners in the nineteenth century.

The piano, too, underwent a wholesale transformation during the first half of the nineteenth century, also made possible by the improved technology of the Industrial Revolution. The older wooden frame was replaced by a cast-iron one which allowed for greater tension on the strings, which, in turn, necessitated thicker strings—all leading to an instrument with greatly increased power. At the same time the hammers were covered with felt which made the instrument "sing" with a mellow tone rather than softly

FIGURE 12–3

A fanciful illustration of the impact of the industrial revolution and the steam engine on the nineteenth-century symphony orchestra.

larger orchestras

bigger pianos

FIGURE 12–4

Orchestral forces needed for performances of Mozart's Symphony No. 40 (1788) and Wagner's Prelude to *Tristan und Isolde* (1865). Listening Exercise 28 asks you to compare your responses to each of these two orchestral works.

MOZART (1788)	WAGNER (1865)
1 flute	1 piccolo
2 oboes	3 flutes
2 clarinets	2 oboes
2 bassoons	1 English horn
2 French horns	2 clarinets
1st violins (8)[†]	1 bass clarinet
2nd violins (8)	3 bassoons
violas (4)	4 French horns
cellos (4)	3 trumpets
double basses (3)	3 trombones
	1 tuba
Total: 36	1st violins (18)[†]
	2nd violins (16)
	violas (12)
	cellos (10)
	double basses (8)
	timpani
	triangle
	cymbals
	harp
	Total: 91

† Number of string players estimated according to standards of the period

FIGURE 12–5

The grand piano made by C. Bechstein (Berlin, 1864) at which Richard Wagner composed the opera *Tristan und Isolde* (1865), now preserved in the Yale University Collection of Musical Instruments. It is a vastly larger and more powerful instrument than Mozart had at his disposal (see page 154).

"ping" as had the older pianos of Mozart's day. The range of the instrument was extended both high and low, approaching the eight octaves of our modern piano. Finally, a **sustaining pedal** was added which allowed the strings of one chord to hold on into the next. The blurred effect that resulted was especially useful when creating, for example, the dreamy mood of Schumann's *Träumerei* (*Dreaming*, see page 266) or the romantic haze of a Chopin nocturne (see page 269).

With its increased power, range, and capacity for special effects, the piano of the nineteenth century became a worthy rival of the orchestra. Indeed, many popular orchestral works—symphonies, overtures, concertos—were transcribed, or arranged, so they could be played as piano solos at home. In the days before radio and the phonograph, the **piano transcription** was the principal means by which the listening public became familiar with the major works composed for orchestra.

Technical Virtuosity

Appropriate for an era that glorified the individual, the nineteenth century was the age of the solo virtuoso. Of course, there had been instrumental virtuosos before—Bach on the organ, Mozart on the piano, to name just two—but now enormous energy was expended by many musicians to raise their

FIGURES 12–6 AND 12–7

(left) Niccolò Paganini (right) *Pagani-ni and the Witches,* a lithograph by an unknown author. Paganini's extraordinary powers on the violin led some to believe he was in league with the devil. The fourth string of his violin was said to be made of the intestine of his mistress whom he had murdered with his own hands. None of this was true, and Paganini undertook several libel suits to disprove it.

performing skills to an unprecedented height. Pianists and violinists in particular practiced long hours just on technical exercises—arpeggios, tremolos, trills, and scales played in thirds, sixths, and octaves—to develop wizardlike hand speed on their instrument. Naturally, some of what they played for the public was lacking in musical substance, tasteless show pieces designed to appeal immediately to the large audiences that packed the ever-larger concert halls. Pianists developed tricks of playing to make it appear they had more hands than two. Franz Liszt (1811–1886) sometimes played at the keyboard with a lighted cigar between his fingers. The Italian Niccolò Paganini (1782–1840) secretly tuned the four strings of his violin in ways that would allow him to negotiate with ease extraordinarily difficult passages (see Example 12–4). If one of his strings broke, he could play with just three; if three broke, he could continue apace with just one. The era of the musical showman had arrived. Fortunately, as we shall see, some of these showmen were also gifted composers.

EXAMPLE 12–4: Paganini, Caprice, Opus 1, No. 5

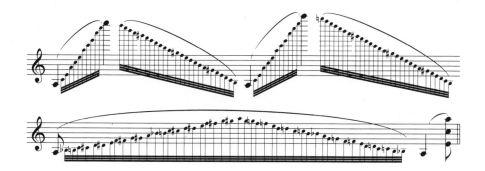

Forms: Monumental and Miniature

The musical forms that had earlier served Haydn and Mozart continued to satisfy the needs of the nineteenth-century composer. Sonata–allegro form, in particular, remained useful because its flexible format could accommodate any number of individual solutions. What developed, then, was not a rush to invent new forms but a trend to extend the existing ones. As composers laid out broad, sweeping melodies, indulged in gigantic crescendos, and reveled in the luxurious sound of the enlarged orchestra, the length of individual movements increased dramatically. Mozart's G minor symphony (1788) lasts about twenty minutes, depending on the tempo of the performance. But Brahm's Symphony No. 1 (1876) takes nearly forty-five minutes, and Mahler's Symphony No. 2 (1894) nearly an hour and a half. Perhaps the longest of all musical works is Richard Wagner's four-opera *Ring* cycle (1853–1876), which continues some seventeen hours during the course of four evenings. In these extended visions the Romantic composer seems to be saying along with the poet: "Romanticism is beauty without bounds—the beautiful infinite."

colossal symphonies

Yet, paradoxically, Romantic composers were fascinated by miniature forms as well. In brief works of a scant minute or two, they tried to capture the essence of one single mood, sentiment, or emotion. Such a miniature was called a **character piece.** It was usually written for the piano and often made use of simple binary **(AB)** or ternary **(ABA)** form. Because the character piece passes by in a twinkling of an eye, it was sometimes given a whimsical title such as bagatelle (a trifle), humoresque, arabesque, musical moment, caprice, intermezzo, or impromptu. Schubert, Schumann, Chopin, Liszt, Brahms, and Tchaikovsky all enjoyed creating these musical miniatures, perhaps as antidotes to their lengthy symphonies and concertos.

brief character pieces

N EW GENRES: THE SYMPHONIC POEM AND THE ART SONG

The Classical genres of the symphony, concerto, string quartet, piano sonata, and opera remained fashionable, though somewhat altered in appearance, throughout the nineteenth century. The symphony, as we have seen, now grows in length, embodying the widest possible range of expression, while the concerto becomes increasingly virtuosic, as an heroic soloist does battle against an orchestral mass. In addition, two new genres of music are created during the Romantic century, specifically, the symphonic poem and the art song.

The advent of the symphonic poem (discussed shortly) is tied to the broad development of program music generally in the nineteenth century. **Program music** is a piece of instrumental music, usually for symphony orchestra, that seeks to recreate in sound the events and emotions portrayed in some extramusical source: a story, a play, an historical event, or even a painting. The theory of program music rests on the obvious fact that specific kinds of music can evoke particular feelings and associations. A lyrical melody may recall memories of love, harshly dissonant chords may create a sense of conflict, rapidly flowing notes may produce a vision of a mountain stream, distant trumpet calls may suggest the imminent arrival of a hero. The urge to make music tell a story or play out a theatrical drama is a natural development in the nineteenth century, given the literary tenor of the age.

program music

Some Romantic composers, notably Johannes Brahms (1833–1897) and Anton Bruckner (1824–1896), resisted the allure of program music and continued to write what came to be called **absolute music**—symphonies, sonatas, quartets, and other instrumental music without extramusical or programmatic references. But most composers succumbed to the temptation to make their instrumental works take on an overtly pictorial or narrative character, to depict a scene or recount a story. The programmatic influence crept into established genres like the overture and symphony. It also gave rise to an entirely new genre, the symphonic poem. The principal kinds of nineteenth-century program music can be defined as follows:

Symphonic poem (also called the tone poem*): A one-movement work for orchestra that gives musical expression to the emotions and events associated with a story, play, political occurrence, personal experience, or encounter with nature. It is usually a lengthy piece composed in any one of several forms including sonata–allegro, theme and variations, and rondo. Examples include Liszt's *Les Préludes* (1854), Modest Musorgsky's *Night on Bald Mountain* (1867), Tchaikovsky's *Romeo and Juliet* (1869), and Richard Strauss's *Don Juan* (1888).

Program symphony: A symphony with the usual three, four, or five movements, but now the individual movements together tell or depict a succession of specific events or scenes drawn from some extramusical work or story. Examples include Berlioz's *Symphonie fantastique* (1830) and Liszt's "Faust" Symphony (1857).

Overture (to an opera or a play): A one-movement work, usually in sonata–allegro form, which foretells in music the essential dramatic events that will follow in an opera or a play. Many overtures became popular with the listening public and came to be performed by themselves. Examples include Rossini's Overture to his opera *William Tell* (1829) and Mendelssohn's Overture to Shakespeare's play *A Midsummer Night's Dream* (1826).

Concert overture: Similar to the overture but *not* designed to precede an opera or play; thus, an independent one-movement work of programmatic content originally intended for the concert hall. Examples include Brahms's *Academic Festival Overture* (1880) and Tchaikovsky's *1812 Overture* (1880). In point of fact, there is little difference between the symphonic poem and the concert overture. Both are one-movement programmatic works intended for the concert hall.

Incidental music: Music to be inserted between the acts or during important scenes of a play to add an extra dimension to the drama. Examples include Mendelssohn's incidental music to Shakespeare's *A Midsummer Night's Dream* (1843) and Edvard Grieg's music to Henrik Ibsen's play *Peer Gynt* (1875).

About 1850 Franz Liszt, a leading advocate of program music, said that an explicit program gave the composer "a means by which to protect the listener against a wrong poetical interpretation and to direct his attention to the poetical idea of the whole." Soon we will hear and discuss three imaginative examples of program music: Berlioz's *Symphonie fantastique* (a program symphony), Mendelssohn's Overture to *A Midsummer Night's Dream* (an over-

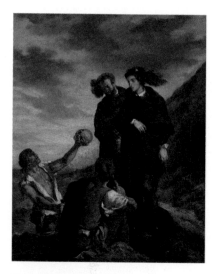

FIGURE 12–8

The nineteenth-century fascination with Shakespeare can be seen in the works of the painter Eugène Delacroix who recreated scenes from *Romeo and Juliet, Hamlet,* and *Macbeth.* Here Hamlet and Horatio gaze on the skull of the late, lamented Yorick in the famous graveyard scene of *Hamlet.*

types of program music

ture to a play), and Tchaikovsky's *Romeo and Juliet* (a symphonic poem). You will be able then to judge whether the existence of a program makes the composer's musical poetry easier to follow and increases the enjoyment of listening.

The other new musical genre that flourished in the nineteenth century was the art song. An **art song** is simply a piece for solo voice and piano accompaniment with high artistic aspirations. Of course, there had been songs of artistic merit for voice and accompanying instrument since the Middle Ages. But one of the hallmarks of the Romantic movement, as we have seen, was a quickening interest in literature and especially in poetry. The Romantic poets like Wordsworth, Keats, Shelley, and Byron burst upon the English scene in the early 1800s, and they had their counterparts in Germany in the person of the great Goethe and the gifted Heinrich Heine (1797–1856). Literally thousands of odes, sonnets, stanzas, ballads, and romances poured from their pens and those of lesser talent. Swept up in this new-found enthusiasm for poetry, composers set many of these texts for voice and piano, believing that music could intensify poetic sentiments by expressing things words alone could not. Because the art song was cultivated mainly in German-speaking lands, the genre is also called the **Lied** (plural **Lieder**), German for "song." The first important composer of the *Lied* was Franz Schubert (1797–1828), and it is to his music and that of the other early Romantics that we now turn.

LISTENING EXERCISE

| 28 | Comparing Orchestral Works of the Classical and Romantic Periods |

Listen again to the first movement of Mozart's Symphony No. 40 in G minor (1788) (CD 2/15; 6–Tape 2B; 2–Tape 1B) and compare it with the Prelude to Richard Wagner's opera *Tristan und Isolde* (1865) (CD 4/12; 6–Tape 4B).

1. Which work has a greater range of dynamic expression (louds and softs)? _____

2. Which work uses a larger, more colorful orchestra? _____

3. Which work has a faster tempo, or pace, to it? _____

4. Which work is more sectional? That is to say, which work has sections that are clearly different in mood, style, and function, one from another?

   _____

5. Which work is introspective in that it continually repeats and turns back upon itself? _____

6. Which work is more progressive in that it moves purposefully and without delay from one section to another? _____

7. Does Mozart make use of trumpets? _____ If not, why not? (See page 191.)

8. Does Wagner have his brasses introduce and carry the melodies or merely support and amplify the strings and woodwinds?

   _____

9. In different ways both Mozart and Wagner wish to express passion in their respective compositions. Describe how the passion, or intensity of feeling, is different in the two works.

   _____

   _____

   _____

10. How does each composer create his special sort of passion? In specific terms, describe what each does in his music to make you feel the way you do about his music.

    _____

    _____

    _____

    _____

KEY WORDS

absolute music	*Lied*	sustaining pedal
art song	overture	symphonic poem
character piece	piano transcription	tone poem
concert overture	program music	
incidental music	program symphony	

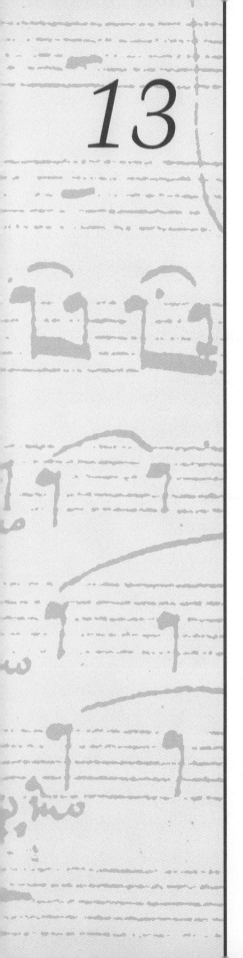

13

THE EARLY ROMANTICS

The decade 1803–1813 was perhaps the most auspicious in the history of music. In this short span of time were born the composers Hector Berlioz (1803), Felix Mendelssohn (1809), Frédéric Chopin (1810), Robert Schumann (1810), Franz Liszt (1811), Giuseppe Verdi (1813), and Richard Wagner (1813). Add to this the shining figure of Franz Schubert (born 1797) and this brilliant galaxy of musical geniuses is complete. We call them Romantics because they were part of, indeed they created, the Romantic movement in music. But with the possible exception of Mendelssohn, they were very unconventional people. Their lives typify all that we have come to associate with the Romantic spirit: self-expression, passion, excess, the love of nature and literature, as well as a certain selfishness, irresponsibility, and even a bit of lunacy. Not only did they create great art but life, and how they lived it, became an art.

THE ART SONG

The genre of the art song, or *Lied*, for solo voice and piano became a popular type of musical expression during the early 1800s. The enormous outpouring of the Romantic poets was matched by the creative enthusiasm of the Romantic composers who set hundreds of ballads, odes, and romances to music. Franz Schubert was the greatest of these composers. His special talent was to fashion music that captures both the spirit and detail of the text, creating a sensitive mood painting in which the voice and accompaniment express every nuance of the poem. Each song is a unique, self-contained, artistic experience.

Franz Schubert (1797–1828)

Franz Schubert was born in Vienna in 1797. Among the great Viennese masters—Haydn, Mozart, Beethoven, Schubert, Brahms, and Mahler—only he was native-born to the city. Schubert's father was a schoolteacher, and the son, too, was groomed for that profession. Yet the boy's obvious musical talent made it imperative that he also have music lessons, so his father taught him to play the violin and his older brother, the piano. At the age of eleven Schubert was admitted as a choirboy in the emperor's chapel, and this simultaneously allowed him to enroll in the excellent boarding school associated with the court. Proximity to the royal palace brought young Schubert into contact with Antonio Salieri, erstwhile rival of Mozart and still imperial court composer (see page 161). He began to study composition with Salieri in 1810. Soon Schubert was composing his own musical works at an astonishing rate.

After his voice changed in 1812, young Franz left the court chapel school and enrolled in a teacher's college. He had been spared compulsory military service because he was below the minimum height of five feet and his sight so poor that he was compelled to wear the spectacles now familiar from his portraits (Fig. 13-1). By 1815 he had become a teacher at his father's primary school. But he found teaching demanding and tedious and so, after three unpleasant years, Schubert abandoned this profession to give himself over wholly to music.

"You lucky fellow; I really envy you! You live a life of sweet, precious freedom, can give free rein to your musical genius, can express your thoughts in any way you like." This was Schubert's brother's view of the composer's newfound freedom. But as many Romantics would find, the reality was harsher than the ideal. Aside from some small income he earned from the sale of a few songs, he lacked a means of support. Schubert, unlike Beethoven, kept no company with aristocrats and thus received no patronage from them. Instead, he lived a Bohemian life, helped along by the generosity of his friends with whom he often lodged when he was broke. His mornings were consumed passionately composing music; his afternoons were passed in cafes discussing literature and politics; and his evenings were often spent playing his songs and dances before friends and admirers.

While Schubert was coming to his artistic maturity, the era of the great aristocratic salon was drawing to an end. Its place, as a focus for artistic expression was taken by the middle-class parlor or living room. Here in less pretentious surroundings, groups of men and women with a common interest in music, the novel, drama, or poetry would meet to read and hear all that was new in these arts. The gatherings at which Schubert appeared, and at which only his compositions were played, were called **Schubertiades** by his friends. It was in small, purely private assemblies such as these (Fig. 13-2), not in large public concerts, that most of his best songs were first performed.

In 1822 tragedy struck the composer: He contracted syphilis. During the years that remained before his premature death in 1828, he created some of his greatest works: the song cycles *Die Schöne Müllerin* (*The Pretty Maid of the Mill*, 1823) and *Winterreise* (*Winter Journey*, 1827), the "Wanderer" Fantasy for piano (1822), and the great C major Symphony (1828). Yet despite his struggle, the ravages of the disease affected his creative output. For example, the sensitive composer apparently could not endure the psychological pain he associated with the sounds of his Symphony in B minor, the so-called Unfinished Symphony; he wrote the first and second movements in the fateful year 1822, but then stopped work on it completely. In 1827 Schubert

Figure 13–1

Franz Schubert

a Bohemian life

FIGURE 13–2

A Schubertiade as depicted in water colors in 1821. The composer, seated at the piano, entertains his friends.

premature death

Schubert's Lieder *and song cycles*

served as one of the torchbearers at Beethoven's funeral. The next year, he too was dead, the youngest of the great composers.

In his brief life of thirty-one years, Franz Schubert wrote eight symphonies, fifteen string quartets, twenty-one piano sonatas, seven Masses for chorus and orchestra, and four operas—a sizable *oeuvre* by any standards. Yet in his day Schubert was known almost exclusively as a writer of art songs. Indeed, he composed more than six hundred works of this genre, many of them minor masterpieces. In a few cases, Schubert chose to set several texts together in a series. In so doing he created what is called a **song cycle**—a collection of individual songs that tell a story or treat a single theme. *The Pretty Maid of the Mill* (twenty songs) and *Winter Journey* (twenty-four songs), both of which relate the sad consequences of unsuccessful love, are Schubert's two great song cycles.

ERLKING (1815)

To gain an idea of Schubert's extraordinary musical talent, we need only to listen to his song *Erlkönig (Erlking)* written when he was just seventeen. The text itself is a ballad—a dramatic story told in alternating narrative verse and dialogue—from the pen of the famous poet Goethe. It relates the tale of the evil King of the Elves and his quest for the soul of a young boy, for legend had it that whosoever was touched by the King of the Elves would die. According to the account of one of Schubert's friends, the composer was reading a book of Goethe's poetry, pacing back and forth in his room. Suddenly, he sprang to the piano and, as fast as he could write, set the entire ballad to music. From there Schubert and his friend hastened to the composer's college to play it for a few kindred spirits. In his lifetime *Erlking* became Schubert's best-known song, one of the few that brought him any money.

FIGURE 13–3

A contemporary painting of the Erlking legend, showing the evil king, the father and son, and the king's comely daughters.

The opening line of the poem sets the frightful, nocturnal scene: "Who rides so late through night and wind?" With his feverish son cradled in his arms, a father rides at breakneck speed to an inn to save the child. Schubert captures both the general sense of terror in the scene and the detail of the galloping horse; he creates an accompanying figure in the piano that pounds on relentlessly just as fast as the pianist can make it go:

EXAMPLE 13–1

The specter of death, the Erlking, beckons gently to the boy. He does so in seductively sweet tones, in a melody with the gentle lilt of a popular tune:

EXAMPLE 13–2

(Thou dearest boy, come go with me!)

The frightened boy cries out to his father in an agitated, then chromatic line:

EXAMPLE 13–3

(Dear father, my father, say, did'st thou not hear the Erlking whisper promises in my ear?)

This cry is heard again and again in the course of the song, each time at a successively higher pitch and with increasingly dissonant harmonies. In this way the music mirrors the growing terror of the boy. The father tries to calm him and does so in low tones that are steady, stable, and repetitive. Thus, each of the three characters of the story is portrayed with a specific musical quality. This is musical characterization at its finest, the melody and accompaniment not only support the text but intensify and enrich it as well. Suddenly, the end is reached. The hand of the Erlking has touched his victim. The accompaniment figure is abruptly choked off as the narrator announces with controlled emotion: "But in his arms, lo! his child lay dead!"

musical characterization

LISTENING GUIDE

Franz Schubert
Art song, *Erlking* (1815)

CD 4/1
6–Tape 4A
2–Tape 2A

0:00	Introduction by piano accompaniment; pounding triplets in the right hand and an ominous minor motive in the left		

Narrator

0:19		Wer reitet so spät durch Nacht und Wind? Es ist der Vater mit seinem Kind. Er hat den Knaben wolh in dem Arm, er fasst ihn sicher, er hält ihn warm.	Who rides there so late through night so wild? A loving father with his child. He clasp'd his boy close with his fond arm, and closer, closer to him warm.

Father

0:52		"Mein Sohn, was birgst du so bang dein Gesicht?"	"Dear son, what makes thy sweet face grow so white?"

Son

1:00	With agitated leaps	"Siehst, Vater, du den Erlkönig nicht? Den Erlenkönig mit Kron' und Schweif?"	"See, father, 'tis the Erlking in sight. The Erlking stands there with crown and shroud?"

Father

1:16	In low, calming tones	"Mein Sohn, es ist ein Nebelstreif."	"Dear son, it is some misty cloud."

Erlking

1:26	With a seductive melody	"Du liebes Kind, komm, geh' mit mir! gar schöne Spiele spiel' ich mit dir; manch' bunte Blumen sing an dem Strand, meine Mutter hat manch' gülden Geward."	"Thou dearest boy, come go with me! And many games I'll play with thee; where varied blossoms sing on meadows fair and my mother has golden garments to wear."

Son

1:50	Tension depicted by tight chromatic movement in voice	"Mein Vater, mein Vater und hörest du nicht, was Erlenkönig mir leise verspricht?"	"Dear father, my father, say, did'st thou not hear the Erlking whisper promises in my ear?"

Time	Description	German	English
2:03	In low, steady pitches	"Sei ruhig, bleibe ruhig, mein Kind, in düren Blättern säuselt der Wind."	**Father** "Be calm, stay calm, my child, Through wither'd leaves the wind blows wild."
2:14	With a happy, lilting tune in major	"Willst, feiner Knabe, du mit mir geh'n? Meine Töchter sollen dich warten schön, mein Töchter führen den nächtlichen Reih'n, und wiegen und tanzen und singen dich ein."	**Erlking** "My handsome young lad, will you come with me? My beauteous daughter does wait for thee, With her you would join in the dance every night, and lull you with sweet song to give you delight."
2:31	Same intense chromatic notes as before, but now a step higher; minor key	"Mein Vater, mein Vater und siehst du nicht dort Erlkönigs Töchter am düstern Ort?"	**Son** "Dear Father, my father, don't you see there the face of the Erlking's daughter in yonder dark place?"
2:44	Low register, but more leaps (agitation) than before	"Mein Sohn, mein Sohn, ich se' es genau, es scheinen die alten Weiden so grau."	**Father** "Dear son, dear son, the form you there see, is only the aging gray willow tree."
3:02	His music is no longer seductive but now threatening and in minor key	"Ich liebe dich, mich reizt deine schöne Gestalt; und bist du nicht willig, so brauch' ich Gewalt."	**Erlking** "I love you well, with me thou shalt ride on my course And if thou are unwilling, I'll seize thee by force!"
3:13	Piercing cries in highest range	"Mein Vater, mein Vater jetzt fasst er mich an! Erlkönig hat mir ein Leids gethan!"	**Son** "Dear father, my father, hold me tight and quick, the Erlking has seized me by his trick."
3:28	With a rising and then falling line	Dem Vater grausets; er reitet geschwind, er hält in den Armen das ächzende Kind. Erreicht den Hof mit Müh und Noth:	**Narrator** His father shudder'd, his pace grew more wild, he held to his breast his poor feverish child. He reach'd the inn with toil and dread,
	Piano stops, recitative	in seinen Armen das Kind war todt!	but in his arms, lo! his child lay dead!

Tension in Schubert's *Erlking* rises continually from the beginning up to the very end. As the story is told the music, too, unfolds continually without repetition of material, though the cries of the son provide something of a constant refrain. Compositions made up of ever-changing music are called **through composed**. *Erlking* is thus a through-composed art song. For texts that do not tell a story or project a series of changing moods, however, **strophic** form is often preferred. Here a single poetic mood is maintained from one stanza, or strophe, of the text to the next. Accordingly, the same

through composed and strophic forms

music is repeated, again and again, for each strophe, as in a hymn or a folk song. Schubert used strophic form, for example, when setting a prayer found in Sir Walter Scott's *The Lady of the Lake*. The result was his immortal *Ave Maria* (1825), a song in which the music for each of three strophes is identical, note for note.

THE TROUT (1817)

Schubert's *Die Forelle (The Trout)* shows how both the Romantic poet and musician were attracted to the charms of nature. Picture in your mind's eye a fresh mountain stream where a trout darts happily about. Schubert captures this vision with a lively tune and a bubbling accompaniment figure in the piano—whether a spinning wheel, a rippling stream, or a galloping horse, Schubert knew better than anyone how to create the musical equivalent of such graphic details. The poem is composed of three eight-line stanzas, each with the rhyme scheme ABABCDCD. The first sets the scene of the crystal-clear stream, the second introduces a fisherman on the opposite bank, and the third tells how the invader tricks and catches the trout. Each strophe is set to the same music with one exception. At the beginning of the third stanza, where the fisherman tricks the trout by muddying the stream, the bubbling accompaniment figure is replaced momentarily by minor chords. Such a change within the basic strophic form produces **modified strophic** form. It allows the composer to highlight a particular detail without disturbing the overall structure of strophic form.

modified strophic form

Unlike the dramatic *Erlking* of Goethe, the lyrical text of *The Trout* (by one Daniel Schubart) is in no way exceptional as a poem. What is remarkable is the way that Schubert can make even the most ordinary verse into a song of extraordinary beauty.

LISTENING
GUIDE

Franz Schubert
Art song, *The Trout* (1817)

CD 4/2
6–Tape 4A

0:00   Piano introduces the rippling
        accompaniment figure in bright
        major key

0:07	First strophe	In einem Bächlein helle, Da schoss in froher Eil' Die launische Forelle Vorüber wie ein Pfeil. Ich stand an dem Gestade Und sah in süzer Ruh' Des muntern Fischleins Bade Im klaren Bächlein zu.	A streamlet clear and sunny With ripples all about, Was once the bath for pretty For gentle little trout. On shore I stood observing With exquisite delight, The happy little creature It was a lovely sight.
0:39	Second strophe: exact repeat of music of first strophe	Ein Fischer mit der Rute Wohl an dem Ufer stand Und sah's mit kaltem Blute, Wie sich das Fischlein wand. Solang dem Wasser Helle, So dacht ich, nicht gebricht, So fängt er die Forelle Mit seiner Angel nicht.	A fisher with his angle Stood on yonder shore Trying to entangle The fish from water's floor. I thought if clear the water Still races all about, He'd never, never capture My lovely, little trout.
1:13	Third strophe: minor replaces major; chords replace rippling figure; return to major tonality and rippling figure	Doch endlich ward dem Diebe Die Zeit zu lang. Er macht Das Bächlein tückisch trübe, Und eh' ich es gedacht. So zuckte seine Rute, Das Fischlein zappelt dran, Und ich mit regem Blute Sah die Betrog'ne an.	Yet the robber had no patience To while away the time He made the brook all muddy Ere I sensed the crime. His line went inward reeling My little fish so sweet, Then saw I with raging feeling The cheated and the cheat.

THE "TROUT" QUINTET (1819)

In the summer of 1819, two years after he wrote his song *The Trout*, Schubert decided to vacation in the hills west of Vienna, to enjoy the stunning beauty of the Austrian countryside. There an amateur cellist asked the composer to arrange for string quartet his charming song about a fish. Schubert accepted the challenge but changed the medium of performance. He decided to add a fifth instrument, a piano, to the ensemble (making it a piano quintet) and to replace the usual second violin of the quartet with a double bass. This would give added weight to the bass line and allow the piano to roam with little competition in the upper register. Having selected his instrumental forces, he then composed a five-movement piano quintet, the "Trout" Quintet, perhaps the most lyrical of all works of chamber music.

a theme and six variations

The fourth movement of Schubert's "Trout" Quintet makes prominent use of the lovely tune of the *Lied* and does so in the form of a theme and six variations. The two phrases of the melody (**A** and **B**) are stated and immediately repeated within each variation, though the repeat of **B** extends only to the last four bars (**B'**). Each instrument has its turn to present the melody—the piano does so in variation 1, the viola in variation 2, and the double bass, cello, and violin in variations 3, 5, and 6, respectively. Variations 4 and 5 take us away from the bright tonic key of D major, to D minor and B♭ major, but variation 6 returns us to the tonic major.

Schubert was fond of making use of the melodies of his songs in his instrumental chamber music. The "Trout" Quintet shows that he was not merely a songsmith but could also compose instrumental music with the sort of lyricism, fluidity, and grace that even Mozart might have envied.

LISTENING GUIDE

Franz Schubert
Piano Quintet in A major, the "Trout" Quintet (1819)
Fourth movement, *Andantino* (gently moving)

CD 4/3
6–Tape 4A

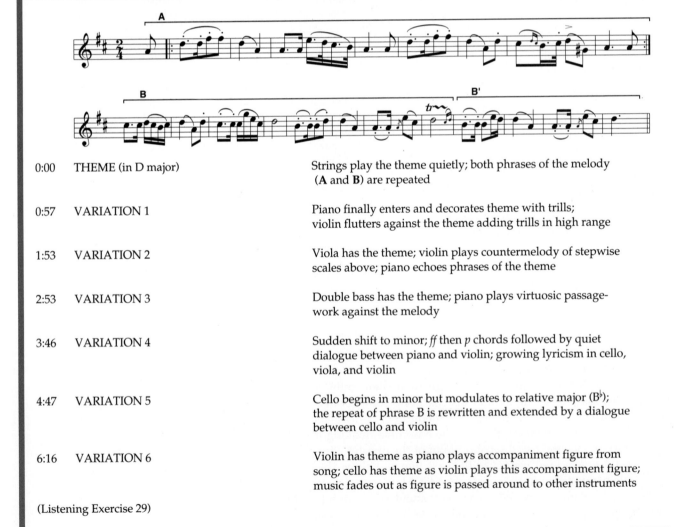

0:00	THEME (in D major)	Strings play the theme quietly; both phrases of the melody (**A** and **B**) are repeated
0:57	VARIATION 1	Piano finally enters and decorates theme with trills; violin flutters against the theme adding trills in high range
1:53	VARIATION 2	Viola has the theme; violin plays countermelody of stepwise scales above; piano echoes phrases of the theme
2:53	VARIATION 3	Double bass has the theme; piano plays virtuosic passage-work against the melody
3:46	VARIATION 4	Sudden shift to minor; *ff* then *p* chords followed by quiet dialogue between piano and violin; growing lyricism in cello, viola, and violin
4:47	VARIATION 5	Cello begins in minor but modulates to relative major (B♭); the repeat of phrase B is rewritten and extended by a dialogue between cello and violin
6:16	VARIATION 6	Violin has theme as piano plays accompaniment figure from song; cello has theme as violin plays this accompaniment figure; music fades out as figure is passed around to other instruments

(Listening Exercise 29)

Program Music[†]

More than any other period, the nineteenth century was a time in which composers sought and received inspiration from sources outside music. An encounter with nature, the impressions of a voyage, a disappointment in love, a popular legend, or an entire play might provide a story, scene, or idea that could be described in music. Of course, music could not actually depict or recreate such extramusical themes. But it could, by using different colors, moods, and sound effects, suggest a particular sequence of happenings and sensations to an attentive listener. To this end composers wrote overtures*, concert overtures*, incidental music*, symphonic poems*, and program symphonies*, which taken together constitute a sizable part of the repertoire of Romantic music. Two of the best composers of this sort of descriptive music were Hector Berlioz and Felix Mendelssohn.

Hector Berlioz (1803–1869)

Hector Berlioz was one of the most original figures in the history of music. He was born in 1803 near the mountain city of Grenoble, France, the son of a local doctor. What he learned of music in the home and at school was scanty: no thorough training in music theory or composition and little exposure to the music of the great masters. Local tutors taught him to play the flute and guitar. Among the major composers of the nineteenth century, he was the only one without fluency at the keyboard. He never studied piano, and could do no more than bang out a few chords.

At the age of seventeen Berlioz was sent off to Paris to study medicine, his father's profession. For two years he pursued a program in the physical sciences, earning a degree in 1821. But Berlioz found the dissecting table gruesome and the allure of the opera house and concert halls irresistible. After a period of soul searching, and the inevitable falling out with his parents over the choice of a career, he vowed to become "no doctor or apothecary but a great composer."

His dismayed father immediately cut off his living stipend, leaving young Berlioz to ponder how he might support himself while studying composition at the Paris Conservatory (the French national school of music). Other composers, finding themselves suddenly on their own, relied on teaching as a means to earn a regular income. Mozart, Haydn, Beethoven, Chopin, and Liszt, for example, all gave piano lessons as young men. But what could Berlioz teach? He had no particular skill on any instrument. So he turned to music criticism, writing reviews and articles for literary journals that poked fun at the French musical establishment. Berlioz was the first composer to earn a livelihood as a music critic, and criticism, not the sale of his music, remained his primary source of income for the remainder of his life.

Perhaps it was only natural that Berlioz wrote about music during the years he learned to compose, for literature had a profound impact on his life and art. As a boy his father had taught him to read Virgil's *Aeneid* in the original Latin; later he would use episodes from this classical epic to form the libretto of an opera called *Les Troyens* (*The Trojans*, 1858). As a young

FIGURE 13–4

Hector Berlioz at the age of twenty-nine.

a music critic

[†]Nineteenth-century program music is discussed more fully on page 242.

FIGURE 13–5

A satirical engraving suggesting the public's impression of Berlioz conducting his vastly enlarged symphony orchestra.

man he read Lord Byron's *Childe Harold's Pilgrimage* and Goethe's *Faust*, works that inspired his concerto for viola called *Harold in Italy* (1834) and his dramatic symphony *The Damnation of Faust* (1846). But of all literary influences, none was greater than that of Shakespeare. As we have seen (page 235), Shakespeare burst upon the consciousness of continental Europe for the first time early in the nineteenth century. Berlioz, like many artists of this period, devoured the English poet's plays and gave musical expression to several. To *The Tempest* and to *King Lear* he wrote concert overtures (see page 243)—independent pieces intended to sum up the spirit of the drama. Berlioz kept a human skull on his desk to remind him of the graveyard scene of *Hamlet* (see Fig. 12–8) and wrote a funeral march (1848) to remember the death of this prince. And he set the main events of *Romeo and Juliet* as a five-movement program symphony, *Roméo et Juliette* (1839), into which a chorus and solo voices intermittently sing Shakespeare's own words.

In these works inspired by literature, as well as in his religious music, Berlioz called for enormous orchestral and choral forces—hundreds and hundreds of performers. He also experimented with new instruments: the ophicleide* (an early form of the tuba), the English horn* (a low oboe), the harp (an ancient instrument now brought into the symphony orchestra for the first time), the cornet* (borrowed from the military band), and even the newly invented saxophone. His approach to musical form was also iconoclastic; he rarely wrote in strict sonata–allegro form or theme and variations, for example. His French compatriots found his compositions "bizarre" and "monstrous" and thought him something of a madman. Increasingly, he crisscrossed Europe to conduct his works before foreigners who more readily appreciated the unique sounds of his music. To London, Bonn, Vienna, Prague, Leipzig, and even Moscow he went to introduce such works as *Symphonie fantastique*, *Damnation of Faust*, *Roméo et Juliette*, or *The Trojans*. He died in Paris in 1869, isolated and embittered. The little recognition he received in his native France came "too late," as he said, to help his career or self-esteem.

SYMPHONIE FANTASTIQUE (1830)

Berlioz's most celebrated work, then and now, is his *Symphonie fantastique*, perhaps the single most influential composition of the entire nineteenth century. Its form and orchestration are revolutionary. But what is more, it tells *a program symphony* in music a vivid story and, as such, is the first complete program symphony. The story surrounding the creation of the descriptive program of the work is as fascinating as the program itself.

In 1827 a troupe of English actors came to Paris to present Shakespeare's *Hamlet* and *Romeo and Juliet*. Berlioz, of course, had read some of Shakespeare's plays in a French translation, but was eager to see these works performed on stage. Though he understood little English, he was overwhelmed by what he saw. The dramatic power, human insights, and touching beauty in Shakespeare's work far surpassed the virtues found in traditional French theater. But Berlioz was not only smitten by Shakespeare; he also fell in love with the leading lady who played Ophelia to Hamlet and Juliet to Romeo, one Harriet Smithson (Fig. 13–6). Like a lovesick adolescent Berlioz swooned at her sight and wrote such violently passionate letters that the frightened starlet refused to meet the student composer. Eventually, his ardor cooled—

for a time he even became engaged to someone else. But the experience of an all-consuming love, the despair of rejection, and the vision of darkness and possible death furnished the stimulus—and story line—for an unusually imaginative symphony. (Ultimately, Berlioz did meet and marry Harriet Smithson, and the two lived miserably together ever after.)

Berlioz wrote the *Symphonie fantastique*, not in the usual four movements of a symphony, but in five, an arrangement that may have been inspired by Shakespeare's use of a five-act format. Movements 1 and 5 balance each other in length and substance, as do 2 and 4, leaving the leisurely third movement as the center of the work. But symmetry is not the only element holding the symphony together. Berlioz creates a single melody which reappears as a unifying force, movement after movement. Earlier, Beethoven had experimented with thematic recall and transformation in his fifth and ninth symphonies. But Berlioz takes this technique one step farther by recalling the melody constantly and by associating it with an object, his beloved. The vision of his loved one, and her attending melody, becomes an obsession. Berlioz called this musical fixation his *idée fixe* ("fixed idea"). As his feelings about the beloved change from movement to movement, so the *idée fixe* is transformed to reflect these various moods. To make sure that the listener has no doubt as to what these moods are, Berlioz prepared a written program to be read as the music is performed.

First Movement: Reveries, Passions

Program: A young musician . . . sees for the first time a woman who embodies all the charms of the ideal being he has imagined in his dreams . . . The subject of the first movement is the passage from this state of melancholy reverie, interrupted by a few moments of joy, to that of delirious passion, with movements of fury, jealousy, and its return to tenderness, tears, and religious consolation.

A slow introduction ("this state of melancholy reverie") prepares the way for the first vision of the beloved, carried forward by the first appearance of the main theme, the *idée fixe*.

EXAMPLE 13–4

The movement unfolds in sonata–allegro form. The "recapitulation," however, does not so much repeat the *idée fixe* as it does transform the melody to reflect the artist's feelings of sorrow and tenderness.

Second Movement: A Ball

The artist finds himself . . . in the midst of the tumult of a party.

A lilting waltz now begins, but it is interrupted by the unexpected appearance of the *idée fixe*, the rhythm changed to accommodate the triple meter of

FIGURE 13–6

The actress Harriet Smithson became an obsession for Berlioz and the source of inspiration for his *Symphonie fantastique*. At the time Berlioz wrote this symphony (1830), she was a good deal more famous than he.

the waltz. Four harps add a graceful accompaniment when the waltz returns, and, toward the end, there is even a lovely solo for cornet. The sequence of waltz–*idée fixe*–waltz creates, once again, ternary form.

Third Movement: Scene in the Country

> Finding himself one evening in the country, the artist hears in the distance two shepherds piping . . . He reflects upon his isolation and hopes that soon he will no longer be alone.

The dialogue between the shepherds is presented by an English horn and an oboe, the latter played offstage to give the effect of a distant response. The unexpected appearance of the *idée fixe* in the woodwinds suggests that the artist has hopes of winning his beloved. But has she falsely encouraged him? The shepherd's tune recurs, but the oboe doesn't answer. There is only the lonely call of the English horn and the empty rumble of distant thunder in the timpani.

Fourth Movement: March to the Scaffold

> Having realized that his love goes unrecognized, the artist poisons himself with opium. The dose of the narcotic, too weak to kill him, plunges him into a sleep accompanied by the most horrible visions. He dreams that he has killed the one he loved, that he is condemned, led to the scaffold, and now witnesses his own execution.

This drug-induced nightmare centers on the march to the scaffold where the artist is to be executed. The steady beat of the low strings and the muffled bass drum sound the steps of the procession. Near the end the image of the beloved returns in the clarinet, only to be suddenly cut off by a *fortissimo* crash by the full orchestra. The guillotine has fallen.

Fifth Movement: Dream of the Witches' Sabbath

climactic fifth movement

> He sees himself at the witches' sabbath surrounded by a troop of frightful shadows, sorcerers, and monsters of all sorts, gathered for his funeral. Strange noises, groans, bursts of laughter, distant cries echoed by others. The beloved melody returns again, but it has lost its noble, modest character and is now only base, trivial, and grotesque. An outburst of joy at her arrival; she joins in the devilish orgy.

a vision of hell

In this monstrous finale Berlioz creates his personal vision of hell. A crowd of witches and other ghouls is summoned to dance around the corpse of the artist on its way to the inferno. Weird sounds are produced by the strings, using mutes, and by the high woodwinds and French horn, playing glissandos*. A piercing clarinet enters with a burlesque parody of the *idée fixe* as Harriet Smithson, now in the garb of an old hag, comes on stage.

EXAMPLE 13–5

She is greeted by a joyous *fortissimo* outburst by the full assembly as all proceed to dance to the now perverted *idée fixe*. Suddenly, the music becomes ominously quiet and, in one of the most strikingly original moments in all of music, great Gothic church bells are heard. Against this solemn backdrop sounds the burial hymn of the medieval Church, the *Dies irae*, played by ophicleides (tubas) and bassoons.

Dies irae

EXAMPLE 13–6

[Di - es i - rae di - es il - la sol - vet   sae - clum   in fa - vil - la]
[Day of anger, day of wrath, on which the ages will be changed to ash]

Not only is the orchestration sensational, the musical symbolism is sacrilegious. Just as he had parodied the melody of the beloved, now Berlioz creates a mockery of one of the most venerable Gregorian chants of the Catholic Church. First the *Dies irae* is played by the horns twice as fast (a process called rhythmic diminution*). Then the sacred tune is transformed into a jazzed-up dance tune played by a shrill, high clarinet, the entire scene now becoming a blasphemous black Mass (see Fig. 12–2).

a mockery of the Church

EXAMPLE 13–7

As the ceremony proceeds, the witches begin to dance. But they do so in an extraordinary way: They enter one by one and create a fugato*, a fugal passage within a symphonic movement. What is a learned fugue doing here in the middle of hell? Presumably because, having just mocked the ancient music of the Catholic Church, Berlioz now decides to ridicule the musical establishment and its strictest form, the academic fugue. But beyond this, the regular entry of more and more voices, or dancing witches, creates the effect of a growing tumult around the corpse of the artist.

a parody of fugue

EXAMPLE 13–8

A climax is reached as the theme, or subject, of the witches, played in the strings, as well as the *Dies irae* melody, played in the brass and woodwinds, sound together, though in different keys, a bizarre example of double counterpoint*. Stranger still is the sound that follows, for Berlioz instructs the violins to play *col legno* ("with the wood")—to strike the strings, not with the usual front of the bow, but with the wooden back, creating a noise something akin to the crackling or burning of hellfire.

col legno *technique*

To the audience that first heard the *Symphonie fantastique* on December 5, 1830, all of this must have seemed incomprehensible: new instruments, novel playing effects, simultaneous melodies in different keys, and a form that is not traditional, like sonata–allegro or rondo, but grows out of the events in a soap-opera–like program. But it all works. Here is a rare example in the history of art in which a creator has not only undertaken to experiment radically but has done so in a way that produces a wholly integrated, unified, and ultimately satisfying work. The separate effects may be revolutionary, momentarily shocking, but they are consistent and logical among themselves when subsumed in the total artistic concept. Had Berlioz never written another note of music, he would be justly famous for this single masterpiece of Romantic invention.

LISTENING GUIDE

Hector Berlioz
Symphonie fantastique (1830)
Fifth movement, Dream of the Witches' Sabbath

CD 4/2
6–Tape 4A
2–Tape 2A

0:00	"Strange noises, groans, bursts of laughter, distant cries" high and low
1:26	Grotesquely transformed *idée fixe* in shrill clarinet
1:34	Joyful, *fortissimo* outburst by full orchestra welcoming the now ugly beloved
1:44	Witches begin to dance to the newly grotesque *idée fixe;* bassoons add raucous counterpoint (1:55)
2:39	Ominous transition
2:57	Funeral bells sound
3:24	*Dies irae* heard in tubas and bassoons
3:46	Horns and trombones play *Dies irae* twice as fast (diminution)
3:56	Woodwinds pervert *Dies irae* chant
4:02	Chant melody, its diminution, and its perversion continue
5:02	Introduction to witches' dance; crescendo
5:19	Witches' dance (fugato) begins with four entries of the subject
5:45	Fugal episode
6:04	Three more entries of the subject
6:20	More strange sounds and cries (transition out of fugato)
7:02	Fragments of the *Dies irae*
7:19	Witches' dance (fugue subject) grows to a rapid climax, then *fortissimo* syncopation (7:47)
8:04	Witches' dance and *Dies irae* combined; trumpets now added
8:30	Violins use wooden back of bow to produce a crackling sound
8:54	*Fortissimo* chords
9:11	Fleeting recall of *Dies irae*
9:30	More chords with a striking harmonic shift
9:36	Final cadential fanfare

(Listening Exercise 30)

Felix Mendelssohn (1809–1847)

Berlioz was a child of the Romantic age: He tried suicide at least twice, ran around Italy with a gang of bandits in imitation of Lord Byron, and married an image, an ideal of a woman, with disastrous consequences. Felix Mendelssohn was an altogether different personality, anything but the stereotype of the rebellious, self-absorbed, struggling artist.

Mendelssohn was born in 1809 into a prosperous, indeed wealthy, Jewish family. His father was a banker, and his grandfather, Moses Mendelssohn (1726–1786), was a noted philosopher. At the family home in Berlin young Felix had every advantage: He studied languages, literature, and philosophy with private tutors, as well as painting, dancing, riding, and even gymnastics. In 1816 Mendelssohn's parents had their four children baptized Christians, partly so they might enjoy full legal equality and move freely in all social circles. Indeed, their home became a gathering place for artists and intellectuals of all sorts: the poet Heine, the philosopher Hegel, and the geographer Humboldt (discoverer of the Humboldt current) were all frequent guests. Because Felix had shown extraordinary musical talent, he was not only given piano lessons but also provided with a small orchestra on Sunday afternoons to try out his youthful compositions. At the age of sixteen he composed a masterpiece, his octet for strings. The next year (1826) witnessed an equally astonishing work, the Overture to *A Midsummer Night's Dream*. As a composer Mendelssohn was even more precocious than either Mozart or Schubert.

Taking advantage of his privileged station in life, Mendelssohn spent the years 1829–1835 traveling across Europe to discover its natural beauty and to meet the great artists of the day. He walked across most of Switzerland, sketching and painting as he went. He met Goethe in Weimar, Berlioz in Rome, Liszt, Chopin, and the painter Delacroix (see page 268) in Paris, and the novelist Sir Walter Scott outside Edinburgh. The itinerant years ended in the spring of 1835 when he was appointed musical director of the Gewandhaus Orchestra in Leipzig, Germany.

Founded in 1781 by the merchants of Leipzig, the Gewandhaus Orchestra ("Clothiers' House" Orchestra) played in the guild hall of that trade association (Figs. 13–8 and 13–9). Mendelssohn recruited better players, increased their salaries, established a pension fund for the orchestra, and conducted as a musical interpreter, not just as a mere time-beater. By so doing he soon made the Gewandhaus Orchestra one of the finest in Europe, a position it has continued to hold down to the present day.

Leipzig was, of course, the city of Bach. The old contrapuntalist had fallen into nearly complete oblivion after his death there in 1750. But his music was adored by Mendelssohn who, in 1829, mounted the first performance of Bach's great *St. Matthew Passion* in nearly a hundred years. ("And to think that it should be a Jew who gives back to the world the greatest of Christian works," he said at the time.) While in Leipzig, Mendelssohn continued to program Bach's music as well as the works of other composers of historical interest: Handel, Haydn, and Mozart among them. This went against the current wisdom which said that the public was interested in hearing only the most up-to-date music. But the idea spread. From this time forward a concert by a symphony orchestra served not only as a forum in which to present new or recent works but also as a museum for the old. Our modern

FIGURE 13–7

Felix Mendelssohn at the age of twenty.

FIGURE 13–8

Exterior of the Gewandhaus in Leipzig as depicted by Felix Mendelssohn. In addition to his talents as a musician, Mendelssohn was also a gifted painter, his preferred medium being water color.

A concert in progress in the Gewand-haus ca. 1840, the hall where Mendelssohn, Liszt, Berlioz, as well as Clara and Robert Schumann frequently performed.

notion that a symphony orchestra exists to preserve a past repertoire, as well as promote a contemporary art, can be traced to Mendelssohn and his contemporaries. Mendelssohn remained in the post of director of the Gewand-haus Orchestra in Leipzig until his premature death by stroke at the age of thirty-eight.

a musical conservative

Given the fact that Felix Mendelssohn led a revival of the music of the eighteenth-century masters, it is not surprising that his own compositions are the most conservative, the most "classical," of the great Romantic composers. His harmonies are colorful but not revolutionary; his orchestration distinctive but not shocking—a light, dancing string sound is his hallmark; and his use of form is traditional, as seen in his heavy reliance on sonata–allegro form. Never does he indulge in startling outbursts of sound. The classical ideals of unity, grace, and formal balance predominate.

influence of nature, travel, and literature

What makes Mendelssohn a musical Romantic is the fact that nature, travel, and literature provided stimuli for so many of his creations. A trip to Italy in 1830–31 gave rise to his "Italian" Symphony, just as a lengthy sojourn in Scotland a year earlier had planted the seeds for the "Scottish" Symphony. On this same northern voyage he visited the windswept Hebrides Islands and soon captured the spirit of the churning sea and rocky coast in his "Hebrides" Overture (1830). Mendelssohn commented on the difficulty he faced when trying to harness a raging ocean within the confines of sonata–allegro form: "The whole development section smells more of counterpoint than of blubber, gulls, and salted cod."

As to literary influences, he heard the voices of Goethe and Shakespeare most clearly. To Goethe's *Faust* the composer owed the inspiration for the *Scherzo* of his early Octet (1825) and several later orchestral works. And to Shakespeare, of course, could be traced the genesis of the music for *A Midsummer Night's Dream*.

OVERTURE TO *A MIDSUMMER NIGHT'S DREAM* (1826)

Mendelssohn began to compose, or "to dream *A Midsummer Night's Dream*," as he says, during July 1826, when he was an impressionable youth of seventeen. His aim was to transform the romantic fantasy of Shakespeare's play into an independent concert overture (a piece for the concert hall, not the theater). Some years later, in 1843, he was commissioned by the king of Prussia to create incidental music (music to be heard during an actual performance) for a production of the play planned for Berlin. Among these incidental pieces is his famous *Wedding March*—originally written to accompany the marriage of the characters Theseus and Hippolyta, now traditionally heard at weddings as the recessional march. *a concert overture*

To enter fully into the enchanted world of Mendelssohn's Overture to *A Midsummer Night's Dream*, we must know something of the play—the program—that inspired it. The drama begins in an imaginary city called Athens where the ruler, Duke Theseus, is about to marry Hippolyta, queen of the Amazons. Nearby is an enchanted forest ruled by Oberon, king of the elves, and his estranged queen, Titania. Into this magical grove come Lysander and Hermia, another pair of would-be lovers. Then enters a group of common craftsmen, led by the blockheaded Bottom, who have come to prepare for the royal wedding. Finally, the hunting party of Theseus and Hippolyta joins the woodland scene. Confusion reigns as an agent of fairy king Oberon, the spirit Puck, administers a love potion to the wrong parties; fairy queen Titania falls in love with the clownish Bottom who is made to wear the head of an ass. Eventually, all is set right and the nobles and gentry return to the court of Athens. The events in the enchanted forest had been no more real than a midsummer night's dream. *Shakespeare's play*

Mendelssohn's Overture closely follows the play. Separate and distinctly different musical colors and styles make the various characters clearly identifiable and the events easy to follow. At the same time, the music unfolds in sonata–allegro form. There is a slow four-chord introduction, a first theme (the dancing fairy music), a transition (royal music of the court of Athens), a second theme (the lovers' music), and a closing theme group (the craftsmen's music and the hunting calls). The fairies dominate the development section *the musical events*

FIGURE 13–10

Oberon, Titania and Puck with Fairies Dancing by the English artist and poet, William Blake (1757–1827).

and, in the coda (or epilogue) have the last word, just as in Shakespeare's play. Mendelssohn's own thoughts best describe the ending: "After everything has been satisfactorily settled and the principal players have joyfully left the stage, the elves follow them, bless the house, and disappear with the dawn. So ends the play, and my overture too."

LISTENING GUIDE	Felix Mendelssohn Overture to *A Midsummer Night's Dream* (1826)	CD 4/5 6–Tape 4A

Program:		*Musical Events:*

EXPOSITION

0:00	Introduction to enchantment	Four sustained chords in the winds (introduction)
0:20	Fairies' music	Rapid, light, staccato notes in violins (first theme)
1:04	Duke Theseus and his court	Full orchestra *fortissimo* (transition)
1:34		Fairies' music mixes into transition
2:08	Lovers' music	Quiet melody in woodwinds and strings grows more passionate (second theme)
3:00	Bottom's music	Raucous motive sounds like braying of a donkey (closing theme, part 1)
3:22	Hunting calls of regal party	Fanfares in brass and woodwinds (closing theme, part 2)

DEVELOPMENT

3:46	Fairies' music developed	Music of the fairies (first theme) worked out in different keys
4:52	Fairies' music extended	String pizzicato and string tremolo
5:27	Lysander and Hermia sleep	Ritard, soft string sound, music seems to come to a stop

RECAPITULATION

5:52	Return to enchantment	Four introductory chords return
6:14	Fairies' music	Dancing fairies' music returns (first theme), but transition is eliminated
6:58	Lovers' music	Lyrical melody in woodwinds and strings (second theme) as before
7:47	Bottom's music	Again raucous *fortissimo* music of the ass (closing theme, part 1)
8:52	Hunting party	Fanfares (closing theme, part 2) serve as ending to recapitulation

CODA

| 9:16 | Epilogue by fairy Puck | Light, quick music of the fairies; toward the end Duke Theseus and the four opening chords are recalled |

(Listening Exercise 31)

THE PIANISTS

By the 1840s the piano had essentially evolved into the instrument we know today (see also, page 239). Its thundering power, rapid action, singing tone, and wide range of expression made it the most popular instrument of the Romantic period. No self-respecting middle-class home could be without one. No education was thought complete without lessons at it. Spurred by the extraordinary vogue of the instrument, a host of virtuoso performers set upon the concert halls of Europe with fingers blazing. What they played was often more a display of digital fireworks—rapid octaves, racing chromatic scales, thundering chords—than of musical substance. Happily, however, several of the greatest piano virtuosos of the nineteenth century were also gifted composers. While these artists sometimes wrote songs, symphonies, or concertos, the piano—and piano style—was at the heart of their creative process.

vogue of the piano

Clara Wieck Schumann (1819–1896)

Clara Wieck Schumann was one of this elite group of outstanding pianists and composers. Critics of the day spoke not only of her flawless technique but also of her great expressivity and interpretive skill. She was born in Leipzig, Germany, in 1819, the daughter of the well-known professor of music Friedrich Wieck (1785–1873). At the age of eleven she gave her debut in the Gewandhaus in Leipzig. Heralded as a child prodigy, she then undertook a concert tour of Europe during which she won the admiration of Mendelssohn, Berlioz, Chopin, and Liszt. Soon she also began to compose: a piano concerto, a number of "romances" for piano, and a few songs. In 1840, against the violent opposition of her father, she married Robert Schumann, who years before had come into the Wieck home in Leipzig to study piano.

a child prodigy

Although Clara Wieck Schumann was much better known on the international music scene than her then obscure husband, Robert, she nonetheless put aside her own career to play the roles of wife and mother to the eight children she soon bore him (one died in infancy). Her development as a composer was hindered not only by the weight of this domestic charge but also by the then widely held belief that no woman could possess musical creativity of the highest order. Clara's ambivalence about the proper calling for an artistically gifted person of her sex can be felt in the entry she made in her diary shortly after her marriage: "I once believed that I possessed creative talent, but I have given up this idea; a woman must not desire to compose. There has never yet been one able to do it. Should I expect to be that one? To believe this would be arrogant, something which my father once, in former days, induced me to do."

FIGURE 13–11

Clara Schumann

In fact, she did not give up composition completely, but continued to produce piano pieces and songs well into the 1850s. Her works are generally marked by a singing melodic line and by intensely chromatic inner parts, a quality derived from her thorough study of the recently rediscovered keyboard music of J. S. Bach. Clara Schumann's artistry will be more widely appreciated when more of her works become accessible on commercial recordings.

FIGURE 13–12

Robert Schumann

art songs and works for the keyboard

Robert Schumann (1810–1856)

Robert Schumann, the gifted but unstable husband of Clara, spent his youth in a typical Romantic pursuit of music and literature. He read Goethe and Lord Byron, wrote poetry, tried his hand at short stories, and learned to play the piano. His mother's plan to have him pursue a program of legal studies, first in Leipzig and then in Heidelberg, met with failure. Schumann was a dreamer and had even less affinity for law than Berlioz had for medicine. In Leipzig, for example, he attended not a single lecture but divided his time between imitating the fashionable writers of the day and improvising on the piano. Obviously, a career in the arts was more to his liking.

With his mother's consent grudgingly gained, Schumann set out in 1830 to make himself into a piano virtuoso under the tutelage of Friedrich Wieck. He practiced long hours to gain the mechanics of a fluid piano technique. But after two years his most noteworthy acquisition was a partially paralyzed right hand, due either to an injury or to mercury poisoning brought on by a treatment for syphilis. With his career as a virtuoso now frustrated, composition and music criticism became the focus of his creative energies. During the 1830s he produced a remarkable series of works for solo piano. He also founded and served as editor for a new musical periodical, the *Neue Zeitschrift für Musik* (*New Journal of Music*). Schumann became the apostle for new music within the German Romantic movement, championing the works of the best and most progressive composers of the day: Berlioz, Chopin, Mendelssohn, Liszt, and the young Johannes Brahms.

Before 1840, the year of his marriage to Clara Wieck, Schumann had written nothing but music for solo piano. Now he decided to spread his wings into the realm of the art song. In the year of union with Clara he brought forth more than 125 songs for solo voice and piano. These include several now-famous song cycles* such as *Dichterliebe* (*Poet's Love*) and *Frauenliebe und Leben* (*Women in Love and Life*), individual songs of which are the equal in quality to the works of the great Franz Schubert in this genre. Clara now encouraged him to extend himself further into the spheres of orchestral and chamber music. But in these larger forms he had only mixed success. His piano concerto (1845) and piano quintet (1842) are supreme accomplishments, but his four symphonies are not uniformly compelling. At heart Schumann was a miniaturist whose creativity was inextricably bound to the keyboard. And unlike his idol Beethoven, who composed on sketch books as he walked through forest and field, Schumann was unable to generate music except at the piano. Touch and sensation were intrinsic to his creative process. His musical style is fundamentally that of a dreamy keyboard improviser.

SCENES FROM CHILDHOOD (1838)

To hear Schumann at his best, let us turn to a set of miniature keyboard pieces he wrote in 1838, *Kinderszenen* (*Scenes from Childhood*). These are not pieces intended for children but musical recollections of events or sensations from childhood—"reminiscences of a grown-up for grown-ups," the composer said. Each of the thirteen works in the set has its own suggestive title, such as *By the Fireside, Catch-as-Catch-Can,* or *Bogeyman's Coming.* Each invites the listener to enter the very private world of the imagination, to make one's own retrospective associations with the sounds. And each is a perfect example of the Romantic character piece[*]—a short work conveying a single character or mood in which that feeling is distilled to its very essence. In their musical form, the scenes are quite uncomplicated, usually in simple ternary structure (**ABA**). What is remarkable is the way in which a vision or sensation is instantly created and then, just as quickly, vanishes. The first of the scenes, *Von fremden Ländern und Menschen (Of Foreign Lands and People)*, may allude to a child's bright eyes seeing far-off places. Another, *Träumerei (Dreaming)*, suggests a child engrossed in a world of dreams. *Dreaming*, incidentally, was the character piece the great pianist Vladimir Horowitz (1904–1989) traditionally played as the last of his encores.

Romantic character pieces for piano

LISTENING GUIDE

Robert Schumann
Character pieces from *Scenes from Childhood* (1838)

CD 4/6–7
6–Tape 4A

Of Foreign Lands and People

0:00	Bright melody in major key with triplet accompaniment	**A**
0:15	**A** section repeated	
0:30	Change to minor key as melody falls and then rises by step	**B**
0:43	Brief fermata (hold)	
0:45	Bright melody returns back in tonic major	**A**
1:00	**B** and final **A** repeated	

Dreaming

0:00	Dreamlike melody in major key rises, falls, and then rises to a climax and falls again	**A**

0:44	**A** section repeated	
1:25	Melody extended through several major and minor keys	**B**
2:04	Dreamlike melody returns but now set in a new harmony	**A**

growing insanity

By all exterior signs, Robert Schumann's life could not have been a happy one. From his earliest years he had shown himself to be what psychiatrists now call a manic-depressive: He exhibited wild swings of mood from elation to despair. Though admired by many of the greatest musicians of the day, there was little popular recognition of his gifts as a composer during his lifetime. For a while he held the post of professor of piano at the Leipzig Conservatory, a chair he obtained with Mendelssohn's aid, and later, in 1850, he became director of municipal music in Düsseldorf, Germany. But he was ineffectual in both positions and his mental health declined. He began to hear voices, both heavenly and hellish, and one morning, pursued by demons, he jumped off a bridge into the Rhine River. Nearby fishermen pulled him to safety, but from that point on, by his own request, he was confined to an asylum where he died in 1856. As his life moved into its final, tragic years, his creative powers dwindled to nothing. As was true with many Romantic composers, most of Schumann's best works were the product of his youth.

Frédéric Chopin (1810–1849)

In the compositions of Frédéric Chopin, the piano and its music have their most perfect union. This "poet of the piano," as he was called, was born near Warsaw, Poland, of a French father and a Polish mother. The father taught at an elite secondary school for the sons of Polish nobility, and it was there that Frédéric not only gained an excellent general education but acquired aristocratic friends and tastes as well. He then moved on to the newly founded Warsaw Conservatory where, between 1826 and 1829, he concentrated on the study of piano and composition. It was during this period that he composed his first major work, a brilliant set of variations for piano and orchestra on Mozart's duet "Là ci darem la mano" ("Give me your hand") from *Don Giovanni* (on the duet, see page 208). Warsaw was now thought to be too small, too provincial, for a young man of his musical talents. So in 1830 he departed to seek his fortune in Vienna and Paris. The next year Poland fell to invading Russian troops, and Chopin never returned to his homeland.

After an unsuccessful year in Vienna, the twenty-one-year-old Chopin arrived in Paris in September 1831. His inaugural concerts caught Parisians' fancy, and his imaginative playing soon became the stuff of legends. But Chopin was not cut out for a life of the public virtuoso. He was introverted, physically slight—weighing little more than a hundred pounds—and somewhat sickly. Consequently, he chose to play at private *musicales* (musical evenings) in the homes of the aristocracy and to give lessons for a fee only the very rich, such as the Parisian Rothchilds, could afford. "I have been introduced all around the highest circles," he said within a year of his arrival. "I hobnob with ambassadors, princes, and ministers. I can't imagine what miracle is responsible for all this since I really haven't done anything to bring it about."

Not only did Chopin become the musical darling of the *haut monde* of Paris but he also was welcomed into the inner circle of an intellectual and artistic elite. Among his friends he numbered the poets Heinrich Heine (1797–1856) and Alfred de Musset (1810–1857), the novelists Honoré de

FIGURE 13–13

A superbly Romantic portrait of Chopin by Eugène Delacroix. Delacroix was a close friend of Chopin and frequently drove him to his concerts.

Balzac (1799–1850) and Victor Hugo (1802–1885), the composers Liszt and Berlioz, and the Romantic painter Eugène Delacroix (1799–1863).

But Chopin's most intense liaison was with Baroness Aurore Dudevant (1803–1876), a writer who under the pen name of George Sand poured forth a steady stream of Romantic novels roughly akin to our Silhouette Romances. She was also an ardent individualist who often dressed in men's clothing and smoked cigars (see cover). In 1838 she became Chopin's friend, lover, and protector. Many of his best works were composed at Nohant, her residence 150 miles south of Paris where the couple spent their summers. After their relationship ended in 1847, Chopin undertook a taxing concert tour of England and Scotland. While this improved his depleted finances, it weakened his delicate health. He died in Paris of tuberculosis at the age of thirty-nine.

Chopin was something of a rarity as a composer because each and every one of his works is written for the piano alone or features the piano in some way, as in the case of his two piano concertos and twenty art songs (in Polish). His compositional style was perfectly suited for the piano, highlighting the very best qualities of the instrument. Light, rapid passage work is placed in the upper register because the piano can sound quickly with no loss of clarity in its high range. Lovely arialike melodies are assigned to the middle register to exploit the instrument's lyrical, singing tone. Chords are broken into harplike arpeggios and set deep into the bass because the piano can provide a powerful, lush harmony to its own melody. And chromatic scales occur everywhere, taking advantage of the fact that these can be played faster on the piano than on any other instrument.

Chopin applied this idiomatic piano style to many different types of music. He transferred to the piano the spirit of three popular dances of the time: the mazurka and the polonaise (both of Polish origin) and the waltz (originally Viennese, by now everywhere in Europe). He wrote three full-length sonatas, but his large pieces usually have more suggestive names such as "fantasy" or "ballad." His shorter works include twenty-one nocturnes, one of which we will examine, and a set of twenty-four preludes—brief character pieces, one in each of the major and minor keys. Perhaps most remarkable is the set of twenty-four *Etudes,* studies which show that in the hands of a genius mere technical exercises can be transformed into pearls of exquisite beauty. While all of his works are highly subjective and intensely expressive, none makes use of a preexisting program or literary theme. Chopin seems to have had no need of external stimuli—his inspiration came from within.

FIGURE 13–14

Portrait of the novelist Aurore Dudevant (George Sand) by Eugène Delacroix. Both the painter Delacroix and the composer Chopin often stayed at her summer home in Nohant.

works for piano

NOCTURNE IN C# MINOR, OPUS 27, NO. 1 (1835)

Just how intensely expressive Chopin's music can be is illustrated by his Nocturne in C# minor written in 1835. A **nocturne** (night piece) is a slow, introspective type of piano music that came into favor in the 1820s and 1830s. It suggests moonlit nights, romantic longing, and a certain painful melancholy, all evoked through bittersweet melodies and softly strumming harmonies.

the nocturne

Chopin's Nocturne in C# minor begins with such a harmony, a C# minor chord spun out as an arpeggio in the bass. The melody **(A)** soon enters above this minor chord but, by means of an added sharp, immediately turns

FIGURE 13–15

FIGURE 13–15

A painting done from memory by the Polish artist Siemiradski shows Chopin playing in the drawing room of Prince Anton Radziwill.

to major. As the opening melody repeats again and again in the course of the work, so, too, do the expressive shifts, twisting back and forth from minor to major, from dark to light. This twisting is one way that intensity of feeling is created.

EXAMPLE 13–9

Soon the opening melody breaks off and a more agitated mood takes hold. A new theme **(B)** enters and the tempo increases. The bass now becomes more animated, playing rapid triplets. Simultaneously, it begins a long and mostly chromatic ascent which creates a feeling of rising tension.

EXAMPLE 13–10

A climax is reached at the peak of this line, emphasized by a remarkable chord change—a chord in E major (four sharps) is immediately followed by one in A♭ major (four flats; see example 12–1). Juxtaposing chords in such radically different keys is a means by which Chopin creates his bold harmonic shifts and rich harmonic colorings. After this climax the agitated **B** melody recommences, once more rising up the scale. Its climax this time yields to yet another new melody **(C)**, which, in turn, culminates with the loudest possible sound *(fff)* and a fermata (hold)—the music stands as if suspended in thin air. A recitative-like passage now pounds forth in the bass, showing off the deep bass range of the newly enlarged piano. This provides a transition back to the original melody **(A)** and tonic key (C# minor).

The return is especially rich and satisfying as the harplike accompaniment and plaintive melody seem to rise from the depths of the fading bass. Chopin's simple formal plan is now clear: statement–digression–return, each section with its own mood or atmosphere. The "lyrical expressive" **(A)** gives way to the "powerful and passionate" **(B)** and **(C)**, which yields finally to the initial lyricism **(A)**. The returning **A** is extended by means of an exquisite little coda which carries the lyrical mood into a heavenly major realm. As the poet Heine said of Chopin, "He hails from the land of Mozart, Raphael, and Goethe. His true home is in the realm of Poetry."

FIGURE 13–16

Daguerreotype (an early photograph) of Chopin a few months before his premature death from tuberculosis in 1849.

LISTENING GUIDE	Frédéric Chopin Nocturne in C# minor, Opus 27, No. 1 (1835)	CD 4/8 6–Tape 4B 2–Tape 2A

0:00	Arpeggiated chords establish harmony in bass	**A**
0:08	Plaintive melody enters quietly in upper register	
0:44	Melody continues	
1:24	Plaintive melody begins again with countermelody now added (1:30) in the middle voice	
2:03	Melody breaks off and accompaniment continues	
2:15	New passionate theme enters and gets louder	**B**
2:43	Rich chords move from four sharps to four flats	
2:51	Passionate theme continues and rises	
3:01	New, more heroic melody enters	**C**
3:17	Very loud repeated chords, then a fermata (hold)	
3:25	Loud, recitative-like passage descending deep into the bass	
3:37	Arpeggiated accompaniment, then plaintive melody reemerges	**A**
4:30	Coda, entirely in major key	**CODA**

the touring virtuoso

the modern piano recital

Franz Liszt (1811–1886)

Franz Liszt was born in Hungary of German-speaking parents. His ambitious father moved the family to Vienna in 1822 so that his gifted son might study with the very best teachers. From Vienna it was on to Paris to establish the boy as the latest child prodigy, the newest infant virtuoso. But some years later, when his father died suddenly of typhoid fever, the sixteen-year-old youth was left in Paris more or less on his own. He gave piano lessons, became something of a religious fanatic, and tried to enter the Paris seminary in hopes of becoming a priest.

But in 1831 Liszt heard the great violin virtuoso Niccolò Paganini (see page 241), and this changed his life. "What a man, what a violin, what an artist! O God, what pain and suffering, what torment in those four strings." Liszt vowed to bring Paganini's technical virtuosity to the piano, and he did. Practicing four to five hours a day—unusual dedication for a prodigy—he taught himself to play on the piano what had never been played before: tremolos, leaps, double trills, glissandos, simultaneous octaves in both hands, all at breathtaking speed. When he returned to the stage for his own concerts, he overwhelmed the audience. He had become the greatest pianist of that era, perhaps of all time.

Then, in 1833, Liszt's life took another unexpected turn. He met the Countess Marie d'Agoult and decided to give up the life of the performing artist in exchange for domestic security. Although she was already married and the mother of two children, she and Liszt eloped, first to Switzerland and then Italy. Residing in these countries for four years, the couple had three children of their own. (Their youngest daughter would become the wife of Richard Wagner, see Fig. 14–9, page 290.) In Switzerland the natural beauty of the land gave rise to several compositions for solo piano. In Italy a painting of Raphael (1483–1529), a sculpture of Michelangelo (1474–1564), and a reading of the *Divine Comedy* of Dante (1265–1321) inspired other pianistic creations. "Raphael and Michelangelo make Mozart and Beethoven more easy for me to understand," he said at the time. Later he completed and revised these character pieces for the piano in a set called *Années de pèlerinage (Years of Pilgrimage)*.

Beginning in 1839, and continuing until 1847, Liszt once more took to the road as a touring virtuoso. He played more than a thousand concerts: from Ireland to Turkey, from Sweden to Spain, from Portugal to Russia. Everywhere he went the handsome pianist was greeted with the sort of mass hysteria today reserved for rock stars. Audiences of three thousand crowded into the larger halls. Women tried to rip off his silk scarf and white gloves. They fought for a lock of his hair. "Lisztomania" swept across Europe.

Despite their obvious sensationalism, Liszt's concerts in the 1840s established the format of our modern-day piano recital. He was the first to play entire programs from memory (not reading from music). He was the first to place the piano parallel with the line of the stage so that neither his back nor full face, but rather his extraordinary side profile, was visible to the audience. He was the first to perform on the stage alone—up to that point concerts traditionally had included numerous performers on the program. At first these solo appearances were called "soliloquies," then "recitals," suggesting they were something akin to poetic recitations.

While concertizing in Russia in 1847, Liszt met another married woman who would profoundly change the course of his life—Princess Sayn-Wittgenstein. (He and Marie d'Agoult had separated in 1844.) This new woman convinced him to give up the life of an itinerant virtuoso and concentrate on composing. Liszt accepted a position at the court of Weimar, Germany, and took up residence with his new mistress. Because a full orchestra was now at his disposal at Weimar, he produced a steady stream of large-scale orchestral works. In 1861 the couple moved to Rome where it was hoped that the princess would secure a divorce. When this was not forthcoming, Liszt entered the lower Holy Orders of the Roman Church, styled himself "Abbé Liszt," and for a while even lived in the Vatican! But he continued traveling and performing to the very end. He died at the age of seventy-five in Bayreuth, Germany, where he had gone to hear the latest opera of his son-in-law, Richard Wagner.

Liszt wrote a dozen symphonic poems*—one-movement works for orchestra that capture the spirit and sentiments of a preexisting story, literary theme or poetic idea—as well as two program symphonies*, and three piano concertos. He also composed more than sixty religious works, including two oratorios*, almost all dating from his stay in Rome. In his instrumental music Liszt developed the idea of "thematic transformation," in which a single main theme and its offshoots dominate an entire movement or all the movements of a work. In this he was carrying forward Berlioz's use of an *idée fixe* (see page 257).

But Liszt was first and foremost a pianist, and it is for his piano music that he is known above all else. If Chopin composed in a way that made the piano sound at its best, Liszt wrote in a style that made him sound best at the piano. He had large hands and unusually long fingers (Fig. 13–17). He could play a melody in octaves when others could play only the single notes

FIGURE 13–18

Marie d'Agoult. She was a novelist in her own right and some of the tracts on music that appeared under Liszt's name, such as his "On the Position of Artists and their Place in Society," were likely penned by her.

FIGURE 13–19

Lisztomania. A recital by Liszt in the mid-nineteenth century was likely to create the sort of sensation that a concert by a rock star might generate today.

of the line. If others could execute a passage in octaves, Liszt could dash it off in more impressive-sounding tenths. So he wrote daredevil music of this sort. His *Transcendental Etudes* and *Hungarian Rhapsodies* are among the most difficult pieces ever written for piano. Only the most advanced virtuosos attempt them.

STORM, FROM *YEARS OF PILGRIMAGE*

As a representative example of Liszt's writing for piano when he was at the height of his dazzling pianistic powers, we turn our attention to *Orage (Storm)*. This is one of the character pieces in the set *Years of Pilgrimage,* begun in 1835–36 during his sojourn in Switzerland with Countess Marie d'Agoult and completed in 1848–52. Not only was wild nature an influence on the Romantic spirit here—a violent Swiss mountain storm was apparently the composer's initial inspiration—but poetry as well. Liszt prefaced *Storm* with a few lines from Lord Byron's Romantic poem *Childe Harold's Pilgrimage.*

> But where of ye, oh tempests! is the goal?
> Are ye like those within the human breast?
> Or do ye find, at length, like eagles, some high nest?

Is the storm atop Alpine peaks or within the human heart? No matter, in either case it is a violent one indeed. There is a frightening introduction, a passionate theme marked *presto furioso*, a tempestuous interlude in which the theme is seen in several new vistas, a return to, and then fade away of, the theme, and finally a great hail of rising and descending octaves to signal the end. If nothing else, *Storm* is an astonishing outburst of pianistic fury. No wonder Liszt left his audiences stunned.

LISTENING GUIDE

Franz Liszt
Storm, from *Years of Pilgrimage*
(sketched 1835–36, completed 1848–52)

CD 4/9
6–Tape 4B

0:00	**INTRODUCTION**	Burst of chords followed by a torrent of rising and falling chromatic scales in octaves in both hands
0:24	**A**	Theme in right hand, rising octaves in the left

0:35	Theme begins again
0:48	Theme extended into high register

1:03	**B**	Cascades of chromatic thirds and then octaves create a "whistling wind" effect
1:26		Theme, now twice as fast, above in right hand with rapid triplets thundering below in the left
1:37		Tremolo, a technique usually used on the violin, played on high by the right hand
2:00		Flashes of the beginning of the theme enveloped in a downpour of parallel octaves
2:11	**C**	Tense, rising chords
2:32		Arpeggios whistle up and down in right hand while theme is heard deep in the bass
3:13	**A**	Theme returns
3:42		Theme dies away
4:13	**CODA**	Burst of chords leads to climactic run of octaves in both hands

LISTENING EXERCISES

29   Franz Schubert   CD 4/3
Piano Quintet in A major, the "Trout" Quintet (1819)   6–Tape 4A
Fourth movement, *Andantino* (gently moving)

This exercise asks you to listen to a movement of Schubert's famous "Trout" Quintet, a good example of chamber music in which there is much give and take among the five instruments. Don't forget that the theme, or melody, for this theme and variations movement is taken from his song *The Trout* (1817). Take one more look at the theme on page 254, and answer the following questions:

Theme (0:00–0:56)

1. Which is the correct schematic representation of the musical form of the theme?   a. **abc**   b. **aba**   c. **aabb′**
2. (0:00–0:56) What does the piano do as the strings present the theme for the first time ?
   a. plays rapid arpeggios   b. plays solid chordal accompaniment
   c. plays nothing

Variation 1 (0:57–1:52)

3. What string technique is the double bass using throughout this variation?   a. pizzicato   b. vibrato   c. tremolo

Variation 2 (1:53–2:52)

4. The viola has the melody in this variation. In what range does it play?
   a. the highest range of the strings
   b. the middle range of the strings
   c. the lowest range of the strings
5. Are both the **a** and **b** portions of the melody each repeated in this variation? _____

Variation 3 (2:53–3:45)

6. Which instrument helps the double bass finish phrase **a** of the melody (at 3:05 and 3:19)?   a. piano   b. violin   c. cello
7. Does this instrument also help the double bass finish phrase **b?** _____

Variation 4 (3:46–4:46)

8. In this variation phrase **a** is exactly repeated (at 4:02). Is phrase **b** also exactly repeated (at 4:35)? _____

Variation 5 (4:47–6:15)

9. Which dynamic level is maintained as the cello plays throughout this variation?   a. *fortissimo*   b. *andantino*   c. *piano*

Variation 6 (6:16–7:30)

10. Toward the very end of this final variation (at 7:18), which instrument brings the movement to a conclusion by twice sounding the accompaniment figure from the song *The Trout* (see page 252)?
    a. violin   b. cello   c. piano

30	Hector Berlioz *Symphonie fantastique* (1830) Fifth movement, Dream of the Witches' Sabbath	CD 4/4 6–Tape 4A 2–Tape 2A

Imagine that you had been among the audience in Paris on December 5, 1830, when Berlioz's *Symphonie fantastique* was first performed. If you had been a dedicated concertgoer up to that time, you might have heard one or two of the late symphonies of Beethoven. This would have been the extent of your exposure to "radical" new music. How would you have reacted? Of course, it is now impossible to gauge the impact of Berlioz's progressive gestures—our ears have become accustomed to them in the music of other, later composers. The following set of questions asks you to focus on a few special aspects of orchestration and form in this astonishing work. As always, be sure that you have read the discussion of this movement in the text (page 258) and have listened to it at least once following the Listening Guide (page 260).

1. (0:00–0:09) The opening sounds eerie because the upper strings are divided into many parts and are playing with a special string technique. What is this technique called?
   a. pizzicato
   b. tremolo
   c. ostinato
2. (0:16–0:19) Now another string technique is employed by the upper strings. Which is it?   a. pizzicato   b. tremolo   c. ostinato
3. (1:26–2:16) The *idée fixe*, now transformed, returns in a high clarinet, is cut off, and then begins again. Previously in the symphony Berlioz has cast it sometimes in duple and sometimes in triple meter. Which meter do you feel here?   a. duple   b. triple

4. (2:39–2:56) The "ominous transition" leading to the introduction of the *Dies irae* chant is a gradual descent. By which family is it mainly carried out?   a. string   b. woodwind   c. brass

5. (3:46) The French horns now play the *Dies irae* theme twice as fast as before. What is this sort of reduction of note values in music called?
   _____

6. (4:26–4:45) In this passage the *Dies irae* melody continues in the low brasses against a pounding sound produced by the bass drum. Which of the following is true?
   a. the low brasses are playing the melody on the downbeat while the bass drum syncopates against it
   b. the bass drum is playing on the downbeat while the low brasses syncopate against it

7. (5:19–5:44) Now the fugato begins. Its structure is made clear, in part, because the composer cuts off the subject each time so as to announce the next entry. He does this by means of a burst of syncopated chords in the brasses. How many times does this occur? _____

8. (7:02–7:18) Which instruments play a reminiscence of the *Dies irae* chant?
   a. bells   b. tubas   c. cellos and double basses

9. (8:04–8:27) Now the *Dies irae* and the witches' dance (fugue subject) are heard simultaneously. How are they orchestrated?
   a. *Dies irae* in violins, witches' dance in trumpets
   b. *Dies irae* in trumpets, witches' dance in violins

10. (8:30–8:46) As the strings produce the crackling sound by playing *col legno* (with the wood of the bow and not the horse hair), a melody is heard in the woodwinds. Which is it?
    a. the *idée fixe*
    b. the *Dies irae* chant
    c. the witches' dance (fugue subject)

	Felix Mendelssohn	CD 4/5
31	Overture to *A Midsummer Night's Dream* (1826)	6–Tape 4B

By now you should have read the discussion of this masterful overture on pages 262–264. Writing descriptive music according to a predetermined program is very much a part of the spirit of the Romantic age, but here the seventeen-year-old Felix Mendelssohn has chosen to do so in traditional sonata–allegro form. As you listen to this piece and answer the questions that follow, try to identify which are the Classical qualities of this overture and which are the Romantic.

1. Appropriately enough, the fairies' music is light and darting. Mendelssohn creates this unique sound, not only by having the strings play fast and quietly, but also by requiring that the notes be detached, sometimes even plucked. Which are the two playing techniques that help produce this sound and which Mendelssohn specifies in his score?
   a. staccato   b. rubato   c. legato   d. pizzicato

2. When the transition begins with the music for Duke Theseus and his court (1:04), the full orchestra enters *fortissimo.* Which is the correct musical term for "full orchestra"?
   a. tremolo   b. toccata   c. tutti

3. Before the lyrical second theme enters quietly in the strings (2:08), there is a brief preparation for it (2:00–2:07). Which family of instruments plays this short introduction? _____

4. Before and during the presentation of Bottom's theme (3:02–3:13), which instruments create the comic quality of this character?
   a. low brasses   b. middle strings   c. high woodwinds

5. Which instruments are most prominent, not surprisingly, in the hunting or fanfare motive that closes the exposition (3:22)?
   a. violas   b. timpani   c. trumpets

6. Between presentations of the hunting calls, a theme from earlier in the movement is also worked in (3:28–4:35). Which one is it? (If you have difficulty remembering, listen again and look at the musical examples on page 264.) _____

7. In the middle of the development there is a long series of pizzicatos in the strings (beginning at 4:52). Which accurately describes the string motion at this point?
   a. pizzicato notes ascending by step
   b. pizzicato notes ascending by octaves
   c. pizzicato notes descending by step
   d. pizzicato notes descending by octaves

8. At the very end of the development (5:27–5:51), the music almost comes to a stop as the violins play a slow solo line. Would you say this is a good example of Classical or Romantic expression in these measures? _____ Why? _____

9. Would you say that the harmony at the end of the recapitulation (9:04–9:14) is active or static? (Can you sing or hum one pitch throughout without creating a dissonance?) _____

10. Which is true about the very end of the overture?
    a. it concludes with the music for Duke Theseus, now in a more lyrical mood
    b. it concludes with the same four chords with which it began
    c. it concludes with the same four chords with which it began, but with a timpani roll added to the last

KEY WORDS

col legno	George Sand	ophicleide
cornet	Gewandhaus	recital
Dies irae	Orchestra	Schubertiade
diminution	Harriet Smithson	song cycle
double	*idée fixe*	through
counterpoint	Lisztomania	composed
English horn	nocturne	

ROMANTIC OPERA

14

T he nineteenth century was a period in which Romantic poetry blossomed, the novel came into its own as a literary genre, and dramas for the stage, especially those of Shakespeare, enjoyed unprecedented popularity. It was also a time in which words and music were tightly allied, as seen in the newly emergent art song and various kinds of programmatic music based on literary texts that came into being. Given this Romantic interest in the union of text and music, it is not surprising that opera also flourished, opera being a genre that combines music, poetry, and drama. Indeed, the nineteenth century has been called "the golden age of opera." It is the century of Rossini, Bellini, Donizetti, Verdi, Wagner, Gounod, Bizet, and early Puccini. Even today about seventy percent of the works produced by the San Francisco Opera Company, the Met in New York, Covent Garden in London, and La Scala in Milan, for example, are operas written during the years 1820–1900.

Italy, of course, is the home of opera. The Italians have an innate love of melody, and their language, with its evenly spaced vowels, is wonderfully suited for singing. While there were important French operas written during the eighteenth century, Italian opera then ruled the European scene. When Handel wrote operas for the London stage in the 1720s, for example, he composed Italian operas, as did Mozart when he created musical theater for the courts of Germany and Austria in the 1770s and 1780s. With the onset of the nineteenth century, however, other peoples, driven by an emerging sense of national pride, developed idiomatic opera in their native tongues. Although Italian opera remained the dominant style, it now had to share the stage, not only with traditional French opera, but with the newer forms of Russian, Czech, and especially German opera as well.

ROMANTIC OPERA IN ITALY

During the early decades of the nineteenth century, the primacy of Italian opera was maintained almost single-handedly by Gioachino Rossini

FIGURE 14–1

Gioachino Rossini

(1792–1868). Surprising as it may seem today, Rossini was the most popular composer of the 1820s, far exceeding in celebrity Beethoven or Schubert. He owed his public favor not only to the charm of his music but also to the fact that the genre of music within which he chose to work—opera—was then the most popular form of public musical entertainment, much more so than the symphony or string quartet, for example. Rossini continued, and indeed brought to a glorious close, the eighteenth-century tradition of comic opera or *opera buffa* (see page 153). Catchy oft-repeating melodies, vivacious rhythms, and rollicking crescendos were his trademark. His best known comic opera, *The Barber of Seville,* has never disappeared from the operatic stage since it first appeared in 1816. Even casual music lovers know a little of this enduring work in the form of the "Figaro, Figaro, Figaro" call from the opening aria for the resourceful barber, Figaro. Rossini could also write in a more serious style, as exemplified in his last opera *William Tell* (1829). This stormy drama, too, has achieved a measure of popular immortality, the overture providing the theme music for the radio and film character of the Lone Ranger.

Italian *Bel Canto* Opera

Whereas German operatic composers would come to emphasize the dramatic power and instrumental color of the orchestra, Italians after Rossini increasingly focused all of their energies on the solo voice and on melody—on the art of beautiful singing, or **bel canto.** The two most gifted of the early creators of this more serious *bel canto* opera were Gaetano Donizetti (1797–1848) and Vincenzo Bellini (1801–1835). In their works there is little orchestral color and almost no counterpoint. The orchestra merely provides a simple harmonic support for the soaring, sometimes divinely beautiful lines of the voice. Look at the opening of the famous aria "Casta diva" from Bellini's *Norma* (1831) in which the heroine sings a prayer to a distant moon goddess. Here the orchestra functions like a giant guitar. Simple chords are fleshed out as arpeggios by the strings while an even simpler bass line is plucked below. All of the musical interest is in the rapturous sound of the human voice. "Opera must make people weep, shudder, die through the singing," Bellini said.

EXAMPLE 14–1

(Chaste goddess, who does bathe in silver light these hallowed, ancient trees)

gen - ti   que - - ste sa - cre, que - ste sa - cre, que-ste sa - cre anti - che pian - te,

Not surprisingly, by placing such importance on the solo singer, *bel canto* opera fostered an environment in which might flourish a star system among the cast. Usually, it was the lyric soprano—heroine and "prima donna"— who held the most exalted position in the musical firmament. By the 1880s, she would be called a "diva" which, as in the aria "Casta diva," means "goddess." Indeed, the goddess of the beautiful female voice would rule Italian opera right through the nineteenth century, from the early *bel canto* operas of Donizetti and Bellini through the mature works of Giuseppe Verdi (1813–1901) and Giacomo Puccini (1858–1924).

cult of the diva

Giuseppe Verdi (1813–1901)

The name Giuseppe Verdi is virtually synonymous with Italian opera. For six decades, from the time of *Nabucco* in 1842 until *Falstaff* in 1893, he had almost no rival for the affections of the opera-loving public in Italy and elsewhere throughout Europe. Even today the best-loved of the twenty-six operas of Verdi are more readily available—in opera houses, in TV productions, and on videotape—than those of any other composer.

Verdi was born near Busseto in northern Italy in 1813, the son of a tavern keeper. He was apparently no musical prodigy, for at the age of eighteen he was rejected for admission to the Conservatory of Music in Milan because he was already too old and his piano technique faulty. But Verdi stayed on in Milan to study composition. He returned to Busseto in 1835 to serve as the town's bandmaster, and then four years later went back to Milan to earn his livelihood as a composer.

To be a composer in nineteenth-century Italy was to be a composer of opera. Verdi's first, *Oberto,* was produced at the famous La Scala Opera House in Milan (Fig. 14–3) in 1839 and it achieved a modicum of success. But his *Nabucco* of 1842 was a popular triumph, receiving an unprecedented fifty-seven performances at La Scala in that year alone. Through subsequent productions in other theaters, Verdi's name was quickly carried throughout Italy, Europe, and America, both north and south. His career was launched.

The text, or libretto*, of *Nabucco,* as well as most of the other operas Verdi composed in the 1840s, concerns the suppression of a people by a cruel foreign power—and by implication the people of Italy by Austria, which then ruled much of the peninsula. Verdi had become a spirited liberal and an Italian patriot. Normally, we do not think of music as expressing political ideas, but opera was such an important part of Italian popular culture that it had the capacity to inspire political revolution. In his libretti Verdi inserted and

FIGURE 14–2

Giuseppe Verdi

FIGURE 14–3

La Scala Opera House about 1830.
Verdi's first four and last two operas
had their premieres at La Scala, the
foremost opera house in Italy.

*Verdi, a voice for Italian
independence*

"a galley slave"

then set for chorus or solo voice such fiery words as "You may have the universe, so long as I keep Italy" and "Long live Italy! A sacred pact binds all her sons." Through his overtly nationalistic music, the composer became an unlikely leader in the Risorgimento, the movement for a united Italy free of foreign domination. In 1861, after that goal had been largely achieved, Verdi was elected to Italy's first parliament, and later, in 1874 to its senate.

But in the late 1840s the drive for Italian independence was far from complete. Indeed, the liberal Revolution of 1848 failed to oust the Austrians from Milan, and Verdi for a time became disillusioned with politics. He now turned his attention to domestic themes and more personal drama, producing a trio of much-admired operas: *Rigoletto* (1851), *La traviata* (1853), and *Il trovatore* (1853). For most of the early-to-mid-1850s, Verdi lived away from the area of Milan, residing in Paris or traveling throughout Europe to oversee the production of his increasingly numerous works. He called these years of toil and intense productivity "my years as a galley slave."

On his return to his homeland in 1857, the pace of Verdi's opera production slackened: He composed only when the subject was of interest or the fee so substantial he couldn't refuse. *La forza del destino* (*The Force of Destiny*, 1861) was written for St. Petersburg for the enormous commission of 60,000 francs; *Don Carlos* (1867) was composed for Paris for an equally large amount; and *Aïda* (1871), written for Cairo shortly after the opening of the Suez Canal, for the astonishing sum of 150,000 francs. Verdi had become more than a little wealthy and he retired to his estate in northern Italy to lead the life of a country squire—or so he thought.

But like a performer who feels he owes the audience more, or has something more to prove to himself, Verdi returned to the theater for two final encores: *Otello* (1887) and *Falstaff* (1893), both exceptionally well-crafted operas based on dramas of Shakespeare. The latter work was written when the composer was on the threshold of eighty, a feat without parallel in music history or the annals of the dramatic stage. He died peacefully at his country home in 1901, a much-respected national institution.

FIGURE 14–4

Verdi's long-time mistress and, ultimately, his wife, Giuseppina Strepponi holding the score of his early opera *Nabucco*.

VERDI'S DRAMATURGY AND MUSICAL STYLE When the curtain goes up on a Verdi opera, the listener will find elements of dramaturgy—how the drama is put together—and musical style that are unique to this composer. For Giuseppe Verdi conflict was at the root of every emotion, and he expressed conflict, whether personal or national, by juxtaposing self-contained, yet clearly differentiated, units of music. A rousing march, a patriotic chorus, a passionate recitative, and a lyrical aria follow one after the other in quick succession. In each vivid number there is no mistaking which emotion is being communicated to the audience. The composer aims not at musical and dramatic subtlety but rather at immediate effect and direct appeal to the listener's sensibilities. The emotional states of the characters are so clearly drawn, sometimes overdrawn, that the drama comes perilously close to melodrama—excessively sentimental or sensational. But it is never dull. There is action, passion, and intensity. "I would be willing to set even a newspaper, or a letter, to music," he said in 1854, "but in the theater the public will stand for anything except boredom."

How is this feeling of relentless intensity in a Verdi opera brought about? It is achieved mainly by changing the nature of the recitative and the vocal quality of the aria. Verdi generally continues to use the former to recite or narrate the action and the latter for expression of feeling. But now the old *secco* recitative, with mere keyboard accompaniment, gives way to orchestrally accompanied recitative *(recitativo accompagnato)*. This allows the action to flow smoothly from orchestrally accompanied aria to orchestrally accompanied recitative and back without a jarring change of texture. Moreover, *recitatives and arias* Verdi is still very much a composer in the Italian *bel canto* tradition of Bellini and Donizetti. The emphasis throughout remains on the solo aria, on a lyrical, beautiful vocal line: No composer had a greater gift for writing simple, memorable melodies that the audience could whistle on the way out of the theater. Yet Verdi also adds intensity and passion to these arias by pushing the singers to the utmost of their range. The tenor is asked to sing up to the B above middle C, the soprano two octaves and more above middle C. The thrilling moments in which the hero (the tenor) or the heroine (the soprano) go right to the top are literally the high points of any Verdi opera.

LA TRAVIATA (1853)

We may measure the high intensity and passion in Verdi's operas by listening to a portion of his *La traviata* (1853). *La traviata* literally means "The Woman Gone Astray." It tells the story of the sickly Violetta Valery, a courtesan, or "kept woman," who resists and then succumbs to the love of a new suitor, the young Alfredo Germont. For a while the couple retires from Paris to lead a quiet life in the country. But without explanation Violetta deserts Alfredo, in truth so that her former life will not bring disgrace upon his *the plot*

Figure 14–5

Marie Duplessis. The end of her brief, scandalous life is the subject of Giuseppe Verdi's opera *La traviata*.

FIGURE 14–6

The great Australian soprano Joan Sutherland singing the role of Violetta and tenor Luciano Pavarotti as Alfredo in Verdi's *La traviata*.

respectable family. The hot-tempered Alfredo now publicly insults Violetta, fights a duel with her new "protector," and leaves Paris. When the nature of Violetta's sacrifice is revealed, Alfredo rushes back but arrives only a short time before she dies.

Verdi first heard this sentimental tale, one that pits passionate love against middle-class morality, when in Paris during the winter of 1852. There he and his mistress, the singer Giuseppina Strepponi (Fig. 14–4), were captivated by a new play of Alexandre Dumas the younger entitled *The Lady of the Camellias,* now known to English audiences simply as *Camille.* The main character of the drama, Violetta Valery, was modeled after a real-life figure, Marie Duplessis (Fig. 14–5), who had been the mistress of playwright Dumas and, briefly, of composer Franz Liszt as well. Like many in this period, she, too, died young of tuberculosis, at the age of twenty-three.

We join *La traviata* toward the end of the first act. A gala party is in progress in a fashionable Parisian salon, and here the dashing Alfredo has finally managed to cut Violetta away from the crowd to profess to her his love. He does so in the aria "Un dì felice" ("One Happy Day") that is lovely, yet somber in tone. The seriousness of his intent is underscored by the slow, square, even plodding accompaniment in the orchestra. When Violetta enters she is supported by the same accompaniment, but the mood of the aria is radically changed to one that is light and carefree. Witness how Verdi's direct musical characterization works: Alfredo's slow melody with a hint of minor is replaced by Violetta's flighty sound of high, rapidly moving notes. Eventually, the two join in a duet: he below somberly proclaiming the mysteries of love; she above making light of them.

After the duet has come to a cadence, a friend, Gaston, briefly interrupts the couple. But soon their voices are once more joined. The tempo of the music increases and so does their growing ardor for each other, shown musically by the way the singers rush in breathlessly on successively higher notes. This rapid second, and final, section of the duet is called a **cabaletta**— the concluding fast section of any two-part aria or duet. The cabaletta was an oft-used dramatic device in Italian opera because the increased speed of the music allowed one or both of the singers to race off stage at the end of a scene or act.

Alfredo has, in fact, kissed Violetta's hand and departed. She is left on stage alone and thinks for a moment that he may be the one her wayward soul has long sought. But in an impassioned recitative ("Folly! Folly! What sort of crazy dream is this"), she jumps to her feet to proclaim that she must always remain free of the entanglements of serious love. This aria "Sempre libera" ("Always Free") is one of the great showpieces for soprano voice. Yet it also helps define through music the character of Violetta—the extraordinary carefree flourishes on the word "pleasure," for example, reinforce her "enjoy-ourselves-while-we-may" approach to life. This declaration of independence is momentarily broken by the voice of Alfredo who from outside her window expresses again his feelings about the mysterious powers of love. Violetta brushes these aside and repeats her vow to be always free. Of course, she does not; she falls fatally in love with Alfredo as acts two and three reveal. Listen now to these two excerpts from Act I of Verdi's *La traviata.* You will have the pleasure of hearing two of the greatest voices of the twentieth century, Joan Sutherland (soprano) and Luciano Pavarotti (tenor).

LISTENING GUIDE

Giuseppe Verdi
La traviata (1853)
Act I, Scenes 4 and 6

CD 4/10–11
6–Tape 4B

Characters: Alfredo, a young man of good standing; Violetta, a kept woman leading a wanton life in Paris
Situation: A party in a Parisian salon around 1850; Alfredo professes his love to Violetta, who at first rejects him.

Aria

0:00

Alfredo (tenor)

Un dì felice, eterea,	One happy day,
Mi balanaste innante,	you appeared to me.
E da quel dì tremante	And from this day, trembling,
Vissi d'ignoto amor.	I have lived in that
Di quell'amor ch'è palpito	unspoken love, in that love
Dell'universo intero,	which animates the world,

Shift to minor

| Misterioso, altero, | mysterious, proud, pain |
| Croce e delizia al cor. | and delight to the heart. |

Violetta (soprano)

1:22 Violetta changes aria to lighter mood through faster tempo and shorter notes

Ah, se ciò èver, fugitemi.	If that's true, leave me.
Solo amistade io v'offro;	Only friendship I offer you.
Amar non so, nè soffro	I don't know how to love
Un cosi eroico amore.	nor suffer such an heroic love.
Io sono franca, ingenua;	I'm being honest and sincere.
Altra cercar dovete;	You must find another.
Non arduo troverete	It won't be difficult.
Dimenticarmi allor.	Just leave me.

Duet

1:46 Alfredo and Violetta together in rapturous duet

Alfredo

Oh amore!	Oh love!
Misterioso, altero,	mysterious, proud, pain
Croce e delizia al cor.	and delight to the heart.

Violetta

Non arduo troverete	It won't be difficult.
Dimenticarmi allor.	Just leave me.

2:48 Exuberant vocal flourishes for both | "Ah" | "Ah" |

Gaston

3:26 Gaston interrupts

| Ebben? che diavol fate? | Well, what the devil's going on? |

Violetta

| Si folleggiava! | Just fooling around. |

Gaston

| Ah, ah, sta ben! restate! | Well then, continue! |

Strains of a waltz heard from ballroom

Duet

3:35 Continues as dialogue

Violetta

Amor dunque non più.	Well then, no more about love!
Vi garba il patto?	Is that a promise?

Alfredo

| Io v'obbedisco. Parto. | I'll obey you. I'm leaving. |

Violetta

A tal giungeste	So it's come to that already?
(Si toglie un fiore	(She takes a flower from
dal seno.)	her bosom.)
Predete questo fiore.	Take this flower.

		Alfredo
	Perchè?	Why?
		Violetta
	Per riportarlo.	So that you can bring it back.
		Alfredo
	Quando?	When?
		Violetta
	Quando sarà appassito.	When it's withered.
		Alfredo
	O ciel! Domani?	Good god, you mean tomorrow?
		Violetta
	Ebben, domani.	Oh well, tomorrow.

Cabaletta

		Alfredo
4:01	Tempo increases	
	Io son, Io son felice!	I'm so happy.
		Violetta
	D'amarmi dite ancora?	Do you still say you love me?
		Alfredo
	Oh! quanto v'amo!	Oh, how much I love you.
	Io son felice.	I'm so happy.
		Violetta
	Partite?	Are you going?
		Alfredo
	Parto.	I'm going.
		Violetta
	Addio.	Adieu.
		Alfredo
	Di più non bramo.	I need nothing more.
	Addio. (esce)	Adieu. (exits)

CD 4/11; 6–Tape 4B; 2–Tape 2A (Act I, Scene 6)

Recitative

		Violetta
0:00	Accompanied by orchestra	
	Follie! Follie! delirio vano è questo! Povera donna, sola, abbandonata, in questo populoso deserto che appellano Parigi. Che spero or più? Che far degg'io?	Folly, Folly! What sort of crazy dream is this! Poor woman, alone, adandoned in this populated desert that they call Paris. What hope have I? What can I do?
0:49	Flights of vocal fancy as she thinks of pleasure	Gioir! Di voluttà ne' vortici perir! Gioir!	Pleasure! Perish in a whirl of indulgence! Pleasure!
1:05	Introduction to aria		

Aria

		Violetta
1:16		
	Sempre libera degg'io Folleggiare di gioia in gioia, Vo' che scorra il viver mio Pei sentieri del piacer.	Always free I must remain to follow from pleasure to pleasure, running my life along the paths of joy.

		Nasca il giorno, o il giorno muoia, Sempre lieta ne' ritrovi, A diletti sempre nuovi Dee volare il mio pensier.	From dawn to dusk I'm always happy finding new delights that make my spirit soar.

Alfredo

2:01	Echoes of his previous aria	Amor è palpito dell'universo, misterioso, altero, croce e delizia al cor.	Love that animates the world mysterious, proud, pain and delight to the heart.

Violetta

2:48	Extravagant flourishes	Follie! Follie! Gioir! Gioir!	Folly! Folly! Pleasure! Pleasure!

Aria returns

3:17	this time even more brilliant in its showy, superficial style	Sempre libera . . .	Always free . . .

(Listening Exercise 32)

ROMANTIC OPERA IN GERMANY

Before 1820 opera was mainly an Italian affair. It was first created in Italy around 1600 and then, during the next two hundred years, was exported to all parts of Europe and eventually to North and South America. But German opera, in comparison, was rather weak and provincial. Before 1820 the only German opera heard outside German-speaking lands was Mozart's *Die Zauberflöte* (*The Magic Flute*, 1791), which owed its widespread appeal to the glories of Mozart's music rather than any fondness for the somewhat primitive conventions of German opera.

What passed as native opera in German-speaking lands went by the name of *Singspiel*. A **Singspiel** ("singing play") is a musical comedy or light musical drama which has, by sheer coincidence, many elements in common with our present-day Broadway musical: plenty of topical humor, tuneful solo songs, energetic choral numbers, and spoken dialogue instead of sung recitative. Mozart, in *The Magic Flute* (1791), and Beethoven, in his only opera, *Fidelio* (1805), each wrote a *Singspiel* in which he tried to bring greater seriousness and unity to the genre. A somewhat younger contemporary of Beethoven, Karl Maria von Weber (1786–1826), likewise attempted to develop a tradition of serious German opera distinct from the Italian style. His *Der Freischütz* (1821) makes use of German folk songs, or folklike melodies, as well as a libretto that delights in magic and the supernatural. (Its most memorable moment is the "Wolf Glen" scene at the beginning of the second act during which magical silver bullets are cast in a Satanic ritual.) The German passion for horror subjects and supernatural tales in the Romantic period can be seen in other works such as Heinrich Marschner's *The Vampire* (1828) and Richard Wagner's *The Flying Dutchman* (1843).

FIGURE 14–7

Richard Wagner

Richard Wagner (1813–1883)

The composer who made the German dream of a truly national opera a reality was the titanic figure Richard Wagner. Wagner was not merely a composer but also a politician, philosopher, propagandist, and bully for his particular vision of dramatic music. For Wagner, opera was the most perfect form of artistic expression and the composer a religious prophet who could reveal a musical kingdom to his congregation, namely, the listening audience. Wagner's music is, indeed, often inspiring. It contains moments of grandeur unmatched by any other composer. His influence on the musical style of other composing musicians at the end of the nineteenth century was enormous. Yet his reception by the musical public at large, then and now, has been divided. Some listeners are immediately converted to adoring Wagnerites at the first sound of the heroic themes and powerful orchestral climaxes. Others are left cold, believing the music long-winded and the operatic plots devoid of real human drama.

Who was this controversial artist who has stirred such mixed feelings within the musical public now for more than a century? Richard Wagner was born into a theatrical family in Leipzig, Germany, in 1813. His first passion was not music but poetry, drama, and the theater. Only in his late teens, when he began to immerse himself in the music of Beethoven, did he begin to consider music as a profession. He made piano transcriptions* of the orchestral music of Beethoven, and took lessons in composition from the cantor of Leipzig's St. Thomas's Church, old Bach's church (see page 128).

early years After a succession of jobs as an opera director in several small German towns, Wagner and his young family moved to Paris in 1839 in hopes of seeing his first opera produced there. Instead of meeting success in Paris, as had Liszt and Chopin before him, Wagner was greeted by thundering indifference. No one could be convinced to produce his work. Reduced to poverty, he spent a brief sojourn in a Parisian prison for nonpayment of debts.

When Wagner's big break came it was not in Paris but back home in his native Germany, in the city of Dresden. His opera *Rienzi* was given a hearing there in October 1842 and generated such an enthusiastic response that the composer was offered the post of opera director for this important city. Dur-

first operas ing the next six years three additional German Romantic operas by Wagner were given there as well: *The Flying Dutchman* (1844), *Tannhäuser* (1845), and *Lohengrin* (1848). In the aftermath of the political revolution that swept much of Europe in 1848, Wagner was forced to flee Dresden, though in truth he took flight as much to avoid his creditors as to escape any repressive government.

Wagner found a safe haven in Switzerland, which was to be his home, on and off, for the next dozen years. Exiled now from the major opera houses in Germany, he began to imagine a complex of music dramas on a vast and

the Ring *cycle* unprecedented scale. What he ultimately created was *Der Ring des Nibelungen (The Ring of the Nibelungs)*, a set of four operas intended to be performed during the course of four successive evenings. *Das Rheingold*, the first, lasts two-and-a-half hours; *Die Walküre* and *Siegfried* each runs nearly four-and-a-half; while the finale, *Götterdämmerung (Twilight of the Gods)*, goes on for no less than five-and-a-half. The thread of a single story runs from beginning to end. But instead of drawing his theme from a play or a set of historical events, Wagner reached back into Germanic legend for his subject matter.

The scene is set in the smoky mists of primeval time, in a land of gods, river nymphs, dwarfs, giants, dragons, and sword-wielding heroes.

Although the plot of the *Ring* is complex in the extreme, it is best viewed as an allegory exploring the themes of power, greed, lust, honor, and bravery in contemporary nineteenth-century society. Power, for example, is symbolized by the ring belonging to the dwarfish Nibelungs, bravery by the exploits of the hero Siegfried. While these are universal themes, they were harmonious with the growing feeling of German national identity. The German philosopher Friedrich Nietzsche (1844–1900), for a time a friend and confidant of Wagner, modeled his concept of the superhero or superman, on Wagner's heroic character. In the twentieth century Adolph Hitler would exploit Wagnerian symbolism to foster the notion of a superior German race, building, for example, a Siegfried Line on the Western Front.

plot of the Ring

Needless to say, publishers and producers were at first reluctant to print or mount the operas of Wagner's *Ring* given their massive scope and fantastic subject matter. They would, however, pay well for the rights to more traditional works by him. So in the midst of his labors on the *Ring* cycle, the always penurious Wagner interrupted the project for a period of years to create *Tristan und Isolde* (1865) and *Die Meistersinger von Nürnberg (The Mastersingers of Nuremberg,* 1868). But these, too, were long and not easy to produce. The bulky scores piled up on his desk.

In 1864 Wagner was rescued from his plight by King Ludwig II of Bavaria who paid off his debts, gave him an annual allowance, encouraged him to complete the *Ring* tetralogy, and helped him to build a special theater where his giant operas could be mounted according to the composer's own specifications. This theater, or Festival House as Wagner called it, was constructed at Bayreuth, a small town between Munich and Leipzig. The first performance of the *Ring* cycle took place there in August 1876 and was an artistic triumph. His last opera, *Parsifal* (1882), premiered there in 1882. After his death the following year, Wagner's remains were interred on the grounds of Bayreuth. To this day the theater at Bayreuth continues to stage the music dramas of Wagner—and only Wagner. Each summer thousands of opera lovers make the pilgrimage to this theatrical shrine to one of art's most determined, and ruthless, visionaries.

FIGURE 14–8

Wagner's "Music Dramas"

With a few very minor exceptions, Richard Wagner wrote only musical works intended for the theater. He did not call these operas, however, but "music dramas." A **music drama** for Wagner was a musical work for the stage in which all the arts—poetry, music, acting, mime, dance, and scenic design—function as a harmonious ensemble. Such an artistic union Wagner referred to as a **Gesamtkunstwerk** ("total art work"). Thus combined, the unified force of the arts would generate real drama. No longer would the dramatic action grind to a halt in order to spotlight the vocal flourishes of a soloist, as often happened in Italian opera.

Indeed, Wagner's music drama differs from conventional Italian opera in several important ways. First, it is not made up of distinct and separate numbers—aria, recitative, duet, and the like—but of an almost seamless flow of undifferentiated solo singing and declamation. Second, ensemble

Bayreuth Festival House, an opera house especially built to produce the music dramas of Richard Wagner—and only Wagner.

singing is almost entirely absent—duets, trios, choruses, and full-cast finales—are rare in the extreme. Finally, the tuneful aria is banished to the wings. Wagner avoids repetition, symmetry, and regular cadences—all things that can make a melody "catchy"—in favor of long-flowing, non-repetitive, not particularly songlike lines. As the tuneful aria decreases in importance, so the role of the orchestra increases.

importance of the orchestra

With Wagner the orchestra is everything. It sounds forth the main musical themes, develops and exploits them, and thereby "plays out" the drama through pure instrumental music. On stage the words and actions of the singers give the audience supplementary clues as to what the musical drama in the orchestra is all about. In the 1850s Wagner drank deeply of the philosophy of Arthur Schopenhauer (1788–1860) who wrote that "music expresses the innermost basis of the world, the essence behind appearances." In music drama what happens on the stage is the appearance, what happens in the orchestra is the reality, the essence of the drama.

Wagnerian tenor and soprano

We have seen that Wagner was one composer of the Romantic era who greatly expanded the size of the orchestra, using triple woodwinds and an enlarged brass section (see page 240). To be heard above an orchestra of nearly a hundred players requires a large, specially trained voice, the so-called Wagnerian tenor and Wagnerian soprano. Yet during moments of climax even these powerful voices are scarcely audible. Imagine an opera of Verdi in which the voice of the hero or heroine cannot be heard. Impossible! But in a music drama of Wagner, the virtual disappearance of the voice does not matter. By design the singer is ultimately consumed by the greater

FIGURE 14–9

Cosima Wagner, daughter of Franz Liszt and Marie d'Agoult, Richard Wagner, and the aged Liszt at Wagner's villa at Bayreuth in 1880. At the right is a young admirer of Wagner, Hans von Wolzogen.

reality of an all-powerful orchestra. Let us see how the orchestra brings this about in Wagner's music drama *Tristan und Isolde*.

TRISTAN UND ISOLDE (1865)

Wagner began to compose *Tristan und Isolde* during 1857 when living in Switzerland and supported in part by a wealthy patron, Otto Wesendonck. Although still married, the composer began an affair with Wesendonck's wife, Mathilde—so fully did Wagner the man live his life as Wagner the artist that it was impossible for him to create an opera dealing with passionate love without being passionately in love himself. Eventually, his own wife, Minne, caused such a scene that the composer fled to Venice. By 1864 Wagner had made his way to Munich for the first production of the now finished *Tristan*. Having long since forgotten both Mathilde and his wife, he now fell in love with Cosima von Bülow, the wife of the man scheduled to conduct *Tristan*. Cosima was the illegitimate daughter of Franz Liszt and Marie d'Agoult (see page 273), and she and Wagner soon produced three illegitimate children of their own. The first of these, a daughter born on the first day of rehearsals for *Tristan,* was christened Isolde.

The story of *Tristan und Isolde* comes from an old Arthurian legend. Briefly, it is the tale of the love of a captive Irish princess, Isolde, betrothed to King Mark of Cornwall (England), and of Tristan, the king's trusted knight. Tristan is sent to conduct the reluctant Isolde to her wedding with King Mark. Wishing only for revenge and then death, Isolde asks for a deadly potion, but her devoted servant instead substitutes a love potion which the unknowing Tristan and Isolde consume. On arrival in Cornwall this passionate, soon adulterous, love is revealed to the court. Despairing of any happy union with Isolde in this world, Tristan allows himself to be mortally wounded in combat and sails off to his native Brittany to die. Isolde pursues him but arrives only in time to have him expire in her arms. Knowing that their union will only be consummated through death, Isolde sings her *Liebestod (Love Death),* an ecstatic vision of their love beyond the grave, and then she, too, expires next to her lover's body. This was the sort of all-consuming, sacrificial love so dear to the hearts of Romantic artists.

Wagner begins *Tristan*, not with a rousing, self-contained overture, but with a simple, yet beautiful, prelude that sets the general tone of the drama and leads directly to the raising of the curtain. The first sound we hear is a plaintive call of the cellos answered by one in the woodwinds. Each is not so much a lengthy theme as it is a short, pregnant motive. Wagner's disciples called each a **Leitmotif,** a brief, distinctive unit of music that is designed to represent a character, object, or idea and that returns repeatedly in order to facilitate the progress of the drama. We have encountered a representational, or programmatic, theme before in the form of Berlioz's *idée fixe* (see page 257). But Wagner's leitmotifs are much shorter than Berlioz's lengthy melody, and there are many more of them. They are usually not sung but only played in the orchestra. In this way an element of the subconscious can be brought to the drama: The orchestra can give a sense of what a character is thinking even when he or she is singing about something else. By developing, extending, varying, contrasting, and resolving these representational leitmotifs, Wagner is able to play out the essence of the drama almost without recourse to his singers.

FIGURE 14–10

Original costume designs for the premiere of Wagner's *Tristan und Isolde,* June 1865.

Leitmotifs in *Tristan* are associated mainly with feelings rather than concrete objects or persons. The Prelude has four such distinctive cells, each of which lends itself to variation and extension.

EXAMPLE 14–2

Notice how both the "Longing" and "Desire" motifs involve chromatic lines, the first descending, the second ascending (see arrows). This sort of

intense chromaticism

linear chromatic motion made it easy for the composer to wind continually through many different keys, not stopping long enough to establish any one as a home base, or tonic. Wagner's intense use of chromaticism loosened the feeling of key and eventually led to the collapse of tonality as the main organizing force in Western music, as we shall later see (page 343). Here he uses twisting chromatic lines for a specific expressive purpose, to convey a sense of the anxiety and pain to be felt by the ill-fated lovers.

As you listen to the Prelude to *Tristan* you can feel the composer trying to draw you into his all-enveloping world of love, longing, and desire. The leitmotifs frequently appear in sequences*, usually moving upward, so as to convey a sense of continual longing and rising tension. Cadences are avoided, thereby increasing the restless mood. And dissonances are placed at points of climax to heighten the feeling of pain and anguish. Throughout there is a gradual ebb and flow of intensity which parallels the emotions of the lovers. When the powerful climax of the Prelude finally arrives, it is, however, evasive and strangely unsatisfying. As we shall see, the real climax, and ultimate resolution of the drama, comes only at the end of the opera.

LISTENING GUIDE

Richard Wagner
Prelude to *Tristan und Isolde* (1865)

0:00   "Longing" and "Desire" leitmotifs presented by cellos and woodwinds, then repeated twice at successively higher degrees of the scale (sequence)

1:30   First climax; "Glance" motif then emerges in cellos

2:23   Another climax; variant of "Glance" motif continues in cellos

3:00   Variant of "Longing" motif played by violins
3:20   "Glance" motif in woodwinds
3:42   Variant of "Glance" motif exchanged between strings and woodwinds and moving up in sequence

4:20   Another climax; variant of "Glance" motif emerges in woodwinds
4:57   Variant of "Longing" motif in woodwinds reaches for successively higher notes of the scale

5:35   "Glance" motif first in strings, then in brasses
6:17   Strings race up to "Deliverance" motif while "Desire" motif is heard in brasses and woodwinds

7:00   Another climax from which continues the "Glance" motif in the violins which push it with great urgency to successively higher pitches
7:37   Final climax as trumpets and then woodwinds blare through with "Desire" motif
8:00   Return to opening sound of "Longing" motif in cellos and "Desire" motif in woodwinds
8:58   Beginning of a lengthy fade out . . .

(Listening Exercise 28)

In the final scene of *Tristan*, Isolde cradles the body of her dying hero and prepares to join him in death. As she sings her justly famous *Liebestod (Love Death)*, three additional leitmotifs appear, each heard previously in the opera. As in the Prelude, the *Liebestod* is in the form of a great dynamic curve with a sublime climax at the apogee. But now the climax, instead of being frustrated through evasion, reaches its fulfillment as Isolde, in a trancelike state of bliss, joins Tristan in death. First listen to the *Liebestod*, concentrating

the Liebestod

on the leitmotifs as they are worked out by the voice, but even more by the orchestra. Then play it once more, this time just drinking in all of Wagner's divinely inspired sound. If there is such a thing as a transcendental quality about Romantic music, you will experience it here.

LISTENING GUIDE

Richard Wagner
Liebestod, from *Tristan und Isolde* (1865)

CD 4/13
6–Tape 4B
2–Tape 2A

Characters: The lovers Tristan and Isolde
Situation: Tristan's castle in Brittany; Isolde cradles Tristan in her arms as she prepares to join him in death.

0:00	Isolde, gazing at Tristan, slowly sings the "Love-Death" leitmotif which is then taken up by the orchestra		

Mild und leise wie er lächelt,
Wie das Auge hold er öffnet—
Seht ihr, Freunde? Seht ihr's nicht?
Immer lichter wie er leuchtet,
Stern-umstrahlet hoch sich hebt?

Oh how mild and gently he smiles
As he opens his eyes—
Do you see, Friends, don't you see it?
Ever brighter, how he shines,
Glowing in starlight raised on high?

1:02   The orchestra continues with the "Love-Death" motif as the singer goes her own way

Seht ihr's nicht?
Wie das Herz ihm mutig schwillt,
Voll und hehr im Busen ihm quillt?

Do you not see it?
How his heart proudly swells,
Full and brave beating in his breast?

1:30   The "Ecstasy" leitmotif enters, not in the voice, but in the high woodwinds and then the violins

Wie den Lippen, wonnig mild
Süsser Atem sanft entweht—
Freunde! Seht!

How from his lips, blissfully mild,
Sweet breath gently flutters—
Do you not see, Friends?

2:08   Reapperance of the ascending, chromatic "Desire" motif from the Prelude

Fühlt und seht ihr's nicht?

Don't you feel and see it?

2:15   "Love-Death" motif returns in voice and orchestra, followed by "Ecstasy" motif and then "Desire" motif in voice

Höre ich nur diese Weise
Die so wundervoll und leise,
Wonne klagend, alles sagend,
Mild versöhnend aus ihm tönend,
In mich dringet, auf sich schwinget,
Hold erhallend um mich klinget?

Do I alone hear this melody
Which, so wonderfully and gently,
Moaning bliss, expressing all,
Gently forgiving, sounding from within
Pierces me, rises upwards,
Blessedly echoing all around me?

3:18   "Transcendent Bliss" leitmotif appears in violins

Heller schallend, mich umwallend,
Sind es Wellen sanfter Lüfte?

Resounding clearly all around me,
Are they waves of gentle air?

3:39	Tension increases as "Desire" motif rises by chromatic steps	Sind es Wolken wonniger Düfte Wie sie schwellen, mich umrauschen, Soll ich atmen, soll ich lauschen? Soll ich schlürfen, untertauchen? Süss in Düften mich verhauchen? In dem wogenden Schwall, in dem tönenden Schall.	Are they clouds of delightful fragrance? As they swell and envelop me, Should I breathe, should I listen? Should I sip them, plunge beneath them? Drink my last in such sweet fragrance? In the growing swell, the surging sound.
4:25	Glorious climax with the "Transcendent Bliss" motif shining forth in the orchestra	In des Welt-Atems wehendem All— Ertrinken, versinken— Unbewusst— Höchste Lust!	In the vastness of the world's spirit To drown, sink down— Unconscious— Supreme bliss!

The orchestra then fades away into silence as the curtain descends

(Listening Exercise 33)

LISTENING EXERCISES

32	Giuseppe Verdi, *La traviata* (1853) Act I, Scene 4: Aria and duet "One Happy Day" Act I, Scene 6: Recitative/ aria "Folly, Folly" / "Always Free"	CD 4/10–11 6–Tape 4B 2–Tape 2A

In *La traviata* Verdi has created what is very much a "singers' opera"—the listener's attention is drawn almost entirely to the voices. The orchestra plays a subordinate role, often limited to setting up a solid accompaniment with simple rhythms and regular meters, all in support of the voices. The following questions illuminate the way in which Verdi makes the voice the center of attention, pausing from time to time to enjoy a moment of vocal bravura, yet still keeps the tempo of the opera moving at a rapid pace.

1. What is the meter of Alfredo's aria "One Happy Day"?
   a. duple   b. triple
2. The "big guitar" effect in the accompaniment (especially evident beginning at 0:38) is created in part because the strings are playing with what technique?   a. tremolo   b. obligato   c. pizzicato
3. When Violetta enters (at 1:22) does the meter change? _____ What happens to the tempo as she enters?
   a. gets faster   b. remains the same   c. gets slower
4. During the vocal high point of this duet, as the singers rhapsodize on the word "Ah" (2:48–3:16), what does the orchestra do? _____ (What better way to call attention to the voices!)
5. How would you describe the tempo and meter of the cabaletta (beginning at 4:01) which concludes this duet?
   a. slow-duple   b. slow-triple   c. fast-duple   d. fast-triple

CD 4/11; 6–Tape 4B; 2–Tape 2A

6. During Violetta's accompanied recitative "Folly, Folly," there is a passage in which she expresses her fear at being merely "a poor woman alone, abandoned in this populated desert that they call Paris" (0:13–0:23). The orchestra helps heighten this feeling of fear by playing:
   a. string tremolo and rising stepwise motion in the bass
   b. string pizzicato and falling stepwise motion in the bass
   c. string obligato and rising stepwise motion in the bass

7. After her recitative, and following some vocal fireworks on the word "gioir" ("pleasure"), Violetta launches into her brilliant aria "Sempre libera" ("Always Free"). Which number has a clear-cut, regular meter?
   a. the recitative "Folly, Folly"   b. the aria "Always Free"

8. At the end of "Always Free" the voice of Alfredo enters (at 2:01) with his familiar refrain "Love that animates the world." Which of the following is true about Alfredo's music?
   a. the tempo speeds up and a guitar accompanies the voice
   b. the tempo slows down and a harp accompanies the voice

9. Now Violetta repeats "Always Free" (3:17), vowing to pursue pleasure and brushing off Alfredo's feelings of true love. Where does the vocal high point of "Always Free" occur—where is the voice pushed to the top of its range?
   a. at the end of the first time Violetta sings the aria (just before Alfredo's voice enters at 2:01)
   b. at the end of the second time she sings it (around 4:40)?

| 33 | Richard Wagner
Liebestod, from *Tristan und Isolde* (1865) | CD 4/13
6–Tape 4B
2–Tape 2A |

Isolde's *Liebestod (Love Death)*, which brings *Tristan und Isolde* to a glorious conclusion, is a unique musical composition. It is written for soprano voice—indeed, for a dramatic Wagnerian soprano—with orchestra, yet it is a very different sort of piece from Giuseppe Verdi's aria "Always Free" from *La traviata* which we have previously heard. The following queries begin by asking for specific responses to the music and conclude with more general questions regarding your reaction to the *Liebestod*.

1. Is there an easily perceptible duple or triple meter in the *Liebestod?*
   _____

2. When the soprano sings the "Ecstasy" leitmotif (2:35–2:57) she does so to what is for Wagner exceptionally "square" poetry—lines of 4 + 4 syllables with internal rhyme. (Try saying the German to yourself.)

   | Wonne klagend, alles sagend | Moaning bliss, expressing all |
   | Mild versöhnend aus ihm tönend | Gently forgiving, sounding from within |

   What is the course of the soprano line during this couplet?
   a. falls   b. falls in a sequence   c. rises   d. rises in a sequence

3. Immediately after (2:58–3:17) the music rises toward a climax to reflect the sentiment of the next couplet:

In mich dringet, auf sich schwinget,   Pierces me, rises upwards,
Hold erhallend, um mich klinget?   Blessedly echoing all around me?

How is this rising tension brought about in the music?
a. tremolos are played by the strings
b. the voice rises up chromatically
c. there is a gradual crescendo
d. all of the above

4. As Wagner now builds to another climax (from 3:39 to 4:25) with the "Desire" leitmotif, he suddenly changes dynamics on the word "lauschen" (listen) (at 4:00). Which does he change to?
a. *pianissimo*   b. *fortissimo*

5. (4:45–5:18) How does Wagner musically depict the final words of Isolde "to drown, to sink down, in supreme bliss"?
a. the vocal line falls, then soars up
b. the vocal line soars up, then falls
c. the vocal line continually falls

6. Which leitmotif from the Prelude is heard softly in the oboes (at 5:36) immediately before the final chord?
a. "Longing"   b. "Desire"   c. "Transcendent Bliss"

7. Who has the "last word" (who is heard at the very end of the *Liebestod*)?
a. the voice   b. the orchestra

8. Which musical force could be omitted without serious loss to the music?
a. the voice   b. the orchestra

9. Is the *Liebestod* through-composed (without large-scale repetition) or in *da capo* aria form? _____

10. From the soprano's point of view, is the *Liebestod* more of a virtuosic, display piece than the aria "Always Free" from Verdi's *La traviata* (see page 286 and disc 4, track 11; 6–Tape 4B; 2–Tape 2A)? _____

11. Do you find this an exceptionally moving musical creation? Are you now a convert to the music of Wagner, a "perfect Wagnerite," to use George Bernard Shaw's phrase? _____

KEY WORDS

accompagnato recitative	*Camille*	*Liebestod*
Bayreuth Festival	diva	Marie Duplessis
House	*Gesamtkunstwerk*	music drama
bel canto	La Scala	*Ring* cycle
cabaletta	leitmotif	*Singspiel*

15

LATE ROMANTICISM

When historians speak of "late Romanticism," they refer to the artistic developments that occurred in the West from about 1870 until 1900–1910, from the time of the Franco–Prussian War (1870) until shortly before the outbreak of World War I (1914). Of course, human activity, artistic or otherwise, rarely occurs within tidy chronological units. As we shall see, a strong anti–Romantic movement developed in France as early as the 1880s. Yet while some progressive artists began to turn away from Romanticism at this early date, other, more conservative ones continued to compose in the late–Romantic style into the 1940s. Romanticism had a strong hold on the consciousness of the listening public, one that it has not entirely relinquished even today.

During the last decades of the nineteenth century, orchestral music, especially German orchestral music, increasingly came to dominate the European musical scene. The continued growth in the size and color of the orchestra made listening to a symphony orchestra the most powerful aesthetic experience that a citizen of the late nineteenth century could enjoy. Not surprisingly, the force of the ever-larger orchestra affected the development of musical genres. We have seen that Wagner wrote operas in which the instrumental ensemble sometimes overwhelmed and absorbed the voice into its rich orchestral tapestry. Similarly, the orchestra began to infiltrate the realm of the art song, so that now the singer of a *Lied** was often accompanied not merely by a piano but by a full orchestra. And all the while the traditional four-movement symphony grew ever longer and more complex, a direct response to the increased number and variety of instruments. Let us review for a moment the development of the symphony during the nineteenth century.

THE ROMANTIC SYMPHONY

Though the symphony came into being during the Classical period, in the orchestral works of Haydn and Mozart, it remained a favorite with nineteenth-century audiences. Romantic composers generally followed the four-movement format inherited from their Classical forebears—fast, slow, minuet or scherzo, fast. But now the third movement might be almost any sort of light, contrasting creation, while the finale increasingly took on a more serious tone. As we have seen (page 242), the movements of a symphony grew in length in the course of the nineteenth century. Perhaps as a consequence of this greater length and seriousness, composers wrote fewer symphonies. Schumann and Brahms composed only 4, Mendelssohn 5, Tchaikovsky 6, Dvorak, Bruckner, and Mahler each 9. No one approached the 40-odd symphonies of Mozart, to say nothing of the 104 of Haydn.

For a Romantic composer contemplating the creation of a symphony, no figure loomed larger than Beethoven. Wagner asked why anyone after Beethoven bothered to write symphonies at all, given the dramatic impact of Beethoven's Third, Fifth, and Ninth. Wagner himself wrote only one, Verdi none. Some composers, notably Berlioz and Liszt, turned to a completely different sort of symphony, the program symphony*, in which an external scenario determined the nature and order of the musical events. But these works sometimes lacked the force, internal unity, and compelling logic of a Beethoven symphony. It was not until the late–Romantic period, nearly fifty years after the death of Beethoven, that someone came forth to claim the title of successor to Beethoven the symphonist. That figure was Johannes Brahms.

FIGURE 15–1

Johannes Brahms

Johannes Brahms (1833–1897)

Brahms was born in the north German port city of Hamburg in 1833. His father was a street musician who also played double bass well enough to enter the Hamburg city orchestra. Although Johannes's formal education never went beyond primary school, his father saw to it that he had the best training on the piano and in music theory. He was fed a heavy diet of the great masters: Bach's *Well-Tempered Clavier* (see page 139), Beethoven's piano sonatas, and Haydn's chamber music. While he studied these by day, by night he played dance music in brothels and bars on the Hamburg waterfront to supplement the modest family income. He gave his first solo piano recital at the age of fifteen and soon began to compose.

Brahms first came to the public's attention in 1853 when Robert Schumann published a highly laudatory article announcing him to be something of a musical Messiah, the heir apparent of Haydn, Mozart, and Beethoven and their great legacy. Brahms, in turn, embraced both Schumanns, Robert and his wife Clara (see page 265), as his musical mentors. When Robert was confined to a mental institution in 1854, Brahms moved into the Schumann home for a period of two years to help Clara raise her seven children. Not surprisingly, his respect and affection for Clara ripened into love, despite the fact that she was fourteen years his senior. Yet for whatever reason—they both later destroyed many of their letters to each other—their mutual affection did not culminate in marriage after Robert's death. Brahms remained a bachelor for the duration of his life.

Clara and Robert Schumann: his mentors

Disappointed first in love and then in his attempts to gain an official position in his native Hamburg, Brahms in 1862 moved to Vienna. He was engaged in one or two minor conducting posts, but for the most part was able to maintain his modest life style—"very un-Wagnerian" he called it— with fees earned as a concert pianist and with royalties accruing from the

FIGURE 15–2

FIGURE 15–2

Brahms's composing room in Vienna. On the wall, looking down on the piano is a bust of Beethoven. The spirit of Beethoven loomed large over the entire nineteenth-century (see also the cover) and over Brahms in particular.

publication of his ever-growing list of compositions. His fame increased dramatically in 1868 with performances of his *German Requiem*, not a setting of the Catholic Mass for the Dead but of texts drawn from the German bible that speak of death, comfort, and peace. Honorary degrees were offered *growing fame* from Cambridge University (1876) and Breslau University (1879). For the latter honor he wrote the *Academic Festival Overture* which begins solemnly enough, but ends with four spirited college songs. Since Brahms himself had never gone to a university, these accolades must have been sweet. After Wagner's death in 1883, he was generally considered the greatest living German composer. His own death, from liver cancer, came in the spring of 1897. He was buried in the central cemetery of Vienna, thirty feet from the graves of Beethoven and Schubert.

Brahms the conservative That Brahms should choose Vienna as his home is not surprising. Brahms was very much a musical conservative, one who perpetuated the traditions of the Viennese masters Haydn, Mozart, Beethoven, and Schubert. He acquired and continued to study, like a musicologist, not only the scores of the Classical masters but also those of the Baroque and Renaissance. He wrote canons* in the style of Palestrina and settings of chorale* tunes à la Bach. Sonata–allegro, rondo, and variation—all traditional forms—provided the structural framework for his large-scale compositions.

Brahms's conservative bent is further evident from the fact that he composed no program music, what to other nineteenth-century musicians like Liszt and Berlioz was the very soul of Romantic music. Instead, Brahms *absolute music* chose to write absolute music*, chamber sonatas, symphonies, and concertos without any sort of program. His chamber music, especially the F minor piano quintet and the three sonatas for violin and piano, is among the most substantive and inventive ever written—music for the true connoisseur. His four symphonies, two piano concertos, and violin concerto are grand works, worthy successors to those of Beethoven. In these, Brahms did not indulge in unrestrained expression as had Berlioz, Liszt, and Wagner, but maintained a sense of balance by articulating his Romantic feelings within the confines of traditional musical forms. Brahms wrote not a single opera but many works for chorus and nearly two hundred songs, or *Lieder*, for voice and piano. With the songs, however, it is as much the richness of the piano accompaniment as it is the vocal line that carries the day. Brahms could write eminently singable melodies, but he was at heart a contrapuntalist and a "developer" in the tradition of Beethoven.

SYMPHONY NO. 1 (1876)

In 1870 Johannes Brahms wrote: "I shall never compose a symphony! You have no idea how the likes of us feel when we hear the tramp of a giant like him behind us." Brahms, of course, was referring to Beethoven. He did go on to write a symphony, indeed, four of them, but he was at first very fearful of doing so. He had tried sketching a symphony as early as 1854. In 1862 he showed a nearly completed first movement to Clara Schumann and then in 1868 parts of the finale. All the while he continued to perfect his technique of writing for a large instrumental ensemble. Finally, in 1876, after twenty-two years, when he was forty-three, Brahms's much-awaited Symphony No. 1 received its premiere. It is a long and serious work that begins fatefully in C minor and ends triumphantly in C major. Like Beethoven's Fifth and Ninth symphonies, which also move from minor to major, it impresses the spirit as a struggle between darkness and light, a progress from adversity to victory.

First movement (*Un poco sostenuto: Allegro;* "Somewhat sustained: Fast"): A dramatic introduction leads to a vigorous first theme that dominates this entire sonata–allegro movement. The intensity, even severity, of the main thematic material is relieved only momentarily by the quiet, pastoral quality of the second theme group. A coda, which matches the introduction in mood and length, ultimately projects a feeling of quiet resignation.

Second movement (*Andante sostenuto;* "Moderately slow, sustained"): This slow, reflective movement is written in ternary form (**ABA′**) plus coda. Rarely with Brahms is there an exact repetition of musical material—he prefers to vary rather than repeat. Here at the restatement of **A** (at **A′**) the returning melody is so changed in pitch content, rhythm, and instrumentation as to be almost unrecognizable. The disguise is even more alluring, more beautiful, than the original face.

Third movement (*Un poco allegretto e grazioso;* "Moderately fast and graceful"): This movement, too, is in ternary form with the return of **A** substantially varied. Just as Beethoven eschewed the stately minuet—the usual third movement of a Classical symphony—in favor of the more vigorous scherzo, so now Brahms leaves behind any lingering influence of the dance. His love of irregular rhythms and metrical displacements was such that he never gives a strong dance beat a chance to get established. What we have here is the musical equivalent of a topsy-turvy frolic in the country.

FIGURE 15–3

The now bearded and rotund Brahms, cigar in mouth, on the way to the Red Hedgehog. This caricature captures the essence of the somewhat eccentric bachelor composer as he heads toward his favorite Viennese pub, the Red Hedgehog.

Fourth movement (*Adagio: Allegro non troppo, ma con brio;* "Slow: Fast, but not too, yet with fire"): The finale of Brahms's Symphony No. 1 is nearly eighteen minutes long and balances the weighty first movement of the symphony. The greater length is caused, in part, by an unusually long slow introduction to the finale. Here Brahms not only sets the mood of the movement but also presents much of its important thematic material, including a glorious solo for French horn at the very climax of the introduction. Brahms had apparently hit on this memorable idea as early as 1868, for he sent the melody to Clara Schumann as a greeting on her birthday that year:

EXAMPLE 15–1

[High on the hills   deep in the   vale   I   greet thee   ten   thou - sand - fold]

successor to Beethoven's Ninth

Only a late–Romantic composer could have written a horn solo like this, just as only a late–Romantic composer could have created the choralelike passage for brass choir that follows it. Yet there is much in this final movement that harkens back to the earlier style of Beethoven: the use of an expanded sonata–allegro form, the explosion of rhythmic energy at the end of the development section, and the tight connection between all sections brought about by motivic unity. Perhaps most obvious is the similarity of the stepwise main theme (see Listening Guide at 5:20) to the main theme of the finale of Beethoven's Symphony No. 9, the famous *Ode to Joy* (see page 230). So similar in spirit are these hymnlike melodies that the wags who first heard Brahms's new symphony in Vienna in 1876 dubbed it "Beethoven's Tenth"!

LISTENING GUIDE

Johannes Brahms
Symphony No. 1 (1876) Fourth Movement
Adagio: Allegro non troppo, ma con brio (slow: fast, but not too, yet with fire)

CD 5/1
6–Tape 5A

INTRODUCTION

0:00   Important six-note motive announced

0:42   Accelerating pizzicatos
1:09   Six-note motive returns, then the pizzicatos in the strings
2:05   Growing tension and uncertainty in the strings
2:43   Timpani roll announces French horn call against silvery string tremolo

3:31   Flute repeats horn call on high
4:12   Brass choir, featuring trombones, plays church choralelike passage
4:37   Horn returns with call

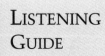

EXPOSITION

5:20	Six-note motive expanded into hymnlike first theme

6:25	Transition with two prominent themes
7:10	Flowing second theme, part 1
7:35	Oboe plays second theme, part 2
8:06	Violins reach upward presenting second theme, part 3
8:41	Closing theme

DEVELOPMENT

9:15	Begins with unaltered repeat of hymnlike first theme
10:24	Transition theme 1 returns
10:48	Transition theme 2 used in imitative counterpoint
11:30	Both transition themes developed
12:10	Rhythmic climax using abrupt syncopation
12:23	Transition that suggests reappearance of French horn call

RECAPITULATION

12:38	Horn call returns
13:26	Second theme group
14:59	Closing theme

CODA

15:26	Eerie modulations
15:41	Six-note motive in bass, which then begins to rise by step
16:05	Tempo becomes faster (*più allegro*) and new rhythmic motive emerges from six-note cell
16:21	Climax with return of church chorale passage in brass
16:53	Syncopation; then the new rhythmic motive drives quickly to the end

(Listening Exercise 34)

FIGURE 15–4

Peter Tchaikovsky

FIGURE 15–5

Nadezhda von Meck was the widow
of an engineer who made a fortune
constructing the first railroads in Russia during the 1860s and 1870s. She
used her money, in part, to support
composers like Tchaikovsky and,
later, Claude Debussy.

LATER PROGRAM MUSIC

Program music, as we have seen (pages 242–244), was at the very heart of
the creative works of the early Romantics like Berlioz, Mendelssohn, and
Liszt. While Brahms later held fast to the Classical ideal of absolute music,
most late–Romantic composers continued to yield to the allure of music
inspired by some sort of extramusical element—a play, an experience with
nature, even a painting. The late-nineteenth-century composer who
achieved the greatest popular success in writing program music, as well as
illustrative ballet music, was Peter Tchaikovsky.

Peter Tchaikovsky (1840–1893)

Tchaikovsky was born in 1840 into an upper-middle-class family in provincial Russia. He showed a keen ear for music in his earliest years, and by the
age of six could speak fluent French and German (an excellent musical ear
and a capacity to learn foreign languages often go hand in hand). As to his
career, it was determined that law would provide the most rapid advance-
ment for young Peter. Thus, he spent seven years, 1852–1859, at the School
of Jurisprudence in St. Petersburg and four more years as a clerk in the Min-
istry of Justice. Then, like Robert Schumann before him, he realized that it
was music, not law, that fired his imagination. He made his way to the St.
Petersburg Conservatory of Music, from which he was graduated in 1866,
and then, that same year, to the newly formed Moscow Conservatory, where
he assumed the position of professor of harmony and musical composition.

In truth, it was not his official position in Moscow that supported
Tchaikovsky during most of his mature years, but rather a private arrangement with an eccentric patroness, Madame Nadezhda von Meck (Fig. 15–5).
This wealthy, music-loving widow furnished him an annual income of six
thousand rubles on the condition that she and the composer never meet—a
requirement not always easily fulfilled since the two sometimes resided at
the same summer estate. In addition to this annuity, Tsar Alexander III in
1881 awarded Tchaikovsky an annual pension of three thousand rubles in
recognition of his importance to Russian cultural life. Being a man of independent means meant not only that Tchaikovsky was able to travel exten-
sively in Western Europe, and even to America, but could also enjoy the
freedom he found so necessary to creative activity.

Tchaikovsky's creative output touched every genre of nineteenth-century
music: opera, song, string quartet, piano sonata, concerto, symphony, and
symphonic poem. It is, however, his large-scale works for orchestra that
have best stood the test of time. Tchaikovsky's musical strengths—sweeping
melodies, colorful instrumentations, dramatic contrasts, and grand gestures—could only be fully expressed by a large symphony orchestra. Not
surprisingly, he also achieved unparalleled success as a composer of orchestral music for ballet, a type of music in which short bursts of colorful sounds
and evocative rhythms are necessary to create distinctly different moods for
each new scene. His *Swan Lake* (1876), *Sleeping Beauty* (1889) and *Nutcracker*
(1892) are the most popular works in the entire repertoire of grand Romantic
ballet, beloved by young and old alike.

Despite his considerable popular success, Tchaikovsky's life was not a happy one. He was a manic–depressive, a neurotic, and a hypochondriac. He was also a homosexual. He died under suspicious circumstances in 1893 at the age of fifty-three. One theory has it that he took his own life by arsenic poisoning to avoid exposure for a liaison with the nephew of a Russian nobleman.

SYMPHONIC POEM, *ROMEO AND JULIET* (1869)

Tchaikovsky was at his best when writing illustrative music for large orchestra, whether a program symphony, a one-movement symphonic poem*, or music for ballet. He called his most overtly programmatic works sometimes simply "overture," sometimes "overture fantasy," and sometimes "symphonic fantasy." We may broadly group these one-movement programmatic pieces in the general category of symphonic poem. As with Berlioz, Mendelssohn, and Liszt before him, it was the plays of Shakespeare that provided the strongest extramusical stimulation. Of his three symphonic poems based on works of Shakespeare—*Romeo and Juliet* (1869), *The Tempest* (1877), and *Hamlet* (1888)—the earliest is best. Indeed, it was his first masterpiece.

his program music

Just as Mendelssohn captures the spirit, not the letter, of Shakespeare's *Midsummer Night's Dream* (see page 262), so Tchaikovsky offers a free, not literal, presentation of the principal dramatic elements of *Romeo and Juliet*. In fact, he distills these into just three musical themes: the compassionate music of the kindly Friar Laurence whose plan to unite the lovers goes fatally awry; the fighting music which represents the feud between the Capulets and Montagues; and the love theme which expresses the passion of Romeo and Juliet. Once again, it is sonata–allegro form that is the arena in which the musical drama will be played out. The introduction presents the music of Friar Laurence, then anguished dissonant sounds in the strings and French horn, and finally a succession of beautifully mysterious chords with strumming by a harp, as if Friar Laurence, like a medieval bard, was about to narrate a tragic tale. When the exposition begins, we hear angry, percussive music, racing strings, and syncopated cymbal crashes: This is the violent world of the Capulets and Montagues. Soon the fighting subsides and the love theme emerges. As appropriate for a pair of lovers, it is in two parts, each of which has the capacity to grow and become more passionate when pushed upward in ascending sequences:

EXAMPLE 15–2A

EXAMPLE 15–2B

The brief development pits the feuding families against the increasingly adamant pleas of Friar Laurence. The recapitulation, true to sonata form, begins with the feud music, but moves quickly to an expanded, more ecstatic presentation of the love theme (part 2 first, then part 1), which is eventually cut off by a noisy return of the feuding clans. The beginning of the dramatic coda is announced by a foreboding *fortissimo* roll on the timpani. As we hear the steady drumbeats of a funeral procession and fragments of the broken love theme, we know that Romeo and Juliet are dead. A celestial hymnlike passage (a transformation of the love theme) suggests the lovers have been united above, a feeling then confirmed by the return of the love theme in high violins. There only remains to bring the curtain down on the story of the star crossed lovers, which Tchaikovsky does with seven *fortissimo* hammer strokes for full orchestra, all on the tonic chord.

Shakespeare wrote *Romeo and Juliet* as a tragedy: "For never was a story of more woe/Than this of Juliet and her Romeo," say the final lines of the play. By incorporating a "celestial conclusion" into his coda—a hymnlike choir of angelic woodwinds followed by the transcendent love theme on high in the violins—Tchaikovsky has changed the final import of the play. True child of the Romantic age, he suggests that the love-death of Romeo and Juliet was, in fact, not a tragedy but their spiritual triumph.

| LISTENING GUIDE | | Peter Tchaikovsky
Symphonic poem, *Romeo and Juliet* (1869) | CD 5/2
6–Tape 5A
2–Tape 2B |

INTRODUCTION

0:00   Friar Laurence theme sounding organlike in the woodwinds

0:36   Anguished, dissonant sound in strings and French horn
1:25   Harp alternates with flute solo and woodwinds
2:07   Friar Laurence theme returns with new accompaniment
2:34   Anguished sound returns in strings and French horn
3:23   Harp strumming returns
3:56   Timpani roll and string tremolos build tension; hints of Friar Laurence theme in woodwinds
4:31   Anguished sound again returns, then yields to crescendo on repeating tonic chord

EXPOSITION

5:01   Feud theme in agitated minor; angry rhythmic motive in woodwinds, racing scales in strings

5:48   Crashing syncopations (with cymbal) running against scales
6:19   Gentle transition, with release of tension, to second theme

6:57   Love theme (part 1) played quietly by English horn and viola

7:13   Love theme (part 2) played quietly by strings with mutes

7:51   Love theme (part 1) returns with growing ardor in high woodwinds while French horn plays counterpoint against it
8:51   Lyrical closing section in which cellos and English horn engage in dialogue against backdrop of gently plucked chords in harp

DEVELOPMENT
9:52   Feud theme against which horn soon plays Friar Laurence theme (10:04)
10:11   String syncopations, again against Friar Laurence theme
10:38   Feud theme and Friar Laurence theme continue in opposition
11:23   Cymbal crashes signal climax of development as trumpet blares forth with Friar Laurence theme (11:30)

RECAPITULATION
11:58   Feud theme in woodwinds and brass against racing strings
12:21   Love theme (part 2) softly in woodwinds
13:00   Love theme (part 1) sounds ecstatically with all its inherent force and sweep
13:41   Love theme begins again in strings with counterpoint in brass
14:01   Fragments of Love theme in strings, then brass
14:28   Love theme begins again but is cut off by Feud theme; syncopated cymbal crashes (14:36)
14:43   Feud theme and Friar Laurence theme build to a climax
15:43   Timpani roll announces coda

CODA
15:52   Timpani beats a funeral march while strings play fragments of Love theme
16:38   Love theme (part 2) transformed into the sound of a heavenly chorale played by woodwinds
17:43   Transcendent Love theme sounds from on high in violins
18:18   Timpani roll and final chords

(Listening Exercise 35)

MUSICAL NATIONALISM

Tchaikovsky was the first Russian composer whose music achieved any currency in the West. This was due partly to the fact that Tchaikovsky's music was as much European as it was Russian. That is to say, his symphonies, symphonic poems, and ballets were as much a reflection of the German symphonic style, which then dominated European music, as they were expressions of native Russian musical idioms. Yet there were national styles of music emerging in Russia and elsewhere in the late nineteenth century, a movement historians call musical **nationalism.**

Musical nationalism was not an isolated phenomenon but part of a broad nineteenth-century development which saw various national groups achieve greater political unity and cultural identity. Instead of hundreds of small

political nationalism

principalities or city–states owing allegiance to some vague confederation or distant foreign power, Europe was becoming organized into a dozen or so strongly unified, centrally governed nation–states, each with a common language and cultural heritage. After a lengthy struggle Italy achieved full national unification in 1861, with Rome as the capital. Ten years later a German Empire, under the political leadership of Chancellor Otto von Bismarck (1815–1898), was formally recognized following the German victory over the French in the Franco–Prussian War of 1870. Pride in a national culture and character was likewise felt by smaller groups, like the Czechs, Hungarians, Poles, and Finns, each of which was trying to free itself from more powerful countries such as Germany, Austria, and Russia.

artistic nationalism

Glorification of one's own national group was part of the spirit of the Romantic age. It was manifested in a renewed interest in native languages, like Czech and Hungarian. It was also expressed by giving greater prominence to the folk arts, incorporating them into more "serious" forms of music, literature, poetry, and painting. National color in music was communicated by means of indigenous folk elements—folk songs, native scales and dance rhythms, and local instrumental sounds. It also could be conveyed by the use of national subjects—the life of a national hero, for example—as the program for a symphonic poem or as the libretto for an opera.

Russian Nationalism: Modest Musorgsky (1839–1881)

Russia was one of the first countries to develop its own national style of art music, one distinct and separate from the traditions of German orchestral music and Italian or German opera. An early use of Russian subject matter can be found in Mikhail Glinka's opera *A Life of the Tsar* (1836). Glinka's nationalist spirit was passed to a group of young composers whom contemporaries dubbed "The Mighty Handful" or, less grandiosely, the "Russian Five": Alexander Borodin (1833–1887), César Cui (1835–1918), Mily Balakirev (1837–1910), Nikolai Rimsky-Korsakov (1844–1908), and Modest Musorgsky (1839–1881). They believed in writing Russian music, free of Western influence, for the Russian people. Of these, the most original and least Western in musical style was Modest Musorgsky.

FIGURE 15–6

Modest Musorgsky

As with most of the members of the "Russian Five," Musorgsky was not initially destined for a career in music. He was trained to be a military officer, and for a period of four years was commissioned in the Russian army. He resigned his appointment in 1858 in favor of a minor post as a civil servant and more free time to indulge his avocation, musical composition. The next year he said: "I have been a cosmopolitan, but now there's been some sort of regeneration. Everything Russian is becoming dear to me." Unfortunately, his brief, chaotic life was marked by increasing poverty, depression, and alcoholism. During those few periods of creative productivity that Musorgsky enjoyed, he managed to compile a small *oeuvre* which includes a boldly inventive symphonic poem, *Night on Bald Mountain* (1867), an imaginative set of miniatures for piano, *Pictures at an Exhibition* (1874), and an operatic masterpiece, *Boris Godunov* (1874), based on the life of a popular sixteenth-century Russian tsar. Many of Musorgsky's works were left unfinished at the time of his death in 1881.

PICTURES AT AN EXHIBITION (1874)

The genesis of *Pictures at an Exhibition* can be traced to the death of Musorgsky's close friend, the Russian painter and architect Victor Hartmann, who had died suddenly of a heart attack in 1873. As a memorial to Hartmann, an exhibition of his paintings and drawings was mounted in Moscow the next year. Musorgsky was inspired to capture the spirit of Hartmann's works in a series of ten short pieces for piano. To provide unity within the sequence of musical pictures, the composer hit on the idea of incorporating a recurring interlude which he called "Promenade." This gave the listener the impression of enjoying a leisurely stroll through a gallery, moving from one of Hartmann's paintings to the next each time the Promenade music was heard. Though originally composed as a work for piano, the imaginative sounds of the ten musical pictures begged for orchestration, a task that several composers later undertook. *Pictures at an Exhibition* is best known to us today in the brilliantly orchestrated version by Maurice Ravel completed in 1922.

Promenade Here the composer projects himself, and by extension the listener, as wandering through an exposition of Hartmann paintings. Immediately, we are transported musically into a world of purely Russian art. The tempo is marked "Fast but resolute, in the Russian manner;" the meter is irregular, as in a folk dance, mixing groups of five beats with those of six; and the melody is built on a folk-influenced scale, called **pentatonic**, which uses only five notes instead of the usual Western scale of seven, here B♭, C, D, F, and G:

FIGURE 15–7

Victor Hartmann's vision *The Great Gate of Kiev* which inspired the last of the musical paintings in Musorgsky's *Pictures at an Exhibition*. Note the bells in the tower, a motif that is featured prominently at the very end of Musorgsky's musical evocation of this design.

EXAMPLE 3

Now begins a musical depiction of ten paintings. We focus our gaze on numbers 4 and 10.

Picture 4: Polish Ox-Cart Hartmann's scene is a view of a rickety ox-cart seen lumbering down a Russian dirt road. The rocking of the cart is suggested by a two-note ostinato*. Notice in this brief composition how music has the capacity to project a sense of time and movement in a way that a painting cannot. Here the viewer remains stationary as the cart appears in the distance *(pp)*, moves closer and closer by means of a crescendo (reaching *fff*), and slowly disappears in the distance as the orchestra is gradually reduced to a single bass instrument (playing *ppp*).

Picture 10: The Great Gate of Kiev The stimulus for the majestic conclusion to *Pictures at an Exhibition* was Hartmann's design for a new and grandiose gate to the ancient Russian city of Kiev. Musorgsky disposes his thematic material to give the impression of a parade passing beneath the giant gate, and he does so in what is tantamount to rondo form (here **ABAB-CA**). The majestic vision of the gate **(A)** alternates with religious music for a

procession of Russian pilgrims **(B),** and even the composer–viewer walks beneath the gate as the Promenade theme **(C)** appears before a final return to a panoramic view of the gate **(A)** now with Hartmann's bells ringing triumphantly.

In this climactic final tableau, the full orchestra is able to give more powerful expression to all of the local color and grandeur inherent in Musorgsky's original music for piano, just as Musorgsky's musical creation is a far more powerful artistic statement than was Hartmann's design for the gate of Kiev (Fig. 15–7).

LISTENING GUIDE

Modest Musorgsky
Pictures at an Exhibition (1874)
(orchestrated by Maurice Ravel, 1922)

CD 5/3
6–Tape 5B
2–Tape 2A

Promenade

0:00   Solo trumpet begins Promenade theme

0:07   Full brass respond
0:15   Trumpet and full brass continue to alternate
0:30   Full strings and then woodwinds and brass enter
1:21   Brass briefly restate Promenade theme

Track 4; 6–Tape 5B

Picture 4: *Polish Ox-Cart*

0:00   Solo tuba plays Ox-Cart melody against backdrop of a two-note ostinato

0:51   Strings and soon full orchestra join in
1:33   Full orchestra plays Ox-Cart theme (note rattle of tambourine)
1:54   Tuba returns with Ox-Cart theme
2:24   Diminuendo and fadeout

Track 5; 6–Tape 5B

Picture 10: *The Great Gate of Kiev*

0:00   **A**   Gate theme in full brass

1:05   **B**   Pilgrims appear in woodwind choir
1:35   **A**   Gate theme in brass with running scales in strings
2:10   **B**   Pilgrims reappear in woodwinds
2:42   **X**   Exotic sounds
3:21   **C**   Promenade theme returns in trumpet
3:59   **A**   Gate theme in full glory with bells added toward the end

(Listening Exercise 36)

The Orchestral Song

We began our discussion of Romantic music with two art songs* of Franz Schubert (pages 246–252), and we end it with two orchestral songs, one by Gustav Mahler (1860–1911), the other by Richard Strauss (1864–1949). This is not an inappropriate framework in which to experience Romantic music, for the nineteenth century was marked throughout by an exceptionally strong union between music and poetry. If poetry had the power to communicate feelings of love, grief, pain, or longing, these typically Romantic sentiments could not fail to be intensified when set to music. Thus, the art song came into being in the early nineteenth century. At about the same time, Beethoven incorporated song into the finale of his Ninth ("Choral") Symphony (1824) as Berlioz and Liszt would later do in their programmatic symphonies. Naturally, it was only a matter of time before the genres of art song and symphony began to interact and influence each another, producing something new: the orchestral song. In its simplest form the **orchestral song** was an art song in which the full orchestra had replaced the piano as the medium of accompaniment. Yet because the orchestra could supply more color and add a greater number of contrapuntal lines, the orchestral song grew to be longer, denser, and more complex than the piano-supported art song. Berlioz, Brahms, and Wagner all experimented with the orchestral song in various ways, but not until Gustav Mahler did this hybrid musical genre reach maturity.

Gustav Mahler (1860–1911)

Gustav Mahler was born in 1860 into a middle-class Jewish family in Bohemia, then part of the Austrian Empire but now encompassed by Czechoslovakia. At the age of fifteen he was admitted to the prestigious Vienna Conservatory of Music where he studied musical composition and conducting. Mahler felt his mission in life was to conduct—to interpret—the works of the masters ("suffer for my great masters," he said). Like most young conductors, he began his career in provincial towns, gradually working his way to larger and more important musical centers. His itinerary as resident conductor took him along the following route: Bad Hall (1880), Laibach (1881–1882), Olmütz (1883), Kassel (1883–1884), Prague (1885–1886), Leipzig (1886–1888), Budapest (1888–1891), Hamburg (1891–1897), and finally back to Vienna.

In May 1897 Mahler returned triumphantly to his adopted city as director of the Vienna Court Opera, a position Mozart had once coveted. The next year he also assumed directorship of the Vienna Philharmonic, then and now one of the world's great orchestras. But Mahler was a demanding autocrat—a musical tyrant—in search of an artistic ideal. That he drove himself as hard as he pushed others was little comfort to the singers and instrumentalists who had to endure his wrath during rehearsals. After ten stormy but artistically successful seasons (1897–1907), Mahler was dismissed from the Vienna Opera. About this time he received and accepted a call to come to New York to take charge of the Metropolitan Opera and, eventually, the

FIGURE 15–8

Gustav Mahler

FIGURE 15–9

Three silhouettes of Gustav Mahler conducting in the orchestral pit of the Vienna Court Opera. Mahler earned his living as a conductor and was free to devote himself to composition only during the summer months.

New York Philharmonic as well. Here, too, there was both controversy and acclaim. And here, too, at least at the Met, his contract was not renewed after two years, though he stayed on longer, until February 1911, with the Philharmonic. He died in Vienna in May 1911 of a lingering streptococcus infection that had attacked his weak heart—a sad end to an obsessive and somewhat tormented life.

Mahler is unique among composers in that as a mature artist he wrote only orchestral songs and symphonies. These he managed to create during the summers when freed of his conducting duties. His five orchestral song cycles* typically contain settings of four, five, or six poems by a single author. *Kindertotenlieder* (*Children's Death Songs*, 1901–1904), for example, is a collection of five songs for voice and orchestra to words by Friedrich Rückert (1788–1866). They express the poet's overwhelming grief on the loss of two young children to scarlet fever. By tragic coincidence, no sooner had Mahler finished setting Rückert's painfully personal memorials than his own eldest daughter died at the age of four of scarlet fever, a loss from which the intensely sensitive composer never recovered.

songs and symphonies

What is also so unique to Mahler is the extent to which he borrowed from his own orchestral songs when he sat down to compose a symphony. It is as if the songs served as a musical repository or vault to which the composer could return for inspiration while wrestling with the problems of a large, multimovement work for orchestra. Mahler's First Symphony (1889), though entirely instrumental, makes use of melodies already present in his song cycle *Lieder eines fahrenden Gesellen* (*Songs of a Wayfaring Lad*, 1885). His Second (1894), Third (1896), and Fourth (1901) symphonies incorporate various portions of the *Wonderhorn Songs* (1892–1899) as solo vocal parts within the symphony. Symphonies Five (1902) and Six (1904) are again purely instrumental, but once more incorporate preexisting melodies, in this case from *Children's Death Songs* and *Five Rückert Songs* (1901–1902). Altogether Mahler wrote nine symphonies, seven of which make use of his own orchestral songs or other preexisting vocal music.

Life Among the Artists

In 1901 middle-aged Gustav Mahler married the dazzling Viennese beauty Alma Schindler (1879–1964). She was the daughter of a noted Austrian landscape painter and was in her own right a talented pianist and budding composer. As a precondition to their marriage, however, Mahler insisted that Alma give up her own career in music to serve his art. Given this infringement of her liberty and the fact that she was just slightly more than half Mahler's age, it is not surprising that their marriage was not a tranquil one. At one point, in 1910, Mahler consulted the famous Sigmund Freud, father of psychoanalysis, in hopes of coming to a better understanding of himself and his union with Alma. (Freud declined to treat Mahler, apparently for fear of destroying the latter's creative process.) After the composer's death in 1911, Alma went on to have affairs with the conductor Bruno Walter and the painter Oskar Kokoschka (see Fig. 17–2), and later to marry the architect Walter Gropius and the novelist Franz Werfel. Obviously, Alma Schindler had a keen eye for talent. Her tongue was equally sharp, as can be seen in the following extracts from her memoirs *And the Bridge Was Love*, which describe Mahler's work habits at their lakeside summer home in southern Austria.

"Mahler got up at six or six-thirty every day. As soon as he was awake, he rang for the cook, who promptly prepared his breakfast and carried it up a steep, slippery trail to his forest study, two hundred feet above the house. (She was forbidden to use the regular road, lest he meet her on his way up; before work, he could not stand seeing anyone.) The study was a one-room brick hut with a door

Alma Mahler in 1902, shortly after her marriage to Gustav Mahler.

and three windows, a grand piano, a bookshelf with the collected works of Kant and Goethe. No music but Bach's. About noon he came down, changed, and went for a swim. . . . Our afternoons were spent walking. Rain or shine, we walked for three or four hours, or rowed around the gleaming, heat-spewing lake. . . . Often he stopped and stood with the sun burning down on his hatless skull, drew out a notebook, wrote, thought, wrote some more. Sometimes he beat time in the air before writing the notes down. This could go on for an hour or more, with me sitting on a tree trunk or in the grass, not daring to look at him. Mahler made sure that everything in his personal life revolved around his own genius."

But to Mahler a symphony was much more than just an extended orchestral song. "The symphony is the world; it must embrace everything," he once said. And so he tried to embrace every sort of music within it. There are folk dances, popular songs, military marches, off-stage bands, bugle calls, and even Gregorian chant at various points in his symphonies. What results is a collage of sound on the grandest scale, one achieved, in part, by employing massive forces and a greatly extended sense of time. Mahler's Symphony No. 2, for example, calls for ten horns and eight trumpets, and lasts an hour and a half. The first performance of his Symphony No. 8 in Munich in 1910 involved 858 singers and 171 instrumentalists. With good reason it has been nicknamed the "Symphony of a Thousand."

"Symphony of a Thousand"

Gustav Mahler was the last in the long line of great German symphonists which extended back through Brahms, Schubert, and Beethoven to Mozart and, ultimately, to Haydn. What had begun as a modest instrumental genre with a limited emotional range had grown in the course of the nineteenth

FIGURE 15–10

Mahler spent his summers at various villas in the Austrian mountains, but he made sure that each was supplied with a "forest hut" where he could go each morning to compose without distraction. The last of these composing chalets, at Alt-Schluderbach, is today one of the more accessible ones.

century into a monumental structure, the musical equivalent, in Mahler's view, of the entire cosmos.

ORCHESTRAL SONG, *I AM LOST TO THE WORLD*, FROM THE *FIVE RÜCKERT SONGS* (1901–1902)

It is the everyday world, not the grand cosmos, that concerns Mahler in his setting of Friedrich Rückert's *Ich bin der Welt abhanden gekommen (I Am Lost to the World)*. Rückert was a minor German Romantic poet whose verse, nonetheless, enjoyed favor with Schubert, Schumann, and Brahms because of its structural regularity. During the summers of 1901 and 1902, Mahler chose to set five among the many hundreds of poems by Rückert. The subject of these five verses was dear to the composer because it expresses in various ways his outlook on life and on art.

Romantic solitude

I Am Lost to the World speaks of the artist's growing remoteness from the travails of everyday life and of withdrawal into a private, heavenly world of music, here signified by the final word *Lied* (song). Although the poem has three stanzas, Mahler chose not a strophic setting*, but a through-composed* one. The first strophe sets the mood of the song as a mournful English horn begins to play a halting melody, one then picked up and extended by the voice. The second stanza moves to a faster tempo and more rapid declamation in the voice, as if the mundane world should be quickly left behind. The final strophe returns to a slow tempo. It also sets the notes of the bass on the beat and on the roots of triads*, all of which help project a settled, satisfied feeling—the self-absorbed poet–composer has withdrawn into the peaceful world of art. Toward the end Mahler shows how music has the capacity to sum up in a few brief sounds the entire progress of the poem, the movement from the dissonance of the world to the peace of the inner self. First the strings (at 6:23) play an extended dissonance (F against E♭) which resolves to a consonance (E♭ against E♭), and this is repeated at the very end (6:39) by the English horn, "dying out expressively" as the composer requests.

I Am Lost to the World has been called Mahler's best orchestral song. That he made use of much of this same music in the beautiful slow movement of his Symphony No. 5 suggests that these musical ideas were important to him and express, as he said at the time, "his very self." Both song and symphony have a certain world-weariness about them, as if Mahler had a premonition that both the artist's life and the Romantic era were coming to an end.

LISTENING GUIDE

Gustav Mahler
Orchestral song, *I Am Lost to the World,*
from the *Five Rückert Songs* (1901–1902)

CD 5/6
6–Tape 5B

0:00	English horn haltingly rises with the melody		
1:00	Voice enters and extends the melody	Ich bin der Welt abhanden gekommen, mit der ich sonst viele Zeit verdorben; sie hat so lange nichts von mir vernommen, sie mag wohl glauben, ich sei gestorben!	I am lost to the world, in which I've squandered so much time; it has known nothing of me for so long, it may well think that I am dead!
1:56	English horn returns with the melody		
2:34	Triplets in harp; faster tempo, recitative quality in the voice	Es ist mir auch gar nichts daran gelegen, ob sie mich für gestorben hält. Ich kann auch gar nichts sagen dagegen, denn wirklich bin ich gestorben der Welt.	I don't really care, if it takes me for dead. Nor can I contradict, for really I am dead to the world.
3:39	Melody returns in English horn; slow, peaceful conclusion	Ich bin gestorben dem Weltgetümmel und ruh' in einem stillen Gebeit! Ich leb' allein in meinem Himmel, in meinem Lieben, in meinem Lied.	I am dead to the world's commotion, and rest in a world of peace. I live alone in my own heaven, in my love, in my song.
5:47	English horn returns with melody		
6:23	Dissonance–consonance in violins		
6:39	Dissonance–consonance in English horn		

(Listening Exercise 37)

Richard Strauss (1864–1949)

Richard Strauss and Gustav Mahler were the two most renowned composer–conductors in Europe at the turn of the century. But Strauss was German, not Austrian like Mahler. And despite his name and frequent association with Vienna, Richard Strauss was no relation to the famous "waltzing" Strauss family of Vienna, led by the "Waltz King" Johann Strauss Jr. (1825–1899). Rather, he was from Munich. His mother was the daughter of a Munich brewer, and his father a French horn player in the orchestra there. Reared in a favorable musical environment, the younger Strauss developed

FIGURE 15–11

Richard Strauss

FIGURE 15–12

Strauss's opera *Salome*, based on Oscar Wilde's lurid play, was an enormous success but was banned for a time in Chicago and New York. Cartoonists here and abroad delighted in this *succès de scandale*.

Salome goes on tour.

Salome: *'Wait and see, John, they're going to chop your head off!'*
John: *'That's not as bad as being made into an opera by Strauss!'*

so quickly that by the time he was twenty he had already heard his compositions performed in Vienna, Berlin, and Cologne. But Strauss was more than a composer. He, too, became a virtuoso conductor, and, indeed, it was mainly in that capacity that he earned his living. At various times he directed the Munich Court Opera (1886–1898), the Berlin Royal Opera (1898–1918), and the Vienna State Opera (1919–1924). During these same years his own operas and symphonic poems had unprecedented popular success. He became, especially after the death of Mahler in 1911, the foremost composer in Europe.

When the Nazis came to power in 1933, they tried to exploit the reputation of this international figure for political purposes: Strauss's name was synonymous with German music. Adolph Hitler had him elected president of the *Reichsmusikkammer* and wrote him personal messages. At first Strauss eagerly collaborated, giving pro–Nazi speeches. But when members of his own family were threatened by German anti–Semitism (his daughter-in-law was Jewish and his only two grandchildren half-Jewish) he began to speak out, however meekly, and thereupon became himself persona non grata to the National Socialists. After the war Strauss and his wife Pauline fled to neutral Switzerland for fear of being prosecuted as Nazi war criminals. It was there that he wrote his final compositions, including his *Four Last Songs*. Eventually, he was exonerated and early in 1949 he returned to his home in Garmisch, Germany (Fig. 15–14), where he died in September at the age of eighty-five.

Strauss's most successful works were composed around the turn of the century. In the decade before 1900 he produced a succession of six symphonic poems. They bring to a brilliant conclusion the tradition of the one-movement programmatic work for orchestra established by Liszt in the 1850s and perpetuated by Tchaikovsky in the 1870s and 1880s. As their titles suggest, these tone poems* follow programs taken from literature (*Thus Spake Zarathustra*, 1896, and *Don Quixote*, 1897), folklore (*Till Eulenspiegel's Merry Pranks*, 1895), legend (*Don Juan*, 1889), and Strauss's own imagination (*Death and Transfiguration*, 1889, and *A Hero's Life*, 1898). Without exception, these are exuberant works with flashy, energetic themes making use of the largest, most colorful sort of late–Romantic orchestra. They place enormous technical demands on the players, a challenge to even the best symphony orchestra.

After 1900 Strauss turned to opera. In quick succession he created *Feuersnot* (1901), *Salome* (1905), *Elektra* (1909), and *Der Rosenkavalier* (*The Cavalier of the Rose*, 1911). His fame as an opera composer rests mainly on *Salome*, a frenetic, dissonant setting of Oscar Wilde's scandalous play (including opera's only striptease act, the "Dance of the Seven Veils"), and *Der Rosenkavalier*, a melodious farewell to grand Romantic opera. In all of these it is the soprano voice that dominates. After World War I (1914–1918), Strauss composed other operas but never matched the originality, or sensationalism, of either *Salome* or *Der Rosenkavalier*. His reputation began to wane and he had doubts about his importance as a creative musician. "I may not be a first-rate composer," he said in 1947, "but I *am* a first-class second-rate composer." As you listen to one of his last compositions, *Im Abendrot (Red Glow of Sunset)*, you might come to feel that Strauss could at times be not only funny but also excessively modest.

FIGURES 15–13 AND 15–14

(left) Strauss and his wife of fifty-four years, Pauline de Ahna. She was an operatic soprano who had made a career singing in music dramas at Bayreuth. She was also, according to contemporary reports, her husband's harshest critic. (right) Within a year of its premiere, Strauss's opera *Salome* had been given at fifty opera houses around the world. With the royalties from these performances, he built this splendid villa in the Bavarian Alps. It was here that he died in 1949.

ORCHESTRAL SONG, *RED GLOW OF SUNSET*, FROM THE *FOUR LAST SONGS* (1948)

How can a song written in 1948 still be a piece of Romantic music? Simply said, musical epochs know no clear-cut boundaries; composers are not obliged to change styles in lockstep when a new century or half-century begins. The aged Richard Strauss continued into the 1940s to compose in the style that he knew best, the late–Romantic style of the 1890s. That these last songs have enjoyed enormous popular favor suggests something more: The listening public has never lost its fondness for the Romantic sound. Sentiment, grandeur, richness, imagination, escapism—these are not only specific Romantic qualities but they are also things we generally associate with the very essence of music.

Red Glow of Sunset is an orchestral song that sets verse by the Romantic poet Joseph Eichendorff (1788–1857). Strauss composed it in May 1948 and later, after his death, it was published among a collection called *Four Last Songs*. Though the music is through composed*, the poem itself has a repeating structure of four four-line stanzas. It treats the familiar Romantic themes of love and death, isolation and solitude, and nature—a mountain sunset is the setting for an aged couple's final journey. The warm glow of Romanticism is everywhere to be heard in the instruments: the huge, coloristic orchestra; the sweeping, if sentimental, opening melody in the strings; the dense chromatic counterpoint reminiscent of Wagner; and the musical depiction of nature—we see the larks take wing through the fluttering of the flute, then soar on high in the violin. As the music leads to the final question "Can this perhaps be death?" it descends and turns more somber.

Not only is *Red Glow of Sunset* Richard Strauss's personal valediction to the world and his wife of fifty-four years, the soprano Pauline de Ahna, but it is also a fitting farewell to German music's most gloriously expressive period, the Romantic era.

LISTENING GUIDE

Richard Strauss
Orchestral song, *Red Glow of Sunset*, from the *Four Last Songs* (1948)

CD 5/7
6–Tape 5B

0:00	Sweeping string melody enriched by French horn

1:26	Wir sind durch Not und Freude gegangen Hand in Hand, vom Wandern ruhen wir nun überm stillen Land.	Through joy and travail we have gone hand in hand, tired from the journey we now rest above the still land.

2:24	String melody returns as bridge to second stanza

2:33	Rings sich die Täler neigen, es dunkelt schon die Luft, zwei Lerchen nur noch steigen nacträumend in den Duft.	The valleys below yield, as the air grows dark, only two larks still soar dreamlike in the soft air.

2:57	Flute and violin depict flight of the larks

3:24	Music turns darker with use of minor chords	Tritt her, und lass sie schwirren, bald ist es Schlafenszeit, dass wir uns nicht verirren in dieser Einsamkeit.	Come here, and let them fly about, soon it will be time for sleep, we must not go astray in this solitude.
4:16	Rich chord changes	O weiter, stiller Friede! so tief im Abendrot, wie sind wir wandermüde— ist dies etwa der Tod?	O spacious, tranquil peace! so deep in the red glow of sunset how world-weary we are— is this perhaps death?

6:10	Orchestral postlude using fragments of the string melody and the music of the larks; a divine example of the richness of Romantic harmony

LISTENING EXERCISES

34

Johannes Brahms
Symphony No. 1 (1876) Fourth Movement
Adagio: Allegro non troppo, ma con brio

CD 5/1
6–Tape 5A

In the finale of this Symphony No. 1, Johannes Brahms employs sonata–allegro form to shape the course of musical events. But like his Classical predecessors, Brahms rarely follows sonata form in all its particulars—he sometimes deviates from the norm because the natural flow of his material seems to dictate some kind of change. In this finale Brahms thwarts the listener's formal expectations in two ways: (1) He repeats without change (or development) the first theme at the beginning of the development, (2) He omits entirely the first theme at the beginning of the recapitulation. The following questions are intended to show how a Romantic composer like Brahms can make something new and exciting out of tried-and-true Classical sonata–allegro form.

Introduction

1. (0:00–2:42) What is the purpose of the first half of the introduction?
   a. to recapitulate the themes of the previous movements
   b. to suggest the beginning of the main theme and build anticipation
2. (2:43–5:19) What is the order of events in the second half of the introduction?
   a. French horn call–flute repeat–church chorale softly in brass–French horn call
   b. French horn call–church chorale softly in brass–flute repeat–French horn call

Exposition

3. (5:20–5:53) Which family of instruments presents the hymnlike first theme?　a. strings　　b. woodwinds　　c. brass
4. (5:54–6:23) Which family of instruments repeats the first theme?
   a. strings　　b. woodwinds　　c. brass
5. (5:54–6:23) What are the strings doing during this repeat?
   a. playing tremolo　　b. playing vibrato　　c. playing pizzicato

　　6:25 Transition begins

6. (7:03–7:09) At the end of the transition there is a brief reminiscence of which theme?　　a. French horn call　　b. hymnlike first theme

　　7:10 Second theme group begins

7. (9:03–9:14) How would you describe what happens at the joint or seam between the end of the exposition and the beginning of the development?
   a. full cadence and then brief transition
   b. brief transition then full cadence

Development

8. (9:15) The hymnlike first theme is now repeated, almost note for note, but has the orchestration changed? Is the order of presentation still strings (9:15) and then a woodwind repeat (9:54)?　　a. yes　　b. no

　　10:24 Development of transitional themes

Recapitulation

9. (12:38) The recapitulation begins with which theme?
   a. French horn call　　hymnlike first theme　　c. second theme group
10. Brahms omits the first theme and the transition themes in the recapitulation. Why?
    a. first theme and transition material *never* return in sonata–allegro form
    b. they were used extensively in the development

Listen now to the conclusion of the symphony. The coda, with the surprise return of the chorale passage, is stunning.

	Peter Tchaikovsky	CD 5/2
35	Symphonic poem, *Romeo and Juliet* (1869)	6–Tape 5A
		2–Tape 2B

Peter Tchaikovsky might be called the quintessential Romantic composer, given his brilliant orchestrations and sweeping, if sometimes sentimental, melodies. Tchaikovsky was not a "developer" in the tradition of Haydn, Beethoven, and Brahms, but usually chose instead to repeat large sections of music. These repetitions he would often partly disguise by means of a new and different orchestration. The following questions focus your attention on various aspects of Tchaikovsky's use of repetition in the symphonic poem *Romeo and Juliet*.

Introduction
1. (0:00–0:35) The opening woodwind passage, which sounds faintly religious, is a musical depiction of the kindly Franciscan monk, Friar Laurence. How would you describe it?
   a. monophonic   b. polyphonic   c. homophonic

   0:36–1:05 Anguished dissonances in strings and French horn

2. (1:25–2:06) We hear solo flute and harp strumming. How many times does the harp play its sequence of strumming chords?
   a. once   b. twice   c. three times
3. (2:07–2:33) The Friar Laurence theme now returns. In what way is it different?
   a. bassoon plays in unison with the melody in woodwinds
   b. trumpet plays fanfare against the melody in woodwinds
   c. strings provide pizzicato counterpoint to the melody in woodwinds

   2:34–3:04 Repeat of anguished dissonances in strings and horn

4. (3:23–3:55) The harp strumming returns. In what way is it different?
   a. solo flute has been replaced by high violins
   b. flute now plays pizzicato
   c. Friar Laurence theme now heard as a counterpoint

5:01 *Exposition* begins with Feud theme

5. (6:19–6:40) Which sentence best describes what occurs in the transition between the Feud theme and the Love theme?
   a. woodwinds gradually descend and there is a release of tension
   b. strings ascend and there is a release of tension
   c. strings descend and there is a release of tension
6. (7:51–8:10 and again 8:33–8:50) As the love theme is played passionately by the woodwinds, the French horn provides a counterpoint. How would you describe it?
   a. two-note phrases that gradually ascend by step
   b. two-note phrases that gradually descend by step
   c. three-note phrases that gradually ascend by step

   8:51–9:46 Lovely closing section

9:52–11:57 Development

7. Is the Love theme anywhere to be heard in the development?
   a. yes   b. no

Recapitulation

8. (11:58–12:21) Has the transition music from the exposition (6:19–6:40) been eliminated here in the recapitulation?   a. yes   b. no
9. (13:00) When the Love theme returns in its full glory, why does it this time sound so much more passionate and powerful?
   a. because the melody is now played by sweeping strings
   b. because the melody in now played by full brass section
   c. because woodwinds now play the melody louder
10. (13:00–14:00) Does the French horn also return again with its counter-point against the Love theme?   a. yes   b. no

---

36	Modest Musorgsky *Pictures at an Exhibition* (1874) (orchestrated by Maurice Ravel, 1922)	CD 5/3 6–Tape 5B 2–Tape 2A

This work by Musorgsky is a colorful set of ten musical pictures connected by a musical Promenade. Musorgsky's particular use of scales, rhythms, and textures gives his music a decidedly Russian flavor, one that sometimes sounds exotic to our ears. The following questions deal with the Promenade and two of the ten pictures.

Promenade

1. How would you describe the instrumental color and texture of the beginning of the Promenade?
   a. monophonic trumpet followed by polyphonic brass choir
   b. monophonic trumpet followed by homophonic brass choir
2. (1:21–1:38) What is the texture in the brass choir at the end of the Prom-enade?   a. polyphonic   b. homophonic

Track 4; 6–Tape 5B

Picture 4: *Polish Ox-Cart*

3. What is the meter of this picture?   a. duple   b. triple
4. What is the mode?   a. major   b. minor
5. Which graph (or picture) best represents the dynamic course of this movement?
   a.   b.   c.

Track 5; 6–Tape 5B

Picture 10: *The Great Gate of Kiev*

6. (0:00–1:04) How would you describe the texture and mode at the beginning?
   a. polyphonic and major   b. homophonic and major
   c. polyphonic and minor   d. homophonic and minor
7. (1:05–1:34) When the pilgrims **(B)** return, do the strings provide a counterpoint?   a. yes   b. no
8. (2:42–3:19) Describe two ways these exotic sounds are created.
   a. _____
   b. _____
9. (3:59–4:50) As the brasses present the Gate theme in the final grand presentation, what do the strings do to fill out the orchestral texture?
   a. play mainly a rapid pizzicato
   b. play mainly a shimmering tremolo
   c. play mainly a basso continuo
   d. all of the above
10. Why do you suppose Musorgsky chose not to end his work with the Promenade theme as he began it? _____
    _____

	Gustav Mahler	CD 5/6
37	Orchestral song, *I Am Lost to the World*, from the *Five Rückert Songs* (1901–1902)	6–Tape 5B

Gustav Mahler's orchestral song *I Am Lost to the World* exploits both the richness of the human voice and the color of the late–Romantic orchestra. Listen to this lovely composition and respond to the following questions.

1. At the very beginning, which instrument provides a bass accompaniment below the melody in the English horn?
   a. French horn   b. viola   c. harp
2. Which is the voice that enters?
   a. an alto   b. a tenor   c. a baritone
3. (2:16–2:32) How is the word "gestorben" ("dead") treated?
   a. there is a vocal flourish which is answered by the French horn
   b. there is a French horn flourish which is answered by the voice
4. At the end of the second stanza (after "gestorben der Welt"), which musical device is used?
   a. an ascending pizzicato in the violins
   b. a descending sequence in the violins
   c. an ostinato in bass
5. For the beginning of the third and final strophe, how would you describe the range of the voice?
   a. falls to the singer's lowest register
   b. continues up to a climax in the singer's highest register

6. The last line of the poem is a fitting epitaph for the entire Romantic era: "in meinem Lieben, in meinem Lied" ("in my love, in my song"). Which is the more correct description of the musical treatment of these two alliterative phrases?
   a. music climaxes on "Lieben" and dies out on "Lied"
   b. starts quietly on "Lieben" and climaxes on "Lied"
7. What role do the brasses play here in Mahler's orchestral song?
   _____

Now listen to the next work on your CDs or tapes, the orchestral song *Red Glow of Sunset* by Richard Strauss. You may view this as a burden, but don't. In this assignment you are privileged to hear two of the most beautiful works of art you will ever experience.

8. In which of the two songs is the orchestra bigger and the orchestral texture denser?   a. the Mahler song   b. the Strauss song
9. Name two other ways in which these songs differ:
   a. _____
   b. _____
10. It is perhaps impossible to say which of these orchestral songs is the "more" beautiful. They are both gorgeous. But which did you prefer?
    _____ Why? _____
    _____

KEY WORDS

absolute music	nationalism	the Russian Five
Joseph Eichendorff	orchestral song	tone poem
Nadezhda von Meck	pentatonic scale	Victor Hartmann

16

FROM ROMANTIC TO MODERN: IMPRESSIONISM

R omantic music reached its apogee during the late nineteenth century in the grandiose works of Wagner, Tchaikovsky, Brahms, Mahler, and Strauss. But by 1900 this German-dominated musical empire was in danger of crumbling, shaken by forces both within and without. Some composers outside the mainstream of Romanticism were becoming downright hostile toward the German style, epitomized by the music of Wagner. Not surprisingly, the most powerful anti–German sentiment was felt in France. (France and Germany went to war in 1870 and would do so again in 1914.) After first embracing Wagner during the 1870s and 1880s, the avant-garde of French music had, by the 1890s, turned antagonistic. It began to ridicule the sentimentality of Romanticism in general and the monumental structures of the Germans in particular. German music was said to be too heavy, too pretentious, too bombastic. Wagner's system of obvious leitmotifs* was now deemed overly simplistic— just as clumsy as one of his Nordic giants. True passion, they said, might be expressed in more subtle ways, in something other than sheer volume of sound and epic length.

I MPRESSIONISM IN PAINTING AND MUSIC

The movement that arose in France in opposition to German Romantic music has been given the name Impressionism. We are, of course, more familiar with this term as a designation for a school of French painters living and working in Paris during the last decades of the nineteenth century. The group included Claude Monet (1840–1926), Edgar Degas (1834–1917), Camille Pissaro (1830–1903), Berthe Morisot (1841–1895), Alfred Sisley (1839–1899), and Auguste Renoir (1841–1919). Impressionist painters were not overtly anti–German like their musical counterparts. There was no need to be, for French painting had a long and secure tradition (Figs. 6–4, 8–7 and 13–13), one not subject to threat of foreign domination. Their rebellion was against the traditional, academic style of painting of their native land.

The Impressionist movement in painting began in the early 1870s when Monet and his colleagues were forbidden to show their canvases in the offi-

FIGURE 16–1

The painting that gave its name to an epoch: Claude Monet's *Impression: Sunrise* exhibited at the first group exhibition organized by Monet, Renoir, Degas, and Pissarro in Paris in 1874. The ships, rowboats and other elements in the early morning light are more suggested than fully drawn. Said the critic Louis Leroy derisively of this painting at the time: "Wallpaper in its most embryonic state is more finished than that seascape."

cial Parisian Salon. Consequently, they launched their own exhibition. In the uproar that followed, the artists were jeeringly called "impressionists" for the sometimes vague quality of their art. The painters accepted the name, partly as an act of defiance against the establishment, and soon the term was universally adopted.

It is ironic that this style of French painting generated such controversy, for no school of painters is now more popular with the general public than the Impressionists. Indeed, judging by museum attendance and the number of books and reproductions sold, there is an almost limitless enthusiasm for the works of Monet, Degas, Renoir, and their associates—precisely the paintings that the artists' contemporaries mocked and jeered. But what is it about the Impressionist style that then caused such a furor?

The Impressionists were the first to turn against representational art, the idea that a painting should exactly represent an object, as in a photograph. Instead, they tried to recreate the impression that the object produced on their senses. The key here is light: The Impressionists saw all objects as awash in vibrant rays of light and sought to capture the aura that the light-bathed object created in the eye of the beholder. To accomplish this they covered their canvases with small, dablike brushstrokes in which light was broken down into spots of color. This creates a sense of constant movement and fluidity. Shapes are not clearly defined but blurred, more suggested than delineated. Minor details disappear. Sunlight is everywhere and everything shimmers (Fig. 16-2).

As impressions and sensations became paramount for these painters, it is not surprising that they showed an intensified interest in music. What art form is more elusive and suggestive? What medium allows the receiver—

FIGURE 16–2

Claude Monet, *The Bridge at Bougival* (1869). The illuminated clouds, the shadows on the bridge, and reflection on the water, all impart a vibrant sense of light as the rays of the sun project down from the sky and across the bridge.

painters and musicians allied

the listener—more freedom to interpret the sensations he or she perceives? Painters began to speak in musical terms. Paul Gauguin (1848–1903) referred to the harmonies of line and color as the "music of painting." Paul Cezanne painted an "overture"in homage to Wagner, while James Whistler (1834–1903), an American who worked in Paris in the 1860s and 1880s, created "nocturnes" and "symphonies." The artist envied the musician's good fortune to work in a medium in which flux and change could be continually expressed—rather than one that required that artist to seize the moment and fix it on canvas. At the same time Claude Debussy, the musician whose work most consistently displayed the Impressionist style in music, found inspiration for his work in the visual arts. He called various collections of his pieces *Sketches, Images,* and *Prints.* Rare are the moments in history when the aesthetic aims of painters and musicians were as closely allied.

FIGURE 16–3

Claude Debussy

Claude Debussy (1862–1918)

Claude Debussy was born in 1862 into a modest family living in a small town outside Paris. Since neither of his parents were musical, it came as a surprise when their son demonstrated talent at the keyboard. At the age of ten he was sent off to the Paris Conservatory for lessons in piano, composition, and music theory. Owing to his skills as a performer he was soon engaged for summer work in the household of Nadezhda von Meck, a wealthy patroness of the arts and the principal supporter of Tchaikovsky (see page 304). This employment took him, in turn, to Italy, Russia, and Vienna. In 1884 he won the Prix de Rome, an official prize in composition supported by the French government, one which required a three-year stay in Rome. But Debussy was not happy in the Eternal City. He preferred the Bohemian life of Paris, the atmosphere of the bistros and the cafes.

Returning to Paris more or less permanently in 1887, the young Frenchman continued to learn his craft and search for his own independent voice as a composer. He had some minor successes, and yet, as he said in 1893, "There are still things that I am not able to do—create masterpieces, for example." But the next year, in 1894, he did just that. With the completion of *Prélude à L'Aprés midi d'un Faune (Prelude to the Afternoon of a Faun)*, he gave to the public what has become his most enduring orchestral work.

Debussy spent his time in the company of poets as well as painters. His *Prelude*, in fact, was inspired by a poem, *Afternoon of a Faun*, written by his friend and mentor Stéphane Mallarmé (1842–1898; Fig. 16-4). It may be just coincidence that Debussy's musical creation has 110 measures and Mallarmé's poem 110 lines. But Debussy does not set the words of the text. Nor does he directly tell a story in music, as might occur in a Romantic tone poem[*]. His music serves only to evoke the general mood of the poem, to create in sound its mysterious sensations. As Mallarmé said when he first heard this sensuous musical impression of his poem, "I was not expecting anything like this. This music prolongs the emotion of my poem, and evokes the scene more vividly than color."

FIGURE 16–4

The poet Stéphane Mallarmé, author of *Afternoon of a Faun*, as painted by the great predecessor of the Impressionists, Edouard Manet (1832–1883). Mallarmé was a friend and artistic mentor of the composer Debussy.

CLOUDS, FROM THE THREE *NOCTURNES* (1897–1899)

Musical color also pervades Debussy's next major orchestral work, the *Nocturnes* written 1897–1899. *Nocturnes* is a set of three pieces, *Clouds*, *Festivals*, and *Sirens*, each of which exploits distinctive instrumental timbres to create a vivid musical painting. The title *Nocturnes* was not inspired by the Romantic night pieces, called *Nocturnes*, of Chopin, but rather by those of the American Impressionist painter James Whistler whose works Debussy knew and loved. Whistler created his nocturnes on canvas by evoking an atmospheric scene through the use of one or two special colors. His *Nocturne in*

FIGURE 16–5

Mallarmé's *Afternoon of a Faun* created something of a sensation among late nineteenth-century French artists. This painting by Ker–Xavier Roussel (1867–1944) is just one of several such representations of the Faun surrounded by woodland nymphs.

FIGURE 16–6

The American artist James Whistler (1834–1903)—perhaps best known to us for his painting of his mother—actually spent most of his career in London and Paris. His "nocturnes," such as this *Nocturne in Black and Gold, The Falling Rocket* (1874), prefigure much of the work of the Impressionists and were greatly admired by Debussy.

Black and Gold (Fig. 16-6) and *Nocturne in Blue and Silver* are representative of these suggestive mood paintings. Debussy, in turn, used the language of the painters to describe what he intended to create musically in *Clouds*, the first of his three nocturnes: "*Clouds* renders the immutable aspect of the sky and the slow, solemn motion of the clouds, fading away in gray tones lightly tinged with white."

Debussy begins by suggesting the "slow, solemn motions of the clouds" in alternating fifths and thirds in the clarinets and bassoons. They seem to float, not being anchored securely in any one key. Next the English horn enters (0:21) with a brief theme that sounds bleak and desolate. After the return of the fifths and thirds (0:48), the music suddenly cascades downward (1:02). This descent in an exceptional moment, an example of what is called **parallelism** in music. This distinctive sound is created because all of the parts are moving, locked in step, in the same direction. Here we have the opposite of counterpoint, the traditional musical technique in which two or more lines continually move against each other. Parallelism was an innovation of Debussy, and it was one way he expressed his opposition to the German school of Wagner and Brahms so heavily steeped in counterpoint:

parallel motion

EXAMPLE 16–1

Soon the bleak theme of the English horn returns (1:37), followed in quick succession by a two-note French horn motive (1:47) and a second two-note gesture in the cellos and double basses (1:49). These brief splashes are not themes, but rather dashes of instrumental color—the musical counterpart to the Impressionist painter's rapidly applied dabs of color on canvas. After another parallel descent in the strings (2:11), the woodwinds lead a stepwise ascent that reaches a subdued climax (3:11). Now a two-note ostinato* begins in the strings which serves as a backdrop for further presentations of the English horn and French horn motives. We have noted how Debussy employs repeating patterns to create the feeling that time remains suspended. Here the use of an ostinato contributes to the sensation that the music is suspended on high.

dabs of musical color

EXAMPLE 16–2

Eventually, the ostinato runs out of energy (4:15) and there are more parallel descents (4:33). Then suddenly, in a magical moment, the music is again borne aloft, carried on high by the flute (4:50). The wonderfully transparent sound **(B)** is created by Debussy's novel orchestration. The flute is doubled by the airy plucking of a harp, while the strings create a shimmering sound, by playing tremolo*, as they quietly suspend a single chord. Notice that the flute and harp melody is not built on the usual seven-note major or minor scale, but on a five-note pattern. This is called a pentatonic scale*. There are only five notes within each octave, here the five notes corresponding to the black keys on the piano. We have seen before that the pentatonic scale is often found in folk music (see page 309). In Debussy's case he first encountered it in the Indonesian music he heard at the Paris International Exhibition of 1889. Here in *Clouds* the pentatonic scale gives an ethereal, otherworldly quality to this theme:

pentatonic scale

EXAMPLE 16–3

As the celestial tones of the flute and harp fade away, we conclude section **B** of *Clouds* and return to the music of section **A.** Yet there is no climax, no strong V–I cadence, no pause to signal a sectional division. In fact, the English horn commences the return to **A** before the flute has finished **B.** The composer fuses their sounds much as a painter of the period might blur the distinction between two shapes or figures (see Fig. 16–1, for example). As this final section proceeds, all of the themes of the work are heard again but in a fragmentary state, broken down and disassembled. They are now mere wisps of melody that dissolve into thin air, just as clouds reform, disintegrate, and disappear. Subdued climaxes, wandering harmonies, floating ostinatos, shimmering strings, coloristic dashes, wisps of themes, these are the qualities of Debussy's musical Impressionism, and nowhere are they more beautifully and imaginatively displayed than in *Clouds.*

LISTENING GUIDE		Claude Debussy *Clouds,* from the three *Nocturnes* (1897–1899)	CD 5/8 6–Tape 5B 2–Tape 2B

	A	Opening section made up of two themes and several motives	
0:00		Cloud theme in alternating fifths and thirds	
0:21		Bleak theme in English horn	
0:28		Quiet roll in timpani	
0:48		Cloud theme in violins	
1:02		Descending parallel motion in the strings	
1:16		Quiet interlude in the strings	
1:37		Bleak theme in English horn	
1:47		Splash of color in French horn and then low strings	
1:57		Bleak theme in English horn	
2:04		French horn motive	
2:11		Parallel descent in strings	
2:32		Long stepwise ascent in the woodwinds	
3:11		Subdued climax	
3:19		Ostinato supports Bleak theme and French horn echoes	
4:01		Bleak theme dies out	
4:15		Cloud theme returns now accompanied by solo viola	
4:33		More parallel descents	
	B	Middle section dominated by a striking melody and texture	
4:50		Flight theme enters in flute and harp	
5:18		Flight theme extended by strings	
5:38		Flight theme returns in flute and harp	
	A	Fragments of themes and motives return	
6:00		Bleak theme emerges once again in English horn	
6:12		French horn echoes along with string tremolos	
6:36		Quiet roll in the timpani with English horn solo	
7:04		Hints of Cloud theme in bassoons	
7:29		Suggestion of the Flight theme	
7:36		French horn echoes	
7:38		Quiet tremolo and isolated pizzicato notes in strings	

(Listening Exercise 38)

Debussy's *Clouds* belongs to the Romantic tradition in which composers drew inspiration from the mysteries of nature. Yet Debussy was more of a modernist than a romantic, partly because of his approach to harmony (see below) and partly because of his use of musical color.

Claude Debussy was the first composer to use musical timbre as something other than an element by which to reinforce and highlight melody. Think back to the orchestral music of Beethoven, Brahms, or Tchaikovsky. When a new theme enters in their works, it is almost invariably presented and carried forward by a new instrument or group of instruments. Instrumental color thus reinforces and gives profile to the theme. Yet it is the succession of themes, working in conjunction with harmony and texture, that creates the musical form. With Debussy, on the other hand, color becomes nearly independent of theme. Instruments enter with a distinct color but with no easily discernible theme. Color begins to replace melody as the primary agent in the creation of musical form. The revolutionary figures of modern music who use color exclusively to generate form—among them Varèse, Webern, Messiaen, and Penderecki (see Chapter 17) found a precedent for their approach to musical form in the compositions of the Impressionist Claude Debussy.

color independent of melody

PRELUDES FOR PIANO (1910, 1913)

Debussy's last and most far-reaching attempt at descriptive writing in music is found in the two books of *Preludes* for piano that he published in 1910 and 1913. Here the challenge to create musical impressions was all the greater, for the piano has a more limited musical palette than the multicolor orchestra. The evocative titles of some of these short pieces allude to their mysterious qualities: *Steps in the Snow, The Sunken Cathedral, What the West Wind Saw,* and *Sounds and Perfumes Swirl in the Night Air.* Timbres and textures can be produced in music, and images and events can be suggested, if not actually depicted. But can music really stimulate our sense of smell? Can it create perfume? Presumably not. That Debussy suggests it might shows how intent he was to create an ideal sort of music, one involving all the senses. As he says of this perfect music, "It would involve a mysterious collaboration of the air, of the movement of leaves and of the perfume of flowers along with music; music would serve to bind all these elements in a way so natural that their unity would seem to grow from all of them."

Voiles (*Sails*), from the first book of *Preludes*, takes us to the sea. In our mind's eye is implanted the vision of a boat rocking gently on becalmed waters. The sails flap listlessly in a fluid descent, mostly in parallel thirds. The hazy, languid atmosphere is created in part by the special scale Debussy employs, the **whole-tone scale.** All the notes of the whole-tone scale are a whole step apart:

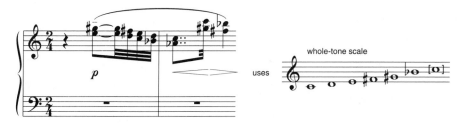

FIGURE 16–7

Claude Monet's *Sailboats on the Seine* (1874). The gentle rocking of the boats is suggested by the exaggerated reflections on the water.

whole-tone scale

EXAMPLE 16–4

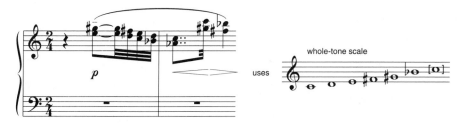

Because in the whole-tone scale each note is the same distance from its neighbor, no one pitch is heard as the tonal center—they all seem equally important. The composer can stop on any note of the scale and it will sound no more central, or final, than any other note. The music floats without a tonal anchor.

In *La Cathédrale engloutie (The Sunken Cathedral),* also from the first book of *Preludes,* the image of a water-engulfed cathedral is created in large measure by the piano's sustaining pedal. The pedal allows the high and low strings of the piano to sound continuously so as to create a wash of sound:

EXAMPLE 16–5

In the midst of this blur, the cathedral slowly rises in parallel chords, "gradually emerging from the fog," as Debussy says in his directions to the pianist. A Gregorian chantlike theme, which had been suggested at the beginning, now emerges fully formed (2:25). Once again Debussy chooses to construct his melody on an unusual scale:

EXAMPLE 16–6

mixolydian scale

seventh chords

Appropriate for a vision of a medieval cathedral is his selection of one of the old medieval church modes, the mixolydian scale, an early type of scalar pattern used in Gregorian chant. In the mixolydian scale, just as in the whole-tone scale and in the pentatonic scale, there is no leading tone[*] and consequently little pull to the tonic. Soon the pentatonic scale is also heard, as are Debussy's familiar parallel descending chords. This time they are all parallel **seventh chords,** four-note chords consisting of a triad with another third on top:

EXAMPLE 16–7

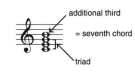

Ultimately, the Gregorian chant theme returns in a final statement (5:09), now engulfed by a muddy, undulating bass. The cathedral has once more returned to the depths.

LISTENING GUIDE

Claude Debussy
The Sunken Cathedral, from *Preludes*, Book I (1910)

CD 6/1
6–Tape 6A

0:00	Parallel chords rise from the murky deep

0:40	Slower moving parallel octaves
1:10	More parallel chords
1:22	Bass begins to move in triplets as the cathedral "rises from the fog"
1:40	Gradual crescendo to a climax
2:04	Bells are sounded as descending parallel octaves
2:25	Gregorian chant theme enters *ff* in parallel chords

3:26	Gradual diminuendo and fadeout
3:50	Quiet melody (on pentatonic scale) enters, grows louder and higher
4:43	Parallel seventh chords, mostly descending
5:09	Murky ostinato enters in the bass as echo of Gregorian chant theme is heard above
6:04	Rising parallel chords as at the beginning
6:19	Final sustained chords

FIGURE 16–8A-C

Three of the thirty paintings of the west facade of the cathedral of Rouen that Claude Monet created between 1892 and 1894. Monet tried to show the facade of the church bathed in different sorts of light, just as Debussy tried to create different musical views of his *Sunken Cathedral.*

Debussy's novel harmony

Debussy's *Cathedral* depicts three different views of this mythical church: the cathedral rising from the ocean floor in the early morning mist, sparkling in the radiant light of the noonday sun, and sinking again into the vapors of evening darkness. His method is not dissimilar to that of the painter Claude Monet who sought to capture, at various times during the day, the effect of fleeting rays of light on the west face of the cathedral of Rouen (Fig. 16–8). While it required a whole set of canvases for Monet to show the effect of light on a single object, the continuous quality of music allowed Debussy to encompass his ever-changing scene within a single composition.

If *Clouds* from the three *Nocturnes* shows Debussy to be a modernist in his use of musical color, his *Preludes* reveal more clearly his forward-looking approach to harmony. Debussy was the first composer to move beyond the traditional system of major and minor tonality. Yes, Richard Wagner had loosened tonality's hold on music in his heavily chromatic harmony, but Debussy made a more radical and complete break with the tonal past. By using the pentatonic scale, whole-tone scale, and mixolydian mode, for example, he lessened the force of the major–minor system in music. By using static harmonies and avoiding V–I cadences, he eliminated the purposeful pull of functional chord progressions as well as a clearly defined key. These harmonic factors contribute to the vague, wandering sound of his music. Debussy's novel approach to harmony helped lay the foundation for "atonal" music which, as we shall see (page 352), would come to dominate much twentieth-century music.

Illness and the outbreak of World War I (1914) brought Debussy's musical productivity to a virtual standstill. It was left to others to pursue his innovations in musical color and harmony. Debussy died of cancer in the spring of 1918 while the guns of the German army were shelling Paris from the north.

THE EXOTIC IN MUSIC

Maurice Ravel (1875–1937), Emmanuel Chabrier (1841–1894), and Paul Dukas (1865–1935), all natives of France, and the Englishman Frederick Delius (1862–1934) are also commonly referred to as "Impressionists." Yet their creations are brimming with what might be called the "exotic"in music. This passion for the exotic was part of the widespread movement in the arts at the turn of the century that sought delight in the mysterious and the far-off.

The painters of the period were most obviously affected. Claude Monet felt the attraction of Japanese colors and designs, as can be seen, for example, in his startling portrait of his wife in traditional Japanese costume (Fig. 16–9). Modernists like Pablo Picasso (1881–1973) and Georges Braque (1882–1963) began collecting African art in Paris about this time. Some historians believe that the Cubist movement in painting (see page 341) was born of Picasso's interest in African sculpture and ceremonial masks. Paul Gauguin (1848–1903) followed his passion for non–Western art farthest afield. His love of Oceanic colors and costumes took him to Martinique, Tahiti, and the nearby Marquesas Islands where he died in 1903 (Fig. 16–11).

The composer Claude Debussy, of course, had not been immune from the influence of foreign sounds. As we have seen, in 1889 Debussy attended the International Exhibition in Paris, the world's fair for which the Eiffel Tower was constructed (Fig. 16–10). There he not only saw newfangled inventions like electric lighting and electric powered elevators but he also heard the colorful sounds of a gamelan* orchestra from Java (Indonesia). This stimulus caused him to experiment with the non–Western pentatonic scale and with static, nonfunctional harmonies. It also encouraged him to think differently about time in music—a musician could create a sound and repeat it endless-

FIGURES 16–9 AND 16–10

(left) Claude Monet, *La Japonaise (Madame Camille Monet in Japanese Costume)* (1876). America and Europe began to show an enthusiasm for things Japanese after the opening of trade with Japan in the 1850s. Fashionable Parisian women wore kimonos and furnished their homes with oriental furniture, painted scenes, and other *objets d'art.* (right) The Cambodian Pagoda at the International Exposition in Paris in 1889. Here Debussy heard the music of Cambodia, China, and Indonesia, and he bagan to formulate a musical aesthetic different from the prevailing German symphonic tradition.

ly without being compelled to move on. Later Debussy would write a piano piece entitled *Pagodas* (1903) and an Egyptian ballet called *Khamma* (1912). In these the influence of authentic Cambodian or Egyptian music is slight. Rather, Debussy drew inspiration from the visual arts of these countries and from what his fancy told him this music ought to sound like. Unlike the painter Gauguin, Debussy's imagination was greater than his will to travel.

Maurice Ravel

The music of Maurice Ravel has many of the same qualities as Debussy's. Ravel's hour-long ballet based on an ancient Greek story, *Daphnis et Chloé* (1912), is full of Impressionist gestures: rippling harp glissandos, parallel descents, ostinatos, shimmering string tremolos, and arabesques for solo flute. Yet Ravel's textures are clearer, his forms more distinct, and his harmonies more inclined to move in purposeful progressions. Ravel, too, had a fondness for the exotic as can be seen in works such as *Shéhérazade* (1903), which hints at the music of the Middle East, and *Songs of Madagascar* (1926) with their African flavor. We have already seen how Ravel captured the spirit of a seductive Spanish dance in his ever-popular *Bolero* (1928) (pages 8–12).

Two other composers who sought musical inspiration beyond the confines of Europe were Albert Roussel (1869–1937) and Giacomo Puccini (1858–1924). In his orchestral *Evocations* (1911) and opera–ballet *Padmâvatî* (1914), Roussel carried to new heights the musical treatment of exotic motifs by making use of Hindu scales from India. Puccini looked for subjects even farther afield, to China, Japan, and the American West, in his operas *Turandot* (1924), *Madam Butterfly* (1904), and *The Girl of the Golden West* (1910).

The love of the exotic, the foreign, and the mysterious were all part of a final expression of Romanticism in the arts. The Romantic writer, beginning with Lord Byron (see page 235), had taught that a free spirit must experience all that the world has to offer. Reality could be found in different forms and in many different lands. The Romantic spirit would go forth to embrace them all. But these distant visions, exotic fantasies, and escapist desires could not last long in the face of global warfare. Such late–Romantic sentiments were soon pushed aside by the grim events of the twentieth century.

FIGURE 16–11

The painter Paul Gauguin went farthest afield in a quest for the exotic, spending much of the last twelve years of his life in the South Seas. His painting *Musique barbare* (1892) is a rendering of an Indonesian gamelan orchestra. Three years earlier, Debussy came under the sway of Indonesian music in Paris.

LISTENING EXERCISE

38 Claude Debussy
Clouds, from the three *Nocturnes* (1897–1899)

CD 5/8
6–Tape 5B
2–Tape 2B

Now let's enjoy a wonderful example of Impressionism in music, the lovely orchestral painting *Clouds* by Claude Debussy (1862–1918). Debussy is exceptionally effective here in using the colors of the various instruments of the orchestra to create the gray mood that he wished to evoke in this "cloudscape." Be sure you have read the discussion of *Clouds* (pp. 327–329) and listened to it following your Listening Guide (p. 330). Listen to it once again and answer the following questions which mainly deal with instrumental color.

1. (0:00) Clarinets and bassoons play the Cloud theme. Which of these two instruments is playing the lower, more chromatic line? _____

2. (0:21) An English horn enters with the Bleak theme. In tone quality (timbre), the English horn is related to the
   a. flute   b. French horn   c. oboe

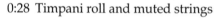

0:28 Timpani roll and muted strings

0:48 Cloud theme returns in violins

3. (1:02) Descending chords: This is a good example of
   a. parallelism   b. counterpoint
4. (1:37) Bleak theme returns in English horn and is answered by two quick notes in the French horn. How many times here do the English horn and French horn play this material? _____

2:11 Descending chords again, now louder and more insistent than before.

5. (2:32) Music rises, mostly by step. As the woodwinds approach the top of this ascent (3:01), the pattern is repeated at successively higher degrees of the scale. The repetition of a motive at successively higher or lower degrees of the scale is called a melodic _____ .
6. (3:19) Bleak theme again returns, this time with a "ticking clock" accompaniment in the strings. Circle the two terms listed below which accurately describe this accompaniment.
   ostinato   libretto   pizzicato   vibrato   tremolo   concertino
7. (4:01) The theme in the English horn dies away while the strings quietly alternate between two notes (up, down; up, down; etc.). What is the interval between these two notes. (This is a difficult question, but try singing to yourself the two notes the strings are playing. Are they close together or far apart?)   a. a whole step   b. a fifth   c. an octave

4:15 Cloud theme returns in the woodwinds, now with a new counterpoint played by a solo viola

4:33 Descending chords again

8. (4:50) A new theme, the Flight theme now enters in the flute and harp. This is a wonderful moment, one created because of the unusual orchestration: flute and harp together and a shimmering sound underneath. Debussy creates this shimmering effect in which of the following ways?
   a. strings hold one chord measure after measure
   b. English horn plays an ostinato
   c. a cymbal sounds in the background

   5:18 Flight theme now in strings

   5:38 Flight theme repeated by flute and harp

9. (6:00) Bleak theme returns in English horn along with echo in French horn. Which instruments are sustaining a single chord underneath?
   a. trumpets   b. clarinets   c. trombones

   6:20 Again, Bleak theme returns with the same instruments holding below

   6:36 Recollection of Bleak theme, now in fragments with timpani roll underneath

   7:04 Cloud theme returns, first in the bassoons and then in the cellos

10. (7:29) Flight theme is suggested. Which instrument plays it this final time?   a. flute   b. harp

---

KEY WORDS

Impressionism	parallelism	whole-tone scale
mixolydian scale	seventh chord	

EUROPEAN MODERNISM

By the standards of any age, the twentieth century must be seen as an eventful, even calamitous, period. Two world wars, a worldwide depression, the extermination of millions of people, the atomic bomb, the cold war, and biological weapons have marked its progression. At the same time, scientific advances have improved the quality and length of life: the automobile and airplane, antibiotics, organ transplants, computers, satellite communications, and radio and television have had a profound impact on our daily lives. Some inventions—the radio, magnetic tape recorder, long-playing records, and the compact disc—have greatly affected our musical culture, bringing serious music to a much larger segment of the general populace and stimulating the growth of popular and commercial music in an unprecedented way. Thus, the tenor of the age has been one of discovery as well as of fear and anxiety brought about by the constant threat of war and nuclear annihilation. During the first half of the twentieth century in particular, scarcely a family in Europe and America went untouched by the Depression and two world wars. All of the composers whose works are discussed in this chapter had their lives drastically altered by one or other of the wars and the rise of facism in Europe. The anxiety and disjunction that you will feel in much of the music of Stravinsky, Schoenberg, Bartók, and the others is an artistic expression of the social upheavals and underlying uncertainties of the twentieth century.

MODERNISM: DIVERSITY AND EXPERIMENTATION

Given all the good and ill that has marked the last hundred years, it is hardly surprising to find that in matters of culture the twentieth century has experienced great diversity and what appears to be a corresponding lack of cohesion. Where is its artistic core? What have been the main artistic currents? What will be the mainstream for the future?

In previous periods in the history of music, each era seems to have developed a single musical style that constituted a sort of synthesis of what that age believed to be the norm, or model, for the music of that time. There was, or appears to have been, little in the way of radical experimentation with the accepted notion of what music was to be. The style of Palestrina in the late Renaissance, of Bach and Handel in the late Baroque era, and of Haydn and Mozart in the late Classical period might be seen as representing these musical norms. But in the modern period a consensus has yet to be reached. No one style has emerged as dominant and lasting. We have seen a bewildering variety of styles come and go: atonal music, twelve-tone music, electronic music, chance music, neo-Classicism, and minimalism have all enjoyed favor at one time or another. We will discuss each of these styles in this and the following chapter, but no one of them can be said to be the mainstream of musical modernism. From a vantage point at the end of this century, the last hundred years appears as a time of alienation, fragmentation, experimentation, and diversity. It is the radically experimental quality of this music, and of our culture in general, that allows us to call it modern or avant-garde.

Radical experimentation in music began shortly before World War I (1914–1918). The new music was not a further evolution of the German-dominated symphonic style of late Romanticism but a sharp turning away from it. It renounced the notion that music should be beautiful and pleasing, expressive or elevating, that it should delight or comfort the listener. Instead, it resorted to distortion, even violence, of sound, to shock the listening audience. Arnold Schoenberg's early experiments with dissonance were received with hoots by a hostile public in Vienna in 1913; Igor Stravinsky's dissonant chords and pounding rhythms caused a riot at the first performance of *Le Sacre du printemps (The Rite of Spring)* in Paris the same year. The intent of the avant-garde composer was to shake the listener out of a state of cultural complacency, just as the artist of the period offended middle-class sensibilities by means of radical visual distortions.

Indeed, there are clear parallels between the music and art of the early twentieth century. The increasingly angular melody and discontinuous rhythm of the new music found analogous expression in an artistic style

FIGURES 17–1 AND 17–2

(left) One of the first statements of Cubist art, Picasso's *Les Demoiselles d'Avignon* (1907). The ladies of the evening are depicted by means of geometric shapes on a flat, two-dimensional plane. Like much avant-garde music of the time, Cubist paintings reject the emotionalism and decorative appeal of nineteenth-century art. (right) *The Wind's Bride* (1914) by Oskar Kokoschka—an Expressionist self-portrait of the artist and Alma Mahler (see page 313), with whom the painter lived following the death of the composer Gustav Mahler in 1911. The painter's introspective look into the subconscious has its analogue in Schoenberg's hyperexpressive works written before World War I.

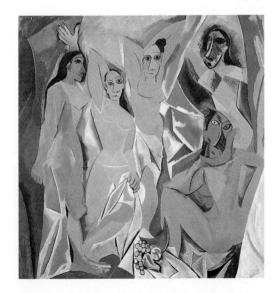

called **Cubism.** A Cubist painting is one in which the artist fractures and dislocates formal reality into geometrical blocks and planes, as in Pablo Picasso's (1881–1973) famous *Les Demoiselles d'Avignon* (1907) where the female form has been recast into angular, interlocking shapes. During the 1910s and 1920s, Picasso and Stravinsky were friends and occasional artistic collaborators in Paris. So disjointed did the musical line become in the works of Arnold Schoenberg that melody as we know it all but disappeared. At that very time a group of painters working mainly in Germany, called Expressionists (see page 353) because they expressed intense internal feelings, so distorted formal reality that objects in their paintings were sometimes barely recognizable. A man and woman are discernible in Oskar Kokoschka's *The Wind's Bride* (1914, Fig. 17–2), but where is the audience in Wassily Kandinsky's *Concert* (1911, Fig. 17–3)? Even more shocking art was produced by the Dadaists (a movement begun in Zurich in 1916) and the Surrealists (formed in Paris in 1922), the latter group glorifying the mysteries of the subconscious (Fig. 17–4). Cubism, Expressionism, Dadaism, Surrealism, and later Abstract Expressionism, Optical art, and Pop art are a few of the diverse artistic movements that have left their mark on the twentieth century. Diversity and radical experimentation are hallmarks of modern art no less than modern music.

FIGURES 17–3 AND 17–4

(left) Wassily Kandinsky's *Impression III (Concert)* (1911). Kandinsky was one of the founders of the Expressionist movement, which was centered in Vienna and Munich. This painting of an audience at a concert does not so much portray a scene as it does convey a psychological state, the audience's reaction to the concert. (right) Like the Expressionists, the Surrealists sought to probe the subconscious mind where unexpected associations might lurk. René Magritte's *Portrait* (1935) calls into question our belief in the reality and the visible object. Does the eye in the midst of a piece of ham make this still life a portrait?

TWENTIETH CENTURY MUSICAL STYLE

Despite its diversity, there are, nonetheless, several constant qualities of modern music that create a consistent musical style. These are most forcefully expressed in the elements of melody, harmony, rhythm, and tone color.

Melody: *More Angularity and Chromaticism*

Music in the Romantic era focused on melody—long sweeping lines that tended to unfold in balanced phrases. The Romantic melody was generally conjunct* in its motion (moving more by steps than by leaps) and built on the notes of the diatonic* scale, though chromatic notes became increasingly frequent toward the end of the nineteenth century. By the early twentieth century, however, this sort of controlled, balanced melody was completely out of fashion. The young avant-garde composers now favored themes that were more asymmetrical, fragmented, and angular. They bent over backward to avoid writing conjunct, stepwise lines. Rather than moving up a half-step from C to D♭, for example, they were wont to jump down a major seventh to the D♭ an octave below. Avoiding a simple interval for a more distant one an octave above or below is called **octave displacement** and it is a feature of modern music. So, too, is the heavy use of chromaticism. In the following example by Arnold Schoenberg (1874–1951), notice how the melody makes large leaps where it might more easily move by steps and also how several sharps and flats are introduced to produce a highly chromatic line:

octave displacement

EXAMPLE 17–1

Unlike the melodies of the Romantic period, many of which are song-like in style and therefore easily sung and remembered, there are very few themes in twentieth-century music that the listener goes away humming. In fact, melody per se is less important to the avant-garde composer than is a pulsating rhythm, an unusual texture, or a new sonority.

Harmony: *More Dissonance, New Chords, New Systems*

Throughout the Baroque, Classical, and Romantic eras, the basic building block of music was the triad*—a consonant, three-note chord. Dissonance was inserted in order to provide tension and variety, but like a hot spice it had to be used sparingly and resolved to a consonance. By the late-Romantic period, however, composers like Richard Wagner (1813–1883) began to enrich their music with more and more chromaticism. This, in turn, created greater dissonance simply because the added chromatic notes generated more and more chords that were not consonant triads. By the first decade of the twentieth century, some composers such as Arnold Schoenberg were using so much chromaticism that the triad all but disappeared. Dissonance became so frequent that it was almost as common as consonance—the exception was becoming the norm. As Igor Stravinsky (1882–1971) said about this reassessment, "Dissonance is now no more an agent of disorder than consonance is a guarantee of security." Hence, the music of the early avant-garde composers took on a harsher, more strident sound, one that has been maintained in modern music, with rare exception, down to the present day. In the course of time we have simply come to accept a greater level of

dissonance as common as consonance

dissonance in the music that we hear, not only in art music but also in popular idioms like film scores and heavy metal rock.

In addition to creating dissonance by chromatically obscuring the triad, twentieth-century composers created dissonance by means of new chords. This was done mainly by superimposing more thirds on top of the consonant triad. In this way were produced not only the seventh chord* (a seventh chord spans seven letters of the scale, from A to G, for example) but also the ninth chord and the eleventh chord. The more thirds that were added on top of the basic triad, the more dissonant the sound of the chord:

seventh, ninth and eleventh chords

EXAMPLE 17–2

eleventh chord

Some composers, including Stravinsky, Béla Bartók (1881–1945), and Aaron Copland (1900–1991), created new dissonant chords by stacking one triad or seventh chord upon another to create a **polychord**. A very dissonant sound was produced if the bottom notes of the two triads were at a dissonant interval from each other, say a major or a minor second away:

polychords

EXAMPLE 17–3

C major triad   D major triad   dissonant polychord

Polychords help create the jarring, clashing sound that is so much a part of modern music.

But perhaps the most challenging harmonic issue facing composers of the twentieth century was the question, "What do we do without tonality?" As we have seen, both Richard Wagner and Claude Debussy in different ways moved away from major–minor tonality, a system that had ruled music for nearly two hundred years. Tonality, with its network of closely related keys, provided a structure for music. Without it composers had to find a new basis for structure. The long ostinati* of Stravinsky and the twelve-tone* method of Schoenberg (both discussed later in the chapter) are modern responses to this need to impose musical structure in the absence of traditional tonality.

dissolution of tonality

Rhythm: *New Asymmetrical Rhythms and Irregular Meters*

Most art music before the twentieth century, and indeed all of our pop and rock music down to the present day, is built on regular patterns of duple (2/4), triple (3/4), or quadruple (4/4) meter. Romantic music of the previous generation of composers had many qualities to recommend it: direct expression, broad themes, powerful climaxes, and moments of tender lyricism, to name a few. But only rarely was it carried along by an exciting, vital rhythm, preferring instead to stay within the comfortable confines of regular accents and duple or triple meter.

At the turn of the century composers of art music began to rebel against the rhythmic and metric regularity that had governed much of nineteenth-century music. In abandoning the traditional structures of rhythm and meter, they were no different from modern poets, like Gertrude Stein (1874–1946) and T. S. Eliot (1888–1965), who dispensed with traditional poetic meters and repeating accents in favor of free verse. Musicians such as Stravinsky and Bartók began to write music in which syncopations and measures with odd numbers of beats made it all but impossible for the listener to feel regular metrical patterns. Accents moved from one pulse to another, meters changed from measure to measure. The following passage from Stravinsky's *Petrushka* (1911) gives a sense of how unpredictable modern meter and rhythm can be. Notice how measures with five pulses per unit appear alongside the more traditional measures with two or three, and note how the meter changes for each bar:

EXAMPLE 17–4

polyrhythms and polymeters

In addition, **polyrhythms** (two or more rhythms at once), **polymeters** (two or more meters at once), and rhythmic ostinatos (continually repeating rhythms) now all came into vogue. Each of these is explained in greater detail on page s 348–349. For the moment, it is enough to observe that rhythm in the twentieth century assumed an energy and drive that had not been heard since the Baroque era. But unlike Baroque music, which rejoiced in rhythmic and metric regularity, much of the great force and tension in modern music, its excitement and flamboyance, comes from its irregular rhythms and meters.

Tone Color: *New Sounds from New Sources*

Twentieth-century composers have created a brave new world of sound. This came about mainly because many musicians were dissatisfied with the string-dominated tone of the Romantic symphony orchestra. The string sound, with its lush vibrato, was thought to be too expressive, perhaps too mushy and sentimental for the harsh realities of the modern world. So the strings, which had been the traditional melody carriers, relinquished this

more percussive sounds

role to the sharper, crisper woodwinds. Instead of playing a sweeping melody, the violinists might now be called on to beat on the strings with the wooden part of the bow or to take their hands and strike the instrument on its sound box. This preference for percussive effects was also expressed in the new importance assigned the instruments of the percussion family. Entire pieces were written for them alone. Instruments such as the xylophone*, glockenspiel*, and celesta* were added to the group (Fig. 3–12), and objects that produced an unfixed pitch, like the cow bell, brake drum, and police siren were also heard on occasion. The piano, which in the Romantic era had been favored for its lyrical "singing" tone, came to be used as an orchestral instrument prized for the decisive way in which the hammers could be made to bang into the strings. The voice, too, was often asked to abandon its traditional lyrical tone and to replace it with declamatory speech, hisses, whoops, cries, grunts, and other novel sounds. What is more, by mid-century an entirely new way of generating and processing sound had been developed, by means of the electronic synthesizer. This allowed for even more new and different tone colors, ones that could not be produced on traditional acoustical instruments.

Producing new tones in novel ways, whether by new "instruments" or by traditional instruments using new playing techniques, is only part of the story of sound in modern music. A more fundamental development is the new way of thinking about musical color, or timbre, as an independent element in music. During the Classical and Romantic periods, sounds of different colors and different volumes had been used mainly as a way to highlight the progress of the themes and thus to articulate the form of a composition. When the second theme entered in sonata–allegro form, for example, it was usually assigned to a new instrument to tell the listener that this was, in fact, a new theme; when a final climax was near, more and more instruments, including the powerful brasses, were usually added to increase the level of sound, signaling that the end was close at hand. The use of tone color and volume as mere servants of melody came to an end at the turn of the twentieth century. Claude Debussy (see page 331) was the first to use color, independent of melody, to give form to a work. But this development was carried to radical lengths in the compositions of modernists such as Edgard Varèse (1883–1965), Olivier Messiaen (b. 1908), and John Cage (b. 1912) whose pieces sometimes do nothing except progress from bright tones spaced far apart to dark tones densely grouped together. There may be no melody or harmony as we usually think of these, but only clusters or streams of sounds with changing colors. This approach to color and line is, of course, similar to the one followed by abstract painters who deemphasize recognizable objects in favor of pure or abstract line and color (see Fig. 17–3). Whether in music or painting, the "meaning" of such compositions is expressed through the interplay of these abstract elements rather than real or concrete objects. There is no obvious story to tell, no plot or program to develop.

timbre independent of melody

T HE COMPOSERS

Faced with the extraordinary diversity of modern music, today's conductors and performers have a difficult time selecting a musical repertoire for the listening public. What kinds of modern music should be performed and how much of it? Audiences are notorious for preferring the tried and true "chestnuts" of the Classical and Romantic periods to any sort of new or experimental music. The masterpieces by the composers that follow are not only compelling works of art in themselves, they also have offered answers for other, later composers in regard to the fundamental question of modern music—how to create cogent new music in a world marked by increasing cultural diversity and artistic fragmentation. All of these works have now become accepted into the standard repertoire of concert music, though not all of the composers have become icons of popular culture like Beethoven or Mozart.

Igor Stravinsky (1882–1971)

Igor Stravinsky is arguably the most significant composer of the twentieth century, both for the music he produced as well as his influence on other composers. He created masterpieces in many different genres: opera, ballet, symphony, church Mass, and cantata. His versatility was such that he could write a ballet for baby elephants (*Circus Polka*, 1942) just as easily as he could set to music a Greek classical drama (*Oedipus Rex*, 1927). Throughout his long life he traveled with the fashionable set of high art. Although reared in St. Petersburg, he later lived in Paris, Venice, Lausanne, New York, and Hollywood. Forced to become an expatriate by the Russian Revolution (1917), he took French citizenship in 1934, and then, having moved to the United States at the outbreak of World War II, became an American citizen in 1945. He counted among his friends the painter Pablo Picasso (1881–1973), the novelist Aldous Huxley (1894–1963), and the poets Dylan Thomas (1914–1953) and T. S. Eliot (1888–1965). On his eightieth birthday, in 1962, he was honored by President John Kennedy at the White House and, later in the same year, by Premier Nikita Khrushchev in the Kremlin. He died in New York in 1971 at the age of eighty-eight.

an international celebrity

Stravinsky rose to international fame as a composer of ballet music. In 1908 some of his early work caught the attention of the legendary impresario (producer) of Russian opera and ballet, Sergei Diaghilev (1872–1929). Diaghilev wanted to bring Russian ballet to Paris, at that time the artistic capital of the world. So he formed a company, called the *Ballets russes* (Russian ballets), and hired, over the course of time, the most progressive artists he could find: Pablo Picasso and Henri Matisse for scenic designs, George Balanchine (later the force behind the New York City Ballet) as a choreographer, and Debussy, Ravel, Strauss, and Stravinsky, among others, as composers. Stravinsky soon became the principal composer of the company, and the *Ballets russes* became the focus of his musical activity for the next ten years. Accordingly, the decade 1910–1920 has become known as Stravinsky's

the Ballets russes

FIGURES 17–5 AND 17–6

(left) Igor Stravinsky (right) Sergei Diaghilev was a cultural impresario who exported Russian art, opera, and ballet to the West. His greatest talent was recognizing and encouraging the genius of artists like Picasso, Matisse, Stravinsky, and Ravel.

Russian ballet period. He would have others—a neo–Classical period (1920–1951) when he returned to Classical forms and a smaller orchestra, and a twelve-tone period (1951–1971) during which he adopted the so-called "serial style" of composing (see page 356)—but his fame was made through his early ballets. Motion, whether of dancers or of musical performers, was always foremost in his mind's eye . As Stravinsky said in his autobiography, "I have always had a horror of listening to music with my eyes shut, with nothing for them to do. The sight of the gestures and movements of the various parts of the body . . . is fundamentally necessary if music is to be grasped in its fullness."

The three most important ballets Stravinsky wrote for Diaghilev's company were *The Firebird* (1910), *Petrushka* (1911), and *The Rite of Spring* (1913). All are built around stories taken from Russian folk tales—a legacy of musical nationalism*—and all make use of the large, coloristic orchestra of the late nineteenth century. Unlike symphonic music, however, music for ballet does not explore, or develop, carefully integrated musical themes. Rather, the composer creates a succession of short, independent vignettes designed to express the action being danced and mimed on the stage. The dance of Diaghilev's *Ballets russes* is not the elegant, graceful classical ballet in the French and Russian tradition, the sort that we associate with Tchaikovsky's *Swan Lake* (1877) or *The Nutcracker* (1892). It is a new modern style of dance influenced by "primitive" folk dancing and folk art; it is heavier, more physical, more driving. Rhythm becomes the driving force of these Russian ballets and in Stravinsky's music in general.

his early ballets

The Firebird and *Petrushka* charmed the sophisticated Parisian audience in 1910 and 1911. But *The Rite of Spring* had an entirely different effect, when first performed on May 29, 1913. The pounding rhythms, harsh dissonances, and strange choreography proved too much. Some members of the audience hissed, others shouted abuse, and minor fisticuffs broke out between those who approved of the Russian's brand of modern art and those who did not. Within a year the music of *The Rite of Spring* had been removed from the ballet itself and played as a separate concert piece, the music alone now recognized as an important, if controversial, artistic statement. Later, in 1941, the score of *The Rite of Spring* furnished the music for a large part of Walt Disney's full-length cartoon film *Fantasia,* and in this form many more people were exposed to Stravinsky's radical statement of musical modernism.

The Rite of Spring

PETRUSHKA (1911)

Less controversial than *The Rite of Spring,* but no less modern, is Stravinsky's first masterpiece, the ballet *Petrushka.* It is scored for a large orchestra with an enormous percussion section consisting of bass drum, cymbals, gong, triangle, tambourine, snare drum, xylophone, glockenspiel, two harps, piano, and another small keyboard instrument called a celesta (on the xylophone, glockenspiel, and celesta, see Fig. 3–12, as well as the glossary). The music rushes by in a flurry of pulsating rhythms and colorful, if somewhat harsh and metallic, sounds. When we listen to *Petrushka,* we sense that we are hearing something new and distinctive. Stravinsky creates this novel, modern sound by employing the following musical procedures.

Polyrhythms   The rhythm of *Petrushka* is highly complex, partly because the composer often superimposes two or more independent rhythms at one time. Look at the reduced score given in example 5. Every instrument seems to be doing its own thing! In fact, six distinctly different rhythms can be heard.

EXAMPLE 17–5

Polymeters   Stravinsky's rhythms can be so independent that each sometimes has its own separate meter and requires a separate time signature, either written or implied. Notice in example 5 that the piccolos and oboes play in 7/8 time, the harps and piano are in 4/4, the cellos and basses in 2/4, and the others in 3/4.

Irregular Accents   Even when all of the parts are playing one and the same rhythm, the music can still sound disjunct because an accent > is placed on a different beat in each measure:

Example 17–6

Polychords The harsh, biting sound that is heard throughout much of *Petrushka* is often created by having two triads sound simultaneously. In Scene 2, for example, the music that accompanies the movements of the puppet Petrushka is constructed from one major triad on C and another on F#. Combining one triad from the white notes of the piano (C major) with one from the black notes (F# major) is a brilliant way to represent the split personality of Petrushka—sometimes puppet, sometimes man. It gives the music a biting, sarcastic quality that is part of Petrushka's character:

Example 17–7

Ostinato Figures A musical figure that repeats over and over is called an ostinato*. We first encountered the ostinato when discussing the music of the early Baroque period (see page 111 and also page 10). But composers of the twentieth century made frequent use of it as well, especially Stravinsky and his older colleague Debussy. Look at the reduced score of *Petrushka* in example 5 and notice how many of the instruments are repeating a two-note pattern (horns and violins), an eight-note pattern (piano and harp), and even a thirteen-note pattern (harp). These ostinatos give the music its incessant, driving quality, especially in the sections with fast tempos. They also help establish a tonal center in a musical style that no longer has recourse to functional chord progressions.

Stravinsky's *Petrushka* is a ballet in four scenes, all of which center around a puppet show at a fair in old Russia. The main character is a wooden puppet, an impish, hard-luck character named Petrushka, the Russian counterpart of our Pinocchio. In Scene 1 we hear the sounds of the swirling holiday crowd, the incessant call of a carnival barker, the song of vodka-sodden revelers, and tunes of itinerant street musicians. Then a drum sounds and an old magician steps out of the puppet theater to play a strange tune on his flute. Suddenly, the tiny curtain opens to reveal three puppets—Petrushka, a Ballerina, and a Moor. When the magician touches them with his flute, they dance to life, at first dangling on strings, but then moving freely among the astonished crowd.

the plot of Scene 1

FIGURE 17–7

The original design for the stage backdrop of Scene 1 of Stravinsky's ballet *Petrushka*, first performed in Paris by Diaghilev's *Ballets russes* in 1911.

To give musical coherence to the diverse elements of this opening scene, Stravinsky makes use of an age-old musical form, the rondo (here **ABACABA** and **ABABA**), which he sets on either side of the mysterious awakening of the puppets.

Scene 1

Section 1 (rondo) The crowd	Section 2	Section 3 (rondo) The puppets' Russian dance
A Crowd and barker **B** Drunken revelers **A** Crowd and barker **C** Street musicians **A** Crowd and barker **B** Drunken revelers **A** Crowd and barker	Flute solo animates the puppets	**A** Russian dance **B** Russian folk song **A** Russian dance **B** Russian folk song **A** Russian dance

Russian flavor

To add a bit of local color to section 1, the composer incorporates a Russian folk song into the music of the drunken revelers **(B)**, just as he uses Russian popular tunes to help create the music of the street musicians **(C).** Similarly, in section 3 a Russian folk song **(B)** alternates with the rhythms of a Russian dance **(A).** By means of these melodies and rhythms—and his own musical imagination—Stravinsky is able to evoke the sights and sounds of a Russian carnival, from the chatter of the barker, to the street musician's barrel organ, to the herky-jerky motion of the dancing puppets.

LISTENING GUIDE

Igor Stravinsky
Petrushka (1911)
Scene 1

CD 6/2
6–Tape 6A
2–Tape 2B

SECTION 1 (Vivace): The crowd

0:00	**A**	Leaping, agitated music of the crowd
0:31		Barker's cry marked by a single, repeated, syncopated pitch
0:49	**B**	Russian song played by full orchestra including percussion
1:07		Russian song played by smaller orchestra (no brass)
1:28	**A**	Agitated music of the crowd returns in woodwinds
1:38		Organ grinder (clarinet) plays Russian popular tune
1:55		Organ grinder's tune continues
2:12	**C**	Flutes play street dancers' music with trumpet added
2:33		Another organ grinder (bell-like sound of celesta)
2:58		Flutes return with street dancers' music, now with bells and strings
3:08	**A**	Agitated music of the crowd and barker breaks in
3:33	**B**	Russian folk song played by full orchestra
3:51		Russian song played by smaller orchestra
4:02	**A**	Incessant call of the barker and agitated music of the crowd
4:27		Barker's syncopated accents become louder and more forceful
4:55		Snare drum brings an end to section 1 by calling attention to the old magician and the puppet theater

SECTION 2 (Lento): The old magician brings the puppets to life with his flute

5:03	Bassoons creep in; strange cascades of sound in violins, harp, and celesta
5:30	Flute solo
6:10	More strange cascades and dissonant sounds
6:42	Piccolo chirps in as the old magician animates puppets

SECTION 3 (Allegro): Puppets' Russian dance

6:48	**A**	Theme of the Russian dance with prominent percussion, especially piano and xylophone
7:00	**B**	Russian folk song briefly heard in clarinet and oboe
7:14		Rising ostinato in all parts
7:27	**A**	Russian dance with even more bright percussion
7:36		Russian folk song in oboe punctuated by percussive descents in piano
7:51	**B**	Piano plays folk song
8:04		Violin plays folk song
8:17		Xylophone hints at return of Russian dance
8:24		Tempo slows down, clarinets and oboes slowly hint at Russian dance
8:44	**A**	Piano plays Russian dance
9:03		Piano plays ostinato figure against string pizzicatos; polyrhythms
9:12	**Coda**	Sharp, accented syncopations in percussion and brass
9:25		Trumpet, snare drum, and clarinet conclude with mock solemnity

(Listening Exercise 39)

FIGURE 17–8

Arnold Schoenberg, *Self Portrait* (1910).

Like *The Rite of Spring*, *Petrushka* is rarely mounted today as a ballet. Instead, Stravinsky's music is heard by itself in the concert hall, one of the few pieces of modern music to have earned a permanent place in the standard orchestral repertoire.

Arnold Schoenberg and The Second Viennese School

If Paris was the artistic capital of Europe before the First World War, Vienna was second in importance. The city of Mozart and Beethoven was blessed with strong musical traditions and a large, if conservative, audience. But the musical expectations of the Viennese were now challenged by a trio of native composers who were to take modern music on a radically different course: Arnold Schoenberg (1874–1951), Alban Berg (1885–1935), and Anton Webern (1883–1945). The close association of these three innovative musicians has come to be called "The Second Viennese School," the first, of course, being that of Mozart, Haydn, and Beethoven.

Arnold Schoenberg, the leader of this group, almost single-handedly thrust modern music on a reluctant Viennese public. Schoenberg was from a Jewish family of modest circumstances and was largely self-taught as a musician. As a young man he worked as a bank clerk during the day, but studied literature, philosophy, and music at night, becoming a competent performer on the violin and cello. He came to know the music of Brahms, Wagner, and Mahler, mostly by playing their scores and attending concerts. Having "left the world of bank notes for musical notes" at the age of twenty-one, he earned a modest living by conducting a men's chorus, orchestrating operettas—the Viennese counterpart of our Broadway musicals—and giving lessons in music theory and composition. Eventually, his own compositions began to be heard in Vienna, though they were usually not well received.

Schoenberg's earliest works are written in a typical late-Romantic style, with rich harmonies, chromatic melodies, expansive forms, and programmatic content. But by 1908 his music had begun to evolve in unexpected directions. Having been strongly influenced by Wagner's chromatic melodies and harmonies, Schoenberg started to compose works in which there was no tonal center. If Wagner could write winding chromatic passages that temporarily obscured the tonality, why not go one step farther and create fully chromatic pieces in which there is no tonality? This Schoen-

atonal music

berg did, and in so doing created what is called **atonal** music—music without tonality, music without a key center.

But Schoenberg not only abandoned music with a tonal center—a stable point of reference for the listener—he also dispensed with the triad as the basic building block of music. Earlier, tonal music had unfolded in chord progressions built mainly of consonant triads. Dissonance, which adds an element of tension and anxiety, was carefully controlled and required to resolve to a stable consonance, usually a triad. With Schoenberg's new atonal music, however, dissonance is freed from the necessity of resolving to consonance—it can wander off chromatically to another dissonance and then yet another. We have, in Schoenberg's words, "the emancipation of dis-

"the emancipation of dissonance"

sonance." Most listeners today are at first hostile to atonal music, in part because there is no tonal center but more so because it is so highly dissonant.

Expressionism and Atonality

Arnold Schoenberg and his students Alban Berg and Anton Webern were not alone in creating a radically new style of art. As we have seen, there appeared at this same time a powerful movement in the visual arts called Expressionism. Expressionism was initially a German–Austrian development that arose in Berlin, Munich, and Vienna. Its aim was not to depict objects as they are seen but to express the strong emotion that the object generated in the artist; not to paint a portrait of an individual but to create an expression of the subject's innermost feelings, anxieties, and fears. Realistic representation gave way to highly personal and increasingly abstract expression. Artists such as Oskar Kokoschka (1886–1980) and Wassily Kandinsky (1866–1944) used harsh colors, macabre images, and distorted figures to show intense psychological states, sometimes with shocking results (see Figs. 17–3 and 17–9). Schoenberg, a personal friend of both Kokoschka and Kandinsky, was himself a painter and exhibited his works with the Expressionists in 1912 (Figs. 17–8 and 17–10). In fact, the music and art of this movement can be described in rather similar terms. The clashing of strong colors, the disjointed shapes, and the jagged lines of the painters have their counterparts in the harsh dissonances, asymmetrical rhythms, and angular, chromatic melodies of Schoenberg and his followers. It is likely not an accident that Schoenberg moved from tonality to atonality in music (1908–1912) at precisely the time Kandinsky and others turned away from realistic representation to abstract expression.

Small wonder that in Schoenberg's day some Viennese musicians refused to play his atonal music, or that when they did the audience's reaction was sometimes violent to the point that police had to be called out to restore order. Despite the hostility, Schoenberg remained true to his own artistic vision:

> Whether one calls oneself conservative or revolutionary, whether one composes in a conventional or progressive manner, whether one tries to imitate old styles or is destined to express new ideas—whether one is a good composer or not—one must be convinced of the infallibility of one's own fantasy and one must believe in one's own inspiration.

PIERROT LUNAIRE (MOONSTRUCK PIERROT, 1912)

Moonstruck Pierrot, Schoenberg's best-known composition, is an exemplary work of Expressionist art. It is a setting for chamber ensemble and female voice of twenty-one poems by Albert Giraud. Here we meet "Moonstruck Pierrot," a white-faced clown from the world of traditional Italian pantomime and puppet shows. Yet in this Expressionist poetry, the fun-loving clown suffers the endless anxiety of a sensitive artist-lover whose only confidant is the moon. Pierrot's inner feelings are projected by means of a new vocal technique invented by Schoenberg called **Sprechstimme**—"speechvoice." *Sprechstimme* requires the vocalist to declaim the text more than sing it. The voice is to produce exact rhythmic values but rises and falls to only approximate pitch levels. This removes all vocal lyricism but adds a new intensity, even an element of hysteria, to the voice, an appropriate feature for this hyperexpressive text.

Poems 5, 6, and 7 of *Moonstruck Pierrot* reveal three different aspects of the clown's feverish state of mind. In number 5 Pierrot assumes the image of the sickly artist, in this case the composer Chopin; in number 6 he offers a poem

FIGURE 17–9

This Viennese theater poster by Oskar Kokoschka of 1909 shows the Expressionist affinity for the dramatic and grotesque. The effect is created by the use of strong, almost crude, lines and bold contrasting color.

of solace to the suffering Madonna; and in number 7 he projects upon the face of the moon his own love pains. Each poem is cast as a *rondeau*, an old musical and poetic form characterized by the use of a refrain (see pages 79–80). Traditionally, composers had used the appearance of a textual refrain to repeat part or all of the melody as well. This helped create a unity of text and music and gave the work formal coherence. But Schoenberg, true to his iconoclastic ways, avoids musical repetition in his atonal works. His music unfolds in an ever-varying continuum, like a stream of consciousness. His dissonances, disjunct rhythms, changing textures, and nonrepeating melodies place unprecedented demands on the listener. Your first reaction to the seemingly formless flow of dissonance in *Moonstruck Pierrot* may be decidedly negative. Yet with repeated listenings the force of the jarring elements of the atonal style begins to lessen and a bizarre, eerie sort of beauty emerges, especially if you are sensitive to the meaning of the text.

Number 5, *Valse de Chopin (Waltz of Chopin)*, is scored for flute, clarinet, piano, and voice. Certainly, this is no waltz in the traditional sense, for the rhythm is highly disjunct, and the strong–weak–weak pattern of the 3/4 waltz never emerges. Rather, the piece follows a broad arc of intensity—a gradual increase in the activity of the instruments and the density of the texture, culminating on the words "Heiss und jauchzend" ("Hot and joyous"), followed by a corresponding decrease in activity and density up to the end. Here musical texture, rather than musical themes, creates form. The lurid image of lips smudged with blood is likely inspired by the fact that Chopin died of tuberculosis.

FIGURE 17–10

As a young man Schoenberg was undecided whether his future in the arts lay in music or painting. Like many Expressionist paintings before World War I, his *Red Gaze* (1910) gives a sense of the subject's inner terror.

CD 6/3; 6–Tape 6A; 2–Tape 2B

Valse de Chopin

Wie ein blasser Tropfen Bluts	**As a faint drop of blood**
Färbt die Lippen einer Kranken	**Stains the lips of a consumptive**
Also ruht auf diesen Tönen	So there dwells in these tones a
Ein vernichungssüchtger Reiz.	Destructive allure.
Wilder Lust Accorde stören	Chords of wild lust break
Der Verzweiflung eisgen Traum—	the despair of the icy dream—
Wie ein blasser Tropfen Bluts	**As a faint drop of blood**
Färbt die Lippen einer Kranken.	**Stains the lips of a consumptive.**
Heiss und jauchzend,	Hot and joyous,
süss und schmachtend	sweet and yearning
Melancholisch düstrer Walzer	Dark, melancholy waltzes
Kommst mir nimmer aus den Sinnen	Never leave my senses
Haftest mir an den Gedanken	Lodged in my imagination
Wie ein blasser Tropfen Bluts!	**As a faint drop of blood!**

Number 6, *Madonna,* draws its inspiration from the vision of the sorrowful Mother of Christ at the Cross. The traditional association of the image of the Cross with musical chromaticism, one extending at least back to Bach, may have given rise to the ascending chromatic line, played pizzicato, in the cello. The angular movement of the voice is typical of Schoenberg's atonal melodic line:

EXAMPLE 17–8

CD 6/4; 6–Tape 6A

Madonna

Steig, O Mutter aller Schmerzen	**Arise, O Mother of all sorrows**
Auf den Altar meiner Verse!	**On the altar of my verse!**
Blut aus deinen magern Brüsten	Blood from your thin breast
Hat des Schwertes Wut vergossen.	Has spilled the rage of the sword.
Deine ewig frischen Wunden	Your eternally fresh wounds
Gleichen Augen, rot und offen,	Like eyes, red and open,
Steig, O Mutter aller Schmerzen	**Arise, O Mother of all sorrows**
Auf den Altar meiner Verse!	**On the altar of my verse!**
In den abgezehrten Händen	In your thin and wasted hands
Hälst du deines Sohnes Leiche	You hold the body of your Son
Ihn zu zeigen aller Menschheit,	To show him to all mankind,
Doch der Blick der Menschen meidet	Yet the look of men avoids
Dich, **O Mutter aller Schmerzen.**	You, **O Mother of all sorrows.**

Number 7, *Der kranke Mond (The Sick Moon),* is a soliloquy for voice and accompanying flute. As do the Expressionist painters, here the poet transfers to the object (the moon) the internal feelings of the subject (the artist–Pierrot). Thus, as Pierrot speaks, the moon begins to reflect his inner turmoil, becoming feverish, tormented, death-sick with love. The silvery tones of the flute help evoke an aura of moonlight, "death-sick" as it may be.

CD 6/5; 6–Tape 6A

Der kranke Mond

Du nächtig todeskranker Mond	**You nocturnal, death-sick moon**
Dort auf des Himmels	**There on heaven's**
schwarzem Pfühl,	**dark couch,**
Dein Blick, so fiebernd übergross	Your look, so feverishly swollen,
Bannt mich wie fremde Melodie.	Charms me like a foreign melody.
An unstillbarem Liebesleid	In unending pain of love
Stirbst du, an Sehnsucht, tief erstickt,	You die, in yearning consumed,
Du nächtig todeskranker Mond	**You nocturnal, death-sick moon**
Dort auf des Himmels	**There on heaven's**
schwarzem Pfühl.	**dark couch.**
Den Liebsten, der im Sinnenrausch,	The lover who, with love-drunk heart,
Gedankenlos zur Liebsten geht,	Steals to the beloved without a care,
Belustigt deiner Strahlen Spiel,	Rejoices in your play of light,
Dein bleiches, qualgebornes Blut,	Your pale, tormented blood,
Du nächtig todeskranker Mond.	**You nocturnal, death-sick moon.**

Needless to say, this music of the extreme avant-garde did not sit well with the anti-intellectual Nazis who took power in Germany in 1933 and Austria in 1938. Hitler and his National Socialists not only harbored a hatred of Jews but they also made it virtually impossible for "degenerate" modern art like *Moonstruck Pierrot* to be seen or heard. So Schoenberg fled the German lands, as did thousands of other progressive spirits, including Thomas Mann (1875–1955), Kurt Weill (1900–1950), and Albert Einstein (1879–1955). He ultimately made his way to this country and to Los Angeles where he died peacefully in 1951 at the age of seventy-six.

SCHOENBERG'S TWELVE-TONE METHOD When Arnold Schoenberg and his followers did away with tonal chord progressions and the use of recurring melodies, they found themselves facing a serious artistic problem:

what to do without tonality?

how to write large-scale compositions in the new atonal style. The repetition of themes and a clear tonal plan gave rise to formal structures, like fugue and sonata–allegro form, that were useful to the composer and most welcome to the listener seeking to make sense of a new musical composition. But Schoenberg's chromatic, atonal, nonrepeating melodies made traditional musical forms all but impossible. What other formal plan might be used? If all twelve notes of the chromatic scale are equally important, as is true in atonal music, why choose any one note at a given spot in a piece and not another?

By 1923 Schoenberg had solved the problem of formal anarchy—or abscence of form—caused by total chromatic freedom. He had discovered a new way of creating music which he called "composing with twelve tones." **Twelve-tone composition** is a method of writing that employs each of the twelve notes of the chromatic scale following a fixed, predetermined order. The composer chooses the succession of twelve notes to achieve the desired "melody" and places them in a row. Throughout the composition the twelve notes must come in the same order. Music in which elements such as pitch

twelve-tone music

or timbre come in a fixed series is called **serial** music. In twelve-tone music the twelve-note series may unfold not only as a melody but also as a melody with accompaniment, or simply as a progression of chords, since two or more notes of the row may sound simultaneously. Moreover, in addition to appearing in its basic form, the row might go backward (retrograde*) or upside down (inversion*) or both backward and upside down at the same time (retrograde inversion). While such arrangements might seem wholly artificial and very unmusical, we should remember that composers such as J. S. Bach in the Baroque era and Josquin Desprez in the Renaissance had subjected their melodies to similar permutations. The purpose of Schoenberg's twelve-tone method was to create musical unity by basing each piece on a single, orderly arrangement of twelve tones, and thereby guarantee the perfect equality of all pitches so that none would seem like a tonal center. Here is the twelve-tone row Schoenberg chose for his *Suite for Piano* (1924), his first piece to make use of the twelve-tone method exclusively:

Row

E F G D♭ G♭ E♭ A♭ D B C A B♭

1 2 3 4 5 6 7 8 9 10 11 12

Retrograde

B♭ A C B D A♭ E♭ G♭ D♭ G F E

12 11 10 9 8 7 6 5 4 3 2 1

Inversion

E E♭ D♭ G D F C F♯ A G♯ B B♭

1 2 3 4 5 6 7 8 9 10 11 12

Retrograde-inversion

B♭ B G♯ A F♯ C F D G D♭ E♭ E

12 11 10 9 8 7 6 5 4 3 2 1

The row or one of its permutations might begin on any pitch, so long as the original sequence of intervals is maintained, and, of course, the rhythms in which the notes appear can also be changed for the sake of variety. In the following example from Schoenberg's *Suite for Piano,* the row itself begins on E but is also allowed to start on B♭, which is also true for the inversion:

EXAMPLE 17–9

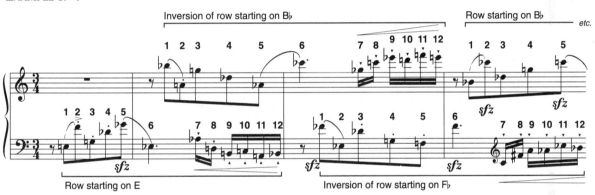

The discovery of the twelve-tone method of composition allowed Schoenberg to construct longer compositions for larger forces. In 1932 he completed most of a full-length opera, *Moses and Aron,* and in 1947 he finished a cantata*, *A Survivor from Warsaw,* in which the story of a survivor of Nazi atrocities in Poland is fused with the text of an ancient Hebrew prayer. Both works are twelve-tone in style throughout. But the listening public never embraced Schoenberg's twelve-tone music. The style is still very much that of dissonant, atonal music, and the rows and their various permutations pass by much too quickly for all but the keenest musical ear to hear. Schoenberg, however, remained convinced to the end that time would vindicate his method of composition—that the listening public would come to appreciate the dissonant universality of twelve-tone music: "One should never forget that contemporaries are not final judges, but are generally overruled by history."

Béla Bartók (1881–1945)

The music of the Hungarian composer Béla Bartók is decidedly modern, yet distinctly different in sound from that of Stravinsky or Schoenberg. While it can be atonal, like the music of Schoenberg, it is often highly tuneful, making use of sweeping melodies. And while it is frequently percussive and

FIGURE 17–11

Béla Bartók

highly rhythmic, like the motor-driven sounds of Stravinsky, Bartók's rhythmic force derives mainly from folk music. Bartók's creative imagination was fired by folk materials of his native Hungary. He saw the return to the simple, direct style of folk music as a way to counter the tendency in Romantic music toward ostentation and sentimentality.

The life of Béla Bartók was strongly affected by the turbulent events that occurred in Eastern Europe during the first half of the twentieth century. He was born in 1881 in Hungary, but in a part of that nation that was later given over to Rumania at the end of World War I. Throughout his life he was an ardent Hungarian nationalist, and chose to develop his obvious musical talents at the Academy of Music in Budapest rather than at the German-dominated Vienna Conservatory where he had also been admitted. As a student at the Academy in Budapest he studied composition and piano, quickly acquiring a reputation as a concert pianist of the highest quality. By the 1920s he had achieved an international reputation both as a pianist and a composer of music in the modern vein. His tours even carried him to the western part of the United States, where one newspaper alerted the public to his coming with the following headline: "Hungarian Modernist Advances upon Los Angeles." As both a Hungarian modernist and nationalist, Bartók was an outspoken critic of the supporters of Nazi Germany who gained control of the Hungarian government in the late 1930s. He called the fascists "bandits and assassins," cut off ties with the German firm that published all his music, and banned the performances of his works in Germany and Italy, thereby losing considerable performance fees. Ultimately, in 1940, he fled to the United States. Bartók died of leukemia in New York City in 1945, and not until 1988 were his remains returned, at the request of his sons, to his beloved Hungary.

Bartók and folk music

Béla Bartók is unique among composers in that he was as much interested in musical research, specifically in the study of Eastern European folk music, as he was in musical composition. He traveled from village to village in Hungary, Rumania, Bulgaria, Turkey, and even North Africa using the newly invented recording machine of Thomas Edison (Fig. 17–12). In this way his ear became saturated with the driving rhythms and odd-number meters of peasant dances, as well as the unusual scales on which the folk melodies of Eastern Europe were constructed. If the cosmopolitan Stravinsky took his folk melodies from printed anthologies, Bartók found his among the people.

The musical heritage of Eastern Europe is heard continually throughout Bartók's music, from his first string quartet (1908) to his great final works for orchestra: *Music for Strings, Percussion and Celesta* (1936), *Divertimento for Strings* (1939), and *Concerto for Orchestra* (1943). This last-named work is probably Bartók's best-known composition. Certainly, it is among his most alluring creations.

CONCERTO FOR ORCHESTRA (1943)

a modern-day concerto grosso

The title of this composition, as Bartók wrote in the program notes for its first performance, "is explained by [the work's] tendency to treat the single orchestral instruments in a 'concertante' or soloistic manner." Instead of having one unchanging group function as soloists, as in a Baroque concerto grosso*, Bartók's group of soloists has a continually revolving membership,

FIGURE 17–12

Béla Bartók recording folk songs among the peasants of Czechoslovakia in 1908. The performers sang into the megaphone of a wax cylinder recording machine invented by Thomas Edison.

drawing at various times on different instruments of the orchestra. Now one, now another instrument or combination of instruments steps forward to display its distinctive tonal color against the backdrop of the full orchestra. There are five movements: The first is "written in a more or less regular sonata form," as the composer says, and makes use of the folklike pentatonic* scale; the second is a colorful parade of pairs of instruments; the third is an atmospheric nocturne, an example of what is called Bartók's "night music," in which the woodwinds slither around chromatically above a misty tremolo in the strings; the fourth is an unusual intermezzo; while the fifth is a vigorous peasant dance in sonata–allegro form. Let us focus our attention on the fourth movement, *Intermezzo interrotto (Broken Intermezzo)*.

An **intermezzo** (Italian for "between piece") is a light musical interlude intended to separate and thus break the mood of two more serious surrounding movements. But here, as the title *Broken Intermezzo* indicates, the light intermezzo is itself rudely interrupted by contrasting music. A sophisticated mood is first established by a charming theme in the oboe. As is usual for Bartók, this melody shows the influence of the Hungarian folk song both in its pentatonic construction (the five notes that make up the scale of the melody are B, C#, E, F#, and A#) and in the way it switches back and forth between an even 2/4 and an odd 5/8:

EXAMPLE 17–10

After the tune is passed around several wind instruments, an even more ingratiating melody emerges in the strings. It, too, is Hungarian in style. In fact, it is Bartók's idealized reworking of the song *You Are Lovely, You Are Beautiful, Hungary.*

EXAMPLE 17–11

But the nostalgic vision of the homeland is suddenly interrupted by a new, cruder theme in the clarinet, and it also tells a tale. Bartók took this clarinet melody from the Russian composer Dimitri Shostakovitch's Symphony No. 7, a programmatic work depicting the German invasion of Russia (1942). Bartók borrowed the theme Shostakovitch had written to signify the invading Germans, believing its simple quarter-note descent to be appropriately heavy and trite.

EXAMPLE 17–12

Thus, Bartók's intermezzo can be heard as an autobiographical work in which, as the composer related to a friend, "the artist declares his love for his native land in a serenade which is suddenly interrupted in a crude and violent manner; he is seized by rough, booted men who even break his instrument." Bartók tells us what he thinks of these "rough, booted men" by surrounding them with rude, jeering noises in the trumpets and woodwinds. Ultimately, he brings back the idyllic vision of the homeland by returning to the opening two themes. The main events of the *Broken Intermezzo* are enumerated in the short Listening Guide that follows. A more detailed description of the piece will emerge as you complete Listening Exercise 40.

LISTENING GUIDE		Béla Bartók *Concerto for Orchestra* (1943) Fourth Movement, *Broken Intermezzo*	CD 6/6 6–Tape 6A 2–Tape 2A

0:00		Four-chord introduction	
0:06	**A**	Oboe introduces theme	
1:07	**B**	Violas introduce theme	
1:49	**A**	Oboe briefly plays theme	

2:14	C	Clarinet introduces theme (borrowed from Shostakovich)
2:22		Rude noises in trumpets and woodwinds
2:36	C	Parody of theme in violins
2:44		More rude noises
2:52	C	Theme played in inversion by the violins
2:56		More rude noises
3:04	B	Theme returns in violas
3:23	A	Theme returns in English horn, flute, and clarinet

(Listening Exercise 40)

Olivier Messiaen (b. 1908)

If the music of Bartók can be said to be a blend of modernism and national-ism, that of the French composer Olivier Messiaen can be called eclectic. Messiaen's music borrows from such diverse sources as Gregorian chant, African and Hindu rhythms, bird songs, and, in at least a few pieces, the twelve-tone method of Arnold Schoenberg. Now well in his eighties, Messi-aen is a man whose life has been an endless search for new and sometimes exotic sounds to express what he perceives to be the limitless beauty of music.

Olivier Messiaen was born in southern France in 1908, the offspring of parents with strong literary interests. His mother was a well-known poet and his father a teacher of English who produced a respected French transla-tion of the complete works of Shakespeare. As a child he demonstrated an extraordinary ear for sounds of all sorts, picking out Mozart and Berlioz on the piano from the scores he received as Christmas gifts. At the age of eleven he was enrolled in the Paris Conservatory of Music, and upon graduation in 1931 he assumed the important post of organist at the Church of the Holy Trinity in Paris, a position he has now occupied for more than sixty years.

When World War II broke out, Messiaen enlisted in the French army but was captured by the invading Germans during the summer of 1940. Shipped off to a prisoner of war camp in eastern Germany, he somehow managed to carry with him scores of Bach, Beethoven, Stravinsky, Ravel, and Alban Berg. During his captivity he acquired music paper from a sympathetic Ger-man officer and composed *Quatuor pour la fin du temps (Quartet for the End of Time)*. The work is scored for clarinet, violin, cello, and piano, the instru-ments that Messiaen had access to in the camp. On January 15, 1941, it was performed before an enthusiastic audience of five thousand shivering camp inmates—Frenchmen, Poles, and Belgians.

FIGURE 17–13

Olivier Messiaen transferring bird-songs into musical notation.

QUARTET FOR THE END OF TIME (1941)

Given the fact that civilization as Messiaen knew it had just been overrun by invading German tanks, it is reasonable to see in the title *Quartet for the*

End of Time a pronouncement of the end of the world. But, in fact, the title comes from a passage in the Book of Revelation, the last book of the New Testament, which refers to an Angel who descends upon earth, lifts his hands to the heavens and proclaims "there shall be time no longer." What Messiaen understood by this decree is that the frightening abyss of unending time would be no more. "My only wish was to advance my desire for the dissolution of time." Removing the terror of endless time must have been a wish shared by many faced with the ceaseless boredom of a prisoner-of-war camp.

The *Quartet for the End of Time* is marked by two important innovations: first, the introduction of birdcalls (a practice almost unique to Messiaen among modern composers), and second and more important, a new method of projecting musical rhythm that conveys the composer's feelings about infinity or endless time. For Messiaen, endless time in music was the relentless march of repeating meters and rhythms set within regularly recurring bar lines. Messiaen intended to replace this usual sort of meter and rhythm with ones that are "free and unequal in length." He accomplished this by creating nonrepeating units of varying lengths, making it impossible for regular patterns of time to establish themselves. The *Quartet for the End of Time* comprises eight movements:

1. *Liturgy of Crystal*
2. *Vocalise of the Angel Who Announces the End of Time*
3. *Abyss of the Birds*
4. *Intermezzo*
5. *Praise to the Eternity of Jesus*
6. *Dance of Fury for the Seven Trumpets*
7. *Cluster of Rainbows for the Angel Who Announces the End of Time*
8. *Praise to the Immortality of Jesu*s

The fifth movement, *Praise to the Eternity of Jesus,* uses only two of the four instruments of the quartet. It is an expressive meditation for cello accompanied by the piano softly playing chords. As Messiaen says, "Jesus is considered here to be the Word. A long, infinitely slow phrase in the cello magnifies with love and reverence the eternity of this powerful yet mild Word 'whose years shall not be consumed.'" The expansive phrase of the cello is somewhat chromatic but by no means atonal—both melody and accompaniment are solidly grounded in E:

EXAMPLE 17–13

Here we clearly see Messiaen's new approach to musical time. Instead of regular groups based on recurring multiples—2 X 2 (2/4 or 4/4), 3 X 2 (3/4), or 2 X 3 (6/8), those usually found in Western music—Messiaen adopts a pattern originating in Hindu India which consists of units of 4, 4, 4, 2, 3, and 2 beats per group. The composer can arrange these numbers of beats in several different orders. He can also add groups together to form even larger units of different lengths, but they are never placed so as to create regular, recurring patterns. In movement 5, the units of varying length sound clearly as chords in the piano, while above these the cello gives forth its soaring melody. Notice in the example how there is no meter (time) signature—a time signature would be useless because the number of beats per measure is continually changing. In this way Messiaen has put an end to regular, consuming "time" as we usually think of it. As you listen you will hear a very slow pulse. Follow the nonrepeating patterns, easily audible in the piano, and see if you do not feel a sense of timelessness.

LISTENING GUIDE	Olivier Messiaen *Quartet for the End of Time* (1941) Fifth movement, *Praise to the Eternity of Jesus*	CD 6/7 6–Tape 6A
0:00	Cello solo	
0:23	Piano accompaniment begins	10 + 7 + 10 + 4 + 8
1:13	Cello solo begins again	
1:36	Piano accompaniment reenters	10 + 7 + 10 + 4 + 8
2:22	Crescendo	
2:25	Falling line in cello	15 + 15
3:08	Cello line continues to fall	4 + 5 + 4 + 5 + 4 + 4
3:30	Piano rises chromatically by half step with crescendo	2 + 2 + 2 + 4 + 2
3:42	Gradual descent of the melody in cello	9 + 4 + 7 + 17
4:22	Rising in thirds in both instruments with crescendo	4 + 4 + 4 + 4 + 4 + 4 + 10
4:58	Climax with rising stepwise motion and crescendo	2 + 1 + 2 + 2 + 2 + 1 + 2 + 4 + 12
5:28	Sudden *pianissimo* as opening melody returns in cello	13 + 4 + 4 + 4 + 8 + 4 + 8
6:20	Pedal point in the piano on the dominant note B	26
6:50	Contrary motion: piano descends by step, cello rises in thirds	4 + 4 + 4 + 4
7:10	Final E major chord	8 + 6 + 4

We have seen how Bach expressed his Lutheran beliefs in the cantata *A Mighty Fortress* (page 129) and Schoenberg his Jewish faith in *A Survivor from Warsaw* (page 357). Likewise in his *Quartet for the End of Time*, Olivier Messiaen has given expression to a deeply held religious belief. As this composer has said, "A number of my works are dedicated to shedding light on the theological truths of the Catholic faith. That is the most important aspect of my music . . . perhaps the only one I shall not be ashamed of in the hour of death."

music as expression of faith

FIGURE 17–14

Krzysztof Penderecki

Krzysztof Penderecki (b. 1933)

The revival of religious expression in the music of postwar Europe is also evident in the work of Poland's most important contemporary composer, Krzysztof Penderecki. But Penderecki's music is not only spiritual, it is often highly moral in tone. Among his major works are *Threnody* (*Lament*, 1960), dedicated to the victims of the bombing of Hiroshima, *Dies irae* (*Day of Wrath*, 1967), commemorating those exterminated at Auschwitz, and *Lacrymosa* (1981), commissioned by Lech Walesa and the Solidarity labor movement in honor of twenty-eight Polish workers killed in the shipyard riots in Gdansk. As the composer has said, "I am very much concerned with these topics . . . in an essentially moral and social way, not in either a political or a sectarian religious way."

Throughout his career Penderecki has sought new means of expression to convey his intense feelings about the spiritual and moral issues of the contemporary world. In his *Threnody*, for example, he has the violins produce not merely half steps (the smallest interval on the piano) but also quarter steps, or quarter tones. At various times he asks them to play *glissandi* (slides) up and down all four strings at once or strike the soundboard of the instrument with the fingertips. In both vocal and instrumental works Penderecki creates **tone clusters**—dense, chromatic chords that include all, or nearly all, the half steps within a given interval. These clusters he then expands and contracts, like a folding fan, producing a band or block of sound that can grow or diminish, becoming more or less dense. In all of this Penderecki is not so much concerned with creating melody or rhythm as he is with constructing new musical textures, densities, colors, and shapes:

tone clusters

EXAMPLE 17–14

STABAT MATER (1961)

Penderecki's *Stabat Mater* (1961) is a setting of selected stanzas of a centuries-old text which speaks of the grieving Virgin Mary before the Cross (the same subject as *Madonna* in Schoenberg's *Moonstruck Pierrot;* see page 354). *Stabat Mater* is an *a cappella** motet*—that is, a sacred work for voices unaccompanied by instruments. The singers are grouped into three choirs, each with sopranos, altos, tenors, and basses. At the outset Penderecki creates an innovative sound. The tenors of Choir 1 intone "Stabat Mater dolorosa" ("The grieving Mother stood") in a phrase reminiscent of Gregorian chant*. Then the basses of the three choirs repeat that text in staggered entries on a single low A, each presenting one syllable of text in turn. The effect of the staggered entries, long notes, and low register is very much like that of a group of Buddhist monks chanting in a Tibetan monastery. The texture gradually becomes more dense as the altos enter with the same text but declaim it three times faster than the basses. Next the tenors appear and produce two tone clusters, one centered on F and the other on the B♭ above.

EXAMPLE 17–15

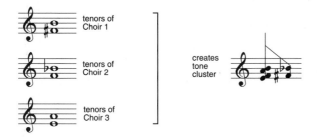

Finally, the sopranos come in with a piercing cry of "Quis" ("Who"), the beginning of the phrase "Who is the man who does not weep seeing the Mother of Christ in such despair?" The bulk of this text is then proclaimed using several unusual vocal techniques—first falsetto* (singing in a higher and "false" head voice as opposed to deeper and natural chest voice), then declamation without singing, and finally whispering and hissing. These techniques add realism to the scene and increase the sense of urgency—the crowd of witnesses to the Crucifixion has come alive. A measure of calm returns with the line "Eia, Mater, fons amoris" ("Oh, Mother, fountain of love"). The voices now enter in imitation, just as in a Renaissance motet (see page 87), but here the intervals of the entering motives are highly chromatic and dissonant, a sure sign that this is modern music. The imitative section works to a climax on the word "Christe," which is shouted *fortissimo* as a giant tone cluster, each choir producing all twelve notes of the chromatic scale at once. This is demanding music for the listeners, but even more so for the singers, each of whom must produce the right pitch in the midst of a broad, chromatic spectrum of sound. More spoken text and shouts of "Christe" in tone clusters eventually give way to the imitative motive once more. Gradually, the texture again becomes increasingly dense until yet another twelve-note cluster is attained. Then, on the final word "gloria," the composer brings off a stroke of genius: The densely packed, dissonant cluster is replaced by a bright, clear D major triad, a stunning, shining affirmation of the glory of the Lord. Penderecki has so accustomed the listener's ear to dissonant clusters that here the age-old consonant triad sounds like a brilliant novelty.

LISTENING GUIDE

Krzysztof Penderecki
Stabat Mater (1962)
(Part 1)

CD 6/8
6–Tape 6B

0:00   Tenor intonation "Stabat Mater dolorosa" ("The grieving Mother stood")

0:13   Basses produce low, hollow sound for same text

0:54   Basses begin to move to new pitches

0:58   Altos enter with same word in repeating notes but higher and faster; they add text "Juxta Crucem lacrimosa, Dum pendebat Filius" ("Near the sorrowful Cross where the Son was hanging")

1:12   Tenors enter with tone clusters

1:37   Sopranos cry "Quis" ("Who")

1:45   Sharp cries and dissonant entries in many voices and in many registers for text "Qui non fleret matrem Christi si videret" ("Who would not weep at the sight of the Mother of Christ")

2:23   Declamation and then whispering become more pronounced for text "In tanto supplicio" ("In such despair")

2:44   Altos of Choir 1 begin calmer, imitative section with motive

E - ia, Ma - ter,   fons a-mo-ris,   Ma - ter   Ma-ter, fons a -   mo- ris,

"Eia, Mater, fons amoris,   "Alas, Mother, fountain of love,
me sentire vim doloris   make me feel the force of sadness
fac, ut tecum lugeam.   that I may be cleansed with you.
Fac, ut ardeat cor meum   Make my heart burn
in amando Christum Deum,   in the love of Christ the Lord
ut sibi complaceam."   that I may find comfort with him."

2:56   Tenors enter with same motive but inverted

3:08   Basses enter with motive

3:20   Altos enter with motive inverted

3:35   Voices of Choir 1 continue to present motive and its inversion

4:14   Voices of all three choirs enter with the motive as texture grows thicker and sound more dissonant

4:50   Shouted tone cluster of twelve half steps "Christe"

4:55   Quiet declamation of a religious congregation

"Christe, cum sit hinc exire,   "Christ, at the hour of my death,
da per Matrem me venire   may the palm of victory come
ad palmam victoriae."   from the Mother's hand."

5:04   Three shouted tone clusters of twelve half steps "Christe"

5:10   More quiet declamation

5:25   Imitative motive enters rapidly and *forte* in all voices

5:37   Brief pause

5:40   Voices enter one by one; some slowly repeat one pitch, others move back and forth in half steps

"Quando corpus morietur,   "When death weighs upon my body,
fac, ut animae donetur   may my soul receive
paradisi gloria."   the glory of Paradise."

6:10   Texture grows denser and volume increases

6:57   Final major triad

LISTENING EXERCISES

<table>
<tr><td>39</td><td>Igor Stravinsky
Petrushka (1911)
Scene 1, The Crowd (first rondo)</td><td>CD 6/2
6–Tape 6A
2–Tape 2B</td></tr>
</table>

The music Igor Stravinsky composed to accompany the ballet *Petrushka* is remarkably colorful and inventive. Every character and important event is supplied with distinctive music. Before attempting this assignment, listen to the music for the first scene of *Petrushka* and follow the Listening Guide on page 351. Try to become familiar with the themes, especially those associated with the Crowd and the Barker, which are given below. Then, answer the following questions which deal only with the music of the first rondo (0:00–5:02).

Rondo sections **A** and **B**

1. The music begins with the crowd theme played at the top range of the orchestra by what instrument?
   a. trumpet
   b. oboe
   c. flute

2. When the Barker enters (0:31) with his distinctive, repeated-note cry, what family of instruments plays the theme?
   a. strings   b. woodwinds   c. brass
3. After the Russian song (0:49 and 1:07), the Barker returns (1:18) and is now more insistent. What family of instruments plays his repeated-note theme this time?   a. strings   b. woodwinds   c. brass

Rondo section **C**

4. In this more subdued, less frenzied section, Stravinsky incorporates two Russian popular songs and a Parisian dancehall tune. Between them, elements from the first section try to break in. In the blanks in the following time log, indicate which music tries to assert itself:
   a. the music of the Crowd
   b. of the Barker
   c. of the Drunken Revelers with the Russian song

1:38   Organ grinder (clarinet)

1:44   _____

1:52   _____

1:55   Organ grinder (clarinet) plays more

2:12   Flutes play street dancers' music

2:27   _____

2:33   Organ grinder (clarinet) and competing theme in celesta (bells)

2:58   Flutes play street dancers music again

3:08   _____ (The return of this music signals the return to section **A** of the rondo.)

5. The tuneful street dance in the flutes (2:12 and 2:58) is one of the rare moments in *Petrushka* when the listener hears a strong, regular meter. In what meter is the melody written?   a. duple   b. triple

Return of the rondo section **A** and **B**

6. After the Russian folk song of the Drunken Revelers, what musical gesture is used (4:00) to signal the return of Barker (4:04)?
   a. a ritardando   b. a crescendo   c. a diminuendo

7. In his final return (4:27), the Barker sounds even more demanding. How does the composer create this effect? _____

_____

	Béla Bartók	CD 6/6
40	*Concerto for Orchestra* (1943)	6–Tape 6A
	Fourth Movement, *Broken Intermezzo*	2–Tape 2A

The fourth movement of Bartók's *Concerto for Orchestra* is entitled *Intermezzo interrotto (Broken Intermezzo)*, and this title may be seen as a metaphor for Bartók's life in his native Hungary, broken or interrupted by the arrival of Nazi troops. The movement incorporates three themes: the first **(A)** is rather light and playful and marked by three staccato notes; the second **(B)** is a lush, lilting Hungarian melody played by the strings; while the third **(C)**, representing the German soldiers, is a straight quarter-note descent, spiced with triplets, introduced by the clarinet. The themes are given below. Study them and become familiar with the general outline of each. Then listen to the movement and compile a time log for it. Remember that the movement unfolds **ABACBA** with the second appearance of **A** being very brief.

Theme **A**

Theme **B**

Theme **C**

0:00 Brief introduction

_____ **A** in oboe

_____ **A** in flute

_____ **A** in clarinet

_____ **A** in French horn

_____ **A** in oboe with counterpoint in flute

_____ **B** enters in violas

_____ **B** heard again more forcefully in violins

_____ **A** returns briefly in oboe

_____ **C** enters in clarinet
(rude noises)

_____ **C** in strings varied by means of repeating notes
(more rude noises)

_____ **C** now ascends (rather than descends) in violins
(more rude noises)

_____ **B** returns in strings

_____ **A** returns in English horn

_____ Cadenza by flute

_____ Reminiscences of **A** lead to quiet end

KEY WORDS

atonal music	ninth chord	seventh chord
Ballets russes	octave displacement	*Sprechstimme*
Cubism	polychord	tone cluster
eleventh chord	polymeter	twelve-tone
Expressionism	polyrhythm	composition
intermezzo	serial music	

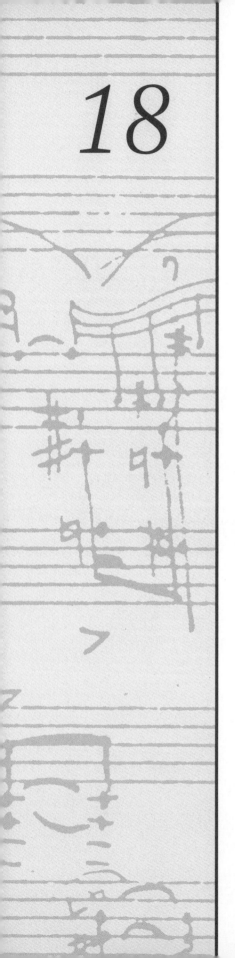

18

AMERICAN MODERNISM

W e are the heirs of a colonial people, and because for so long we imported cultural riches from overseas, it became traditional for Americans to think of art as something purchased abroad." In these words the composer Aaron Copland (1900–1990) sums up the American attitude toward art and music during most of the early history of this country and Canada as well. To be sure, frontier North America was not a musically cultured land by any standards. There were few concert halls or opera houses, no schools or conservatories where gifted young musicians might be trained, and no entrenched aristocracy that might serve as patrons for composers of serious music. What art music there was was imported, first mainly from England and then, beginning in the second half of the nineteenth century, from Germany. As the music of Wagner and Brahms came to dominate the international stage, young composers from the United States increasingly went to Germany to pursue their musical studies and became more Teutonic in style than American. The strength and vitality of American music in the eighteenth and nineteenth centuries lay not in this country's art music but in its popular music (see Chapter 19).

By the 1920s, however, all this had changed. There were now more and better symphony orchestras, several prominent schools of music, concert series devoted not only to American but also to modern American music, publishers who specialized in the "cultivated" style, and many more people with accumulated capital who were willing to spend it on art, domestic as well as imported. A composer of serious music now had a reasonable chance of earning a living through commissions from wealthy patrons and from publishing royalties. Moreover, the upheavals in Europe during the 1930s soon brought the three most important figures of continental modern music—Stravinsky, Schoenberg, and Bartók—to these shores. Their presence gave a new prominence and prestige to modern music in general. By the outbreak of World War II, America had come to rival Europe as the most important wellspring of modern music, just as New York rivaled and then supplanted Paris as the capital of the art world.

EUROPEAN STYLE AND AMERICAN POPULAR MUSIC

American composers of serious music adopted all of the elements of musical style displayed by their European counterparts—atonality*, polyrhythms*, harsh dissonances, and twelve-tone* procedure, for example. At the same time, a distinctly American quality is evident in the modern music produced in this country: It is strongly influenced by, makes use of, and sometimes merges with popular music. Charles Ives (1874–1954) quotes a steady stream of American hymn tunes, patriotic songs, and marches in his orchestral works; George Gershwin (1898–1937) and Aaron Copland (1900–1990) smoothly blend the learned style with elements of jazz in several of their compositions; Leonard Bernstein (1918–1990) could write a broadway musical one year and a symphony the next; just as Philip Glass (b. 1937) will take a breather from composing opera to produce an album of songs with the help of Paul Simon and Linda Ronstadt. In sum, the line between art music and popular music is less clearly drawn in America than in Europe, and composers here have found it easier to "cross over" from one style to the other.

"cross over" of musical styles

Charles Ives (1874–1954)

Charles Ives was an American pioneer in music, a true American nationalist. His music is as brusk, independent, and rough-hewn as the New England settlers from which he was descended. Ives was born in Danbury, Connecticut, the son of George Ives (1845–1894), a bandleader in the Union Army who had served with General Grant during the Civil War. The senior Ives gave his son a highly unorthodox musical education, at least by European standards. There was the obligatory study of the Three Bs—Bach, Beethoven, and Brahms—along with harmony and counterpoint, as well as lessons on the violin, piano, organ, cornet, and drums. But young Ives was taught how to "stretch his ears" by singing a tune such as *Swanee River* in E♭ while his father accompanied him on the piano in the key of C. And he learned to appreciate new and unusual sounds as his father experimented with violin strings stretched over a clothes press, a piano tuned in quarter tones*, and drinking glasses set at equally small intervals. He was not a product of a music conservatory but spent his time on the ballfield (Fig. 18–1), on the parade ground, and in the church choir loft. The sounds that stuck in his ears were those of marches, popular and patriotic songs, fiddlers' jigs, minstrel tunes, and church hymns.

Since his forebears had gone to Yale, it was decided that Charles should enroll there, too. At Yale he took courses in music with Horatio Parker (1863–1919), a composer of some capability who had been trained in Germany. But Ives's youthful, independent ideas about how music should sound clashed with Parker's traditional European notions of harmony and counterpoint. The student learned to leave his more radical musical experimentations, such as a fugue with a subject entering in four different keys,

FIGURE 18–1

Young Charles Ives in the baseball uniform of Hopkins Grammar School, New Haven. A better baseball player than student, Ives needed a year of preparatory school before he entered Yale. At Hopkins he studied English, German, Latin, and Greek, but not music.

FIGURE 18–2

Charles Ives and his staff at the office of Ives and Myrick in lower Manhattan. Ives formulated a new and "scientific" method of estate planning, for which he is known in the industry even today.

outside Parker's classroom. Ives became heavily involved in extracurricular activities, including fraternity musicals, and maintained a D-plus average (a "gentleman's" mark before the days of grade inflation).

When he graduated with the class of 1898, Charles Ives decided not to pursue music as a profession. He realized that the sort of music he had in his head was not the kind the public would pay to hear. As he later said, "If [a composer] has a nice wife and some nice children, how can he let the children starve on his dissonances—answer that!" Ives couldn't, and so headed to New York to become an insurance agent. In 1907 he and a friend formed the company of Ives and Myrick (Fig. 18–2), an agency that sold insurance as a subsidiary of Mutual of New York (MONY). Ives and Myrick grew to become the largest insurance agency in the United States, and in the year in which Ives retired, 1929, had sales of $49 million.

Ives the insurance agent

But Charles Ives led two lives: insurance executive by weekday, frantic composer by night and weekend. During the twenty years between his departure from Yale (1898) and the American entry into World War I (1917), Ives composed the bulk of his 43 works for symphony or band, 41 choral pieces, approximately 75 works for piano solo or various chamber ensembles, and more than 150 songs. Almost without exception they went unheard. Ives made little effort to get his music performed, and when he did, his compositions were greeted with either hisses or laughter.

a dissonant synthesis of new sounds

The music of Charles Ives sounds like that of no other composer. It is wild, heroic, naive, vital, dissonant, and perhaps a bit crazy. Ives wanted to reinvigorate music by embracing new sounds, sounds he might then fuse together to form a new, higher musical synthesis. He did so by giving vent to the abundance of material that had accumulated in his head since his boyhood—sounds such as two bands playing two tunes in different keys and meters at once, a church choir singing one chord while the organist mistakenly plays another, a honky-tonk pianist playing an out-of-tune wreck. These he brings together to produce a jumble of melody, an ear-splitting dissonance, and rhythms of such complexity they are almost impossible to play. In his quest to find fresh musical resources, Ives discovered most of the innovations of modern music about the same time as the European modernist. Atonality*, quarter tones*, polychords*, whole-tone scales*, and tone clusters* are all present in his scores before 1914. He was a prophet crying in the American wilderness.

FIGURE 18–3

Charles Ives photographed in the 1940s during his retirement. He kept tinkering with his musical compositions to the end of his life.

THE FOURTH OF JULY (1911–1913)

No piece could be more representative of Ives's distinctly American brand of musical modernism than *The Fourth of July*. Ives's own words best capture the panoramic vision of a small-town Fourth of July that inspired this one-movement orchestral work.

> Cannon on the Green, Village Band on Main St., fire crackers, shanks mixed on cornets, strings around big toes, torpedoes, Church-bells, lost finger, fifes, clam-chowder, a prize-fight, drum-corps, burnt shins, parades (in and out of step), saloons all closed (more drunks than usual), baseball game (Danbury All-Stars vs. Beaver Brook Boys), pistols, mobbed umpire, Red, White and Blue, runaway horse,—and the day ends with the sky-rocket over the Church-steeple, just after the annual explosion sets the Town-Hall on fire.

The Fourth of July is a piece of program music*, but program music of a different sort. Instead of a logical sequence of musically described events, as occurs in Tchaikovsky's *Romeo and Juliet*, for example, Ives superimposes many musical references at once to create a giant collage of sound. Marching bands, army buglers, sailors, country fiddlers, and church choirs can all be heard more or less simultaneously. They are depicted musically by the more than fifteen patriotic songs, hymns, sea chanties, and marches that Ives borrowed to fashion this hodgepodge. The most prominently quoted tune is *Columbia, the Gem of the Ocean* written in 1843 (see example 18–1), but snippets of *The Battle Hymn of the Republic, The Battle Cry of Freedom,* and *Reveille* can also be heard. Most of the borrowed melodies, however, including *Yankee Doodle* and *Dixie*, are inaudible in the midst of the incredible din of twisted melodies, harmonies, and rhythms. The cacophony comes to a climax with the burst of the skyrocket toward the end. In listening to *The Fourth of July*, don't become frustrated if you cannot clearly identify all the popular tunes. Ives heard the American pageant as a complex, dissonant, sometimes muddled melting pot of sound.

a collage of songs and marches

EXAMPLE 18–1

LISTENING GUIDE

Charles Ives
The Fourth of July (1911–1913)

CD 6/9
6–Tape 6B

0:00	Violins play slow variation of *Columbia*
0:36	Basses do the same
0:55	Tuba joins the basses
1:37	Piccolo plays variation of *Columbia*
1:46	Strings play dissonant variation of *Columbia*
2:04	Piccolo plays variation of *Columbia*
3:01	Strings and winds play *Battle Hymn of the Republic*
3:12	Horns play *The Battle Cry of Freedom*
3:20	Horns and trumpet play *Reveille*
3:31	Trombone plays *Columbia*
3:41	A march begins with the entry of the drums
3:51	Piccolo sneaks in phrase of *The Girl I Left Behind Me*
4:01	Orchestral explosion: the fireworks have begun
4:25	March begins again with *Columbia* in the French horns
4:34	Fragments of many tunes are played in various instruments including *Columbia* (trombones), *Battle Hymn of the Republic* (cornet), *Dixie* (piccolo), and *Yankee Doodle* (piano and xylophone), but most can't be heard
5:27	Pause before the strings carry the skyrocket over the church steeple
5:50	Remnants of the rocket quietly fizzle back to earth

In 1918 Charles Ives suffered a heart attack which more or less brought his activity as a composer to an end. He stored his many unplayed compositions in the barn of his Connecticut farm and devoted what energies he had left to his insurance business. But word of his unusual creations gradually spread to a few American composers, among them Aaron Copland, who arranged for performances of Ives's music in New York, California, and Europe. By 1939 critics called it "the greatest music by an American composer," and in 1947 he was awarded the Pulitzer Prize in music for his Third Symphony, one he had written forty years earlier! In his usual gruff, eccentric way, Ives told the members of the Pulitzer committee, "Prizes are for boys. I'm grown up."

Aaron Copland (1900–1990)

Aaron Copland is often described as our most American composer because of his extensive use of native elements in his music and his conscious attempt to communicate directly with his fellow citizens. Copland was born in Brooklyn of Jewish immigrant parents, his father having arrived there from Poland by way of London and his mother from Lithuania via Texas.

There was little music in the Copland home: "Music as an art was a discovery I made all by myself," he says of his youth. "No one ever talked music to me or took me to a concert." He dug into musical scores at the New York Public Library and took himself to concerts of the New York Symphony.

At the age of twenty Copland set sail for Paris to broaden his artistic horizons. In this he was not alone, for the City of Light at this time attracted young writers, painters, and musicians from across the world including Stravinsky, Picasso, James Joyce (1882–1941), Gertrude Stein (1874–1946), Ernest Hemingway (1898–1961), and F. Scott Fitzgerald (1896–1940). After three years of study Copland returned to the United States determined to compose a kind of music that was distinctly American. Like other young expatriate artists during the 'twenties, he had come to know who he was by learning who he was not: "In greater or lesser degree, all of us discovered America in Europe."

At first Copland sought to forge an American style by incorporating into his music elements of jazz, recognized the world over as a uniquely American creation. His debt to the Jazz Age is especially apparent in his *Piano Concerto* (1926) written two years after George Gershwin's *Rhapsody in Blue for Jazz Band and Piano*. Then, beginning in the late 1930s, Copland turned his attention to a series of projects that had rural and western America as their subjects. The ballet scores *Billy the Kid* (1938) and *Rodeo* (1942) are set in the West and make use of classic cowboy songs like *Goodbye, Old Paint* and *The Old Chisholm Trail*. Another ballet, *Appalachian Spring* (1944), recreates the ambience of the farm country of Pennsylvania, and his single opera, *The Tender Land* (1954), is set in the cornbelt of the Midwest.

In these distinctly American works, Copland's musical voice is unique and consistent. He uses folk and popular elements to soften the dissonant harmonies and disjunct melodies of European modernism. Copland's melodies tend to be more stepwise and diatonic than those of other twentieth-century composers, perhaps because Western folk and popular tunes are fundamentally conjunct and without chromaticism. His harmonies are almost always tonal and often slow moving in a way that can evoke the vastness and grandeur of the American landscape. The triad, too, is still important with Copland, perhaps for its stability and simplicity, but he frequently uses it in a modern way, as we shall see, by having two triads sound simultaneously, creating mildly dissonant polychords. But perhaps the most important component in the distinctive "Copland sound" is his clear, luminous orchestration. He does not mix colors to produce rich Romantic blends, but keeps the four families of instruments (strings, woodwinds, brasses, and percussion) more or less to their own group. And he distributes the instruments of the orchestra so as to construct a solid bass, a very thin middle, and a top of one or two high, clear tones. It is this separation and careful spacing of the instruments that creates the fresh, wide-open sound so pleasing in Copland's music.

his musical style

The clarity and simplicity of Aaron Copland's music is not accidental. During the Great Depression of the 1930s, he became convinced that the gulf between modern music and the ordinary citizen had become too great—that dissonance and atonality had little to say to most music lovers. "It made no sense to ignore them and to continue writing as if they did not exist. I felt that it was worth the effort to see if I couldn't say what I had to say in the

music for the common citizen

FIGURE 18–4

Aaron Copland conducting one of his scores at a recording session at CBS.

simplest possible terms." Thus, he not only wrote appealing new tonal works like *Fanfare for the Common Man* (1942) but also was attracted to traditional tunes such as *The Gift to Be Simple* which he uses in *Appalachian Spring.*

APPALACHIAN SPRING (1944)

Appalachian Spring is a one-act ballet that tells the story of "a pioneer celebration of spring in a newly built farmhouse in Pennsylvania in the early 1800s." A new bride and her farmer–husband express through dance the anxieties and joys of life in pioneer America. The work was composed in 1944 for the great lady of American choreography, Martha Graham (1893–1991), and it won Copland a Pulitzer Prize the following year. It is divided into eight connected sections that differ in tempo and mood. Copland has provided a brief description of each of these orchestral scenes.

Section 1: "Introduction of the characters one by one, in a suffused light." The quiet beauty of the land at daybreak is revealed as the orchestra slowly spaces out the notes of the tonic and then dominant triad.

EXAMPLE 18–2

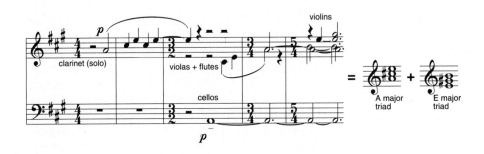

While this simultaneous presentation of two triads should be heard as a polychord, the effect is only mildly dissonant because of the slow, quiet way in which the notes of the two chords are introduced. The serene simplicity of the introduction sets the tone for the entire work.

Section 2: "A sentiment both elated and religious gives the keynote of this scene." The early calm is suddenly broken by a lively dance with a salient rhythm played aggressively in the strings. As the dance proceeds, a more restrained, hymnlike melody emerges in the trumpet.

Section 3 is a dance for the two principals, in ballet parlance a *pas de deux,* accompanied by lyrical writing for strings and winds. *Sections 4* and *5* are musical depictions of the livelier aspects of country life, with *4* including a toe-tappin' hoedown, while *Section 6* recalls the quiet calm of the opening of the ballet.

Section 7: "Calm and flowing. Scenes of daily activity for the Bride and her Farmer-husband." For this section Copland chose to make use of a traditional tune of the Shakers, an extreme religious sect that prospered in the

FIGURE 18–5

A scene from Martha Graham's ballet *Appalachian Spring* with music by Aaron Copland.

Appalachian region in the early nineteenth century and whose members showed their spiritual intensity in frenzied singing, dancing, and shaking. The tune, as Copland first presents it in the clarinet, is given in example 18–3. Since the action of the ballet at this point concerns "scenes of daily activity," the original text of the Shaker song is harmonious with what is occuring on stage:

EXAMPLE 18–3

'Tis the gift to be simple,
'Tis the gift to be free,
'Tis the gift to come down where we ought to be,
And when we find ourselves in the place just right,
'Twill be in the valley of love and delight . . . .

Thereafter come five variations in which *The Gift to Be Simple* is not so much varied as it is clothed in different instrumental attire.

Section 8: "The Bride takes her place among her neighbors." Serenity returns to the scene as the strings, then woodwinds, and then strings and woodwinds together play a slow, mainly stepwise descent "like a prayer." The hymnlike melody from section 2 is heard again in the flute, followed by the quiet landscape music from the beginning of the ballet. Darkness has again descended on the countryside leaving the young pioneer couple "strong in their new house" and secure in their community.

LISTENING GUIDE

Aaron Copland
Appalachian Spring (1944)
Sections 1, 2, 7, and 8

CD 6/10–13
6–Tape 6B
2–Tape 2B

SECTION 1 (track 10; 6–Tape 6B)

0:00	Quiet unfolding of triads by clarinet and other instruments
0:45	Soft violin melody descends
1:11	More triads in woodwinds and trumpet
1:36	Oboe and then bassoon solos
2:19	Clarinet plays concluding triad

SECTION 2 (track 11; 6–Tape 6B)

0:00	Percussive rhythm (♩♪ ♩ ♩♪ ♩) in strings and rising woodwinds
0:19	Rhythm gels into spritely dance
0:43	Trumpet plays hymnlike melody above dance
1:13	Rhythmic motive scattered but then played more forcefully
2:09	Hymn heard in strings with flute counterpoint above
2:36	Rhythmic motive skips away in woodwinds

SECTION 7 (track 12; 6–Tape 6B; 2–Tape 2B)

0:00	Clarinet presents Shaker tune
0:36	Variation 1: Oboe and bassoon play tune
1:06	Variation 2: Violas play tune at half its previous speed
1:51	Variation 3: Trumpets and trombones play tune
2:16	Variation 4: Woodwinds play tune more slowly
2:31	Variation 5: Final majestic statement of tune by full orchestra

SECTION 8 (track 13; 6–Tape 6B)

0:00	Serene, stepwise string music
0:44	Woodwinds continue placid mood
0:58	Strings and winds together play more loudly
1:20	Flute enters with hymnlike tune from section 2
2:14	Clarinet plays triad from the beginning of ballet
2:29	Soft, mild, polychords in strings

(Listening Exercise 41)

ELECTRONIC MUSIC

One of the universal qualities of modern music, in America as well as Europe, is its insatiable appetite for new sounds. New vocal techniques such as Schoenberg's *Sprechstimme** (speech-voice) and Penderecki's whispers and hisses, and new percussion instruments such as the glockenspiel and xylophone used by Stravinsky, Ives, and Copland, are all part of this continual search for novel sonorous effects. After World War II rapid advances in three areas of electronic technology expanded the horizons of musical sound. The first of these was the invention of magnetic tape for recording sound (tape recording as we know it), which allowed the composer not only to record a musical idea but also to alter it radically by copying (dubbing), mixing, and splicing. The second was the development of the synthesizer, a machine that could create its own sounds electronically. And the third and most recent was the advent of the computer, which gave the composer the capacity not only to create new sounds but to control precisely all the parameters of sound as well—pitch, duration, volume, tone color, and attack and decay. Composing music with each of these inventions involves a union of technology and inspired fantasy.

Edgard Varèse (1883–1965)

Edgard Varèse was an early proponent of electronic music. Although born in France, Varèse is viewed as an American composer since all of his surviving compositions postdate his arrival in New York City in 1915. Appropriately enough, his first work following his emigration was *Amériques* (1921), a piece for large orchestra with an unusual percussion section that makes use of a glockenspiel, xylophone, siren, rattle, sleighbells, castanets, and assorted drums. Then, in 1931, Varèse wrote *Ionization*, a piece for percussion instruments alone, thirty-seven different ones played at various times by thirteen performers. This fascination with percussive sounds reflects Varèse's view that pitch is not the primary element of music. Rather, he is concerned almost exclusively with rhythm, texture, and color. This radical shift of emphasis—from lines of melody and accompanying harmony to blocks of rhythmically animated sounds and colors by themselves—is one of the important developments initiated by the more experimental composers of modern music in America.

Varèse's initial training had been in engineering and mathematics, and this scientific bent likely accounts for his interest in electronic music. As early as 1927 he had been encouraging electronic engineers at laboratories of the Bell Telephone Company to create machines that would make the modern, synthetic sounds he wanted to hear. When magnetic tape recorders became available in the early 1950s, Varèse was one of the first to take advantage of them. In 1954 he helped perfect a type of electronic music called *musique concrète* ("concrete music"). **Musique concrète** is so called because the composer works directly, or concretely, with sounds recorded on magnetic tape, not with intermediary symbols (musical notation) and middlemen (performers). Musical tones or everyday sounds from the real world—a car horn, a dog's bark, a dish falling on the floor—are captured on tape, doctored in some way, and then reassembled to form an unexpected montage of sound. The great contribution of *musique concrète* was to show that any sort of sound or noise might serve as building material in a musical composition. The next step, taken in the late 1950s, was to add or mix in sounds produced electronically by means of a synthesizer (see boxed essay).

FIGURE 18–6

Composer Edgard Varèse surrounded by a light sculpture.

The Electronic Synthesizer

The **electronic synthesizer** is a machine that has the capacity to produce, transform, and combine (or synthesize) electronic sounds. A traditional, acoustical musical instrument generates sound by setting a string in motion, by passing air through a tube, or by striking a skin or some other wooden or metal object. A synthesizer, however, creates sound by means of an oscillator. An **oscillator** is a device that, when activated by an electronic current, pulses back and forth, producing an electronic signal that can be converted by a loudspeaker into sound. Before it passes through a speaker and becomes audible, however, the electronic signal can be modified in various ways: It can be made higher or lower, not just by a tone or semitone, but by every small fraction of an interval in between; its color (timbre) can be changed—a clarinet sound turned into a trombone, a violin tone into that of a police whistle—by modifying the waveform and the relative prominence of the overtones*. The electronic synthesizer, then,

places at the fingertips of the user a new range of hitherto-fore unknown and unimaginable sounds. Wails, sirens, clangs, crashes, swooshes, and thousands of other audible phenomena have been and will be added to the accepted vocabulary of music. Equally important, a single keyboard can now produce the sounds of many different instruments.

The first synthesizer was built in the 1950s for RCA at a studio in New York City. But it was bulky and awkward to use, making the production of new sounds a time-consuming, costly process. Subsequent developments in microchips and integrated circuitry produced more powerful, flexible, "user friendly" machines. Some smaller varieties of synthesizers, like the Yamaha SY-22, are portable yet can generate a surprisingly wide range of tones. They are now used by musicians of all stripes, from "serious" composers to rock performers.

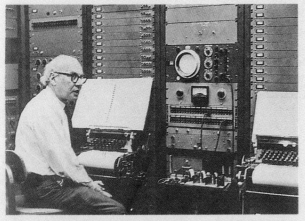

An early electronic music synthesizer, the RCA Mark II which occupies walls of a studio in New York City. During the 1950s a composer might spend hours at such a machine trying to generate a mere minute of electronic music.

A composer can create almost the same music in a fraction of the time with the use of the more modern Yamaha SY-22 electronic synthesizer.

POÈME ÉLECTRONIQUE (1958)

Edgard Varèse's *Poème électronique* is an early landmark in the medium of synthetic music. It is a composite of *musique concrète*—including taped sounds of a siren, a train, an organ, church bells, and a human voice, all altered or distorted in some imaginative way—plus a few new electronic *"poem for the electronic age"* sounds generated by synthesizer. Varèse created this "poem for the electronic age" to provide music for a sound and light show inside the pavilion of

FIGURE 18–7

The Philips pavilion at the 1958 Brussels World's Fair. It was designed by the celebrated Swiss architect Le Corbusier (1887–1965) and housed a sound and light show with music by Edgard Varèse, his *Poème électronique*.

the Philips Radio Corporation at the 1958 World's Fair in Brussels (Fig. 18–7). This eight-minute creation was recorded on tape and then played on 425 speakers, again, and again, to the fifteen or sixteen thousand persons who visited the Philips pavilion daily.

As you listen to *Poème électronique* you may have one or several of the many reactions experienced by those visitors to the Philips pavilion in 1958: anger, fear, revulsion, curiosity, or awe at the sheer variety and novelty of the sound. Startling tones come in rapid succession and quickly disappear; large, dense masses of sound are suddenly succeeded by very thin, airy ones. Three mysterious pitches rise chromatically. Squawks, honks, swoops, and animal noises come one after the other. What is the artist trying to say? Like many composers, Varèse was reluctant to talk about the "meaning" of his music. But in his typically laconic fashion he did remark about *Poème électronique*: "I wanted to express tragedy—an inquisition." Does this work convey the feeling of a tragedy to you? If not, what associations, if any, are produced in your mind as you listen? Perhaps more important, is this really music or is it just ingeniously contrived noise? If it is merely noise, then what is music?

what is noise?
what is music?

LISTENING GUIDE	Edgard Varèse *Poème électronique* (1958) (beginning)	CD 6/14 6–Tape 6B

0:00	Large bell, squibbles and zaps, sirens
0:41	A driplike noise, squawks
0:55	Three-note chromatic ascent sounded three times
1:10	Low sustained noise with rattle, siren, more squawks
1:32	Three-note chromatic ascent, squawks and chirps
2:02	Percussion instruments, siren
2:33	Large bell returns, sustained tones
2:57	More drips, large low crescendo, rattles and zaps

Computer Music

Computer music, the most recent development in electronic music, couples the computer to the electronic synthesizer. The principle of computer music is this: All aspects of musical sound—pitch, duration, color, volume, attack and decay—can be measured and expressed quantitatively in binary numbers. Such numbers can be stored and manipulated by computer and, on command, can be turned into electrical voltages that can then be pushed through speakers to produce audible sound. Computers offer the musician two attractive advantages. First, they make the storage and retrieval of sounds infinitely faster and hence more manageable—musical events can be saved for future recall and the composer can reenter and add to the musical file at whatever spot is desired, just as one enters a word-processing file. Second and more important, computers possess the capacity to define and reproduce in much greater detail the physical properties of any sound, musical or otherwise. Thus, they not only open an entire new world of sound and noise but can also duplicate with greater fidelity than can the synthesizer alone the sounds of traditional acoustical instruments like the violin and trumpet. Today the computer-driven synthesizer can produce a tone quality that is virtually indistinguishable from the recorded sound of a symphony orchestra, if this is what the composer wishes. The impact of this development on the musical world has been enormous. Composers of art music can generate directly for broadcast on compact disc or tape an original musical composition without bothering with an orchestra and listening audience that may be indifferent or even hostile to modern music. Similarly, commercial musicians writing for radio, television, and film can more or less duplicate every nuance of a full eighty-piece orchestra without the enormous expense an orchestra usually entails. The "orchestra" that furnishes the soundtrack for *"Miami Vice,"* for example, is nothing more than a computer-driven synthesizer sitting in the home of the composer, Jan Hammer. Just as "talking pictures" put large numbers of theater organists and theater orchestras out of work in the 1930s, so the computer-synthesizer has displaced countless recording studio musicians in New York, Nashville, and Los Angeles.

Composer Jonathan Berger at work in a computer music studio at Yale University.

CHANCE MUSIC

Most musical compositions sound more or less the same each time we hear them. This is because musical notation makes it possible for the composer to prescribe carefully every aspect of the music. The performer merely follows the composer's blueprint. But in the 1950s a new approach to composition emerged in which the composer gives only the most general sort of outline, creating an artistic framework but leaving it to the performer to determine the sounds that occur within. More radical still, sometimes random noise from the outside world is permitted to enter and exit freely a work of art as it passes through time. What results is a random, indeterminate music called simply **chance music.** Its most forceful advocate is a mild and gentle man named John Cage.

John Cage (b. 1912)

John Cage was born in Los Angeles, the son of an inventor. He was graduated valedictorian of Los Angeles High School and spent two years at nearby Pomona College before going to Europe to learn more about art, architecture, and music. Arriving in New York in 1942, he worked variously as a wall washer at the YWCA, teacher of music and mycology (the science of mushrooms) at the New School of Social Research, and as music director of a modern dance company.

From his earliest days as a musician, Cage has had a special affection for percussion instruments and the unusual sounds they can create. His *First Construction (in Metal)* (1939) has six percussionists play piano, metal thunder-sheets, oxen bells, cowbells, sleigh bells, water gongs, and brake drums, among other things. By 1941 he had collected three hundred percussion objects of this kind—anything that might make an unusual noise when struck or shaken. Cage's tinkering with percussive sounds led him to invent the **prepared piano:** a grand piano outfitted with screws, bolts, washers, erasers, and bits of felt and plastic all inserted between the strings (Fig. 18–9). This transformed the piano into a one-man percussion band which could produce a great variety of sounds and noises—twangs, zaps, rattles, thuds, and the like—no two of which were exactly the same in pitch or color. In creating the prepared piano, Cage was merely going farther along the experimental trail first blazed by his spiritual mentor, Edgard Varèse: "Years ago, after I decided to devote my life to music, I noticed that people distinguished between noises and sounds. I decided to follow Varèse and fight for noises, to be on the side of the underdog."

FIGURE 18–8

"I have nothing to say and I am saying it." John Cage.

FIGURE 18–9

John Cage's "prepared piano." By putting spoons, forks, screws, paper clips, and other sundry objects into the strings of the piano, the instrument is changed from one producing melodic tones to one generating percussive impacts.

FIGURE 18–10

The *Campbell's Soup* (1965) painted by Andy Warhol (1930–1987) asks the fundamental question: "What is art?"

Cage's glorification of everyday noise began in earnest during the 1950s. Rather than engage in a titanic struggle to shape the elements of music like Beethoven, he decided to sit back, relax, and just let noises occur around him. In creating this sort of purposeless, undirected music, Cage invented what has come to be called chance music, the ultimate in musical experimentation. In chance music, musical events are not carefully predetermined by the composer but come in an unpredictable sequence as the result of using astrological charts, tossing coins, throwing dice, or shuffling the pages of music any which way. In *Musical Walk* (1958), for example, one or more pianists connect lines and dots in any fashion to create a musical "score" from which to play. Such "scores" only suggest in the most vague way what the musician is to do. The musical "happening" that results is the sort of spontaneous group experience that was to flower during the 1960s. More radical still is Cage's work 0'00" (1962) which allows the performer total artistic freedom. When performed by Cage himself in 1962, he sliced and prepared vegetables at a table on a stage, put them through a food processor, and then drank the juice, all the while amplifying and broadcasting the sound of these activities around the hall. In a funny way, Cage's attempts to elevate the random, ordinary noise of food processing to the level of art is rather like Andy Warhol's glorification of the Campbell's soup can (Fig. 18–10).

Naturally, music critics have called Cage a joker and a charlatan. Most would agree that his "compositions" in and by themselves are not of great musical value. But he does have a philosophy about music that he articulates by means of challenges and indirect questions. By focusing on the chance appearance of ordinary noise, Cage aggressively asks us to ponder the fundamental principles that underlie most Western music. Why must sounds of similar range and color come one after the other, why must music have form and unity, why must it have "meaning," why must it express something, why must it develop and climax, why must it be goal oriented as is so much of human activity in the West?

4'33" (1952)

The "composition" of Cage that causes us to focus on these questions most intently is his *4'33"*. Here one or more performers carrying any sort of instrument come out on the stage, seat themselves, open the music, and play nothing. For each of the three carefully timed movements there is no music but only the indication *tacet* ("it is silent"). With no organized sound to be heard during the four minutes and thirty-three seconds of silence that follows, the listener gradually becomes aware of the background noise in the hall—a creaking floor, a passing car, a dropped paper clip, an electrical hum. It turns out there is no such thing as absolute silence.

Needless to say, we have not filled your tapes and CDs with four minutes and thirty-three seconds of background noise. You can create your own, and John Cage would like that. Listen to *4'33"* with the following guide and note what you hear. Perhaps this experiment will make you more aware of how important conscious organization is to the art we call music. If nothing else, Cage makes us realize that music, above all, is a form of communication from one person to the next and that random background noise can do nothing to express or communicate ideas and feelings.

LISTENING GUIDE		John Cage *4′33″* (1952)

0:00–0:30	First movement—silence (?)
0:31–2:53	Second movement—silence (?)
2:54–4:33	Third movement—silence (?)

MINIMALISM

John Cage's *4′33″* involves a minimal amount of music—in fact, its actual musical content is zero. In the 1960s this desire to cut away the technical complexities and emotional conflicts inherent in most modern art music led to a new movement in composition called minimalism, one that originated in, and seems confined to, the United States.

Minimalism is a style of modern music that takes a very small amount of musical material and repeats it over and over to form a composition. A three-note melodic cell, a single arpeggio, or two alternating chords is the sort of small, "minimal" element a composer will introduce, reiterate again and again, modify or add to, and then begin to repeat once more. The basic material is usually simple, tonal, and diatonic. By incessantly repeating these minimal figures, the composer lures the listener into a dreamlike, hypnotic state, where atonality, dissonance, and mathematical systems may never penetrate. Then suddenly the music will shift, by means of a new chord, new melodic figure, or new instrumental color, to a different but equally trance-inducing mood. By stringing together a few or many of these short repeating figures, compositions can be created that are anything but minimal in length, however. *Einstein on the Beach* (1976) by Philip Glass and *Nixon in China* (1987) by John Adams (b. 1947) are two full-scale minimalist operas—both last several hours and have been successfully staged by the Metropolitan Opera in New York.

Philip Glass (b. 1937)

Although there are many composers producing attractive pieces in the minimalist style, Philip Glass has pursued this idiom more consistently and with greater success than the others. Glass had the sort of traditional musical education thought proper for a rising young composer: five years at the Julliard School of Music in New York followed by two years of private study in Paris. But while in Paris, Glass took a job as a music copyist for the great Indian sitar* player Ravi Shankar (see page 416), and this gave him an appreciation of the importance of the principle of "change within repetition" in Indian music. Back in New York in 1967, Glass formed his own ensemble in order to perform the unorthodox sort of music he now had in his ear. The Philip Glass Ensemble (Fig. 18–11) is composed of a half-dozen musicians, including Glass himself, who play electronic keyboard synthesizers and var-

FIGURE 18–11

The Philip Glass Ensemble with the composer at the lower right. The group plays mainly acoustical woodwind instruments and electronic keyboard synthesizers.

ious woodwind instruments. Glass drove a cab by day and rehearsed with his group at night until his original, highly unusual style of composition caught on.

When it did, it did so more with the general listening public than with the music critics, perhaps because the sound of electronically amplified keyboards and simple, repeating chords gave the music of Glass a certain affinity to rock. And in fact, Glass has intentionally tried to cultivate a simpler, *minimalism and pop music* more accessible style, thereby to lure the general populace back to the concert hall. Indeed, so popular has the simple, repetitive style of minimalism become that it now pervades the realm of pop music, rock, TV commercials, and films. Within the last decade Glass himself has written music for the award-winning movie *The Thin Blue Line* (1988), has produced a collection of songs, *Songs from Liquid Days* (1986), in collaboration with Paul Simon and Linda Ronstadt, and has indirectly influenced the style of such rock groups as U2, Tangerine Dream, Pink Floyd, and Talking Heads. Nevertheless, Glass is quick to point out the difference between the serious composer (the "concert musician" as he says) and the pop artist:

> There's one important distinction between pop and concert music; I think it's the only important distinction. When you talk about concert musicians, you're talking about people who actually invent language. They create values, a value being a unit of meaning that is new and different.

FLOE, FROM *GLASSWORKS* (1983)

The album Glassworks by Philip Glass was released in 1983 by CBS Records to introduce his music to the listening public at large. We will concentrate on one of the six pieces of the album, a work for a small ensemble called *Floe*. Here, immediately, we can sense Glass's fondness for consonant sonorities, slow harmonic changes, and endlessly repeating rhythms and pitches. Small rhythmic and melodic cells move—indeed, move faster and faster—but this rapid motion occurs within long blocks of static harmony. (The piece is apparently entitled *Floe*, as in "ice floe," because of these slow moving blocks.) There is no carefully directed progress toward some distant goal, no climax, no well-prepared conclusion. *Floe* simply stops as if in mid-stream—a deafening silence. Listen to Glass's *Floe* and see what you think of this radically different approach to musical sound and time. Most persons have a strong reaction to minimalist music—they either yield willingly to its hypnotic powers or become bored by the endless repetition.

LISTENING GUIDE	Philip Glass *Floe*, from *Glassworks* (1983)	CD 6/15 6–Tape 6B

0:00	French horn plays four-note motive in 3/4 meter
0:28	Woodwinds and electronic keyboards play rapid arpeggios, slowly alternating between two chords
1:17	Horns enter this two-chord arpeggiated environment
1:56	Horns play repeating triplets
2:20	Horns add new repeating rhythm (♩ ♪ ＇ ♩ ♪ ＇)
2:54	Horns add yet another repeating rhythm (♪ ＇ ♪ ＇ ♪ ＇ ♪ ＇)
3:18	Two horn rhythms alternate
3:52	Sudden return to opening horn motive
4:16	Woodwinds and keyboard instruments return
4:59	Triplets grow louder in woodwinds and keyboards
5:56	Music stops abruptly

(Listening Exercise 42)

THE CURRENT SCENE: MUSICAL PLURALISM

American composers of more recent times, from the 1960s on, have faced a perplexing question: Where is the mainstream of musical modernism? Should they follow the star of Philip Glass and compose in the minimalist style? Should they embrace Arnold Schoenberg's dissonant twelve-tone* method and create works in which all aspects of melody and harmony are strictly predetermined? Or should they head in the opposite direction and travel the freely experimental route of John Cage, though this more chancey path can sometimes lead to musical happenings that border on the silly? At the moment it seems as if composers are doing all of these and more. John Adams has entered a "postminimalist" phase in his controversial new opera (*The Death of Klinghoffer*, 1991), produced in conjunction with avant-garde director Peter Sellars. Milton Babbitt (b. 1916) and his students at Princeton continue to compose twelve-tone serial music*. David Del Tredici (b. 1937)

FIGURES 18–12 AND 18–13

(left) John Adams studied music at Harvard and has taught at the San Francisco Conservatory of Music. His most recent opera, *The Death of Klinghoffer* (1991), will be performed in San Francisco, Los Angeles, Brooklyn, Brussels, Glyndebourne, Lyons, and Vienna over a two-year period. (right) Ellen Taaffe Zwilich studied at Florida State and Julliard, and has had works commissioned by the New York Philharmonic, the Cleveland Orchestra, the Boston Symphony, and the Chicago Symphony. Her Symphony No. 1 was awarded the Pulitzer Prize in 1983.

and Jacob Druckman (b. 1928) write in a neo-Romantic idiom making use of traditional functional harmony. Ellen Taaffe Zwilich (b. 1939) creates a neo-Classical style using a traditional orchestra and the traditional forms, if not the syntax, of the music of the Baroque and Classical periods. There is also microtonal music (Ben Johnson), quotation music (George Crumb), environmental music (Max Neuhaus), feminist music (Pauline Oliveros), and ethnic music (Michael Tenzer), the latter integrating sonic materials from areas of the third world with the musical traditions of the West. Given our closeness to the events, it is impossible to say which, if any, of these new directions will prove to be the beacon of the future. For the moment the listener must simply be satisfied to delight in the great variety of auditory experience that the new musical pluralism makes possible.

Conclusion: The Character of American Music

America is a country that has always placed a premium on scientific discovery and technology. It is thus no surprise that electronic music and its latest offshoot, computer music, should thrive in this environment. So, too, this country has always taken pride in its independent thinkers. That John Cage's radical chance music might take root here is thus likewise not surprising, since he poses revolutionary questions regarding the very meaning of music. But above all, we are a nation of diverse ethnic groups, each with its own folk songs and traditional music. Because almost no art music was composed in America before 1900, folk music and popular music gained a permanent hold on the American psyche. Not only did folk and popular music influence art music—as in the works of Ives and Copland, as we have seen—but art music influenced popular music—the minimalists have had a profound impact on "new wave" rock groups like the Talking Heads, to cite just one recent example. Indeed, the line between high art and popular art in America has always been a thin one, and it is to the subject of American popular music that we turn in Chapter 19.

LISTENING EXERCISES

<table>
<tr>
<td>**41**</td>
<td>Aaron Copland
Appalachian Spring (1944)
Sections 1, 2, 7, and 8</td>
<td>CD 6/10–13
6–Tape 6B
2–Tape 2B</td>
</tr>
</table>

As we usually ask you to do, go back and review the discussion of this piece on pages 376–378. Then answer the following questions which deal with musical themes, textures, and colors.

Section 1 (track 10; 6–Tape 6B): Introduction

1. Which family of instruments provides the bulk of the soloists for this opening section?
   a. strings   b. woodwinds   c. brass   d. percussion
2. (1:59) As the oboe gently descends, do the strings also descend or do they rise in contrary motion against the oboe?
   a. descend   b. rise
3. (2:19) As the clarinet rises to end the opening section, what do the strings do?
   a. continue with the melody
   b. play a dissonant chord above the clarinet
   c. hold a single note below

Section 2 (track 11; 6–Tape 6B): Joys and anxieties of pioneer life

This section is composed of two musical ideas: an energetic dance theme and a more restrained hymnlike tune (see examples on page 378).

4. The dance theme begins in the strings (at 0:19) and then the hymnlike tune enters in the trumpet (0:43). Which is moving in longer note values (and hence sounds slower)?   a. dance theme   b. hymnlike theme
5. (1:20–2:07) Now the lively dance theme dominates. Identify three qualities of the music you hear in this passage that are reminiscent of the music of Igor Stravinsky, a composer whom Copland greatly admired.
   a. violent, percussive strokes in the timpani, piano, and xylophone
   b. a rhythmic ostinato in the flutes and harp
   c. a sweeping melody in the cellos
   d. tone clusters in the brasses
   e. strong, irregular accents

Section 7 (track 12; 6–Tape 6B; 2–Tape 2B): Variations on a Shaker tune *The Gift to Be Simple* (see example 18–3 on page 377)

   0:00 Tune in the clarinet
   0:36 Oboe and bassoon present variation 1
   1:06 Violas and then violins present variation 2

6. During variation 2 (1:06–1:41) what do the woodwinds and percussion (piano, harp, and glockenspiel) do?
   a. play a flowing countermelody
   b. establish an ostinato as a sonorous backdrop

7. At the end of variation 2 there is a brief transition (1:46) to variation 3 (1:51). Which of the following occurs in this transition?
   a. a rising scale in trombone and trumpet that produces a modulation to a new, higher key
   b. a descending scale in dotted notes in the strings but no modulation

   1:51 Trumpets and trombones present variation 3 against which the violins and violas interject running scales as counterpoint

8. In variation 3 (1:51–2:13) the Shaker tune appears in note values that are played in what speed?
   a. twice as fast as the previous variation
   b. the same as the previous variation
   c. twice as slow as the previous variation

   2:16 Woodwinds quietly carry the tune in variation 4

9. (2:31) The full orchestra offers the fifth and final variation. How would you describe what the strong bass line is doing in this statement?
   a. descending slowly, mainly by step
   b. descending quickly in large intervals
   c. rising slowly, mainly in large intervals

Section 8 (track 13; 6–Tape 6B): "Like a prayer"

This begins with a quiet interlude in which all the strings play a slow, mainly stepwise descent. This is repeated by all the woodwinds (at 0:44) and then by both strings and woodwinds together (at 0:58).

10. (1:20) The hymnlike melody from section 2 returns in the flute. The orchestration of this passage is quite marvelous and rather unusual. The flute is on top, and quiet strings are in the middle. What instrument, surprisingly, provides the firm bass line?
    a. timpani   b. trombone   c. harp

| 42 | Philip Glass
Floe, from *Glassworks* (1983) | CD 6/15
6–Tape 6B |

Floe is performed by the Philip Glass Ensemble, a chamber group consisting of woodwinds and electronic keyboards, here supplemented by two French horns. The piece begins with the two horns playing in 3/4 time. The first horn sounds a four-note motive, each note of which comes on the downbeat and lasts throughout the measure. The second horn enters on beat 2 in most of the measures.

1. Which is an appropriate melodic graph for the four-note motive played by the first horn?

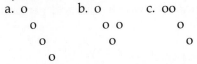

2. How many times is this four-note motive played by the horn? _____
   At 0:28 the winds and electronic keyboards enter playing rapid arpeggios in contrary motion which outline two chords. You should be able to sense a beat and the presence of duple meter in this section.

   As the instruments play rapidly, the chords change very slowly.

3. How many beats are there between chord changes? How many beats do you count between one chord and the next? _____

4. (1:17–1:55) Now the horns reenter. Do they play with the keyboards and woodwinds on a strong beat or against them on a weak beat in syncopation?
   a. with the keyboards and woodwinds
   b. against the keyboards and woodwinds

5. (1:17–1:55) Are the horns playing chords or arpeggios in this section?
   a. chords   b. arpeggios

6. (1:56) The horns now change to a new rhythmic pattern. Which figure correctly represents what they are playing?

   a. ♫ ♩   b. ♩ ♫   c. ♩ ♩ ♩

   At 2:20 the horns switch to the following pattern, ♩ ♪ ᵞ ♩ ♪ ᵞ and at 2:25 this begins to alternate with the triplets.

   At 2:54 the horns introduce the following rhythmic pattern:
   ♪ ᵞ ♪ ᵞ ♪ ᵞ ♪ ᵞ

7. (3:52) Now there is a sudden return to the opening four-note motive in the horns. Have the arpeggios in the woodwinds and keyboards disappeared?   a. yes   b. no

8. How many times is the horn motive heard before the arpeggios return at 4:16? _____

9. (4:59) What rhythmic figure is heard here in the keyboard and woodwinds?   a. ♫ ♩   b. ♩ ♫   c. ♩ ♩ ♩

10. Does the piece end on a downbeat?   a. yes   b. no

KEY WORDS

chance music	Martha Graham	oscillator
computer music	minimalism	prepared piano
electronic music	*musique concrète*	synthesizer

19 AMERICAN POPULAR MUSIC: BLUES, JAZZ AND ROCK

W hat is popular music? Is it music for all the people? Is it music more loved or favored than some other types of music and hence "popular" like a movie star or political figure? Is it a commodity that can be mass produced and sold everywhere, like a pair of blue jeans? Is it a fashionable sort of music whose favored status can quickly fade like the once-popular wide tie or mini-skirt? With qualifications, we may confidently say "yes" to all of the above. Although lovers of classical music can be just as passionate about Beethoven, for example, as those of rock music can be about the Rolling Stones or Bon Jovi, obviously, popular music is enjoyed by a much larger segment of society than is more "serious" music. Popular music is heard everywhere—on radio and television, in the supermarket, and in the dentist's chair. It is "broadcast" in the literal sense of the word. Popular records, tapes, and CDs outsell classical selections by about nine to one. For the most part, popular music is simple and direct. It requires little or no formal training in music to appreciate. Rarely does popular music aspire to be art. It is made to be enjoyed for the moment without concern about its lasting value.

Popular music is similar, but not identical, to folk music. Folk music, too, is enjoyed by all of society. But, unlike popular music, different kinds of folk music are known to different groups. A cowhand in west Texas, or a farmer in Blue Earth, Minnesota, for example, may never have heard the ballads sung by a coal miner in Harlan, Kentucky. Each community and each ethnic group has its own folk music that is passed along from one generation to the next. True folk music is created by the local community. It is never written down, and exists only when sung or played from memory. Popular music, on the other hand, is not only written down but also is intended to be reproduced and sold as a commodity to a mass audience, whether in the form of sheet music or recordings. The homespun folk singer who chants a centuries-old ballad—like *The Streets of Laredo* (see page 31)—is a far cry from the professional pop singer who performs his or her latest hit in Madison Square Garden. Yet from the folk music of both white and black America have sprung our most distinctive genres of popular music: blues, jazz, and rock.

B LUES

Why, where, and how the blues originated is a story that will probably never be fully told. We cannot even hazard a guess as to who gave this style of singing the name "blues," though the expression "the blue devils" had been used to describe a melancholy mood since Shakespeare's time. All that can be said with certainty is that the **blues** are a form of black folk song that originated in the South sometime during the 1880s and 1890s. Like all true folk music, the blues were passed along by oral tradition, one performer learning directly from another without benefit of written music. Comparisons with other forms of folk music suggest that the blues had two immediate ancestors. First and most important was the work song and field holler (or cry) of the black laborers, which bequeathed to the blues a vocal style, a particular scale (see below), and a body of subjects or topics for singing the blues. The second was the Anglo–American folk ballad which imparted the regular, predictable pattern of chord changes that characterize the blues. Blues were first printed as sheet music in 1912 (*The Memphis Blues* and *The Dallas Blues)*, and the first blues recordings, all made by black artists, were cut in 1920.

origins

A singer sings the blues to relieve a melancholy soul, to give vent to feelings of pain and anger. Poverty, loneliness, oppression, family troubles, infidelity, and separation are typical subjects of the blues. The lyrics are arranged in a succession of stanzas, usually three to six to a song, and each stanza is made up of three lines. The second line normally repeats the first, and the third rounds off the idea and concludes with a rhyme. At the end of each line an instrument inserts a short response, called an **instrumental break,** as a way of replying to the cry of the voice. Thus, the blues perpetuates the age-old African performing style of "call and response," the form of which is shown in the following blues stanza:

a succession of three-line stanzas

Call	Response
The moon looks lonesome when	
it's shining through the trees.	(instrumental break)
Yes, the moon looks lonesome,	
shining through the trees.	(instrumental break)
And a man looks lonesome when	
his woman packs up to leave.	(instrumental break)

By the turn of the century the guitar was the accompanying instrument favored by blues singers. It could not only supply a solid harmonic support but could also provide an expressive "second voice" to answer in the instrumental break after the previous call in the vocal line. "Bending" the guitar strings at the frets produced a whining, mournful sound in keeping with the general feeling of the blues.

guitar accompaniment

The object of the blues is not so much to tell a story, as in the white folk ballad, but to express emotion. The voice sometimes moans and sometimes shouts, it is often raspy or frayed, and it always twists and bends the pitch. Instead of hitting a tone directly, the singer usually approaches it by slide from above or below. In addition, a particular scale, called **blues scale,** is used in place of a major or minor scale. The blues scale has seven notes, but

blues scale

the third, fifth, and seventh are sometimes flat, sometimes natural, and sometimes in between. The three "in between" tones are called **blue notes**. The blues scale is an integral part of virtually all Afro-American folk music including the work song and spiritual as well as the blues:

EXAMPLE 19–1

= blue note

Good blues singers indulge in much spontaneous expression, adding and subtracting text and improvising around the basic melody as the spirit moves them. Such liberties are possible because these mournful songs are built above the bedrock of a twelve-bar harmonic pattern which repeats, over and over, one statement for each stanza of text. Singing the blues means singing in a slow 4/4 above this simple I–IV–I–V–I chord progression in the following manner[†]:

Vocal lines:	Line 1		break		Line 2		break		Line 3		break	
Chord:	I————————————				IV———		I———————		V———————		I———————	
Measure:	1	2	3	4	5	6	7	8	9	10	11	12

Sometimes additional chords are inserted between the basic ones for greater harmonic interest. Yet the simplicity of the pattern is its greatest resource. Thousands of tunes have been constructed over this basic harmonic progression, by solo singers, by solo pianists, by Dixieland jazz combos, and by rock 'n' roll bands.

Bessie Smith (1894–1937)

Although there have been and are many great blues singers—Blind Lemon Jefferson, Ledbelly, Muddy Waters, and B. B. King, to name just a few—perhaps the greatest of them all was Bessie Smith, called the "Empress of the Blues." A native of Tennessee, Bessie Smith was "discovered" singing in a bar in Selma, Alabama, and brought to New York to record for Columbia Records. The blues recordings she made between 1924 and 1927 catapulted her to the top of the world of popular music. In her first full year as a recording artist, her disks sold more than two million copies, and she became the highest paid black artist, male or female, of the day. In fact, all of the great blues singers who achieved recording success during the 'twenties were women, perhaps because so many of the texts of the blues have to do with male–female relations and are written from the woman's perspective. Tragically, Bessie Smith's career was cut short by a fatal automobile accident in 1937.

Lost Your Head Blues, recorded in 1926, reveals the huge, sweeping voice of Bessie Smith. She was capable of great power, even harshness, one moment, and then in the next breath could deliver a phrase of tender beauty. She

FIGURE 19–1

Bessie Smith, the "Empress of the Blues," was a physically powerful woman with an exceptionally flexible, expressive voice.

[†]Chord progressions of this sort are discussed on page 32.

could hit a note right on the head if she wanted to, or bend, dip, and glide into the pitch, as she does, for example, on the words "days," "long," and "nights" in the last stanza of *Lost Your Head Blues.* In this recording Bessie is backed by Fletcher Henderson (piano) and Joe Smith (trumpet), and they begin with a four-bar introduction. Then the voice enters and the twelve-bar blues harmony starts up, one full statement of the pattern for each of the five stanzas of text. Each time Bessie Smith sings her melody above the repeating bass, she varies it slightly by means of vocal inflections and off-key shadings. Her expressive vocal line, the soulful, improvised responses played by the trumpet, and the repeating twelve-bar harmony carried by the piano are the essence of the blues.

LISTENING GUIDE

Lost Your Head Blues
sung by Bessie Smith (recorded in New York, 1926)

CD 6/16
6–Tape 6B
2–Tape 2B

0:00   Four bar introduction
0:11   Line 1: I was with you baby when you did not have a dime. (trumpet)
         Chords: I————————————————————————————————
0:22   Line 2: I was with you baby when you did not have a dime. (trumpet)
         Chords: IV————————————————————— I ———————————
0:32   Line 3: Now since you got plenty money you have throw'd your good gal down. (trumpet)
         Chords: V————————————————————— I ———————————

(For the next three stanzas the chord changes and instrumental breaks continue as above; in the last stanza the breaks come in the middle of the lines as well as at the end.)

Once ain't for always, two ain't for twice.
Once ain't for always, two ain't for twice.
When you get a good gal, you better treat her nice.

When you were lonesome, I tried to treat you kind.
When you were lonesome, I tried to treat you kind.
But since you've got money, it's done changed your mind.

I'm gonna leave baby, ain't gonna say goodbye.
I'm gonna leave baby, ain't gonna say goodbye.
But I'll write you and tell you the reason why.

Days[†] are lonesome, nights are long[†].
Days are lonesome, nights[†] are so long.
I'm a good gal, but I've just been treated wrong.

[†]Note the vocal "slides" here.

(Listening Exercise 43)

The impact of the blues on the popular music of the twentieth century has been enormous. In addition to being in itself a genre of music of great feeling and power, the blues gave to jazz a much-used harmonic pattern and an expressive style of playing. All the jazz greats, from Louis Arm-

influence of the blues

strong (*Gut Bucket Blues*), to Duke Ellington (*Ko-Ko*), to Charlie Parker (*Parker's Mood*) improvised around the blues in one style or another. Equally important, it was from the blues and its offspring, rhythm and blues, that rock 'n' roll was born.

JAZZ

Jazz has been called the only truly American contribution to the world of music. It is a mixture of many different musical streams from the New World including the marches of John Philip Sousa (1854–1932), the fiddle tunes and jigs of white Appalachia, and, most important, the spirituals and blues of American blacks in the South. The four-square sense of phrasing and strong, regular harmonies of the Anglo-American styles merged with the complex rhythms, percussive sounds, and flexible vocal production of *origins* Afro–American music to produce a dynamic new sound. Jazz originated about 1910 almost simultaneously in many southern and midwestern cities: New Orleans, St. Louis, Kansas City, and Chicago, to name a few. Because its style was different from city to city and because various other styles of jazz would later evolve—swing*, bebop*, cool*, and third stream* among others—jazz must be defined in rather general terms.

Jazz is lively, energetic music with pulsating rhythms and scintillating syncopations, usually played by a small instrumental ensemble (a combo) or a somewhat larger group (a big band). Jazz tends to be polyphonic as several instruments play independent lines. And it also includes a strong element of improvisation which gives individual performers the freedom to *jazz style* follow their own flights of musical fancy. Tension and excitement are created as virtuosic soloists play off against a regularly changing harmony and a steady beat provided by the rhythm section (usually drums, piano, and a string bass). During its earliest years, jazz was music meant to be danced to, but today it is heard mostly in supper–clubs, cafes, and concert halls. Jazz has become not only the most significant and lasting form of American popular music, producing such figures as Louis Armstrong (1898–1971), Duke Ellington (1899–1974), Benny Goodman (1909–1986), and Charlie Parker (1920–1955), but it has also influenced the styles of European and American composers of art music including Debussy, Stravinsky, and Copland.

Ragtime: A Precursor of Jazz

Ragtime music was an immediate precursor of jazz and shares with it many of the same rhythmic features. To black musicians, "to rag" meant to play or sing music in a heavily syncopated, jazzy style. Ragtime music originated in brothels, saloons, and dancehalls during the 1890s—the "gay 90s"—and the jaunty, upbeat sound of ragtime captured the spirit of that age. Most rags were written by black pianists who played in houses of ill-repute because it was difficult in those years for black musicians to find employment elsewhere. Piano rags, the first of which was published in 1897, took America by storm, more than two thousand being printed by the end of World War I. Sold as sheet music of a thin page or two, piano rags quickly moved from the saloon into middle-class homes where musically literate amateurs played them on the parlor piano.

The undisputed "King of Ragtime" was Scott Joplin (1868–1917). The son of a slave, Joplin managed to acquire for himself a solid grounding in classical music while he earned a living playing in honky-tonk bars in and around St. Louis. In 1899 he published *Maple Leaf Rag* which sold an astonishing one million copies. Though he went on to write other immensely popular rags such as *The Entertainer* and *Peacherine Rag*, Joplin gradually shed the image of barroom pianist and moved to New York to compose rag-oriented opera.

The *Maple Leaf Rag*, which was all the rage at the turn of the century, is typical of the style of Joplin and his fellow ragtime composers. Its form is similar to that of a traditional military march, consisting of a succession of sixteen-bar units, each of which is repeated. And its harmonies are also European in origin, moving purposefully from chord to chord with slight chromatic inflections—Joplin knew his Schubert and Chopin! But what makes ragtime so infectious is its bouncy, syncopated rhythm. Syncopation, of course, is the momentary displacement of an accent from on the beat to off the beat. In piano ragtime the left hand keeps a regular "um-pah, um-pah" beat, usually in 2/4 meter, while the right hand lays on syncopations against it. In the following example from the *Maple Leaf Rag*, syncopation (S) occurs when long notes (either an eighth note or two sixteenth notes tied together) sound off (between) the steady eighth-note beats of the bass:

FIGURE 19–2

One of the few surviving photographs of ragtime composer Scott Joplin.

EXAMPLE 19–2:

New Orleans (Dixieland) Jazz

Although jazz sprang up almost simultaneously in towns up and down the Mississippi River, its focal point and probable place of origin was New Orleans. Not only was New Orleans the home of many of the early jazz greats—King Oliver (1885–1938), Jelly Roll Morton (1890–1941), and Louis Armstrong (1898–1971)—but it enjoyed an exceptionally lively and varied musical life that encouraged the development of new musical styles as well. Culturally, New Orleans looked more toward France and the Caribbean than it did to the Anglo–American north. The city air was filled with opera tunes, marches, and ballroom dances from imperial France but also Afro–American blues and ragtime and Cuban dance rhythms. The end of the Spanish–American War (1898) brought a flood of used military band

FIGURE 19–3

A New Orleans street band in the 1930s. The tradition of jazz being made in the streets of New Orleans, at parades, funerals, and functions of fraternal orders, extends back to the late 1800s and continues today.

instruments into second-hand shops in New Orleans at prices that were affordable even to impoverished blacks. Musicians, black and white alike, found ready employment in ballrooms of the well-to-do, in the bars and brothels of Storyville (a thirty-eight-square-block red-light district in the center of the city), at parades, picnics, and weddings and funerals associated with the many New Orleans societies and fraternal orders. Music was everywhere. Even today in New Orleans bands of various sorts, some good, some bad, can be heard on the streets of the city's French Quarter at almost any hour, day or night.

What did the early jazz musicians of New Orleans play? Their repertoire consisted of syncopated or jazzed-up marches and popular songs, ragtime music, and blues. The structure of each of these genres was square and predictable. The rag had phrases (strains) of sixteen bars, many popular songs of the period had four four-bar phrases, and the traditional blues, as we have seen, consisted of a steady stream of twelve-bar units. Within the strict formal confines of these four-, eight-, twelve- and sixteen-bar patterns, the New Orleans jazz combo found a security that allowed the solo instruments the greatest sort of freedom of expression. The melody was usually played *Dixieland style* in some jazzed-up way by a cornet or trumpet; a clarinet supported this lead instrument and further embellished the tune; a trombone added a counterpoint against the melody in a lower range; down below a tuba set the harmonies if the group was marching, but if it did not, that job was handed over to a string bass, piano, banjo, and/or guitar; these same instruments (tuba, string bass, piano, banjo, and guitar) along with the drums formed the **rhythm section** because they not only set the harmony but also helped the drums give out the beat in a steady fashion.

playing without written music   New Orleans–style bands, then and now, never play from written music. They count, or feel, where they are in the four-, eight-, twelve- or sixteen-bar phrase; they sense when the chords should change within each phrase; and they improvise and refashion the tune, but always so that it fits the regularly changing chords. Teamwork (each musician has a specific role to play according to his instrument) and individual creativity, precision and spontaneity, regularity and happy abandon are the hallmarks of classic Dixieland jazz.

Louis Armstrong (1898–1971)

The brothels and gambling houses of the red-light district of New Orleans were closed by the U.S. Navy in 1917—the corrupting influence of Sodom and Gomorrah was thought to imperil a large navy base nearby. As a consequence, many places of employment for jazz musicians disappeared and the players began to look elsewhere for work—in New York, Chicago, and even Los Angeles. One of those who eventually made his way to Chicago was Louis "Satchmo" ("Satchelmouth") Armstrong. Armstrong was born in New Orleans in 1898, and in 1923 followed his mentor, King Oliver, to Chicago to join the latter's Creole Jazz Band. By this time Armstrong was already recognized by his peers as the best jazz trumpeter alive. He soon formed his own band in Chicago, The Hot Fives, to make what was to become a series of landmark recordings. When the vogue of classic New Orleans–style jazz gave way to the sound of the swing band around 1930, Armstrong moved to New York where he "fronted"—played as featured soloist—in a number of large bands. He invented the practice of "scat singing"—singing nonsense syllables in jazz style, and eventually became known as much for the gravelly sound of his voice, in songs such as *Hello*

FIGURE 19–4

Louis Armstrong (seated) with his band The Hot Fives at a recording session sometime during 1925–1926. The songwriter and pianist Lillian Hardin, who became Armstrong's wife, is at the right.

Dolly and *Mack the Knife*, as for his trumpet playing. His last years were spent in almost continual travel, sent around the world by the State Department as "Ambassador Satchmo." He died at his home in Queens, New York, in 1971.

Although cut in Chicago, the recordings that Louis Armstrong made with his group The Hot Fives beginning in 1925 are classics of New Orleans–style jazz. In fact, four of the five players in this all-star combo were natives of New Orleans and had played together there. The exception was Lillian Hardin, a pianist and songwriter from Tennessee. *Droppin Shucks* is Hardin's composition that The Hot Fives play in traditional Dixieland style. The tune here is only sixteen bars long but it appears seven times, each time varied in some way according to the mood of the players. In a jazz piece of this sort each presentation of the tune is called a **chorus,** whether played by a soloist or the entire ensemble. Although there are three melody instruments here, trumpet, trombone, and clarinet, it is Armstrong's strong, clean trumpet sound that dominates the group. He is also heard as a vocalist in choruses 3 and 4, a jilted lover who has had "shucks" dropped on him by an unfaithful woman, but who is about to drop some of his own.

Listening Guide

Droppin' Shucks, a song by Lillian Hardin
played by Louis Armstrong's The Hot Fives (recorded in Chicago, 1925)

CD 6/17
6–Tape 6B

0:00	Introduction (minor-key sound)
0:24	Chorus 1—full ensemble
0:48	Chorus 2—piano (Lillian Hardin) and banjo (Johnny St. Cyr)
1:11	Chorus 3—vocal (Louis Armstrong)
1:34	Chorus 4—vocal
1:51	Chorus 5—clarinet (Johnny Dobbs)
2:16	Chorus 6—trombone (Kid Ory)
2:39	Chorus 7—full ensemble

Big Bands and Swing

The recordings of Louis Armstrong and The Hot Fives sold as fast as they could be pressed. Jazz became the rage of the 1920s, just as ragtime had been the craze at the turn of the century. It was, in the words of the novelist F. Scott Fitzgerald, the "Jazz Age." So popular did jazz become that it was now performed in ballrooms, large dancehalls, and movie theaters in addition to the smaller bars and supper–clubs where New Orleans–style jazz had its home. And just as the small supper–club gradually gave way to the ballroom, so too did the small jazz combo cede pride of place to the big band—for to be heard above the stomping and swaying of many hundreds of pairs of feet, an ensemble larger than the traditional Dixieland combo of five or seven players was needed. Thus was born the big-band era, the

glory days of the bands of Benny Goodman (1909–1986), Duke Ellington (1889–1974), Count Basie (1904–1984), and Glenn Miller (1904–1944).

Though not "big" by the standard of today's marching band, the **big band** of the 1930s and 1940s was at least double the size of the New Orleans–style jazz combo. In 1943, for example, Duke Ellington's orchestra consisted of four trumpets, three trombones, five reed players (men who played both clarinet and saxophone), plus a rhythm section of piano, string bass, guitar, and drums—a total of sixteen players (Fig. 19–6). Most big-band compositions were worked out ahead of time and set down in written arrangements called "charts." The fact that jazz musicians now for the first time had to play from written scores suggests that a more disciplined, polished, orchestral sound was desired. The addition of a quintet of saxophones gave the ensemble a more mellow, blended quality. The new sound has little of the sharp bite and wild syncopation of the earlier New Orleans–style jazz. Rather, the music is mellow, bouncy, and flowing. In a word, it "swings." **Swing,** then, can be said to be a popular style of jazz played by a big band in the 1930s and 1940s.

Bebop

The craze for big-band swing jazz reached its peak immediately before and during World War II. It had become, in effect, the popular music of America. Swing jazz was heard at home on the radio, on juke boxes, at college proms, in hotel ballrooms, in theaters, and even in New York's Carnegie Hall, the hallowed home of classical music. Then, for reasons that are not fully known, it fell out of favor. One cause was that many of the best young performers found that playing from written big-band charts limited their freedom and creativity. They wanted to return to a style of playing where improvisation was more important than composition and where the soloist, not the ensemble, was king. Choosing their playing partners carefully, they worked or "jammed" in small, elite groups in clubs in midtown Manhattan

FIGURES 19–5 AND 19–6

(left) Benny Goodman, the "King of Swing," during a radio broadcast in the early 1940s. (right) Duke Ellington (seated at the piano) and his big band in 1943. Unlike other band leaders of this time, Ellington was as much a composer and arranger as he was a performer.

return of the jazz combo

a hard-driving, dissonant style

and in Harlem, and in so doing created a new virtuosic style of jazz called bebop.

Bebop is a complex, hard-driving style of jazz played by a small combo without written music. Typically, it involves a quintet of trumpet, saxophone, piano, double bass, and drums. The best players, among them saxophonist Charlie Parker (1920–1955) and trumpeter Dizzy Gillespie (b. 1917), had astonishing techniques and played at breakneck speeds. Their love was improvisation, and the solos they created were more complex than those heard in either swing or New Orleans–style jazz. They overlaid the melody with so much rapid, jarring embroidery that the tune soon became unrecognizable. They also changed chords more rapidly than earlier jazzmen and went to more remote keys. Only the most gifted performers could keep up and "make the changes"—anticipate the changing harmonies and instantly improvise an appropriate melody. Gillespie has said that he and Parker intentionally made the harmonies overly difficult to discourage less-talented performers from jamming with them. Bebop was for an elite few.

Charlie "Bird" Parker (1920–1955)

Perhaps the most gifted of the bebop artists was Charlie "Yardbird" or "Bird" Parker, the subject of Clint Eastwood's movie *Bird* (1988). Parker was a tragic figure, a drug-addicted, alcoholic, antisocial man whose skills as an improviser and performer, nonetheless, were greater than all other jazz musicians save Louis Armstrong. Indeed, the lives of Armstrong and Parker make an interesting comparison. Both were born into the extreme poverty of the ghetto, Armstrong in New Orleans and Parker in Kansas City, and both rose to the top of their profession through extraordinary talent and hard work. But Armstrong was an extroverted person who viewed himself as a public entertainer as much as an artist. Parker didn't care whether people liked his music or not, and he managed to alienate everyone around him including, finally, his friend and longtime playing partner, Dizzy Gillespie. He died of the effects of his many excesses, alone and broke, at the age of thirty-four. Parker's life may have been a mess, but his rapid, inventive style of playing irrevocably changed the history of jazz.

In 1950 Parker and Gillespie recorded a bebop version of a sentimental love song called *My Melancholy Baby* (1911). Like many popular tunes from the early part of this century, *My Melancholy Baby* is sixteen bars long and divided into four four-measure phrases (here **ABAC**). After a four-bar introduction by pianist Thelonious Monk, Parker plays the tune more or less "straight," with only moderately complex elaborations. But when Dizzy Gillespie enters for the second chorus, the ornamentation becomes more complex by means of running thirty-second notes and continues to do so through the third and final chorus which Monk and Parker divide. Notice, as you listen to *My Melancholy Baby*, that there is none of the teamwork or intricate counterpoint found in classic Dixieland jazz where three solo lines would sound simultaneously in the choruses for the full group. Here in bebop are brilliant solos for a single instrument against the backdrop of the rhythm section, but no ensemble improvisation. Try to follow the original tune as each soloist embroiders it.

FIGURE 19–7

Charlie "Bird" Parker about 1950. Parker developed a fast, snapping, syncopated style of playing that often sounds like the word "bebop" said quickly.

Although *My Melancholy Baby* is more accessible than most bebop-style jazz, it still has little in the way of a beat. The drummer in bebop, contrary to Dixieland and swing, does not pound the bass drum regularly on beats one and three of the 4/4 measure, but brushes every beat quietly and without accent on the cymbal. And the melody instruments (trumpet and saxophone) constantly shift the accent from one beat to another during their improvisatory solos, confusing the beat. What results is a music more for listening than for dancing. As a consequence, bebop has never achieved a wide popular following. Instead, it serves as a sort of "chamber music" of jazz, a somewhat esoteric style that thrills a small number of connoiseurs.

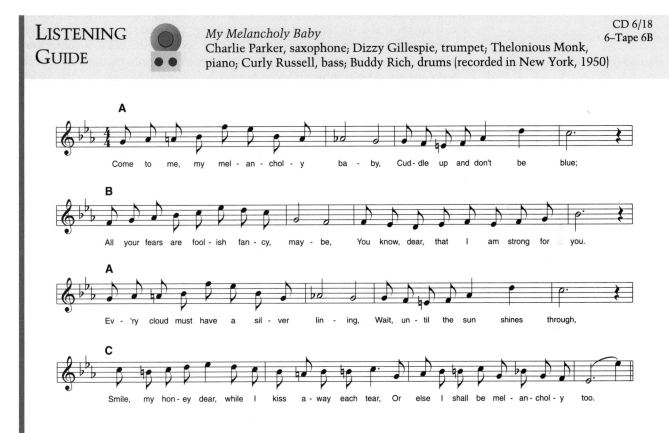

LISTENING GUIDE

CD 6/18
6–Tape 6B

My Melancholy Baby
Charlie Parker, saxophone; Dizzy Gillespie, trumpet; Thelonious Monk, piano; Curly Russell, bass; Buddy Rich, drums (recorded in New York, 1950)

A Come to me, my mel-an-chol-y ba-by, Cud-dle up and don't be blue;

B All your fears are fool-ish fan-cy, may-be, You know, dear, that I am strong for you.

A Ev-'ry cloud must have a sil-ver lin-ing, Wait, un-til the sun shines through,

C Smile, my hon-ey dear, while I kiss a-way each tear, Or else I shall be mel-an-chol-y too.

0:00   Four-bar introduction
0:13   Chorus I—**ABAC,** saxophone
1:12   Chorus II—**ABAC,** trumpet (with mute)
2:13   Chorus III—**AB,** piano
2:40   . . . . **AC,** saxophone
3:05   ritard and tag (short coda) by saxophone and trumpet

(Listening Exercise 44)

Jazz Styles since 1950

proliferation of jazz styles

The heyday of bebop (1945–1955) marked the beginning of a decline in the popularity of jazz. If you couldn't dance to it, why listen? The decade also saw the beginning of a fragmentation and proliferation of jazz styles—no one type of jazz was able to capture the public's imagination. **Cool jazz,** sometimes called "soft bebop" because of its more relaxed, less-frenzied solos, grew out of bebop and gained a modest following in the 1950s. Its main practitioners were trumpeter Miles Davis (1926–1991) and saxophonists Gerry Mulligan (b. 1927) and Stan Getz (1927–1991). Their delivery was soft, gradual, and nonaggressive, a welcome change of pace to the dramatic, hard-driving sound of bebop. The early 'fifties also witnessed the advent of **third–stream jazz,** a mixture of jazz and classical styles. The hope was that the music of one stream (jazz) might blend with that of another (classical) to produce an alternative direction for progressive jazz. The term "third–stream" was first coined by Gunther Schuller (b. 1925), a composer, conductor, and French horn player who in the 1950s moved back and forth between the Metropolitan Opera House and recording "gigs" with Miles Davis.

rock and jazz

If jazz in the 1960s turned toward classical music, by the 1970s it was headed in a radically different direction, toward rock. The cause of this about-face, simply said, was money. Jazz recordings, whether in bebop, cool, or third–stream style, were not selling. What was selling was rock. So jazz musicians, driven by economic reality, began to adopt the rhythms of the rock drummer and the simple, repetitious harmonies outlined by the Fender bass guitar. Young trumpeters such as Lou Soloff (b. 1943) and Chuck Mangione (b. 1941) stopped playing like Miles Davis and went off to form jazz–rock bands such as Blood Sweat and Tears, Chicago, and the Chuck Mangione Ensemble. They have made great music—and gotten rich—by fusing the driving rhythms and harmonies of rock with the big-band brass sounds and the virtuosity of the jazz improviser. The moral of this story, as it pertains to the history of jazz and its listening public, is that any popular music without a catchy tune or a foot-stomping beat won't be popular for long.

R OCK

Bursting on the scene in the mid–1950s, rock 'n' roll (and its later manifestation, rock) revolutionized popular music in America and indeed throughout the world. Its style is well known to all—the pounding beat, the heavy, amplified guitar sound, the driving bass, and the simple, repetitive harmonies. There is, to be sure, much harmonic repetition, noisy filler, and electronic distortion. But, of course, rock involves much more than just music. The style of dress of the rockers, their sometimes outrageous manner of behavior, both on and off the stage, and their social or political beliefs are just as important to rock culture as is the music they produce. Rock was born as a music of protest and rebellion directed against the established musical and social order.

The origins of rock can be found in a style of music called rhythm and blues that came out of the South around 1950. Like the blues, **rhythm and blues** makes use of the twelve-bar blues pattern and an expressive style of singing. But here the 4/4 meter and usually slow tempo of the blues is changed to a faster 4/4, upbeats and downbeats are made stronger, a saxophone is added to the basic guitar sound, and the text is shouted as much as sung. All of this produces a raw, driving, highly danceable kind of music. At first rhythm and blues was created and played exclusively by black musicians for a black audience. But as many of these musicians and listeners moved to the urban centers of the North in the 1950s, a white audience began to hear and dance to this energized black music, mostly over the radio. Indeed, the term "rock 'n' roll" was first coined in 1951 by a white disk jockey in Cleveland, Alan Freed, who championed black rhythm and blues. Soon black artists like Chuck Berry (*Maybellene* and *Roll Over Beethoven*), Bo Diddley (*Bo Diddley*), Fats Domino (*Blueberry Hill*), and Little Richard (*Tutti Frutti* and *Lucille*) found that there was a demand for their music in the white market. And white musicians like Bill Haley (*Rock around the Clock*), Carl Perkins (*Blue Suede Shoes*), Jerry Lee Lewis (*Great Balls of Fire*), and Elvis Presley (*Jail House Rock*) began to copy the black sound. Perkins, Lewis, and Presley had grown up in the South in the environment of black rhythm and blues. Presley's first manager said that he was simply "looking for a white boy who could sing colored."

Elvis Presley (1935–1977) became the "King of Rock 'n' Roll"; his singing electrified a white audience only then coming to know the sounds of black rhythm and blues. Presley's first hit, *Heartbreak Hotel* (1955), and subsequent *Love Me Tender* (1956) were in the tradition of the white country ballad, though sung in an expressive, throbbing style. But his *Hound Dog* (1956) and *Jail House Rock* (1957) continued the development of hard-driving rhythm and blues. Indeed, *Hound Dog* had been borrowed from blues singer Big Mama Thornton. Within two years of his first hit, Presley had become a national obsession, his every gyration the object of scrutiny by the media. But the public Elvis was very much a creation of the tabloids and Presley's clever managers. Though on stage he projected an image of the youthful rebel, the hard-guy rocker, exuding sexual confidence and suggestiveness, in reality he was very much a pampered mama's boy and timid about sexual matters. He died young of drug abuse, a bloated caricature of himself. The sad part is that, in spite of the rhinestones, the Cadillacs, and all the other silliness that attended his life, he was highly musical and blessed with an exceptionally rich and wide-ranging baritone voice. His was by far the best voice of any of the male rock singers, then or now.

By the early 1960s much of the initial energy and freshness of early rock 'n' roll had been lost. Sentimental tunes directed at the hordes of teenagers of the postwar baby boom (*Teenager in Love* and *Teen Angel*, for example) began to dominate the market. But American rock soon received a shot in the arm from an unexpected source, Great Britain. The reason for this is clear. England had recently become infatuated with the sounds of American bluesmen like Muddy Waters as well as rhythm and blues singers like Chuck Berry and Bo Diddley, some of whom had toured there. As foreign imitators, British pop musicians embraced the new styles with greater fidelity to the original than did their American cousins. The pounding,

FIGURE 19–8

Chuck Berry, one of rock 'n' roll's early stars. He along with Bo Diddley and Little Richard transformed rhythm and blues into rock 'n' roll.

FIGURE 19–9

The "King is Dead, Long Live the King." The hysteria surrounding Elvis has diminished only slightly. Since his death in 1977, Elvis "sightings" are reported almost weekly in the tabloids. One recent television special had him alive and well, living under the F.B.I.'s witness protection program.

FIGURE 19–10

The Beatles's *Sergeant Pepper's Lonely Hearts Club Band* was one of the first to establish "album oriented" rock in which tunes in a variety of styles are selected and arranged to form a single, unified collection.

swaggering style of Mick Jagger and his Rolling Stones is very much in the tradition of "shouting" rhythm and blues from Louisiana and Mississippi. And The Who, led by guitarist Pete Townshend, adopted the same heavy amplification and driving bass, but added more varied chord changes, notably in their "rock opera" *Tommy* (1968). But of all the British groups, the most adaptive and most successful was the Beatles.

The Beatles were formed in Liverpool, England, in 1960 and achieved an overnight success in that country with their first recording (*Love, Love Me Do*, 1962). In 1964 they took America by storm, first with their best-selling single *I Want to Hold Your Hand* and then in person through a sold-out national tour. "Beatlemania" was born. But unlike the equally popular Elvis, a dynamic performer but not a composer, each of the Beatles was a songwriter in his own right. And two of them, bass guitarist Paul McCartney and rhythm guitarist John Lennon, were exceptionally creative. They wrote fresh lyrics and unpredictable tunes that the parents as well as the kids could enjoy. What is most remarkable about the Beatles is the variety of musical styles that they adopted and made their own: rhythm and blues (*Roll Over Beethoven* and *Twist and Shout*), country blues (*Oh, Darling*), church hymns (*Let It Be*), British music-hall songs (*When I'm Sixty-Four*), Broadway show tunes (*The Long and Winding Road*), novelty songs (*Octopus's Garden*), and psychedelic rock (*Lucy in the Sky with Diamonds*). In 1970, after a decade of unprecedented popularity and financial gain, the Beatles disbanded, though each of them ultimately returned, with differing degrees of success, to the field of popular music with his own band.

folk-rock and protest-rock

While America was held captive to Beatlemania, a newer, softer style of rock music, called folk–rock, emerged on these shores. **Folk–rock** was a mixture of the steady beat of rock with the forms, topics, and styles of singing of the traditional Anglo–American folk ballad (see page 392). The folk ballad had survived in the South and West in the form of the country–western ballad. Folk music, in general, enjoyed a revival beginning with the

Kingston Trio's recording of the ballad *Tom Dooley* (1958) and with the work of Peter, Paul, and Mary, and of Joan Baez. But the sources of the new folk–rock were more city than country, and the primary artists urban Jewish rather than Appalachian Protestant. The labor movement, the civil rights movement, and protests against the Vietnam War were supported by these artists. Bob Dylan, who sang accompanied only by his guitar and harmonica, inaugurated this urban folk style with protest songs such as *Blowin' in the Wind* (1963). Paul Simon, the creative force behind Simon and Garfunkel, started in the footsteps of Dylan but quickly developed his own folk–rock manner with *The Sounds of Silence* (1964), *Bridge over Troubled Water* (1969), and *Slip Slidin' Away* (1977). More recently, Simon has combined the rock beat with the choral sounds of native folk artists of South Africa in his antiapartheid album *Graceland* (1986). James Taylor, Judy Collins, and Joni Mitchell are three other folksingers who occasionally incorporate rock idioms in their music. The beat is there, but they sing accompanied by the sound of the quieter acoustical guitar rather than an electrically amplified instrument.

Rock (and its progenitor rock 'n' roll) is now nearly fifty years old but shows no signs of losing its popular following. Each time one rock style gets stale, two others emerge to take its place. In the last twenty years we have seen the rise of acid rock (The Grateful Dead), disco (The Bee Gees), pop–disco (Madonna and Michael Jackson), working-class hard rock (Bruce Springsteen and John Cougar Mellencamp), electric folk (The Pogues), blues revival (Steve Winwood), punk rock (Kiss), symphonic rock (Pink Floyd), new wave (Talking Heads), heavy metal rock (Metallica), and Euro–pop (Enigma). Yet at the same time the "oldies but goodies" of the mid-1950s keep going strong and are reissued in CD format; Beatles songs remain popular, and Paul McCartney, George Harrison, and Ringo Starr continue to record individually; and Mick Jagger and the Rolling Stones, and Pete Townshend and The Who enjoy "comeback" tours even though they never really went away. What began as a youthful rebellion is now the accepted mainstream of American popular music. Only a few extreme styles, like punk rock and heavy metal, exist on the countercultural fringe. A half-century of hearing the "sinful" beat of rock 'n' roll has mollified even the most reactionary ears. And impossible as it seems, the kids who grew up buying Chuck Berry and Elvis 45s are now middle-aged and beyond.

from rebellion to mainstream

LISTENING EXERCISES

43	*Lost Your Head Blues* sung by Bessie Smith (recorded in New York, 1926)	CD 6/16 6–Tape 6B 2–Tape 2B

Lost Your Head Blues tells the tale of a "good old gal" who has "just been treated wrong." In a treatment typical of the blues, here Bessie Smith belts out five stanzas of text, each with three lines. After each line, trumpeter Joe Smith enters to offer an instrumental comment on the sentiments just expressed by the singer. Complete the following time log by entering the times at which the voice begins each line and the trumpeter begins the instrumental breaks.

Stanza 1

0:11	I was with you baby when you did not have a dime.	:
:	I was with you baby when you did not have a dime.	:
:	Now since you got plenty money you have throw'd your good gal down.	:
		:

Stanza 2

0:44	Once ain't for always, two ain't for twice.	:
:	Once ain't for always, two ain't for twice.	:
:	When you get a good gal, you better treat her nice.	:

Stanza 3

1:16	When you were lonesome, I tried to treat you kind.	:
:	When you were lonesome, I tried to treat you kind.	:
:	But since you've got money, it's done changed your mind.	:
		:

Stanza 4

1:49	I'm gonna leave baby, ain't gonna say goodbye.	:
:	I'm gonna leave baby, ain't gonna say goodbye.	:
:	But I'll write you and tell you the reason why.	:

In the final stanza the trumpet is more fully integrated with the voice. Here just listen to the extraordinarily powerful and flexible voice of Bessie Smith.

Stanza 5

2:20   Days are lonesome, nights are long.
Days are lonesome, nights are so long.
I'm a good gal, but I've just been treated
wrong.

---

44   Bebop-style Jazz   CD 6/18
My Melancholy Baby   6–Tape 6B
Charlie "Bird" Parker, saxophone; Dizzy Gillespie, trumpet
(recorded in New York, 1950)

Bebop is a highly complex style of progressive jazz with difficult chord changes and dizzying flights of instrumental virtuosity. What makes *My Melancholy Baby* easy to follow is the form: a short introduction, three sixteen-bar choruses, and a short coda. The form is made clear to the listener because there is a change to a new solo instrument at the beginning of each chorus. From one chorus to the next, however, the playing becomes progressively more complex, and the tune more heavily disguised by ornamentation. The first five questions that follow help illuminate the musical form, while the second five concentrate on aspects of the bass line.

1. (0:00–0:12) Which instrument solos during the introduction?
   a. saxophone   b. trumpet   c. piano
2. (0:13–1:11) What does the piano do during Charlie Parker's solo in chorus 1? _____
3. (1:12–2:12) During the trumpet solo of chorus 2, is Parker's saxophone heard?   a. yes   b. no
4. (2:13–3:04) During chorus 3, is Gillespie's trumpet heard?
   a. yes   b. no
5. Which of the forms that we have studied is embodied in this piece?
   a. rondo
   b. sonata–allegro
   c. theme and variations
6. Is the bass instrument that plays in this quintet the double bass of the symphony orchestra or the electric bass guitar? _____
7. Does the player use a bow or play pizzicato? _____
8. Which figure more accurately reflects the rhythm of the bass?
   a.   b.

   or

9. Which statement correctly describes the bass line?
   a. moves mainly in stepwise motion in regular, even notes
   b. moves by leaps in highly varied rhythms
10. This sort of bass line, then, can be said to be similar to which musical procedure of the Baroque era?
    a. the ostinato* bass
    b. the walking bass*
    c. the pedal point*

---

45 | Listening to Contemporary Rock

This book was written as a text for music appreciation courses in colleges and universities. Although the author played piano in a rock 'n' roll band many years back, he is certain that you, the college student, are more familiar with the contemporary rock scene than he. This last listening exercise gives you the chance to demonstrate your expertise. Your task is to choose a piece of contemporary rock music, analyze it, and write a brief report. As you listen, you may wish to consider the following questions as a way of focusing your thoughts:

1. What instruments are playing?
2. Are they acoustical musical instruments or electronically amplified ones?
3. Most rock pieces are in a major key and in duple meter. Is yours?
4. Does the voice sing the melody, or tune, alone or is it doubled by one of the instruments?

5. Is the mood and style of the music well suited to this particular text, or might this music be used just as well for another set of lyrics?

6. What do you think is the single most important element in your piece? Is it the text, a catchy melody, a satisfying harmonic pattern, a driving rhythm, or something else?

7. What instrument is playing the bass line? Does the bass stand out in any special way? Is it, for example, played louder than the other parts? If so, why?

8. What about the form of your rock song: Is it through-composed* like Schubert's *Erlking* (page 250) or strophic* like *Lost Your Head Blues* as sung by Bessie Smith (page 395)? Many pop tunes are strophic but each stanza ends with a refrain. Is yours arranged in this fashion?

9. What do you think is the relationship between music and noise in your piece? Is there any "electronic filler?" If so, what purpose does it serve?

10. How inventive is your work? Is it fresh and innovative, or is it simply a repackaging of the clichés of popular music? Will your selection stand the test of time to become a classic? If so, why; if not, why not?

KEY WORDS

bebop	cool jazz	ragtime
big band	folk-rock	rhythm section
blue note	folk song	swing
blues	instrumental break	third-stream jazz
blues scale	jazz	

CONTRASTS: WESTERN MUSIC AND NON-WESTERN MUSIC

20

T he music we have discussed in this book has been mainly Western European art music. It is a musical tradition that originated in Europe and spread both east and west, to Russia and gradually to North and South America. In many ways our operas, concertos and symphonies have become the international currency of art music. They are heard in many cities throughout the world, east and west, north and south. Symphony orchestras in Tokyo and Rio play the works of Beethoven almost as often as do those in Paris, Rome, St. Louis, and Cleveland. Young students from Korea, China, Singapore, and Japan flood the conservatories of London and New York to develop their considerable talents as performers on Western-style instruments. Added to this is the enormous influence of American and British popular music, which has infiltrated, and in some cases overwhelmed, local traditional musics throughout the world.

But the music of the West, both classical and popular, is by no means the only music of the world. Great masses of people remain wholly or mostly unaffected by it. For example, China, with a quarter of the world's people, India, with 800 million citizens, and Indonesia, the fifth most populous nation on earth, with 200 million inhabitants, all retain their native musical traditions independent of the West. The sounds of each of these cultures is radically different, one from the other, just as they are each unrelated to the music of Bach, Mozart, and Beethoven. And while we cannot here enjoy anything more than a tantalizing taste of these foreign delights, they will be enough to highlight the ways in which our own art music of the West is different, indeed unique among the musics of the world.

Gamelan Music of Bali

Bali is an island, about the size of Delaware, that belongs to a chain of islands forming the southeast Asian country of Indonesia (see Fig. 20–1). It is an island of swaying palm trees, fertile rice fields, and hundreds of small villages, each with its own vital and distinctive musical tradition. For the more

FIGURE 20–1

The sub-continent of Asia, Southeast Asia, and the Pacific rim.

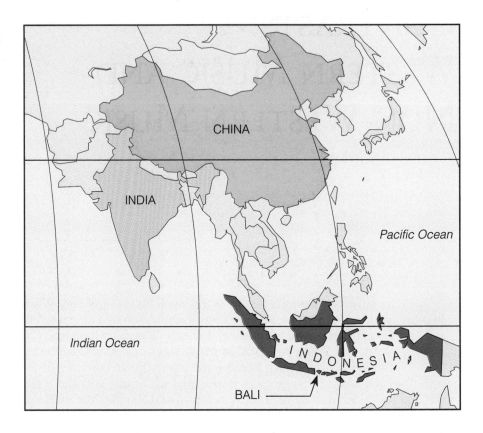

FIGURE 20–1

The sub-continent of Asia, South-east Asia, and the Pacific rim.

than two million inhabitants of Bali, music is an integral part of their daily lives, for music is intimately bound up with religion and folklore. Hindu deities and local spirits must be honored daily in the temple and in the home. Larger ceremonies are invariably celebrated to the accompaniment of music performed by a gamelan.

the gamelan

A **gamelan** is a collection of as many as twenty-five musical instruments played together as an orchestra. The ensemble, however, sounds very unlike our Western orchestra, for the dominant family of the gamelan is not the strings, but the percussion: metallophones (xylophone-like instruments with bronze keys and bamboo resonators), tuned gongs, gong-chimes, cymbals, and drums, along with an occasional flute. So, too, the gamelan employs a different approach to generating musical lines. In the Western orchestra a single instrument is responsible for providing a melody or counter-melody, or creating a single instrumental color. In gamelan music, however, players of several instruments continually contribute bits of music which, when taken together, form a composite line of distinctive color. In the example that follows, notice how the parts are interlocking and mutually interdependent. It is only their composite sound, not the individual parts, that is conveyed to the ear of the listener. In gamelan music, solos are rare. What sound like solos are actually passages played by small groups. There is a strong commitment to group interaction, with each performer doing his or her part for the benefit of the whole. The effect is that of a well–polished, well–disciplined musical machine—a source of pride for the local village.

FIGURE 20–2
A Balinese gamelan fronted by a set of gongs tuned to a pentatonic scale and mounted horizontally.

Indeed, most gamelans are organized as community or village clubs, and they draw heavily on the local populace for performers.

EXAMPLE 20–1

A striking example of Balinese gamelan music is the piece *Jaya Semara*. In a way similar to Britten's *The Young Person's Guide to the Orchestra*, *Jaya Semara* begins by exploring the colors and textures of the various instruments and instrumental families of the Balinese orchestra, all the while showing off the extraordinary virtuosity of the performers. Only midway through the piece (at 2:10) does a melody enter and a steady rhythmic pulse assert itself.

As with every piece of Balinese music, *Jaya Semara* was taught to the performers, a group from the town of Denpasar, by a master teacher, or guru. The teacher played and explained each part, bit by bit, until finally the entire composition was learned. Though the music is extraordinarily complex, no notation was used. On Bali, everything is taught, learned, and performed entirely by ear.

oral teaching and learning

LISTENING GUIDE

Jaya Semara
a piece for Balinese gamelan
(recorded in Denpasar, Bali, Indonesia in 1989 by Michael Tenzer)

Introduction to Listening
tape: side B, band 2

0:00	Full gamelan with "solos" by high gongs, drums, and then metallophones
0:26	High gongs dominate
0:41	Full gamelan
0:47	High metallophones dominate
1:00	High gongs return
1:24	Single deep gong
1:30	Tempo increases; full gamelan enters
1:37	Drum beat begins
1:47	Drum solo
2:10	Full gamelan with bamboo flute plays repeating melody and ostinato rhythmic patterns
3:17	Tempo increases; then rhythmic patterns break down
3:37	Final gong

Music for a Chinese String Orchestra

China is arguably the oldest and richest continuing civilization in the world. Many of the inventions and products that altered the course of Western history—gunpowder, printing, paper, silk, the nautical compass, and the dictionary, for example—were first developed in China. China also has a musical history that extends back thousands of years. A mathematical theory for generating all musical pitches was known in the third century B. C.; orchestras with twenty and more performers played at court during the Ta'ng dynasty (618–907); and full-fledged opera developed during the Yuan period (1271–1368) and continues to be popular today.

In a country with many distinct ethnic groups and over 300 forms of regional theater, there is, naturally, no one uniform musical style. But a common denominator of all Chinese music is the importance given to the string instruments. They are played alone as solo instruments and, as in the West, they form the nucleus of the Chinese orchestra. Traditionally the Chinese orchestra is much smaller than its Western counterpart, and the tones it produces are totally different. The **pipa** (a four-string lute), the **qin** (a seven-string zither), and the **erhu** (a two-string fiddle) usually provide the dominant sound. While the strings of the pipa and qin are plucked, those of the erhu (see Fig. 20–3) are made of silk and are played with a bow. A vibrato-rich sound results, a strange, veiled tone of great beauty.

We hear the sound of the erhu prominently in the orchestral piece *The Moon Mirrored in the Pool*. As with most Chinese music, here melody is paramount. The task of the player of the erhu and the other bowed instruments is to perform it with great subtlety of color and infinite gradations of pitch. There is little harmony in Chinese music. What there is usually results from two instruments playing different versions of the melody simultaneously. Sometimes the melody is simply doubled at the octave or in unison

an ancient art

FIGURE 20–3

Lui Man-Sing performing on the erhu.

with tremolos*, a technique that produces a shimmering effect. Typical of Chinese music, the scale used in *The Moon Mirrored in the Pool* is a pentatonic* one (here G, A, B, D, E, [G]). But these five notes are merely a point of departure for the astonishingly beautiful erhu, which plays as much between pitches as on them.

LISTENING GUIDE		Hua Yanjun (1890–1950) *The Moon Mirrored in the Pool* (performed by the Central Broadcasting Traditional Instruments Orchestra of China)	Introduction to Listening tape: side B, band 3

0:00	Bamboo flute plays introduction
0:07	Full orchestra introduces melody
0:30	Erhu continues with melody
0:39	Pipa amplifies and extends melody
1:06	Erhu plays variation of melody against background of tremolos on the main notes of the melody
1:42	Crescendo
2:24	Bowed strings play melody with tremolo by plucked strings
2:45	Erhu and pipa play different versions of the melody together
3:16	Prominent "Western-style" bass emerges in low register
3:32	High bowed strings and plucked strings play melody in unison
3:52	Lower bowed strings and plucked strings play melody
4:15	Erhu returns with melody; duple meter accompaniment plucked in background
4:50	Erhu plays fragments of melody

Music for the Indian Sitar

Stretching from the towering Himalayan mountains in the north to the tidal mud flats of the south, India is a vast land full of contrasts: the beauty of the Taj Mahal and the squalor of the urban slums; the wealth of the maharajas and the abject poverty of the untouchables; the jewels on the neck of a prince who, for religious reasons, wears no shoes. It is also a land of many ethnic and religious groups, with the Moslems strong in the north and the Hindus dominating the south. Indian music, too, is divided somewhat along regional lines. What is called **Hindustani** style music is heard in the north, while **Karnatak** style prevails in the south. Among the many differences between the two is the fact that Karnatak music is almost always sung, whereas Hindustani music frequently makes use of an instrument called the sitar.

Hindustani and Karnatak styles

The **sitar** is a large lutelike instrument with as many as twenty strings, some of which are used to play a melody, some simply to vibrate sympathetically with the melody strings, and some to provide a drone*. At each end of the instrument is a large, semicircular gourd which serves as a resonator to amplify the sound of the strings. With this impressive array of strings, the sitar is capable of producing a variety of timbres, dynamic levels, and special effects when in the hands of a gifted performer. A performance on the sitar is invariably accompanied by a **tabla,** a double drum. The right-

the sitar and tabla

FIGURE 20–4

Ravi Shankar performing on the sitar.

hand end of the tabla is tuned to the tonic, dominant, or subdominant note of the sitar melody, while the left-hand end can produce almost any low pitch depending on the amount of pressure the drummer applies. With these two instruments alone, gifted Indian musicians can create a performance that is stunning in its virtuosity and exhilarating in its effect.

Every piece of traditional Indian music makes use of a raga. A **raga** is a basic scale and a basic melodic pattern, but it is more. A raga expresses the feeling, the mood of the piece. It has been called "the mystical expressive force" at the heart of every Indian composition. The raga that we shall hear, Raga Jogeshwari, makes use of a six-note scale which rises and falls as it descends and ascends.

EXAMPLE 20–2

From the scale of Raga Jogeshwari is derived a basic theme which is presented here at the beginning of the piece three times in quick succession. Thereafter the work unfolds in a series of presentations of the theme and increasingly elaborate improvisations upon it. As you will hear, not only are the notes of the scale of the raga played, but also microtones between pitches, as the performer manipulates the strings of the sitar to "bend" the pitches. Bending the pitch adds subtlety and expressive power to the music. The texture becomes increasingly saturated with such ornaments, and, toward the end, the tempo increases to heighten the sense of progress.

Perhaps more than any other musical culture, Indian music relies exclusively on a single melody for musical expression. There are no contrapuntal lines and no harmony other than the constant drone on the tonic and dominant notes of the melody. For an Indian performer, chords are thought to create too much sound at once and to detract from what is truly important: the expressive nuances of the melody and the intricate rhythmic interplay between the sitar and the tabla.

The performance of Raga Jogeshwari that you will hear is by Ravi Shankar, one of India's finest sitar players. Shankar personifies the ideal of Indian music in which composer and performer are one and the same person. Indeed, Raga Jogeshwari is his own creation. Yet each new performance of this raga results in a new composition because so much of the performance is improvised. For an Indian musician, composition, improvisation, and performance are three simultaneous manifestations of the urge for creative expression.

LISTENING GUIDE		Raga Jogeshwari Gat II (Theme II) (performed by Ravi Shankar, sitar, and Alla Rakha, tabla)	Introduction to Listening tape: side B, band 4

0:00   Scale of raga played as quick arpeggio

0:08   Sitar presents theme three times against beat in the tabla

0:45	Alternations of the theme with free improvisations
1:17	Ascending and descending improvisations upon the scale of the raga
2:11	A strong cadence for the tabla
2:40	More elaborate patterns repeated on successive degrees of the scale
4:18	Tempo increases
4:45	Strumming on the drone strings of the sitar
5:00	Sitar explores half steps that naturally occur in ascending version of the raga
5:50	Tabla mimics rhythmic patterns of the sitar

Contrasts

From this brief tour of three non-Western musical cultures, it is easy to hear that the beautiful and sometimes exotic sounds of the music of Indonesia, China, and India are distinctive, indeed unique. Each of these three great musical traditions is very different from the other. Yet they also have many things in common that separate them from the musical practices and traditions of the West. The following are among the more important contrasts between Western and non-Western musical practices:

The importance of melody and rhythm, and the absence of harmony: Non-Western musics are marked by gradations and subtleties of pitch that are far more sophisticated than those in Western melodies, which tend to move directly from one well-defined pitch to the next. Rhythms, too, are generally more complex and rhythmic interaction between the parts is more complicated. Yet at the same time, harmony as we in the West know it, is virtually nonexistent. Of all the musical cultures of the world, only the West has emphasized the simultaneous sounding of several pitches. The harmony which results adds richness and depth to the sound, but often at the expense of melodic and rhythmic features.

Improvisation: Spontaneous improvisation is a musical practice that occurs, in varying degrees, in virtually all musical traditions except that of Western classical music. A singer of the Ashanti people in Ghana, West Africa, is expected to vary a tribal song and add sections to it, just as the Indian sitar player is expected to ornament and extend a traditional raga, after years of patient study of the ornamental art. A performer's worth is measured in terms of his or her ability to create music that is new and imaginative within the confines of a traditional form. We in the West have a similar type of music, American jazz, but the strong emphasis on improvisation in jazz only serves to show that this style of music is African, not European in its roots.

Oral teaching and learning: As we have seen, each of the three musical cultures explored in this chapter relies exclusively on oral transmission, not written notation, as the means by which to communicate music. The Indian guru will teach the secrets of the ragas to the young student by rote. The master explains and plays, the student imitates and practices, year after year. Musical notation has no place in the process. There is musical notation in India, China, and Bali, but it is usually used in learned discussions of the theory of music, not in practical music making. This is true everywhere throughout the non-Western world.

The importance of musical notation in the West: Western musical culture is the only one to rely on notation as a means of preserving and passing on its musical heritage from one generation to the next. It is also the only culture where performers play by reading written symbols. Working from notation has advantages and disadvantages. It allows the composer to prescribe in great detail exactly what he or she wishes to express. It is possible to have a very clear and unchanging notion of what a particular work of art is to be. Yet as a result, each successive performance of that work tends to be rather similar to the last—there is little room for spontaneous creativity.

Composer and performer as one: The use of musical notation in Western classical music has given extraordinary powers of control and authority to the composer. He or she can dictate every small detail of a composition, and it is up to the performer to carry out precisely these instructions. The performer is very much the servant of the composer. Non-Western cultures have a more balanced relationship between composer and performer. Indeed, the composer and performer, like Ravi Shankar, are usually one and the same person. A piece of music comes into being only at the time of performance. It has no life outside of performance. It is not thought out in advance in someone's head. It is not written down in musical notation. There is not composer and performer, only musician. Similarly, there is no conductor in non-Western cultures, no one who directs but does not perform. Even in the large Balinese gamelan, where many instrumental parts have to be coordinated, the leader is one of the performers, usually one of the drummers.

Concerts and audience response: Public performance of music in non-Western cultures occurs in a freer, more relaxed environment. In Africa it is not uncommon to see a group of expert musicians surrounded by people who join in by singing, clapping, playing rattles, and dancing with the music. Concerts in Bali usually occur in open-air pavilions where the audience crowds around, laughs, talks quietly, and encourages the performers. Interaction between the performers and the community is an important part of the music-making process. Prior to the nineteenth century, concerts in the West were similar to this freer, more interactive experience. Not until the Romantic era, when composers made a musical composition a revered "work of art," was the audience required to sit in respectful, meditative silence.

Conclusion

The contrasts between Western and non-Western musical traditions have implications that extend far beyond the world of music. For music reflects the way a society thinks and what it values. From the preceding view of non-Western music, we can begin to see how much we are a society of musical spectators, rather than participants. We divorce the individual performers from the group experience. We value a single creator who determines all elements of the musical composition. We have turned away from improvisation and spontaneous creativity, preferring instead precise planning and faithful duplication at the moment of performance. The work of art is given an exalted position. It is fixed in notation and unalterable. It does not grow and evolve to reflect the changing needs and desires of the community. Finally, we have transformed what is at heart an oral and physical means of communication into one of visual relationships through a heavy reliance on musical notation. We have replaced sound with visual symbol. We have also gradually replaced the musician with two individuals, the performer and the composer. More recently, with the advent of computer music in this century, we have replaced the composer with the computer programmer. Today, as arguments about "multiculturalism" swirl around us, even a cursory study of non–Western music suggests why such an experience is important. Not only do we learn something about the music of other people, we find out even more about ourselves.

KEY WORDS

erhu	pipa	sitar
gamelan	qin	tabla
Hindustani music	raga	
Karnatak music	Ravi Shankar	

GLOSSARY

absolute music: instrumental music free of a text or any pre-existing program

a cappella: a term applied to unaccompanied vocal music; originated in the expression *a cappella Sistina*, "in the Sistine Chapel" of the pope where instruments were forbidden to accompany the singers

accelerando: a tempo mark indicating "getting faster"

accent: emphasis or stress placed on a musical tone or a chord

accidental: a sharp, flat, or natural sign which alters the pitch of a note a half step

accompagnato: see *recitativo accompagnato*

acoustical instruments: instruments that produce sounds naturally when strings are bowed or plucked, a tube has air passed through it, or percussion instruments are struck

adagio: a tempo mark indicating "slow"

Alberti bass: instead of having the pitches of a chord sound all together, the notes are played in succession to provide a continual stream of sound

aleatoric music: see *chance music*

allegretto: a tempo mark indicating "moderately fast"

allegro: a tempo mark indicating "fast"

allemanda: see *allemande*

allemande: a stately dance in 4/4 meter with gracefully interweaving lines

alto (also contralto): the lower of the two female voice parts, the soprano being higher

andante: a tempo mark indicating "moderately moving"

andantino: a tempo mark indicating "moderately moving" yet slightly faster than *andante*

antecedent phrase: the opening, incomplete-sounding phrase of a melody; often followed by a consequent phrase which brings the melody to closure

anthem: a composition for chorus on a sacred subject; similar in design and function to a motet

aria: an elaborate lyrical song for solo voice

arpeggio: the notes of a triad or seventh chord played in direct succession and in a direct line up or down

arioso: a style of singing and a type of song midway between an aria and a recitative

art song: an accompanied song or ayre with artistic aspirations

atonal music: music without tonality, music without a key center; most often associated with the twentieth-century avant-garde style of Arnold Schoenberg

augmentation: the notes of a melody held for longer, usually double, their normal duration

ballad: a traditional song, or folk song, sung by a soloist that tells a tale and is organized by stanzas

ballet: an art form that uses dance and music, along with costumes and scenery, to tell a story and display emotions through expressive gestures and movement

Ballets russes: a Russian ballet company of the early twentieth century led by Sergei Diaghilev

banjo: a five-string plucked folk instrument of Afro-American origin

bar: see *measure*

baritone: a male voice part of a middle range, between the higher tenor and the lower bass

bass: the lowest male voice range

bass clef: a sign placed on a staff to indicate the notes below middle C

bass drum: a large, low sounding drum struck with a soft-headed stick

bass viol: see *viola da gamba*

basso continuo: a small ensemble of at least two instrumentalists who provide a foundation for the melody or melodies above; heard almost exclusively in Baroque music

basso ostinato: a motive or phrase in the bass that is repeated again and again

bassoon: a low, double-reed instrument of the woodwind family

Bayreuth Festival House: an opera house in the town of Bayreuth, Germany, constructed exclusively for the music dramas of Richard Wagner

beat: an even pulse in music that divides the passing of time into equal segments

bebop: a complex, hard-driving style of jazz which emerged shortly after World War II; it is played without musical notation by a small ensemble

bel canto: (Italian for "beautiful singing") a style of singing and a type of Italian opera developed in the nineteenth century that features the beautiful tone and brilliant technique of the human voice

big band: a mid- to large-size dance band that emerged in the 1930s to play the style of jazz called swing

binary form: a musical form consisting of two units (**A** and **B**) constructed to balance and complement each other

blue note: the third, fifth, or seventh note of the blues scale that can be altered to be sharper or flatter; helps produce the wail of the blues

blues: an expressive, soulful style of singing that emerged from the Afro-American spiritual and work song at the end of the nineteenth century; its texts are strophic and harmonies simple and repetitive

blues scale: a seven-note scale in which the third, fifth, and seventh pitches are sometimes flat, sometimes natural, and sometimes in between

bolero: a popular, suggestive Spanish dance for a soloist or couple often performed to the accompaniment of castanets

bourée: a fast dance in 2/2 with a quick upbeat and rapidly running eighth notes

Brandenburg concertos: set of six concerti grossi composed by J. S. Bach between 1711 and 1720, and subsequently dedicated to Margrave Christian Ludwig of Brandenburg

brass family: a group of musical instruments traditionally made of brass and played with a mouthpiece; includes trumpet, trombone, French horn and tuba

bridge: see *transition*

bugle: a simple brass instrument that evolved from the valveless military trumpet

cabaletta: the concluding fast section of any two-part aria or duet; a useful mechanism to get the principals off the stage

cadence: a musical resting place at the end of a phrase

cadenza: a showy passage for the soloist appearing near the end of the movement in a concerto; it usually incorporates rapid runs, arpeggios, and snippets of previously heard themes into a fantasy-like improvisation

canon (also round): a contrapuntal form in which the individual voices enter and each in turn duplicates exactly the melody that the first voice played or sang

cantata: a term originally meaning "something sung;" in its mature state it consists of several movements, including one or more arias, ariosos, and recitatives; cantatas can be on secular subjects, but those of J. S. Bach are primarily sacred in content

caprice: a light, whimsical character piece of the nineteenth century

castrato: a boy or adult singer who had been castrated to keep his voice from changing so that it would remain in the soprano register

celesta: a small percussive keyboard instrument using hammers to strike metal bars, thereby producing a bright, bell-like sound

cello (also violoncello): an instrument of the violin family but twice its size; it is played between the legs and produces a rich, lyrical tone

chamber music: music, usually instrumental music, performed in a small concert hall or private residence with just one performer on each part

chamber sonata: see *sonata da camera*

chance music (also aleatory music): music that involves an element of chance (rolling dice, choosing cards, etc.) or whimsy on the part of the performers; especially popular with avant-garde composers

chanson: a French term used broadly to indicate a lyrical song from the Middle Ages into the twentieth century

character piece: a brief instrumental work seeking to capture a single mood; a genre much favored by composers of the Romantic era

chorale: the German word for the hymn of the Lutheran church; hence a simple religious melody to be sung by the congregation

chord: two or more simultaneously sounding pitches

chord progression: a succession of chords moving forward in a purposeful fashion

chorus: a group of singers, usually including sopranos, altos, tenors, and basses, with at least two and often many more singers on each vocal part; also, in jazz, the full tune

chromaticism: the frequent presence in melodies and chords of intervals only a half step apart; in a scale the use of notes not part of the diatonic major or minor pattern

church sonata: see *sonata da chiesa*

clarinet: a single reed instrument of the woodwind family with a large range and a wide variety of timbres within it

clavier: a general term for all keyboard instruments including harpsichord, organ, and piano

clef sign: a sign used to indicate the register, or range of pitches, in which an instrument is to play or a singer is to sing

coda: (Italian for "tail") a final and concluding section of a musical composition

col legno: (Italian for "with the wood") an instruction to string players to strike the strings of the instrument not with the horsehair of the bow, but with the wood of it

collegium musicum: a society of amateur musicians (usually associated with a university) dedicated to the performance of music, nowadays music of the Middle Ages, Renaissance, and Baroque era

color (also timbre): the character or quality of a musical tone as determined by its harmonics and its attack and decay

comic opera: a genre of opera that originated in the eighteenth century portraying everyday characters and situations, and using spoken dialogue and simple songs

computer music: the most recent development in electronic music; couples the computer with the electronic synthesizer to imitate the sounds of acoustical instruments and to produce new sounds

concert overture: an independent one-movement work of programmatic content originally intended for the concert hall and not designed to precede an opera or play

concertino: the group of instruments that function as soloists in a concerto grosso

concerto: an instrumental genre in which one or more soloists play with and against a larger orchestra

concerto grosso: a three-movement concerto of the Baroque era that pits the sound of a small group of soloists (the concertino) against that of the full orchestra (the tutti)

conjunct motion: melodic motion that proceeds primarily by steps and without leaps

consequent phrase: the second phrase of a two-part melodic unit which brings a melody to a point of repose and closure

consonance: pitches sounding agreeable and stable

continuo: see *basso continuo*

contrabassoon: a larger, lower-sounding version of the bassoon

cool jazz: a style of jazz that emerged in the 1950s that is softer, more relaxed, and less frenzied that bebop

cornet: a brass instrument that looks like a short trumpet; it has a more mellow tone than the trumpet and is most often used in military bands

cornetto: a woodwind instrument that developed during the late Middle Ages and early Renaissance that sounds like a hybrid of a clarinet and trumpet

corrente: see *courante*

counterpoint: the harmonious opposition of two or more independent musical lines

courante: a lively dance in 6/4 with an upbeat and frequent changes of metrical accent

crescendo: a gradual increase in the volume of sound

cross over: the phenomenon whereby a classical musician moves into the sphere of popular music, or a popular musician enters the realm of classical music or that of another popular style

cymbals: a percussion instrument of two metal disks; they are made to crash together to create emphasis and articulation in music

da capo aria: an aria in two sections with an obligatory return to and repeat of the first; hence an aria in ternary **(ABA)** form

dance suite: a collection of instrumental dances each with its own distinctive rhythm and character

development: the center-most portion of sonata-allegro form in which the thematic material of the exposition is developed and extended, transformed, or reduced to its essence; it is often the most confrontational and unstable section of the movement

diatonic: pertaining to the seven notes that make up either the major or the minor scale

Dies irae: a Gregorian chant composed in the thirteenth century and used as the central portion of the Requiem Mass of the Catholic Church

diminished chord: a triad or seventh chord made up entirely of minor thirds and producing a tense, unstable sound

diminuendo: a gradual decrease in volume of sound

diminution: a reduction, usually by half, of all the rhythmic durations in a melody

disjunct motion: melodic motion that moves primarily by leaps rather than by steps

dissonance: a discordant mingling of sounds

diva: (Italian for "goddess") a celebrated female opera singer; a prima donna

dominant chord: the chord built on the fifth degree of the scale

dotted note: a note to which an additional duration of fifty percent has been added

double bass: the largest and lowest-pitched instrument in the string family

double counterpoint: counterpoint with two themes that can reverse position, the top theme moving to the bottom and the bottom to the top (also called invertible counterpoint)

double exposition form: a form originating in the concerto of the Classical period in which first the orchestra and then the soloist present the primary thematic material

downbeat: the first beat of each measure; it is indicated by a downward motion of the conductor's hand and is usually stressed

drone: a continuous sound on one or more fixed pitches

dynamics: the various levels of volume, loud and soft, at which sounds are produced in a musical composition

electronic instruments: machines that produce musical sounds by electronic means, the most widespread instrument being the keyboard synthesizer

electronic music: sounds produced and manipulated by magnetic tape machines, synthesizers, and/or computers

eleventh chord: a chord comprised of five intervals of a third and spanning eleven different letter names of pitches

English horn: an alto oboe, pitched at the interval a fifth below the oboe, much favored by composers of the Romantic era

episode: a passage of free, nonimitative counterpoint found in a fugue

erhu: an ancient two-string Chinese fiddle

étude: (French for "study") a musical composition that aims to improve the technical facility of the performer

exposition: in a fugue the opening section in which each voice in turn has the opportunity to present the subject; in sonata-allegro form the principal section in which all thematic material is presented

falsetto voice: a high, soprano-like voice produced by adult male singers when they sing in head voice and not in full chest voice

fantasy: a free improvisatory-like composition in which the composer follows his or her whims rather than an established musical form

fermata: a mark in the music indicating that the performer(s) should hold a note or chord for an extended duration

fiddle: a popular term for the violin

figured bass: a numerical shorthand placed in the music that tells the player which unwritten notes to fill in above the written bass note

finale: the last movement of a multi-movement composition, one that usually works to a climax and conclusion

flat: a symbol in musical notation that lowers a pitch by a half step

flute: a high–sounding member of the woodwind family; the instrument was initially made of wood but more recently, beginning in the nineteenth century, of silver or even platinum

folk-rock: a mixture of the steady beat of rock with the forms, topics, and styles of singing of the traditional Anglo-American folk ballad

folk song: a song originating from an ethnic group and passed from generation to generation by oral tradition rather than written notation

form: the purposeful organization of the artist's materials; in music, the general shape of a composition as perceived by the listener

forte (f): a dynamic mark indicating "loud"

fortepiano (also pianoforte): the original name of the piano

fortissimo (ff): a dynamic mark indicating "very loud"

free counterpoint: counterpoint in which the voices do not all make use of some pre-existing subject in imitation

French horn: a brass instrument that plays in the middle range of the brass family; developed from the medieval hunting horn

French overture: a two-part musical form of the Baroque era consisting of a slow first section in duple meter with dotted rhythms and a fast second section with imitative counterpoint

fugato: a "little fugue," meaning usually the exposition (only) of a fugue set in some other musical form like sonata-allegro or theme and variations

fugue: a composition for three, four, or five parts played or sung by voices or instruments, which begins with a presentation of a subject in imitation in each part, continues with modulating passages of free counterpoint, and further appearances of the subject

full cadence: a cadence that sounds complete, in part because it usually ends on the tonic note

gallant style: a light, graceful, ornamental style of music that developed at the beginning of the Classical period

gamelan: the traditional orchestra of Indonesia consisting of as many as twenty-five instruments, mostly gongs, chimes, drums, and metallophones

gavotte: a moderate dance in 2/2 with full upbeat and prominent rhythm

Gesamtkunstwerk: (German term for "total art work") an art form that involves music, poetry, drama, and scenic design; often used in reference to Richard Wagner's music dramas

Gewandhaus Orchestra: the symphony orchestra that originated in the Clothiers' House in Leipzig, Germany, in the eighteenth century

gigue: a fast dance in 6/8 or 12/8 with a constant eighth-note pulse that produces a galloplike effect

glissando: a device of sliding up or down the scale very rapidly

glockenspiel: a percussion instrument made of tuned metal bars which are struck by mallets

grave: a tempo mark indicating "very slow and grave"

great staff: a large musical staff that combines both the treble and bass clefs

Gregorian chant (also plainsong): a large body of unaccompanied monophonic vocal music, set to Latin texts, composed for the Western Church over the course of fifteen centuries, from the time of the earliest Fathers to the Council of Trent

ground bass: the English term for *basso ostinato*

half cadence: a cadence at which the music does not come to a fully satisfying stop but stands as if suspended on a dominant chord

half step: the smallest musical interval in the Western major or minor scale; the distance between any two adjacent keys on the piano

harmonics: the secondary tones above a fundamental pitch that taken in sum help form the totality of that sound

harmony: the sounds that provide the support and enrichment—an accompaniment—for melody

harp: an ancient plucked string instrument with a triangular shape

harpsichord: a keyboard instrument, especially popular during the Baroque era, that produces sound by depressing a key which drives a lever upward and forces a pick to pluck a string

Hindustani style music: the traditional, or classical, music of northern India

homophony: a texture in which all the voices, or lines, move to new pitches at roughly the same time; often referred to in contradistinction to polyphony

horn: a term generally used by musicians to refer to any brass instrument, but most often the French horn

idée fixe: literally a "fixed idea," but more specifically an obsessive musical theme as first used in Hector Berlioz's *Symphonie fantastique*

pentatonic scale: a fiv
  and non-Western n
phrase: a self-contain
pianissimo (pp): a dy
piano (p): a dynamic
piano: a large keyboa
  ous dynamic levels
  strings
piano transcription: t
  orchestral score, ar
  great staff for playi
pianoforte: see *fortepi*
piccolo: a small flute;
  wind instrument
pickup: a note or two
  piece intending to g
  beat
pipa: an ancient four-
pitch: the relative po
pizzicato: the proces
  of an instrument ra
plainsong: see *Gregor*
point of imitation: a
  in turn by each voi
polychords: the stack
  another so they so
polymeters: two or n
polyphony: a musica
  neously sounding
  and create counter
polyrhythms: two or
popular music: a bro
  a large section of t
  contradistinction t
  sical music
prelude: an introduc
  gives the performe
  for a more substar
prepared piano: a pi
  erasers, and bits o
  ment from a melo
prestissimo: a tempo
presto: a tempo mar
prima donna: (Italia
  singer in an opera
program music: a pi
  symphony orches
  events and emotic
  source: a story, pl
program symphony:
  or five movement
  together tell a tale
  or scenes
Proper of the Mass:
  texts that vary wi

imitation: the process by which one or more musical voices, or parts, enter and exactly duplicate for a period of time the music presented by the previous voice
imitative counterpoint: a type of counterpoint in which the voices or lines frequently use imitation
incidental music: music to be inserted between the acts or during important scenes of a play to add an extra dimension to the drama
instrumental break: in the blues or in jazz, a short instrumental passage that interrupts and responds to the singing of a voice
intermezzo: (Italian for "between piece") a light musical interlude intended to separate and thus break the mood of two more serious surrounding movements or operatic acts or scenes
interval: the distance between any two pitches on the scale
inversion: the process of inverting the musical intervals in a theme or melody; a melody that ascended by step, now descends by step, and so on

jazz: a lively, energetic music with pulsating rhythms and scintillating syncopations, usually played by a small instrumental ensemble

Karnatak style music: the traditional, or classical, music of southern India
key: a tonal center built on a tonic note and making use of a scale; also, on a keyboard instrument, one of a series of levers that can be depressed to generate sound
key signature: a preplaced set of sharps or flats used to indicate the scale and key
Kyrie: the first portion of the Ordinary of the Mass and hence usually the opening movement in a polyphonic setting of the Mass

La Scala: the principal opera house of the city of Milan, Italy, which opened in 1778
largo: a tempo mark indicating "slow and broad"
leading tone: the pitch a half step below the tonic which pulls up and into it, especially at cadences
leap: melodic movement not by an interval of just a step but usually by a jump of at least a fourth
legato: an articulation mark indicating that the notes are to be smoothly connected; the opposite of staccato
Leitmotif: a brief, distinctive unit of music that is designed to represent a character, object, or idea; a term applied to the motives in the music dramas of Richard Wagner
lento: a tempo mark indicating "very slow"
libretto: the text of an opera
Liebestod: (German for "love death") the famous aria sung by the expiring Isolde at the end of Richard Wagner's opera *Tristan und Isolde*
Lied: (German for "song") the genre of art song, for voice and piano accompaniment, that originated in Germany ca. 1800

London symphonies: the twelve symphonies composed by Joseph Haydn for performance in London between 1791 and 1795; Haydn's last twelve symphonies (Nos. 93–104)
lute: a six-string instrument appearing in the West in the late Middle Ages

madrigal: a popular genre of secular vocal music that originated in Italy during the Renaissance
madrigalism: a device, originating in the madrigal, by which key words in a text spark a particularly expressive musical setting
major scale: a seven-note scale which ascends in the following order of whole and half steps: 1-1-1/2-1-1-1-1/2
Mass: the central religious service of the Roman Catholic church, one which incorporates singing for spiritual reflection or as accompaniment to sacred acts
measure (also bar): a group of beats, or musical pulses; usually the number of beats are fixed and constant so that the measure serves as a continual unit of measurement in music
melisma: in singing, one vowel luxuriously spread out over many notes
melody: a series of notes arranged in order to form a distinctive, recognizable musical unit; it is most often placed in the treble
metallophone: a percussion instrument consisting of keys made of tuned metal bars which are struck by hammers or sticks
meter: the gathering of beats into regular groups
metronome: a mechanical device used by performers to keep a steady tempo
mezzo-soprano: a female vocal range between the alto and soprano
middle C: the middle note on the modern piano
minimalism: a style of modern music that takes a very small amount of musical material and repeats it over and over to form a composition
Minnesinger: a secular poet-musician who flourished in Germany during the twelfth through fourteenth centuries
minor scale: a seven-note scale which ascends in the following order of whole and half steps: 1-1/2-1-1-1/2-1-1
minuet: a moderate dance in 3/4, though actually danced in patterns of six steps, with no upbeat but with highly symmetrical phrasing
mixolydian scale (mixolydian mode): a seven-note scale often used in Gregorian chant, one different from the major and minor scale
mode: a pattern of pitches forming a scale; the two primary modes in Western music are major and minor
moderato: a tempo marking indicating "moderately moving"
modified strophic form: strophic form in which the music is modified briefly to accommodate a particularly expressive word or phrase in the text

modulation: the proces
changes from one ke
for example

monophony: a musical
music with no accom

motet: a composition fc
gious, devotional, or

motive: a short, distinc

mouthpiece: a detachal
which the player blo

movement: a large, ind
mental work such as
quartet, or concerto

music: the rational org
they pass through ti

music drama: a term u
Wagner

musique concrète: mu
directly with sounds
musical notation an

mute: any device that i
ment; on the trumpe
inside the bell of the

nationalism: a movem
in which composers
ities in their music k
scales, dance rhythr

natural: a symbol in n
or flat

neo-Classical: a move
seeks to return to th
Baroque and Classi

ninth chord: a chord s
constructed by supe

nocturne: a slow, intrc
harmonies and poig
during the 1820s an

nonimitative counterr
lines that do not im

oboe: an instrument c
pitched of the doub

octave: the interval cc
the major and minc
similar because the
pitch is exactly twi

octave displacement:
melody whereby a
distant, and the me
next note up or do

opera: a dramatic wo
their parts; it usual
costumes

rubato: (Italian for "robbed") a temp mark indicating that the performer may take, or steal, great liberties with the tempo

sackbut: a brass instrument of the late Middle Ages and Renaissance; the precursor of the trombone

Sanctus: the fourth section of the Ordinary of the Mass

sarabande: a slow, elegant dance in 3/4 with a strong accent on the second beat

scale: an arrangement of pitches that ascends and descends in a fixed and unvarying pattern

scherzo: (Italian for "joke") a rapid, jovial work in triple meter often used in place of the minuet as the third movement in a string quartet or symphony

Schubertiade: a social gathering for music and poetry that featured the songs and piano music of Franz Schubert

score: a volume of musical notation involving more than one staff

secco recitative: dry recitative accompanied only by the harpsichord

sequence: the repetition of a musical motive at successively higher or lower degrees of the scale

serenade: an instrumental work for a small ensemble originally intended as a light entertainment in the evening

serial music: music in which some important component—pitch, dynamics, rhythm—comes in a continually repeating series; see also *twelve-tone composition*

seventh chord: a chord spanning seven letter names and constructed by superimposing three thirds

sharp: a musical symbol that raises a pitch by a half step

shawm: a double reed woodwind instrument of the late Middle Ages and Renaissance; the precursor of the oboe

sinfonia: (Italian for "symphony") a one-movement (later three- or four-movement) orchestral work that originated in Italy in the seventeenth century

Singspiel: (German for "singing play") a musical comedy originating in Germany with spoken dialogue, tuneful songs, and topical humor

sitar: a large lutelike instrument with as many as twenty strings, prominently used in the traditional music of northern India

snare drum: a small drum consisting of a metal cylinder covered with a skin or sheet of plastic that when played with sticks produces the "rat-ta-tat" sound familiar from marching bands

solo: a musical line sung or played by a single performer

solo concerto: a concerto in which an orchestra and a single performer in turn present and develop the musical material in the spirit of harmonious competition

sonata: originally "something sounded" on an instrument as opposed to something sung (a "cantata"); later a multimovement work for solo instrument or instrument with keyboard accompaniment

sonata-allegro form: a dramatic musical form of the Classical and Romantic periods involving an exposition, development, and recapitulation, with optional introduction and coda

sonata da camera (chamber sonata): a suite for keyboard or small instrumental ensemble made up of individual dance movements

sonata da chiesa (church sonata): a suite for keyboard or small instrumental ensemble made up of movements indicated only by tempo marks such as *grave, vivace, adagio,* etc.; originally intended to be performed in church

song cycle: a collection of several songs united by a common textual theme or literary idea

soprano: the highest female vocal part

Sprechstimme: (German for "speech-voice") a singer declaims, rather than sings, a text at only approximate pitch levels

staccato: a manner of playing in which each note is held only for the shortest possible time

staff: a horizontal grid onto which are put the symbols of musical notation: notes, rests, accidentals, dynamic marks, etc.

stanza: a poetic unit of two or more lines with a consistent meter and rhyme scheme

step: the interval between adjacent pitches in the diatonic or chromatic scale; either a whole step or a half step

string bass: see *double bass*

string instruments: instruments which produce sound when strings are bowed or plucked; the harp, guitar, and the members of the violin family are all string instruments

string quartet: a standard instrumental ensemble for chamber music consisting of a first and second violin, a viola, and a cello; also the genre of music, usually in three or four movements, composed for this ensemble

strophe: see *stanza*

strophic form: a musical form often used in setting a strophic, or stanzaic, text such as a hymn or carol; the music is repeated anew for each successive strophe

style: the general surface sound produced by the inner action of the elements of music: melody, rhythm, harmony, color, texture, and form

subdominant chord: the chord built on the fourth, or subdominant, degree of the major or minor scale

subject: the term for the principal theme in a fugue

swing: a mellow, bouncy, flowing style of jazz that originated in the 1930s

symphonic poem (also called the tone poem): a onemovement work for orchestra of the Romantic era that gives musical expression to the emotions and events associated with a story, play, political occurrence, personal experience, or encounter with nature

symphony: a genre of instrumental music for orchestra consisting of several movements; also the orchestral ensemble that plays this genre

symphony orchestra: the large instrumental ensemble that plays symphonies, overtures, concertos, and the like

syncopation: a rhythmic device in which the natural accent falling on a strong beat is displaced to a weak beat or between the beats

synthesizer: a machine that has the capacity to produce, transform, and combine (or synthesize) electronic sounds

tabla: a double drum used in the traditional music of northern India

tempo: the speed at which the beats occur in music

tenor: the highest male vocal range

ternary form: a three-part musical form in which the third section is a repeat of the first, hence **ABA**

terraced dynamics: a term used to describe the sharp, abrupt dynamic contrasts found in the music of the Baroque era

texture: the density and disposition of the musical lines that make up a musical composition; monophonic, homophonic, and polyphonic are the primary musical textures

theme and variations: a musical form in which a theme continually returns but is varied by changing the notes of the melody, the harmony, the rhythm, or some other feature of the music

The Well-Tempered Clavier: two sets of twenty-four preludes and fugues written by J. S. Bach between 1720 and 1742

third-stream jazz: a mixture of jazz and classical styles that originated in the 1950s

through composed: a term used to describe music that exhibits no obvious repetitions or overt musical form from beginning to end

timbre: see *color*

timpani (also kettle drums): a percussion instrument consisting usually of two, sometimes four, large drums that can produce a specific pitch when struck with mallets

time signature (also meter signature): two numbers, one on top of the other, usually placed at the beginning of the music to tell the performer what note value is carrying the beat and how the beats are to be grouped

tonality: the organization of music around a central tone (the tonic)

tone: a sound with a definite, consistent pitch

tone cluster: a dissonant sounding of several pitches, each only a half step away from the other, in a densely packed chord

tone poem: see *symphonic poem*

tonic: the central pitch around which the melody and harmony gravitate

transition (also bridge): in sonata-allegro form the unstable section in which the tonality changes from tonic to dominant (or relative major) in preparation for the appearance of the second theme

treble: the uppermost musical line, voice, or part; the part in which the melody is most often found

treble clef: the sign placed on a staff to indicate the notes above middle C

tremolo: a musical tremor produced on a string instrument by repeating the same pitch with quick up and down strokes of the bow

triad: a chord consisting of three pitches and two intervals of a third

trill: a rapid alternation of two neighboring pitches

trio: an ensemble, vocal or instrumental, with three performers; also, a brief musical composition, much like a minuet, that follows the minuet in symphonies, string quartets, and sonatas of the Baroque and Classical periods; it was originally performed by just three instruments

trio sonata: an ensemble of the Baroque period consisting actually of four performers, two playing upper parts and two on the *basso continuo* instruments

triplet: a group of three notes inserted into the space of two

trombone: a brass instrument of medium to low range that is supplied with a slide allowing a variety of pitches to sound

troubadour: a secular poet-musician who flourished in southern France during the twelfth and thirteenth centuries

trouvère: a secular poet-musician who flourished in northern France during the thirteenth and early fourteenth centuries

trumpet: a brass instrument of the soprano range

tuba: a brass instrument of the bass range

tune: a simple melody that is easy to sing

tutti: (Italian for "all") the full orchestra or full performing force

twelve-tone composition: a method of composing music devised by Arnold Schoenberg that has each of the twelve notes of the chromatic scale sound in a fixed, regularly recurring order

unison: two or more voices or instrumental parts singing or playing the same pitch

upbeat: the beat that occurs with the upward motion of the conductor's hand and immediately before the downbeat

vibrato: a slight and continual wobbling of the pitch produced on a string instrument, or by the human voice

viola: a string instrument; the alto member of the violin family

viola da gamba (bass viol): the lowest member of the viol family; a large six- or seven-string instrument played with a bow and heard primarily in the music of the late Renaissance and Baroque eras

violin: a string instrument; the soprano member of the violin family

virtuosity: extraordinary technical facility possessed by an instrumental performer or singer

vivace: a tempo mark indicating "fast and lively"

vocal ensemble: in opera a group of four or more solo singers, usually the principals

voice: the vocal instrument of the human body; also a musical line or part

volume: the degree of softness or loudness of a sound

walking bass: a bass that moves at a moderate pace, mostly in equal note values, and often stepwise up or down the scale

waltz: a popular, triple-meter dance of the late eighteenth and nineteenth centuries

whole step: the predominant interval in the Western major and minor scale; the interval made up of two half steps

whole-tone scale: a six-note scale each pitch of which is a whole tone away from the next

woodwind family: a group of instruments initially constructed of wood; most make their sound with the aid of a single or double reed; includes flute, piccolo, clarinet, oboe, English horn, and bassoon

word painting: the process of depicting the text in music, be it subtly, overtly, or even jokingly, by means of expressive musical devices

xylophone: a percussion instrument consisting of tuned wooden bars, with resonators below, that are struck with mallets

zither: a folk instrument consisting of a wooden box on which are stretched a number of strings of different pitches

CREDITS

Text

84 Marsilio Ficino, "The Golden Age in Florence," in *The Portable Renaissance Reader,* ed. James Bruce Ross and Mary Martin McLaughlin, New York, The Viking Press, 1953, p. 79.

87 Edward Lowinsky, *Music in the Culture of the Renaissance and Other Essays,* ed. Bonnie J. Blackburn, Chicago, The University of Chicago Press, 1989, vol. I, p. 87.

93 Palestrina, *Pope Marcellus Mass,* ed. Lewis Lockwood, New York, W. W. Norton and Company, 1975, p. 12.

118 Walter Kolneder, *Antonio Vivaldi: Documents of his Life and Works,* New York, C. F. Peters Corporation, 1981, p. 43.

158 *Music in the Western World: A History in Documents,* ed. Piero Weiss and Richard Taruskin, New York, Schirmer Books, 1984, p. 299.

159 "Haydn," in *The New Grove Dictionary of Music and Musicians,* ed. Stanley Sadie, London, Macmillan, 1980, vol. VIII, p. 344.

162 *The Letters of Mozart and his Family,* ed. Emily Anderson, London, Macmillan, 1938, vol. III, p.1187.

183 A & M Records, SP–3735.

198 Alfred Einstein, *Mozart: His Character, His Work,* London, Oxford University Press, 1945, p. 300.

213 Conrad Fischer and Erich Koch, *Ludwig van Beethoven,* London, Macmillan, 1958, p. 28.

313 Alma Mahler Werfel, *And the Bridge was Love,* New York, Harcourt Brace, 1958, pp. 25–27.

353 Arnold Schoenberg, "The Composition with Twelve Tones," in *Composers on Music,* ed. Sam Morgenstern, New York, Pantheon Books, 1956, p. 380.

373 Charles Ives, *The Fourth of July,* ed. John Kirkpatrick, New York, Associated Music Publishers, 1974, p. 1.

386 Robert Palmer, liner notes to Philip Glass, *Einstein on the Beach.*

Illustrations

cover Bildarchiv preussischer kulturbesitz, Berlin; **2** © Ken Biggs; **3 (top)** Alexander Teshin Associates; **bottom** T. Hoffmeyer; **4** Alexander Teshin Associ-

INDEX